SOCIAL PROBLEMS

Michael McKee
University of Cincinnati

Ian Robertson
King's College

 Random House
New York

SOCIAL PROBLEMS

Credits for chapter opening photos: (1) Paolo Koch; (2) Donato Leo/DPI; (3) Bruce Roberts/Rapho Guillumette; (4) Elliot Erwitt/Magnum; (5) Courtesy, CBS News; (6) DPI; (7) Tim Eagan/Woodfin Camp; (8) Ken Heyman; (9) Leonard Freed/Magnum; (10) Harvey Stein; (11) Mimi Forsyth/Monkmeyer; (12) Tim Eagen/Woodfin Camp; (13) Hella Hammed/Rapho Guillumette; (14) Charles Gatewood; (15) Ken Heyman; (16) Leonard Freed/Magnum; (17) Paul Conklin/Monkmeyer.

First Edition
987654321
Copyright © 1975 by Random House, Inc.

Library of Congress Cataloging in Publication Data

McKee, Michael R   1938–
  Social problems.

  Includes bibliographies.
  1. Sociology. 2. Social problems. 3. United States—Social conditions. 4. Social psychology. I. Robertson, Ian, joint author. II. Title.
HM51.M198   309.1'73   74-32068
ISBN 0-394-31895-1

Cover illustration: Detail from *The City* by Fernand Léger, courtesy of The Philadelphia Museum of Art, The A. E. Gallatin Collection.

Designed by Meryl Sussman Levavi.

Manufactured in the United States of America.
Composed by American Can Co., Printing Division, Clarinda, Iowa.
Printed and bound by the Kingsport Press, Kingsport, Tennessee.

Preface

In writing this book, we have sought to provide a social problems text that will be pedagogically useful, enjoyable to read, and distinctive. We have attempted to achieve these objectives in a number of ways.

Our treatment is a specifically sociological one; therefore, we have paid due attention to sociological theories and perspectives. We believe that too many social problems texts are atheoretical, leaving the student with some understanding of the scope of current problems but with no tools for the analysis of fresh problems that might arise in later years. Our theoretical approach is a flexible and eclectic one; we do not believe that any single perspective can adequately explain the immense variety of problems faced by American society. We have relied primarily on three theoretical perspectives—social disorganization, value conflict, and deviance—and we have systematically applied one or more of these perspectives, as appropriate, to each problem. Each perspective is carefully outlined in the first chapter and then integrated into the succeeding chapters. In addition, every chapter concludes with a "Theoretical Review," containing a further summary of the relevance of sociological theory to the problem in question.

This text is action-oriented; a social problems text is, in effect, a course on "sociology in action." We have been careful not to treat each problem as merely a catalog of woes—the ultimate purpose of studying social problems is not to define them, nor even to simply understand them, but to be able to seek and evaluate possible solutions. Each chapter, therefore, contains an analysis of various solutions that have been proposed for the problem under discussion.

We have tried to avoid the usual adherence to an institutional analysis of social problems and have attempted to combine an institutional perspective with recognition of the importance of social values and attitudes in the creation and solution of society's problems. We believe that this approach reflects a growing sense among sociologists of the inadequacy of a purely institutional analysis of complex social phenomena.

We have attempted to make the book thoroughly contemporary and relevant, not only by using the most up-to-date sources and research findings, but also by stressing the importance of those "new" problems that are taught in many classrooms but still ignored in many social problems texts: environment and resources, mass media, the life cycle, sex roles, government and corporations, work and alienation.

We have provided a systematic organization for each chapter in the belief that it will greatly help the student to develop a meaningful way of approaching each new problem. Each chapter opens with a section on "The Nature and Scope of the Problem," in which the basic outline of the problem is presented. The next section, entitled "Approaching the Problem," contains theoretical and historical, or other, perspectives that will be of use in substantive analysis. Subsequent sections deal with major aspects of the problem under consideration, and a final section on "Prospects for the Future" surveys likely trends in the problem area and outlines potential solutions.

Finally, we have attempted to provide a text that is easily readable and jargon-free. Pictures, graphs, and tables have been carefully selected for their functional value and are used liberally throughout the book. A number of boxed "interest items" have also been included in each chapter to complement and add relevance to the text, and every chapter contains a list of suggestions for further reading.

We are glad to acknowledge the assistance of Peter Crawshaw, whose wise and insightful comments were particularly appreciated; Alice Mohr, William Feigelman, and Edward McDonagh, who read the entire manuscript and offered many valuable suggestions for improvement; and Jane Ferrar, Julia Hall, Floyd Hammack, Stanford Lyman, Denton Morrison, Edward Sagarin, and Charles Winick, who also read individual chapters and offered useful comments. Naturally, the authors accept full responsibility for any shortcomings that might remain. Some others who contributed their efforts are: Jeanne Carnevale, Mary Dorn, Frank Etch, Deborah Gorenflo, Judi Fox Middleton, Paul Moore, Jim Stemler, Jo Ann Storey, Bob Vincent, and Pat Wahl.

We would also like to thank several people at Random House: Deborah Drier, Walter Kossmann, Mary Schieck, and above all our editor, Linda Baron, whose editorial skills, splendid efficiency, and unfailing good humor have contributed so much to the book.

Contents

part one

Introduction

1

The Sociology of Social Problems

We are a restless society—pioneering social and technological change at a rate unprecedented in human history, torn by conflicts over basic social goals and directions, yet always sustained by the vision of a bright future as the last, best hope of mankind. And we are a society of para-doxes—a nation committed to human equality yet tolerating profound inequalities; a country of spectacular natural beauty, but with the worst pollution problem in the world; a society of high ideals and dedica-tion to peace, but with a long and harsh record of social injustice and violence; a people of unprecedented material affluence for the many, but dire poverty and malnutrition for the few.

This is the stuff of which social problems are made. Our society is often dislocated by the uneven rate of social change; it contains a het-erogeneous population whose differing backgrounds and interests cre-ate fundamental conflicts; and it includes various minorities which, despite their loyalty to the common culture, renounce and deviate from some basic social beliefs and practices. All societies have social prob-lems, but it seems that these basic features of our own society generate problems that are more complex and more numerous than those that most other nations must confront. Yet we are an optimistic people, deeply convinced of our collective ability to resolve our problems and transform our society. As we shall see, the discipline of sociology has contributed significantly to this sense of our capacity to change the so-cial environment, and it continues to contribute to the design of actual plans and programs for change.

THE NATURE OF SOCIAL PROBLEMS

What exactly is a social problem, and how does it differ from other social conditions? Here is a definition:

A social problem exists when a significant number of people, or a number of significant people, perceive an undesirable difference between social ideals and social realities, and believe that this difference can be eliminated by collective action.

This definition actually contains several distinct ideas, and the nature of a social problem will become clearer as we look at each of these ideas more closely.

1. *Social problems involve the subjective perception of an objective condition.*

For a social problem to exist, there must be a real, *objective* condition, such as crime, drug abuse, or government corruption. But the mere existence of such a condition is not enough to make it a social problem. There must also be a *subjective* response in people's minds: they must perceive the condition as presenting a problem. Sometimes a condition can persist for decades or even centuries before it is perceived as a social problem. For example, inequality of opportunity for women has always existed in America, but it is only recently that large numbers of people have subjectively perceived this objective condition as an undesirable one. The combination of the objective condition and the subjective response in this case has made the status of women a social problem in contemporary America. It is likely that many of our social conditions that are not currently perceived as problems will become social problems in the years ahead. Sociologists sometimes attempt to identify these "latent" problems and so to predict the social concerns of the future.

Public perception of a social problem naturally depends to a great extent on the visibility of the condition in question. For this reason, groups that are newly aware of their disadvantaged status often take dramatic action to bring their plight to public attention. Movements such as civil rights, women's liberation, and gay liberation have all attempted to attract public attention by unusual methods, for their adherents realize that unless the situation they complain of is widely perceived as a social problem, no social action will be taken to solve it. The visibility of a social problem depends, too, on the willingness of the mass media to devote publicity to it. The media play an important, agenda-setting function in our society: by focusing on newsworthy actions of aggrieved groups, they increase public awareness of undesirable social conditions. The media in the United States, moreover, do not merely report events; they also engage in commentary and investigative reporting, and so uncover latent social problems that might otherwise have escaped attention. The Watergate affair is one recent example of a condition that was first exposed by the press and that even then might have been forgotten but for constant media coverage. Public opinion often lags behind the exposures of the media, however; it took well over a year of press and TV coverage of Watergate before opinion polls showed that a majority of Americans perceived the reality of government corruption to be a social problem in the United States.

2. *Social problems involve a gap between social ideals and social reality.*

All social problems involve a widespread perception of the difference between the real—what is—and the ideal—what ought to be. The ideals of any society are based on the values and attitudes of its people. *Values* are shared ideas about what is desirable, such as a belief in free speech, the sanctity of marriage, or equal opportunity. *Attitudes* are predispositions to respond favorably or unfavorably toward particular people, events, or situations—such as a feeling of prejudice against an ethnic group, or a benevolent view of the police force. Naturally, values and attitudes vary a great deal through history, among different societies, and among different groups and individuals within a society. Because social values and attitudes are continually changing, the gap between particular social ideals and particular social realities also changes—sometimes closing, sometimes widening—with the result that new social problems emerge and old ones disappear.

The problem of environmental pollution provides an example of how changing values and attitudes contribute to the emergence of a new social problem. There is nothing new about the ravaging of the American environment: it has been an accepted feature of the American scene for almost two hundred years. But social ideals have suddenly leaped ahead of social reality. We are now painfully aware of environmental pollution and take a very unfavorable attitude toward industrial polluters. The result is that environmental pollution, a subject that did not appear in social problems textbooks a few years ago, is now regarded as a critical social problem for American society. The problem of poverty provides another example. In the late forties, about 27 percent of the American people lived below the poverty line, but poverty was commonly perceived as a fact, not as a problem, and social problems textbooks ignored the subject. Today a much lower proportion of the population—about 11 percent—lives below the poverty line, but government has declared a "war on poverty," and the problem is now on the agenda for national action. The social reality of poverty in America is less severe, but our social ideals have changed, and poverty is consequently perceived as a social problem.

On the other hand, some social conditions that were perceived as major problems a few decades ago have become less significant, not because the reality is any different, but because our values and attitudes have accommodated to the reality. For example, premarital sexual activity was regarded as a major problem in the forties and fifties, but today values relating to sexual conduct are less rigid, and attitudes toward premarital sexuality are much more tolerant. The gap between the ideal and the real has closed, and the issue is not considered a social problem to any great extent in the seventies.

Social conditions, then, acquire meaning through people's attitudes and values. Over half the college students in the United States have smoked marijuana. Does this mean that the laws should be made more strict or that they should be repealed? If there is an urban riot, does this mean that we need more law and order or that efforts must be made to redress the grievances that led to the disturbance? The answer to such questions depends on social attitudes and values, which are subject to change in time and which are rarely shared by an entire population. The resulting potential for conflict often makes social problems considerably more difficult to solve.

3. *Social problems must be perceived as problems by a significant number of people or by a number of significant people.*

No matter how undesirable a social condition may seem to a few people, it cannot be regarded as a social problem until it is subjectively perceived as such either by a significant proportion of the population or by a number of people who occupy positions of power and influence in the society. For example, the "desecration" of the Sabbath by Sunday commercial and sports activities is not generally regarded in America as a social problem. Although the practice is repugnant to some people, they are not sufficiently numerous nor do they occupy enough positions of power and influence in society. Society contains many such groups that find some social condition or other undesirable, but unless this attitude is widely shared or is endorsed by influential individuals or groups, the society will not dignify the condition concerned with the status of a social problem.

The history of the development of opposition to the war in Southeast Asia reveals the importance both of significant numbers of people and of numbers of significant people in leading public opinion to perceive a social condition as a social problem and then to confront that problem by collective action. Initially the war was opposed by a very small number of citizens who perceived a gap between the reality of the war and American ideals. The numbers of the protesters gradually grew, and they won more support, but by the mid-sixties opinion polls showed that their view was still rejected by the great majority of Americans. However, around that time a number of people occupying positions of great power and influence started to campaign against the war — people such as congressmen and senators, editors of major newspapers, religious leaders, and heads of commercial corporations who believed the war to be economically damaging. With this new impetus, opposition to the war developed so rapidly that by 1968 President Johnson's reelection was in jeopardy and he withdrew from the campaign. Richard Nixon was able to win election largely on a promise to end a

Power and status are unequally distributed in society. Some individuals have much more influence than others in defining social problems and in determining public policy toward the problems. *(Charles Gatewood)*

war which had been endorsed by most Americans (including himself) only two years previously.

A few highly significant individuals—a president or a pope—can place a "new" social problem before a population in a single speech. Most social problems, however, seep more slowly into the public consciousness as increasing numbers of people define the condition concerned as undesirable and capable of solution.

4. *Social problems must be regarded as capable of solution through collective action.*

A social condition that is believed to be incapable of solution is not regarded as a social problem. All societies experience social conditions that they recognize as undesirable, such as disease, war, or famine. But it is only when people believe that they have the capacity to do something about these conditions that the conditions are regarded as social problems. If the conditions are defined as part of the natural order—an unavoidable feature of earthly existence, an act of God, or an inevitable consequence of the brutish nature of man—then they are not regarded as social problems, and people make no collective effort to change them.

Many of our currently recognized social problems once fell into this category. Mental disorders, for example, were variously attributed to genetic defects, moral deficiencies, or even possession by evil spirits, and so people did not feel that social action could influence the nature, incidence, or distribution of mental disorders in society. Today, on the other hand, it is widely believed that at least some mental disorders result from pressures of the social environment, and so mental disorders are perceived as a social problem that can be confronted by social action. Similarly, poverty was once regarded as natural and inevitable, and the poor were often believed to be shiftless, idle, and entirely responsible for their plight. Today, poverty is seen largely as a consequence of a particular social structure and its system for distributing wealth; people feel that if the appropriate social changes were made, poverty could be alleviated or even eliminated. Consequently poverty is now defined as a social problem capable of solution through collective action.

Collective action may take many forms. In the extreme case, it can involve public demonstrations, violence, or even revolution, but more commonly it involves the efforts of interest groups to inform the public of the issues at stake and to persuade those in positions of authority to make the necessary changes. Sometimes those in authority take the initiative themselves; usually, however, pressure of public opinion is necessary to provoke specific changes. Solutions to social problems are rarely based on any one strategy or approach, but legislative action is often a vital element in the process.

THE SOCIOLOGICAL APPROACH

There are many different ways of looking at social problems. For example, the theologian, the economist, the painter, the psychologist, the novelist, and the political scientist all look at a social problem from the viewpoint of their own disciplines. But because the problems are *social*, it is the sociologist who is primarily concerned with their comprehensive analysis. Sociology is the scientific study of human society; it is the task of the sociologist to make systematic analyses of social behavior. The sociologist may, of course, utilize perspectives and information from other disciplines; historical facts, psychological theories, or economic data may serve to illuminate a particular problem. But ultimately the sociologist analyzes social problems within a framework of theory and research that is distinctively sociological.

All *social* problems fall within the boundaries of the discipline of sociology, even though at first sight they may appear to be purely *individual* in their causation or effects. One of the most important of all sociological insights is that of the relationship between the plight of the apparently isolated individual and the overall social context in which he or she lives. It was one of the founders of modern sociology, Emile

Private troubles and public issues are inextricably linked. The heroin addict's problem may seem purely personal—but it can only be fully understood in terms of social pressures toward addiction and social opportunities for becoming an addict. *(Bob Combs/Rapho Guillumette)*

Durkheim, who first graphically illustrated this connection.[1] Durkheim chose to study suicide, perhaps the most highly individual act of which any person is capable. If someone commits suicide, we tend to seek an explanation in terms of individual psychology—that is, the particular stresses to which the person was subjected and their impact on his or her particular personality. Such an explanation may be adequate for many purposes, but it is not a complete one. Durkheim painstakingly studied suicide statistics for different regions and countries, and found that the incidence of suicide varied between areas and between populations in a consistent fashion over the years. For example, people in urban areas were more likely to commit suicide than people in rural areas; men were more likely to commit suicide than women; Protestants were more likely to commit suicide than Catholics; single people were more likely to commit suicide than people living in family groups. In other words, particular social contexts affect the incidence of suicide. In our society, suicide is disapproved under all circumstances. But among the ancient Romans and among traditional Japanese to this day, institutionalized suicide has been regarded as a highly honorable act in certain circumstances. These social values and attitudes inevitably affect individual behavior. So although an individual suicide may be explained in psychological terms, the total incidence of suicide must be

[1]Emile Durkheim, *Suicide* (Glencoe, Ill.: Free Press, 1964).

explained with reference to the society in which the suicides take place.

The same is true for any other social problem: alcoholism, sexism, violence, crime, variant forms of sexual behavior, overpopulation, or racial discrimination. These problems all affect individuals, but the form they take and their degree of prevalence in a given population varies in relation to the social context in which they occur. As the sociologist C. Wright Mills observed, it is fundamental to the sociological perspective that one should be able to perceive this essential connection between "private troubles" and "public issues."[2]

Basic Concepts in the Study of Society

Social problems occur within the context of society, and in order to analyze these problems it is necessary to understand the basic workings of human society. A *society* is a system of individuals and groups interacting with one another in social relationships. Every society has an underlying pattern of regularities, or *social structure*, which the sociologist can analyze through the use of four basic concepts: *culture, norms, roles,* and *socialization.*

Culture. Each society develops its own distinctive culture. The term signifies all the human products of a society, both material and nonmaterial, such as language, hair styles, philosophy, clothing, government, sex roles, values, art, religion, and modes of transportation. An individual born into a culture normally grows up to take that culture for granted, as part of the "natural" order. He or she tends to view other cultures and their practices as strange, somehow odd, perhaps bizarre, or even "wrong." A fundamental tenet of sociology is that our concept of reality is socially constructed—that is, that we do not all perceive the same universe, but rather, our perceptions are colored by the society in which we happen to live and by our particular position within that society. In the Middle Ages, men "knew" that the earth was flat. Likewise, we "know" that it is round, not because we have conducted personal experiments to discover whether it is flat or round, but because the roundness of the earth is part of the information that our culture provides and that we automatically accept. Within some cultures there are *subcultures,* groups that participate in the overall culture but which have their own distinctive life styles and values as well. Membership in a subculture also colors perception of reality: a subculture of Wall Street stockbrokers probably takes a markedly different view of American reality than a subculture of Chicago Hell's Angels. Most people remain "imprisoned" within the viewpoint of their own culture or subculture and implicitly assume that it is superior to and more "normal" than the viewpoint of other groups. This type of thinking is termed *eth-*

[2]C. Wright Mills, *The Sociological Imagination* (New York: Oxford University Press, 1959).

nocentrism. Ethnocentric attitudes prevent understanding and communication between different groups and often aggravate social problems.

Norms. Every human society constructs its culture out of an infinite range of possibilities that exist in every field, from musical form to clothing styles. While each particular culture includes only a small segment of this infinite range, its members view this segment as appropriate and all the possibilities outside this segment as inappropriate. The judgment of what is appropriate or "correct" is guided by social norms, informal rules that indicate what is to be considered "normal" within the culture or subculture in question. Norms vary a great deal in the degree to which deviance from them is permitted. Some norms are relatively weak, such as saying "hello" when answering the telephone; these are termed *usages.* Other norms are stronger, such as eating with utensils rather than with fingers; these are termed *conventions.* Others are stronger still, such as covering certain parts of the body with clothing in public; these are termed *mores.* The strongest norms of all, such as not having sexual intercourse with close blood relations, are termed *taboos.* Deviance from norms may be penalized by anything from mild social disapproval to reactions of outrage. When important norms are violated by individuals or groups in society—for example, property norms by criminals or chastity norms by prostitutes—the deviations are liable to be defined in the dominant culture as social problems. In such cases the variation in norms between subculture and subculture or between a subculture and the dominant culture may be the source of severe social tensions.

Roles. Within each society, people occupy different roles. A role is simply a set of expected patterns of behavior relating to a specific status or position in society, such as the role of mother, pupil, teacher, president, sick person, or hippie. The norms surrounding a particular role designate the appropriate or "normal" behavior for the person in the specific situation concerned. Thus two people who are assuming the temporary roles of student and professor behave toward one another in a way rather different from the way they would behave if they were occupying other, perhaps less formal, roles—if, for instance, they were volunteers for the same political cause or sat on a jury together. The complex web of interaction in any society or social situation is based on the particular norms and roles that are operating at the time. When social roles are prescribed on the basis of rigid and irrational criteria—such as the allocation of menial roles to people on the basis of their color or sex—severe social problems may result.

Socialization. How does an individual born into a culture learn to abide by the culture's norms and behave appropriately in particular roles? The learning process is termed socialization—a lifelong process through which, day by day, the individual internalizes the norms of the

Socialization is the process by which members of society learn the norms that govern appropriate behavior in that society. The socialization process differs from group to group, depending on many factors such as social class or ethnic group. *(Peter Simon)*

society, taking social customs, attitudes, and values into his or her own developing personality. Man's capacity for socialization is unparalleled in the animal world. The behavior of the lower animals is governed almost entirely by instinct; a worm learns virtually nothing during its life. But at higher levels in the animal kingdom instinct has less and less influence on behavior, and learning becomes more and more important. In the case of man, learning is supremely important, accounting for most human thought and conduct. Apart from a few very basic impulses—for food, sex, and self-preservation—we have virtually no instinctual behavior. Our personalities, behaviors, knowledge, attitudes, and values depend largely on the learning experiences offered by the society into which we are born. Various agencies of socialization—parents, media, peer groups, schools—all operate, deliberately or otherwise, to socialize each individual into the behavior patterns appropriate for his or her particular social location, until this behavior comes to seem "natural" and "normal."

In a large and complex society, with its wide range of subcultures and economic classes, the process and content of socialization vary considerably from individual to individual and from group to group. One important consequence of this differential socialization is that different people in different social locations perceive and experience so-

The Sociological Imagination

It is by means of the sociological perspective that men now hope to grasp what is going on in the world and to understand what is happening in themselves as minute points in the intersection of biography and history within society. In large part, contemporary man's self-conscious view of himself as at least an outsider, if not a permanent stranger, rests upon an absorbed realization of social relativity and of the transformative power of history. The sociological imagination is the most fruitful form of this self-consciousness.

SOURCE: C. Wright Mills, *The Sociological Imagination* (New York: Oxford University Press, 1959).

cial problems in very different ways and in accordance with very different attitudes and values. Thus there may be considerable dispute as to the causes, consequences, and possible solutions of social problems.

C. Wright Mills writes of the scientific understanding of society as "the sociological imagination."[3] To Mills, sociology is a form of greater human awareness, a transcendence of ethnocentrism, a profoundly liberating experience: it enables the individual to comprehend for the first time the social surroundings that he or she had always taken for granted. The sociological imagination enables its possessor to grasp the fact that countless cultural elements and social conditions that seem laws of nature are really laws of man—conditions created by men and women in the past and capable of being modified by men and women now and in the future. Thus social ills are suddenly perceived afresh, as something to be dealt with rather than something to be simply endured.

THEORETICAL PERSPECTIVES ON SOCIAL PROBLEMS

Sociology, like all sciences, includes two interrelated elements, theory and research. Both are essential to the sociological enterprise. Theory without research may become little more than abstract speculation unrelated to the real world, while research without theory can become a collection of almost meaningless facts that resist interpretation. Let us look first at the theoretical perspectives that sociologists use to analyze social problems and then at the basic methods of social problems research.

A theory is essentially a statement that attempts to explain a relationship between two or more concepts or facts, commonly termed *variables*—for example, between suicide and social class. Thus we might

[3]Ibid.

theorize that people who have lost their jobs and cannot find employment might be more likely to commit suicide than people whose status remains constant, because the former group are likely to experience the change as psychologically stressful. A theory that has not been verified by research is termed a *hypothesis;* a hypothesis states a probable but unproven relationship between two or more variables.

Some theories are rather restricted in scope and are merely statements about very specific situations. Other theories are more abstract and serve to orient the sociologist in a much more general way to the problems he is studying by providing an overall perspective on society. Several such theoretical perspectives are available to the sociologist who studies social problems. It is unlikely, however, that any single perspective will be appropriate for all social problems, and therefore two or more approaches will often be used in combination. In general, a sociologist attempting to analyze and interpret a social problem will use one or more of the following three broad perspectives: *social disorganization, value conflict,* and *deviance.*

Social Disorganization

From this theoretical perspective, society is regarded as an organized system whose parts are integrated in an ordered, coherent pattern. Social problems arise when the social system, or some part or parts of it, becomes disorganized, with the result that the system operates less effectively. Thus social disorganization involves the breakdown of the organizational structure; the various elements in society become "out of joint," and the influence of social norms on particular groups or individuals is weakened. The result is that the collective purposes of society are less fully realized than they could be under a different, better organized system. Social disorganization can lead to personal disorganization, such as mental illness, drug abuse, or criminal behavior.

Many theorists working from a social disorganization perspective take a *functionalist* view of society. They regard society as a fairly stable, well-integrated system, based on a general consensus of values and organized in such a way that each part functions to maintain the balance of the system as a whole. Social change tends to be disruptive unless it is relatively slow, because the entire system must adapt slightly in order to accommodate changes in any one of its components. All elements in the social system — such as the schools, the family, the churches, and important values and norms — have ongoing *functions* in preserving social equilibrium. As the functionalist theorist Robert K. Merton has pointed out, these social elements may function in a "manifest" (that is, obvious and recognized) manner or in a "latent" (that is, concealed and unrecognized) manner.[4] Social welfare payments, for

---

[4]Robert K. Merton, "Social Problems and Social Theory," in *Contemporary Social Problems,* 3d ed., eds. Robert K. Merton and Robert Nisbet (New York: Harcourt Brace Jovanovich, 1971), pp. 793–845.

example, have the manifest function of maintaining a substantial section of the community above starvation level, but they may also have the latent function of preventing the crime and civil disturbance that might ensue if the poor had no other source of income. Elements in the social system may also have "anticipated" functions and "unanticipated" functions. The schools, for example, have the anticipated function of educating the young, but they also have the unanticipated function of segregating them from society and so encouraging the development of youth subcultures. Social disorganization and social problems arise when one or more of the elements in the social system fails to meet specified functional requirements and instead produces ongoing *dysfunctions* by disrupting the social equilibrium. Often these dysfunctions result from latent or unanticipated effects of elements that are otherwise functional. Industry, for example, has the manifest and anticipated function of raising living standards, but it is also dysfunctional in that it is polluting the environment and depleting natural resources in a way that was not anticipated — and doing so to such an extent that a major social problem has resulted.

There can be many reasons for social disorganization: norms may break down because of inadequate socialization; the social system may be poorly related to its physical environment; or the social structure may be such that many members are arbitrarily prevented from attaining their goals. Underlying most social disorganization, however, is the phenomenon of rapid social change. The most dramatic examples of social disorganization resulting from rapid social change may be seen when modern technology is introduced into one of the few remaining preliterate communities of the world. For these traditional societies, which have lived for many generations in a comparatively static culture, the sudden impact of technology is usually shattering. The norms, roles, and socialization processes that were once functional for these small communities are now hopelessly inadequate, and severe social disorganization almost inevitably results.

American society is also very vulnerable to social disorganization resulting from rapid change. Not only is our society highly complex and thus more easily disorganized, but furthermore it is changing at a rate probably unprecedented in human history. Anthropologist Margaret Mead argues that the speed of cultural change in the United States is now so great that, in a sense, our parents have no children and our children no parents; so extreme is the discontinuity between the cultures into which each generation is born that they live in what are virtually two different worlds.[5]

Why does change generate social disorganization and social problems? The main reason is that change tends to be uneven, resulting in what the anthropologist William F. Ogburn has termed *culture lag*.[6] Some areas of society change faster than others, with the result that

[5]Margaret Mead, *Culture and Commitment* (New York: Natural History Press, 1970).
[6]William F. Ogburn, *Social Change* (New York: Viking, 1950).

Social Change and Social Problems

Many of our current dilemmas and change "syndromes" result from the fact that we have had more radical transformations of the human condition in the past one hundred years than may have occurred in all recorded history. Within three generations, massive series of scientific, technological, social, and economic changes have impacted one upon the other. Humanity has been thrust into a new world. Those ranges of scale, magnitude, and frequency of change have no reliable historical precedents or guidelines for their assessment and control.

As industrial civilization has expanded in this relatively brief period to encompass the entire planet, so have the problems that threaten human existence. Many of the problems themselves are not new nor are they intrinsically linked to the change processes which have occurred. What is new, and increasingly urgent, is their expanded dimensions. Their sheer size and complexity have, in many cases, been paradoxically compounded by the very measures which man has developed to combat them. By making humanity more secure against hunger and disease, we have added astronomically to our numbers; by shrinking the physical distance between peoples, we have increased the critical and complex interdependence of all human society; by communicating the material possibilities of a better life, we have enormously increased the expectations and demands by all people for access to these possibilities; and by the prodigal exploitation of our physical environs, we have now produced many grave imbalances in our life-sustaining natural environment.

SOURCE: John McHale, *World Facts and Trends,* 2d ed. (New York: Collier Books, 1972).

the parts of the system no longer mesh as a whole. In general, technological changes take place more rapidly than changes in other institutions and in values—humanity accepts new tools more readily than new ideas. Industrialization, for example, has proceeded much faster than the development of social controls over the pollution that industrialization generates—and so we have a social problem. Similarly, while developments in medical science have led to a global population explosion, religious prohibitions of artificial means of birth control have not been modified, nor, in most parts of the world, has there been any change in the traditional favorable attitude toward a large family. In the past, these attitudes were functional in maintaining population numbers; today, however, they are highly dysfunctional and aggravate a serious social problem. Change in some areas, accompanied by fail-ure to change in others, always offers a potential for social problems.

Some social problems may actually stem from the unanticipated re-sults of efforts to solve other problems. The best-known example is Prohibition, which was designed to end alcohol consumption in the United States. In fact, it did little to reduce consumption rates. More serious, however, was its dysfunctional result—that of making potential criminals of millions of citizens and yielding vast profits for organized crime. Another example is the construction of expressways from city centers to the suburbs. Originally designed to solve the problem of traffic congestion, these new roads in fact made it possible for the mid-dle class to desert the city centers and commute to work, thus destroy-ing the tax base of the cities and plunging them into their present state of decay. A more recent example was the 1970 Operation Intercept mounted by the federal government against the smuggling of drugs into the country. The campaign, particularly through its blockade of the border between the United States and Mexico, successfully reduced the amount of marijuana entering the country. However, the resulting sharp rise in the price of available marijuana brought about a highly undesirable consequence: numerous young people who could not buy marijuana switched to heroin, a much more dangerous drug, but one more easily smuggled into the country and more profitable to organized crime. By the time the dysfunctional consequences of the costly opera-tion were perceived and the project abandoned, patterns of drug use had already shifted, and the United States had a much more serious social problem on its hands than before.

The fundamental tenet of the social-disorganization perspective, then, is that society can be regarded as an integrated, coherent organ-ization, but that if for any reason it becomes disorganized, dysfunc-tions may arise and social problems may result.

Value Conflict

This theoretical perspective is based on rather different assumptions. Its basic tenet is that society is composed of many groups and interests that, having different values, are consequently liable to be in continual conflict with one another. Social problems stem from the basic incom-patibility of the interests of the various social groups. Conflict may range in intensity from mere discontent to outright violence. If kept within reasonable limits, however, this conflict is considered beneficial to society, for it is viewed as the mechanism by which needed changes are brought about, thus preventing society from lapsing into organized stagnation.

From the value-conflict perspective, many social problems are cre-ated, aggravated, or maintained by the actions of special interest groups working for their own advantage. Pollution in the United States is much worse than it need be, and the prospects for its effective con-

Because different members of society are socialized into different roles, they view and experience social problems in different ways. Intense value conflicts are consequently a recurring element in the origin and solution of social problems. *(Charles Gatewood)*

trol much diminished, because a number of powerful corporations earn large profits from the production of pollutants or save large sums by not taking antipollution measures. The imposition of restrictions on the use of the noxious chemical DDT was delayed for years as a result of lobbying and political pressure by the manufacturers of the chemical. Cigarette manufacturers have campaigned long and successfully to prevent antitobacco legislation, despite the acknowledged danger that their product poses to the health of tens of millions of Americans. The American Medical Association has spent millions of dollars over many years in its campaigns against national health care programs, even to the extent of pouring money into elections to defeat congressional candidates pledged to programs of socialized medicine. In pursuing their own interests, the physicians have compounded the social problem of unequally distributed and unnecessarily expensive health services.

Why are such value conflicts so common in modern American society? One cause lies in the heterogeneity of the society, which we mentioned earlier; with so many different sets of values in circulation, collisions are inevitable. In a small traditional community, by contrast, there is a considerable degree of consensus on values: people share the same beliefs and interests, and so the potential for conflict is limited. But a complex modern mass society, with its wide spectrum of opinions, occupations, life styles, classes, and minorities, offers great potential for clashes of values and interests. As we have seen, people in different positions in society are socialized differently and therefore experience social problems in different ways. Their attitudes and values depend on such factors of socialization as class, education, income, and personal history. Furthermore, each group is involved in a social problem in a different way; in every conflict there are groups that stand to gain and groups that stand to lose. The potential for conflict is further enhanced by the fact that in a rapidly changing society, values and attitudes may change rapidly also. A group that has long been submissive to discrimination (like blacks, Chicanos, American Indians, homosexuals, or women) may determine in the space of a few years that its disadvantaged status is the result of remediable injustice rather than of unalterable circumstance – and a new social problem emerges.

In addition to the heterogeneity of the society and the rapidity of social change, another major source of value conflicts is social inequality. People simply do not have equal access to power or wealth, and the relative few who do occupy powerful positions have much more influence than the others in defining social norms and values, in determining which social problems warrant a remedy, and in deciding on the appropriate course of action in each case. Like any other group, people in positions of power tend to regard certain groups or values more favorably than others, and these attitudes are reflected in the ordering of social priorities and in the allocation of scarce resources. The positions of authority in American society are those at or near the top of the hierarchy in politics, media, corporations, and government bureaucracies. These positions are generally held by individuals who are male, middle-aged, Protestant, white, of Anglo-Saxon background, and wealthy. These people do not of course act as a "conspiracy" in any sense, but like any other group of individuals who share similar attitudes and values, they tend to take the correctness of their own viewpoints for granted and to assign priority to their own interests. Their interests, however, may frequently conflict with those of subordinate groups, whose members have been socialized into different values, though they lack the influence to make these values affect social policy. Seeing their interests ignored, and powerless to do anything about it, the subordinate groups may then become deeply discontented and resentful.

Sociologists who take a value-conflict perspective on social problems often reject the social-disorganization approach, with its functionalist emphasis. They point out that an element in society which is functional for one group, or even for overall social stability, may be highly dysfunctional for another, less privileged group, and they question whether social organization is preferable to social disorganization under all circumstances, since an effective organization may also be an unjust one. In short, the functionalist perspective, with its central concern for overall social stability, is sometimes criticized as an inherently conservative approach. Other sociologists, however, take a flexible, nondoctrinaire approach; they are willing to adopt either perspective, or a combination of the two, depending on the social problem under consideration. The problem of environmental pollution, for example, may be seen as involving both value conflict (between polluters and environmentalists) and social disorganization (resulting from a lack of effective social controls over pollution).

The value-conflict perspective, then, regards the differing values and interests of various groups as the basis for social problems. Conflict is seen as inevitable and often as a necessary impetus for desirable social change.

Deviance

From the deviance perspective, some social problems are regarded as the consequence of behavior that departs significantly from important social norms. Deviance becomes a social problem because most people, having internalized the dominant norms, experience deviant behavior as repugnant and threatening—as an affront to their values and even as a danger to the continuing stability of society.

Earlier in the century, sociologists tended to blame deviants for most social problems. Deviance was believed to be an intrinsic attribute of the deviants themselves—there was something "wrong" with them. This was a rather ethnocentric notion, however, for it took the values, attitudes, and norms of the middle-class America of the time for granted, as unquestionable absolutes, and then viewed any deviation from them as "sick," or pathological. This attitude, according to which the deviant is held largely responsible for some "abnormal" condition that generates social problems, remains to this day the dominant one in the popular mind. It is less common among modern sociologists, though it still reappears occasionally. One modern book on social problems, for example, offers the following explanation of social problems in such varied fields as sexuality, the media, and politics:

> Persons who have a deviant personality organization . . . are maladjusted people whose neurotic compulsions, enthusiasms, hates, and determination involve them deeply in social problem situations. Such people, with their fanaticism, help to create social problems. . . .

> Young unmarried men and women, students and clerks, aspiring musicians, writers, and artists dwell in the shabbiness of nondescript rooming-houses where landlords are unconcerned about the informal sleeping arrangements of many of their tenants. These practically nameless young people make a fetish out of being emancipated. . . . For weeks or months or years they dwell in a world apart. Theirs is a way of life foreign and almost unbelievable to outsiders. . . .

There are deviant persons who are somewhat of a nuisance — those who write crank letters to the editor, and who pester radio stations with complaints and demands. . . . Occasionally, a deviant person will secure control of a newspaper or radio station and seek to use it to promote his intemperate views. . . . In the newspaper world, the neuroticism of an owner, or of a columnist, probably accounts for some of the more notorious abuses of press responsibility. . . .

Most extremists are deviants. Most extremists show a fanatical preoccupation with their "cause," a suspicious distrust of other people in general, a disinterest in normal pursuits, recreations, and small talk, and a strong tendency to divide other people into enemies and allies. These are symptoms of an unhappy, neurotic personality.[7]

The problem with this approach is that behavior that seems deviant in one context may be perfectly normal, acceptable, and appropriate in another. Indeed, any group's way of life may, and often will, seem "unbelievable to outsiders." The authors of the above quotations obviously place a high value on "normal pursuits," on "small talk," on formal sleeping arrangements, on "temperate" views (which they implicitly equate with their own), and on an unwillingness to pester radio stations with complaints. But millions of other Americans might regard these very attitudes as deviations from their own norms, as intolerant expressions of an "uptight" mentality. Accordingly, most sociologists are careful to use the term "deviant" in a strictly neutral way to refer to individuals, groups, or situations that do not conform to specified social norms, usually (but not necessarily) those of the dominant culture. Used in this way, the term does not carry any moral judgment as to whether either the established or the deviant norm is "right" or "wrong."

Sociologist Robert K. Merton, who adopts this approach, has developed an influential account of deviance in terms of *anomie* — that is, a situation in which dominant norms cease to be meaningful or effective.[8] In his view, deviance results from a discrepancy between socially approved goals and socially approved means of achieving them. For example, we have a socially approved goal of becoming rich, but not everyone has access to socially approved means of doing so. If a person deprived of such means should still embrace the goal but cease to care about conforming to norms regarding proper or lawful behavior — that is, if he is anomic — then the person may pursue the goal by methods that are disapproved of or even criminal. Much deviance is thus related to the established values of society: in America we place an extremely high value on private property, but we are thereby inviting a correspondingly high crime rate among people who have internalized the social value of the desirability of property but have rejected

[7]Paul B. Horton and Gerald R. Leslie, *The Sociology of Social Problems,* 4th ed. (New York: Appleton-Century-Crofts, 1970), pp. 37, 443, 478, 591.
[8]Robert K. Merton, *Social Theory and Social Structure,* 2d ed. (New York: Free Press, 1968), pp. 184–248.

the social norms specifying the legitimate means of acquiring property. Other forms of deviance, according to Merton, are generated in the same way.

Another extremely influential view is that deviance is not a characteristic of "deviants" but rather a *label* which one group applies to another. Howard S. Becker, one of the main proponents of the labeling theory, claims that the deviant is simply someone to whom the label of "deviant" has been successfully applied.[9] In his view, there is no such thing as deviance as such, since everyone is a deviant from someone else's norms and values: it just depends on whose vantage point you take. In general, however, the vantage point is that of the dominant culture rather than that of a particular subculture. The dominant culture's view of marijuana use, for example, is that it is a social problem caused by deviant drug users. From the point of view of the marijuana smokers, on the other hand, the social problem is that other people have defined them as a problem. Similarly, pornography and prostitution are usually defined as social problems of sexual deviance, while from the viewpoint of pornographers, prostitutes, and their customers, the problem is that other people are imposing their values on them. When in the nineteenth century the Mormons in Utah officially practiced polygamy, this deviation from monogamous norms was seen as a grave social problem. But to the Mormons, the real social problem was the attitude of the rest of society toward the Mormon family structure.

The deviance perspective, then, whether it assigns values or not, views many social problems as the result of deviation from established social norms. While there are not many sociologists who remain loyal to the traditional ethnocentric notion of deviance, neither are there many who could endorse without reservation the extreme relativism of Becker's labeling theory. The deviance perspective is often found in combination with the social-disorganization perspective or the value-conflict perspective. Most sociologists would acknowledge that some degree of deviance is functional to society; it provides the opportunity to reassert social values through negative sanctions and so to define the limits of what is acceptable. But few would deny that other forms of deviance, such as violence and crime, present serious social problems.

RESEARCH ON SOCIAL PROBLEMS

Theories about the origins, consequences, and solutions of social problems are of little use without facts. The sociologist uses research both to gather facts and to test hypotheses to determine whether they fit the facts. As more facts come to light, theories can be further refined, and as theories are refined, research findings can be further illuminated.

[9]Howard S. Becker, *Outsiders* (New York: Free Press, 1964).

Research Methods

Research in sociology generally uses one of three methods. Each method has its own advantages and disadvantages, and each is more appropriate for some problems than for others. Often two or even all three methods can be applied to the same problem, for, like the theoretical perspectives, they are not necessarily mutually exclusive. The three research methods are the case study, the sample survey, and the experiment.

The case study. A case study involves the intensive examination of a particular individual, group, or situation over a period of time. The researcher closely studies the subject, often as a participant observer, and maintains careful records of significant events and observations. He or she may conduct long, probing interviews with selected individuals whose attitudes, values, and experiences might throw light on the problem. The researcher then analyzes the data and draws certain conclusions, which are intended to apply to other, similar cases as well. For example, in a study on racial discrimination, a single high school in the process of racial integration may be selected as the case study. The researcher will collect statistics, interview students, parents, teachers, administrators, and local politicians, and, if possible, do some observing in the school itself. Finally, in the report, the researcher will provide a history of the integration effort, an account of the attitudes and effects it generated, and a theoretical analysis of the findings, touching upon the matters of school integration and racial discrimination in general.

The case-study method has the significant advantage that it can inexpensively provide rich insights and "real-life" information that other techniques may overlook. However, the method also has a number of disadvantages. One is that it relies very heavily on the insights and sensitivity of the particular researcher concerned, and it is therefore subject to distortions introduced by his or her conscious or unconscious bias. Another disadvantage is that the findings from a single study, or even a few selected studies, are usually an inadequate basis for proving anything; the cases may have been exceptional, and therefore generalizations are not necessarily valid. The findings of case studies can be used, however, to formulate hypotheses about the general problem in question, after which the hypotheses can be tested more rigorously by other methods.

The sample survey. In the sample survey, a representative group of people is chosen from a particular "population" — a school, an ethnic or occupational group, or even the whole nation. If the people who are included in the survey are chosen by careful statistical methods, their responses can be used as a valid indication of the attitudes of the entire group in question. The subjects in the survey may be given relatively brief interviews, or they may be asked to complete questionnaires about a particular topic. The information from these surveys may then be fed into a computer and various correlations established between particular items — say, educational background and degree of social mobility. Thus in the case of a social problem such as racism, it might be possible to establish the kinds of attitude which particular populations have toward particular minority groups and also to establish what the correlates of these attitudes are — income, years of schooling, age, attitudes toward other ethnic groups, and so on.

The sample survey is not as useful as the case study for the penetrating analysis of social problems, and it can be relatively expensive to conduct, but it is an indispensable source of information and data on social behavior, values, and attitudes. The method is also especially valuable for measuring changes in these variables over a period of time, as the questionnaires or interviews can be repeated at intervals.

The experiment. The experimental method provides the opportunity for a carefully controlled examination of the relationship between two variables. In order to achieve this, one variable is kept constant while the other is varied; any changes in the constant variable can then be explained in terms of a cause-and-effect process. If, for example, we want to check the effects of different sources of information on people's political attitudes, we may take three groups, each similar in all significant respects, and present the first group with political information on a TV screen, the second group with the same information on a radio, and the third group with the same information in a newspaper. The groups can then be tested afterwards to see to what extent their attitudes now differ. By varying the sources of information, we are able to establish which type of medium is the most effective in changing attitudes, other things being equal.

A basic technique of the experimental method is to have two groups of subjects, one of which, the "experimental" group, is subjected to the experiment, while the other group, the "control" group, is not subjected to the experiment but is otherwise similar to the experimental group in all significant respects. Thus we might show a film on racism to the experimental group but not the control group and then give both groups a questionnaire to establish their racial attitudes. If the attitudes of the group that has seen the film differ significantly from the attitudes of the group that has not seen the film, we are then justified in concluding that the film was responsible for the change of attitude.

The experimental method is especially valuable in that it allows a controlled scientific analysis of problems that cannot be adequately studied in the course of everyday life, where so many other influences intervene that might distort the processes involved. But the method is useful only for rather narrowly defined issues. And there is always the possibility that people may behave rather differently in the real world than in the social scientist's laboratory.

The Problem of Bias

The sociologist is profoundly aware of how attitudes, values, and norms change with time, and he or she will accordingly take a much more critical and detached view of the values of any group than the members themselves will take. To the individual members concerned, their norms and values are often unquestioned absolutes. But to the sociologist, they are merely responses to a particular set of social conditions and are therefore relative. The sociologist is all too well aware of how new, fashionable values fail to stand the test of time, of how the current, established norms of one era become the outworn myths of the next, and of how the heresies of today become the truisms of tomorrow.

Yet paradoxically, this critical detachment often opens the sociologist to the charge of bias. If the sociologist's conclusions support the established view, the charge of bias is rarely made, for most people take this view for granted: the established view is by definition "correct." But if the sociologist's findings lead toward a different view, a view which does not support the interests of the dominant culture, he or she is likely to be accused of bias. Howard S. Becker, the proponent of the labeling theory of deviance, speaks of a "hierarchy of credibility":

> We provoke the suspicion that we are biased in favor of the subordinate parties . . . when we tell the story from their point of view. . . . We provoke this charge when we assume, for the purposes of our research, that subordinates have as much right to be heard as superordinates, that they are as likely to be telling the truth as they see it as superordinates, that what they say about the situation has a right to be investigated and have its truth or falsity established, even though responsible officials assure us that it is unnecessary because the charges are false.
>
> We can use the notion of a *hierarchy of credibility* to understand this phenomenon. In any system of ranked groups, participants take it as given that members of the highest group have the right to define things the way they really are. . . . Therefore, from the point of view of the well-socialized participant in the system, any tale told by those at the top intrinsically deserves to be regarded as the most credible account obtainable. . . . We are, if we are proper members of the group, morally bound to accept the definition imposed on reality by a superordinate group in preference to the definitions espoused by subordinates.[10]

In applying theories and research methods, the sociologist also encounters the problem of personal bias on his own part. Like everyone else, the sociologist's attitudes and values are influenced by the time and place in which he or she happens to live; sociologists are not exempt from socialization. Can the sociologist avoid unconscious bias?

[10]Howard S. Becker, "Whose Side Are We On?" *Social Problems* (Winter 1967).

The Sociologist

. . . a person intensively, endlessly, shamelessly interested in the doings of men. His natural habitat is all the human gathering places of the world, wherever men come together. . . . His consuming interest remains in the world of men, their institutions, their history, their passions. And since he is interested in men, nothing that men do can be altogether tedious for him. . . . Nobility and degradation, power and obscurity, intelligence and folly—these are equally interesting to him, however unequal they may be in his personal values and tastes. Thus his questions will lead him to all levels of society, the best and the least known places, the most respected and the most despised.

SOURCE: Peter Berger, *Invitation to Sociology: A Humanistic Perspective* (New York: Doubleday, 1963).

At present there is no general consensus among sociologists on this point. Most sociologists, however, believe that absolute objectivity is not possible. No matter how scrupulously detached the sociologist tries to be, some unconscious values and assumptions will intrude into research and theorizing. Personal values might determine, for example, what subjects the sociologist chooses to investigate, which theoretical perspectives will be used to analyze them, and how the findings will be evaluated. Some sociologists, in fact, argue that no attempt should be made to eliminate bias and that the social scientist should make definite value judgments and conduct research in accordance with his or her personal values and social commitments. However, the majority of sociologists probably reject this view, and consider that so long as the sociologist abides by three basic rules, research will be guarded against gross distortions of reality. First, the sociologist must make every effort to be aware of his or her own personal biases and to exclude them from research if necessary. Second, the sociologist must rigorously distinguish between fact and opinion in research. And third, the sociologist must make his or her research methods, data, and findings available for the critical scrutiny of the public and other members of the profession so that the work can be meticulously checked and the experiments repeated by other investigators to see if they get the same results.

FURTHER READING

Becker, Howard S., *Outsiders: Studies in the Sociology of Deviance*, 1963. Becker presents a series of studies of different kinds of "deviance." In each case his analysis is based on the "labeling" theory—that deviance is not so much a characteristic of the people in question as a social process by which some individuals are labeled as deviant by others.

Berger, Peter L., *Invitation to Sociology: A Humanistic Perspective*, 1963. A short and elegantly written introduction to sociology. The book includes an absorbing analysis of what Berger terms "the sociological perspective."

Glaser, Daniel, *Social Deviance*, 1971. A brief treatment of some of the main forms of deviance in the United States, with an analysis of their origins and the social mechanisms for their control.

Horowitz, Irving L., ed., *Society*. A useful journal containing highly readable articles on a variety of sociological topics, including many social problems. It provides an up-to-date means of complementing texts and other course materials.

Huff, Darrell and Irving Geis, *How to Lie With Statistics*, 1954. A readable little volume on the use and misuse of statistics. Huff and Geis alert the reader to the many ways in which statistics can be misleadingly presented or interpreted.

Lemert, Edwin M., *Human Deviance, Social Problems, and Social Control*, 1972. A stimulating discussion of various forms of social deviance by a leading social problems theorist.

Mead, Margaret, *Culture and Commitment*, 1970. A famous anthropologist examines the impact of rapid technological change on modern society. She places particular emphasis on generational conflict: each generation is socialized into a very different world, she argues, so that the old have little to teach the young.

Merton, Robert K., "Social Problems and Social Theory," in *Contemporary Social Problems*, eds. Robert K. Merton and Robert Nisbet, 3d ed., 1971. A sophisticated theoretical discussion of social problems from a functionalist perspective.

Mills, C. Wright, *The Sociological Imagination*, 1967. A book written from a conflict perspective, which has become a classic introduction to sociology. Mills analyzes the distinctive nature of the "sociological imagination" and also elaborates the connection between "private troubles" and "public issues." There is included a "behind the scenes" account of precisely how the sociologist goes about his or her work.

Spear, Mary Eleanor, *Plotting Statistics*, 1969. A short and clearly written account of charts and graphs and how to interpret them.

Toffler, Alvin, *Future Shock*, 1969. Toffler argues that the pace of social change is now almost beyond our comprehension and is resulting in increasing anomie and social disorganization. He offers a number of suggestions for coping with these problems.

U.S. Bureau of the Budget, *Statistical Abstract of the United States*, published annually by the U.S. Department of Commerce. Contains a great deal of easily accessible data on many aspects of American society. The abstract is a very useful source of statistics on a variety of social problems.

part two

Society in Transition

Social change has always been a central force in society. The very discipline of sociology grew out of the efforts of nineteenth-century thinkers to understand the various changes that were disrupting society in that period. For many generations prior to that time, the social world was almost static. There were changes, of course, but they were few in number and took place over decades, if not centuries. The Industrial Revolution shattered forever the old, secure order and thrust industrial nations into a world of rapid and incessant change. Our ancestors expected that their children would inhabit much the same world as their grandparents; they regarded change as abnormal, as an unwelcome interruption of a stable existence. Today we accept change as an inevitable fact of life; we take for granted the continuous changes in our environment and hardly dare speculate about the kind of world our children will grow up in.

Contemporary sociologists generally agree that ours is a society in transition, but there is no consensus on the kind of society we are becoming. There is not even agreement on what terms to use in describing our society. Some sociologists call it "post-modern," some refer to it as "post-industrial" or "post-capitalist," and others call it "techno-tronic." The rapid change that characterizes the modern nations can, however, be traced back to the emergence of the industrial system, vastly increased living standards, and the transition from predominantly rural to predominantly urban influence. The rapidly changing modern industrial state offers many advantages compared to life in some traditional communities, but a society in transition is also characterized by many social problems that are not found to a significant extent in more static societies. In this section, we examine some of these problems.

Population growth is one such problem. Changes in living standards and advances in medical knowledge have generated a population problem that has overtaken us so rapidly that many people still do not recognize the issue as a problem at all—although many other observers believe that overpopulation may be the doom of our species.

The ravaging of the environment and the depletion of resources is another social problem of which we have only recently become aware —even though the United States has long been the main culprit in this process. Our industrial system demands an ever-increasing supply of natural resources and generates an even greater amount of pollution. There is an intrinsic tension between our desire for a high level of consumption and our hope for an unspoiled environment.

The city is another relatively recent historical phenomenon. Large-scale urbanization is based upon sophisticated technology that frees most of the population from agricultural toil. But the modern environment has generated a host of new social problems, and these problems have been aggravated by yet another social trend—the flight of the American middle class and its tax money to the affluent suburbs.

One of the most important consequences of mass literacy and new communications technology has been the emergence of the mass media —now a major agency of socialization, an important transmitter of information, and a crucial influence on public opinion. The implications of the emergence, content, and current organization of the mass media are not yet fully understood, and they are controversial.

The nature of work is also changing. Conditions of work have improved radically in the United States during the course of the last century, yet the workers often seem alienated—that is, they draw no identity from their occupations, and they experience this significant part of their lives as oppressive or meaningless. In a society whose economy is founded on a "work ethic," this development is highly problematic.

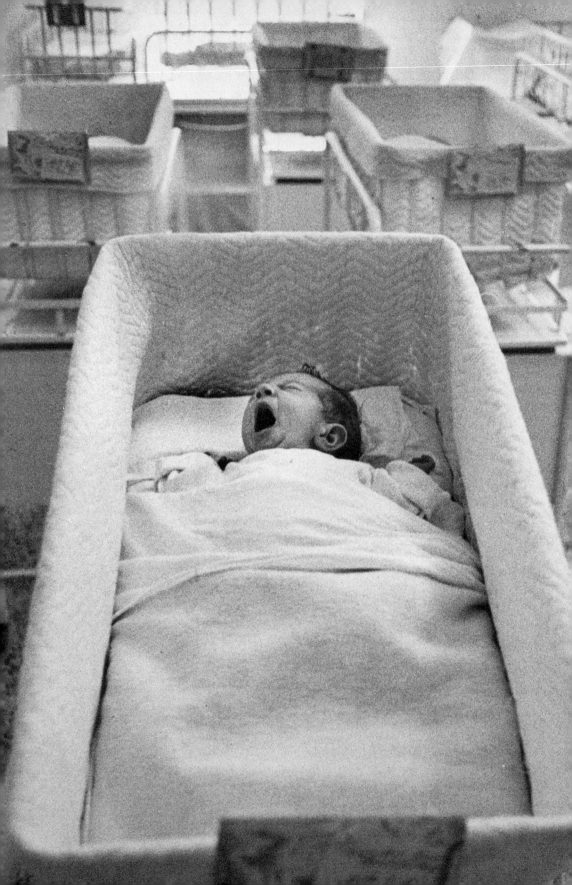

2

Population

THE NATURE AND SCOPE OF THE PROBLEM

In approximately the time it takes you to read this sentence, four people, most of them children, will die of starvation. There are some 3.8 billion people on earth. About 2 billion of these are malnourished or undernourished, and they are currently starving to death at the rate of about 10 million each year. The number of the underfed is rising, both relatively and absolutely, and the death rate from famines is expected to reach tens of millions each year before the end of this century. The problem is that the earth's human population is growing at an unprecedented rate — it is actually doubling itself every thirty-five years. One out of every twenty humans who has ever lived is alive today, and many doubt that our planet has the resources to support such a population. If the present rate of increase were to be maintained, there would be a hundred people for every square yard of the earth's surface within nine hundred years. Obviously, the limited capacity of the planet to support an indefinitely expanding human population will put a catastrophic stop to population growth long before that point.[1]

Rapid population growth is one of the most urgent social problems of the twentieth century. There can be no question that, unless expansion is checked, our standards of living and our very way of life are liable to

[1]See Henry Borgstrom, "The Dual Challenge of Health and Hunger," *PRB*, selection no. 31 (Washington, D. C.: The Population Reference Bureau); Shirley F. Hartley, *Population Quantity Versus Quality* (Englewood Cliffs, N.J.: Prentice-Hall, 1972), pp. 106–142.

a fundamental and unwelcome change. Many experts believe it may already be too late to avert a catastrophe. Their pessimism stems from the fact that the population problem, to a greater extent than most other social problems, is certain to grow more serious the longer we wait to take effective action. Even if we applied drastic methods now and achieved a planetary growth rate of zero, the present population would continue to expand for at least one generation as today's children matured and reproduced. Moreover, the effects of population growth can be more serious, far-reaching, and irrevocable than those of most other social problems. As we shall see, the consequences touch directly or indirectly on practically every aspect of personal and social life.

Yet, paradoxically, one of the most serious obstacles to solving the problem of population growth is the fact that many people simply do not perceive the issue as a problem at all.

Differing Attitudes Toward Population Growth

To some people in the United States, and to many governments abroad, the population problem just does not exist. Their reasons are many, but these are some of the more recurrent ones:

Values. Throughout history, large families and growing tribes have been regarded as a fundamentally good thing, and it is difficult for societies to change their value orientations in the course of a few decades. Social customs in many parts of the world encourage early marriage, regard a large family as an economic asset, and stress the domestic role of women as mother and child-rearer. Moreover, human reproduction and family size have traditionally been regarded as a private affair and the prerogative of the family. Any suggestion of interference tends to be resisted as an invasion of liberty and privacy.

Nationalist feelings. Many nations or ethnic groups believe that their military strength or influence is enhanced by a large population. Some countries even regard themselves as underpopulated and fail to see their situation in a global context. This is particularly true of the less developed countries in the third world. Argentina, for example, is attempting in the supposed interests of economic growth to double its population by the end of the century, and early in 1974 the government issued a decree to restrict the use of contraceptives. In the overpopulated and desperately poor country of Bangla Desh, the first minister of family planning was a father of eighteen children who was opposed to family planning in principle. His first official act was to curtail family planning programs. Many citizens of Bangla Desh feel that their country can only be secure if it has as many people as China—a country with sixty-seven times the land area and incomparably greater natural resources. At present Bangla Desh budgets only six cents per person per year for family planning activities in a program calculated to reach about 1 percent of the population.[2]

Religious objections. Attitudes to population growth and birth control are often affected by religious values. Several religions have traditionally objected to sex for pleasure rather than procreation, and both governments and populations are influenced by these religious precepts. The Roman Catholic church, which is influential in many overpopulated areas, has historically been opposed to both contraception and abortion.[3] In the Middle East and North Africa, the Islamic religion often tends to be opposed to birth control, and there is opposition to family planning in several traditionalist Arab societies. "To have many children is to be blessed by Allah," an old proverb runs. Hinduism and Buddhism, however, are generally noncommittal on the subject and are not doctrinally opposed to birth control.

Preoccupation with other problems. It is all too easy to overlook possible indirect effects of rapid population growth, for they do not come labeled as such. They may appear, rather, as poverty, unemployment, illiteracy, disease, crime, or other social problems that are perhaps more readily identified. In their concern for these immediate and more visible problems, people may fail to see the significance of anything so distant and abstract as world population trends. In particular, many citizens of economically developed countries see little connection between their own population structures, which may sustain high standards of living, and the plight of millions elsewhere in the world. Politicians, too, often tend to think in terms of immediate results and the next election—there are few votes and little popularity to be gained by designing policies for the next generation, let alone the next century—and so population growth is placed low on the agenda of national priorities.

Population Growth: A Glimpse of the Future

The general public has seemed so unconcerned about population growth that when writers in the fifties and sixties became convinced of the gravity of the problem, they often adopted a "doomsday" approach in order to alert popular attention. The titles of their books are suggestive: *Standing Room Only, Our Crowded Planet, The Challenge to Man's Future, The Population Bomb.*[4]

Isaac Asimov has calculated that at current rates of increase the total mass of the human population would equal the mass of the earth by

[2]"World Environment Newsletter," *World* (May 8, 1973), p. 38.
[3]"Birth Control Blues," *Time* (February 4, 1974), p. 54. There is current disagreement among members of the Roman Catholic church on the question of contraception. Surveys indicate that 60 to 75 percent of U.S. priests and laity do not consider artificial birth control sinful.
[4]Karl Sax, *Standing Room Only: The World's Exploding Population* (Boston: Beacon Press, 1960); Fairfield Osborn, ed., *Our Crowded Planet: Essays on the Pressures of Overpopulation* (New York: Doubleday, 1962); Harrison Brown, *The Challenge to Man's Future* (New York: Viking, 1954); Paul R. Ehrlich, *The Population Bomb* (New York: Ballantine Books, 1968).

Overpopulation—The Wrong Problem?

Some social scientists believe that the focus on "overpopulation" is misdirected; instead, we should concentrate on how our resources are distributed among nations and people. Otto Fredrich states: "children are not just transients in the world's boarding-house, to be welcomed or turned away at the convenience of the older boarders. And if it is true that every newborn child should have a right to its share of food, it is also true that those who control the food supply should think twice before declaring that they no longer have enough for strangers and newcomers. In other words, the essence of the population problem—so far, at least—is not that mankind has propagated too many children but that it has failed to organize a world in which they can grow in peace and prosperity. Rich nations and poor alike have grossly misused the world's resources, both material and intellectual; neglected them, wasted them, and fought each other over how to share them. Thus the basic question is not how many people can share the earth, but whether they can devise the means of sharing it at all."

SOURCE: Otto Fredrich, "Population Explosion: Is Man Really Doomed?" *Time* (September 13, 1971).

3530 A.D. and the mass of the entire universe by 6826 A.D.[5] What, he asks, are the outside limits of population that we can realistically reach? Since the life-sustaining capacity of the earth is limited by the amount of sunlight available to plants, and since the limit of animal life is determined by the availability of plant food, he hypothesizes a situation in which the entire planet is fully occupied by humans and their plant food. All other animals are extinct, and the only remaining plant is that which can be consumed in its entirety by man—single-celled algae. The algae in turn feed on human wastes and finely chopped human corpses. Under these circumstances (and ignoring *all* other factors) the earth could theoretically support a population of 40 trillion, or about 200,000 persons per square mile. He calculates that we will reach that number by 2436 A.D., less than five hundred years from now.

These calculations do not take into account other factors such as energy requirements, pollution, or the increasing breakdown of social structure that might result from the progressively more intense crowding of people into less and less space.[6] Cities are growing even faster than total population; and crowding has been implicated as a possible factor in some forms of social disorganization. Many writers such as

[5]Isaac Asimov, "The End," *Penthouse Magazine*, vol. 2, no. 5 (January 1971), pp. 26–28, 56.
[6]See Chapter 4, "Cities," for population distribution and density; see Chapter 3, "Environment," for a more complete treatment of environmental factors.

Paul Ehrlich believe that, given the current rate of population increase, the human species has only about one generation to stop the growth in population. This would be very fast action under even the most favorable conditions — and conditions are far from favorable.

APPROACHING THE PROBLEM

There are several pitfalls to avoid in any study of the population problem. One is that we may become so obsessed with gloomy predictions that we feel the situation is hopeless and make no effort to resolve the problem. The danger here is that this attitude may become a self-fulfilling prophecy — that is, people may believe in the prediction so much that they act as if it were already proved valid. By doing so, they unconsciously assure that it *does* become valid.

A second pitfall is that we may react too optimistically, believing that somehow the issue is a false alarm and that the danger will miraculously fade. There are many experts who believe that future scientific and technological developments will provide a means of sustaining a large human population at a reasonable standard of living. These hopes may prove well founded — but they also may not, and it would be unwise to place too much confidence in them.

A third pitfall is that we may tend to narrow our focus to the question: "How many people can the earth support?" This is an important question. But it implies that our goal is to grow to the maximum number that our planet can sustain at a minimum level of subsistence. We might instead ask, "What size of population is compatible with an acceptable standard of living?" The quality of life may, at least temporarily, have to be regarded as secondary to the issue of survival, but it should not cease to be our ultimate concern.

The Elements of Population Growth

Demography is the study of the size, composition, growth rates, and distribution of populations. It provides a way of looking at the dynamics and history of population growth: how it came about, what variables affect it, and how much an understanding of the past and present can help us in predicting and guiding the future. Accurate information on population trends is important to many aspects of planning in modern societies, and the demographer is trained to assemble the relevant statistics, explain them, compare them, and then make projections. Recently one of the more important demographic concerns has been population growth — how and why rapid population growth has occurred, and what techniques might be employed to control it.

The two most important variables directly affecting population are *birth rate* and *death rate*. (A third factor, *migration rate,* may also be significant in specific populations.) These rates are expressed in statistical measures: the crude birth rate is the number of births per year per thousand members of the population: the crude death rate is the number of deaths per year per thousand members of the population. The *growth rate* of a population, representing births minus deaths, is usually expressed as an annual percentage.

By applying these measures to a particular country, we can gain an idea of its demographic structure and trends. For example, India in 1973 had a birth rate of 42 per thousand, a death rate of 17 per thousand, and an annual growth rate of 2.5 percent. The United States, in contrast, had a relatively low birth rate of 15.6, a death rate of 9.4, and a growth rate of only 0.8 percent. A few parts of Europe actually have a negative growth rate, meaning that their population is shrinking rather than expanding.[7]

In fact, there are striking and consistent differences between the population growth rates of the developed and the developing countries of the world. The low birth rates — those below 20 — are found exclusively in the developed areas of North America, Europe, and Japan. Birth rates over 35 are characteristic of the large developing nations, with the smaller nations of Africa, Asia, and Latin America somewhere in between.

A useful concept in the analysis of population growth is that of *doubling time* — the number of years required for a given population to double its size. Until recently, doubling time has been a matter of centuries. Today, in most nations, it takes less than a single lifetime. Demographers have made rough estimates of the population of the human species at various points in history. For example, during the Stone Age, when man was hunting and foraging for subsistence, the total human population was probably not more than 10 million. By the beginning of the Christian era, however, the number had grown to about 250 million, with a growth rate of about 0.6 percent. A thousand years later, the total population was about 300 million, and by 1650 it had risen to half a billion. In the two centuries to 1850, it doubled to a billion. The next doubling, to the 2 billion mark, took only eighty years and was completed around 1930. The current doubling to 4 billion is almost complete in less than fifty years. If present rates continue, the next doubling will take thirty-five years. This rapid growth rate means that by the year 2000, within the lifetime of many readers of this book, the earth will be supporting a population of approximately 7 billion: close to three times as many as when most of these readers were born.[8]

Why is population growth accelerating in this way? Increased birth rates over death rates are part of the answer, but there is another factor as well. Suppose we had a population of 10,000, increasing at 3 percent per year. In ten years the population would have increased, not by 30 percent to 13,000, but by about 34 percent, to 13,400. The increase in each year is not 3 percent of the original total, but 3 percent

[7]Figures taken from the *1973 World Population Data Sheet* (Washington, D.C.: The Population Reference Bureau, 1973).

[8]Rufus E. Miles, Jr., "Man's Population Predicament," *The Population Bulletin*, vol. 26, no. 2 (April 1971), p. 5.

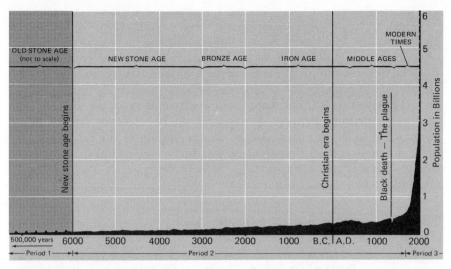

Population through history. "What conclusion would you draw if you observed a population curve similar to that of man in any other organism? We would be terrified. In fact, there is no doubt that we would instantly summon every control measure from 1080 to the Bomb to save the globe from being eaten alive." (Paul B. Sears, as quoted in Robert Rienow and Leona Rienow, *Moment in the Sun* [New York: Ballantine Books, 1967], p. 118.) (GRAPH SOURCE: Population Reference Bureau, Inc., "How Many People Have Ever Lived on Earth?" *The Population Bulletin,* vol. 18, no. 1 [February 1962], p. 5.)

of the *new* total. The number of people added each year at a constant rate of increase is therefore greater than the number added the year before. Thus a population with a 3 percent growth rate will double itself in twenty-three years. At 2 percent—the current world rate—it will double itself in thirty-five years. And even at 1 percent—slightly more than the present U.S. rate—a population will double in seventy years.

It follows that population growth cannot be instantly stopped, any more than a speeding car stops as soon as one puts on the brakes. Even if we could ensure that from this moment on, parents would have only enough children to replace their own generation, all the children who are not yet parents would still bear their own offspring before the momentum of growth would cease. This fact is one basis for the urgent mood among advocates of population control. Given the best efforts and most effective programs we can devise, world population is virtually certain to reach at least 7 billion, and might easily go as high as 10 billion, before it can be brought to a halt. And there are very few signs that such efforts are being made.

The Causes of Recent Population Growth

Why has population recently grown at such a high rate? The main reason is a sharp change in the ratio of births to deaths: we have been very successful at controlling the death rate but not so successful at controlling the birth rate. As we have seen, the global population has been fairly stable during most of the time that man has lived on earth. Both birth rates and death rates were high and tended to balance one another. Life was, in the words of the philosopher Thomas Hobbes, "poor, nasty, brutish, and short." Life expectancy in the Bronze Age was an estimated eighteen years, and in the Roman Empire about twenty-five to thirty years. But by the beginning of the twentieth century, the average life expectancy was forty years, and in the United States today it is approximately seventy-five years.[9] This vastly increased life expectancy is a major factor in the population growth rate.

Population Growth in Selected Countries, 1973

COUNTRY	TOTAL POPULATION (millions)	BIRTH RATE	DEATH RATE	RATE OF POPULATION GROWTH (percent)	YEARS TO DOUBLE PRESENT POPULATION
United States	210.3	15.6	9.4	0.8	87
Canada	22.5	15.7	7.3	1.2	58
United Kingdom	57.0	14.9	11.9	0.3	231
France	52.3	16.9	10.6	0.6	117
Sweden	8.2	13.8	10.4	0.3	231
East Germany	16.3	11.7	13.7	−0.2	–
West Germany	59.4	11.5	11.7	0.0	–
USSR	250.0	17.8	8.2	1.0	70
India	600.4	42.0	17.0	2.5	28
Pakistan (including Bangla Desh)	151.7	51.0	18.0	3.3	21
China	799.3	30.0	13.0	1.7	41
Japan	107.3	19.0	7.0	1.2	58
Taiwan	15.0	27.0	5.0	2.2	32
South Korea	34.5	31.0	11.0	2.0	35
Mexico	56.2	43.0	10.0	3.3	21
Cuba	8.9	27.0	8.0	1.9	37
Brazil	101.3	38.0	10.0	2.8	25
Ireland	3.0	22.4	11.2	0.5	139

SOURCE: Adapted from the *1973 World Population Data Sheet* (Washington, D.C.: The Population Reference Bureau, 1973).

Life expectancy is rising very rapidly in the developing nations, which have been propelled with dramatic suddenness from the traditional to the modern world. The developed regions of the world improved their medical and agricultural techniques in a slow process extending over centuries, but this knowledge has been extended to the developing nations in the course of a generation or two. Birth rates were always very high in these countries, because so many children died in infancy and a large number of births was necessary merely to maintain population size. The death rates have now dropped sharply, while birth rates in general have remained very high. There has not

[9]Robert C. Cook, "How Many People Have Ever Lived on Earth?" *The Population Bulletin*, vol. 18, no. 1 (February 1962), p. 15.

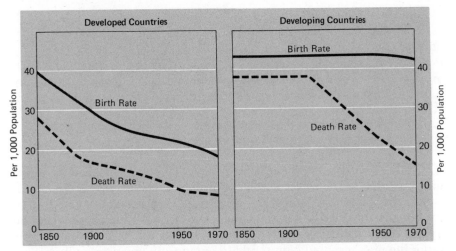

Birth rates and death rates in developed and developing countries. In the developed countries, the decline in the death rate over the past century has been accompanied by a parallel decline in the birth rate. In the developing countries, however, there has been a rapid decline in the death rate during the course of this century, but the birth rate has remained almost constant. The result is massive population growth in the developing countries. (SOURCE: International Demographic Statistics Center, Bureau of the Census.)

been time for the changes in attitudes that seem to have been responsible for the decline in birth rates in the already developed countries. As a result, the overall rate of natural population increase in the developing world exceeds 2 percent — a rate sufficient to increase the populations of these countries ten times in 116 years.[10]

A complicating factor is that rapid population growth began in the developing nations at a time when they already had a much larger population, especially in Asia and Latin America, than Europe and North America had at the time of their expansions centuries earlier. This means that the high growth rate will increase the absolute numbers of people much more rapidly than it did in Europe and North America. If a developing nation is already working close to the limit of its available agricultural and economic resources, the high rate could push it over the brink into disaster.

Recognizing the Danger: Malthus and His Principle

It was an eighteenth-century English parson, Thomas Malthus, who gave the first warning of the implications of population growth. His theories were actively debated at the time and proved most unwelcome; both the theories and their originator were widely vilified and ridiculed. Two centuries later the controversy continues.

Malthus lived at the height of the Industrial Revolution in England. It was an age of boundless optimism. The dominant idea at the time was

[10]*The World Population Situation in 1970,* United Nations Department of Economic and Social Affairs, Population Studies, no. 49 (New York: United Nations, 1971), p. 40.

"the perfectibility of man" — the notion that man's history was essentially an evolution, via industrialism, to a golden age of abundance, bliss, and human perfection In his famous book, *Essay on the Principles of Population,* published in 1898, Malthus formulated a principle which appeared to destroy, utterly and irredeemably, the possibility of any future golden age. It was a very simple principle:

> Population, when unchecked, increases in geometric ratio. Subsistence only increases in arithmetic ratio.[11]

In other words, the natural tendency of population growth, when unchecked, is to increase in powers of two: 1, 2, 4, 8, 16, 32, 64 — a *geometric* ratio. But food supply depends on a fixed amount of land and so cannot possibly increase in the same ratio. At best, food supply can be increased in a steady, additive fashion: 1, 2, 3, 4, 5, 6, 7 — an *arithmetic* ratio. Inevitably, population tends to outrun the means of subsistence. Necessarily, some factors intervene to keep population within the limits set by food supply — those factors being war, pestilence, and famine. To Malthus, the logical conclusion was that mankind would always tend to increase, press against the limits of the food supply, and then be forced back by the unalterable facts of nature. Misery, hunger, and poverty would therefore be the unavoidable lot of the majority of the human race.

Reactions to the Malthusian Theory

The idea was an unpalatable one, discordant with the spirit of the age, and it was received accordingly. Malthus became known as the "gloomy parson"; a critic called his theory "that black and terrible demon that is always ready to stifle the hopes of humanity."[12] One of Malthus's biographers notes that "for thirty years it rained refutations."[13] But the thesis was difficult to refute. There was the brutally simple logic of the principle; there was the national census three years after publication of the *Essay* showing that the British population had increased 25 percent in thirty years; and there was the unquestionable fact of increasing poverty among the masses.

Malthus's theory quickly became associated with political conservatism, largely because of his attitude to the poor. He was not hostile to the lower classes, but he did believe that they were responsible for their own condition and for most of the population increase. If population growth were to be checked, it would have to be checked primarily among the poor, and to this end Malthus recommended the abolition of poor relief and state support of pauper children To those who made the laws, this seemed a very sound doctrine, and in fact English poor laws were modified accordingly. For the rest of the population,

---

[11]Judy K. Morris, "Professor Malthus and His Essay," *The Population Bulletin,* vol. 22, no. 1 (February 1966), pp. 16–17.
[12]Robert Heilbroner, *The Worldly Philosophers,* 3d ed. (New York: Simon & Schuster, 1967), p. 76.
[13]Ibid., p. 76.

Malthus recommended "moral restraint" — people were to refrain from marriage until later in life and to refrain from sexual intercourse until marriage.

Artificial methods of birth control, however, were repugnant to Malthus, although ironically, the principle of birth control came to be termed "neo-Malthusianism." And Malthus did not foresee a need to halt population growth entirely; the need was simply to slow down population growth so that food supply could catch up.

Malthus's gloomy predictions were not fulfilled for the region with which he was concerned — Europe and, to a lesser extent, North America. He did not foresee the rapid drop in birth rates that followed a few decades later, nor the improvement in agricultural methods that vastly increased crop yield from a fixed area of land. Both Europe and the United States grew in numbers and affluence, and it seemed that Malthus had been proved wrong. What was not realized until comparatively recently was the extent to which the continued prosperity and growing population of the developed countries depended on the importation of resources from the less developed nations of the world.

THE DEVELOPING NATIONS: A MALTHUSIAN TRAP?

Today we can no longer be so sure that mankind has escaped from "the Malthusian trap."

Overpopulation and Global Malnutrition

Despite the euphoria over "the Green Revolution" in agricultural techniques, the fact is that more, not fewer, people are suffering from malnutrition every year. As Dr. Henry Borgstrom points out:

> If all the food in the world were equally distributed and each human received identical quantities, we would *all* be malnourished. If the entire world's food supply were parcelled out at the U.S. dietary level, it would feed only about one third of the human race. The world as a global household knows of no surpluses, merely enormous deficits. . . .

> Already short of food, the world is adding 70 million people to its feeding burden each year — the equivalent of the entire United States population every three years. The annual increase is itself growing at a rapid pace; it is outstripping the gains in world food production despite all the triumphs of agriculture and fisheries. . . .[14]

By the end of the sixties, ten out of every twenty children born in the developing countries perished in childhood from hunger or malnutrition. Of the remaining ten, seven suffered physical or mental retardation.[15] Malnutrition can not only kill and cripple the body; it can also

[14]Borgstrom, "The Dual Challenge of Health and Hunger," pp. 1, 2.
[15]Heilbroner, *The Worldly Philosophers*, p. 83.

Literally millions of people are expected to starve to death on the Indian subcontinent between now and the end of the century. Although India cannot feed her present population—only one citizen in fifty has an adequate diet—the total population of the country will exceed 1 billion by the year 2000 unless birth rates are reduced. (Marilyn Silverstone/Magnum)

permanently damage the brain. The brain of an infant grows to 80 percent of its adult size in the first three years of life. If supplies of protein are inadequate in this stage, the brain stops growing. The damage is irreversible. Undernourishment is rampant in the developing countries: in India, for example, only one person in fifty has an adequate diet. Yet every year 70 million more people are being added to the global population, mostly in the developing countries. The fastest rates of increase are usually in the poorest countries—Rwanda, for example, with an annual population growth rate of 2.9 percent, has an annual per capita income of sixty dollars.[16] Merely to feed the present population of the earth adequately would involve doubling present agricultural production, although most cultivable land is already being farmed.

Overpopulation and Economic Development

Population growth can also be disastrous for a developing country because a vicious circle develops between demographic and economic factors. Industrialization is a prerequisite for the economic development that will bring about rising standards of living for all members of the population. But in order for a country to industrialize, it has to invest capital in basic necessities such as factory machines, transportation systems, and technical education. In a society in which population remains constant, about 3 to 5 percent of the national income has to be invested each year to create a 1 percent increase in the per capita income. But if the population is growing at the rate of about 3 percent, as

[16]Figures taken from the *1973 World Population Data Sheet.*

is the case with most developing nations, the investment must be between 12 to 20 percent. Such levels of investment are quite impossible for poor countries, in which lack of investment capital is often the main barrier to economic advance.

The poor countries are increasing their populations twice as fast as the rich ones, but they have the least need of large populations and can least afford them. Any economic advances they do make are used to accommodate more people, rather than to improve living standards. A country whose population is doubling every twenty years has to double its national income in that period — a staggering task — merely to remain where it was. Not only does increased population absorb economic gains, it also increases pressure on land already densely settled, thus possibly retarding agricultural production. The large numbers of children become heavy burdens on the working population; in the less developed countries of Asia, Africa, and Latin America, children under fifteen constitute about 40 percent of the population.[17] These children are often obliged to work to support themselves and their families. The result is mass illiteracy and critical shortages of trained personnel.

The gap between the living standards of the developed and the developing world is wide and getting wider. The annual per capita gross national product in the United States in 1973 was $4,760; in many developing countries, it is below $100.[18] In 1958 the developed countries, with only 32 percent of the world's population, produced 82 percent of the world's goods and services. Ten years later, in 1968, the developed countries had only 30 percent of the global population, but they produced 87 percent of the goods and services. Despite foreign aid efforts, the gap is steadily widening, and population increase is a major cause of this trend. In fact, it is unlikely that many of the developing countries will ever be able to approach the standard of living of the United States; the planet simply does not have enough natural resources to support vast populations at the present American level.

Demographic Transition: A Way Out?

The population of the industrialized nations of the world has tended to level off after an earlier rapid increase. This historical sequence of population growth in the Western world and in Japan has led some demographers to consider whether the same pattern might repeat itself with other peoples. Research on the question has led to the hypothesis of *demographic transition* — the theory that the growth rate of a population tends to stabilize as a society perceives the problems of overpopulation. According to the theory, people will tend on the whole to have as many children as they think they can adequately support, given existing and expected conditions. The high population growth rate in the developing world is attributed to the fact that people's attitudes have

[17]Hartley, *Population Quantity Versus Quality*, p. 36.
[18]Figures taken from the *1973 World Population Data Sheet*.

not yet caught up with their actual circumstances, which have altered rapidly under the impact of modernization.

In other words, the concept of demographic transition is not a law, but rather an empirical generalization about how people might be expected to behave in the long run when confronted with a generally similar pattern of conditions. The theory provides us with a fairly simple model, which many societies seem to fit, and which appears to suggest a fairly reliable ongoing process with a favorable outcome. But there are some difficulties.

One problem is that the concept of demographic transition is merely a theoretical model. Human events seldom conform to neat schemas, and the fact that some societies have a certain demographic history does not necessarily mean that all societies will repeat the same process. It is conceivable that other factors, such as religion, could "freeze" a society at a certain stage. We do not know what the key determinants of the transition process are, or to what extent it depends on specific cultural institutions and values.

The Japanese demographic transition, for example, took place in a much shorter time, by very different methods, and in accordance with rather different values than the Western transition. Before World War II the Japanese population was growing rapidly, but at the end of the war there was a general consensus in Japan that population control was necessary. Japan had a long tradition of toleration of abortion and did not view it as fundamentally immoral as Western societies did at the time. In the ten years from 1947 to 1957, the Japanese birth rate dropped from 34 per thousand to 14 per thousand, the most rapid decline in birth rate ever recorded. But during this period, half of the conceptions in Japan were terminated by abortion. As Irene Taeuber observes:

> A major contribution of the Japanese experience to the assessment of future experience elsewhere is the fact that growth was not predictable. . . . The means whereby the transition proceeded, perhaps even its course and speed, were associated intimately with the indigenous and developing culture of the Japanese. Perhaps cultural factors will give distinctive dimensions to other transitions.[19]

At the very least, we should be wary of anticipating that other societies will follow the demographic patterns established in Europe and North America. But there is evidence of some demographic transition in a few of the developing countries. Dudley Kirk[20] points out that between World War II and the early sixties, virtually all nations fell into one of two categories—either with birth rates under 25 or with birth rates over 35. Since that time, however, a number of nations with high

[19]Irene B. Taeuber, "Japan's Demographic Transition Re-examined," *Population Studies,* vol. 14, no. 1 (July 1960), p. 39.
[20]Dudley Kirk, "A New Demographic Transition?" in *Rapid Population Growth: Consequences and Policy Implications,* prepared by a Study Committee of the National Academy of Sciences (Baltimore: Johns Hopkins Press, 1971), pp. 123–147.

Direct Means of Fertility Control

Withdrawal	Major method historically; widespread in Western countries until quite recently.
Douche, foam, cream, etc.	Minor methods, relatively ineffective and outmoded; extent of use unknown but primarily among lesser educated in developed countries.
Rhythm	Primarily used by Catholics, but in the United States only about 14 percent of Catholics used this method in 1970.
Condom	Widely used throughout the world, and particularly in Japan, Western Europe, and the United States (about 15 percent of all users).
Diaphragm	Sharp fall in use since oral pill in the United States in the 1960s; minor method now.
Intrauterine devices	Innovation of early 1960s, now various versions, growing use throughout world, particularly in developing countries.
Oral pill	Major innovation of 1960s; most widely used contraceptive in developed countries (e.g., about 25 percent in the United States).
Sterilization	Both male and female users throughout world, but seldom equally (United States an exception in this regard, where about 10 percent now thus protected).
Abortion	In mid-1960s, may well be the most widely used single method, legal and illegal. Today legal for half the world's population.

As a rough indication of magnitude, these direct means of fertility control are used at a given time by about 65–70 percent of couples in the reproductive ages in the advanced countries, by 30–40 percent in the transitional, and by 5–15 percent in the traditional.

SOURCE: Bernard Berelson, "World Population: Status Report 1974," *Reports on Population/Family Planning,* no. 15 (January 1974).

birth rates have been moving into an intervening range. Kirk argues that once a sustained reduction of the birth rate has begun in the developing nations, it proceeds at a much more rapid pace than it did historically in Europe and North America. The key factors in initiating the decline vary from region to region, but Kirk believes that there is always a definite connection with some "threshold" level of socioeconomic development, with education and per capita income as the major factors. On this basis, there is reason to hope that the demographic transition will be achieved in all countries – if the necessary level of socioeconomic development can be reached. However, most of the newly transitional countries have relatively small populations; the largest and poorest countries are still struggling with birth rates of 35 and up – in some cases over 50. Overpopulation drains their economic resources, and there seems no immediate prospect of their achieving socioeconomic levels that might reduce these rates.

A more pessimistic view of the demographic transition hypothesis has been voiced by Paul Ehrlich and John Holdren.[21] They argue that even if all nations do industrialize, create better socioeconomic conditions, and initiate a demographic transition, the population problem will still be acute. They estimate that even if we achieve this global industrialization process within fifty years – a spectacular accomplishment – a rapid drop in birth rates would begin only around the year 2020, and world growth rates would decline to the present U.S. level only by about 2050. By that time the global population would already be four times the present level, and it would still continue to double itself every seventy years.

The theory of demographic transition, then, provides some hope, but certainly not a solution. Only if certain doubtful preconditions are met might population stabilize, and even then the absolute number of people involved might outstrip the carrying capacity of the earth.

Let us examine the actual population problem in specific countries to gain a clearer understanding of the practical problems involved in reducing birth rates.

India: Population Growth and Population Policy

"India is the bellwether." So asserted William and Paul Paddock in a 1967 consideration of population growth and food supply:

> India is the case in point. It is the bellwether that shows the path which the others, like sheep going to the slaughter, are following. The hungry nation that today refuses to heed India's history will be condemned to relive it.[22]

The successes and failures of India are of vital significance to the

[21]Paul R. Ehrlich and John P. Holdren, "Avoiding the Problem," *Saturday Review* (March 6, 1971), p. 56.

[22]William Paddock and Paul Paddock, "Today Hungry Nations, Tomorrow Starving Nations," in *The American Population Debate*, ed. Daniel Callahan (New York: Doubleday, 1971), p. 127.

developing world. India is one of the world's largest nations. It is also one of the poorest. Within an area about one-third the size of the United States, India crowds a population nearly three times as large as ours. Unless the current growth rate is reduced, India will have a population of well over a billion by the year 2000. The likelihood that such a nation could ever clothe and feed itself, let alone develop beyond a subsistence economy, is rather slender. An India of such proportions would be constantly on the brink of famine and disaster.

The Indian birth rate declined from 52.4 at the start of the century to 40.0 in the fifties. But the death rate declined also, from 46.8 to 22 in the same period.[23] The death rate has continued to fall while the birth rate has not, so the gap is growing steadily wider. The effects on living standards are severe. The average Indian has a food intake of about 2000 calories, as against an estimated minimum requirement of 2300–2500. (The average U.S. intake is 3000–3400.) It is not, by any means, that the Indian government is not trying; the massive population increase simply swallows up what might have been substantial progress.

In 1952 India became the first country to adopt an official family planning program. The program was initially very poorly funded – in 1956, for example, total expenditures amounted to 1 cent for every twenty persons. By 1970 the figure had risen to 7.7 cents per capita. That 7.7 cents per capita represented 1 percent of the entire government budget for the year, and is the highest percentage ever budgeted for family planning by any nation. Partly because officially sponsored family planning was an innovation, India's program moved slowly in the first years. The principle means of contraception promoted by the program was the rhythm method, but by the early sixties it became clear that this means would not suffice. In 1965 two new techniques were introduced: male sterilization (vasectomy) and the more recently developed intrauterine device (IUD). An extensive network of urban and rural centers was established and mobile teams toured the countryside, explaining the benefits of family limitation and recruiting clients. When oral contraceptives became available, they were added to the arsenal. But the IUD and vasectomy have remained the preferred methods.

In the first year of the reorganized program, over 600,000 men accepted sterilization and over 800,000 women received IUDs.[24] The number rose the following year, but started to decline toward the end of the sixties. One reason was probably that the initial surge of clients included those most receptive to contraception; those who were approached later required more persuasion. More importantly, the program encountered more religious and other opposition than had been expected. Local practitioners of native medicine, who had been bypassed by the official system, deeply resented it. So did the suppliers of illegal abortions, who saw their market threatened. Rumors about the

---

[23]S. Chandrasekhar, "India's Population: Fact, Problem, and Policy," in *Asia's Population Problems*, ed. S. Chandrasekhar (New York: Praeger, 1967), p. 80, Table 7.
[24]"India: Ready or Not, Here They Come," *The Population Bulletin*, vol. 25, no. 5 (November 1970), p. 7.

undesirable effects of contraception were encouraged, magnified, and spread through the population. In 1971 it was calculated that only about 13 percent of all couples in the reproductive ages (fifteen to forty-four) were using any of the methods of family planning provided by the government progam and only 1.6 percent were using the IUD.[25] Vasectomy rates are still low, although there has been some success with the use of "vasectomy camps," which concentrate resources for a few weeks on a single intense campaign in one district. The 1971 to 1972 sterilization total for the entire country was 2.2 million. The figure seems large, but given the size of India's population problem it is relatively insignificant, especially when it is remembered that many of those accepting sterilization had already had as many children as they wanted.

India's family planning program has been hampered over the years by unexpected snags, bureaucratic inefficiency, lack of funds, poor planning, and the sheer size of the task. The program has suffered from its own inbuilt assumptions. Goals were unrealistically set; it was hoped to reduce the birth rate from forty to twenty-five in ten years, to achieve a growth rate of only 1 percent. There was a failure to anticipate opposition, and it was assumed that private and public interest would coincide. The medical-clinical emphasis of the program may have been misplaced in a country where appropriate facilities are scarce, and it might have been possible to utilize more fully other private, international, and even commercial organizations. Nevertheless, India is making some progress. Since 1973, the birth rate has dropped to 37.6. In urban areas it has dropped more sharply, to 32.0. But this means that fifty-seven thousand new babies are born every day. Time may be running out for India: in 1974 a panel of Indian social scientists issued a government report predicting that if current trends continue, half the Indian population will be homeless by the year 2000 and the country will be denuded of its resources for fuel and food.[26]

China

It is easy to gain the idea that the Indian population growth rate is the highest in the world, but in fact it is somewhat lower than several other developing countries. In 1973 almost thirty countries had a growth rate of 3 percent or more.[27] Doubling time at that rate is a mere nineteen years. There is one country whose population problem, for sheer size alone, dwarfs that of India: China. Not even the Chinese know exactly how large their population is; official estimates range from 750 million to 830 million.[28] At the current rate of increase, the Chinese population is projected to climb to a phenomenal 2.9 billion within sixty years.

[25]Dorothy Nortman, "Population and Family Planning Programs: A Factbook," *Reports on Population/Family Planning*, 2 (September 1972), p. 24, Table 4.

[26]Bernard Weinraub, "The Year 2000 in India: Experts Paint Grim Picture," *New York Times* (June 19, 1974).

[27]Figures taken from the *1973 World Population Data Sheet*.

[28]"World Environment Newsletter," *World* (May 8, 1973), p. 38. The last census in China was in 1953 and indicated that there were 583 million Chinese.

China, a poor and overpopulated country, has achieved considerable success in reducing the birth rate. The reduction has been made possible, however, only by the willingness of the Chinese masses to dutifully obey the injunctions of their leaders. The Chinese seem to have abided by Mao's exhortations to abstain from premarital intercourse, to delay marriage, and to limit families through contraception. *(René Burri/Magnum)*

The Chinese are making major efforts to reduce their birth rate, and their task is made easier by a social structure that emphasizes obedience to politically determined norms. Marxist doctrine does not sanction population control as a means of combating poverty; it attributes poverty not to overpopulation but to defects in the social order. Thus, the campaign for birth control is based officially on the view that population control will improve the health and living conditions of young people, and in particular will liberate women from the traditional restrictions they have suffered in China. Propaganda posters remind women that a good career and education are easier to achieve with a small family.

The Chinese have made extensive use of the "barefoot doctor," who after three months of intensive training becomes a local family planning propagandist and worker. These paraprofessionals may distribute various contraceptive devices, give advice on birth control, and perform abortions. There is very strong pressure on couples to have no more than two children; to have a larger family is regarded as disrespectful to party and country. Chairman Mao has asked men and women not to marry until the ages of twenty-six and twenty-three respectively, and there is every indication that this injunction is being observed. Premarital sexual intercourse is illegal, and by all accounts young Chinese are exceptionally chaste before marriage. The Chinese claim that in Peking at least, the rate of natural population increase has been reduced to 0.1 percent. There has not been such a dramatic reduction in births in rural areas, where most Chinese live, but the Chinese do claim that their overall birth rate is dropping steadily.[29]

DOES THE UNITED STATES HAVE A POPULATION PROBLEM?

What about the United States? The richest country in the world has one of the lowest population growth rates. Do we have anything that could honestly be labeled a population problem?

In 1970 Congress established a Commission on Population Growth and the American Future to inquire into this question. When the commission submitted its report in the spring of 1972, its answer was a considered yes. There is a problem — not as desperate or dramatic as that of India, but a problem nonetheless, and one that needs prompt, intelligent action. The commission reported that what is central to the issue is the quality of life and "if this country is in a crisis of spirit — environmental deterioration, racial antagonisms, the plight of the cities, the international situation — then population is part of that crisis."[30]

Growth and Its Problems

Population growth is nothing new to the United States. In the first half of the nineteenth century, population increased by 30 percent each decade as immigrants streamed across the Atlantic to the New World. But as the immigration slackened at the start of the twentieth century, the birth rate also declined, reaching a low in the depression years during the thirties. At the end of World War II came the celebrated and unanticipated "baby boom" that peaked in the mid-fifties and ended in about 1960. The birth rate then began to decline again, until in the early seventies the media began speaking of a "baby bust." Again, the decline was unexpected — just when the children of the baby boom reached adulthood and the rate was expected to soar once more, it fell: from 18.2 in 1970 to a record low of 15.0 in 1974.[31] One theory for the baby bust is that the present generation of young adults is postponing the age at which it begins child-rearing; when the childbearing age stabilizes, the rate may rise again. A second reason is that young people today expect to have fewer children than people a few years their senior. According to the 1971 Census Bureau survey, married women

[29]"China: Population in the People's Republic," *The Population Bulletin*, vol. 27, no. 6 (December 1971).
[30]*Population and the American Future: The Report of the Commission on Population Growth and the American Future* (Washington, D.C.: U.S. Government Printing Office, 1972), p. 12.
[31]Harold M. Schmeck, Jr., "Birth, Fertility Rates at a New Low in U.S.," *New York Times* (April 16, 1974), p. 1.

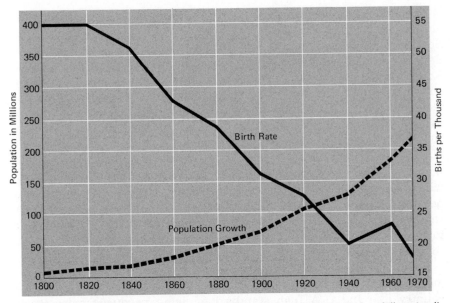

U.S. population and birth rate, 1800–1970. Although the U.S. birth rate has fallen steadily for 150 years, the size of the population has continued to increase. The main reason is that the death rate has been reduced by improvements in medical science and public health standards. (SOURCE: Adapted from Robin Elliott, Lynn C. Landman, Richard Lincoln, and Theodore Tsuoroka, *U.S. Population Growth and Family Planning: A Review of the Literature* [New York: Planned Parenthood—World Population, n.d.], p. vii.)

aged eighteen to twenty-four expect to have an average of 2.4 children. Not everyone will marry, but couples often have more children than they planned for, so the figure may be higher. It appears there is little prospect as yet for a zero growth rate.

What kind of problems did the Commission on Population see as stemming from population growth in the United States? One is the pressure on the schools and colleges, and ultimately on the job market: youth unemployment is at its highest levels in many years. Crime rates are highest for persons aged twenty-five and under, and increased crime rates may be related to the increase in the relative size of this age group. Housing suffers pressure as young adults move out of their parents' homes and form families of their own. Demands for all sorts of commodities and services grow, and, if the supply cannot easily be increased, prices may rise and inflation follow. Metropolitan areas expand, along with the need for urban services—police and fire protection, sanitation, water supply, public transportation, recreational facilities. Government administration also becomes more complex and costly: by far the largest employer in New York City is the city itself, with a civil service roster of some 250,000. None of these difficulties is insurmountable, but they are pressures on the society and the economy, and they can become material and psychological strains on individuals.

The effects of population growth on resources and environment must also be considered. Water is a resource already in short supply in the Southwest, and the shortage will spread north and east in the coming decades. We have already felt the consequences of an energy shortage. Food production may also become a problem, especially if we follow a sound environmental policy that restricts the use of pesticides and some chemical fertilizers. Within the next thirty-five years, we will need 30 million more acres of farmland to feed our population. An additional 300 million more acres of forest land must be found to satisfy our demands for lumber and paper; the average American consumes 450 pounds of wood and paper each year. Already the "great outdoors" in which Americans have long camped, hunted, fished, and played may be lost to most of us. Some national parks have already decided to restrict admissions, and during hunting season many favored patches of forest are apt to contain more hunters than deer. Many of our resources of forests, open space, water, and minerals are dwindling.

Pollution will probably increase – and this is a problem which may be more serious in a rich country like the United States than in a poor country like India. A high standard of living produces more waste products per person – more auto emissions, more industrial waste flowing into lakes and rivers, more smog, more plastic bottles and disposable beer cans littering the countryside and filling city dumps. Some of these pollution problems might be substantially alleviated with present or foreseeable technology, but technology requires energy for its application, and energy is in short supply. Moreover, the production of energy usually causes thermal or atmospheric pollution. Even if we are in no imminent danger of starvation, the quality of our lives may deteriorate in important respects as our population increases.

Still, there are many who feel that the United States can afford to take a relatively leisured view of the situation. They argue that our land and resources can support a considerably greater population with little adverse effect on living standards, provided we make sensible and imaginative use of what we have. In part this attitude stems from a concern that the "population crisis" not be used as an excuse for neglecting other pressing social problems. But the spirit of optimism may also derive from a tendency to consider the United States in isolation from the rest of the world. Many people feel that because we are not yet seriously overcrowded, because we can feed ourselves, and because our technology seems able to take care of our future requirements, we are all right. But one critical fact calls this optimism into question: the global interdependence of nations. We depend on other parts of the world for raw materials and those places, in turn, depend on us for food. The United States and Canada are the only countries that usually produce a considerable surplus of staple grains. When serious food shortages threaten elsewhere, it is mainly our surplus that can make the difference between starvation and survival for the threatened nations. If the U.S. population becomes so numerous that we need all the food for ourselves, the rest of the world may no longer have this safety margin.

In addition, the United States consumes so much of the world's resources that a single new American baby represents, in global terms, a greater ecological threat than thirty Asian babies. With 6 percent of the world's population, we consume 35 percent of the earth's energy and material resources. Each American baby consumes during his or her lifetime approximately 26 million gallons of water, 21,000 gallons of gasoline, 10,000 pounds of meat, and 28,000 pounds of milk and cream. Even at our present low rate of population growth, our numbers will have increased to 420.3 million in a hundred years. The impact on the rest of humanity continues to be enormous.

United States Population Policy

Birth control and family planning have been common in the United States for decades, but until 1971, federal law still classified contraceptives as "obscene or pornographic materials." Another law, dating back to 1873, had outlawed the importation, mailing, and transporting in interstate commerce of "any article whatsoever for the promotion of contraception."[32] State laws were similarly condemnatory, and even as late as the sixties there were prosecutions under these laws. On the whole, however, the laws were widely disregarded, even though doctors who prescribed contraceptives, pharmacists who sold them, and people who purchased them rendered themselves technically liable to prosecution. Today, government-sponsored family planning programs are operating in every state, and the federal government has a number of agencies specifically concerned with family planning and population research.

U.S. concern about population growth became evident in the early sixties, but it was first directed toward other countries. Beginning in 1963, U.S. aid provided for family planning in developing nations as a part of general aid to economic development. Soon after, however, legislators and administrative agencies realized that many people in the United States itself were nearly as disadvantaged as any Asian peasant when it came to the availability of contraception. Middle-class women could go to their private physicians for information and to their pharmacists for supplies, but poor women did not have private physicians, and the clinics to which they might go for medical care were not offering contraceptive information. When the war on poverty began in 1964, one of its strategies was to make family planning as available to the poor as it already was to the rest of the population. A few years later, Congress made use of one of the means by which social reforms have frequently been urged on reluctant states. In 1967 Congress required that, in order to qualify for federal funds for maternal and child health services, each state must undertake to extend family planning

[32]*Population and the American Future*, p. 98.

services to all of its population by 1975. At this stage, however, there was still no connection made between private family planning and national population control. Birth control, at home as well as abroad, was simply one weapon in the war against poverty.

In 1969 the population factor was finally made explicit. Senator Ernest Gruening became deeply concerned by the population growth and conducted lengthy congressional hearings on the question. The media took up the issue, and for the first time a general public awareness of the danger developed. In July of that year President Nixon issued a special message on population:

> One of the most serious challenges to human destiny in the last third of this century will be the growth of the population. Whether man's response to that challenge will be a cause for pride or for despair in the year 2000 will depend very much on what we do today.[33]

Soon after, in 1970, the Commission on Population Growth and the American Future was established to study the implications of population growth and make recommendations for future policy. Its report, published in 1972, unequivocally supported the goal of a stabilized American population and urged a number of measures to achieve it.

Family planning services remain the core of population policy in the United States, but the Center for Population Research, a group of scientists within the National Institute of Health, has given some attention to other social and institutional factors, such as the role of women in American society and the usual assumption that their "career" will be in the home, raising children. Very little emphasis is placed on population education outside the provision of family planning services, however. Many legislators and appointed officials wish to avoid controversy on sex education, and so there is usually no systematic attempt to educate young people in contraceptive techniques.

There have also been some unfortunate side effects of the predominantly poverty-related emphasis of government family programs in the United States. Among the middle class, the tendency has been to emphasize the comfortable assumption that the poor are the largest contributors to population growth. But this is simply not so. In proportion to their numbers, those families with an income below the poverty level do have relatively more children. In absolute terms, however, it is the group composing the remaining socioeconomic levels who contribute most to population growth.[34] A further unfortunate effect is that poor people and racial minorities have sometimes gained the impression that the purpose of the programs is not to help them but to eliminate them. Even today, most white Americans remain unaware of the fear of genocide among some American blacks.

[33]Ibid., p. 3.
[34]Jack Rosenthal, "Birth Rates Found in a Sharp Decline Among Poor Women," *New York Times* (March 5, 1972).

Many American parents are able to provide for their large families and so tend to believe that they are not really contributing to the population problem. But this view neglects the global impact of more Americans: in terms of the resources they will consume and the pollution they will generate, these eight American children represent a greater ecological threat to the planet than 240 Asian children. *(Vivienne/DPI)*

The existing population structure of the United States also portends another unprecedented problem. At present our population is a young one, due to the post-World War II baby boom. Since that time, however, the birth rate has been declining. This means that in a few decades when the baby-boom children pass middle age, the average American will be much older than he is today, and our population structure will be top-heavy with the aged. This will necessarily involve major changes in social policy and priorities. The provision of adequate old-age homes and geriatric hospitals, for example, may become more important than the building of schools and colleges. Already, some elementary schools are standing empty for lack of pupils, baby-food manufacturers report declining sales, and the baby-service industry is now pitching new products to teen-agers and adults.

POPULATION GROWTH: AN OVERVIEW

Rapid population growth has many consequences that give rise to a variety of social problems. Let us review some of the more serious consequences.

Ecological consequences. Populations need raw materials, and the higher their standard of living, the more raw materials are needed for each individual. All our natural materials—food, fibers, fuels, minerals—are limited in quantity. So is living space; as populations increase, more and more of the countryside will be despoiled, and many species may face extinction. As folk singer Joni Mitchell has succinctly put it:

> They paved paradise
> And put up a parking lot[35]

Pollution of the environment will probably increase as expanding populations demand more goods and dispose of more wastes. This is particularly true of the industrialized countries—and almost every country in the world hopes one day to be fully industrialized. If the global population runs to many billions, the ecological effects will be incalculable.

Economic consequences. Overpopulation need not always predict or accompany poverty, but in practice the two are usually closely linked. A poor country with a growing population is hampered by the ratio of dependent to productive persons. Economic gains tend to be absorbed in the increased population, so that individuals are no better off than before. It becomes almost impossible for these countries to accumulate the investment capital they need to industrialize and improve living standards. Even wealthy countries may find it increasingly difficult to provide their citizens with the rising standard of living that they expect.

Political consequences. In an age of rising expectations a large poor population is a political hazard. A population that is hungry and miserably clothed and housed is likely to be restless and politically unstable. Law and order too often come to look as though they have been designed to protect the interests of the rich—among nations as well as among individuals. Overpopulation can pose a persistent threat of strife within nations and perhaps even conflict between nations.

Educational consequences. The age structure of a fast-growing population involves a very high proportion of children of school-going age and a rapid increase in their absolute numbers. The financial burden on a poor country of increasing the amount of education—let alone the quality—is almost insupportable. The result is that, in many countries, a majority of school-age children simply do not go to school. Despite massive international campaigns against illiteracy in the last few decades, there are now more illiterate people in the world than at any time in history. Social mobility is restricted and millions of individuals are denied the opportunity to fulfill their human potential.

Health consequences. Overpopulation often means malnutrition or

---

[35]Joni Mitchell, "Big Yellow Taxi," *Ladies of the Canyon*, (Reprise).

even outright starvation. It limits medical resources, for as the population increases, services are spread more thinly than before. Poor nutrition directly affects the body and the mind; and it contributes indirectly to many other diseases in that the individual's resistance to infection is drastically lowered. The standard of public hygiene and sanitation in many overpopulated countries is also generally low and thus further contributes to sickness and even epidemics.

Overcrowding consequences. In many animal species, overcrowding results in pathological behavior, even if food supply is adequate. There is as yet no proof that overcrowding has the same effect on humans, but high population density has been indirectly implicated in a variety of social problems.

PROSPECTS FOR THE FUTURE

What can be done about population growth? There are three basic methods which, when utilized separately or in combination, can reduce the birth rate: family planning, economic or social incentives, and outright coercion. All existing programs are based primarily on family planning, although some programs make minor use of incentives (such as gifts of radios to those who accept sterilization). Many authorities feel that the family planning approach is inadequate to meet the urgency of the situation and that it may be necessary to create additional incentives—or even to impose some compulsory limit on the number of children a family may have.

Family Planning

In Asia, most of the larger nations and many of the smaller ones have policies explicitly aimed at reducing population growth. In Africa, where densities are lower and ethnic rivalries are often strong, neutrality or even permissiveness toward population growth is much more common. Several countries actually fear underpopulation. In Latin America, family planning is likely to emphasize health considerations rather than overpopulation. Yet, in a few places the programs have been instrumental in significantly reducing the birth rate, notably in Taiwan, Singapore, South Korea, and Hong Kong.

But there is no country in which family planning programs alone have brought population growth to a halt, and there is a feeling among some demographers that alone, these programs never will. The main reason lies in a key principle of family planning: that couples should be encouraged to have the number of children they want—no more, and no less. But what parents want and what a country needs cannot necessarily be counted on to coincide. There are several other reasons for the relative failure of family planning techniques as well. In many cases, the programs are inadequately funded, and neither the information nor the contraceptives are available to more than a fraction of the population. Many programs have hesitated for political, moral, or ideological reasons to use other methods such as sterilization and abortion. Yet if unwanted births alone could be eliminated, population growth would be slowed considerably. A 1970 study by Larry Bumpass and Charles Westoff of births in a representative sample of fifty-six hundred American women found that one-fifth of all births and one-third of births to black women were reported to be unwanted at the time of conception.[36]

Incentives

If family planning alone is inadequate, what role can incentives play and what kind of incentives can be used? The most frequently proposed incentives are financial, and several countries have experimented with cash rewards for sterilization or even the acceptance of intrauterine devices. Other proposals are to allow tax exemptions for only the first two children or even to impose an additional "child tax" on families with more than a certain number of offspring. The chief argument against these financial penalties is that they would fall most heavily on the poor. The result could be that the children in large, poor families would suffer further as a result of the financial burdens imposed on their parents.

Other incentive proposals are more far-reaching and would involve more basic changes in social values and attitudes. Kingsley Davis[37] has urged the adoption of social and economic policies that would change the prevailing, probirth bias of our society. The intention would be to change social norms so that it would be considered undesirable to have large families. New means would be provided through which people could find other forms of satisfaction and personal fulfillment. Couples would still be free to make the final decision but attitudes and values would be altered and couples might be reluctant to plan for families of more than two children. And if the relative roles of men and women were altered, women would become less dependent on home and children for personal fulfillment. Any measures that make the labor market more hospitable and attractive to women would tend, in the long run, to reduce the birth rates.

Coercion

But if family planning and social incentives fail, governments may eventually be obliged to exercise some form of compulsion to limit births. It is at this point that the discussion assumes Orwellian overtones. Most people believe that government interference in such a pri-

[36]Larry Bumpass and Charles Westoff, "Unwanted Births and U.S. Population Control," *Family Planning Perspectives,* 2 (October 1970), p. 4.

[37]Kingsley Davis, "Population Policy: Will Current Programs Succeed?" *Science* (November 10, 1967), pp. 730–739.

vate matter would be tyranny. Moreover, a compulsory system of population control would be vulnerable to abuse and discrimination and would be exceedingly difficult to enforce. Nevertheless, there have been various suggestions offered. One is that every woman of childbearing age could be issued a child licence entitling her to have two children or whatever the zero-growth number happens to be.[38] She could transfer her rights to another woman if she did not want to use them, so that a family that wanted a larger number of children would be able to purchase that right without affecting absolute numbers of births. The idea at least avoids some of the evils of uniform enforcement; but it might favor the affluent over the poor. Other more hypothetical proposals involve the administration of a chemical inhibitor to the entire population.[39] Such an agent would be designed to reduce fertility but not eliminate it; the dosage would be regulated so that only the desired number of children would be conceived each year. The usual suggestion is for some chemical that could be added to the water supply. Another suggestion, less subtle, is that all couples should automatically be sterilized after the birth of their second child.

The question of whether governments have the right, under any circumstances, to compel people to limit the number of their children is a highly debatable one. Do individuals have absolute rights, or are all personal rights ultimately subject to the good of society? Much of the history of social and personal legislation—child labor laws, antidiscrimination laws, and the like—has been based on the principle that one man's right to swing his fist ends where another man's nose begins. Is the freedom to bear children subject to this principle too?

Paul Ehrlich, author of *The Population Bomb*, considers that the whole question of "freedom" has become confused and irrelevant. In an interview with *Playboy* magazine, he said:

> People aren't sufficiently aware that their freedoms are rapidly disappearing *because* there are more and more people. As population grows, we find that there are more and more restrictive laws on where we can drive, whether we can own a gun, whether we can fly an airplane, where we can throw our garbage, whether we can burn leaves. And as conditions become more crowded, even stricter and more comprehensive Government controls and regulations will be implemented.[40]

In any event, if compulsory population control does ever become necessary, it may not take a particularly flexible and humane form. By that time, the emergency may be so acute that personal rights will have to be subordinated to social survival.

Responding to the challenge of the population problem will surely

---

[38]Kenneth E. Boulding, *The Meaning of the Twentieth Century: The Great Transition* (New York: Harper & Row, 1964), pp. 135–136.

[39]Melvin M. Ketchel, "Fertility Control Agents as a Possible Solution to the World Population Problem," *Perspectives in Biology and Medicine*, 11 (Summer 1968), pp. 687–703.

[40]Paul R. Ehrlich, "Interview: Dr. Paul Ehrlich," *Playboy Magazine*, vol. 17, no. 8 (August 1970), p. 58.

Population: A Theoretical Review

The social problem of rapid population growth represents the gap between a *social ideal* of humanity free from hunger, want, and overcrowding and the *social reality* of a galloping increase in human numbers which, unless checked, may have disastrous effects on our living standards and on the global environment. Rapid population growth has so many effects in other areas of society that many social and natural scientists consider it to be the most serious social problem confronting the world today.

The *social-disorganization* perspective provides a particularly fruitful way of looking at the problem. From this perspective, the problem of rapid population growth stems from the fact that some elements in the social system have changed at much faster rates than others, resulting in a fundamental and dysfunctional imbalance between human numbers and the resources available to support them. Throughout most of human history the death rate has been very high, particularly among infants and children. A very high rate of reproduction was therefore a functional necessity if a society was to survive. Social norms, attitudes, and values which encouraged large families and a high birth rate were functional in maintaining stable populations. But modern scientific and technological developments, especially in the field of medicine, have had a great impact on the human death rate. The average life span has been extended by several decades, and the mortality rate among infants and children has been drastically reduced. The excess of births over deaths, particularly in the developing nations, has meant an increasing population growth. A high rate of reproduction is now dysfunctional along with the attitudes, values, and norms that support it. But changes in the social attitudes, values, and norms relating to family size and the social role of women have not kept pace with changes in technology and medical science. The inconsistency between social norms and the reality of overpopulation has resulted in a serious disorganization of society, and the achievement of many other social and economic goals, such as the elimination of poverty, is imperiled.

Rapid population growth does not only stem from social disorganization, it also contributes to further disorganization. Overpopulation leads to overcrowding; it leads to strong pressures on already inadequate educational, housing, welfare, and other facilities; it means that economic resources are used merely to keep pace with population increases rather than to better the living standards of a stable population; it causes additional demands on the dwindling natural resources of the planet; and it inevitably leads to more and more pollution, which is already endangering the ecological systems of the earth.

From the *value-conflict* perspective, much of the population problem stems from fundamental conflicts in values between various societies and between various groups within particular societies. Although many people are anxious to see restraints placed on family size, many others are strongly committed to the view that family size is a matter of personal choice. Large families have traditionally been viewed as a blessing, and in many parts of the world parents still gain economic benefits from having their children at work. Several religions have traditionally opposed sex for any purpose other than procreation, and in many cases religious movements are opposed to birth control and even more strongly opposed to abortion. Many countries consider themselves underpopulated, and do not see their population structure in relation to the overpopulation of the world as a whole. Other countries believe that a large population will give them military strength. Still other countries contend that the poverty of their inhabitants is the result not of their own overpopulation, but of a global imbalance in the distribution of wealth: if they had a greater share of the wealth now concentrated in the hands of a few industrialized societies, their large populations would not be such a problem. Even among those who acknowledge that we are currently overpopulated in relation to our resources, there is often a deep conviction that technological advance will provide a solution. Some people believe the population problem is a "phony" issue, and that there are other pressing social problems to which we should attend first. Value conflicts, then, are unavoidable in viewing the problem of population increase and in any policies designed to solve it. Many sociologists, however, regard this value conflict as necessary and useful because it may provide a mechanism through which attention can be focused on problematic issues and through which needed changes can be accomplished.

The *deviance* perspective is of only limited use in the analysis of the population problem. It should be noted, however, that in the past, couples who chose not to have children, women who chose a career role instead of a motherhood role, or women who chose abortions were regarded as social deviants. These attitudes still predominate but are slowly changing: there is already a tendency to regard parents of large families as deviant.

involve major changes in society. To many, this is not a palatable idea. Yet if we refrain from action, far more unpalatable changes may be forced on us by circumstances beyond our control. Fortunately humans, unlike other animals, have the ability to manipulate their environment and plan their futures. Population expert Frank Notestein sees in this capacity some grounds for hope:

> A discussion of the crisis of population growth must be organized around two sharply contrasting themes: one, of almost unrivaled dangers; the other, of new hope that it may be resolved during the remainder of this century. It is difficult to overstate the importance of either theme. The dangers threaten . . . a catastrophic loss of life. The hope lies in the fact that there is now reason to think that, if the world is willing to bend its energies toward solving the problems, it can go far toward doing so. . . .
>
> We must assume that the future will bring an accelerated pace of change. We have already moved from a position of public apathy to one of deep concern by many people. . . . Our estimate of the future possibilities should be based on the premise that we are at the beginning of an accelerating trend. Almost all the work, national and international, remains to be done. If our efforts are commensurate with our opportunities, however, we have reason to believe that by the end of the century the spectre of poverty by population growth can be lifted from the earth.[41]

But if we fail to use our opportunities, then, as Paul Ehrlich points out, we could even go the way of most other species that have ever existed on earth—to total extinction:

> There are many species that have vanished because they could not adapt. It's not at all inconceivable that man will follow these creatures into extinction. If he continues to reproduce at the present soaring rate, continues to tamper with the biosphere, continues to toy around with apocalyptic weapons, he will probably share the fate of the dinosaur. If he learns to adapt to the finitude of the planet, to the changed character of his existence, he may survive. If not, nothing like him is ever likely to evolve again.[42]

---

[41]Frank W. Notestein, "The Population Crisis: Reasons for Hope," *Foreign Affairs*, vol. 46, no. 1 (October 1967), pp. 167, 180.
[42]Ehrlich, "Interview: Dr. Paul Ehrlich," p. 154.

FURTHER READING

Berelson, Bernard, ed., *Population Policy and Developed Countries,* 1974. A useful examination of the population policies of the industrialized nations. The author gives special attention to social and economic policies that might affect demographic trends in the future.

Callahan, Daniel, *Ethics and Population Limitation,* 1971. A discussion of the moral issues involved in the population debate. Callahan looks at population growth from the perspective of three main values, which are not necessarily compatible: individual freedom, justice, and survival.

Ehrlich, Paul R., *The Population Bomb,* 1971. A best seller written for the general public rather than an academic audience. Ehrlich traces the course of population growth and surveys its impact on food, energy, and other resources. He makes an urgent plea for drastic changes in public policy and private attitudes.

Ehrlich, Paul R. and Anne H. Ehrlich, *Population/Resources/Environment: Issues in Human Ecology,* 1972. A readable, passionate, and comprehensive account of the interrelationship between population growth, resources, and environmental pollution.

Meadows, Donella H., et al., *The Limits to Growth: A Report for the Club of Rome's Project on the Predicament of Mankind,* 1972. A recent summary of the main findings of a research team's computer projection on the future interaction of population, resources, and pollution. The report is a basic reference source for any serious discussion of the population problem.

National Academy of Sciences, *Rapid Population Growth: Consequences and Policy Implications,* 1971. A scholarly and sober approach to the population problem; the implications of overpopulation and of various public policy alternatives are explored in a dispassionate manner.

Osborn, Fairfield, ed., *Our Crowded Planet: Essays on the Pressures of Overpopulation,* 1962. Contains a number of essays by experts in various fields relevant to the population problem. The book focuses on the many ways in which population generates social problems.

Population and the American Future: The Report of the Commission on Population Growth and the American Future, 1972. A report on current population trends in the United States and their potential implications.

Reid, Sue T. and David R. Lyon, eds., *Population Crisis: An Interdisciplinary Perspective,* 1972. A book of readings covering a wide range of perspectives on the population problem from many disciplines in both the natural and social sciences.

Wrong, Dennis H., *Population and Society,* rev. ed., 1967. A short introduction to demography, with a clear account of the dynamics of population growth.

3

Environment and Resources

THE NATURE AND SCOPE OF THE PROBLEM

Most mammal species do not survive for more than 600,000 years before becoming extinct. Man, however, has already inhabited the planet for at least 1,000,000 years. One of the main reasons for this achievement is man's unique capacity to alter the environment to suit himself. In recent decades, however, man has been altering the environment at such a rate and on such a scale that his former asset could turn into a severe and potentially fatal liability. Our demands for a rising standard of living and for an increasing supply of natural resources seem infinite—but the earth is finite. We are running out of resources and energy, and we are running out of space in which to put ourselves and our waste products.

The effects of the environmental crisis are all around us. City dwellers choke in smog. Oil spills ruin beaches. Childhood swimming holes become open sewers. Mercury poisoning makes tuna fish inedible. Nuclear reactors leak deadly radiation. Lake Erie is dying, its clear waters transformed into a noxious chemical brew. Our body tissues contain high concentrations of DDT and other toxic insecticides. A tenth of our annual bill for health services goes for treating illnesses that result from environmental pollution.[1] Sewage sludge dumped in the Atlantic creeps steadily back to the East Coast, and is expected to arrive on the beaches later this decade. Our rivers reek of industrial wastes, sewage, detergents, and dead fish. Aircraft, traffic, and machinery pollute the environment with incessant noise. Billboards and advertising signs clutter the roadways and offend the eye. And to com-

[1]*New York Times* (October 7, 1970).

pound our problems there is a growing global shortage of basic resources — meat, oil, gasoline, grains, paper, wood, minerals — with
accompanying world-wide price increases.

The problems of pollution and resource depletion are international,
but they concern the United States more than any other country. With
only 6 percent of the planet's population, the United States consumes
40 percent of the natural resources and contributes about half of the
industrial pollution. As one writer notes:

> The average American uses more electric power than fifty-five
> Asians or Africans. The generation of electric power is a prime pro-
> ducer of pollution. A single American accounts for more detergents,
> pesticides, radioactive substances, fertilizers, fungicides, and defoli-
> ants in the rivers and oceans than are produced by a thousand
> people in Indonesia — a nation that is generally cited as a prime
> example of human overcrowding. One American is responsible for
> putting more carbon monoxide and benzopyrene in the air than 200
> Pakistanis or Indians. One American consumes three times more
> food than the average person who comes from places that account
> for two-thirds of the world's population. The average American is
> responsible for 2,500 pounds of waste per year — many times the
> world average. If abandoned refrigerators, automobiles, and other
> bulky objects were included, the figure would be astronomically
> higher. The United States . . . accounts for almost 30 percent of the
> poisons being dumped into the sky and the seas. The notion, there-
> fore, that Americans are less of a drain on the Earth than Chinese or
> Indians, because there are so many fewer of us, is an absurdity and
> a dangerous one.[2]

The environmental crisis has been generated by a complex interplay
of several factors, primarily population growth, industrialization, and
pollution. The rise of industrial civilization has made possible high
standards of living for an increasing human population. As more and
more people demand greater and greater quantities of goods, industry
digs ever more voraciously into the environment for the necessary raw
materials and thus steadily depletes the supply of nonrenewable resources. Industrial production generates air, water, and land pollution,
and the consumption of the products compounds the problem as wastes
are returned to the environment. The delicate balance of nature is being upset to the point where there is severe doubt as to whether population, industrialization, and pollution can continue on their present
course of growth without globally disastrous consequences.

Values, Attitudes, and Interests

The problems posed by a deteriorating environment will not easily be
solved, for they are rooted in the very structure of our civilization.

[2]Norman Cousins, "Affluence and Effluence," *Saturday Review* (May 2, 1970), p. 53.

Large and powerful interests, including corporations and governments, have some stake in the careless exploitation of the environment; and so do most individuals. The problem of the environment can only be understood in terms of the dominant values and attitudes of our society, particularly those concerning economic growth and the mastery of nature. Attempts to resolve this social problem are therefore likely to present difficult choices and to excite severe conflicts over values, attitudes, and interests.

In many small-scale, preliterate communities, the inhabitants regard themselves as an integral part of nature, an element in an integrated system in which nature influences man as much as man influences nature. But beyond these societies, people tend to take a different view. This is especially true of the Western tradition. The Book of Genesis teaches that man was made in the image of God, who gave him "dominion over the fish of the sea and over the fowl of the air, and over the cattle, and over all the earth, and over every creeping thing that creepeth upon the earth." The image of man struggling against nature is far more common in our literature, art, and culture than the image of a joint venture between the two.

Particularly in America, the relationship between man and nature has been one of subjugation and exploitation. When the first settlers set foot on Plymouth Rock, they found "a hideous and desolate wilderness, full of wilde beasts and wilde men."[3] But this wilderness was also a land of seemingly unlimited abundance that would richly reward the efforts of any industrious man or woman.

Drawn by the promise of land and the opportunity to start a new life, great tides of immigrants came from the Old World, bringing with them the values, attitudes, and technology that would transform the New. Convinced that the wilderness was to be remade, the pioneers acted on this attitude; the image of the rugged, individualist frontiersman dominated that era and persists to this day. The new military and agricultural technology spelled the end of the American Indians' way of life. Lumbermen cut down whole forests and moved on. Oilmen opened gushers that spewed oil at the rate of thousands of barrels a day from wells that seemed limitless. Cattle barons bred herds that stripped the plains of grass, creating badlands. Farmers plowed up turf in the dry plains states, and the wind blew the topsoil away. Hunters almost wiped out the buffalo, often butchering the animals for the tongue — a delicacy — and leaving the rest of the carcass to rot. Alaskan seals were slaughtered down to 3 percent of their former numbers. The passenger pigeon, whose numbers represented a third of the entire bird population of the United States, and which darkened the skies for several days during its annual migrations, was hunted to total extinction.

Abundance encouraged waste; if the resources of one area were exhausted, there was plenty more. Growth was considered a blessing:

[3]Stewart L. Udall, *The Quiet Crisis* (New York: Holt, Rinehart & Winston, 1963), p. 3.

the man or woman who produced more was rewarded, not the man or woman who preserved the surrounding natural beauty. Not all Americans, of course, shared the myth of inexhaustible resources. The efforts of men and women of conscience and foresight were responsible for the conservation movement, the creation of national and state parks, and ultimately the legislation that, by the beginning of this century, had put an end to the most blatant and irresponsible plundering of natural resources. But the dominant contemporary American creed still reflects many of the early values—rugged individualism, a striving for material goods, a frontier ethic which justifies the subjugation of nature to man.

Robert Rienow and Leona Train Rienow have suggested that American values contain little commitment to environmental conservation:

> Americans have come to accept as a right an ignominious premise: that waste disposal is an essential use of surface water—that a basic function of a crystal stream or wholesome lake is to accept as much sewage and industrial filth as it can possibly handle without losing so much oxygen that it turns into a festering foul-smelling cesspool. On this premise we have built our whole national economy. . . .
>
> We are led inexorably to the following considerations: 1) So great has economic pressure on our resources become that we must now make conscious choices between practical utility and the preservation of such beauty as remains to us. 2) The ethics and values that we have always proclaimed as a nation contain no commitment whatever to beauty. Indeed, we have been committed to its undeviating destruction.[4]

Thus, although environmental awareness has soared during the past decade, most Americans, including many who consider themselves environmentally conscious, carry on in the tradition of the early frontiersmen and resource raiders. They drive enormous cars that pollute the environment and squander valuable resources, they consume tons of plastics and paper packaging, they waste water and electricity. Business corporations often confine their environmental awareness to their advertisements and focus more on public relations than on antipollution measures. In some cases corporations have proudly advertised their achievements in reducing pollution without mentioning that these measures were forced on them by laws they lobbied against.

No change in American environmental policies will come about without changes in these attitudes and values. And such changes will be resisted by many powerful interests and by many individuals and groups when they realize the costs of conserving the environment in terms of increased taxes, reduced profits, and other inconveniences. We face many choices, but it is unlikely that we can have both an unspoiled environment and increasing industrialization. The debate over

[4]Robert Rienow and Leona Train Rienow, *Moment in the Sun* (New York: Ballantine Books, 1969), pp. 131, 161.

The roadsides and highways of America have been made ugly through the unregulated profusion of garish advertising signs and billboards. Conservationists are now broadening their objectives to include an attack on this visual pollution of the landscape. *(Dennis Brack/Black Star)*

the Alaskan oil pipeline illustrated this conflict between our demands for resources and our demands for environmental conservation. For years, environmentalists were able to delay construction of the pipeline by pointing to the devastating effects it might have on the wildlife and environment of Alaska. But as soon as an oil shortage developed in 1973, public opinion swung rapidly against the conservationists, and legislation to permit construction of the line was rushed through Congress. The nation opted for economic growth and exploitation of resources despite the environmental costs. Similarly, there are strong demands that the requirements of the Federal Clean Air Act be eased. In the interests of reducing air pollution, the act required that emission controls be applied to auto exhausts. But one effect of the controls is to increase gasoline consumption by at least 7 percent, and as newer, more stringent controls are applied, the mileage obtainable from a gallon of gas has grown even less. Again, social priorities will have to be determined: do we want more miles per gallon, or less fumes in the atmosphere?[5]

Although most social and natural scientists regard the environmental crisis as a real and pressing social problem, there remain some critics who believe that the issue is a false one or that our efforts and attention are being misdirected. The attitudes of these critics fall into three main categories:

[5]*Newsweek* (January 22, 1973), p. 54.

Value Conflict: Exploitation of Resources or Conservation of Environment?

Often man upsets the habitat to which a creature is highly attuned. Consider the giant California condor—the "Thunderbird" of Indian lore—whose dark bulk once soared lazily over many parts of the Western sky. The condor must have cliffs for nests, where he is provided with just the right air currents to bear his heavy body aloft in his search for carrion. Brooking no violation of his privacy, he will abandon a nest should human traffic come within earshot.

Because he demands a tiny but inviolate corner of this world for himself, the condor seems doomed. Poisoned and hunted elsewhere, the forty remaining birds have retreated to the Sespe Wildlife Refuge of 53,000 acres, which man reluctantly assigned them in 1951. Even here he is being threatened. There are those who think we need another impoundment of water on the Sespe River more than we need the condor. In this case we cannot claim that we did not know the ecology of the species; we are simply—and callously—ignoring it.

We can put in our dam and create still another undistinguished development and drive the condor to extinction. For some unfathomable reason we think this makes us richer than the Indian who stood in silent awe as the Thunderbird soared far overhead, then floated, with its weird and Harpy grace, into the canyon's swirling mists.

SOURCE: Robert Rienow and Leona Train Rienow, *Moment in the Sun* (New York: Ballantine Books, 1969).

1. *There is no crisis at all.* A few experts contend that the prophecies of environmental doom are mere exaggerations. For example, John D. Maddox takes the optimistic view that energy is more plentiful and cheap than it has ever been; that pollution is relatively minimal; and that the small quantities of insecticides found in Antarctic birds are indications that the poison spreads very slowly, rather than that it threatens the world.[6]
2. *A technological solution will be found.* Some experts believe that future technological discoveries will provide a solution. Economist Harold J. Barnett, for example, recalls that there have been many gloomy predictions in the past, but man has always triumphed through the application of new technologies: new fertilizers, new weed-killers, the power saw, long-distance pipelines, strip mining.

[6]John D. Maddox, *The Doomsday Syndrome* (New York: McGraw-Hill, 1972), pp. 4–5.

The pace of technological innovation is such, he believes, that radically new methods will be found to solve our problems.[7]

3. *The environmental crisis is a diversion.* A number of critics, including many radicals, regard concern for the environment as a middle-class luxury. Social-science professor Matthew A. Crenson, for example, takes the view that outcries over pollution are louder not because we have more pollution, but because our ideals are higher. Environmental concerns, he feels, are merely esthetic; the real problems of our society are those such as crime, poverty, narcotics addiction, and racial discrimination, and these should receive priority.[8]

APPROACHING THE PROBLEM

Sociologists often study the problem of the environment in terms of social disorganization caused by rapid technological change. From this perspective, our society is regarded as disorganized to the extent that our capacities to control pollution no longer match our capacities to generate pollution, and to the extent that our values and attitudes favoring the wholesale exploitation of the environment are no longer consistent with the reality of scarce resources. Our industrial system is highly functional for the creation of rising living standards, but is proving dysfunctional, in ways that were never seen or intended, through the creation of a ravaged environment. In analyzing the problem of the environment, sociologists have drawn on data from other disciplines outside the field of the social sciences—notably from the work of ecologists who study the biological aspects of the environment, and from the work of futurologists who make mathematical projections of existing economic, demographic, and other relevant trends.

The Science of Ecology

Life on earth exists only in the biosphere, a thin film of air, soil, and water at or near the surface of the planet. Within this biosphere, and particularly in the region immediately above and below sea level, countless species of organisms live in a delicately balanced and infinitely complex relationship with one another. The study of this interlocking web of life is only a few decades old and is termed *ecology* (from the Greek word for "home"). Ecology is the science of the mutual relationships between organisms and their environment. It embraces all forms of life in their natural settings—from the worm to the tree to man—and, more importantly, it attempts to trace how these organisms function in their distinctive environments, both alone and together. The ecological perspective has given us the notion of "Spaceship Earth"—the idea of

[7]Harold J. Barnett, "The Myth of Our Vanishing Resources," *Trans-action*, vol. 4, no. 7 (June 1967), pp. 7–10.
[8]*New York Times* (April 20, 1971).

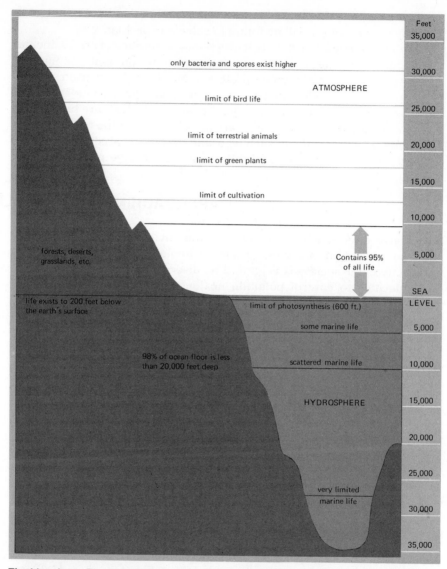

The biosphere. The biosphere is a thin film of life-sustaining air, soil, and water at or near the surface of the earth. The biosphere, with its countless interdependent organisms, is the largest of all ecosystems, but it is fragile and easily disrupted. (SOURCE: John McHale, *World Facts and Trends* [New York: Macmillan, 1972], p. 9.)

our planet as a massive, life-sustaining vessel in the void of the universe with finite, endlessly cycling resources. As biologist René Dubos emphasizes:

> The expression "Spaceship Earth" is no mere catch phrase. Now that all habitable parts of the globe are occupied, the careful husbandry of its resources is a sine qua non of survival for the human

species, more important than economic growth or political power. We are indeed travelers bound to the earth's crust, drawing breath from its shallow envelope of air, using and reusing its limited supply of water. Yet we collectively behave as if we were not aware of the problems inherent in the limitations of Spaceship Earth. . . . All over the world, technological civilization is threatening the elements of nature that are essential to human life, and the values that make it worth living.[9]

The concept of the ecosystem. At the heart of the science of ecology is the concept of an *ecosystem,* a self-sustaining community of organisms within its inorganic environment. The largest ecosystem of all is the biosphere itself, but an ecosystem may be as small as a drop of pond water, teeming with its microscopic yet interdependent inhabitants. There are four main elements in any ecosystem:

1. *Energy and inorganic matter.* Life can exist only in the presence of energy and inorganic (nonliving) matter. Energy is drawn primarily, though often indirectly, from the sun. Inorganic matter includes substances such as water, oxygen, carbon dioxide, nitrogen, and various other nutrients. These sources of energy and nutrition, in the appropriate balance, provide the environment that sustains life processes.
2. *Plants (or producers).* These are the trees, shrubs, grasses, and other green plants, which take energy from the sun and nutrients from the soil and atmosphere and convert them into organic, living material. The producers range in size from microscopic phytoplankton, such as algae, to huge redwoods.
3. *Consumers.* These are the higher organisms that feed on the producers. Some—the primary consumers or herbivores—feed directly on the plants, as in the case of deer and rabbits. Others—the secondary consumers or carnivores, such as foxes and lions—feed on other animals. Food chains can become very complex; for example, man is both a primary and a secondary consumer, while a mosquito that feeds on man is a tertiary consumer.
4. *Decomposers.* These are tiny creatures—insects, bacteria, fungi— that abound in the soil, atmosphere, and bodies of dead plants and animals. They break down the organic material of the dead organisms and so release their nutrients back into the ecosystem. Even these lowly, invisible microorganisms, unmourned when they are exterminated, are essential to life on earth.

Each component in the ecosystem interacts with others in an astonishingly complex network of interlocking energy and chemical cycles. Although growth and decay are taking place continuously and simulta-

[9]René Dubos, "The Human Landscape," *Bulletin of the Atomic Scientists,* vol. 26, no. 3 (March 1970), pp. 31–37.

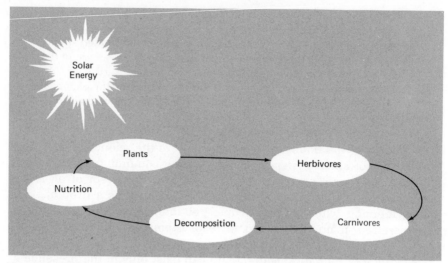

The cycle of life. Life on earth depends on a delicately balanced cycle involving energy, plants, animals, and nutrition sources. Disruption of the cycle at any point can have severe effects elsewhere in the process.

neously in an ecosystem, they balance each other in the long run: the ecosystem tends to equilibrium. All living things, including man, depend on the stability of these processes which constitute the chain of life. As Alan Devoe points out:

> All creatures are in a common brotherhood . . . interconnected with everything else. . . . There is a bond between a man and a mouse, or a tree and a fox, or a frog and a raccoon. . . . We are one small ingredient in a whole of unimaginable vastness . . . a part of a general and embracing interdependence. . . . We are supported by starfish. An owl props us. Earthworms minister to hold us upright.[10]

Human interference in the ecosystem. Interference at any point in these cycles can have unforeseen and even disastrous consequences. Man first began to interfere with the ecosystem around ten thousand years ago at the time of the Agricultural Revolution. He learned to domesticate animals and plants, replacing the complex ecosystem with a simple one in which nearly all the energy and chemical cycles were directed at supporting the human species alone. Since that time, technological progress has been spectacular, and so has the accompanying rate of increase of the human population. Within a relatively short period after the development of organized agriculture, the first urban societies were founded, and within less than ten thousand years, man was walking on the moon. Today, we add to our numbers every month the equivalent of the human population at the time of the Agricultural

[10]Quoted in Rienow and Rienow, *Moment in the Sun*, p. 45.

Breaking the Chain of Life

Fishermen in northwest Missouri, ignoring the thrill that the annual migrations of the fresh-water white pelicans gave the observers and resentful of having to share fish with them, organized raids on the birds' island nests and decimated the population. Today the white pelicans are on the critical list for survival.

But so are the game fish, unfortunately. It so happens that the diet of the pelican is largely rough fish; with the pelican all but wiped out, the rough fish are increasing and crowding out the game fish, ruining the fishermen's sport.

In a less direct fashion we have the now classic story of the boy who set out to trap the skunks in the vicinity of his duck pond. After a while his ducks began to vanish mysteriously, one by one. It took an old woodsman who understood the web of life to explain to the boy that skunks eat snapping turtle eggs, and that when the skunks are killed off the turtles increase and quietly pick off the ducks. Akin to this ecological ring is the grasshopper-prairie dog chain, described recently by zoology Professor George M. Sutton of Oklahoma University. Burrowing owls feast on grasshoppers and similar pests. But they use the burrows of prairie dogs for their nests. When ranchers, seeing the prairie dogs nibbling at their pastures, persuaded federal agents to start a full-scale chemical warfare against the prairie dogs, the burrowing owl population decreased. Soon armies of grasshoppers and other insects began to take over and the end is not yet come.

SOURCE: Robert Rienow and Leona Train Rienow, *Moment in the Sun* (New York: Ballantine Books, 1969).

Revolution, and we are capable of, and are achieving, large-scale interference in the global ecological balance. Again and again we disrupt the web of life by shutting out sunlight with smog, increasing the amount of atmospheric carbon dioxide by burning fuels, killing off decomposers with insecticides, polluting water sources with chemical effluents, or simply hunting species to extinction.

To biologist Paul Ehrlich, the main reason for the reckless human intervention in the planetary ecosystem is overpopulation, which causes massive and increasing depletion of resources and also environmental pollution.[11] Others, like ecologist Barry Commoner, believe that faulty technology constitutes the major environmental threat. Common-

[11]Paul R. Ehrlich and Anne H. Ehrlich, *Population/Resources/Environment: Issues in Human Ecology,* 2d ed. (San Francisco: W. H. Freeman & Co., 1972).

er points out that pollution has increased more than 2,000 percent since World War II, a far greater increase than the increase in population. The real problem, he argues, is that "productive technologies with intensive impacts on the environment have displaced less destructive ones."[12] For example, high-polluting detergents have largely replaced low-polluting soap; truck freight haulage, with high environmental impact, has replaced rail haulage, with its relatively low environmental impact; synthetic, nondegradable fibers have replaced natural fabrics; plastics have replaced wood. Our productive circles have broken out of the circles of the ecosystem, producing a counterecological pattern of growth: "Human beings have broken out of the cycle of life . . . to survive, we must close the circle."[13]

The Limits to Growth

In 1970 the Club of Rome, a private international group of eminent social and natural scientists, decided to investigate the effects of continued industrial and population growth on the human future. With the aid of large foundation grants, they commissioned a detailed and intricate study of the likely effects of sustained growth patterns. The study was conducted by a research team at the Massachusetts Institute of Technology (MIT), where a complex computer model was used to generate projections extending well into the next century. The report of the research team, entitled *The Limits to Growth*, was published in 1972.[14] It made international headlines and immediately became a focal point in the debate on population growth, industrialization, resources, and pollution. In clear language, and with the backing of sophisticated statistical models and reams of computer print-outs, the researchers concluded that mankind probably faces an uncontrollable and disastrous collapse of society and economy within a hundred years—and possibly a good deal sooner—unless we quickly establish a global equilibrium in which population growth and industrial output remain constant. If the human population continues to multiply, industrialize, consume resources, and pollute at its present rate, then the environmental system of the planet will be so devastated as to be incapable of sustaining industrial civilization or large human numbers.

Projections for the world ecosystem. The research team studied the dynamic interactions over time of five factors in a simulated computer model of the world ecosystem. They traced the effects that population increase, food production, depletion of natural resources, industrial output, and pollution have on one another. They found that in each of these factors, growth is not linear, but rather exponential. Linear growth is a simple, additive type of growth—like putting away a penny

[12]Barry Commoner, *The Closing Circle* (New York: Knopf, 1971), p. 177.
[13]Ibid., pp. 299–300.
[14]Donella H. Meadows, et al., *The Limits to Growth* (New York: Signet, 1972).

The Hazards of Exponential Growth

Common as it is, exponential growth can yield surprising results — results that have fascinated mankind for centuries. There is an old Persian legend about a clever courtier who presented a beautiful chessboard to his king and requested that the king give him in return 1 grain of rice for the first square on the board, 2 grains for the second square, 4 grains for the third, and so forth. The king readily agreed and ordered rice to be brought from his stores. The fourth square of the chessboard required 8 grains, the tenth square 512 grains, the fifteenth required 16,384, and the twenty-first square gave the courtier more than a million grains of rice. By the fortieth square a million million rice grains had to be brought from the storerooms. The king's entire rice supply was exhausted long before he reached the sixty-fourth square. Exponential increase is deceptive because it generates immense numbers very quickly.

A French riddle for children illustrates another aspect of exponential growth — the apparent suddenness with which it approaches a fixed limit. Suppose you own a pond on which a water lily is growing. The lily plant doubles in size each day. If the lily were allowed to grow unchecked, it would completely cover the pond in thirty days, choking off the other forms of life in the water. For a long time the lily plant seems small, and so you decide not to worry about cutting it back until it covers half the pond. On what day will that be? On the twenty-ninth day, of course. You have one day to save your pond.

SOURCE: Donnella H. Meadows, et al., *The Limits to Growth* (New York: Signet, 1972).

every day for a month. At the end of thirty days, you will have thirty pennies. Exponential growth, however, is based on a fixed doubling time and involves increasingly rapid growth — like putting a penny away on the first day of the month, doubling it on the second, doubling that on the third, and so on. The exponential growth would result in a sum of over $10 million at the end of the month. The last day alone would yield more than $5 million, because at the moment of the last doubling time, growth leaps from half the limit to the ultimate limit. The MIT report implies that mankind stands on the brink of that last, fatal doubling.

At first the MIT research team built a standard world model, in which they assumed that current trends would continue unchanged. In such a situation, they found, a shortage of natural resources would eventually destroy the industrial base, which would collapse and take with it the services and agricultural systems on which we depend. Food shortages and lack of health services would lead to a massive increase in the death rate.

The MIT team tried to find a way out of this predicament by running dozens of hypothetical variations through the computer. It was assumed, for example, that vast, hitherto undiscovered natural resources might be found and exploited. What would happen? The computer showed that in such a case, industrialization would rapidly accelerate, and the resulting pollution would ravage public health, reduce agricultural production, and overwhelm the environment. What if technology provided new means of controlling the pollution? In that case, responded the computer, population would soar and outstrip the capacity of the land to produce food. No matter how the factors were varied, growth would always invite a circular process leading to a situation in which human populations starve, raw materials are exhausted, or pollution surpasses livable limits. All growth projections ended, sooner or later, in collapse. All these projections took no account of the social stresses and even wars that might result from overcrowding and desperate shortages of food and resources.

The MIT group found only one possible solution: maintaining population and industrialization in a steady state of global equilibrium. This would involve a deliberate antigrowth policy. Birth rate would equal the death rate, and investment in new industrial equipment would not exceed the retirement of old equipment. If exponential growth in population and industrialization could be brought to a screeching halt, this would automatically end the exponential growth in pollution, resource depletion, and food requirements. Even so, the poor countries of the world may have no realistic hope of matching the present living standards of the rich countries, whose pollution and natural resource load on the ecosystem is twenty to fifty times as great per person. Since there are far more people in the poor countries, their attainment of the living standards of the rich countries would increase the planetary load at least tenfold, and the earth simply does not have the capability to sustain such a rise in mass living standards. In fact, observes the report, an equalization of standards is far more likely to be caused by a decline in the economic standards of the rich countries; wealthy industrial societies may be "self-extinguishing."

Major changes would be required in a no-growth society, such as a shift in emphasis from the acquisition of goods to the enjoyment of services. The MIT group acknowledges that their proposal would necessitate radical changes in values and attitudes and that their antigrowth suggestion strikes at the very foundations of our most cherished beliefs about the inevitability of progress, the desirability of growth, and the virtues of free enterprise. But as Professor Dennis L. Meadows, director of the MIT study, points out:

> Our view is that we don't have an alternative — it's not as though we can choose to keep growing or not. We are certainly going to stop

growing. The question is, do we do it in a way that is most consistent with our goals, or do we just let nature take its course?[15]

Reactions to the *Limits to Growth* report. The *Limits to Growth* report has had its critics, and its methods and findings have been challenged on many fronts. Rudolph Klein has attacked the very idea of a computer model of the ecosystem:

> Futurology is . . . the latest model off the assembly line. . . . It is desparately important that complex problems should not be reduced to the simple symmetry required by systems analysis. . . . The inevitable result is to produce an equally simple answer whose very simplicity makes it unfit as a guide to action.[16]

Dr. Henry C. Wallich charges that a no-growth economy is hard to imagine, much less achieve, and might lock poor people into perpetual poverty:

> The only way to make it stable is to assume that people will become very routine-minded, with no independent thought and very little freedom, each generation doing exactly what the last did. I can't say I'm enamored with that vision. . . . Can you expect billions of Asians and Africans to live forever at roughly their standard of living while we go on forever at ours?[17]

Carl Kayson argues that technology will come to our aid and avert the predicted environmental collapse:

> Advancing technology . . . brings down the costs of using existing resources and literally creates new resources by bringing within the bounds of cost feasibility materials which formerly lay outside it. . . . The advance of technology, like the growth of population and industry, has also been proceeding exponentially. . . . There are no credible reasons for believing that the world as a whole cannot maintain a fairly high rate of economic growth (though not necessarily the present one) over a long period of time into the future.[18]

But the MIT report did win the support of thirty-three leading European scientists from various disciplines, who endorsed a statement, "Blueprint for Survival," published in the same year as *The Limits to Growth*.

> The principal defect of the industrial way of life with its ethos of expansion is that it is not sustainable. . . . We can be certain . . . that sooner or later it will end (only the precise circumstances are in

[15]*New York Times* (February 27, 1972).
[16]Rudolf Klein, "Growth and Its Enemies," *Commentary*, vol. 53, no. 6 (June 1972), pp. 37–44.
[17]*New York Times* (February 27, 1972).
[18]Carl Kayson, "The Computer That Printed W*O*L*F," *Foreign Affairs*, vol. 50, no. 4 (July 1972), pp. 663–666.

doubt), and that it will do so in one of two ways: either against our will, in a succession of famines, epidemics, social crises and wars; or because we want it to . . . in a succession of thoughtful, humane, and measured changes.

By now it should be clear that the main problems of the environment do not arise from temporary and accidental malfunctions of the existing economic and social systems. On the contrary, they are the warning signs of a profound incompatibility between deeply rooted beliefs in continuous growth and the dawning recognition of the earth as a space ship, limited in its resources and vulnerable to thoughtless mishandling. The nature of our responses to these symptoms is crucial. . . . If a strategy for survival is to have any chance of success, the solutions must be formulated in the light of the problems. . . . If we plan remedial action with our eyes on political rather than ecological reality, then . . . very surely, we will muddle our way to extinction.[19]

THE DETERIORATING ENVIRONMENT

From the time that our ancestors threw gnawed bones into the nearest gully, man has assumed that the wind, water, and sheer space of nature would swallow his wastes and render them innocuous. But now man's numbers and technology are overwhelming the capacity of the natural environment to cope. A soaring population, armed with destructive technologies—automobiles, jet aircrafts, detergents, nuclear reactors—is making a greater and greater impact on the ecosystem. Man is fouling his environmental nest and in doing so he is causing havoc elsewhere in the ecosystem. Many complete smaller ecosystems that took millennia to evolve have been irreparably damaged. Entire species are no more than memories, existing only as stuffed specimens in museums or faded prints in old travel books. Such familiar creatures as whales, polar bears, and tigers are on the danger list.

Let us look at some of the ways in which multiplying industrial man is despoiling the environment and threatening the planetary ecosystem.

Air Pollution

A citizen on the streets of New York inhales into his lungs the equivalent in toxic materials of thirty-eight cigarettes a day.[20] Atmospheric pollution cuts down on the amount of sunlight reaching New York by up to 25 percent. Other cities are worse off, however; pollution cuts out up to 40 percent of Chicago's sunlight.[21] And it is not only the cities that are affected. Smog generated in urban and industrial areas has been

---

[19]Edward Goldsmith, et al., "Blueprint for Survival," *The Ecologist*, vol. 2, no. 1 (January 1972), pp. 2–6.
[20]Rienow and Rienow, *Moment in the Sun*, p. 141.
[21]Ehrlich and Ehrlich, *Population/Resources/Environment*, p. 146.

An electricity generating plant pollutes air and water. The environmental impact of this plant illustrates a basic American dilemma: the more energy and resources we consume, the more pollution we create. Ultimately, we may have to choose between high consumption and a livable environment. *(Arthur Tress/Photo Researchers, Inc.)*

sighted over the oceans and even over the North Pole. At present, the United States dumps more than 200 million tons of wastes into the atmosphere every day—almost a ton per day per person.[22]

Air pollution comes from four main sources: transportation, power generation, industry, and waste incineration. By far the most serious contributor to air pollution is the private automobile. Each year our 90 million cars spew forth some 66 million tons of carbon monoxide, 1 million tons of sulfur oxides, 6 million tons of nitrogen oxides, 12 million tons of hydrocarbons, 1 million tons of particulate matter, and a variety of other poisonous substances.[23] Areas such as Los Angeles show a concentration of lead in the air that is fifty times greater than that in rural areas.[24] Asbestos particles from brake linings pollute the city air and are believed to be carcinogenic (cancer-causing) in sufficient amounts. As Ehrlich comments, "translated into daily amounts, the figures mean that each day American cars exhaust into our atmosphere a variety of pollutants weighing more than a bumper-to-bumper

[22]Kenneth Auchincloss, "The Ravaged Environment," *Newsweek* (January 26, 1970).
[23]Ehrlich and Ehrlich, *Population/Resources/Environment*, p. 147.
[24]John McHale, *World Facts and Trends,* 2d ed. (New York: Macmillan, 1972), p. 16.

line of cars stretching from Cleveland to New York."[25] Air pollution from automobiles is actually becoming worse. New automobiles are being added to our already clogged highways at such a rate that by 1980 the gains made by antipollution devices in improving the quality of our air will actually be reversed.[26] In any case, antipollution measures are directed at only a very few constituents of auto exhausts. The remaining gases and particles produce a variety of different chemicals, depending on climatic conditions at the time; warm sunlight turns the atmosphere over our cities into a photochemical brew whose content varies from hour to hour.

Power generation produces many noxious chemicals, particularly sulfur oxides (about 3 million tons a year) derived from the burning of high-sulfur coal. Industry produces an almost infinite range of atmospheric pollutants, including a further 2 million tons of carbon monoxide, 9 million tons of sulfur oxides, and 3 million tons each of nitrogen oxides and particulate matter.[27] Waste incineration, even when done properly, produces millions of tons of particulates and nitrogen oxides, and when done improperly, produces carbon monoxide as well.

Air pollution on this scale poses a grave threat to public health. Deaths due to lung cancer and bronchitis are doubling every ten years, and emphysema, a lung disease, is the fastest growing cause of death in the United States. Air pollution has been directly implicated in these trends. Dr. Paul Kotin, director of the National Institution of Environmental Health Services, estimates that a tenth of the nation's annual bill for health services goes to treating illness resulting from environmental pollution, mostly atmospheric.[28] Under the particular climatic condition known as a thermal inversion (a layer of warm air above a layer of cold air, trapping smog near the surface), air pollution has been known to kill numbers of people outright. The most notorious example was the 1952 smog in London which killed four thousand people in the space of four days. There have been several less dramatic instances in the United States. On Thanksgiving Day, 1966, an inversion layer trapped fumes in New York City and caused an estimated 168 deaths. Los Angeles now declares frequent "smog days," on which conditions are so dangerous that schoolchildren are not allowed to engage in activities that might involve deep breathing.

The U.S. Public Health Service predicts that sulfur dioxide emission will increase from its 1960 level of 20 million tons to 35 million by the year 2000; nitrogen oxide emission will rise from 11 million to 30 million tons, and particulates from 30 million to over 45 million tons. The number of automobiles is projected to quadruple in the same period.[29] The prospects for cleaner air are not encouraging — especially when the

[25]Ehrlich and Ehrlich, *Population/Resources/Environment*, p. 147.
[26]R. Stephen Berry, "The Chemistry and Cost: Perspectives on Polluted Air — 1970," *Bulletin of the Atomic Scientists*, vol. 26, no. 4 (April 1970), p. 2.
[27]Ehrlich and Ehrlich, *Population/Resources/Environment*, p. 147.
[28]*New York Times* (October 7, 1970).
[29]Ehrlich and Ehrlich, *Population/Resources/Environment*, p. 152.

auto manufacturers and gasoline producers constitute such powerful interests in American society and when American attitudes and values place such emphasis on the virtues of the private car in preference to low-polluting mass transit systems.

Water Pollution

The United States has the unique, if dubious, distinction of being the only country in the world to contain a river which has been declared a fire hazard. The river in question is the Cuyahoga in Ohio, and it has twice caught fire when the industrial chemicals, oils, and other combustible pollutants that it carries were accidentally ignited. None of our other rivers has yet burst into flame, but many of them are heavily polluted with contaminants—treated and untreated sewage, detergents, pesticides, agricultural fertilizers, chemical wastes, high-temperature industrial effluents. All over the United States, communities depend for their domestic water supplies on the contaminated water flushed out of the communities upstream. Immense sums are invested in making this water safe to drink, though not always successfully. At the end of the last decade over sixty American cities were listed by the Public Health Service as having water supplies that were "unsatisfactory" or "a potential health hazard."[30]

Many of our lakes, too, are in danger. Lake Erie is now almost dead, its bottom covered with a layer of effluent that is up to 125 feet thick in places. The other Great Lakes are also threatened by an accelerated process of aging called "eutrophication." Under natural conditions, eutrophication occurs slowly. A lake starts out cold and almost lifeless, but as streams carry in nutrients from the surrounding drainage basin, the fertility of the water increases, encouraging the growth of plants and animals. Organic material piles up on the lake bottom, and the water becomes shallower and warmer. The edges fill in, marsh intrudes, and swampy forests take over until the lake disappears completely. The Great Lakes were very young when the first Europeans discovered them—cold, deep, extremely pure, created by a glacier a mere twenty thousand years ago. But in the past fifty years, the enormous amount of pollution has speeded up the eutrophication process—in the case of Lake Erie, by the equivalent of fifteen thousand years. The lake is probably unsalvageable and seems destined to appear on future maps as a gigantic, man-made swamp.[31]

Much of the pollution that falls out of the atmosphere or enters rivers finally ends up in the oceans. Even the vast oceans (which contain four-fifths of the planet's animal life and the bulk of its vegetation) cannot absorb the mounting deluge of contaminants. Explorer Thor Heyerdahl, crossing the Atlantic on a small raft, found the surface of the

[30]Ibid., p. 157.

[31]Charles F. Powers and Andrew Robertson, "The Aging of the Great Lakes," *Scientific American,* vol. 215, no. 5 (November 1966), pp. 95–104.

ocean littered like a city beach with plastic bottles, old shoes, and gobs of tar. Half a million tons of crude oil are leaked or dumped into the oceans every year.[32] Rivers that would normally carry about 200,000 tons of phosphates to the sea each year now carry more than 6,500,000 tons, mostly in the form of agricultural fertilizers. Lead is being washed into the sea at a rate thirteen times higher than under natural conditions. The oceans are the ultimate accumulation site for as much as 25 percent of the DDT and other pesticides sprayed onto the land; as a result, large numbers of fish have been condemned for human consumption because of the high concentration of man-made poisons in their flesh.[33] It is often held that man can solve his food problem by increased exploitation of the oceans, but this belief neglects the fact that:

> The open sea — 90 per cent of the ocean and nearly three-fourths of the earth's surface — is essentially a biological desert. It produces a negligible fraction of the world's fish catch at present and has little or no potential for yielding more in the future.[34]

The reason is that the nutrients that sustain oceanic life are concentrated in coastal waters. These nutrients are introduced into the seas from the rivers, which are now laden with poisons as well as nutrients. Pollution may kill off much of this anticipated food resource, and render a good deal of the remainder largely inedible.

Again, the problems raised by water pollution require some hard choices. Can we maintain a high population and a high standard of living without producing billions of tons of pollutants? And if we do not dump them into the rivers and seas, where do we put them?

Despoiling the Land

Man is despoiling the land in countless ways. He has done so since the Agricultural Revolution, often devastating vast expanses by counter-ecological activities. The Sahara desert, for example, is partly man-made; beneath the thick layers of sand are to be found traces of dense forests that existed less than two thousand years ago. Morocco was once covered with dense woods, which have disappeared as a result of overgrazing by domesticated sheep and goats. Today, forests are being cut down throughout the tropics, in order to make way for more economically rewarding activities such as cattle raising. Again, the ecological consequences are unforeseeable — both for the regions concerned and for the global environment that depends on these forests to remove large quantities of carbon dioxide from the atmosphere. Exploitation and despoilation of land resources occur all over the United States in the construction of highways and parking lots, in the development of

---

[32]McHale, *World Facts and Trends*, p. 27.
[33]Goldsmith, et. al., "Blueprint for Survival," p. 3.
[34]John H. Rhyther, "Photosynthesis and Fish Production in the Sea," *Science*, 166 (October 3, 1969), pp. 72–76.

Our consumer society generates millions of tons of waste products every year. Some of the waste is burned, polluting the air; some is dumped at sea, polluting the ocean; but most is left to rust and rot on the land. *(Bruce Davidson/Magnum)*

projects such as the Alaskan pipeline, and in the use of the strip-mining technique for coal extraction, which is leaving ugly scars across the landscape at such a rate that by 1980 over 5 million acres will have been defaced, many of them in western areas of spectacular natural beauty.

Another way in which we despoil the land is by dumping our garbage on it. An urban population of 1 million needs dumping space for five thousand cubic feet of garbage and refuse every day. Each year we junk over 3.5 billion tons of wastes, including 7 million automobiles and 20 million tons of paper.[35] As Ehrlich notes:

> Each year in the United States we must dispose of 55 billion cans, 26 billion bottles and jars, 65 billion metal and plastic bottle caps, and more than half a billion dollars worth of other packaging materials. Seven million automobiles are junked each year, and the amount of urban solid wastes (trash and garbage) collected annually is approximately 200 million tons. Every man, woman and child in the United States is, on the average, producing nearly a ton of refuse annually. In addition to junked cars, some 10 million tons of iron and steel are

[35]McHale, *World Facts and Trends*, p. 22.

scrapped each year, more than 3 billion tons of waste rock and mill tailings are dumped near mine sites, and huge amounts of slag, ash, and other wastes are produced by smelters, power plants, other industries, and agriculture.[36]

Solid wastes are unpleasant, odorous, and ugly. They pollute water that percolates through them, they pollute the atmosphere if they are incinerated, and they provide breeding grounds for a wide range of noxious pests. The pollutants can also have devasting effects on the local ecosystems of the soil. Millions of tiny invertebrates live in each acre and sometimes in each square meter of soil, and these organisms and microorganisms are vital to continuing fertility. But all these pollutants and wastes exist only because there is a demand, a market, a profit for the original products. Our own attitudes and values as a society have led inevitably to the despoilation of the land. We are all "against pollution"—but we are the polluters.

Chemicals and Pesticides

American women carry in their breasts up to ten times more of the toxic insecticide DDT than the maximum level permitted in dairy milk for human consumption. Every morsel that we eat, even "organic" foods, is tainted with pesticides. The soil and water of the planet have been contaminated with these chemicals, which are very stable and resist decomposition for decades after they are first used. DDT is found everywhere on earth, even in the tissues of Antarctic penguins, on a continent where the chemical has never been used. And there is growing evidence that many pesticides are carcinogenic (cancer-causing) substances. The spread of DDT and other toxic chemicals serves to illustrate the manner in which we have surrounded ourselves with hundreds of thousands of new compounds about whose potential effects we know virtually nothing. Neither we nor any other species on the planet has had any evolutionary experience with the new substances, and we have had no opportunity to evolve natural defenses against potential damage that they might do to our biological systems. Most of the chemicals may well prove innocuous to man, if not to other species; but many, such as chlorinated hydrocarbon insecticides or the tranquilizer thalidomide (which induced birth deformities when administered to pregnant women), can have severe and unintended consequences on mankind.

How have DDT and the other insecticides spread throughout the ecosystem, and why are they found in such high concentrations in consumers such as man? The chemicals enter the ecosystem when farmers or governments spray them on the land. Some of the substance remains in the soil, some is blown into the atmosphere, and some is

[36]Ehrlich and Ehrlich, *Population/Resources/Environment*, p. 159.

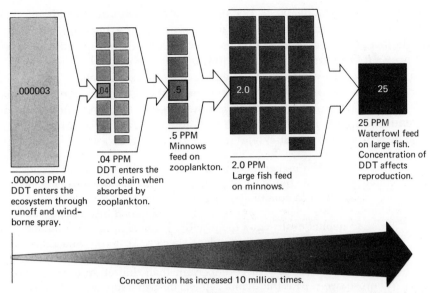

Magnification of DDT in parts per million (PPM). DDT, like many other pesticides, is an extremely stable compound that does not decompose for many decades. It is readily absorbed into the tissues of plants and animals, and when numbers of these organisms are consumed by another, the concentration of the chemical is magnified at each step. Animals at the top of the food chain may absorb lethal quantities of a pesticide that was applied many years previously and hundreds of miles away. (SOURCE: John McHale, *World Facts and Trends* [New York Macmillan, 1972], p. 21.)

washed into the rivers and seas. The chemical contaminates animals and plants, which are eaten by other animals, that may in turn end up on our dining tables. DDT and many other pesticides are cumulative poisons. They tend to be retained in the tissues of organisms that consume them, rather than excreted back into the environment. The concentration of DDT increases at each level in the food chain; concentrations in animals at the top of the chain are sometimes as much as ten million times higher than concentrations in animals lower down. Thus aquatic plants may contain low concentrations of the chemical; dozens of these plants are eaten by small fish, so the concentration is increased; thousands of these small fish are eaten by larger predator fish during their lifetime, so the concentration is increased again; and numbers of the latter fish are eaten by birds of prey, which may finally die of poisoning, their bodies decomposing to release the DDT into a fresh cycle through the ecosystem. The chain of life thus becomes a chain of death.

Pesticides have been effective against agricultural pests, but only to a limited and steadily diminishing extent. Some 250 pest species are resistant to one group of pesticides or another, while others require increasing applications of poison to keep their populations within manageable proportions. Other previously innocuous creatures have actually become major pests because of the unintended eradication of their natural predators. Mites, for example, have become significant pests largely because insecticides have killed off the insects that used to prey on them and keep their numbers under control. The toxic substances spread everywhere, affecting creatures that were never the target of the exterminators. This has been the fate of the American eagle, our national emblem, which is now faced with imminent extinction because the DDT in its eggs often prevents them from hatching.

The "Blueprint for Survival" report states the problem clearly:

> There are half a million man made chemicals in use today, yet we cannot predict the behavior or properties of the greater part of them (either singly or in combination) once they are released into the environment. We know, however, that the combined effects of pollution and habitat destruction menace the survival of no less than 280 mammal, 350 bird, and 20,000 plant species. To those who regret these losses but greet them with the comment that the survival of homo sapiens is surely more important than that of an eagle or a primrose, we repeat that homo sapiens himself depends on the continued resilience of those ecological networks of which eagles and primroses are integral parts.[37]

So far, the United States has released about 1 billion pounds of DDT into the environment, and we continue to use over 100 million pounds per year. Annual world production of the chemical, which is only one of many similar pesticides, is 1,300 million pounds.[38]

Radioactive Wastes

An explosion at any one of the nation's forty-two operating nuclear power plants could result in the release of large quantities of atomic radiation. The explosion itself would not be large, but the nuclear fallout could be the equivalent of hundreds of Hiroshima-sized atomic bombs. In May 1974 the Atomic Energy Commission admitted that in the previous year, all forty-two plants had suffered "abnormal occurrences," including 371 "potentially significant" incidents, of which 12 involved the release of radioactivity outside the power plants. Thirteen of the plants had to be shut down for extended periods.[39]

Nuclear power plants generate radioactive nuclear wastes. These wastes emit radiation which in small doses can cause cancers or birth deformities, and in large doses, death. The wastes are particularly dangerous because many of them remain radioactive for tens, hundreds, or even thousands of years. The problems posed by nuclear power plants are likely to increase as the United States constructs new "breeder" reactors—a development program to which high priority has

[37]Goldsmith, et. al., "Blueprint for Survival," p. 6.
[38]McHale, *World Facts and Trends*, p. 21.
[39]*Village Voice* (July 4, 1974).

been assigned following the mid-seventies energy shortage. Each breeder reactor will hold one to three tons of plutonium 239; a piece of this substance the size of a grapefruit could, if equally distributed, supply a lethal dose to the entire human race. One prototype breeder reactor was built outside Detroit in 1966; it recently closed down after a "near miss" accident that fell outside the "maximum credible accident" anticipated in the Atomic Energy Commission's specifications for the installation.[40] The fact that such a highly dangerous and experimental plant could have been built in close vicinity to a densely populated industrial area is itself a cause for concern and for criticism of the AEC. After the accident, the AEC illegally refused to file an official statement on the environmental impact of the breeder reactor program. Private conservationist groups thereupon hauled the AEC before a federal court, which declared that the "program presents unique and unprecedented environmental hazards to human health for hundreds of years."[41]

The disposal of nuclear wastes is a major problem. Some wastes are buried in covered trenches. Other wastes—the most lethal, such as strontium 90 and plutonium—are buried underground in sealed concrete tanks. These tanks contain millions of gallons of concentrated radioactive waste, which is so hot that it boils by itself for years and will be utterly lethal for thousands of years. The sealed tanks, located in Richland, Washington, have leaked at least sixteen times since 1968; in 1974 a leak continued for fifty-one days, flooded 115,000 gallons of the contents into the ground and raised the radiation count high above the maximum measurable levels of the underground radiation detectors. The tanks, which were built to last for decades, not thousands of years, are already showing signs of stress. The AEC has entertained various proposals for the ultimate disposal of the wastes, ranging from firing them into space in rockets to converting them into solids and storing them in the deepest abandoned mines that can be found. Meanwhile, the largest insurance companies in the Western hemisphere have refused, even as a joint venture, to underwrite more than 1 percent of the potential liability for a major nuclear power plant accident.

The AEC has been strongly criticized before Congress on the grounds that there is

> a serious AEC credibility gap. It seems apparent that the AEC isn't nearly as certain about nuclear safety as it ought to be. It has suppressed unwelcome research of possible hazards that have been discovered by its own researchers. When the researchers have pressed their doubts on higher officials, the AEC suppressed their reports and terminated their experimental programs, and sometimes researchers have been fired.[42]

[40]Ehrlich and Ehrlich, *Population/Resources/Environment*, p. 173.
[41]*Village Voice* (July 4, 1974).
[42]William Nelson Peach, *The Energy Outlook for the 1980's: A Study Prepared for the Use of the Subcommittee on Economic Progress of the Joint Economic Committee, Congress of the United States* (Washington, D.C.: U.S. Government Printing Office, 1973).

In 1973 the Environmental Protection Administration determined to set stricter safety standards for the AEC. The AEC appealed to President Nixon, who removed authority for the setting of standards from the EPA and gave it to the AEC itself. Ehrlich comments on this development:

> The ultimate folly in our development of nuclear energy is that the AEC is charged with the inherently contradictory responsibilities of developing nuclear power generation as expeditiously and as inexpensively as possible, *and* safeguarding the public against the hazards involved in this development. In any industrial process, one buys safety at the expense of time and money.[43]

Why is the AEC being permitted to embark on a program with acknowledged risks of potentially catastrophic consequences over hundreds of years? Again, the issue is one of values, attitudes, and resulting priorities. If the United States is to achieve its goal of becoming capable of meeting all its growing energy requirements within a decade without any reliance on foreign imports, then programs such as the construction of further breeder reactors seem necessary, regardless of their potential environmental impact.

Changing the Weather

Man is altering the weather. Some of his alterations are relatively minor: cities, for example, are "heat islands," 10 to 20 degrees warmer than the surrounding countryside. The concrete and asphalt of an urban area absorb the heat like a giant storage battery during the day, and continue to warm the air after sunset. Automobile engines and industrial production add to the heat. When the warm air covering the city comes into contact with a cold front, the result is rain, fog, or cloud, so that cities have more wet weather than neighboring rural areas.[44]

But man is altering the global climate as well, with consequences that are not yet fully understood. We know that the main agent of this alteration is air pollution, but the ultimate impact is difficult to ascertain. On the one hand, man is increasing the amount of carbon dioxide in the atmosphere – partly by burning solid fuels and wastes, partly by destroying the forests and vegetation which convert carbon dioxide into oxygen. Since 1880 the carbon dioxide content of the atmosphere has increased by about 12 percent. Carbon dioxide is transparent to radiation in the form of light, but not to radiation in the form of heat. As a result, the sun's rays pass through the carbon dioxide and warm up the earth, but the heat is trapped by the carbon dioxide on its way back into space – the so-called greenhouse effect. The effect, at least up to 1945, has been a progressive warming of the earth's atmosphere. If the

[43]Ehrlich and Ehrlich, *Population/Resources/Environment*, p. 174.
[44]*U.S. News & World Report* (September 17, 1973), pp. 47–48.

global temperature rises by as little as another 4 or 5 degrees, the polar icecaps will begin to melt, raising sea levels as much as three hundred feet and flooding coastal cities all over the world. But since the mid-forties, and in spite of the increase in atmospheric carbon dioxide, there has been a slight decrease in global temperature. The reason seems to be that other pollutants—industrial emissions, particulates, dust from mechanized agriculture and trails of high-flying jet aircraft—are blocking out some of the sun's rays and reflecting them back into space before they can warm up the earth.[45] If we are lucky, these two man-made but contradictory pressures—one toward the melting of the polar icecaps, the other toward the creation of a new Ice Age—will balance one another out. But we simply do not understand the full implications or potential consequences of our interference with the weather.

ENERGY AND RESOURCES

Energy

The United States found itself, in the mid-seventies, in an "energy crisis." Political events in the Middle East led to a shortage of oil and a sharp rise in the price of gasoline and heating fuels, and for the first time the American public realized how very vulnerable our industrial society is to energy shortages. With 6 percent of the world's population, we account for about a third of the world's energy consumption. The average American lives on about ten thousand watts of energy per day, while most of the rest of the world survives on little more than a hundred watts. And the U.S. consumption rate is increasing by 2.5 percent annually.[46]

The energy crisis had been predicted for several years, but the institutions that might have made a difference largely ignored the problem. The lights were on, the bills were low, and few people cared. Government energy policy was almost nonexistent; even though 10 percent of our national economic activity is devoted to extracting, refining, distributing, and consuming fuel, there was no separate government department to oversee energy problems until very recently. The natural gas industry urged consumption of energy with advertisements declaring that "Gas heats best," but by 1972 natural gas was so scarce in twenty-one states that no new customers were accepted.[47] Electric companies urged that the American home be all-electric, but in 1973 they were urging the consumer to "Save a watt!" Gasoline companies made the highways of America ugly with billboards and advertisements promot-

[45]Peter V. Hobbs, Halstead Harrison, and E. Robinson, "Atmospheric Effects of Pollutants," *Science*, 183 (March 8, 1974), pp. 911–912.

[46]S. Fred Singer, "Human Energy Production as a . . . ," *Scientific American*, vol. 223, no. 38 (September 1970), p. 175.

[47]*New York Times* (February 10, 1974).

U.S. Fuel Reserves: How Many Years Will They Last?

FUEL	PROVEN RECOVERABLE RESERVES	ESTIMATED NUMBER OF YEARS
Natural gas	52 billion barrels	19
Uranium	3,000 trillion cubic feet	11
Oil	450,000 tons	13
Shale oil	160–600 billion barrels (recoverable only if crude oil prices rise 150%)	35–120
Coal	1.5 trillion tons	500

SOURCE: U.S. Geological Survey in *Newsweek* (January 22, 1973), p. 53.

ing their product, but in 1974 they were urging the motorist to conserve fuel.

The United States has blundered into the energy crisis. Cars have grown steadily bigger and more greedy for gas. The United States has nearly half of the world's passenger cars and consumes well over half of the world's gasoline. World consumption of oil is increasing at such a rate that during the 1970s more oil will be consumed than was used during the entire hundred years from 1870 to 1970, and in the decade of the 1980s, these demands will double again.[48] Supplies of oil and other fossil fuels – coal and natural gas – are steadily being depleted; eventually the point will be reached at which the deposits still remaining will be so low grade that it will no longer be technologically or economically feasible to extract the deposits still remaining.

We can continue to meet our growing energy requirements for a considerable time, however, but only at the cost of further environmental deterioration. The burning of fuel to generate electricity pollutes the atmosphere. It is believed that there are billions of gallons of oil beneath the waters of the Atlantic coast, but their exploitation would pose immense ecological risks. There are huge deposits of coal in the American West, but they would have to be strip-mined, laying waste vast surface areas and polluting water with sulfur washed by rain from the exposed coal face. Nuclear breeder reactors could be built to provide energy, but they also generate deadly radioactive wastes, for which we can find no safe storage space. Corporate interests have been quick to exploit the energy crisis in their campaigns against strict environmental legislation. Frank N. Ikard, president of the American Petroleum Institute, has highlighted some of the oil industry's complaints: conservationists delayed the construction of the Alaska pipeline for six years after the discovery of enormous gas and oil reserves; they halted drilling in the Santa Barbara channel for five years after it was discovered that 4 million barrels of crude oil awaited exploitation; and they induced the government to impose "unrealistic" schedules for emission controls

[48]Stewart L. Udall, "The Last Traffic Jam," *Atlantic Monthly,* 230 (October 1972), p. 72.

on new cars, and so increased gasoline consumption by 15 million gallons a day.[49]

Resource Depletion

The energy crisis seems to herald the start of an era of shortages. Many key minerals and other raw materials are in short supply, both in the United States and in the world as a whole. Up to World War II, the United States was a net exporter of raw materials, but it has been a net importer ever since. The United States, in fact, is presently consuming about a third of the raw materials produced in the entire world. Americans use more than 60 percent of the world's natural gas, more than 40 percent of the aluminum and coal, more than 33 percent of the nickel, petroleum, platinum, and copper, and about 25 percent of the gold, iron, lead, mercury, silver, tin, zinc, and tungsten. But according to the projections made by the MIT research team in *Limits to Growth*, current exponential growth patterns will exhaust existing known reserves of aluminum in 31 years, chromium in 95 years, copper in 21 years, iron in 93 years, lead in 21 years, nickel in 53 years, tin in 15 years, and zinc in 18 years.[50]

New mineral reserves will be discovered, of course, but it is worth noting that, despite intensified efforts, "the rate of new discoveries and the development of reserves is declining for a wide range of minerals."[51] Advances in technology may also make it possible for low-grade deposits to be exploited: it is not economically feasible to extract such deposits at the moment, but it might become worthwhile as shortages increase and prices of raw materials rise sharply, as they inevitably will. The extraction of minerals from very low-grade ores will have far greater environmental impact than existing processes, however, because of the much greater volume of material that will have to be mined, crushed, treated with chemicals, heated, cooled, and dumped.

We will face increasing shortages of many other raw materials — wood, paper, and foods of various types. World food production is currently inadequate to sustain the present human population, and famine is already widespread in several parts of the world. The United States, which habitually produced an annual agricultural surplus, can no longer be confident of doing so. Nearly all the cultivable land on earth is now being used for agricultural production, and although the use of mechanization and fertilizers might increase output up to a point, these methods would have other undesirable environmental consequences. The United States will also face a severe water shortage later in the century. In 1900 Americans used 40 billion gallons of water annually; in 1970 they used 350 billion gallons, and by the end of the century they

[49]*New York Times* (February 28, 1974).
[50]Meadows, et al., *The Limits to Growth*, pp. 64–67.
[51]Edmund Faltermayer, "Metals: The Warning Signals Are Up," *Fortune*, 86 (October 1972), p. 109.

will require between 700 and 1,000 billion gallons. Yet even with "optimum foreseeable developments in purification and engineering," not more than 650 million gallons will be available, and the actual figure is likely to be significantly lower.[52] In many parts of the western United States, the dependable water flow is already inadequate.

The growing shortage of resources has two significant implications. First, the United States is consuming and has already consumed so large a proportion of the world's nonrenewable resources that the extractable reserves that would be needed to raise the rest of the world to the present U.S. standard of living probably do not exist.[53] Second, even the United States will be incapable of maintaining its present style of living indefinitely in the face of dwindling natural resources, although technological developments may postpone the day of reckoning.

PROSPECTS FOR THE FUTURE

When the nation celebrated the first Earth Day in 1970, many people suspected that "the environment" was destined to be yet another instant crisis that would be almost as instantly forgotten. And it is true that many social problems fester unattended until they are suddenly upon us in crisis proportions, only to fade from public consciousness when some new crisis captures the popular attention. But despite all the trappings of a fad — bumper stickers, slogans, speeches, posters, popular articles, petitions — it is evident that the dramatically worsening quality of our air, water, and land and our voracious consumption of natural resources constitute a genuine and grave threat to the human future. As *The New York Times* editorialized after Earth Day, "Concern with ecology is fashionable nowadays. But if the fad dies, we die with it."[54]

What social action can be taken to ameliorate the environmental problems that face us? There are several immediate steps we can take.

The reduction of wastage. We waste staggering quantities of energy and resources. Some of the problems are technological; we waste in the form of useless heat a full five-sixths of the energy used in transportation, two-thirds of the fuel consumed to generate electricity, and nearly one-third of the fuel used for other purposes. This amounts to a wastage of more than 50 percent of the energy used in the United States. The answer here is a refinement of technology. Other forms of waste are more easily curtailed, for example, by putting insulation in our homes or by conserving our domestic and industrial energy use. We also squander other resources in a highly irresponsible manner. It is quite feasible to build cars that would last for decades; instead, they

[52]*Population Bulletin*, vol. 26, no. 2 (Washington, D.C.: Population Reference Bureau, Inc., 1970).
[53]Ehrlich and Ehrlich, *Population/Resources/Environment*, p. 73.
[54]*New York Times* (April 23, 1970).

Goals for Spaceship Earth

Perhaps the major necessary ingredient that has been missing from a solution to the problems of both the United States and the rest of the world is a goal, a vision of the kind of Spaceship Earth that ought to be and the kind of crew that should man her. Society has always had its visionaries who talked of love, beauty, peace, and plenty. But somehow the "practical" men have always been there to praise the smog as a sign of progress, to preach "just" wars, and to restrict love while giving hate free rein. It must be one of the greatest ironies of the history of the human species that the only salvation for the practical men now lies in what they think of as the dreams of idealists. The question now is: can the "realists" be persuaded to face reality in time?

SOURCE: Paul R. Ehrlich and Anne H. Ehrlich, *Population/Resources/ Environment: Issues in Human Ecology* (San Francisco: W. H. Freeman & Co., 1972).

are deliberately built with a "planned obsolescence" that sends them to the junk heap in a few years, while social attitudes and values prize newer automobiles. We waste more resources on a variety of useless or near-useless products and unnecessary packaging and wrapping materials. Rising prices, however, are likely to provide a strong incentive for us to conserve energy and resources in the future.

Development of new energy. Energy has been so plentiful in the past that there has been little incentive for us to develop new sources. Several cheap, nonpolluting sources exist, if we can apply technology to harness their potential. Among these sources are solar energy, hydrogen gas derived from electrolysis, the exploitation of temperature differentials between different areas, wind power, or geothermal energy from subterranean fissures in the earth's crust. Future energy policies are unlikely to be based on any one or two major sources; instead, there is likely to be considerable diversification depending on the resources that are most readily exploitable in particular areas. Fossil fuels would still be used, but more sparingly—both to conserve the fuels and to protect the atmosphere against pollution.

The limitation of population. As we have already noted, an expanding human population is a major threat to the environment, especially if the population is maintaining a high standard of living and hence consuming resources and polluting the environment at a very high rate. Efforts must be made to stabilize the U.S. population as soon as possible and to aid other countries around the world in campaigns to reduce their birth rates. Famine conditions are likely to provide global incentives to reduce birth rates, but developing nations will need economic, medical, and technical assistance in applying birth control measures.

Legislation against pollution. State and federal legislation will be necessary to eliminate some of the most serious pollutants from the environment. Limited progress has already been made: through the Clean Air Act, for example, or through the restrictions that have been imposed on the use of DDT and other pesticides. Stronger measures will probably be necessary, however, such as stiff penalties for polluters. Industry could be required to install new pollution controls, although ultimately it is the consumer or taxpayer who will foot the bill. A pollution tax could also be introduced on such items as "throwaway" containers, high-sulfur fuel, inefficient municipal incinerators, or even the gasoline-powered automobile; the tax would encourage the development of nonpolluting alternatives. Federal and state regulatory bodies, such as the Environmental Protection Agency, could be given wider powers to monitor pollution and to establish and enforce environmental standards.

Changes in attitudes and values. Most difficult of all, but perhaps most necessary to a solution of our environmental problems, will be to change the attitudes and values that are largely responsible for the environmental crisis. Our conventional, free-market economy and our dedication to unplanned growth seem incompatible with our demands for a clean environment. We will have to learn that environmental considerations must sometimes come before the profit motive and that endless economic growth may be ultimately counterproductive: it brings not only dollars and cents, but also smoke and garbage and auto exhausts. Nothing, perhaps, typifies the conflict between our traditional values and our environmental needs so much as the automobile. It poisons the air, devours gasoline, consumes mineral resources, kills and maims tens of thousands of citizens each year, defaces the country with concrete and gas stations, and ultimately becomes junk on the landscape; yet to many people, it seems to represent the heart and soul of the American way of life. Moreover, what the *Wall Street Journal* calls the "highway-auto-petroleum complex" employs one out of every five American workers. Many corporations and many citizens, in fact, have a stake in the economic activities that generate pollution, and their private interests are reflected in their attitudes and values. Although scientists consider that the automobile constitutes the greatest threat to clean air, the automobile manufacturers, not surprisingly, disagree. New York City public health officials believe that cars create half the city's air pollution problem, but the head of General Motors' emissions research laboratories believes that cars are responsible for less than a tenth of the problem. New York vehicle pollution control officials be-

Young people take part in community action to clean up the effects of an oil spill on a California beach. But the aim of community action groups in the future must be to prevent pollution rather than fight the endless battle of clearing it up. *(George Hall/Woodfin Camp)*

lieve that emission controls are not working, but General Motors believes that they have resulted in a "major reduction" of pollution.[55]

Attempts to change public attitudes and values may be expected to meet with strong opposition from the big polluters, who represent one of the largest power coalitions in the United States. Industry is naturally organized to resist any changes that will cost money, including pollution controls. Big polluters have not only attempted to safeguard their interests through private lobbying against antipollution legislation; they have even succeeded in installing themselves on the boards of environmental policy-making bodies. Many state panels set up to regulate air pollution under the provisions of the Clean Air Act are now largely or almost entirely composed of persons representing industry, agriculture, or the municipalities. The big corporations represented on these boards include Union Carbide, U.S. Steel, Bethlehem Steel, Dow Jones Chemical, and Regis Paper—all of them corporations that have been repeatedly cited as major polluters of the environment. Senator Edmund Muskie, a leading proponent of environmental legislation, has commented acidly that "the Clean Air Act was never intended to allow

[55]*New York Times* (May 23, 1971).

Environment and Resources: A Theoretical Review

The social problem of the environment and its resources represents the gap between a *social ideal* of an unspoiled natural environment with an adequate supply of natural resources and the *social reality* of an increasingly polluted planet with a growing shortage of raw materials and energy. The problem is a grave one because indications are that, if pollution and resource depletion continue to increase exponentially, the environment may become virtually uninhabitable and basic resources may be so scarce that industrial civilization will collapse within a few generations. The problem is compounded by the fact that there is a built-in tension between our desire for more resources and our desire for less pollution, because the extraction and consumption of resources is itself the main contributor to pollution.

The *social-disorganization* perspective provides a useful way of looking at the problem. From this perspective, the problem of the environment and its resources stems from the disorganization caused by rapid technological change. Humanity first interfered with the ecological systems of the planet several thousand years ago, at the time of the agricultural revolution, but this interference had a relatively minor impact on the environment and resources. Since the Industrial Revolution, however, we have been radically changing many aspects of our environment, often without any appreciation of the possible consequences. Our industrial system is highly functional for providing rising living standards, but it has had many unanticipated dysfunctions as well. The environment has been ravaged, species have been driven to extinction, nonrenewable resources have been consumed at an increasing rate, and poisons of various kinds have been introduced into the biosphere. The problem has been aggravated by another unintended consequence of industrialization: rising living standards and better health care have led to an exponential growth in the size of human population, so that there are far more people demanding raw materials and polluting the environment.

Our society is disorganized, then, in that our attitudes and values stress economic and industrial development—a desire that is inconsistent with the reality of scarce resources and the inevitable pollution that economic and industrial growth generates. Society is further disorganized in that our mechanisms for social control over pollution have not kept pace with the development of our capacities to pollute the environment: many ecosystems are already irreparably damaged, and many others are still being damaged simply because we have not had the will or the means to exercise control over the despoilation of the environment. The exercise of this control will continue to present problems in the future because of the underlying imbalance between our commitment to growth and consumption of resources and our hopes for the conservation of the environment.

The *value-conflict* perspective also provides a useful way of looking at many of the problems of environment and resources. The most obvious conflict is that between the conservationists, who are dedicated to the preservation of an unspoiled natural environment, and those economic interests that directly benefit from the exploitation of resources or the pollution of the environment. This conflict involves some of the most powerful interests in American society, notably the large industrial and commercial corporations. Pollution controls are expensive, and the large corporations are naturally reluctant to undertake any expense that they consider an unnecessary drain on their profits. But this conflict is not limited to conservationist organizations and large corporations; it is found among ordinary citizens. Nearly all our citizens favor a reduction of environmental pollution, but a great many of them are not willing to bear the costs—in increased taxation or higher prices—of establishing effective pollution controls.

The problem of the environment and its resources is marked by many other value conflicts. Some people believe that the benefits of industrial progress justify the environmental costs of economic growth. This view is commonly held in the developing nations, where clean air, fresh rivers, and unspoiled landscapes may seem a luxury when compared with the reality of widespread poverty. Other people believe that technological progress will solve the problem by making possible the use of resources which cannot be economically extracted at present or by providing new and inexpensive methods of pollution control. Others believe that a "no growth" economy would be plagued by even more problems than those currently generated by a growing one. Value conflicts recur in any analysis of the problem, but they may encourage a confrontation with the issues and the development of new solutions.

The *deviance* perspective is of limited usefulness in analyzing the problem, but it should be noted that, whereas our values were indifferent to environmental despoilation in the past, those who needlessly ravage the environment are increasingly regarded as deviants.

polluters to regulate themselves."[56] Other corporations and public bodies have a vested interest in the development of particular energy resources, so that, for example, the petroleum industry and the Atomic Energy Commission spend large sums each year in public relations efforts to generate favorable public attitudes to their respective products and programs. Solving the problems of the environment will inevitably involve conflict of values and interests in America. And the problems will not be solved at all if traditional values and attitudes persist.

The environment is likely to remain as a major social problem throughout this century. It raises many profound questions about the relationship between the rich and poor countries, about the consequences of world population growth, about the virtues of economic growth and industrialism, and about the very values and destiny of our civilization. But the battle for a sound environment is by no means a hopeless one. Much of the problem stems from a state of social disorganization that need not be permanent. Our industrial system is having environmental effects we had not anticipated, and our attitudes, values, and capacity to control our technology have not yet caught up with this change. Young people in particular are very aware of the issues and are deeply concerned about the environment. They seem determined to close the gap between the ideal of a sound environmental policy and the reality of our careless exploitation of our planet.

[56]*New York Times* (December 13, 1972).

FURTHER READING

Borland, Hal, et al., *The Crisis of Survival*, 1970. A collection of essays that question our commitment to continuing economic growth. The writers argue that our political and economic systems tend to encourage and camouflage rather than eliminate pollution.

Caudill, Harry M., *My Land is Dying*, 1973. A brief account of strip-mining and the devastation of the land that it causes.

Commoner, Barry, *The Closing Circle*, 1971. Commoner argues that population growth is not the main factor in the ravaging of our environment. The real culprit, he contends, is our "counter ecological" technology. Changes in technology, he believes, could go a long way toward solving the problem.

Ehrlich, Paul R. and Anne H. Ehrlich, *Population/Resources/Environment: Issues in Human Ecology*, 1972. A comprehensive and readable book tracing the interaction of population growth, resource depletion, and pollution. The authors present a mass of information in very readable form and argue that the environmental crisis is the most serious problem facing the planet today.

Goldsmith, Edward, et al., "Blueprint for Survival," *The Ecologist*, vol. 2, no. 1 (January 1972). An important statement on the environmental crisis by a group of eminent European scientists. They contend that we must act now to halt economic and population growth—or we will "muddle our way to extinction."

Maddox, John D., *The Doomsday Syndrome*, 1972. The author presents a strong argument that the environmental crisis is much exaggerated and suggests that concern over "ecology" is simply another fad.

McHale, John, *World Facts and Trends*, 2d ed., 1972. A collection of tables, graphs, and statistical information on international trends in population growth, resource depletion, and pollution. McHale provides a running commentary on the significance of these trends.

Meadows, Donella H., et al., *The Limits to Growth: A Report on the Club of Rome's Project on the Predicament of Mankind*, 1972. A summary of the MIT research team's findings on the potential consequences of continued population growth, pollution, and consumption of nonrenewable resources. An essential source for any analysis of the problem.

Ramparts Magazine eds., *Eco-Catastrophe*, 1970. A radical view of the environmental problem; the authors contend that effective environmental reform is impossible without sweeping changes in the social and political system.

Rienow, Robert and Leona Train Rienow, *Moment in the Sun*, 1969. A passionate and very readable account of the destruction of the American environment. The authors contend that the underlying problem is our value system, which favors technological advances over the preservation of natural beauty.

4

The Cities

THE NATURE AND SCOPE OF THE PROBLEM

America today is a predominantly urban nation, and the problems confronting most Americans are the problems of the city. According to the 1970 U.S. census, over 70 percent of Americans live in metropolitan areas, and demographers now predict that the proportion will have risen to 90 percent by 1980. The national Commission on Population Growth and the American Future predicts that by the year 2000, some 60 percent of Americans will live in metropolitan areas of a million inhabitants or more.[1]

The American future, then, is an urban one. But Americans have mixed feelings about this prospect, for many of our cities are in a state of decay and the reality of "city life" falls far short of American ideals. The city was once considered the crowning achievement of humanity. To the ancient Greeks it was almost synonymous with civilization itself; Aristotle described the city as "a common life to a noble end." Today there are genuine doubts in America as to whether our cities can survive as a habitable environment at all. In 1968 President Johnson sent a special message on "The Crisis in Our Cities" to Congress and appealed for concerted national action to save our urban areas. But since then, despite some remedial measures, the situation has often grown steadily worse. The very word "city" can evoke images of bad housing, riots, addiction, crime, poverty, and deteriorating public and social services. The urban area is the home of most Americans, and it is also the locus of our more intractable social problems.

[1]*Population and the American Future: The Report of the Commission on Population Growth and the American Future* (Washington, D.C.: U.S. Government Printing Office, 1972), p. 34.

The Development of the City

Large urban settlements were an impossibility before the domestication of plants and animals. Organized agriculture made possible a surplus production of food, freeing individuals from the land and allowing them to engage in specialized, nonagricultural activities. About 3000 B.C. distinctly urban settlements arose in the Indus River valley, in the Persian Gulf, and on the shores of the Mediterranean. These settlements were, by modern standards, very small—the walls of Babylon bounded an area of only 3.2 square miles, and the famous biblical city of Ur occupied only 220 acres. But the cities rapidly became the center of political and religious influence, the natural crossroads for communication and ideas, and the source of technological innovation. The Greek city-state became the home of the democratic ideal, and the Roman Empire spread the planned, formally administered urban form throughout the known world. With the development of international trade hundreds of years later, new cities, such as Venice in Italy, arose at the mercantile centers of the world.

The modern city, however, is essentially a product of the Industrial Revolution, which made possible a vastly different ratio of urban workers to the agricultural laborers who sustained them. Before 1800 little of the world was really urban, but thereafter, urbanization took place at an increasing rate. By the beginning of the nineteenth century the population of London had reached 1 million; by the middle of the century 4 cities had passed the million mark; by the beginning of the twentieth century 19 cities had done so; and in the sixties there were 141 cities of over a million inhabitants. At the end of this century there may be 500 cities with populations of over 1 million, and several are expected to contain over 25 million people. By the year 2000 some four-fifths of the world's population may live in cities.[2]

The American City

The urbanization of the United States has been equally rapid. In 1790, at the time of the first census, 95 percent of the American population lived on farms. The census showed only twenty-four urban settlements, of which only two had populations of more than 25,000. But the cities expanded rapidly under the impact of waves of immigrants: a hundred years after the first census, 30 percent of the population was urban, and five cities had over a million inhabitants. In this century, internal migration, such as that of black Americans from the rural South, has further increased the size of the cities.[3] Nearly three-quarters of the national population now lives in urban areas, and only 5 percent of Americans are engaged in farming. This unprecedented ratio of agri-

[2]Kingsley Davis, "The Urbanization of the Human Population," *Scientific American*, vol. 213, no. 3 (September 1965), pp. 41–53.
[3]B. Drummond Ayres, Jr., "Blacks Return to South In a Reverse Migration," *New York Times* (June 18, 1974), p. 1. A significant number of blacks are moving from the North to the South, but it is too early to assess the significance of this trend.

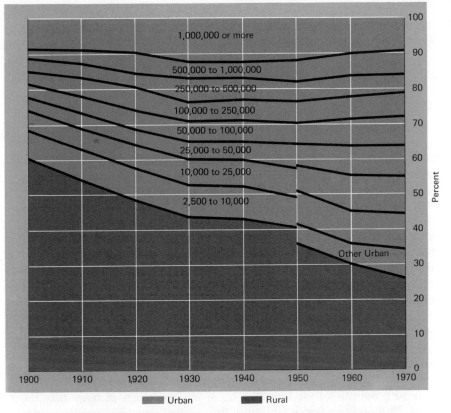

| | | | | | | | | 100 |

1,000,000 or more

500,000 to 1,000,000

250,000 to 500,000

100,000 to 250,000

50,000 to 100,000

25,000 to 50,000

10,000 to 25,000

2,500 to 10,000

Other Urban

Percent

1900 1910 1,920 1930 1940 1950 1960 1970

Urban   Rural

Population in urban and rural areas, 1900–1970. The United States has been transformed in the course of this century from a predominantly rural to a predominantly urban nation. Most urban dwellers, however, still reside in relatively small towns and suburbs. (SOURCE: Bureau of the Census; Executive Office of the President: Office of Management and Budget, *Social Indicators, 1973* [Washington, D.C.: U.S. Government Printing Office, 1973], p. 242.)

cultural to urban workers — which can still periodically yield an embarrassing food surplus — is largely the result of the highly industrialized and technological nature of American society.

The problems of the city are not new. The complaints made by writers and public officials in the last century have a familiar ring. In the 1830s a former mayor of New York described his city as "one huge pigsty," and in 1840 one resident in seven was classified as a pauper.[4] In 1880 the Chicago *Times* complained that "the river stinks. The air stinks. People's clothing, permeated by the foul atmosphere, stinks. . . . No other word expresses it so well as stink."[5] Junius Henry Brown wrote of New York in 1869:

[4]Dushkin Publishing Group, *American History*, vol. 2 (Guilford, Conn.: Dushkin Publishing Group, 1973), p. 136.
[5]Ibid., p. 141.

> Hundreds of outrages are committed daily in this City, by notorious
> roughs; and yet the arrests are so very few as scarcely to deserve
> mention. . . . Men are robbed in broad daylight; women are violat-
> ed in the street cars; stores and dwellings are set on fire; houses are
> entered by burglars, corpses are thrown into the river; mysteriously
> murdered persons are sent to the morgue.[6]

Although many of the problems sound the same, the attitudes toward
them were different. Most citizens of that era believed in the inevitability of progress and felt that the city could only improve with the passage of time.

The Metropolis and the Megalopolis

Although most Americans are said to be urban dwellers today, this
does not mean that they live in the central cities. In fact, a majority of
urban inhabitants are now living in the suburbs, and many others live
in relatively small cities. The Bureau of the Census defines any locality
with over twenty-five hundred inhabitants as an urban area, even if the
residents themselves do not regard it as such. And the bureau pur-
posely ignores the political boundaries of cities and suburbs — which
are technically separate but in fact inseparably linked — by the use of its
concept of a *Standard Metropolitan Statistical Area.* An SMSA covers
any area that includes one city (or two or more close cities) and its surrounding counties that together have a population of over fifty thousand. The massive urbanization of the central cities has overflowed into
these metropolitan areas, and there are now 267 SMSAs,[7] containing 69
percent of the American population.[8] The growth of the suburbs and
the decline of the central city is one of the most significant developments in American society during this century.

Los Angeles, one of the few major cities to develop after the advent
of the automobile, is often cited as a possible prototype for the sprawl-
ing metropolitan area of the future. The area contains a small central city, a county of nine other cities, and sixty-seven smaller self-
governing communities. This great sprawl has often been termed a
"group of suburbs in search of a city." Space is squandered so that public transport is expensive and often nonexistent. The exhaust of the
automobiles so pollutes the atmosphere that airline visitors first glimpse
the city as a gray pall intermittently pierced by mountaintops. Yet the
city boasts excellent police and fire departments and other facilities
and offers a distinctive life style to which millions of its citizens are
devoted; they would not choose to live anywhere else. This modern
metropolis excites widely varying reactions. The architect Frank Lloyd

---

[6]Junius Henry Brown, *The Great Metropolis: A Mirror of New York* (Hartford, Conn.: American Publishing Co., 1869), pp. 24, 74.
[7]U.S. Bureau of the Census, *Statistical Abstract of the United States, 1973*, 94th ed. (Washington D.C.:
U.S. Department of Commerce, 1973), p. 849.
[8]*Population and the American Future*, p. 25.

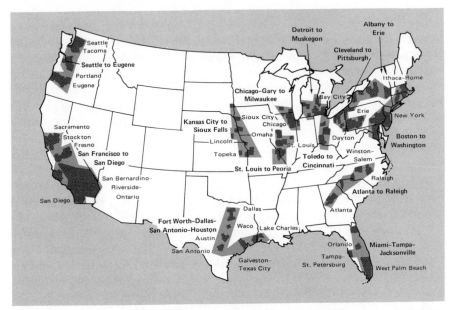

Thirteen major megalopolises in the United States. In several parts of the United States, spreading urban areas are merging with one another to form continuous, densely populated tracts. These megalopolises are expected to grow larger and more numerous in the future. (SOURCE: Department of Commerce, Bureau of the Census.)

Wright recommended that urban renewal in Los Angeles should consist of the demolition and rebuilding of the entire city; the British town planner Fred J. Osborn termed the area "the hashish dream of a fanatical motorist"; the novelist Aldous Huxley gave a more balanced view when he wrote that Los Angeles had the greatest potential of any place he had known—though whether it was a potential for horror or fulfillment, he could not tell.[9]

Another major development is the gradual linking of a series of metropolitan areas into what has been termed the *megalopolis*—a vast unbroken area of cities and suburbs. The most outstanding megalopolis is the great chain of cities and suburbs on the eastern seaboard, from Boston to Virginia—an area containing 40 million people in an almost continuous urban tract. Other incipient examples of the megalopolis are to be found in southern California, Texas, and the Great Lakes area. Ultimately, most Americans may live in areas such as these.

APPROACHING THE PROBLEM

Sociologists have been anxious to establish exactly what urbanism means to people, and the ways in which urban life differs from that of the traditional community.

[9]Ralph Tomlinson, *Urban Structure* (New York: Random House, 1969), p. 305.

The Meaning of Urbanism

One early but influential statement was that of the German sociologist Ferdinand Tönnies, who in 1887 made a classical distinction between the *Gemeinschaft* (community) and the *Gesellschaft* (association). In the *Gemeinschaft* there are close interpersonal relationships, and the solidarity of the community is based on traditional shared values and the communal feelings of the entire group. Such communities exist primarily in the context of the traditional village or the very small town. In the *Gesellschaft,* on the other hand, relationships between people are distant and impersonal: most individuals are strangers to one another and such solidarity as they experience is based on the functional need that people have for each other. The large modern city is the preeminent example of this type of social organization.

Tönnies's theory strongly influenced sociologists at the University of Chicago during the earlier part of this century. These sociologists were particularly interested in urban problems and attempted to develop an *ecological* approach to the city. That is, they sought to analyze urban life as a pattern of self-sustaining relationships between human beings and their social and physical environment. The classic statement of the "Chicago school" was contained in an essay by Louis Wirth.[10]

To Wirth, the essential features of the city are its size, population density, and social diversity. These features lead to a distinctive type of relationship between the inhabitants, who are much more isolated and anonymous than their rural counterparts. The individual is reduced to virtual insignificance in the large, complex mass of people in the city: he cannot know more than a tiny proportion of his fellows personally, and so the nature of his social relationships is profoundly different from that of the villager. The urban man may have more acquaintances, but he knows them in a much more superficial and impersonal way, and interacts with them in "segmental" roles—as a bank clerk, perhaps, or a fellow commuter—rather than as whole people. Relationships are often predatory because they tend to be based on utility rather than affection, with the role each person plays in relation to the others being a means toward achieving his own ends—usually economic. The city thus consists of a vast mass of people living in close proximity but without deep sentimental bonds with one another.

Wirth points out that diverse populations tend to inhabit compact settlements in the city and thus become segregated from one another, usually along class or ethnic lines. In addition, the urban division of labor leads to a proliferation of specialized tasks, so that the city contains many areas which have specific functions and distinctive characteristics (such as Broadway, Wall Street, or Fifth Avenue). The result is a juxtaposition of divergent personalities and modes of life, which tends to produce a considerable tolerance of differences among individuals. City dwellers are thus more likely than rural dwellers to develop a rela-

[10]Louis Wirth, "Urbanism as a Way of Life," *American Journal of Sociology,* 44 (July 1938), pp. 8–20.

Modern American cities contain very heterogeneous populations, but the various groups tend to settle in specific areas and thus become segregated from one another, usually along ethnic or class lines. Nonwhites tend to be concentrated in the city centers in the most-depressed areas. *(Bruce Davidson/Magnum)*

tivistic perspective, that is, they may no longer take their own attitudes and values for granted as unquestioned absolutes and instead acknowledge the validity of other viewpoints and life styles. Individuals in the city are, however, subordinated to categories in the mass urban environment, and civic institutions organize their facilities for the average person rather than for particular people.

A more recent analysis of urbanism by sociologist Herbert J. Gans[11] suggests that Wirth's analysis is no longer relevant to the outlying metropolitan areas, but may still have some relevance to the inner city. Gans closely analyzes the population of the inner city and distinguishes five categories of inhabitants. The *cosmopolites* are students, artists, writers, intellectuals, and professional people who live in the city in order to have easy access to its unequaled cultural facilities. The *unmarried or childless* are mostly young people who come to the city and rent apartments to be close to job opportunities, but who tend to move to the outer suburbs when they get married. The *ethnic villagers* are ethnic groups who are isolated from significant contact with the rest of the city, but maintain traditional ways of life (particularly kinship patterns) within their own areas. The *deprived* are the very poor, the handicapped, the emotionally disturbed, and the nonwhite population.

[11]Herbert J. Gans, "Urbanism and Suburbanism as Ways of Life," in *Human Behavior and Social Processes*, ed. Arnold M. Rose (Boston: Houghton Mifflin, 1962), pp. 625–648.

The *trapped* are people who are downwardly socially mobile, people who are old and living on fixed incomes, and people whose neighborhood is being invaded by commerce, industry, or other ethnic groups, but who cannot afford to move out. The first two categories are in the city by choice; the third category by tradition and to some extent by necessity; and the last two categories are in the inner city because they cannot leave it.

Other empirical studies of urbanism have shown that in relation to rural areas cities have a higher number of foreigners, a higher general level of educational attainment, more working women, higher average incomes, smaller families, less stable marriages, greater social mobility, and smaller residential quarters. The reported incidence of all forms of social behavior of a "pathological," nonconformist, or "deviant" nature is also much greater in urban than in rural areas. Burglary rates are three times as high, rape rates are twice as high, robbery rates are six times as high. Chronic alcoholism rates are twice as high, suicide rates in cities of over ten thousand population are twice as high, and hard-drug addiction is primarily a problem of large metropolitan areas.

The Flight to the Suburbs

The single most important factor in the decay of the American central cities has been the flight of the middle class to the suburbs, a process that began after World War II and that has been ruinous for the tax base of the cities. The growth of the suburbs has been recent but rapid. Seventeen percent of the American people lived in the suburbs in 1920, 19 percent in 1930, 20 percent in 1940, and 24 percent in 1950. But then came the great exodus; 33 percent of the population lived in the suburbs in 1960 and 37 percent in 1970.[12] The 1970 census showed that, for the first time, more Americans live in the suburbs than in the cities. During the sixties the suburban population increased by 15 million, while the population of the central cities remained virtually unchanged.

In many of the cities of the world, the wealthy are concentrated in the city center and the poor in slums on the outskirts. The opposite is rapidly becoming true of American cities. The middle class has fled from the problems of the city—its crime rate, its lack of space, its high tax rates—and established homes in the more appealing suburbs. The bulk of the remaining population is poor, although the very rich do sometimes maintain residences—often apartments—in the center city in the few exclusive residential areas remaining.

The flight to the suburbs has been facilitated by several factors. One is the development of mass private ownership of the automobile, which has made it possible for workers to commute relatively long distances; federally subsidized highway programs, too, have made commuting much easier for the suburban resident. Another factor is the postwar

[12]E. J. Kahn, Jr., *The American People* (New York: Weybright & Talley, 1973), pp. 107–121.

The surburban life style has been much criticized and even satirized for its alleged materialism, status-consciousness, homogeneity, and artificiality in social relationships. But millions of middle-class Americans have found in the suburbs the ideal compromise between urban and rural living. *(Paul Sequeira/Rapho Guillumette)*

boom in the American economy, which made home ownership a possibility for millions of Americans; and low-cost mortgages were available through the Federal Housing Authority and the Veterans Administration. A further factor is the tendency of industry and commerce to relocate to the suburbs, where rates and taxes are lower; modern industrial production techniques demand horizontal expansion, but only vertical expansion is possible in the crowded city.

Suburban living has been much satirized and criticized: the suburbs are often alleged to be socially homogeneous, deadly dull, and isolated from reality; the concerns of the inhabitants are said to revolve around washing the car, mowing the lawn, attending parties, driving to the school and supermarket, and gearing personal behavior and material consumption to the expectations of the neighbors. This picture is of course much overdrawn, and there is often great heterogeneity in the suburbs (many of which are predominantly working class and substantially populated by ethnic minorities). It is clear, however, that the suburban life style differs a great deal from that of the city centers and that many Americans have found in the suburbs the ideal compromise between rural and urban living.

The effects on the central city of the flight to the suburbs have been devastating. Industry and commerce are relocating to the suburbs to gain access to the suburban labor market; many shops also follow their customers from the central cities. New highways cut through central city residential areas so that suburban commuters can travel more quickly to and from their places of work. The town houses vacated by the middle class are quickly subdivided into apartments or rooming houses; overcrowding follows, and areas tend to degenerate into slums. White and middle-class children disappear from the city schools, and educational standards fall far below those in the suburbs. The suburban middle class often pays no city taxes, may pay lower taxes in the suburbs, and yet makes full demands on the fire, police, transport, and other urban services for which the poor, the minorities, and the working class of the cities have to pay.

As we look more closely at the problems of the central cities, we find again and again that a major source of contemporary urban problems is the flight of the middle class to the metropolitan suburbs.

THE PROBLEMS OF THE CENTRAL CITIES

The city is a complex social organization, and it is not, as was once thought, a self-sustaining one. As Daniel Patrick Moynihan has forcefully argued, the cities are not "self-restorative" without outside aid; but assistance must be in accordance with an overall plan rather than on the basis of piecemeal intervention. There are, argues Moynihan, four vital aspects of city organization—housing, transport, industry, and social services—and effective city planning must deal with them as a systematic whole. In the past, interventions in only one area have led to undesirable effects in the others—highway programs, for example, have facilitated the flight to the suburbs and worsened the plight of the central cities; attempts to make industry assume a greater share of the city tax burden have simply encouraged industrial enterprises to move to outlying areas.[13]

Finances

Much of the decay of the city centers is a result of their financial strangulation. Cities derive about three-quarters of their income from property taxes. These taxes take an average of 7.6 percent of individual income in the cities, compared to about 5.6 percent in the suburbs, yet the suburbanite gets more for his tax dollar. The reason is that the city has extra burdens—its crime rates are higher, so it needs more police; its population is poorer, so it needs more welfare services; its daytime population is far higher than the number of its residents, so it needs more transport; its buildings are more dilapidated, so it needs more fire

[13]Daniel P. Moynihan, "Toward a National Urban Policy." *The Public Interest*, 17 (Fall 1969), pp. 3–20.

protection. Yet taxes cannot be raised too much; most citizens of the central city are poor, and more industry will relocate to the cheaper suburbs if there are no incentives for remaining in the city. Higher taxes can also be an incentive to the neglect of property; old property is usually more lightly taxed than new, but if property is renovated, the taxes on it rise. As a result, residents and landlords are inclined to allow property to deteriorate. Higher taxes would probably accelerate the process of deterioration and encourage the spread of slums.

The suburbs, already benefiting financially from their relationship with the central city, are also able to use their zoning regulations to exclude the poor. Undeveloped land in the suburbs can be zoned for large residential lots of several acres each, thus earmarking them for large expensive homes that the poor cannot afford. These expensive homes provide about as much tax revenue to the suburb as would a number of smaller, more inexpensive homes, but the zoning gives the suburb fewer and richer families, and hence less children to educate and less welfare recipients to look after. The same tax dollar therefore goes a good deal further in the suburbs, while the poor remain trapped in the city, a burden to its straining finances.

Housing

Housing is one of the most serious problems of the central city, and it is one that has been aggravated rather than helped by federal programs. The Federal Housing Association and the Veterans Administration facilitate single-family home construction and mortgages for home ownership, but nearly all the homes built or bought under these programs have been in the suburbs. Over 5 million private homes have been built under federal programs that have benefited the suburban middle class, but only 600,000 units of low-income public housing have been constructed.[14] If federal housing programs have benefited the affluent at the expense of the poor, programs for urban renewal have had an even more disastrous effect. These programs were officially intended to eliminate the slums from the city centers, but little thought was given to what would replace them. Federal funds were used to buy up inner-city land, which was then sold to private developers. These developers used the property for the most profitable forms of construction — office blocks and luxury apartment buildings. Little provision was made to rehouse the displaced lower-income occupants; by the late sixties, urban renewal had demolished 404,000 units of housing, mostly in the central cities, but had constructed less than 40,000 replacement dwellings. The result has been further pressure on the remaining slum housing, which has forced up rents. The National Commission on Urban Problems found that nearly half the residents in central cities are either ill-housed or pay more than a fifth of their annual income in rent. Lower-income whites pay on average between a quarter and a third of

[14]Nathan Glazer, "Housing Problems and Housing Policies," *The Public Interest,* 7 (Spring 1970), p. 30.

their income for housing, and blacks pay the most—an average of 35 percent, far above that of the middle-class suburbanite.[15]

Another effect of unplanned urban renewal has been to destroy the "ethnic villages," the local neighborhoods in which various ethnic groups maintain their traditions, speak their original languages, and develop close interpersonal ties. Herbert J. Gans has studied in detail the urban renewal of Boston's North End, which shattered the traditional Italian community in the area, disrupting friendships and a whole way of life. The renewal did not seem to benefit the local inhabitants, who opposed it; only the speculators and property developers rejoiced.[16]

Jane Jacobs, an ardent critic of poorly planned urban renewal programs writes:

> There is a wistful myth that if only we had enough money to spend—the figure is usually put at a hundred billion dollars—we could wipe out all our slums in ten years, reverse decay in the great, dull, gray belts that were yesterday's and day-before-yesterday's suburbs, anchor the wandering middle class and its wandering tax money, and perhaps even solve the traffic problem.
>
> But look what we have built with the first several billions: Low-income projects that become worse centers of delinquency, vandalism and general social hopelessness than the slums they were supposed to replace. Middle-income housing projects which are truly marvels of dullness and regimentation. . . . Luxury housing projects that mitigate their inanity, or try to, with a vapid vulgarity. Cultural centers that are unable to support a good bookstore. Civic centers that are avoided by everyone but bums, who have fewer choices of loitering place than others . . . Promenades that go from no place to nowhere and have no promenaders. Expressways that eviscerate great cities. This is not the rebuilding of cities. This is the sacking of cities.[17]

Urban Ghettos

Perhaps the most serious problem of the central cities today is the concentration within them of impoverished and isolated minority groups, particularly blacks. The 1970 census showed that 74 percent of the black population of 23 million live in metropolitan areas. In fact, 40 percent of the black population are concentrated in twenty of these areas, and 4 million blacks are concentrated in the four cities of New York, Philadelphia, Chicago, and Detroit. The black population of New York—1,666,636, or 21.2 percent of the city's total population—is the largest concentration of black people on earth. Of the blacks who live

[15]Dushkin Publishing Group, *American Government '73/'74* (Guilford, Conn.: Dushkin Publishing Group, 1973), pp. 415–416.
[16]Herbert J. Gans. *The Urban Villagers* (New York: Free Press, 1962).
[17]Jane Jacobs, *The Death and Life of Great American Cities* (New York: Random House, 1961), p. 4.

in metropolitan areas some 80 percent live in the central city, mostly in black ghettos.[18]

These ghettos are often the locus of some of the city's worst problems. Employment opportunities are scarce; most new jobs are opening up in the suburbs, and blacks are excluded from these by the barriers of economics and prejudice. The black population is increasing far faster than housing is becoming available. As a result, large, older properties are rapidly converted to multiple-tenant occupancy, and the resulting overcrowding tends to generate slum conditions. Attempts to rehouse ghetto occupants elsewhere in the metropolitan area have consistently met with strong opposition from the local white communities. Meanwhile, the median black income is only 58 percent of that of whites; unemployment rates are double those of whites; and nearly a quarter of black families have a female head (which usually means a reduced family income), compared with 8.9 percent of white families. Social problems such as crimes, addiction, and poverty are rife in the ghettos; the President's National Advisory Commission on Civil Disorders described these areas as "an environmental jungle."[19]

Education

Education also suffers in the central cities. Racial segregation in the schools is one obvious consequence of the segregated residential patterns of the metropolitan area. But equally important is the fact that education in the United States, unlike education in most other parts of the world, is financed by local community taxes rather than by national resources. The result is a great disparity in per capita pupil expenditure, usually to the disadvantage of the central-city child. Even within states these discrepancies are striking. Wyoming contains a school district with the highest per capita expenditure in the nation—$14,554; but it also contains a school district that spends $617 per capita. South Dakota has a district that spends $6,012, but also one that spends $175.[20] Per capita expenditure in the thirty-six largest metropolitan areas averages some 30 percent less than in the surrounding suburbs. The children most in need of high-quality schooling receive some of the worst schooling in the nation.

Government

One major obstacle to urban reform is the fragmented and obsolete system of urban government. Many cities have suprisingly little control over their destinies. They rely heavily on the federal government for grants, and they are often subject to state laws on such matters as their

---

[18]Kahn, *The American People*, p. 111.
[19]*Report of the National Advisory Commission on Civil Disorders,* chap. 16 (New York: Bantam Books, 1968), pp. 390–408 (abridged).
[20]"A Profile of the U.S. Education System," *Congressional Digest* (August–September 1972).

right to raise money—even by installing parking meters. More importantly, there is often a tremendous overlap and duplication of effort among the various local authorities in any metropolitan region. The result is that a metropolitan area comprising several autonomous localities will have perhaps dozens of police chiefs, fire chiefs, health officers, and so on—a duplication that frequently represents little more than a wastage of public money. Most cities were originally established when they were merely clusters of people surrounded by the countryside, but the incipient megalopolis of today strains the original charters to the limit. A Bureau of the Census study showed that the SMSAs contained an average of eighty-seven governmental units each: St. Louis had 439 such units, New York 555, Pittsburgh 806, Philadelphia 963, and Chicago 1,060.[21]

Citizens have to pay for all this duplication of services. Yet the political boundary lines of cities and suburbs are largely irrelevant when we consider such services as metropolitan transport, freeways, water supplies, sanitation, food inspection, or pollution control. But little progress has been made toward the reorganization of metropolitan governments. The wealthier suburbs find that the situation is much to their liking since many of their services are subsidized by the central city, and local communities, in general, are extremely reluctant to surrender their own spheres of authority. Although most countries treat education, housing, highways, and welfare services on a national basis, the United States has a tradition of community control over these areas, and demands for more uniform and centralized administration run counter to deeply entrenched values and attitudes concerning the virtues of local democracy. This is particularly true of such sensitive issues as "community control" of education by local ethnic neighborhoods.

The problems of city governments are compounded by the fact that state legislatures have traditionally tended to represent rural rather than urban interests. In 1960 there were thirty-nine states in which the urban population represented a majority, but there was not a single state in which the urban population controlled the state legislature. In 1965 about three-quarters of the state legislators were elected by little more than a quarter of the people. This disparity stems from old electoral boundaries that have traditionally overemphasized rural interests. Some states have recently begun to correct the situation, but others have not reapportioned their local boundaries for half a century, and several continue to ignore federal and Supreme Court orders to redraw their precinct lines. As a result of the influence of rural areas in state legislatures, many state programs often show a marked bias against the cities. Urban residents generally pay more in taxes than they receive in benefits, and cities have to request permission from the state to make minor alterations in their own affairs—even down to raising the fees on dog licences.[22]

[21]U.S. Bureau of the Census, "Governmental Organization," *U.S. Census of Governments, 1962* (Washington, D.C.: U.S. Government Printing Office, 1963), p. 11.
[22]Tomlinson, *Urban Structure*, p. 259.

PROBLEMS OF CROWDING

Some years ago, a woman named Kitty Genovese was attacked and murdered outside her New York apartment house. The attack lasted for at least half an hour, during which time she was beaten, kicked, and strangled by her assailant. Her screams brought at least thirty-eight of her neighbors to their windows. They watched in horror—but not one of them did anything about it, even to the extent of calling the police.

The behavior of these onlookers was an extreme example of what is known as "bystander apathy," the unwillingness of people to "get involved" in the problems of others. This apathy seems to be directly related to the number of bystanders involved; if there are several, each seems to assume that someone else will accept responsibility for helping in the situation.[23] Anyone who has walked around the downtown areas of a large city will be familiar with the sight of an individual sprawled on the sidewalk against a building—maybe drunk, maybe asleep, maybe ill, maybe dying, maybe dead—while crowds of people pass by with scarcely a glance. In a small village, however, one would expect the sight of someone in this condition to evoke an immediate response from passers-by.

How are we to account for bystander apathy in its aggravated urban form? It seems that the urban resident, unlike his rural counterpart, risks being overwhelmed by the number of potential interpersonal relationships that exist in his environment. Accordingly, he "screens out" many stimuli and concentrates instead on the small number of relationships—in work, home, and circle of friends—that is important to him. When implicit demands are made on him by someone in a state of distress, and if there are several other people in the vicinity, he will tend to ignore the situation, especially if the other people are ignoring it also. If he is the only person in the vicinity, however, and cannot evade responsibility for taking action, he is more likely to respond.

Many social scientists have felt that the anonymity of the city may be a major contributing factor to the high degree of antisocial and aggressive behavior found in urban areas. To test this hypothesis, Philip Zimbardo chose two very different locations—the small California community of Palo Alto and New York City—and left a car unattended for sixty-four hours in each place. Both cars were made to look abandoned by the removal of licence plates and the raising of the hood, and both were kept under observation for the entire period. The Palo Alto car was not touched during its abandonment except once: when it began to rain, a passer-by lowered the hood so that the engine would not get wet. In New York City, however, the car was vandalized within ten minutes of its abandonment. Yet this act was only the first of a grand total of twenty-four separate acts of theft and vandalism; by the end of the sixty-four hours the vehicle had been stripped and virtually de-

---

[23]R. Latané and J. Rodin, "A Lady in Distress: Inhibiting Effects of Friends and Strangers on Bystander Intervention," *Journal of Experimental Social Psychology*, 5 (1969), pp. 189–202.

Bystander Apathy: A Lady in Distress

An experiment by Latané and Rodin clearly illustrates the way in which people will accept more interpersonal responsibility if they are on their own. Three separate experimental situations were used. In the first, the subject was shown into a waiting room by a young woman and requested to complete a questionnaire. The woman then left and went into an adjoining room. A few moments later, the subject heard the sound of furniture falling over, and the woman screaming that she was hurt and trapped beneath the furniture. The incident lasted for a full two minutes. Of the subjects who were waiting alone in the room, some 70 percent came to her aid. In the second experimental situation, the conditions were the same but subjects were shown into the room two at a time. In these circumstances, only 40 percent of the subjects came to her aid. In the third experimental situation, an associate of the experimenters was shown into the room with the subject, and when the incident took place, the associate displayed no concern or reaction whatever. Under these conditions, only 7 percent of the subjects responded and went to the aid of the woman.

SOURCE: R. Latané and J. Rodin, "A Lady in Distress: Inhibiting Effects of Friends and Strangers on Bystander Intervention," *Journal of Experimental Social Psychology*, 5 (1969).

molished. Zimbardo considered that the anonymity of the city, which made it unlikely that thieves and vandals would be recognized or apprehended, was a critical variable in accounting for the different fate of the urban car.[24]

Population density is known to correlate highly with a variety of serious social problems—crime, suicide, juvenile delinquency, physical and mental illness, and infant mortality. Cities are often very densely populated; the United States Civil Rights Commission noted that some blocks in Harlem are so crowded that the entire population of the United States could be fitted into three New York boroughs at the same density. It need not be, of course, that overcrowding as such contributes to these urban problems—poverty is also a correlate of these problems and may be the crucial factor. But social scientists are becoming interested in the effects of overcrowding on human behavior.

Numerous animal studies have shown the severe physical and psychological effects of overcrowding, even in situations where food supply remains adequate. Crowding affects the capacity of animals to cope

[24]Philip G. Zimbardo, "The Human Choice: Individuation, Reason, and Order, Versus Deindividuation, Impulse, and Chaos," in *Nebraska Symposium on Motivation*, eds. W. Arnold and D. Levine (Lincoln, Neb.: University of Nebraska Press, 1969), pp. 237–307.

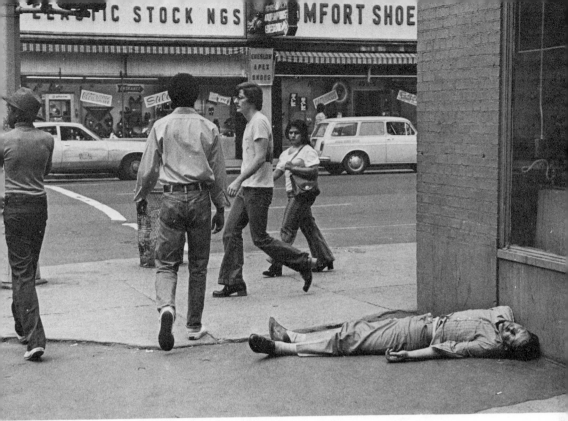

The unwillingness of onlookers to become involved in the troubles of others seems much more common in large cities than in small rural communities. This behavior, known as "bystander apathy," is probably related to the impersonal, anonymous nature of the city. Each individual assumes that the problem is none of his or her business and that someone else will assume responsibility for it. *(Charles Gatewood)*

with stress, affects body size in the development of young animals, and lowers both resistance to infection and reproductive capacity. There are also strong correlations between crowding in animals and physiological changes in the secretion of hormones from various glands; if animal populations are allowed to grow beyond a certain limit, a population collapse inevitably follows as a result of a lowered fertility rate, an increased susceptibility to disease, and mortality from sheer shock caused by overloading of the capacity of the adrenal glands. The overcrowding is usually accompanied by a great increase in aggressive behavior among the animals concerned. The most famous experiment on animal overcrowding was conducted by J. B. Calhoun, who maintained a large number of rats in a confined area with ample food supplies. The result was a social breakdown so severe that Calhoun termed his rat pen a "behavioral sink." Interestingly, however, most rats seemed actually to prefer the excitement and aggression of their crowded area; given the opportunity to migrate to a less crowded area, they remained where they were.[25]

[25]John B. Calhoun, "A Behavioral Sink," in *Roots of Behavior*, ed. E. L. Bliss (New York: Harper & Row, 1962).

Some theorists, particularly in the biological sciences, have attributed many of the problems of urban life to overcrowding, but it must be very strongly emphasized that rats are not human beings and evidence from animal studies provides only suggestive hypotheses—never proof— about the basis of some human behavior. The behavior of humans in cities is explicable in other terms besides overcrowding. The reason for high homicide, addiction, and suicide rates in cities, for example, may be that the city attracts people who are particularly inclined to such behavior, or it may be that other factors in the city, apart from over- crowding, are responsible for such behavior. The evidence from animal studies is interesting, but until we know a great deal more about the relationship between crowding, apathy, anonymity, stress, and brain chemistry, we are in no position to assert that high population density as such is responsible for specific urban problems.

Increasing Population Density

ASSUMED POPULATION DENSITY (persons per square mile)	AREA WITH APPROXIMATE DENSITY ASSUMED	NUMBER OF PERSONS IN CIRCLE OF 10 MILE RADIUS
1	U.S. in 1500	314
50	World in 1960	15,700
8,000	Average central city in metropolitan area in U.S.	2,512,000
17,000	Chicago	5,338,000
25,000	New York	7,850,000
75,000	Manhattan	23,550,000

SOURCE: Philip Hauser, "The Chaotic Society: Product of the Social Morphological Revolution," *American Sociological Review.* vol. 34. no. 1 (February 1969).

Another area of study that has attracted the attention of urban sociol- ogists, social psychologists, and also architects is that of territoriality and aggression. Studies such as those pioneered by the noted ethologist Konrad Lorenz have indicated that many animals disperse their popu- lation by the establishment and defense of territory. The behavior is innate in the animals rather than learned, and the territory is held ei- ther permanently or temporarily by an individual or by a group of indi- viduals against an intruder of the same species. The spacing of birds along a telephone wire is an example of the occupation and defense of temporary space by individuals; the defense of whole areas of land by wolf packs is an example of permanent defense of territory by groups.

That human beings often behave in territorial ways is undisputed; national boundaries, the resentment of intruders in the home, and even the proprietary attitude we assume when sitting on a public park bench are examples of this behavior. It is not clear, however, whether this behavior is innate, as in animals, or simply learned through sociali- zation; most social scientists adopt the latter view. But whatever the origins of the behavior, there is no doubt that humans (unlike other mammals) avoid physical proximity and particularly the touch of other humans unless they are on very familiar terms with them. Cultures vary in this respect, and Americans require more physical distance between individuals than virtually any other people, but all cultures seem to require that there be some physical separation at least between strangers. Crowded streets and subway cars are often experienced as psychologically discomforting and stressful, even when the crowding is not sufficient to be physically uncomfortable. Such crowding may be an important factor in the stress associated with urban living. Sociologist Gerald Suttles has analyzed the behavior of juvenile gangs in terms of aggressive territoriality.[26]

Lack of territorial attitudes, in the view of some architects, is a major reason why high-rise, low-income apartment blocks have rapidly degenerated into vertical slums, with criminals prowling the stairwells where once they would have frequented the back alleys and side streets. Oscar Newman, for example, noted that the crime rate increases in almost direct proportion to the height of a building. High-rise projects, he argues, encourage crimes by fostering feelings of anonymity: the intruder encounters no questioning glances, no territorial attitudes, and feels safe in the vast impersonal space. Newman urges the construction of housing estates in accordance with his idea of "defensible space." A larger number of smaller buildings would be constructed with a layout of buildings and gardens that would give the inhabitants a sense of identity with their surroundings and a feeling of safety and territoriality that would discourage unwelcome trespassers.[27]

The social implications of crowded conditions are still imperfectly understood. Some argue that man is not accustomed to living in large urban settlements. If we understand the history of the human species as beginning about one million years ago, then the time that even a small proportion of mankind has lived in cities is perhaps one-half percent of the entire period of human existence on earth. Man is a highly adaptable animal and it is very probable, but not certain, that he can take this radically changed environment in his stride without undue psychological stress, provided, of course, that other aspects of urban living are tolerable.

PROSPECTS FOR THE FUTURE

In its final report, the National Commission on the Causes and Prevention of Violence painted a gloomy picture of what the future holds for American cities if no urgent remedial action is taken. This is how the commission saw urban living a few years from now:

[26]Gerald Suttles, *The Social Order of the Slum* (Chicago: University of Chicago Press, 1970).
[27]Oscar Newman, "A Theory of Defensible Space," *Intellectual Digest*, 3 (March 1973), p. 5.

In a few more years, lacking effective public action, this is how [our] cities will likely look:

Central business districts in the heart of the city, surrounded by mixed areas of accelerating deterioration, will be partially protected by large numbers of people shopping or working in commercial buildings during daytime hours, plus a substantial police presence, and will be largely deserted except for police patrols during night-time hours.

High-rise apartment buildings and residential compounds protected by private guards and security devices will be fortified cells for upper-middle and high-income populations living at prime locations in the city.

Suburban neighborhoods, geographically far removed from the central city, will be protected mainly by economic homogeneity and by distance from population groups with the highest propensities to commit crimes.

Lacking a sharp change in federal and state policies, ownership of guns will be almost universal in the suburbs, homes will be fortified by an array of devices from window grills to electronic surveillance equipment.

High-speed, patrolled expressways will be sanitized corridors connecting safe areas, and private automobiles, taxicabs, and commercial vehicles will be routinely equipped with unbreakable glass, light armor, and other security features. . . .

Streets and residential neighborhoods in the central city will be unsafe in differing degrees, and the ghetto slum neighborhoods will be places of terror with widespread crime, perhaps entirely out of police control during night-time hours. Armed guards will protect all public facilities such as schools, libraries, and playgrounds in these areas.

Between the unsafe, deteriorating central city on the one hand and the network of safe, prosperous areas and sanitized corridors on the other, there will be, not unnaturally, intensifying hatred and deepening division. Violence will increase further, and the defensive response of the affluent will become still more elaborate.

Individually and to a considerable extent unintentionally, we are closing ourselves into fortresses when collectively we should be building the great, open, humane city-societies of which we are capable.[28]

But such a situation is certainly not inevitable. How can we go about solving the social problem posed by the crisis in our cities? There are no easy answers, but some strategies are available.

Nonresident taxes. A basic requirement must be to place city finances on a more equitable basis. One possibility is for the central cities to ex-

[28]*Final Report of the National Commission on the Causes and Prevention of Violence.*

tract higher revenues from suburbanites who use city facilities but often pay no city taxes. New York and some other cities have attempted this — they impose a tax on all money earned in the central city, regardless of the place of residence of the worker. It might be possible to impose relatively higher taxes on nonresidents than on residents. Cities could also extract taxes from the suburbs by charging higher rates for the various city services that are made available to suburbanites. Cheap parking, for example, attracts traffic to the cities, leading to congestion, road-repair bills, underutilization of public transport, and extra traffic controllers — all costs that the inner-city resident has to pay.

Federal and state aid. A second possibility is to obtain far more federal and state funds for the cities. Again, some progress has been made. Under President Johnson's optimistically entitled Model Cities program, cities are entitled to seek federal funds for a comprehensive attack on their problems; the money may be used for education, construction, antipoverty efforts, medical facilities, sanitation, day care centers, and narcotics-addiction treatment. Yet the amount of federal funds available is strictly limited and inadequate to the needs of the cities.

Another federal program that initially seemed promising is the revenue sharing plan, under which a proportion of the tax revenues collected by the federal government is given back to state and local governments for their use. In 1972 Congress enacted legislation authorizing some 30 billion dollars' worth of expenditures under this program, to be spread over the ensuing five years. The federal government, however, views much of this money as a replacement for funds paid out under its other programs rather than as a supplement to existing ones, so the position of the cities has been only marginally improved.

Annexation of suburbs. A third possibility for different financing of the cities is to extend their boundaries through the annexation of the surrounding suburbs, bringing the entire metropolitan area under central control for some purposes at least. This would not only eliminate many duplications and inefficiencies, but might help to give more residents in the area a larger share of the revenues available for education and other vital services. But although a number of annexations of suburbs by central cities have taken place during this century, it seems unlikely under present conditions that there will be many more. This is because annexation usually involves a referendum in the suburb to be annexed. Suburbanites see no benefits and many disadvantages in becoming part of the city from which many of them have only recently fled, and the results of referenda are likely to be resoundingly negative. More successful metropolitan governments have been established abroad, notably in Toronto and in London. In both cases the central city has been merged for some administrative and fiscal purposes with the entire surrounding region. But the suburbanites of Toronto and London

Freedom in the City

It is necessary to ask ourselves whether we really would prefer to return to the traditional condition of man in which each individual presumably related to the whole personality of a few people rather than to the personality modules of many. Traditional man has been so sentimentalized, so cloyingly romanticized, that we frequently overlook the consequences of such a return. The very same writers who lament fragmentation also demand freedom—yet overlook the unfreedom of people bound together in totalistic relationships. For any relationship implies mutual demands and expectations. The more intimately involved a relationship, the greater the pressure the parties exert on one another to fulfill these expectations. The tighter and more totalistic the relationship, the more modules, so to speak, are brought into play, and the more numerous are the demands we make.

In a modular relationship, the demands are strictly bounded. So long as the shoe salesman performs his rather limited service for us, thereby fulfilling our rather limited expectations, we do not insist that he believe in our God, or that he be tidy at home, or share our political values, or enjoy the same kind of food or music that we do. We leave him free in all other matters—as he leaves us free to be atheist or Jew, heterosexual or homosexual, John Bircher or Communist. This is not true of the total relationship and cannot be. To a certain point, fragmentation and freedom go together.

SOURCE: Alvin Toffler, *Future Shock* (New York: Random House, 1970).

had no say in the matter; the amalgamations were carried out by acts of the respective national legislatures. This type of action would, of course, run contrary to the attitudes and values of many Americans.

Luring back the middle class. Other proposals involve somehow bringing the middle class back to the city. That city life can be appealing for at least some members of the middle class is demonstrated by the remarkable persistence of such middle-class bohemian areas as Greenwich Village in New York, Beacon Hill in Boston, or Nob Hill in San Francisco. There are also indications that many young people reared in the suburbs find suburban living altogether too bland and are returning to the central cities, but whether they will remain there to raise families is another question. One suggestion is that middle-class urban housing should be subsidized in order to lure the middle class back to the cities, but this solution is unlikely to find favor with the urban poor, who understandably claim priority on funds for housing subsidies. Some cities, such as Philadelphia, are attempting to "give away" inner-city proper-

Brasilia, the new capital of Brazil, presents a soaring spectacle of futuristic design. Most of the inhabitants are government bureaucrats whose jobs require them to live there, but they complain that the city has an artificial, formal atmosphere and lacks the "soul" of older, unplanned cities such as Rio de Janeiro. *(Carl Frank/Photo Researchers, Inc.)*

ty: if the new owners will undertake to remodel old buildings, they can have the properties for a nominal cost.

New cities. Another suggestion is that we recognize that existing cities are obsolete and build new ones instead. The only country that has systematically built new towns from scratch is Britain, which has constructed several during the course of the century with such success that it proposes to build many more. The objective is partly to keep the population of large cities down to manageable proportions and partly to rehouse low-income families in existing slum areas. The towns are intended to have about 100,000 inhabitants, and are carefully designed to have adequate areas of "green belt" (areas of unspoiled countryside) and sufficient light industry to provide full employment opportunities.

Brazil has taken the unusual step of building its capital city as a completely new urban settlement. The capital, Brasilia, is situated some six hundred miles from Rio de Janeiro in the Brazilian interior. The intention in choosing this site was to help open up the resources of the Brazilian hinterland by forcing government and commerce to relocate from the coastal cities. The city is designed in the shape of an airplane, with housing on one axis and government, commerce, and recreation facilities on the other. Brasilia is a spectacle of futuristic design, but is generally considered an unpopular place in which to live. Ironically, Brasilia already has slums — built by the workers who were imported to erect the "model" city. There have been a few attempts at constructing new towns in the United States, of which the most successful have been Columbia in Maryland and Reston in Virginia. But although the idea has some attractions, its costs would be prohibitive and it does not really constitute a solution to the contemporary crisis of the existing central cities.

One prerequisite for such a solution must be the careful and controlled planning of urban change. As Moynihan has pointed out, many of the programs that have been designed to improve urban living — highways, urban renewal, federal housing assistance — have merely aggravated the urban crisis through unforeseen side effects. Both the haphazard growth of the cities in the past and the piecemeal planning of recent decades have brought the cities closer to disaster; it seems that they will be rescued only with careful and humane planning.

Attitudes and Values

Yet there is one final obstacle to saving our cities. That obstacle is one of attitudes and values. A deep anti-urban bias has always existed in American life and still influences public policy today. The bias was present at the founding of the Republic: Thomas Jefferson felt that cities were "pestilential to the morals, the health, and the liberties of man." He wrote, "Our governments will remain virtuous for centuries, as long as they are chiefly agricultural."[29] The Jeffersonian vision was of a democracy based on yeomen farmers, sturdy, self-reliant folk who could make mature decisions uninfluenced by the frenzy and self-indulgence that seemed inseparable from city life.

As American cities grew larger, the hostility to them increased. Mark Twain wrote of New York in 1867:

> I have at last, after several months' experience, made up my mind that it is a splendid desert — a doomed and steepled solitude, where a stranger is lonely in the midst of a million of his race. A man walks his tedious miles through the same interminable street every day, elbowing his way through a buzzing multitude. . . . Every man seems to feel that he has got the duties of two lifetimes to accomplish in one, so he rushes, rushes, rushes. . . . All this has a tendency to make the city-bred man impatient of interruption, suspicious of strangers, and fearful of being bored, and his business interfered with.[30]

[29]Murray S. Stedman, Jr., *Urban Politics* (Cambridge, Mass.: Winthrop, 1972), p. 21.
[30]Franklin Walker and G. Ezra Lane, eds., *Mark Twain's Travels with Mr. Brown* (New York: Knopf, 1940), pp. 259–278.

The City: Past and Present

The vast populations of these great cities are utterly divorced from all the genial influences of nature. The great mass of them never, from year's end to year's end, press foot upon mother earth. . . . Wisely have the authorities of Philadelphia labelled with its name every tree in their squares: for how else shall the children growing up in such cities know one tree from another? How shall they even know grass from clover?

The life of great cities is not the natural life of man. He must, under such conditions, deteriorate, physically, mentally, morally. . . . The old healthy social life of village and townland is everywhere disappearing.

. . .

New York is the most exciting city in the world, and also the cruddiest place to be that I can conceive of. The city, where when you see someone on the subway you know you will never see him again. The city, where the streets are dead with the movement of people brushing by, like silt in a now-dry riverbed, stirred by the rush of a dirty wind. The city, where you walk along on the hard floor of a giant maze with walls much taller than people and full of them. The city is an island and feels that way; not enough room, very separate. You have to walk on right-angle routes, can't see where you're going to, only where you are, can only see a narrow part of sky, and never any stars. It's a giant maze you have to fight through, like a rat, but unlike the rat you have no reward awaiting you at the end. There is no end, and you don't know what you're supposed to be looking for.

And unlike the rat, you are not alone. You are instead lonely. There is loneliness as can exist only in the midst of numbers and numbers of people who don't know you, who don't care about you, who won't let you care about them.

SOURCES: Henry George, "City and Country," in *The Complete Works of Henry George,* vol. 3 (New York: Doubleday and McClure, 1898); James S. Kunen, *The Strawberry Statement: Notes of a College Revolutionist* (New York: Random House, 1969).

This anti-urban bias, the feeling that the "authentic" America as captured by Norman Rockwell in his covers for the old *Saturday Evening Post* lies in the small community rather than in the unnatural excrescence of the great city, is still a powerful influence on American attitudes. A recent survey of college seniors found that 43 percent agreed with the statement, "I basically dislike large cities," and 54 percent with the statement, "I don't want my children to grow up in the city."

The Cities: A Theoretical Review

The social problem of the cities represents the gap between a *social ideal* of thriving urban centers, providing a fulfilling life style for all their inhabitants, and the *social reality* of our cities as centers of decay and neglect, in which so many other social problems are primarily located. The problems of the cities are familiar to most Americans because we have become a predominantly urban nation, and the process of urbanization is likely to continue in the future.

The *social-disorganization* perspective provides a particularly useful way of analyzing the problems of the cities. The growth of large cities is a relatively recent historical phenomenon that is associated with other forms of rapid social change—notably industrialism, which freed a high proportion of the population from agricultural activities. Our cities grew rapidly and haphazardly and soon had more than their share of such social problems as crime, alcoholism, and mental illness. But these problems have been severely worsened over the last quarter-century by the flight of the middle class to the new suburbs. Federal housing subsidies and highway programs were functional for their immediate purposes, which were the encouragement of home ownership and the improvement of access to the central cities. But the programs had an unanticipated dysfunction: they made it possible for the middle class to leave the cities, taking with them their skills, sense of civic responsibility, and property tax potential. Industry and commerce have also tended to leave the city centers to settle in the cheaper suburbs. The result is that the city centers are inhabited largely by working-class whites, minority-group members, and others who for reasons of economic status or discrimination are unable to move. The disorganizing effects on the cities have been many. Less tax money is available for education, housing, welfare, and urban services, although the cities are precisely the areas that are most in need of funds for these facilities. Commuters from the suburbs pay no city property taxes, yet make demands on city police, transport, and other services. Even where urban renewal projects have been implemented, the effect has often been to worsen the plight of the cities: traditional ethnic neighborhoods have been shattered, and low-income housing has often been demolished only to be replaced by office blocks or apartment buildings for the wealthy minority. The growth of the suburbs has severely disorganized the finances and general welfare of the central cities.

The *value-conflict* perspective is also very helpful in understanding the problems of the cities. Since the earliest days of colonial America, there has always been a strong anti-urban bias in our society. The small community has been an American ideal, and indeed the flight to the suburbs represents an attempt to re-create the smaller, more intimate community of rural areas and the historic past. Many Americans are more concerned with improving suburban, rural, and small-town life than they are with improving the central cities. Most significantly, those groups and individuals that enjoy the most power and influence in American society are not likely to be residents of the central cities, and so are less inclined than the city dwellers themselves to work for changes in urban policies and particularly in urban financing. Major changes in the financing of the cities would inevitably mean a redistribution of resources from other areas, especially the suburbs; but suburban residents are unwilling to shoulder responsibility for the urban problems from which they have only recently fled. In most state legislatures, rural interests are represented disproportionately in comparison with urban interests, and this fact is frequently revealed by the way the states allocate their resources to different areas. The problems of the cities are aggravated by a continuing conflict of values and interests between the city dwellers—who are often poor minority-group members, and relatively powerless—and the suburban, small-town, and rural residents who are reluctant to accept the financial burden of saving the American cities.

The *deviance* perspective also highlights many of the problems of the cities. Nearly every kind of deviant behavior is more common in urban than in suburban or rural contexts. Drug addiction, suicide, homicide, mental disorders, rape, variant forms of sexual conduct, bystander apathy, robbery, or vandalism all appear to be primarily urban problems. It is not clear why the reported incidence of these forms of deviance is greater in the cities: it may be that urban living encourages deviance, or it may be that the cities attract people with deviant tendencies, or both factors may be involved. It is certain that the city, with its large, heterogeneous, anonymous population, is much more tolerant of deviant forms of behavior than are smaller, more intimate communities. It may also be that the overcrowding and impersonality of the city have a definite psychological impact on some individuals and so contribute to deviant and even pathological behavior. The greater incidence of deviance not only presents the city with extra problems, but may also encourage the departure from the city of those who can afford to leave.

In their classic study of a small town of three thousand residents, Arthur Vidich and Joseph Bensman found that the townsfolk pitied the city people in their nerve-racking and vice-prone environment. The inhabitants believed that the best traditions of America—democracy and individualism— were rooted in small towns and rural areas.[31]

Sociologist Philip Hauser has attributed much of our failure to solve, or even seriously confront, the urban crisis to the anti-urban bias in American life and public policy:

> The urban crisis which afflicts this nation is the product of the gap that exists between the 20th century technological and demographic world we have created and the 19th century and prior century ideologies, values and institutions we have inherited. . . . Our outmoded tenets, values and institutions are paralyzing us in our efforts to deal with our problems.[32]

A similar view was expressed by Senator Joseph S. Clark:

> America's cities are in a state of crisis today, beset by a host of financial, political and environmental problems. But the chief problem in my view, is none of these. It is psychological.
>
> Our basic trouble is that we, as a nation, have gone off to live in the wicked city and we're still ashamed to write home and admit that we like it. . . .
>
> That is not to say we do not have our urban financial, environmental and political problems. We do, in shocking degree. But each of these maladies is related to the fundamental American bias against urban life, as somehow less pure, virtuous and ennobling than life on the farm. . . . We are still torn between our romantic dreams of a rural utopia, and the crying needs of urban life.[33]

Solutions to the problems of America's cities may well require a massive reassessment of national attitudes, values, and priorities and a reallocation of our economic and human resources. But our best efforts can only be successful if the will to save the cities is there.

[31]Arthur Vidich and Joseph Bensman, *Small Town in Mass Society* (Princeton: Princeton University Press, 1958).
[32]Philip M. Hauser, *Cities in the 70's* (Washington, D.C.: National League of Cities, 1970), pp. 15–21.
[33]Testimony before the Subcommittee on Executive Reorganization, August 15, 1966.

FURTHER READING

Banfield, Edward, *The Unheavenly City: The Nature and Future of Our Urban Crisis*, 1970. A controversial statement in which the author contends that our cities, with all their problems, are healthy, vital, and offer unprecedented opportunities for human fulfillment. Banfield argues that we criticize the cities because we expect more of them than ever before—not because urban conditions are worsening.

Clark, Kenneth B., *Dark Ghetto: Dilemmas of Social Power*, 1965. An eminent black social scientist describes life in the black ghettos of the central cities and shows how these conditions are maintained by neglect and by existing social policies.

Gans, Herbert J., *The Levittowners: Ways of Life and Politics in a New Suburban Community*, 1967. An account by a participant-observer of the first two years in the development of a new suburb. On the basis of his research, Gans strongly challenges the stereotype of suburbanites as bored conformists, although he recognizes that suburban living poses many problems.

———, *The Urban Villagers*, 1962. Provides a description of the tightly-knit ethnic communities of our large cities. In a case study of how one such community was shattered by an urban renewal program, no one seemed to benefit except the property speculators.

Jacobs, Jane, *The Death and Life of Great American Cities*, 1961. Presents an indictment of the urban renewal programs in American cities, which, the author contends, have been so badly planned that they have made the cities less habitable than before.

The National Commission on Urban Problems, *Building the American City*, 1968. The report of a federal commission on the problems of the American city. Contains a great deal of information, particularly on the plight of the poorer members of the urban community.

Report of the National Advisory Commission on Civil Disorders, 1968. A report on the ghetto riots of the 1960s. Includes a wealth of information on economic and psychological conditions in urban ghettos.

Suttles, Gerald, *The Social Order of the Slum*, 1970. An account of slum life in a large American city with an analysis of gang warfare and an example of territorial behavior in humans.

Thomlinson, Ralph, *Urban Structure: The Social and Spatial Character of Cities*, 1969. An introductory textbook on urban sociology; contains chapters on most urban social problems.

Wirth, Louis, "Urbanism as a Way of Life," *American Journal of Sociology*, 44 (July 1938). Wirth's classic essay on the nature of the cities remains, to this day, a readable and relevant document.

5

Mass Media

THE NATURE AND SCOPE OF THE PROBLEM

Six thousand years ago, before the invention of writing, human communication was limited in space and time to the strength of a person's voice and the quality of the hearing and memory of his listeners. Today communications satellites transmit messages instantaneously to any part of the world, and even to the moon. Artifacts such as books, films, and computer memory banks retain information indefinitely for the use of future generations. A communications revolution has taken place, especially in the course of the last century, and it has had multiple social consequences that are not yet clearly understood. The average American, for example, spends no less than nine full years of his life watching a television set[1] — with precisely what consequences we do not know. But we do know that the impact of the mass media has made the world a very different place and has had far-reaching effects on the modern consciousness.

Mass Media and Mass Culture

Communication is fundamental to human society. It is through communications that we spread attitudes and values, transmit culture, maintain social order and cohesion, and generate change. Yet we take our mass media — books, newspapers, billboards, comics, radio, television, records, movies — very much for granted. We rely on them for news, for entertainment, for the formation of public opinion, for advertising, and

[1]Jerold M. Starr, "Mass Media," in *Social Structure and Personality,* ed. Jerold M. Starr (Boston: Little, Brown, 1974), p. 246.

Americans may see and hear the President of the United States more often than they meet many of their own friends and relatives. By presenting such shared symbols to the individual members of society, the media play an important part in the creation of mass culture. *(Wide World Photos)*

for the picture of the wider world that we carry around in our heads. In periods of news blackouts, many people experience feelings of great uneasiness, uncertainty, and isolation; they complain of "missing the news," and "not knowing what's going on in the world."[2]

The mass media are a vital element in the modern *mass culture*. Mass culture refers to the distinctive way of life that has developed in the industrialized societies of the world. In these countries vast populations exhibit relatively standardized life styles, values, fashions, and other cultural forms. Such a homogenization of culture would be impossible among such a large number of geographically dispersed people without the influence of the mass media, simply because information about current and emerging cultural forms could not otherwise be so quickly or widely disseminated. Modern mass culture, in fact, overlaps national boundaries to a great extent, and improved communications have made possible considerable similarity in the cultures of the advanced industrial nations. For example, most countries in the world have poorly developed motion picture industries, and a great many of them rely very heavily on American movies for entertainment—and so the Hollywood version of the United States is spread around the globe.

The mass media are an important agency of socialization in any mass

[2]Daniel Katz, et al., *Public Opinion and Propaganda* (New York: Holt, Rinehart & Winston, 1960) pp. 263–271.

culture: they portray social attitudes, values, norms and roles to the developing individual and thus complement the socialization processes that take place in the family, school, and peer group. The media serve to integrate the individual into society, giving him or her a sense of close familiarity with cultural elements that might be distant in space or time: through the media, for example, we may see and hear the American president more often than we see or hear some of our relatives and friends.

Criticisms of the Media

The mass media in America have been under mounting criticism in recent years. Some observers believe that the media are innocent but get blamed for the social problems they portray; others argue that the media have become a social problem in themselves in that they cause or augment a wide range of other social problems. Different individuals and interest groups have different values and attitudes toward the media, and the ways the media exercise their responsibilities vary widely. Some of the more common charges made against the media are these:

1. *Biased reporting.* One allegation, which has been made since the late sixties by the nation's highest elected officials, is that the media have created a "credibility gap" between rulers and ruled through the selective reporting and even deliberate distortion of news. Minority groups have also alleged that their views are distorted by the media and that they are denied access to certain media, particularly broadcasting.
2. *Undesirable role models.* Another charge is that the media provide role models for disapproved deviants by giving publicity to hijackers, rioters, or drug-taking rock stars. Many such problems, it is felt, would "go away" of their own accord if they were not overblown by TV and newspapers.
3. *Vulgarization of culture.* It is often alleged that commercial advertising interests have too great an influence over media content and that consequently the media are vulgarizing American culture and neglecting their responsibility to educate the public and improve popular tastes. The educational potential of the media is said to be grossly neglected.
4. *Offensive content.* The media are often accused of disseminating offensive material that is alleged to be distasteful to many citizens and harmful to many others, particularly children. Two main categories of material are involved: that which portrays violence and aggression; and that which is regarded as obscene or pornographic.
5. *Stereotyped images.* It is alleged that the media and the advertisers who use them create false, stereotyped, and ethnocentric images of

particular classes of people, such as housewives, blacks, or distant preliterate peoples, who are habitually shown in "typical" unflattering roles. In this way, it is charged, the media compound such problems as sexism and racism.

6. *Unattainable goals.* Another charge is that the media create individual maladaptation to reality and hence social disorganization by portraying an imaginary and unattainable world. Since the media are a powerful agency for socialization it may be that people are socialized to some extent into a fantasy existence and are disappointed by, and less able to deal with, their real one.

APPROACHING THE PROBLEM

Mass Media in America

The goals and organizational structure of the American mass media are largely determined by the dominant attitudes and values of American society. The striking feature which distinguishes the American mass media from their counterparts in many other areas of the world is that they are run primarily by commercial enterprises for the purpose of making profits. The profits come either from direct sales, as in the case of movies, or from advertising, as in the case of television and radio, or from both, as in the case of newspapers and magazines. Advertisements occupy up to eighteen minutes per hour of television time; large newspapers devote about 40 percent of their space to advertising, and small newspapers devote about 60 percent.[3] As we shall see, the organization of American mass media along commercial lines has profound effects on the content of newspapers and broadcast programs.

A second feature of the organization of the American media is that there is surprisingly little competition among them; they are coming increasingly under the influence of large conglomerates, many of which own interests in several disparate forms of mass communication. Nearly a third of radio and television stations are affiliated with or owned by newspapers in the same city. In over a third of the cities with only one radio station, that station is associated with the city's only newspaper. The Des Moines area, with its population of 300,000, provides an example of such multimedia concentration of ownership: the Cowles family controls all morning papers, all afternoon papers, and all Sunday papers, and is licencee and owner of one AM station, one FM station, and one TV station.[4] This feature of media organization also has profound implications in many parts of the United States — as political candidates not favored by the media conglomerates in their districts have found to their cost.[5]

[3]Allan Wells, *Mass Media and Society* (Palo Alto, Calif.: National Book Press, 1970), p. 149.
[4]*Editor and Publisher* (January 5, 1974).
[5]See, for example, Gaeton Fonzi, *Annenberg: A Biography of Power* (New York: Weybright & Talley, 1970).

Let us look more closely at newspapers, radio, and television in America to assess the implications of their reliance on advertising and of their concentration of ownership.

Newspapers. Widespread literacy is a comparatively recent phenomenon — in fact, most of the inhabitants of the modern world can still neither read nor write. Although Johannes Gutenberg invented the movable type in the 1450s, the emergence of a genuine mass media using print had to await the development of popular literacy and technological innovations in printing processes and in the manufacture of uniform paper. Early newspapers were written for an educated elite and were confined to local news, literary reviews, and political essays. Initially, they had a small, book-shaped format. The large size of newspaper pages today derives from an English newspaper tax of 1711, which was assessed on the number of pages; editors evaded the tax by increasing page size to the unwieldy proportions that are still used today. It was only in the 1830s that mass newspapers as we know them today first appeared, devoting space to such familiar topics as social events, sports, crimes, and features. The invention of the telegraph in 1837 made the gathering and dissemination of news over great distances much easier. By the end of the century, the great newspaper chains of magnates, such as Joseph Pulitzer, Edward Wyllis Scripps, and William Randolph Hearst, were created.

There are about 1,775 daily newspapers in the United States today with a total circulation of about 162 million. Advertising supplies about two-thirds of their income, and the newspapers aim at providing the readers with what they want in order to increase circulation — not so much for the increased sales revenue as for the increased advertising rates that high circulation brings. The result often is that controversial or minority opinions are not printed for fear of offending readers, and material that advertisers might not like (such as articles recounting consumer complaints against products) is less likely to appear. In addition to the newspapers, there are about ten thousand periodicals, some with very large circulations indeed: the *Reader's Digest* sells 17 million copies of each issue. Some magazines can be successful with a small circulation if their readership is restricted to a particular socioeconomic or interest group that specialist advertisers are particularly keen to reach, such as ski or photography magazines.

The ownership of newspapers is increasingly concentrated in the hands of a few groups. By January 1974 nearly 55 percent of the dailies in America were owned by groups with an average 5.9 newspapers each. There are twenty-one groups that own more than 10 dailies; the largest is Gannett, which owns 56, followed by Thompson with 47, and Scripps with 36. In addition, newspaper groups own 25 percent of all television stations and 8 percent of all AM radio stations, and many also own magazines and publishing companies. In many large metropolitan areas, there are no competing newspapers, and the same company owns

Which Wire Service Did You Read?

PORTSMOUTH, Va. AP–A number of American servicemen now listed as missing in action may be alive in captivity somewhere in south-east Asia, Secretary of Defense Elliot Richardson said Friday.

—AP, MARCH 16

SCOTT AFB, Ill. UPI–With three-fourths of the United States' prisoners of war home, Secretary of Defense Elliot Richardson held out little hope Friday that more than the 562 already identified by the Communists may be found alive.

—UPI, MARCH 16

SOURCE: *Columbia Journalism Review* (May–June 1973).

both morning and evening papers. There are twenty-nine states in which no city has competing daily newspapers.[6]

News is gathered partly by local reporters and special correspondents, but most news—up to 80 percent in some newspapers—is supplied by two great American-based international syndicates, United Press International and Associated Press. The features carried in many newspapers—horoscopes, political columns, crosswords, comic strips, advice columns—are supplied through features syndicates. The result is a high degree of homogeneity among American newspapers, and since space is limited, there is comparatively little opportunity for the publication of views and features that originate outside the syndicate system; many papers are unable to accommodate more than one or two free-lance features in an issue.

Radio. There are more radio sets than people in the United States. Radio reaches 99 percent of all American homes, but television has displaced it from the all-pervasive influence it had in the forties, and it now tends to be used for marginal listening—as an accompaniment to working, reading, or driving. There are some 4,273 AM stations and 2,229 FM stations;[7] the latter have a much shorter broadcast range and are more appropriate for small communities or select audiences.

The influence of advertisers on the content of radio programs is far greater than in the case of newspapers. Unlike newspapers, whose content is determined by the newspaper editorial staff, radio program content is frequently determined by the advertiser and not by the station itself. The advertiser chooses program material that he feels will be appropriate for attracting the kind of audience that he is interested in marketing his product to. Minority or special-interest audiences,

[6]*Editor and Publisher* (February 23, 1974).
[7]U.S. Bureau of the Census, *Statistical Abstract of the United States, 1973*, 94th ed. (Washington, D.C.: U.S. Department of Commerce, 1973), p. 498.

therefore, tend to be neglected unless an advertiser is particularly interested in reaching them.

Unlike the press, however, the broadcasting system is subject to some degree of federal regulation. Radio expanded so rapidly in the twenties that the federal government was obliged to intervene in 1927 to prevent a chaotic overlapping of broadcast frequencies. Regulatory procedures are based on the principle that "the airwaves belong to the people." This is not an ideological position, as in most other countries, but simply a result of the technical restrictions imposed by the limited number of broadcast frequencies available. Control of broadcasting is in the hands of the seven-member Federal Communications Commission; the commissioners are directly appointed by the president. The FCC controls the frequencies, range, and times of radio transmissions and issues licences to broadcast stations. These licences are renewable every three years, in theory on the basis of the past performance and future plans of the stations concerned. The FCC requires stations to devote 5 percent of their broadcast time to news, to regulate time given to commercials, to refrain from using obscene material, to relay a certain amount of public service information, and to give a balanced account of controversial issues. It also allows no single owner to possess more than five stations of a particular kind (TV, AM, and FM), and these stations must be in different geographical areas. The FCC is prohibited from censoring content, although recently it has come very close to doing so: when Vice-President Spiro Agnew alleged in the early seventies that songs by various rock groups made positive reference to the use of drugs, the FCC threatened to revoke licences of stations broadcasting songs with a drug content. The cryptic and sometimes inaudible nature of rock lyrics has made this censorship a difficult task, but many stations have since imposed a musical self-censorship.

The FCC has been strongly criticized in recent years on the grounds that, like many agencies originally established to regulate industry, it has merely become the protector of the industry it is supposed to be regulating. As Harvard economist John Kenneth Galbraith has noted:

> Regulatory bodies, like the people who comprise them, have a marked life cycle. In youth they are vigorous, aggressive, evangelistic, and intolerant. . . . Later they mellow, and in old age – after a matter of ten or fifteen years – they become, with some exceptions, either an arm of the industry they are regulating, or senile.[8]

The FCC has consistently cooperated with the broadcasting industry. It has rubber-stamped applications for licence renewals, even from stations that have made no attempt to meet its minimal requirement of providing a news service. Licence renewal is virtually automatic even where an alternative group has offered comprehensive and innovative proposals in the hope of acquiring a licence from an existing station.

[8]Quoted in Elizabeth Brenner Drew, "Is the FCC Dead?" *Atlantic Monthly,* vol. 220, no. 1 (July 1967), p. 30.

The FCC even refused to hear complaints from listeners and community interest groups at the time of licence renewals until it was ordered to do so by the Supreme Court. The commissioners are generally on intimate terms with the industry, and nine out of ten commissioners leaving the FCC proceed to take lucrative jobs in the broadcasting industry.[9]

Television. Since its widespread adoption in the fifties, television has become the most potent media form in America. It has greatly reduced the importance of radio and is probably responsible for the fact that cinema attendance has dropped by half since the fifties – although Americans now see more movies than ever before on their TV screens. Television has probably also hastened the demise of many general circulation magazines, such as *Life* and *Look,* by diverting their advertising revenue. Television reaches 98 percent of American homes, and a quarter of these homes have more than one set. A television set is switched on for an average of six hours a day in each household,[10] and the statistically average child spends about twenty hours a week watching it.[11] This situation is unparalleled elsewhere in the world – the United States owns more than a third of the world total of 225 million televisions, and in most countries TV broadcasts are limited to a few hours a day on one or two channels.

Like radio programs, local television programs are often selected by commercial sponsors to yield the highest possible audience ratings for the marketing of their products. National TV programs are usually developed by the networks themselves, which then sell the program to commercial interests. Unlike radio and the press, which draw most of their advertising from local sponsors, television gains some 80 percent of its income from national advertising.[12] There are three giant national TV networks – ABC, NBC, and CBS, and most advertising is funneled through them; they therefore indirectly dictate the type and quality of programs that Americans see, particularly during the prime-time evening hours when advertising rates may run as high as fifty thousand dollars per minute. Even more so than in the case of radio and newspapers, television has traditionally disregarded minority interests, deviant viewpoints, and programs of high artistic and intellectual quality; the desire to reach and hold a national audience of many millions obliges the programers to aim at the lowest acceptable common denominator of public tastes and interests. The three major networks are not subject to the authority of the FCC, since the local affiliated stations that run the programs are technically responsible for them.

Television programing has been much criticized for its content. Sober, serious, educative programs tend to be eliminated because they

[9]Ibid., p. 31.

[10]Surgeon General's Report, *Television and Growing Up: The Impact of Televised Violence* (Washington, D.C.: U.S. Government Printing Office, 1972), pp. 82–84.

[11]Wilbur Schramm, et al., *Television in the Lives of Our Children* (Stanford, Calif.: Stanford University Press, 1961), p. 27.

[12]Ben H. Bagdikian, *The Information Machines* (New York: Harper & Row, 1971), p. 172.

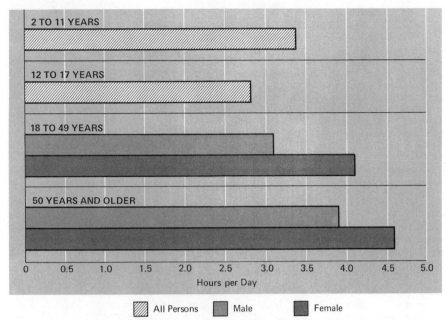

Hours of television viewing by age and sex. The average American watches a TV set for nine years of his life. The youngest and oldest sections of the population spend more time watching TV than the intervening age groups, who must make some time commitment to school and occupation. (SOURCE: A. C. Nielsen Co., Chicago, Ill., *Nielsen Television, '71.* Executive Office of the President: Office of Management and Budget, *Social Indicators, 1973* [Washington, D.C.: U.S. Government Printing Office, 1973], p. 222.)

are believed to be of marginal interest to most viewers — a belief supported by audience surveys that indicate that such programs do not attract large audiences. Advertisers fear that if the content of a program offends, the offense will be transferred to their product, and so controversy, creativity, and social relevance tend to be underplayed. The Alfred I. du Pont – Columbia University Survey Unit on Broadcast Journalism conducted an extensive study on public affairs broadcasting of public events at the end of the sixties. Their report noted that television programs are the major source of current affairs information for 65 percent of the population, but found:

> Across vast distances, at enormous expense and with enormous ingenuity, shallow calls to shallow, morning, noon, and night. To any honest and objective eye . . . most broadcasting must appear a hideous waste of one of the nation's most important resources.[13]

Other critics have pointed to the effects of television advertising on the young and on public life in America in general. Children below the age of about seven do not understand the purpose of commercials and

[13]*New York Times* (November 11, 1969).

Native American children are watching a media characterization of their ancestral history. The media have been much criticized for their role in maintaining ethnocentric and inaccurate stereotypes of minorities and other groups that do not conform to middle-class norms. *(Michal Heron/Woodfin Camp)*

do not separate them from reality, and there are worries as to what effect this socialization into materialism and half-truth may have.[14] Another worry is the effect of the nearly 300 million dollars of annual advertising for a variety of drugs and pills, many of them ineffectual. Senator Frank Moss of Utah has stated the problem:

> The drug culture finds its fullest flowering in the portrait of American society which can be pieced together out of hundreds of thousands of advertisements and commercials. It is advertising which amounts so graphically the message that pills turn rain to sunshine, gloom to joy, depression to euphoria, solve problems, dispel doubt. Not just pills; cigarette and cigar ads; soft drink, coffee, tea and beer ads—all portray the key to happiness as things to swallow, inhale, chew, drink, and eat.[15]

Another problem which is much debated is the impact that television viewing has had on the present college generation—the first in the world to have grown up in the constant companionship of the TV set. The poet Karl Shapiro believes that the new media have thoroughly vulgarized the minds of the young:

> This generation cannot and does not read. I am speaking of university students in what are supposed to be our best universities. Their illiteracy is staggering. We are experiencing a literary breakdown

[14]Aletha Huston Stein, "Television Effects on Children," in *Encyclopedia of Sociology* (Guilford, Conn.: Dushkin Publishing Group, 1974), p. 293.

[15]Quoted in Nicholas Johnson, "The New Consumerism," in *Advertising's Role in Society*, eds. John S. Wright and John E. Mertes (St. Paul, Minn.: West Publishing, 1974), p. 433.

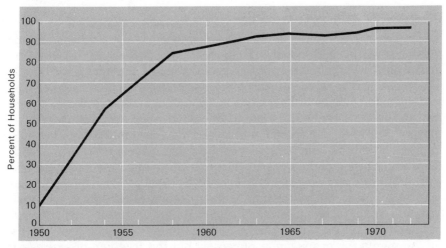

Households with television. Since it became generally available to the public after World War II, TV has rapidly entered most American households. The postwar generation is the first in history to have been reared in the almost daily company of television. (SOURCE: A. C. Nielsen Co., Chicago, Ill., *Nielsen Television '71* and *'73.* Executive Office of the President: Office of Management and Budget, *Social Indicators, 1973* [Washington, D. C.: U.S. Government Printing Office, 1973], p. 221.)

which is unlike anything I know of in the history of letters. It is something new and something to be reckoned with. We have reached the level of mindlessness at which students and the literate public can no longer distinguish between poetry and gibberish. Arrogance and ignorance always go hand in hand and now we are having both shoved at us from both sides. . . . The willful exploitation of primitivism by the media has rendered us insensible and made us a prey to every disease of aesthetic decadence which the lower reaches of the imagination can concoct.[16]

Harry S. Ashmore has argued that the media have severely distorted the perception that young people have of the world:

It is the function of journalism to present a picture of the world upon which men can act. That picture now reaches most of the people as part of a package of broadcast images designed primarily for the senses and only incidentally for the mind. There is evidently a connection between this new aspect of mass communications and the fact that many of the young no longer draw a clear line between reality and romantic fancy. . . .

Thus the American society finds itself quite literally confronted by the first generation weaned on television—a body of restive young people subjected from their earliest years to a torrent of fantasy and violence in which dramatic conflict is neatly resolved by the good-and-evil simplicities of a medieval morality play.[17]

[16]Quoted in Harry S. Ashmore, "Journalism 1970: Uncertain Oracles," *Center Magazine,* vol. 3, no. 6 (November–December 1970), p. 12.
[17]Ibid., p. 12.

The Media Abroad: A Comparison

Commerical ownership of mass media, particularly of broadcasting media, is the exception rather than the rule elsewhere in the world. In most countries, the media are to a greater or lesser extent government-controlled. In the whole of Africa there is no independent radio or television station. There are very few independent stations in Latin America, and in Asia they exist only in Japan, Hong Kong, and the Philippines.[18] Freedom of expression is accordingly very much muted in most of these countries; and in many cases outright government propaganda constitutes much of the content. The use of the mass media for political socialization was first fully appreciated by Stalin in the Soviet Union, and techniques for propaganda were systematically applied with devastating effect in Nazi Germany under Hitler's minister for propaganda, Goebbels. Few countries today go to quite these lengths in the use of the media for propaganda purposes, but the freedom of expression allowed to the American media is unsurpassed anywhere in the world except perhaps in Britain and the Scandinavian countries. The media of the latter countries are subject to somewhat stricter limitations in one respect—the laws relating to libel and to pretrial publicity are much more restrictive. But the media in these countries are inclined to be more critical of public figures than is customary in the United States. Scandinavian or British politicians are subjected to informed and grueling interrogations on television, and American politicans are treated very deferentially in comparison.

Let us look more closely at two contrasting but noncommercial media systems, those of the Soviet Union and Britain.

The Soviet Union. When the Soviet army invaded Czechoslovakia in 1968, international opinion was outraged. News reports and films dealing with the invasion were available to a shocked public around the world. But what did the citizens of the Soviet Union know of the invasion? On August 12, 1968, the news was reported to them in a small, one-paragraph item in *Pravda,* the official organ of the state information agency, Tass. This is what the Russian people learned:

> Tass is authorized to announce that party and state leaders of the Czechoslovak Socialist Republic have appealed to the Soviet Union and other allied states to provide urgent help to the fraternal Czechoslovak people, including help by their armed forces. The fraternal countries firmly and resolutely oppose any outside threat whatsoever in their unshakable solidarity. No one will ever be allowed to wrest a link from the community of socialist states.[19]

Readers seeking more information from the other official Soviet paper, *Izvestia,* would have found exactly the same report in its pages. No

[18]Harold M. Evans, "Is the Press Too Powerful?" *Columbia Journalism Review,* vol. 10, no. 5 (January–February 1972), p. 10.
[19]*Pravda* (August 12, 1968).

other news was available; of the tanks in the streets, the reaction of the world, the dismay of the Czechs — nothing. And throughout the Czech crisis, all Western radio broadcasts to the Soviet Union were jammed.

The Soviet media are entirely controlled by the state. All newspapers are owned by the state or by one of its public organs. The editorial staffers are usually members of the Communist party and practice a form of self-censorship, but in addition, directives from above dictate how the important issues are to be treated in the news. Movies are under the control of the Ministry of Education, and films, like all other art forms — novels, paintings, poetry, songs — are meant to have a strong ideological content. To the Soviets, this is the essence of truth in art, although to Western minds the products seem stereotyped, uncreative, and often boring.

Radio and television are also used as instruments for political socialization. Like the press, they are believed to have two overriding purposes: the elevation of mass culture and the dissemination of information and values supportive of the regime and its ideology. The cultural content of radio and television is designed to improve public taste; about half the total broadcast time, for example, is devoted to classical music, but the works of the Beatles and other modern artists have long been banned. Public affairs reporting does not distinguish fact from opinion or from exhortation. Alternative viewpoints are not presented, and the system of broadcasting most widely in use in the Soviet Union — radio diffusion exchange — eliminates the possibility of Western views intruding into most households. Radio diffusion exchange, unlike regular radio, does not give the listener a choice of programs. Most Russian radios are simply wired receivers without a station selection dial, rather like loudspeakers. They are placed in public places, such as factories and train stations, so that broadcasts can be continuously available outside the home. The system was initially installed for economic reasons, as the receivers cost less than a tenth of a regular radio and give better reception; but more importantly, they restrict the listener to a few, carefully chosen programs.

There are, however, some freedoms. Citizens are encouraged to use the media to criticize the inefficiencies of the administration; *Izvestia* receives some 300,000 letters a year from the public on these issues. There can be no criticisms of policies, but the citizen participation in matters relating to the actual mechanics of the bureaucracy is highly valued. And although the Soviet system appears to us to embody blatant propaganda at its worst and most totalitarian, we might note the official Soviet view of our own system. They consider our media no less biased; theirs might be controlled by the government, but they view ours as controlled by commercial interests that urge us to buy, buy, buy — a form of political socialization into the values of a capitalist system. Our media may be less deliberate and more subtle in their influence, but they do serve to socialize the individual into an acceptance of capitalist values.

Britain. British broadcasting is based on an ideological attitude that the airwaves should be used for the enrichment of popular culture, and although there is a small and carefully regulated independent sector, most broadcasting is operated as a monopoly by the British Broadcasting Corporation. The BBC is established by royal charter as a public body; it is not controlled or operated by any branch of government and there are no political appointees to its board. All the operations of the BBC are financed by licence fees for radio and TV sets. There are four main radio channels, ranging in a hierarchy of cultural quality from light entertainment to very serious intellectual fare. Two main TV channels exist, one of very high cultural and intellectual quality and one more popular. Both present programs uninterrupted by advertising of any kind.

A separate independent system exists, aiming at a more popular audience, but it has been able to attract only a minority of viewers from the BBC network. Even on this system, which is restricted to one channel, the quality of programing is far higher than that of American TV, largely because programs are not directly sponsored by advertisers – the advertiser buys a slot of time but has no influence over program content. Licences in the independent system are periodically reviewed and are revoked if program quality is not high enough. The amount of time devoted to advertising is much less than on American television, and ads are usually shown before and after rather than in the middle of programs. The organization of both the BBC and the independent system reflects the British view that the airwaves are too important an opportunity for public education and cultural enrichment to be entrusted to the hands of purely commercial interests.

INFLUENCE AND EFFECTS OF THE MEDIA

How influential are the media over our minds? Are we manipulated by advertisers? Do our political choices depend on media coverage? Does violence on TV lead to violence in America?

Advertising

Advertisers certainly believe that they can influence us via the mass media; indeed, it is this belief that keeps the media in business. The belief is a well-grounded one: products that are suitably advertised do sell more; products whose sales are falling off can receive a boost through advertising, especially advertising that changes the "image" of the product. But not all advertising will be successful in influencing attitudes and actions; some, in fact, will have the reverse effect to that intended.

Methods of advertising. Advertising and propaganda require special skills. All through history there have been men and women who intuitively understood the human mind and were able to manipulate popular attitudes, but it has taken the development of modern experimental psychology to make truly systematic propaganda methods available. Even so, it is not always clear how or why advertising and persuasion techniques work or fail. A great deal depends on the product or viewpoint that is being promoted: dramatic advertising works best for emotionally neutral products, but gentle persuasion is much better than drama in changing someone's political or religious attitudes—a fact often neglected by the more extreme political or religious groups, whose messages are frequently couched in language that is either meaningless to the hearer or that arouses his or her antagonism.

Much American advertising is, to a greater or lesser extent, dishonest. In extreme cases, claims that have little basis in reality may be made for a product, such as, the alleged nutritional value of some breakfast foods. A more common but very effective technique is that of associating elements that arouse a favorable response with the advertised product, which would normally arouse no response at all. Menthol cigarettes, for example, are commonly advertised in the context of cool mountain streams, and Marlboro cigarette advertisements have very successfully tapped the romantic, frontiersman element of the male psyche by associating the product with images of cowboys and steers silhouetted against a setting sun. The use of the female form, however, is the favorite element in these associative techniques: witness, for example, National Airline's campaign using a series of stewardesses who beseech, "Fly me!" One more insidious technique, which is considered so unethical that it has been banned in the United States and most countries, is subliminal advertising, in which a message is communicated so quickly or so subtly that the conscious mind does not notice it. Early trials yielded varying results but showed the method to be extremely effective in some cases; if an advertisement for ice cream was flashed for a fraction of a second during the course of a movie, ice cream sales soared during the intermission.

Effects of advertising. But we are not mere puppets in the hands of the advertisers and persuaders. There is strong evidence that people are very selective in what they perceive and in what they retain. They respond to material that relates to their interests, is consistent with their attitudes, and is supportive of their values.[20] Smokers, for example, are much less likely than nonsmokers to pay attention to antismoking advertisements: 32 percent of male smokers read them, compared with 60 percent of male nonsmokers.[21] Dramatic evidence for the importance of selective perception and interpretation of messages is provided in a study by Patricia Kendall and Katherine Wolf, who

---

[20]David Krech and Richard S. Crutchfield, "Perceiving the World," in rev. ed., *The Process and Effects of Mass Communications,* eds. Wilbur Schramm and Donald F. Roberts (Urbana, Ill.: University of Illinois Press, 1971), pp. 116–137.

[21]Charles F. Cannel and James C. MacDonald, "The Impact of Health News on Attitudes and Behavior," *Journalism Quarterly,* 33 (1965), pp. 315–323.

studied reactions to a series of antiprejudice cartoons. The cartoons satirized a highly prejudiced character, Mr. Biggott, who was depicted expressing hostile feelings toward minority groups. When the cartoons were shown to a group of 160 men, two-thirds of them misunderstood the message. They missed the point of the satire and believed the intention of the cartoons was to create or intensify racial prejudice. The most important correlate of this misunderstanding was the existence of prior prejudice toward minority groups in the individuals themselves. Three-quarters of the men who misinterpreted the cartoons were found to be already prejudiced.[22] It is quite likely that the popular TV show "All in the Family" is similarly misinterpreted by many viewers.

A comparison of two media campaigns also illustrates the importance of audience attitudes. The first concerns a CBS network program during World War II. A popular entertainer, Kate Smith, conducted an 18½-hour marathon radio program in which she made repeated appeals for people to buy U.S. government bonds. She managed to sell 112 million dollars' worth. The second campaign concerns a six-month-long multimedia effort aimed at presenting information about the United Nations to the population of a large city. The intention of the campaign was to show how, by the use of broadcasts, newspaper articles, posters, speeches, and leaflets, an entire community could be educated about a current affairs topic of major importance. The campaign was a disaster. A random sample of citizens was interviewed before and after the campaign. Before it started, 30 percent of the citizens could not say what the main purpose of the United Nations was and did not know that it had an international peacekeeping function. After the campaign, the number of the uninformed had shrunk only to 28 percent. In the case of the war-bonds campaign, people had felt patriotic and had responded readily to appeals from a popular figure; in the case of the U.N. campaign, they were simply not interested and had screened out the information.[23] The mass media seem more likely to reinforce attitudes, values, and stereotypes than to change them. The effects of media campaigns depend on a whole series of variables: the type of message, the existing public orientation, the type of medium, the nature of the communication situation, and the psychology of the individual.

Political Effects

What of the effect of the mass media on our perception of and attitudes toward political figures?

In the presidential election of 1964, a Hollywood actor was hired by the Republican campaign committee in California to read TV spot ads for Barry Goldwater in the final week of the campaign. The actor was

---

[22]Patricia Kendall and Katherine Wolf, "The Analysis of Deviant Cases in Communications Research," in *Communications Research, 1948–1949*, eds. Paul F. Lazarsfeld and Frank Stanton (New York: Harper & Bros., 1949).

[23]Charles R. Wright, *Mass Communication* (New York: Random House, 1959), pp. 107–110.

Ronald Reagan. Although he had no previous political experience, his television performance was so highly rated that, within days, he launched a successful campaign for the governorship of California.

It seems probable that we may elect quite different people to public office than we would without the influence of television. A candidate who is not good on television is not likely to be elected. This factor was irrelevant before the advent of TV, when other criteria such as oratory, record, and public statements were used in evaluating a political candidate. It is generally believed that television was the crucial factor in John F. Kennedy's hairsbreadth victory over Richard Nixon in the 1960 presidential election—both men believed afterward that Nixon would have won if the two had not engaged in a series of television debates that were watched by up to 75 million people. Commentators agreed that neither candidate had "won" the debates in terms of debating points scored, but Kennedy had appeared as the more photogenic and appealing character—particularly in the first debate, which attracted the largest audience and had the greatest impact on voter preferences. The mass media coverage of Kennedy and his family after the election gave him an almost unprecedented status as a culture hero, and after his assassination his funeral was watched by some 93 percent of all television households in the United States.[24]

Nixon learned the lesson of television well. In the 1968 presidential election a concerted attempt was made to "sell" the candidate on television. Nixon's private surveys revealed that his public image was bad. He was regarded as a "loser," a dirty campaigner, and untrustworthy. His advisors recommended that he campaign not on his record but on the basis that he was a "new Nixon"—a phrase he repeatedly used in the campaign. An expert television producer, Roger Ailes, was hired to orchestrate every detail of his television appearances for maximum effectiveness. Ailes considered that he had a difficult task:

> Let's face it, a lot of people think Nixon is dull. . . . They look at him as the kind of kid who always carried a bookbag. . . . Now, you put him on television, you've got a problem right away. He's a funny-looking guy. He looks like someone hung him in a closet overnight and he jumps out in the morning with his suit all bunched up and starts running around and saying, "I want to be President." I mean, that's how he strikes some people. That's why these shows are important. To make them forget all that.[25]

The entire campaign was carefully packaged by professional advisors, and Nixon defeated Hubert Humphrey by a small margin after outspending him by 12.6 million dollars to 7.1 million dollars in broadcast expenditure. Nixon probably also benefited from unfavorable media coverage of the rioting at the Democratic convention in Chicago.

[24]Harold Mendelsohn and Irving Crespi, *Polls, Television and the New Politics* (Scranton, Pa.: Chandler Publishing, 1970), pp. 266, 272–277.
[25]Joe McGinniss, *The Selling of the President, 1968* (New York: Trident, 1969), p. 103.

The cost of such media advertising has an important implication; wealthy candidates are very much at an advantage over poorer candidates. When Nelson Rockefeller of New York found, from his early polls, that he had only 26 percent popular support for his gubernatorial reelection in 1966, he launched a major media campaign in which he outspent his opponent by 15 to 1. He won easily, but would he have done so without the media impact he was able to buy? The question cannot be answered with certainty, as it seems that media influences work, at least in part, through an indirect process involving other agencies. In a classic study, Paul F. Lazarsfeld, Bernard Berelson, and Hazel Gaudet examined voter decision-making over a period of months with the objective of discovering how radio and newspapers influenced voters. They found that the influence was an indirect one: Instead of coming immediately to their own conclusions, people turned to others whom they knew and trusted for interpretation of the messages they had received.[26] In much the same way, we are more likely to be influenced to see a movie by the recommendation of a friend than by a media advertisement for it, although the advertisement may provoke our initial interest in the possibility of seeing it.

Media Violence

One of the most vexing questions about the media is the potential impact of television violence on the young. Between the ages of five and fourteen, the average child witnesses the annihilation of twelve thousand human beings on television.[27] Children's cartoons contain an average of twenty-five violent acts per hour. About 80 percent of all programs shown at prime viewing times contain at least one violent incident, with an average of 6.7 such incidents an hour. These acts of violence are often presented as approved and useful ways of handling problems.[28] Children's programs feature six times as many violent episodes as the programs for adults. Half of all the leading characters in these programs commit acts of violence, one in ten kills somebody, and one in twenty is killed. This violence is actually required by some advertisers, who insist on it as a means of attracting a large audience. In contracts with writers, advertisers may even specify the number of killings and shootings per program.[29]

At first sight, it seems inevitable that exposure to such slaughter will have an effect on the minds of the youthful viewers and perhaps on their actions as well. But this connection is extremely difficult to prove, because of both the ethical and methodological problems involved in any experiment on the subject. Two main methods are available. The

[26]Paul F. Lazarsfeld, Bernard Berelson, and Hazel Gaudet, *The People's Choice* (New York: Columbia University Press, 1948).
[27]Chris A. De Young and Richard Wynn, *American Education: Foundations in Education,* 7th ed. (New York: McGraw-Hill, 1972), p. 4.
[28]Stein, "Television Effects on Children," p. 293.
[29]Starr, "Mass Media," p. 8.

Numbers and Rates of Violent Episodes

	TOTAL	ABC	CBS	NBC
Number of violent episodes	394	111	127	146
(percent of total)	(100.0)	(28.2)	(34.8)	(37.0)
Rates per program:				
Average for all programs	4.5	5.0	3.9	4.9
Average for programs containing violence	5.5	5.5	5.1	6.1
Rates per hour:				
Average for all hours	6.7	6.3	6.9	7.0
Average for hours containing violence	7.7	6.7	8.6	7.9

SOURCE: Robert K. Baker and S. J. Ball, *Mass Media and Violence*, a staff report to the National Commission on the Causes and Prevention of Violence (Washington, D.C.: U.S. Government Printing Office, 1969).

first would be to compare the attitudes and behavior of children who have been exposed to television during their lives with other children, similar in all other respects, who have not been exposed to television. This method is hardly feasible in the United States, where there is a television in nearly every home, and where homes that do not have television are likely to be very different from homes that do, so that other variables could account for any observed differences in the children. The second method is to expose children to a violent media presentation and then assess their behavior afterward, as compared with a similar group of children who have not seen the presentation. It has been found that under these conditions, children who have been exposed to media violence are temporarily more aggressive. But it is difficult to show whether or not this attitude is sustained over a period of weeks, months, or years in children who have had prolonged experience of media violence, because other intervening factors during that period might account for their behavior.

A government study conducted by the surgeon-general under the auspices of the National Institute for Mental Health concluded that "there is a modest relationship between exposure to television violence and aggressive behavior or tendencies."[30] But the tentative nature of this finding has been strongly criticized on the grounds that the committee studying the question was unduly influenced by the main media networks. The networks were allowed to participate in the nomination of members of the committee and vetoed seven candidates, all of whom had done research on television or spoken sharply against the industry. Five members of the remaining twelve-man committee were industry representatives.[31] The media, which encourage advertisers to believe that what the public views will influence them, are equally adamant in

[30]Surgeon General, *Television and Growing Up*, p. 14.
[31]"TV Violence: Government Study Yields More Evidence, No Verdict," *Science*, vol. 175, no. 11 (February 11, 1972), p. 608.

their insistence that the violence children see has no effect on them whatsoever.

The issue of the impact of violence in the media is still unsettled. Some authorities assert that the violence may even be beneficial in that it can provide a "safety valve" and so prevent, or discourage participation in, violent behavior. Others feel that audiences may imitate the behavior, especially if those who commit violent acts are presented in a favorable, heroic light. It is probable that a great deal depends on the individual and his situation—on the intensity of his attention, on his selective predispositions to what he views, on whether he perceives aggression to be rewarded or punished, on the actual opportunities for violence that exist for him, on his personal character, and on antiviolence feelings in his family and environment. Until more evidence is at hand, acts of homicide will continue to be considered fit for prime viewing time—although interestingly, acts of love are considered obscene, despite the fact that there is no scientific evidence to indicate any adverse effects from exposure to them.

OBJECTIVITY AND MEDIA RESPONSIBILITY

The freedom of the press was established very early in American history, and it has been under attack from one quarter or another ever since. In a crucial court case in 1735, newspaper editor John Zenger was put on trial in New York for publishing "seditious libel" in his weekly journal. On the facts of the case, it was clear that he had broken the law. But the jury decided that the freedom of the press was so singularly important a right that they refused to convict him. Although the issue of the freedom of the press was hotly debated in the early days of the republic, the attitude exemplified by the jury won most popular support, and in 1791 the First Amendment to the Constitution was passed, prohibiting Congress from abridging free speech or freedom of the press.

The White House and the Press

Virtually every president of the United States has had unkind comments to make about the press. Jefferson spoke of the "falsehoods, calumnies, and audacities" of newspapers and of the "malignity, vulgarity, and mendacious spirit" of the editors. Yet he asserted, "I will protect them in the right of lying and calumniating," and claimed that he would rather see newspapers without a government than a government without newspapers. His attitude, stated in 1799, was:

> To the press alone, chequered as it is with abuses, the world is indebted for all the triumphs which have been gained by reason and humanity over error and oppression. . . . To the same beneficient

The First Amendment

Congress shall make no law respecting an establishment of religion, or prohibiting the free exercise thereof; or abridging the freedom of speech, or of the press; or the right of the people peaceably to assemble, and to petition the Government for a redress of grievances.

SOURCE: *The Constitution of the United States.*

source, the United States owe much of the lights which conducted them to the rank of a free and independent nation.[32]

Subsequent presidents often took the press to task. John Quincy Adams alleged that newspapers "pour forth continuous streams of slander . . . no falsehood is too broad, no insinuation too base for them." Lincoln complained bitterly of "customary newspaper exaggeration." Theodore Roosevelt once called the press a "liability to democracy." Harry S Truman accused the press of "distorted editorials and slanted headlines . . . outright misrepresentation . . . distorting of the facts." Dwight Eisenhower objected that the press was "less than gentlemanly" to him, but asserted that he would die to protect its freedom to insult him.[33] John F. Kennedy publicly canceled his subscription to the *New York Herald Tribune* in protest against its reporting; both he and Lyndon Johnson frequently telephoned the television networks to complain about what they felt were biased programs.[34]

In the seventies the attacks on the press from the White House reached new heights. Vice-President Spiro Agnew and President Nixon repeatedly attacked the media for slanted news and unpatriotic reporting. The media, they charged, had fallen into the hands of a small, unelected elite, who controlled the fate of governments through the carefully sifted information that was fed to the public. Two main areas of dispute emerged between the press and the administration—the issue of press responsibility in relation to national security and the question of where to place the blame for the "credibility gap" that existed between government and the people.

The Pentagon papers. The White House became deeply concerned at press reportage of government secrets relating to the Vietnam war, which it alleged was undermining the American military and diplomatic campaign. The media responded that the term "national security" was being used indiscriminately to cover up administration blunders and to deceive the American people. The issue came to a head

[32]Quoted in Pie Dufour, "Press v. President: It's an Old Story," *New York Times* (November 30, 1969).
[33]Quoted in Eric Sevareid, "Candor Towards the Press," *New York Times* (January 21, 1971).
[34]David Wise, *The Politics of Lying* (New York: Random House, 1973), p. 370.

when a secret Pentagon report of the history of U.S. involvement in Vietnam was stolen and published in the *New York Times*. The administration claimed that the leakage of information was highly damaging to the U.S. negotiations at the Paris peace talks, then in session, and took court action against the *Times*. The newspaper retorted that the material in the Pentagon papers was already known to all the participants at the peace talks, but not to the American public, and that the press had a duty to publish the chronicle of blunders and deceptions recounted in the documents. The case finally went to the Supreme Court, which upheld the *Times* appeal by a vote of 6 to 3.

The opposing views of the judges summarize the arguments on both sides of the question. Supporting the administration position, Justice Harry A. Blackmun wrote that if publication caused

> the death of soldiers, the destruction of alliances, the greatly increased difficulty of negotiation with our enemies, the inability of our diplomats to negotiate, to which list I might add the factors of prolongation of the war and of further delay in the freeing of United States prisoners, then the nation's people will know where the responsibility for these sad consequences rests.[35]

Upholding the *Times* appeal, Justice Hugo Black declared:

> In the first amendment, the founding fathers gave the free press the protection it must have to fulfill its essential role in our democracy. The press was to serve the governed, not the governors. The Government's power to censor the press was abolished so that the press would remain forever free to censure the Government. The press was protected so that it could bare the secrets of government and inform the people. Only a free and unrestrained press can effectively expose deception in government. And paramount among the responsibilities of a free press is the duty to prevent any part of the Government from deceiving the people and sending them off to distant lands to die of foreign fevers and foreign shot and shell.[36]

Despite the Supreme Court's ruling, it may be that the administration position is the one that most Americans would support. In 1970, shortly before the publication of the Pentagon papers, CBS conducted a national survey to test the hypothesis that if the Bill of Rights were presented for ratification by the American people today, it would be defeated. CBS decided to poll people on particular issues in the Bill of Rights without using the actual term itself, in case the phrase elicited a preconditioned, unthinking bias. The findings of the poll indicate that a majority of Americans are quite willing to restrict basic freedoms constitutionally guaranteed in the Bill of Rights. About 76 percent of the people interviewed believed that extremist groups should not be

[35]Quoted in Robert Chandler, *Public Opinion: Changing Attitudes on Contemporary Political and Social Issues* (New York: R. R. Bowker & Co., 1972), p. 3.
[36]Ibid., p. 3.

Truth and Politics

Truth and politics are on rather bad terms with each other. No one, as far as I know, has ever counted truthfulness among the political virtues.

Seen from the viewpoint of politics, truth has a despotic character. It is therefore hated by tyrants, who rightly fear the competition of a coercive force they cannot monopolize, and it enjoys a rather precarious status in the eyes of governments that rest on consent and abhor coercion.

—Hannah Arendt

allowed to organize demonstrations against the government, even if there appeared to be no clear danger of violence. Over half the sample—54 percent—would not give everyone the right to criticize the government if the government felt the criticism was damaging to the national interest. Some 55 percent felt that the media should not be allowed to report some stories that the government, in time of peace, felt to be harmful to the national interest. Some 58 percent felt that if the police suspected a person of a serious crime, they should be allowed to hold him without charge until they could gather enough evidence against him. And 20 percent felt the government should be allowed to hold secret trials.[37]

The credibility gap. The second main area of dispute between administration and press is the "credibility gap." Many Americans simply do not believe their government, and they have refused to do so in increasing numbers since the days of the Johnson administration. Indeed, Richard Nixon made the credibility gap one of the issues in his 1968 presidential campaign: he promised to end the gap, to "tell the American people the hard truth," and to provide "an open administration." After his election his press officers, Herb Klein and Ron Ziegler, announced that "truth will be the hallmark of the Nixon administration. . . . We feel that we will be able to eliminate any possibility of a credibility gap in this administration."[38]

During the Watergate scandal, Ziegler added a new usage to the English language by describing his earlier statements as "inoperative," that is, false. And President Nixon became embroiled in the greatest credibility gap in the history of the presidency when, through press statements and televised addresses to the nation, he repeatedly denied any complicity in the Watergate cover-up. Less than a week after he was forced to admit that his statements on Watergate were "at variance"

[37]Ibid., pp. 3–5.
[38]Wise, *The Politics of Lying*, p. 21.

Former presidential aide John Dean accuses the President of the United States of conspiracy to subvert the course of justice in the Watergate affair. Investigative reporting by the media brought several Watergate-related scandals to light, and media exposure of the issue resulted in widespread public perception of government corruption as a major social problem in America. *(Mark Godfrey/Magnum)*

with the facts of the case, Nixon resigned. The fact that the president had systematically lied to the American people for two years threatened a new crisis of confidence in government. In his inaugural address, President Ford assured the nation:

> I believe that truth is the glue that holds government together, not only our Government but civilization itself. . . . I expect to follow my instincts of openness and candor with full confidence that honesty is always the best policy in the end. . . . Our long national nightmare is over.[39]

Ford's aides once more promised an "open administration" and an end to the distrust of government that had profoundly affected traditional political relationships in the United States.

This distrust runs very deep. After the American moon landings in 1970, the Knight newspaper group interviewed 1,721 people in several U.S. cities and asked them if they really believed that the astronauts had gone to the moon and come back. The sample was not a statistical-

---

[39]*Time* (August 19, 1974), p. 13.

ly rigorous one, and the answers did not necessarily reflect public opinion in general, but they were startling nonetheless. In Detroit, 2 percent doubted that the landing had taken place; in Philadelphia, 9 percent; in Charlotte, North Carolina, 17 percent; in Akron, Ohio, 4 percent; in Macon, Georgia, 18 percent. The viewers believed that the TV moonwalk had been faked — possibly it had been filmed in Arizona. Why in their view had the hoax been perpetrated? Three main answers emerged: to fool the Russians or to justify the expenditures of the space program or else to provide entertainment for the American masses and keep their minds off their real problems.[40]

The media allege that the credibility gap exists because of the deceptions of the government, which the media merely report and indeed have a duty to report. The administration alleges that the gap exists because of partisan and distorted reporting by the media. The problem was highlighted by the Watergate scandal. Some people regarded the part played by the media as scurrilous muckraking, others regarded it as responsible and commendable. The Watergate issue became the focus of national and international attention as the result of investigative reporting and media exposure.

Media Objectivity

How objective are the media in America today? The problem of objectivity is a difficult one, for every individual, no matter how scrupulous, will tend to report any event in a different way from anyone else. As Harold Evans, the editor of the London *Sunday Times,* points out:

> Critics of the press sometimes talk as if there is a pure well somewhere, containing information, which is only to be tapped, and which pressmen pollute. There is no such thing. There are of course speeches, court cases, legislative debates to report, but information cannot be packaged untouched by the human hand. Even with the best resolution to be impartial, news cannot be recorded without varying perceptions. No two people ever see the same event and report it in the same detail.[41]

Newspapers. Most American newspapers subscribe to the traditional separation of opinion on the editorial pages from straightforward news on the news pages. Some newspapers, however, feel that personal opinion will inevitably affect the way news is selected and presented and do not attempt a formal separation: this attitude is taken by most underground newspapers and also by such national news magazines as *Time* and *Newsweek.* Of the newspapers that express an editorial policy, how many are liberal and how many conservative? Are they really biased against a conservative administration? Ben Bagdikian has made a study of the question and concludes:

---

[40]Wise, *The Politics of Lying*, pp. 497–498.
[41]Evans, "Is the Press Too Powerful?" p. 10.

The newspapers of this country are out of step with the electorate —
but they are massively out of step in the direction opposite to that
which [some critics] claim. . . . The newspapers are overwhelmingly Republican and conservative.[42]

Of the American dailies that endorsed a presidential candidate in the
Nixon-Kennedy election of 1960, 78 percent endorsed Nixon. In the
Nixon-Humphrey election of 1968, 80 percent endorsed Nixon. And
these were not simply the smaller newspapers — Nixon had 82 percent
of the daily circulation for him in 1960 and 78 percent in 1968. In many
large metropolitan areas, such as Chicago, Los Angeles, Detroit, Philadelphia, and Cleveland, all the major newspapers supported him. This
conservative bias is apparent in congressional as well as presidential
elections. In the 1969 to 1970 Congress there were 222 conservative districts whose members consistently supported conservative measures;
in these districts, there were 430 conservative papers and 88 liberal
ones. There were 202 predominantly liberal districts with liberal congressmen; these had 360 conservative papers and 115 liberal ones.
Conservative members in conservative districts had a 5 – 1 advantage in
newspaper support; liberal members in liberal districts had a 3 – 1 disadvantage. In 79 districts which consistently voted for liberal representatives, there were 130 conservative papers and no liberal papers at
all.[43]

Broadcasting. How biased are the broadcasting media? Radio and television are obliged by FCC regulations to present both sides of any
controversial question and to give equal time to both points of view. A
president has a considerable advantage, too, in that his important statements are guaranteed dissemination, and he can request and receive
prime viewing time whenever he wants to put his own case to the nation. President Johnson used television so often for this purpose that
the networks provided "hot cameras" — teams of technicians constantly
waiting at the White House in case Johnson ever wished to go on national television at a moment's notice. As one NBC executive recalls,
"Once Johnson went on the air so fast that we couldn't put up the presidential seal. When a network technician said we need a second to put
up the seal, Johnson said, 'Son, I'm the leader of the free world, and I'll
go on the air when I want to'."[44] Presidential and other administration
broadcasts are usually followed by a discussion among network commentators. These discussions are also required by the FCC to be balanced and impartial but have been criticised for alleged bias.

Media organization and media bias. But all the media have certain
organizational features that influence their selection and presentation

[42]Ben H. Bagdikian, "The Politics of American Newspapers," *Columbia Journalism Review*, vol. 10,
no. 6 (March – April 1972), p. 8.
[43]Ibid., p. 10.
[44]Wise, *The Politics of Lying*, p. 374.

of news. Newspapers have deadlines, fixed budgets, and restricted space for various categories of news. The final pages are of a precise size and must be ready at a precise moment, so that stories may often be simplified to the the point of distortion or rushed to press without a painstaking check on accuracy. In the case of television, organizational influences have an even greater effect on news presentation. The news has to take a striking and interesting form, as viewers are competitively sought for newscasts and documentaries. If viewers are lost to a rival newscast at 6 P.M., they may remain tuned to another channel throughout the prime hours of the evening. The result is a continuing search for excitement, sensation, and action in the reportage. News tends to focus on confrontations that can be easily characterized, rather than on muddy issues; on areas of general interest rather than minority interest; on trivial items that have news value, rather than on important issues that seem dull. Television has to entertain as well as inform its audience. And so a violent campus confrontation will receive maximum coverage, while a quietly negotiated settlement may be ignored.

The media have often been criticized for their coverage of small, militant groups, whose actions may receive as much attention as a more sober statement by an administration official. But the media coverage of these "pseudo-events" is simply a response to the commercialization of broadcasting and the need to entertain rather than bore the audience. Yippie leaders Jerry Rubin and Abbie Hoffman were well aware of this fact and gleefully created newsworthy pseudo-events—such as throwing dollar bills to the brokers in the chamber of the New York Stock Exchange or threatening to pollute the Chicago water supply with LSD. The Yippies were able to gain instant coverage and national recognition out of all proportion to their numbers and influence at the time; and they became a more formidable political force as a result. In 1974, the Symbionese Liberation Army achieved instant national and international notoriety by kidnapping the daughter of media magnate Randolph Hearst. Of course, the fact that a group is small and militant does not mean that it is necessarily unimportant—the Boston Tea Party was the action of one such group.

PROSPECTS FOR THE FUTURE

Media Innovations

Major innovations in the content of the American media are unlikely to come from the existing press conglomerates or network-based broadcasting stations, all of which are heavily dependent on advertising. There have been several innovations in recent years, however, but these have taken place and will continue to take place outside the framework of existing media organizations. Local radio stations broadcasting on FM frequencies (frequently from college campuses) have provided a radical alternative to the existing radio system. The number of listener-sponsored radio and TV stations has steadily increased, and they provide high-quality, diversified programing. National Educational Television (NET) now operates over two hundred stations. Underground newspapers have proliferated. Some, like *Rolling Stone,* are highly profitable; others mushroom up and disappear. There are probably less than a hundred of these papers regularly appearing at any one time, but in general they are opposed to "establishment" attitudes and values and deal not with news in general but rather with areas of interest to specific groups—the young, the blacks, feminist women, or sexual minorities. None provides a comprehensive alternative to existing daily newspapers. American television could potentially be revolutionized by cable television (CATV). This system is based on the transmission of TV signals via special cables rather than airwaves; the signals can be picked up by a community antenna and then relayed by wire to subscribers' homes. CATV offers several advantages over traditional methods of televising—pictures are clearer and the system can accommodate at least twenty channels. The established networks appreciated the threat that CATV posed to their oligopoly, however, and after they had put pressure on the FCC, the commission determined that CATV should be maintained as a supplementary system only. Unless the FCC reverses its policy, CATV will not develop into a genuinely competitive alternative system. There are at present some 2,770 CATV systems in the United States, reaching nearly one household in ten.

Mass Media and Modern Consciousness

The mass media form an inextricable element in our distinctively modern consciousness. Traditional communities lived isolated in space and time, but through mass communications we have access to an almost infinite range of historical, cross-cultural, and intellectual perspectives. These perspectives can be presented at the push of a button to members of both modern and traditional communities. Media content challenges ethnocentric attitudes, providing images of different life styles and values to people who have never been exposed to ways of life different from their own. In this way the media relativize the social reality that people had once unquestioningly accepted as an absolute. Sociologists Peter Berger, Brigitte Berger, and Hansfried Kellner have written of the "homeless mind" of the modern man or woman, who is thrust into a universe of varying, competing world-views and who is irretrievably detached from the intellectual security of that insular, taken-for-granted cultural reality in which most humans have lived throughout history.[45]

Marshall McLuhan, a Canadian analyst of the social significance of the mass media, has attracted a great deal of attention through his thesis

[45]Peter Berger, Brigitte Berger, and Hansfried Kellner, *The Homeless Mind* (New York: Vintage Books, 1973).

The media can create "instant" heroes and celebrities and may help to popularize and spread their ideas and life styles. The rapid development of a modern youth culture has been acutely dependent on several media, notably rock music, movies, and underground newspapers. *(Dagmar)*

that history is shaped by the type of information technology available at a particular time. The manner in which we receive information through our five senses, he says, determines the pattern of our social relationships. "The medium is the message," because content is less important than the way in which it is presented. Thus when the medium of communication was simply the spoken word, people lived in small-scale communities, and close emotional bonds existed among the inhabitants. The development of printing led to an industrialized, urbanized, specialized society, with personal relationships based more on intellectual than emotional exchange. Today electronic communications have reduced the entire world to a "global village," with far-reaching implications for the gradual homogenization of all human cultures.[46] Sociologists are generally skeptical of McLuhan's argument, which they consider to be too technologically determinist; other factors, they believe, interact to produce changed social circumstances, and the development of different types of communication may be as much a consequence as a cause of changing social structures. But sociologists do recognize the importance of the media in social change through their "agenda setting" function. The media focus attention on social facts—government corruption, drug addiction, racial discrimination—and as a result these issues are catapulted to public attention and recognized as social problems. The media also accelerate social change by the continuous creation of mass culture. The counterculture of the young, for example,

[46]Marshall McLuhan, *Understanding Media* (New York: McGraw-Hill, 1964); Marshall McLuhan and Quentin Fiore, *The Medium Is the Massage* (New York: Random House, 1967).

Mass Media: A Theoretical Review

The social problem of the mass media represents what many people consider to be a gap between a *social ideal* of responsible, objective media and the *social reality* of media that often seem irresponsible, biased, owned by a few partisan interests, dominated by commercial concerns, and apt to vulgarize rather than improve the public taste. The mass media have become an extremely important social influence over the course of the present century. They have played an important role in the development of modern mass culture, and they now complement the family, the schools, and the peer group as a prime agency of socialization in all industrialized countries.

The *social-disorganization* perspective offers several insights into media problems. The structure of the media in the United States is such that ownership of many forms of media is often concentrated in the hands of a few powerful individuals or companies. Given the potential influence of the media, this may be regarded as undesirable. Moreover, the content of the media—particularly the broadcasting media—is largely determined by advertisers. The advertisers are anxious that broadcast material should not offend viewers because some of this offense may "rub off" on to the advertised product. In addition, the advertisers are primarily concerned with reaching the largest possible audience and so tend to select program material that will reach the lowest common denominator of public taste. The result of this domination of the broadcasting media by advertisers is that programs tend to avoid controversial material, and the educational potential of broadcasting is generally neglected. Various minority groups, too, have great difficulty in gaining access to the media to explain their own grievances. It has also been argued by some critics that the mass media contribute to social disorganization by portraying violence, conflict, and other undesirable activities in a favorable light, thereby possibly encouraging the spread of antisocial or illegal behavior.

The *value-conflict* perspective is especially useful in the analysis of media problems. There are many grounds for conflict over what the functions of the media should be and over what sort of material they should present. Many citizens, for example, are concerned about what they believe to be the obscene, pornographic, or immoral content of the media, while other citizens regard such content as perfectly acceptable and do not regard it as immoral in any way. Some citizens are willing to accept some form of media censorship, while others—even while they deplore some of the content of the media—are strongly opposed to censorship in any form. Some people feel that the media tend to vulgarize public tastes by pandering to the widest possible audience and argue that the media have a responsibility to perform an educational function in uplifting popular culture; others believe that this view is snobbish and elitist, and that the media should offer the people what they want. Some groups are anxious to see radical reforms of the media, particularly radio and television, that would take control of content out of the hands of the advertisers and possibly eliminate all advertising from broadcasting; the broadcasting companies and the advertisers naturally resist the suggestion. The objectivity of the media presents a recurring potential for value conflicts. Objectivity is very much in the eye of the beholder, because no two people will report the same event in exactly the same way. Consequently, individuals and groups will continually feel that their newspaper, radio station, or TV channel is presenting a "biased" or "unfair" view of some issue—a charge that the media professionals may deeply resent. The issue of objectivity is frequently raised by politicians. Unlike most other citizens, they are constantly in the public eye and are dependent on continuing public approval for their political success; consequently they are very sensitive about media coverage of their activities. The close scrutiny and strong criticism that the newspapers in particular devote to public figures and to public policies are often a source of bitter conflict between the media on the one hand and the politicians and their supporters on the other. By their very nature, the media often become involved in controversial issues, even when they are seeking to avoid controversy and merely give balanced reportage; and so value conflicts are basic to their role in society.

The *deviance* perspective is of limited use in the analysis of media problems. Some critics have charged, however, that the media encourage deviance by providing role models of deviants of various kinds—drug-takers, rioters, hippies, hijackers—and thereby encourage the spread of deviant behavior in society. These views are controversial; for example, there is as yet no conclusive proof that media violence encourages violence in viewers, and there is very strong evidence that printed pornography does not have any adverse effects on those who are exposed to it, even in adolescence. Many observers, nonetheless, believe that the media unnecessarily increase the incidence of deviant behavior by keeping it before the public eye.

swept through the Western world in a matter of a few years; it was based primarily on one medium — rock music — and propagated rapidly by others — radio, TV, movies, and the underground press.

Yale University social scientist Robert Jay Lifton has pointed to the role of the media in creating what he terms a new "self-process" of psychological exploration. A new type of person is emerging, whom he terms "Protean man." The phrase derives from the Greek god Proteus, who could change his form at will into any person or object he chose, but could never retain the same form for very long. In traditional culture, says Lifton, an individual was willing to be cast into a static role in a static culture — village blacksmith, for example. But today, many individuals seek perpetual personal growth through new experiences, yet they never find full satisfaction in any of them, and are driven to look ever further afield for personal fulfillment. According to Lifton, a major influence in creating Protean men and women is

> the flooding of imagery produced by the extraordinary flow of post-modern cultural influences over mass communication networks. These . . . permit each individual to be touched by everything, but at the same time cause him to be overwhelmed by superficial messages and undigested cultural elements, by headlines and by endless partial alternatives in every sphere of life.[47]

The individual and social consequences of the development of mass media are still imperfectly understood. We do know that their freedom is essential for democracy, and we do know that they profoundly affect our consciousness of the world, yet we do not fully understand the contribution the media make to solving or compounding our various social problems. We should always remember, however, that the media, like all other social phenomena, are not some alien construct, superimposed on society; they are a human creation, and in principle can be modified and controlled by human beings in accordance with social values. As the broadcaster Edward R. Murrow once remarked:

> A communications system is totally neutral. It has no conscience, no principle, nor morality. It has only a history. It will broadcast filth or inspiration with equal facility. It will speak the truth as loudly as it will speak falsehood. It is, in sum, no more nor less than the people who use it.[48]

[47]Robert Jay Lifton, *History and Human Survival* (New York: Random House, 1969), p. 318.
[48]Quoted in Sander Vanocur, "TV's Failed Promise," *Center Magazine*, vol. 4, no. 6 (November–December 1971), p. 46.

FURTHER READING

Christenson, Reo M. and Robert O. McWilliams, *Voice of the People*, 2d ed., 1967. A collection of over one hundred articles covering every aspect of public opinion and propaganda.

Emery, Edwin, et al., *Introduction to Mass Communications*, 3d ed., 1970. An introductory textbook that provides a good and comprehensive introduction to virtually every aspect of the media. It is especially illustrative of the media's social impact.

Johnson, Nicholas, *How to Talk Back to Your Television Set*, 1970. A well-written and stimulating criticism of the FCC and television networks by a renegade member of the FCC. Johnson offers numerous suggestions for media reform.

McGinniss, Joe, *The Making of the President*, 1968. Best-selling account of how Richard Nixon was "sold" to the American people in the 1968 presidential election. The book contains detailed information on how the media were used to present an appealing, specific "image" of the candidate – an image that opinion polls showed Nixon had lacked before.

McLuhan, Marshall, *Understanding Media*, 1964; McLuhan, Marshall and Quentin Fiore, *The Medium is the Massage*, 1970. In these two books, McLuhan presents his distinction between "hot" and "cool" media and his controversial argument that the nature of society is largely determined by the type of communications media it has at its disposal.

Schramm, Wilbur, *Men, Messages, and Media: A Look at Human Communication*, 1973. A comprehensive history of human communication and its influence on society. The author examines most of the main theories of mass communication and predicts the impact of future developments on media technology.

Schramm, Wilbur and Donald F. Roberts, eds., *The Process and Effects of Mass Communications*, 1971. A comprehensive collection of readings covering many aspects of the media, including the effects of advertising and propaganda.

Surgeon General's Report, *Television and Growing Up: The Impact of Televised Violence*, 1972. Provides a survey of existing evidence on the impact of television violence on children. The report tentatively concludes that TV violence may encourage similar behavior in young viewers.

Wise, David, *The Politics of Lying*, 1973. A carefully researched and easily readable book about the credibility gap in the Johnson and Nixon administrations. Wise recounts, in detail, the many clashes between administration officials and the press and argues that both administrations intended to use the media in order to deceive the American people.

6

Work and Alienation

THE NATURE AND SCOPE OF THE PROBLEM

When General Motors opened their new automobile plant in Lordstown, Ohio, they believed they had found a revolution in industrial design. This plant was to be the most efficient, the most highly automated, the most trouble-free auto factory in the world, producing vehicles at the phenomenal rate of 101 finished products per hour. Every conceivable aspect of the production process had been meticulously planned—except, as it turned out, for one factor: the human element. The workers at the new plant were first apathetic, then resentful. They began to sabotage the production line in myriad little ways. And finally, in 1972, they made industrial history by calling a three-week strike—not against low pay, but against the deadening conditions of the assembly line. In the past, workers had walked off the job in order to get more money; this time, to the amazement of employers and even of the labor unions, they sat in at the plant, occupied the machines, and demanded radical changes in the very nature of their work. Since that time, the "alienation" of workers has been perceived as a major social problem in the United States by workers, employers, unions, media, and social scientists.

What exactly is alienation? The term has become a modern catch-all phrase, used to describe a variety of socially created psychological ills, and we must define its meaning more precisely. Essentially, alienation signifies the sense of powerlessness and meaninglessness experienced by people when confronted with social institutions they cannot control and which are felt to be oppressive to basic human needs. Alienation in the contemporary work force is indicated by the fact that workers all over the country are insisting that their lives are their own, even when they are at work; that they are not simply commodities to be bought and sold in the labor market; that the authority of the firm must have strict limitations; and that employees deserve to be consulted on every aspect of the production process.

Perhaps because the notion of worker alienation was originally developed by Karl Marx, the topic has always tended to be neglected in the United States, and other aspects of work have received the main focus of attention. At the start of the century, attention centered on the often violent conflict between workers and management as laborers attempted to form unions and demanded better pay and working conditions. Then came the depression, with widespread poverty and lack of sufficient work, and unemployment was the key issue. Thereafter, the stress was on productivity, with social scientists concentrating on ways in which the findings of sociological and psychological research could be used to enhance worker efficiency and increase output. More recently, automation has been perceived as a major issue: in 1964 a presidential commission was established to study the impact of work automation on the American economy. The report of the commission offered stern warnings about how technological innovation might displace many workers from their jobs, but gave virtually no attention to the alienating potential of automation.[1]

Yet less than a decade after the report on automation, the focus had shifted completely. In 1972, the same year as the Lordstown strike, a special task force prepared a report for the Secretary of Health, Education, and Welfare, and made alienation its main theme. The report, *Work in America,* was widely publicized and had great impact. Its recounting of the phenomena of "blue-collar blues" and "white-collar woes" was immediately recognized by the American public as relating directly to their own work experience. The report outlined the nature of the problem:

> Significant numbers of American workers are dissatisfied with the quality of their working lives. Dull, repetitive, seemingly meaningless tasks, offering little challenge or autonomy, are causing discontent among workers at all occupational levels. This is not so much because work itself has greatly changed: indeed, one of the main problems is that work has not changed fast enough to keep up with the rapid and widescale changes in worker attitudes, aspirations, and values. A general increase in their educational and economic status has placed many American workers in a position where having an interesting job is as important as having a job that pays well. . . . Many workers at all occupational levels feel locked-in, their mobility blocked, the opportunity to grow lacking in their jobs,

---

[1]*Report of the National Commission on Technology, Automation, and Economic Progress* (Washington, D.C.: U.S. Government Printing Office, 1965).

challenge missing from their tasks. Young workers appear to be as committed to the institution of work as their elders have been, but many are rebelling against the anachronistic authoritarianism of the workplace.[2]

The report concluded that American workers are being profoundly influenced by a new spirit that challenges traditional assumptions about work. They are demanding changes in their jobs — a widening of their responsibilities, the elimination of repetitive tasks, the rotation of duties, consultation on matters affecting them, choice of their own hours, a four-day week. Are these attitudes the result of major structural and ideological changes in the past few years? Or is alienation simply a fad issue that will soon vanish from the public consciousness when the media lose interest in the subject? As we shall see, answers to these questions do not come easily; attitudes are sharply divided and the evidence is sometimes ambiguous. In fact, when the *Work in America* report was first published, one Labor Department official declared that the whole problem of worker discontent would "go away if sociologists stopped writing about it." Secretary of Labor James D. Hodgson said that the issue had been "overblown," and that the phenomenon was "the creation of pop sociologists and their media sisters." When Peter J. Brennan appeared before the Senate Labor Committee for confirmation as secretary of labor, he was asked what proposals he had to combat low morale and alienation among the labor force. His suggestion was to get "some go-go girls to entertain male workers. . . . If it's women, we bring in men to dance."

But although alienation is currently a central focus of the social-scientific analysis of work as a social problem, it is by no means the only important issue in the area of work. Many other problems exist which are only indirectly related to alienation. Earlier forecasts that automation would virtually eliminate manual labor have been proved unfounded, but automation and technology continue to play a significant role in displacing workers, causing unemployment, and necessitating retraining. Migrant farm workers continue to be grossly exploited. Older workers find it difficult to change jobs and are particularly vulnerable to dismissal and subsequent unemployment in times of economic depression. Many readers of this volume will soon be facing a labor market unprepared to accommodate the new generation of highly educated workers created by the post–World War II baby boom and the expansion of higher education. To this pressure on employment opportunities will be added the demands of blacks and other minorities for equal opportunity. Women are also likely to add to the pressure on an already tight job market as they seek independent careers and access to occupations traditionally denied to them on grounds of their sex.

[2]*Work in America: Report of a Special Task Force to the Secretary of Health, Education, and Welfare* (Cambridge, Mass.: M.I.T. Press, 1973), pp. xv, xvii.

The problems of work and alienation in America, however, do not occur in isolation from the wider social context. The social structure and particularly the class system influence the nature of the work place, and the nature of the work place influences the lives of workers outside their working hours.

APPROACHING THE PROBLEM

The Meaning of Work

We tend to take our contemporary attitudes and values about work for granted, and forget that social definitions of work — its value, its dignity, its necessity — have varied a great deal through history and across cultures.

Preindustrial society: work as a curse. To the ancient Greeks, for example, work was nothing more nor less than a curse. It was regarded as a thoroughly burdensome and unpleasant way of life, entirely incompatible with the dignity of the citizen. The highest and most distinctively human activity was the cultivation of the mind and the constructive use of leisure. In Greek society, the institution of slavery was justified on the grounds that it freed the citizen to spend his life in cultural enrichment and philosophic contemplation. This attitude toward work may be a reason why the Greeks, despite their highly developed theoretical science, never produced a significant applied technology based on their ideas.

The ancient Hebrews accorded work rather more dignity than had the Greeks before them, but they also regarded it as sheer drudgery. Work, however, was seen as a grim necessity, imposed on mankind by a wrathful God as a punishment for the disobedience of Adam and Eve. Early Christian doctrine generally accepted the Hebrew view of work as a curse of God and saw little inherent virtue in labor. Work was associated not so much with the acquisition of wealth and material goods as with poverty, purification, and self-denial. In fact, many of the heretical sects that arose during the early Middle Ages demanded that their adherents engage in ceaseless labor on the grounds that work was a degrading, humiliating scourge of the sinful flesh. It was quite permissible for monks to go begging rather than work. The only virtue of work lay in the fact that the products of labor could be charitably shared with the poor, thus earning the blessing of God for the giver.

The Protestant Ethic: work as a duty. The great change in values and attitudes toward work came with the Protestant Reformation. In one of the most provocative arguments in all sociology, the German sociologist Max Weber asserted that it was the ideas of puritanism that provided the impulse for the transformation from the medieval to the modern industrial world, in which disciplined labor is seen as the fundamental basis of social and economic life. Protestantism, he argued, had elevated work from a painful necessity to a profound moral obligation, a source of value and self-respect. What was the mechanism for this change? In *The Protestant Ethic and the Spirit of Capitalism*, Weber explains how religious thinkers such as Luther and Calvin had redefined the nature of work. In their Protestant doctrine, work was a duty imposed on man by God. Work was therefore a service to God; all who could work, should work, so that religious devotion and worldly action were united. Work, like devotion, now became a "calling." Individual puritans considered themselves predestined by God, from the beginning of time, to eternal salvation or damnation. No man could tell whether he was destined to be saved or not, but success in worldly works came to be regarded as a sign of God's favor. Ceaseless work therefore became a moral virtue, but since luxury and self-gratification were sins, profits could not be spent on idleness or pleasure. Profits could, in fact, only be reinvested to make more profit, and so the new economic form of capitalism was born. Thus, according to Weber, the modern industrial world was created; and although the original psychological mechanism that drove men to work is now forgotten, its effect lingers on:

> The puritan wanted to work in a calling: we are forced to do so. For when asceticism was carried out of the monastic cells into everyday life, and began to dominate worldly morality, it did its part in building the tremendous cosmos of the modern economic order. This order is now bound to the technical and economic condition of machine production which today determines the lives of all individuals who are born into this mechanism.[3]

Weber believed that there was a master process behind the development of the modern world—*rationalization*. By rationalization he meant the manner in which every aspect of social and economic life becomes more ordered and calculated in its organization, procedures, and ideas. The small craftsman, for example, gives way to the assembly line, the individual tutor to the impersonal multiversity, distinctive architecture to featureless office blocks, and the town market to the department store.

The modern world, he believed, was becoming shallow and materialistic as a result of rationalization. A new human type was emerging, the technical expert or bureaucrat, and our lives were being ordered by men who were "specialists without vision, sensualists without heart." The result was that "the world is disenchanted," and modern man is doomed to live in an "iron cage."

[3]Max Weber, *The Protestant Ethic and the Spirit of Capitalism* (New York: Scribner's, 1958), p. 181.

Rationalization: An Industrial Example

To take an example therefore, from a very trifling manufacture; but one in which the division of labour has been very often taken notice of, the trade of a pin-maker; a workman not educated to this business (which the division of labour has rendered a distinct trade) . . . could scarce, perhaps, with his utmost industry, make one pin in a day. . . . I have seen a small manifactory of this kind where ten men only were employed, and where some of them consequently performed two or three distinct operations. . . . Those ten persons, therefore, could make among them upwards of forty-eight thousand pins in a day. Each person, therefore, might be considered as making four thousand eight hundred pins in a day.—Adam Smith, 1776.

SOURCE: Adam Smith, *The Wealth of Nations* (New York: Modern Library, 1965).

The Meaning of Work in America

The old Protestant work ethic, with its insistence on labor as a moral duty, has persisted almost unchallenged in the United States until quite recently. It has seemed almost heretical to suggest that work is either fundamentally undesirable or that it should be enjoyable in itself. The stress throughout our history has been on the virtues of a good, hard day's work, as an instrumental means toward achieving material ends and as a beneficial experience for the individual. Former President Nixon voiced the feelings of many Americans when he declared in a speech on welfare reform that labor was good in itself, that it accorded with religious teachings, and that it was endorsed by the American tradition. He added: "Scrubbing floors and emptying bedpans have just as much dignity as there is in any work done in this country—including my own. . . . Most of us consider it immoral to be lazy or slothful."

But work in America is more than simply a culturally prescribed, morally valued activity. It is central to the lives of most adults, contributing to their identity and self-esteem, bringing order and meaning to their lives.[4] It is usually necessary to hold a job to gain approval from others—income from welfare brings low status. There is a strong link between pay and personal worth, so that the more highly paid an individual is, the more highly he tends to regard himself and to be regarded in society. The person at the bottom of the pay scale is readily regarded as "worthless," and welfare recipients almost become nobodies in society.

One of the first questions we ask a stranger is "What do you do?"

[4]Curt Tausky, "Meanings of Work Among Blue-Collar Men," *Pacific Sociological Review*, vol. 12, no. 1 (Spring 1969), pp. 49–55.

Many Americans adhere to the traditional "work ethic"—a set of values that many sociologists believe is historically linked to the old Calvinist insistence on lifelong labor as a moral duty. Adherents of the work ethic generally take a poor view of welfare recipients, hippies, and others who are believed to seek instant gratification in preference to dedicated labor. *(Jan Lukas/Rapho Guillumette)*

The answer to this question tells us a great deal about him or her. This is because people are, in a very profound sense, what they do. A person's self-image is largely dependent on and continually reinforced by his work. A congressman makes speeches, runs in elections, gives interviews—activities that constantly reinforce his self-image as an influential public figure. And an assembly-line worker who spends his days attaching a nut to a bolt may come to think of himself as personally insignificant, an interchangeable part in the factory machinery. In fact, the *Work in America* report noted that people in low-status jobs find they can draw no satisfying identity from their occupations, and they reject the unflattering identities that society forces on them. Interviews with blue-collar workers showed that the typical worker has "an overwhelming sense of inferiority: he cannot talk proudly to his children of his job, and feels he must apologize for his status."[5]

Sociologist Peter Berger has argued that it is becoming increasingly difficult for people to derive a full sense of identity from their work:

> Work provided the individual with a firm profile. This is no longer the case with most workers in industrial society. To say, "I am a railroad man" may be a source of pride, but the pride is as precarious as the occupational title. To say, "I am an electroencephalograph technician" means nothing to most people to whom it is said. To say "I am an addressograph operator" means nothing for a different reason, not because people do not understand what kind of work it entails, but because it is next to impossible to derive any

[5]*Work in America*, p. 35.

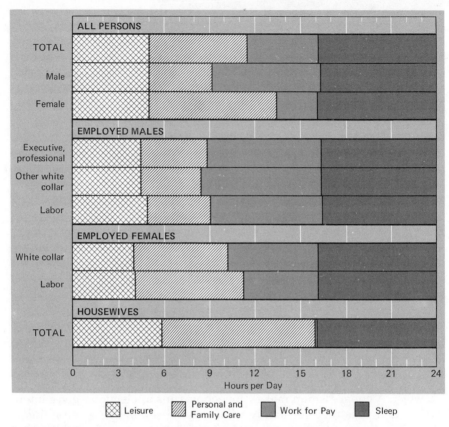

Daily use of time by sex and occupation. The data were collected from a representative urban sample of adults who were asked to record their hourly activities in a diary. Interestingly, white-collar workers work a longer day than blue-collar workers, and housewives claim more leisure time than any other group. (SOURCE: John P. Robinson and Philip E. Converse, "66 Basic Tables of Time-Budget Data for the United States," Survey Research Center, Institute for Social Research, University of Michigan, Ann Arbor, Mich., June 1966. Executive Office of the President: Office of Management and Budget, *Social Indicators, 1973* [Washington, D.C.: U.S. Government Printing Office, 1973], p. 214.)

sort of self-identification from such an occupation, not even the self-identification with an oppressed proletariat that sustained many workers in earlier phases of industrialism.[6]

Berger suggests that work may have one of three meanings for the individual. First, it may be a source of identification and fulfillment. Second, it may be seen as a threat, an indignity, a source of oppression. Third, it may be some "grey, neutral region that one puts up with more or less for the sake of other things supposed to be more important."

[6]Peter L. Berger, "Some General Observations on the Problem of Work," in *The Human Shape of Work*, ed. Peter L. Berger (New York: Macmillan, 1964), p. 215.

The Receptionist: An Interview

(A receptionist at a large business establishment in the Midwest. She is twenty-four. Her husband is a student. "I was out of college, an English Lit. major. I looked around for copywriting jobs. The people they wanted had majored in journalism. Okay, the first myth that blew up in my face is that a college education will get you a job.")

I changed my opinion of receptionists because now I'm one. It wasn't the dumb broad at the front desk who took telephone messages. She had to be something else because I thought I was something else. I was fine until there was a press party. We were having a fairly intelligent conversation. Then they asked me what I did. When I told them, they turned around to find other people with name tags. I wasn't worth bothering with. I wasn't being rejected because of what I had said or the way I talked, but simply because of my function. After that, I tried to make up other names for what I did—communications control, servomechanism. (Laughs.)

You come in at nine, you open the door, you look at the piece of machinery, you plug in the headpiece. That's how my day begins. You tremble when you hear the first ring. After that, it's sort of downhill—unless there's somebody on the phone who is either kind or nasty. The rest of the people are just non, they don't exist. They're just voices. You answer calls, you connect them to others, and that's it. . . .

Until recently I'd cry in the morning. I didn't want to get up. I'd dread Fridays because Monday was always looming over me. Another five days ahead of me. There never seemed to be any end to it. Why am I doing this? Yet I dread looking for jobs. I don't like filling out forms and taking typing tests. I remember on applications I'd put down, "I'd like to deal with the public." (Laughs.) Well, I don't want to deal with the public any more. . . .

I don't know what I'd like to do. That's what hurts the most. That's why I can't quit the job. I really don't think I'd mind going back and learning something, taking a piece of furniture and refinishing it. The type of thing where you know what you're doing and you can create and you can fix something to make it function.

SOURCE: Excerpted from Studs Terkel, *Working* (New York: Pantheon Books, 1972, 1974).

The first and second categories, Berger suggests, are shrinking in favor of the third.

Work confers social status on the individual. The occupation of one's father is the main determinant of social class — which in turn is the main determinant of one's chances in life. Work is also a means by which people sense their personal usefulness and feel their integration into society; retired people often suffer a crucial and shattering loss of identity and purpose. Work is also a place to meet people and form friendships. In our society, it enables the male to maintain his position as breadwinner and hence as head of the family. Work is also, for most people, a matter of sheer economic necessity; other needs cannot be gratified without the economic benefits of labor. And of course for some Americans, work has yet another meaning: it can be inherently satisfying and deeply absorbing.

Work, then, has many interrelated meanings in America. It is clear that these meanings are changing as the technological revolution progresses. Increasingly, workers are being separated from the products of their labor and transformed into machine-watchers engaged in highly standardized tasks that might just as well be performed by anyone off the street. The result is that individuals may find little significance in the activities that take up most of their adult waking lives and so are robbed of a vital source of meaning. Work remains necessary for a livelihood, but the individual simply plays a "role" as worker, conserving his true, authentic self for the precious hours with his family and his few weeks of annual vacation. Work in America can actually seem meaningless — and this is a prime cause of alienation.

The Concept of Alienation

Karl Marx developed the concept of alienation as a broad and sweeping account of the plight of modern man. To Marx, alienation was the process by which man lost his sense of control over the social world, which confronted him as a hostile thing, leaving him as an "alien" in the very world that he had created. Marx applied this perspective to virtually every area of human endeavor — such as government, law, economics, or religion. As applied to religion, for example, the concept of alienation implies that men create various religions; then they lose the sense that religions are socially created and begin to worship in awe the very concepts they have created. Industrial alienation follows a similar course. Men establish systems of economic activity for their own benefit, but then find themselves the powerless victims of the very systems they have created.

Alienated labor. Marx believed that constructive labor was the most distinctive aspect of the human character — more than any other animal, man was creative. Through work, man creates his world, and through work he also creates himself and his culture. His labor enables him to experience himself as a conscious, active being rather than simply one object among others. The great tragedy of history, in Marx's view, is that man has become alienated from his work and thus separated from his products, the natural world, his fellow beings, and from his own essential nature. The main mechanism for this growth of alienation is the division of labor, which develops to its highest degree in the modern capitalist state. As soon as there is a division of labor, each person has a particular, exclusive form of activity forced upon him. The individual no longer uses all his capacities in his work, because the manual and intellectual aspects of his production tend to be separated. Work represents an enforced activity, not a fulfillment of a creative urge:

> It is not the satisfaction of a need, but only a means for satisfying other needs. Its alien character is shown by the fact that as soon as there is no physical or other compulsion, it is avoided like the plague.[7]

The advent of automation, according to Marx, compounds the problem; man creates machines to help him, but instead becomes their slave:

> In the factory, we have a lifeless mechanism independent of the workman, who becomes its mere living appendage. . . . It is not the workman that employs the instruments of labor, but instruments of labor that employ the workman.[8]

The worker is thus separated from the most essential part of his nature as a creative being who takes joy in the construction and mastery of the human environment. He takes part in activity that has no inner meaning for him, that makes him merely part of a process, and that thus leaves him alienated in the most profound sense.

Class conflict. Marx had a solution. He pointed to the class basis of the division of labor, which made it possible for some people to exploit others so that the rewards of work would be unequally distributed. All history, he argued in *The Communist Manifesto,* was the history of class conflict—between master and slave, lord and serf, capitalist and worker. Alienation and class antagonisms would develop to their greatest intensity in the capitalist state, leading to a final confrontation between the opposing classes. The impoverished workers, developing a common sense of their oppression as a class, would rise up in revolt. The result, after an initial temporary period of socialism under a "dictatorship of the proletariat," would be the communist or classless society. In such a society individual men and women would once again feel themselves in control of the social environment, and work would again be-

[7]Karl Marx, *Economic and Philosophical Manuscripts of 1844* (New York: International Publishers, 1964), p. 111.
[8]Karl Marx, *Capital* (New York: Modern Library, n.d.), pp. 461–462.

come a creative, fulfilling activity. The future would be one of abundance in which:

> Society regulates the general production and thus makes it possible for me to do one thing today and another tomorrow, to hunt in the morning, fish in the afternoon, rear cattle in the evening, criticize after dinner, just as I have a mind, without ever becoming hunter, fisherman, shepherd or critic.[9]

Most American sociologists reject Marx's link between the class structure and the alienating effects of industrial production and do not accept the contention that the abolition of classes would eliminate feelings of alienation. The same work might be equally alienating in a classless society. The countries of the Soviet bloc claim to have reached the stage of socialism (communism is still in the distant future, and there is as yet no society in the world that describes itself as communist), but there is no reason to suppose that workers in those countries are immune to the effects of industrial alienation. Most analysts would accept, however, that the nature of a person's work experience affects his social character, his participation as a citizen, and his overall sense of worth and dignity. As Robert Blauner suggests:

> The worker's relation to the technological organization of the work process and to the social organization of the factory determines whether or not he characteristically experiences in that work a sense of control rather than domination, a sense of meaningful purpose rather than futility, a sense of social connection rather than isolation, and a sense of spontaneous involvement and self-expression rather than detachment and discontent.[10]

WORK IN AMERICA

The Composition of the Work Force

The nature of work in America and the structure of the work force have both changed rapidly over the course of the last century. The nation has been transformed from a predominantly rural and agricultural to a predominantly urban and industrial society, with an accompanying surge in material affluence. In 1900 some 37 percent of the labor force were farm workers, and only 18 percent were white-collar workers, but by the end of the sixties only 5 percent of the labor force were on the farms, and white-collar workers had become the largest occupational category. More and more of these white-collar workers are employed

---

[9]Karl Marx and Friedrich Engels, *The German Ideology* (New York: International Publishers, n.d.), p. 22.
[10]Robert Blauner, *Alienation and Freedom* (Chicago: University of Chicago Press, 1964), p. vii.

by large government or commercial organizations, and the number of white-collar individuals who own their own firms is declining sharply. There has been a tremendous diversification in the numbers and in the types of jobs: in the 1850 census, a grand total of 323 occupations was recorded, but by the mid-sixties there were an estimated 23,000 different job titles.[11]

Blue-collar and white-collar workers. Blue-collar workers represent a steadily shrinking proportion of the nation's work force. Although they represented the largest single category as late as the mid-fifties, they will constitute less than a third of the employed in the United States by 1980.[12] One reason for this development is the rapid growth of service industries, with their need for administrative personnel; another is the spread of automation. As of 1971 approximately half of all plants and equipment in the United States were five years old or less.[13] Such a high rate of technological change results in improved productivity, better wages, and a shorter workday; but it also gives rise to problems of dislocation and unemployment, and blue-collar workers have been the main victims of the process. The number of unskilled jobs is unlikely to shrink further in absolute terms, however; it will decline only as a proportion of all jobs. Even in an age of computers and automation, millions of Americans still earn a living by performing tasks which have not changed in centuries—making beds, sweeping floors, collecting garbage. Such jobs tend to be held by the poorly educated, by minority groups, by illegal immigrants, or by other disadvantaged sectors of the population, but are becoming harder and harder to fill. These jobs are now dignified by such titles as "dietary service aides" or "sanitation disposal personnel." But even so, New York City finds it necessary to pay its garbage collectors some $12,886 per year in order to attract men to the job and to keep them there.

It is sometimes suggested that blue- and white-collar occupations are becoming more similar. To some extent this is true. At the beginning of the century, white-collar workers tended to earn much more than manual workers. Today, however, the range of earnings in each group is very wide, and incomes in office and factory jobs crisscross up and down the wage and salary scale. Blue-collar workers, however, start on full wages comparatively early in life. They reach an early plateau in their earning capacity, but their expenses continue to rise as they become homeowners, as their children enter college, and as their parents grow older and require support. Qualitatively, the lives of all workers have improved in many important respects—real earnings, health and living standards, and life expectancy. Conditions in the factory are much better than they were, although conditions in the office,

[11]Seymour Wolfbein, *Work in the American Society* (Glenview, Ill.: Scott, Foresman, 1971), pp. 43–45.

[12]U.S. Bureau of Labor Statistics, *Bureau of Labor Statistics Bulletin*, no. 1673 (Washington, D.C.: U.S. Government Printing Office, 1970), p. 57.

[13]Jack Rasmus, "Another Way to Work," *Social Policy*, vol. 3, no. 5 (January–February 1973), p. 107.

where work is segmented and under authoritarian supervision, often seem more like those of a factory.

Yet despite the improvement in working conditions that has been brought about by the efforts of labor unions and governments, the work place can still be a dirty and dangerous environment. Every year more than fifteen thousand Americans are killed outright on their jobs, mostly in blue-collar occupations. Every year, too, an additional ninety thousand workers are permanently injured. And the toll from latent diseases like occupationally induced cancers probably raises the figure much higher. Exposure to industrial pollutants in the work place causes about a million new cases of occupational disease each year.[14]

Today's blue- and white-collar workers do share some important characteristics, however. They are now sufficiently secure in material terms to question the conditions and purposes of work. They are not, like previous generations of workers, immigrants from backgrounds of poverty, eager and grateful for any work they can get. The younger workers have not, like their parents, known a depression and the misery of permanent unemployment. They are confident of their ability to find work and are willing to move from job to job in search of satisfaction. If their work experience contradicts the American dream of their schooling and early socialization, they are increasingly unwilling to endure it.

Women workers. A division as significant as that between blue- and white-collar workers is that between men and women in the work force. In 1900, only 20 percent of women were in paid employment. The proportion is more than double that today, yet women are still largely confined to the lower-paid, less prestigious forms of labor. The job of secretary is symbolic of the work status of women; there are 9 million secretaries in the United States, representing a third of the female work force. Their work—especially for those in typing pools or operating keypunch machines—is hardly less monotonous than that of the assembly-line worker. The division of labor along sex lines is part of the sexist heritage of our culture, and there is no particular rationale for the way in which work is divided. Work which is defined as appropriate for males in one era may easily be defined as appropriate for females in another, as has happened, for example, with such jobs as schoolteacher, telephone operator, and more recently, bank teller. In other societies, the sexual division of labor may be very different: in many small preliterate communities, for example, the carrying of heavy loads is primarily a woman's job. In the Soviet Union 79 percent of the doctors, 37 percent of the lawyers, 32 percent of the engineers, and 76 percent of the economists are women.

The women's liberation movement has so far had relatively little ef-

---

[14]*Work in America*, p. 26.

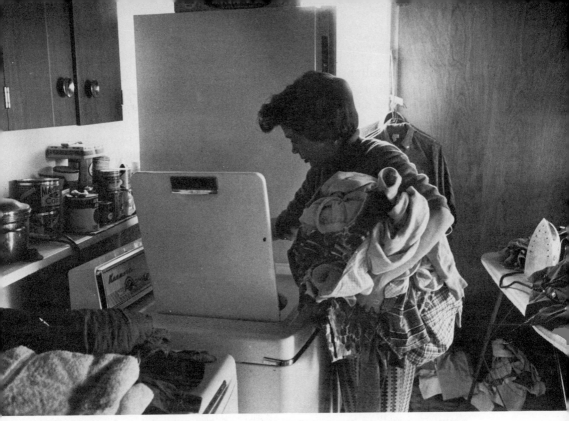

Housework is usually unpaid and, hence, not considered "real" work at all. The low status of housework is intimately linked to the relatively low status of women in American society. Even when workers are hired to perform household duties, wages are very low—domestic servants are among the most poorly paid employees in the nation. *(Inqe Morath/Magnum)*

fect on the role of women in American work. Women still have a secondary status in the labor force, and in fact their income as a percentage of the total is steadily declining. In 1955, women earned 64 percent of the income of similarly employed men; in 1970, they earned only 59 percent. Women also have higher rates of unemployment. In 1969, the female unemployment rate was 4.7 percent compared to 2.8 percent for men; in 1971, it was 6.9 percent for women compared to 5.3 percent for men. Women are still expected to concentrate on housework, which, being unpaid, has low prestige. There is no doubt that the contribution of women to the economy, and the rewards they receive for that contribution, are far below what could be expected in terms of their education, experience, and abilities.

Minority group workers. Minority groups, too, do not play a full role in the economy. The median income for all adult males in the United States at the end of the last decade was $6,429; for minority males it was $3,991. The median income for all women was $3,132; for minority women it was $1,084. Half of the minority males received less than

$4,000.[15] The job prospects for black youth are particularly gloomy. Black teen-age unemployment is far higher than that for whites, even in times of economic prosperity. In recent years the unemployment rate for young black Americans has seldom been less than 33 percent, and it is often as high as 50 percent. The figures may be even higher than this, as many black youths are not counted among the unemployed because they have simply stopped looking for jobs. When they do get work, their jobs offer fewer hours, less pay, less permanence, and fewer prospects for advancement than jobs held by comparable whites. Black women suffer the most, because they face a combined race and sex discrimination. And the situation is likely to grow more serious: blacks will represent an even higher proportion of all new entrants into the labor market in years to come than they have in the past.[16] The position of minority workers may be improved in some respects, however, by federal equal opportunity legislation.

Young workers. The American work force is becoming younger and better educated. Two-thirds of the growth in the work force in the seventies will come from the sixteen-to-thirty-four age group. In the late fifties, some 19.3 million workers, representing over a third of the adult civilian labor force, had completed only eight years or less of formal education. But by the early seventies, this group had been reduced to about 12.5 million, or less than a fifth of the entire labor force. Projections show that the proportion of poorly educated workers will continue to decline to about an eighth of the labor force by 1980 and to about one-sixteenth by 1990.[17] Working-class children are increasingly attending college, and we will have to consider the effect of the relative freedom of college life on these young people as they move into the labor force. The attitudes and values of youth, in fact, may present a real challenge to existing practices in the economic and industrial life of the United States. The young have high expectations as a result of their education; their greater affluence makes them less tolerant of unpleasant work. Numbers of them do not feel any great pressure to work, and their experience of participation in campus decisions and their generally anti-authoritarian attitudes are likely to influence their response to the work place. The corporate economy requires more and more skilled workers, which implies an ever more highly educated labor force. But the experience of higher education is likely to result in an antipathy to hierarchy, authority, and alienating work conditions. Better educated workers are likely to demand greater control over the entire production process—unless job scarcity forces them to conform.

---

[15]Ibid., p. 52.
[16]The Twentieth Century Fund Task Force on Employment Problems of Black Youth, *The Job Crisis for Black Youth* (New York: Praeger, 1971), pp. 3–5.
[17]Denis F. Johnston, "Education of Workers: Projections to 1990," *Monthly Labor Review*, vol. 96, no. 11 (November 1973), pp. 22–31.

The Knowledge Worker

Extending the years of schooling forces us to create jobs that apply knowledge to work. The person who has sat on a school bench until he is eighteen or twenty may not have learned anything. But he has acquired different expectations.

He (or she) expects in the first place a different kind of job, a job that is "proper" for a high school or college graduate. This is first a job with higher pay. But also a job with greater opportunity. A job that gives a "living" is no longer enough. It must offer a "career." But the job for the highly schooled is also a job in which one no longer works with one's hands but by applying one's mind. It is a knowledge job. Long years of schooling make a person unfit for anything but knowledge work. . . .

But the knowledge worker sees himself as just another "professional," no different from the lawyer, the teacher, the preacher, the doctor, the government servant of yesterday. He has the same education. He has more income. He has probably greater opportunities as well.

This hidden conflict between the knowledge worker's view of himself as a "professional" and the social reality in which he is the upgraded and well-paid successor to the skilled worker of yesterday, underlies the disenchantment of so many highly educated young people with the jobs available to them. It explains why they protest so loudly against the "stupidity" of business, of government, of the armed services, and of the universities. They expect to be "intellectuals." And they find that they are just "staff." Because this holds true for organizations altogether and not just for this or that organization, there is no place to flee.

SOURCE: Excerpted from Peter F. Drucker, *The Age of Discontinuity* (New York: Harper & Row, 1968, 1969).

Old workers. One group whose problems are very much neglected in contemporary America are the older workers, who are victims of the myth that they have little to contribute after the age of forty. It is very difficult for these workers to switch from one career to another, and they are unable to compete with younger people for jobs. Yet the workers over forty comprise some 41 percent of the American work force. There is an anti-age-discrimination clause in the federal Employment Act which stipulates that workers must be judged on merit rather than age for the purposes of hiring, promotion, or dismissal, but until recently the law has rarely been enforced. The economic recession of the late sixties and early seventies has attracted more attention to the plight of older workers, however, and the U.S. Labor Department is now in the process of suing over two hundred major companies for millions of dollars on charges of age bias.[18] Many, if not most, firms still discriminate against older workers, however, especially in their hiring practices. It is illegal to advertise a vacancy for someone who is "young" or a "recent college graduate," but it is permissible to ask the age of applicants. Older workers, despite their greater maturity and experience, are often excluded even from job interviews on the grounds of age.

Migrant and child workers. On conservative estimates, there are about 2 million illegal immigrants in the United States, with about a quarter of a million of them in New York alone. (Statistics are obviously largely a matter of guesswork, and some estimates place the total number at 4 or 5 million.) These workers have no welfare or unemployment benefits to fall back on, since application for assistance would make their presence known to the authorities. There is no shortage of employers, however, who exploit their illegal presence and employ them at grossly depressed wage levels. Another exploited group is children. In 1971 the Department of Labor reported that more than a quarter of the country's seasonal farm work force — about 800,000 persons out of 3.1 million — were children under the age of sixteen. Half of them, in fact, were between ten and thirteen years old. Only 22 percent of migrant laborers' children remain in school beyond the sixth grade.[19] Migrant workers and their children are among the most systematically underpaid and exploited workers in the nation.

Job Dissatisfaction

Just how dissatisfied is the American work force? The question is not easily answered. Some studies seem to indicate a deep level of dissatisfaction with work, but others suggest that most workers remain satisfied. The social scientist therefore has to look more closely at the methodology of the various studies — how were the samples drawn, what kind of questions were asked, what did the respondents understand by the questions?

Surveys on job satisfaction. For years social scientists and pollsters have been asking people if they are satisfied with their jobs. And the overwhelming majority have consistently answered yes. Gallup polls, for example, have shown that between 80 and 90 percent of the respondents give a positive answer to this question. Furthermore, when a representative sample of American men were asked, "If by some chance you inherited enough money to live comfortably without work-

---

[18]Lawrence Stassen, "The Ax and Older Workers," *New York Times* (June 23, 1974).
[19]*New York Times* (September 4, 1972).

ing, do you think you would work anyway or not?" some 80 percent replied that they would work anyway.[20]

If we ask the questions rather differently, however, we get different types of answers. For example, when the workers who said that they would continue working even if they did not have to were asked *why* they would stay at work, they were very unclear about the reasons. The main explanation they gave was that they wanted to "keep occupied." The implication of this response is that it was not the pleasures of work which influenced their initial answer, but rather an inability to conceive of an alternative way of spending their free time. Again, if we ask workers the question, "Would you pick the same job over again?" the resulting answers suggest a high level of job dissatisfaction. Of white-collar workers, only 43 percent say they would choose the same jobs, and of blue-collar workers, only 24 percent reply that they would.[21]

Percent of People in Occupational Groups Who Would Choose Similar Work Again

PROFESSIONAL AND LOWER WHITE-COLLAR OCCUPATIONS		WORKING-CLASS OCCUPATIONS	
Urban university		Skilled printers	52
professors	93	Paper workers	42
Mathematicians	91	Skilled autoworkers	41
Physicists	89	Skilled steelworkers	41
Biologists	89	Textile workers	31
Chemists	86	BLUE-COLLAR WORKERS,	
Firm lawyers	85	CROSS SECTION	24
Lawyers	83	Unskilled steelworkers	21
Journalists (Washington		Unskilled autoworkers	16
correspondents)	82		
Church university			
professors	77		
Solo lawyers	75		
WHITE-COLLAR WORKERS,			
CROSS SECTION	43		

SOURCE: *Work in America: Report of a Special Task Force to the Secretary of Health, Education, and Welfare* (Cambridge, Mass.: The M.I.T. Press, 1973), p. 16.

The University of Michigan Survey Research Center has conducted extensive studies of worker attitudes, which also contradict findings of the less sophisticated opinion polls. When workers were asked to rank aspects of work in order of importance, they gave this ranking:

1. Interesting work.
2. Enough help and equipment to get the job done.
3. Enough information to get the job done.
4. Enough authority to get the job done.

[20]Nancy C. Morse and Robert S. Weiss, "The Function and Meaning of Work and the Job," *American Sociological Review*, vol. 20, no. 2 (April 1955), pp. 191–198; *Work in America*, p. 14.
[21]*Work in America*, p. 16.

5. Good pay.
6. Opportunity to develop special abilities.
7. Job security.
8. Seeing the results of one's work.[22]

This study, and others like it, suggests that money is not all-important to workers. They do want to become masters of their immediate environment and resent constant supervision, lack of variety, and feelings of personal powerlessness.

Income is still very important, however. Studies have suggested that about 20 percent of all workers earning less than five thousand dollars a year are dissatisfied; for those earning five to ten thousand dollars, the proportion drops to 10 percent; and for those earning over ten thousand dollars to 8 percent. But dissatisfaction also varies from job to job, independently of income. Among the self-employed in construction, only one in twenty is dissatisfied; in technical, managerial, and professional occupations, the rate is one in ten; and in manufacturing, service, and wholesale occupations, the rate is one in four. Blacks are more dissatisfied than any other workers in the nation: they are twice as likely as whites to be dissatisfied, and 37 percent of them express negative attitudes toward their jobs. The second most dissatisfied workers are those under thirty with some college education; about one in four in this category expresses negative attitudes. Third most dissatisfied are women under thirty. Dissatisfaction becomes progressively greater in the younger age groups. Of those over fifty-five, only 6 percent are dissatisfied; of those forty-five to fifty-four, 11 percent are dissatisfied; of those thirty to forty-four, 13 percent; and of those twenty-nine and under, 25 percent.[23] The young may be becoming even more resentful of authority; studies by Daniel Yankelovich show that, although in 1968 some 56 percent of students said that they would not mind being bossed around on the job, this figure had dropped sharply to 36 percent by 1971.[24] Other studies cited in *Work in America* reveal burgeoning discontent among clerical employees and even in middle-management executives who apparently fear being immobilized in a monolithic structure where their talents will never be recognized or challenged.

The apparent discrepancies between various findings on the question of worker alienation are readily explicable in terms of a model proposed by Frederick Herzberg. He suggests a novel way of looking at the needs of workers through two distinct factors: intrinsic and extrinsic satisfaction. In this model, job satisfaction and job dissatisfaction are not seen, as we usually conceive them, as opposites on the same dimension. Rather, they are viewed as two quite separate phenomena with quite different forces operating to sustain them. Dissatisfaction at work

[22]Ibid., p. 13.

[23]Neal W. Herrick, "Who's Unhappy at Work and Why," *Manpower*, vol. 4, no. 1 (January 1972), pp. 2–7.

[24]Daniel Yankelovich, *The Changing Values on Campus: Political and Personal Attitudes on Campus* (New York: Washington Square Press, 1972), p. 28.

depends on extrinsic factors, such as low pay, poor supervision, or unpleasant working conditions. Satisfaction at work depends on intrinsic factors, such as achievement, accomplishment, responsibility, and challenge.[25] So when a worker is asked, "Are you satisfied with your work?" he may tend to interpret the question as referring to the extrinsic factors and answer, "Yes"; but if the question were designed to tap his attitude toward the intrinsic factors, his response might be entirely different.

Health and job satisfaction. In addition to actual surveys of worker attitudes, there are other measures of worker alienation and its effects. Studies by the University of Michigan's Institute for Social Research have indicated that a variety of health problems are related to job dissatisfaction; this is especially true of psychosomatic illnesses. Arthur Kornhauser, in a major study of the mental health problems of industrial workers, found:

> Poorer mental health occurs whenever conditions of work and life lead to continuing frustration . . . of strongly desired goals which have become indispensable elements of the individual's self-identity as a worthwhile person. Persistent failure and frustration bring lowered self-esteem and dissatisfaction with life, often accompanied by anxieties, social alienation and withdrawal . . . in short, poor mental health.[26]

Another surprising finding that emerged from an impressive fifteen-year-long study of aging is that work satisfaction is the strongest predictor of longevity. The second best predictor was overall "happiness." These two social-psychological measures predicted longevity better than a rating by an examining physician, a measure of the use of tobacco, or a study of genetic inheritance. Controlling these other variables statistically did not alter the dominant role of work satisfaction.[27] Another link between work and longevity is provided by a study of the Abkhasian people of the Soviet Union, undertaken by the anthropologist Sula Benet. Her examination of data showed that 2.5 percent of Abkhasians were ninety years old or older, compared with 0.1 percent for all Russians and 0.4 percent for Americans. This society has a social system in which increased prestige comes with age. But more important, work is literally a lifelong task. Even at the age of one hundred, Abkhasians gladly work in the fields for four hours a day.[28] In our society, in contrast, there is no respected work role for the old. Instead, we offer them little more than a meaningless existence and a sick role that encourages psychosomatic (and genuine) illness.

[25]Frederick Herzberg, *Work and the Nature of Man* (Cleveland: World Publishing, 1966).
[26]Quoted in *Work in America*, p. 84.
[27]Ibid., p. 84.
[28]Sula Benet, "Why They Live to be 100, or Even Older, in Abkhasia," *New York Times Magazine* (December 26, 1971), pp. 28, 29.

The Causes of Worker Alienation

What is the root cause of worker alienation in America? A model proposed by the late American social scientist Abraham Maslow may provide a basis for analysis.[29] Maslow suggested that human needs can be ranked in a hierarchy with each successive step requiring fulfillment only when the previous need has been met. Man's initial need is for the satisfaction of simple physiological requirements—food and a roof over his head. When this need is satisfied, man becomes aware of the need for safety and security. Thereafter, the psychological need for companionship and affection presents itself. The next step in the hierarchy is the requirement for self-esteem and the esteem of others. Then, finally, is the need for self-actualization, the fulfillment of one's deepest potentials. Most people throughout history have led a hand-to-mouth existence, and the final needs in this hierarchy have never become dominant. But in an affluent society, such as the United States, the needs for self-esteem and self-actualization become more pressing psychological requirements. Yet the organization of work systematically stunts the quest for the satisfaction of these humanistic needs.

American industry has traditionally seen the worker as merely part of a process. This attitude is best exemplified in a statement by Frederick Winslow Taylor, father of time-and-motion studies and scientific management at the turn of the century:

> For success, then, let me give one simple piece of advice beyond all others. Every day, year in and year out, each man should ask himself, over and over again, two questions. First, "What is the name of the man I am now working for?", and having answered this definitely, then, "What does this man want me to do, right now?"[30]

Empirical research conducted as early as the thirties should have provided a basis for questioning the assumption that the key to contented workers was simply good pay and physical conditions. The famous experiments at the Hawthorne plant of the General Electric Company consisted of systematically changing aspects of the worker's environment and incentives in order to see which would increase productivity. It was found that productivity increased no matter what changes were made: the workers were responding not to the content of the changes, but to the fact that variety was being introduced into their lives and attention was being paid to them.[31]

The present trend is still toward large corporations and impersonal bureaucracies which typically organize work in such a way that the independence of workers is minimized and control and predictability are maximized. Yet the more aware, democratic, educated, and self-

[29]Abraham Maslow, *Motivation and Personality* (New York: Harper & Row, 1954).
[30]Quoted in *Work in America*, p. 500.
[31]Fritz J. Roethlisberger and William J. Dickson, *Management and the Worker* (Cambridge, Mass.: Harvard University Press, 1939).

affirmative a worker is, the less he or she will stand for boring, dehumanized, authoritarian work conditions. An earlier generation of workers may have found such conditions tolerable, but, as an official of the American Telephone and Telegraph Company lamented in 1973, "We have run out of dumb people to handle these dumb jobs."[32] The dumb jobs stem largely from the way that work has been broken down into smaller components, creating processes that are easy to learn but tedious to operate. This kind of functional specialization reduces job satisfaction: where tasks are so minutely subdivided that the worker performs only a minor operation on his product, he loses all sense of meaning and creativity. Workers feel they are in dead-end positions; they have no interest in doing the job well for its own sake; the work is utterly boring and the only solution is to get out or wait for retirement.

The automobile assembly line has always been the epitome of the rationalized production process, and the signs are that workers are increasingly resisting the discipline required by the industry. The reasons are not hard to find. As one foreman explains it:

> The line here, the moving line, controls the man and his speed. No matter how slow a man is, he has to keep moving. We're all human, we like to go as slow as we can unless we're pushed, and this line controls him perfectly.[33]

And the workers themselves make such comments as these:

> The work isn't hard, it's the never-ending pace. The guys yell "hurrah" whenever the line breaks down.

> On the line you're geared to the line. You don't dare stop. If you get behind you have a hard time catching up.

> The job gets so sickening—day in and day out plugging in ignition wires. I get through one motor, turn around and there's another motor staring me in the face. It's sickening.

> The assembly line is no place to work, I can tell you. There is nothing more discouraging than having a barrel beside you with 10,000 bolts in it and using them all up. Then you get a barrel with another 10,000 bolts, and you know every one of those 10,000 bolts has to be picked up and put in exactly the same place as the last 10,000 bolts.[34]

It is not surprising that absenteeism among the three leading auto manufacturers—General Motors, Ford, and Chrysler—has doubled in the last seven years. On Mondays and Fridays up to 15 percent of the workers in the industry simply fail to turn up. Annual labor turnover

[32]*Washington Post* (January 1, 1973).
[33]Charles R. Walker, Robert Guest, and Arthur N. Turner, *The Foreman on the Assembly Line* (Cambridge, Mass.: Harvard University Press, 1956), p. 11.
[34]Charles R. Walker and Robert Guest, *Man on the Assembly Line* (Cambridge, Mass.: Harvard University Press, 1952), pp. 53–55.

The auto assembly line has come to epitomize the process of rationalization and automation in industry—a process that often involves the subordination of individual human capacities to the demands of mechanized production. Although auto workers are often well paid, the industry has a high labor turnover rate and a long history of labor disputes. *(Ken Heyman)*

has also almost doubled: in fact, Chrysler reported in 1970 that almost half of its workers in the previous year did not complete their first three months on the job.

Of course, only a minority of blue-collar jobs are on the production line, which represents an extreme example of the subordination of man to machine. It remains true that many people do get a certain amount of pleasure out of life at work, even in a mass-production factory. People have a great capacity to adapt themselves, to draw satisfaction from even limited effectiveness at work, to find companionship in their interactions with fellow workers. But throughout the labor force the symptoms and causes of alienation abound. As Robert Sherrill notes:

> Regimentation and repetition may not have nearly as much to do with worker alienation as does the fact that much work just isn't worth doing at all or is basically corrupt. Even the dumbest worker hired to manufacture spray deodorant containers, or plastic plates, or pressed sawdust furniture, or ersatz packaged food, must realize that it wouldn't really matter if his factory closed down forever. So why should he care about his work?[35]

How do we evaluate all this evidence? Is there really a crisis of alienation in the work force, or is the problem largely a creation of excitable

[35]Robert Sherrill, "Review of *Job Power* and *Work in America*," *New York Times Book Review* (July 8, 1973), p. 3.

social scientists and commentators? It seems fair to conclude that there definitely is a high degree of worker dissatisfaction. It may not be as widespread as some have argued, but it is no longer possible to claim that the issue doesn't exist. There is no real way of knowing whether alienation is greater than it was a decade or a quarter of a century or a century ago; certainly working conditions have improved dramatically since that time, but so have our expectations. In Abraham Maslow's hierarchical model, our entire society may be moving into a new phase of quest for self-actualization. And finally, the problem of job dissatisfaction is perceived by many corporations as sufficiently serious that they have begun to experiment with programs to "reduce alienation." Business and administration journals are filled with articles on alienation. Our society is increasingly aware of and concerned with the problem.

PROPOSALS TO REDUCE WORKER ALIENATION

Many ideas have been suggested, and a number have been put into practice, in an effort to reduce alienation in the work place. Although some social scientists argue that alienation can only be combated effectively at the societal level, with major changes in American values and the class structure, most managerial effort has been devoted to structural changes in the work place itself. There is considerable dispute as to what types of changes would be most effective — managers, workers, unions, shareholders, and theorists all have different values and attitudes that are not necessarily compatible, and there is a good deal of mutual suspicion.

The General Foods plant experiment. The kind of changes that have been made so far are well exemplified by an experiment that was conducted at a General Foods plant. The new plant was built because many of the employees in an existing plant manifested such extreme symptoms of alienation that production was being very seriously affected. The workers were casual, indifferent, and apathetic; they had no interest in the quality of the finished product, and there were frequent cases of minor industrial sabotage, leading to waste, shutdowns, and poor labor-management relations. After extensive consultation with academic experts and the workers themselves, the firm built a new plant with the following features:

1. Autonomous work groups. These were self-managing work teams that assumed full collective responsibility for significant parts of the production process.
2. Integrated support functions. Activities typically performed by outside specialists — quality control, maintenance, even sweeping of floors — were built into the operating teams' responsibilities.
3. Challenging job assignments. An attempt was made to design every

set of tasks so that higher human abilities would be involved. Every effort was made to eliminate dull, routine jobs. Those that remained were shared among the team, so that no one individual was permanently stuck with a dull job.

4. Abolition of supervisors. Instead, "team leaders" were substituted, whose task was defined not as giving orders, but rather as facilitating collective decision-making.

5. Sharing of decision rules. The basic rules by which management made economic and production decisions were shared with the operating teams, so that decisions that would normally be made by supervisors were made at operator level.

6. Elimination of differential status symbols. Separate parking lots, cafeterias, types of office furniture, and other status symbols were removed entirely. The aim was to encourage feelings of equality and social contact among all workers.[36]

The results of the experiment were dramatic. It had been anticipated that 110 workers would be needed to run the plant, but the new system was so successful that only 70 were necessary. After eighteen months, the new plant's operating cost was 33 percent lower than the old plant. There was an astounding 92 percent fewer quality rejects, and the absenteeism rate dropped to 9 percent below the industry norm. Annual savings to the firm totaled more than half a million dollars.

Other approaches. Several other experiments have yielded equally encouraging results. At the Bankers Trust Company, typists had repetitious jobs that entailed recording stock transfer data. Production was low, quality of work poor, and morale weak. The workers were encouraged to redesign their own jobs. They did this by eliminating the work of a checker and of a special group that made corrections, and assumed these responsibilities themselves. The new system permitted annual savings of $360,000, with marked changes in worker attitudes. On a Corning Glass assembly line, women workers assembled hot plates, with each individual doing only a tiny part of the entire job. The routine was radically altered so that each woman assembled the entire hot plate, to which her initials were added. The women were encouraged to design their work as a group, and to conduct their own quality checks. Within six months, rejects dropped from 23 percent to 1 percent of output, absenteeism fell from 8 percent to 1 percent and productivity increased by 47 percent.

Other techniques that are being explored include participatory management, profit sharing, and the four-day week. Under participatory management, workers participate in decisions on their own productive methods, on the internal distribution of tasks, on questions of recruitment, on issues of internal leadership, and on when they will work.

[36]Richard E. Walton, "How to Counter Alienation in the Plant," *Harvard Business Review,* vol. 50, no. 6 (November–December 1972), pp. 70–82.

The workers generally do not participate, however, in general economic decisions; these are still made by higher-level management executives. Under profit sharing, efforts are made to satisfy workers that participative management is not simply a device to increase productivity without expense to the company. Profit sharing may be either in the form of payment of stock ownership to the worker or of direct payment of a contracted proportion of company profits. This payment is additional to normal pay and fringe benefits. The four-day week involves the elimination of one working day and the lengthening of the remaining four. Often, employees can choose which four days they wish to work. Between 700 and 1,000 American companies have so far adopted the four-day week, and about 100,000 employees are involved.[37] Initial results are highly encouraging. In a survey of a sample of organizations using the four-day week, it was found that 62 percent reported improved production and only 3 percent reported that output had been reduced. Some 51 percent had higher profits and only 4 percent experienced lower earnings. And 66 percent considered that efficiency had been improved, to only 3 percent which considered it had not.[38]

Not all experiments, of course, have worked. Some new approaches have led nowhere, others have merely led to trouble. In some cases, practical and economic restraints make major redesign of work extremely difficult. As the head of the Ford labor relations department declared bluntly, "You can't stay in the auto assembly business by throwing parts on the floor and saying to the guy, 'Make an automobile out of it'." But many of the experiments have been highly rewarding, leading to greater productivity, better quality, lower absenteeism, and much more satisfied workers. The general trend in the future is likely to be in the direction of further experimentation and more widespread implementation of proven techniques for diminishing worker alienation. As Richard E. Walton of the Harvard Business School notes:

> The roots of worker alienation go so deep that nothing less than comprehensive, radical, systematic redesign of the workplace can sever them.[39]

PROSPECTS FOR THE FUTURE

Alienation and Revolt

The prospect of increasing worker alienation raises the possibility of increased working-class consciousness — something that Marx predicted. In assessing the future of work as a social problem, we must confront the question: Was Marx right? Will class antagonisms increase to the point of revolutionary upheaval, and if not, why not?

[37]*U.S. News and World Report* (March 20, 1972), p. 82.
[38]Ibid, p. 82.
[39]Quoted in the *Washington Post* (January 1, 1973).

Alienation is a pervasive but not a universal feature of work in America. Millions of workers still find in their jobs a source of comradeship, creativity, and personal satisfaction. *(Sherry Suris/Rapho Guillumette)*

Marx prophesied that alienation would end only with the general revolt of the workers. Yet the industrial working class has not yet staged a successful socialist revolution in any country in the world, let alone the United States. All the socialist revolutions of the past — Russia, China, and Cuba, for example — occurred in preindustrial contexts, contrary to Marx's predictions. Was he hopelessly wrong, or might he yet be proved right?

It is important to remember that Marx wrote during an earlier phase of the Industrial Revolution, when a rural peasantry was being transformed into an urban proletariat under conditions of the most humiliating poverty and calculated exploitation. It seemed reasonable to Marx that the capitalists, in their ceaseless pursuit of profit, would tend to grow fewer and richer, with the workers becoming more numerous and poorer and with the middle class being gradually squeezed out of the picture. What Marx could not foresee, however, was the great adaptability that the capitalist system has shown since that time, and the way in which rising affluence has extended the middle class while shrinking the original proletariat.

The American working class today is hardly in the forefront of radical social change. Instead, change in the sixties and seventies has been impelled by militants in minority groups and well-educated young radicals from the white upper-middle class. In the main issues of the day—equality, participation, environment, sexual liberation, community, concern for the quality of life—the blue-collar worker has, if anything, been in the rear guard of the cultural and behavioral revolutions. Alterations in the structure of occupations and incomes, a familiarity with middle-class life styles and consumption patterns, the sense of the possibility of upward social mobility—all these have brought about many changes in the values and attitudes of the American worker. He is more individualistic, less conscious of his class membership, more politically conservative. His labor unions are no longer a radical force in society, but have themselves become part of the establishment. By gaining concessions for the workers, they have reinforced the faith of workers in the system as a whole. Workers often do not feel themselves to be exploited by individual capitalists. It is now difficult to apportion blame for one's economic woes with any precision; the lines between the classes are more blurred than ever, and the worker is likely to be employed not by one man but by a faceless corporation, owned by thousands or hundreds of thousands of shareholders. The very feeling of powerlessness that comes of alienation serves to inhibit action to change the situation.

Ultimately, however, the workers still seem to have a basic faith in American capitalist institutions. The workers in general have a stake in the system Marx expected them to overthrow, and their alienation would have to reach unforeseeable levels before there would be any real possibility of a revolutionary change of the system.

Job Scarcity and the Young

Another problem that will be of burgeoning concern in the future is a specter from the past—unemployment. Since the late sixties, unemployment figures have been rising steadily, and this does not seem to be simply a function of a sluggish economy. In part, increased automation is responsible, though this is less true of the United States than other parts of the world. (Elsewhere, there are growing numbers of "marginal men"—individuals who have reached adulthood and find they have no significant economic role to play, despite their qualifications. In Latin America, for example, urban populations have grown twice as fast as urban jobs, and in many other parts of the world, unemployment rates of 15 to 20 percent are common in urban areas.) The main reason for the growing unemployment in the United States, however, is the baby boom after World War II. Between 1948 and 1953, the number of babies born in America increased by almost half—the largest increase in birth rate ever recorded up to that time anywhere in the world. During each year of the seventies, we will have to find jobs for about 40 percent more people than in each of the last ten years. Chil-

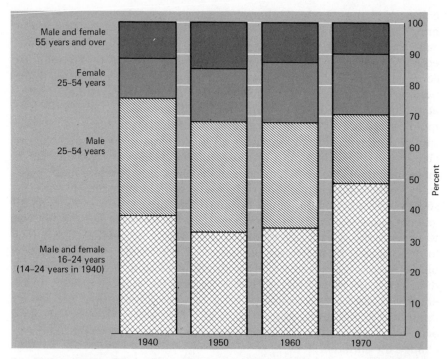

Male and female
55 years and over

Female
25-54 years

Male
25-54 years

Male and female
16-24 years
(14-24 years in 1940)

1940 1950 1960 1970

Percent

Age and sex composition of the unemployed, 1940–1970. The unemployment rate represents the number of unemployed persons as a percentage of the civilian labor force. As the chart shows, young workers are a steadily increasing proportion of the unemployed. (SOURCE: Bureau of the Census; Executive Office of the President: Office of Management and Budget, *Social Indicators, 1973* [Washington, D.C.: U.S. Government Printing Office, 1973], p. 116.)

dren of the baby boom are now entering the work force in large numbers, because so many of them delayed going to work by attending college. The pressure of this new wave of work-seekers could have far-reaching effects, not only on unemployment figures but also on future life styles. As Peter Drucker has suggested, the facts of employment and demography challenge the assumption that the forms of contemporary youth culture, with its antimaterialism and hang-loose, antiwork ethic, are the wave of the future:

> Jobs are likely to be of increasing concern to the young during the next ten years. The shift from "abundant jobs for college graduates" in 1969 is not, as many commentators believe, merely a result of the 1970–1971 mini-recession. It is a result of the overabundance of college graduates, which will continue until the end of the decade even if the economy starts expanding again at a fast clip. . . . The graduates from today's youth culture are likely to find themselves far more worried about jobs and money than they now suspect.[40]

[40]Peter Drucker, "The Surprising Seventies," *Harper's Magazine*, vol. 243, no. 6 (July 1971), pp. 35–39.

The young, like women and blacks, will be entering a labor market with higher expectations than previous generations, but the market is not well prepared to receive them. Many will have to take jobs for which they are overqualified. Others may not find work at all. The uncertainty is this: will their inability to achieve their expectations lead to even higher levels of alienation and revolt against current working conditions, or will they forego their expectations and seek security, being satisfied merely to have a job at all?

The Decline of the Work Ethic

Another problem that will concern us in the future is perhaps, in the long run, the most significant of all. There is a deep and inherent tension in the modern industrial system. The system demands self-denial and discipline from the individual as a worker, yet demands gratification and pleasure from the individual as a consumer. Under these circumstances, the maintenance of the work ethic on which the whole system depends is an inherently fragile enterprise. Already, the adherents of the counterculture have to a greater or lesser extent rejected the traditional work ethic and its demands for endless deferral of gratification and lifelong self-discipline. Part of the dismayed adult reaction to the counterculture was surely based on the realistic perception that if the new values are adopted by the bulk of the population, the industrial system as we know it must change dramatically. The critical tension between the requirements of work and the seductions of pleasure was prophetically expressed by Adriano Tilgher in the thirties:

> In the very homeland of the religion of work a still later religion is growing up, the religion of large buying and of amusements, a religion of comfort, of well-being, of convenience. . . . This has the distinct tendency to relax the tautness of the will to work. . . . The divine madness of labor seems an unbearable chain, binding man to things outside his nature, locking his soul in a narrow prison where its energies are impoverished and weakened.[41]

Recently, Harvard sociologist Daniel Bell has expressed the view that the tension is a growing one, which may constitute the ultimate crisis of our society:

> American capitalism has lost its traditional legitimacy which was based on a moral system of reward, rooted in a Protestant sanctification of work. It has substituted a hedonism which promises a material ease and luxury. . . .
>
> The characteristic style of an industrial society is based on the principles of economics and economizing: on efficiency, least cost, max-

[41]Adriano Tilgher, *Work, What It Has Meant to Men Through the Ages* (New York: Harcourt, Brace and Company, 1930), pp. 142, 147.

Work and Alienation: A Theoretical Review

The social problem of work and alienation represents the gap between a *social ideal* of work as a source of satisfaction, fulfillment, and secure personal identity, and the *social reality* of work as an experience that many citizens consider unsatisfying, meaningless, and oppressive. The concept of alienation is an old one, but has recently come into common usage in the United States. It signifies the sense of powerlessness and lack of meaning that people feel when they are confronted with social institutions over which they have no control: that is, they feel "alien" in the very world that their society has created.

The *social-disorganization* perspective offers a fruitful way of examining the problem of work and alienation. From this perspective, the problem may be seen as the product of rapid changes in both industrial technology and in social values. In preindustrial society, individuals often had much more control over their own working lives. The extended family often functioned as a self-contained economic unit, and people usually worked in small, intimate groups in which every member knew every other member. The worker did not necessarily repeat the same kind of task over and over again, but might assume different duties as the need arose. In addition, the worker had a much more direct relationship to his or her product: the carpenter, for example, made every part of a piece of furniture and had the satisfaction of creating a finished product that bore the stamp of his own personal skills.

Industrialization has radically changed the nature of work. The underlying process behind industrialization is "rationalization," a term that refers to the way in which traditional spontaneous methods are replaced by systematic, calculated, routine procedures. Rationalized work methods are much more efficient and have, therefore, been almost universally adopted in industry, commerce, and administration. Large-scale organizations have replaced small groups as the basic unit in all these areas: the modern factory or office worker may be only one of thousands of other workers in the same building, so that an impersonal environment results. Moreover, the modern worker often does not see his or her finished product: most furniture, for example, is now manufactured on the assembly line, with an individual carpenter contributing an endless series of the same small, standardized part. The office worker, too, may repeatedly type the same forms, year after year, with no sense of overall participation in the affairs of the organization. Work is thus robbed of much of its meaning and satisfaction; people feel themselves to be cogs in a machine rather than autonomous, creative individuals.

Changes in social values and attitudes have worsened the feelings of alienation. In a less affluent society, hard work was a dire economic necessity: good jobs were hard to obtain, and workers were prepared to tolerate harsh conditions. The conditions of labor have improved in many respects, for example, hours are shorter, wages and salaries are higher, and there are safeguards against arbitrary dismissal. But attitudes and values have changed as well. People now have much higher expectations. We live in a society that values human dignity and freedom of choice; we raise our children to expect personal fulfillment and to be autonomous and creative. These early expectations are often frustrated by the experience of work in our society. Unlike their parents or grandparents, today's younger workers are unwilling to accept alienating working conditions. The inconsistency between the reality of work in America and the values into which the young have been socialized contributes further to social disorganization.

The *value-conflict* perspective also provides a useful way of looking at some of the problems of work and alienation in America. There is often a basic conflict of interest between the workers and the management in industry, commerce, and administration. The workers are increasingly concerned with the fulfillment of their human potential, but management's main concern is efficiency and profits. Rationalized work procedures are usually regarded by management as essential if efficiency is to be maintained and if profit levels are to be increased. There is, therefore, an inevitable value conflict between employers and employees in nearly every area of the economy.

Another value conflict stems from the fact that our society places great emphasis on two contradictory values: the work ethic, which stresses self-denial and discipline, and the pursuit of pleasure, which stresses immediate gratification and personal satisfaction. The work ethic can be maintained only by the institutional suppression of the value of pursuit of pleasure, but this can lead to many value conflicts.

The *deviance* perspective is of little relevance to the problem of work and alienation, although those who reject the work ethic are sometimes regarded as social deviants.

imization, optimization, and functional rationality. Yet it is at this point that it comes into sharpest conflict with the cultural trends of the day. The one emphasizes functional rationality, technocratic decision-making, and meritocratic rewards. The other, apocalyptic moods and antirational modes of behavior. It is this disjunction which is the historic crisis of Western society. This cultural contradiction, in the long run, is the deepest challenge to the society.[42]

We have examined alienation within the context of work. But this context is a narrow one. The social forces that give rise to alienation are not restricted to the world of work; the office or factory is merely a focus of attention because of its central role in our lives. The issue of alienation is a far greater one, concerning the impotence of the individual in a society so large, so impersonal, so rationalized and bureaucratized that human institutions seem beyond human control. The protest against alienating conditions in the work place is merely one symptom of a wider cry, heard throughout our social institutions, and succinctly symbolized in the slogan: I AM A HUMAN BEING: DO NOT FOLD, BEND, SPINDLE, OR MUTILATE.

[42]Daniel Bell, "The Cultural Contradiction," *New York Times* (August 27, 1970).

FURTHER READING

Berger, Peter L., ed., *The Human Shape of Work*, 1964. A collection of essays on the human meaning of work. Includes an excellent essay on the subject by Berger himself.

Blauner, Robert, *Alienation and Freedom*, 1964. A sociological analysis of the problem of alienation in American society. Blauner speaks of his own sense of powerlessness as experienced in the workday, but analyzes his problem in the context of a more general social alienation.

Marcuse, Herbert, *Eros and Civilization*, 1955. A radical philosopher's sophisticated argument that industrial civilization is founded on the repression of the pleasure instinct in workers. Workers, he argues, are systematically socialized into a willingness to tolerate the rigid demands of the work place—but only at the cost of their human capacity for spontaneity and the enjoyment of pleasure.

Marx, Karl, *Selected Writings in Sociology and Social Philosophy*, ed. Tom Bottomore, 1964. A selection of Karl Marx's writing drawn from all his major works. The selections include many of Marx's comments on alienation and his passionate denunciation of the alienation of labor.

Terkel, Studs, *Working*, 1974. A fascinating collection of tape-recorded interviews with workers of every kind. Terkel's book rapidly became a best seller as the general public realized the intense human interest in the working lives of these ordinary Americans. Some of the interviewees find fulfillment in their jobs; others, however, are deeply alienated.

Whyte, William H., *The Organization Man*, 1956. A perceptive and controversial account of life as a worker in a large corporation. Whyte argues that the worker becomes almost completely subordinated to the demands of the faceless organization to which he or she dedicates his or her working life.

Work in America: Report of a Special Task Force to the Secretary of Health, Education, and Welfare, 1973. The report that first acknowledged the existence of worker alienation as a major social problem in America. Written in clear, nontechnical language, the report recounts the "blue-collar blues" and "white-collar woes" of millions of American workers.

part three

Inequality
in Society

ver two thousand years ago the Greek philosopher Aristotle made the observation that human populations tend to be divided into three main groups: the very rich, the very poor, and those in between. It seems that little has changed since that time; an upper, a middle, and a lower class are still identifiable in nearly every society, including our own.

An unequal society is one in which the social rewards of power, wealth, and status are unevenly distributed among the members. It is sometimes possible for someone to enjoy one of these rewards without the others: a person may, for example, have status but no power, or power but no wealth. But in practice these three characteristics are usually very closely related—the rich tend to be powerful and to have high status, and the poor tend to be powerless and to have low status. The uneven distribution of these social rewards is often self-perpetuating because the more privileged groups can use their power, wealth, and status to retain and strengthen their position, while the less privileged groups have few resources and so find it difficult to achieve a greater share of social rewards. Inequality is particularly unjust when it is passed on within particular groups from generation to generation because it prevents people from making full use of their talents and arbitrarily deprives them of the opportunities that are so freely available to others.

Our nation was founded on the belief that all men are inherently equal, and even today it remains an important part of the American creed that every citizen should have at least equal opportunity for personal advancement and fulfillment. But, in practice, the United States falls far short of this ideal. We are a very unequal society. Our practices are often inconsistent with our expressed values, and many severe social problems result.

In this section of the book we examine some social problems that are closely linked to inequality. We consider first the problem of government and corporations—those huge organizations that dominate our society. Compared with ordinary citizens, the officials who control these organizations exercise enormous power—but on whose behalf do they use it, and to whom are they accountable? We also look at the problem of poverty in the most affluent society in the world. While super-rich millionaires manage, quite legally, to pay little or nothing in taxes, millions of other Americans live on incomes officially regarded by the federal government as being insufficient to maintain minimum standards of nutrition, clothing, and housing. How can such poverty exist in the midst of such plenty? We also examine a problem that has bedeviled our society since the first contact between white settlers and the American Indians: race and ethnic relations. The United States is composed of many different racial groups, but members of one of them —the whites—enjoy disproportionately more power, wealth, and status than members of any of the other groups. Why is it that inequality seems to be linked to such an irrelevant factor as the color of a person's skin? We also take a look at education because our schools are supposed to provide a channel for social mobility, a means through which a disadvantaged child can gain access to the wealth, power, and status that others enjoy. But the reality of our educational system is very different: the more affluent a child's family is, the better the education that the child receives; the poorer the family, the worse the quality of the education is likely to be. Finally, we look at the problem of sex roles. For generations, it has been taken for granted by the great majority of men and women alike that women are innately inferior to men and that both sexes are born with very different abilities and personalities to complement their physical differences. This view is now being challenged vociferously, yet arbitrary discrimination on the grounds of sex still persists. Why do sexual inequalities remain?

As we look at each of these problems of inequality, it will become clear that they cannot easily be solved. Inequality is rooted deep in the structure of American society, and powerful interests are as willing to defend the status quo as militant elements are to attack it. But it should be remembered that social inequality and its consequences are not a part of the natural order. Inequality is not inevitable: it was created by society, and so, in principle, it can be modified by social action in any way that we wish—if we have the will to make such changes.

7

Government and Corporations

THE NATURE AND SCOPE OF THE PROBLEM

Our lives in America are dominated by large private and public organizations. Private organizations, primarily business corporations, supply most of our consumer needs: health services, banking facilities, clothes, automobiles, television, newspapers. Public organizations, mostly government agencies, provide social services and regulate our lives by offering education and welfare, issuing permits, recording births and deaths, collecting taxes, administering laws. Our lives, and indeed our entire complex civilization, are inextricably dependent on large organizations. Yet these organizations, originally established to satisfy our needs and improve the quality of our lives, are often experienced as oppressive. They seem unresponsive, impersonal, inefficient, and often arrogant. And the suspicion exists that the major organizations in our society sometimes work in concert to advance their own institutional interests rather than those of the people. The lack of public accountability of these large organizations has become a major social problem in American society.

Large organizations are termed *formal organizations* to distinguish them from more informal groups, such as a local club or a gathering of friends. The essence of a formal organization is that it is structured according to a rational design in order to achieve a specified goal with maximum efficiency. In most cases this structure is a *bureaucratic* one, in which there is a hierarchy of officials, all with circumscribed spheres of authority and all working at specific tasks in order to maximize the efficiency of the organization as a whole. To the individual who deals with these organizations, they often seem exasperatingly slow and inefficient, hidebound by red tape and petty regulations. But they remain more effective than any other form of social organization as a means of coordinating large numbers of people to achieve particular objectives. Taxes, for example, could hardly be collected by informal methods: it is only through a system of complex rules and a hierarchy of officials, each with a specialized function, that the massive task is possible at all.

Formal organizations are inseparable from the modern state. Before the rise of the first nation-state in Mesopotamia, they were unknown in human experience. But as soon as a centralized authority arose and attempted to coordinate policies to achieve social goals, the formal organization developed. The concept was spread throughout Europe by the Romans, whose army—an outstanding example of a formal organization—conquered the known world by routing the numerically superior but informally organized armies of opposing peoples. After the political revolution in France and the Industrial Revolution in England, highly sophisticated bureaucracies were developed to meet the new demands for industrial production and government services. Today, it is impossible to imagine society without formal organizations.

Yet millions of Americans are disturbed by the fact that these organizations have only a limited responsibility to the public. As the size of our population has increased and as our society has become more complex, new types of organizations have emerged to meet new social needs. But the development of social controls over these organizations has not kept pace with the increasing size and power of the organizations themselves. Many formal organizations exert great influence in society, but the means are lacking to hold them responsible to the public they are supposed to serve. Large corporations dominate the economy and make decisions that affect the very nature of our society, but they are privately owned and the ordinary citizen has little influence over their affairs. Government bureaucracies and programs have proliferated and grown to such an extent that the elected representatives of the people often have little effective control over them: the task of supervising the vast range of bureaucratic activities is too immense. Especially when technical matters are involved—as in the affairs of the Pentagon—congressional expertise is often inadequate to the task of making informed judgments, with the result that more and more power over important decisions passes to trained government experts in specialized fields. These experts, sometimes termed "technocrats," make more and more of the day-to-day decisions that Congress has neither the time nor the specialized knowledge to question.

Government and corporations are widely distrusted in America. The presidencies of Lyndon Johnson and Richard Nixon were marked by a public feeling that their administrations were deliberately and systematically lying to the people. Corporations are believed to be more concerned with their own profit than with the quality and price of their product or with the truth of their advertising. And there is a pervasive sense that government bureaucracies and private corporations have become so isolated from public accountability that they have lost sight of the interests of ordinary people. Corporate interest groups lobby in Washington, seek passage of legislation to serve their own ends, influence the appointment of officials, and often seem to have more say in the councils of government than the voters. A recent poll showed that three out of five college students believe that "big business has taken the reins of government away from Congress and the Administration," and a University of Michigan survey showed that nearly 60 percent of all Americans think that "government is run by a few big interests looking after themselves."[1]

The Growth of Big Government

The federal government employs more than 3 million civilians, and is growing bigger all the time. The total number of people who work for the federal, state, and local governments is nearly 13 million. A quarter of a century ago, government at all levels employed some 6.4 million workers with an annual wage bill of $43 million, but the annual wage bill is $226.9 million today and is expected to reach $560 billion by 1980. In that year the number of civilian government employees will exceed 18 million Americans.[2]

Big government has come under attack from both liberals and conservatives, although for different reasons. Conservatives have resented the huge federal bureaucracies because they consume tax dollars—often wastefully—and because their very existence seems to imply continuing efforts to meddle in society, to centralize control in state and federal authorities, and to interfere with the free enterprise system. Liberals have resented the bureaucracies because they believe that many of them, particularly the Pentagon, have become self-perpetuating juggernauts that are no longer under democratic control and that squander resources that could be better used elsewhere.

The inefficiency and duplication of effort of the government is almost legendary.

> It is virtually impossible to obtain an accurate count of just how many Federal grant programs exist. Some estimates go as high as 1,500. Despite impressive attempts by individual legislators and by the Office of Economic Opportunity, there is still no agreement on a comprehensive list. . . .
>
> Nine different Federal departments and 20 independent agencies are now involved in education matters. Seven departments and eight independent agencies are involved in health. In many major cities, there are at least 20 or 30 separate manpower programs, funded by a variety of Federal offices. Three departments help

[1]Richard J. Barnet, Ronald E. Müller, and Joseph Collins, "Global Corporations: Their Quest for Legitimacy," in *Exploring Contradictions: Political Economy in the Corporate State*, eds. Philip Brenner, Robert Borosage, and Bethany Weidner (New York: McKay, 1974), p. 72.
[2]*U.S. News & World Report* (June 19, 1972), p. 78.

Big Government

If you took all the corridors in all of the federal buildings in Washington and laid them end to end, and inclined one end slightly and started a billiard ball rolling down, by the time it reached the lower end, the ball would have attained such a velocity that it would hurtle on through space while approaching an infinite mass and thereby destroy the universe. This is not likely to happen because such coordination is unheard of among federal agencies.

SOURCE: Matthew P. Dumont, "Down the Bureaucracy!" *Trans-action* (October 1970).

develop our water resources and four agencies in two departments are involved in the management of public lands. Federal recreation areas are administered by six different agencies in three departments of government. Seven agencies provide assistance for water and sewage systems. Six departments of the government collect similar economic information — often from the same sources — and at least seven departments are concerned with international trade. . . .[3]

During the decade that ended in 1971, there were only four states in which jobs in private industry increased at a faster rate than jobs in government.[4] One reason for this growth is that Americans are demanding an ever greater range of services from their government. But once a department or agency is established, it is difficult to abolish. Members of its staff develop a vested interest in keeping their jobs and programs going and in increasing the range of their activities and the size of their budgets. If a social problem emerges, such as drug addiction in the sixties, the immediate response is to establish federal and state programs to confront the problem. But the resulting bureaucracies seem to become self-perpetuating, and continue to grow and extend their areas of jurisdiction even when the original problem is checked or disappears. Matthew P. Dumont observes of the government bureaucracy: "It is a vast, indestructible mollusk that absorbs kicks and taunts and seductions and does nothing but grow."[5]

The Rise of the Corporation

The American economy is today dominated, even controlled, by giant corporations. The corporation is a relatively new type of commercial

[3]Richard M. Nixon, "State of the Union Address, January 22, 1971," quoted in the *New York Times* (March 25, 1971).
[4]*U.S. News & World Report* (June 19, 1972), pp. 78–79.
[5]Matthew P. Dumont, "Down the Bureaucracy!" *Trans-action*, vol. 7, no. 12 (October 1970).

organization that emerged in the late nineteenth century. Unlike those business enterprises that are owned by an individual or a partnership, the corporation is owned by stockholders. These stockholders may include hundreds of thousands of individuals and also other corporations; in fact, most corporate stocks are owned by corporate investors and not by private citizens. The corporation is run by a professional management appointed by a board of directors who are elected by the stockholders. In theory, the stockholders exercise control over the affairs of the corporation, but in practice the board usually becomes a self-perpetuating body whose recommendations, including nominations for new board members, are ratified as a matter of course by the stockholders.

The basic objectives of these corporate enterprises are profit and growth. They achieve these objectives by ever more efficient means of production, heavy investment in technological innovation and research, and a quest for expanding markets and fresh sources of cheap raw materials. The largest corporations are no longer bounded by a single country, but extend their operations over many parts of the world; indeed, the activities of these multinational corporations have become a cause for international concern—especially after one of them, the International Telephone and Telegraph Company (ITT), was accused of conspiring to bring down the government of a foreign country, Chile. The larger corporations have also tended to consume one another through a process of mergers and takeovers. As competition between the survivors declines, their products grow more and more similar and are distinguished more through advertising gimmicks than qualitative differences—consider the similarity between the products of General Motors and Ford. One common use of advertising is the creation of a market for a product where no demand for it existed before, such as the demand for electric toothbrushes or electric carving knives.

The largest one hundred corporations own half of all the manufacturing assets in the United States. The two largest corporations are General Motors with annual sales of over $35 billion and Standard Oil of New Jersey with annual sales of over $25 billion. The budget of General Motors is larger than that of any government in the world other than the United States and the Soviet Union. Of the world's one hundred largest economic entities, more than half are corporations, nearly all of them American.[6]

Within the corporate world there is a high degree of concentration of ownership and influence. The large banks occupy a central position in the American economy; the largest, BankAmerica, has assets of nearly $50 billion and has over one thousand branches spread around the world. With trust funds of over $400 billion for investment, the banks have considerable power on the stock market and in the internal affairs of the corporations whose stocks they own. Institutional investors,

[6]Mark J. Green, "The High Cost of Monopoly," *The Progressive*, 36 (March 1972), pp. 15–19.

The Fifteen Biggest Corporations in the World

RANK	COMPANY	SALES (millions)	NET INCOME (millions)
1	General Motors	$35,798	$2,398
2	Standard Oil (N.J.)	25,724	2,443
3	Ford	23,015	907
4	Royal Dutch/Shell	18,672	1,789
5	Chrysler	11,774	255
6	General Electric	11,575	585
7	Texaco	11,407	1,292
8	Mobil Oil	11,390	849
9	Unilever	11,010	423
10	International Business Machines	10,993	1,575
11	International Telephone and Telegraph	10,183	528
12	Gulf Oil	8,417	800
13	Philips Lamp	8,108	323
14	Standard Oil (Calif.)	7,762	844
15	British Petroleum	7,726	761

SOURCE: "The World's Fifty Biggest," *Time* (August 19, 1974).

such as banks and insurance companies, hold over $1 trillion of corporate stocks with just forty-nine commercial banks accounting for 60 percent of this sum.[7] Of the stocks that are not owned by institutions, some 82.4 percent are held by a mere 1.6 percent of the American public, a fact that suggests that control of the corporate system is concentrated in a very few hands. In fact, the same individuals frequently sit on several boards of directors. The House of Representatives banking committee has surveyed forty-nine banks in ten major cities and found more than 8,000 cases, involving 6,500 firms, in which the officers of the banks sat on boards of other companies or vice versa. When the Penn Central Company went bankrupt, it was found that sixteen of its twenty-three directors served also as directors of nineteen banks. Seventeen of the top thirty stockholders in Penn Central were banking institutions, many of which had loaned millions of dollars to the company. The same pattern of interlocking interests is found throughout the upper levels of the corporate economy.[8]

Many economists have argued that this concentration of the ownership of wealth and manufacturing capacity undermines the free enterprise system that is so highly valued in the United States. In the traditional model of free enterprise, each individual freely pursues his own economic self-interest. These competing interests produce an overall balance, and so serve to maximize the economic benefits to society as a whole and to prevent domination of the economy by any one interest. A system of informal checks and balances is thus essential for the effective operation of the free enterprise system. But if more and more power is concentrated in the hands of a few interlocking corporations, the balance is upset. Economic competition is reduced and the corpo-

[7]Thomas Ford Hoult, *Sociology for a New Day* (New York: Random House, 1974). p. 245.
[8]Gabriel Kolko, *Wealth and Power in America* (New York: Praeger, 1962), pp. 60, 68.

rate sector of society dominates noncorporate businesses and the private sector.

Economist John Kenneth Galbraith takes this view when he contends that modern corporate industry is so large, so technologically complex, and involves so great an investment of time and capital that it can no longer afford the hazards of a free market—the stakes are too high for any real risk to be tolerable.[9] The consequence, he argues, is that government and corporations cooperate in managing what is in effect a planned economy, with very little competition among the dominant enterprises. The only remaining capitalists in America, suggests Galbraith, are those people engaged in the professions, vice, retail trade, repair work, handicrafts, and personal services. Morton Mintz and Jerry Cohen take the view that the United States contains an industrial and financial complex that is, for economic purposes at least, almost an independent government, with the Pentagon—the greatest spender of funds and main support of corporate capitalism—at its core.[10] Theodore Roszak considers that we no longer have free enterprise, but rather an oligopoly, that is, a control of the market by a few:

> We call it "free enterprise." But it is a vastly restrictive system of oligopolistic market manipulation, tied by institutionalized corruption to the greatest munitions boondoggle in history and dedicated to infantilizing the public by turning it into a herd of compulsive consumers.[11]

The modern corporation has excited a particular dislike among many young people, who see it as the outstanding example of the rationalized, technocratic, joyless formalism that they reject in modern society. Corporations are well aware of this antipathy; prominent corporate businessman Jacques Maisonrouge has declared:

> If I were asked to describe the current stereotype of the corporation held by the young, I would be compelled to say: A corporation is a business structure whose sole reason for existence is the earning of profits by manufacturing products for as little as possible and selling them for as much as possible. It does not matter whether the product does good or evil; what counts is that it be consumed—in ever-increasing quantities. Since everything the corporation does has, as its ultimate goal, the creation of profit, it offers its workers no deep personal satisfactions, no feeling of contributing anything worthwhile to society, no true meaning to their activities. Go to work for a corporation and you are, through good salaries and various fringe benefits, installed as a faceless link in the lengthening chain—completing the circle by becoming one more consumer of all that junk. And, like all circles, the whole structure signifies nothing.[12]

[9]John Kenneth Galbraith, *The New Industrial State*, 2d rev. ed. (Boston: Houghton Mifflin, 1971).
[10]Morton Mintz and Jerry Cohen, *America, Inc.: Who Owns & Operates the United States* (New York: Dell, 1973).
[11]Theodore Roszak, *The Making of a Counter Culture* (Garden City, N.Y.: Doubleday, 1969), p. 16.
[12]Quoted in Barnet, Müller, and Collins, "Global Corporations: Their Quest for Legitimacy," p. 73.

APPROACHING THE PROBLEM

The social problem posed by government and corporations in America may be seen as stemming from both social disorganization and value conflict. American society can be considered disorganized in that formal organizations have grown and proliferated at a much faster rate than the means to exercise social control over their activities. Although giant corporations and large government bureaucracies are functional for their own purposes, and for countless socially valuable purposes as well, they also have the unanticipated dysfunction of reducing the individual's control over the forces affecting his life. A value-conflict perspective highlights the fact that there are major differences in values, attitudes, and interests between those in the upper levels of the giant organizations and the ordinary consumers and citizens. The distribution of power in society favors one group of interests, so the potential for discontent and conflict is increased.

Sociologists studying the problems posed by government and corporations often make use of classic theories developed earlier in this century to account for the phenomenon of bureaucracy and the phenomenon of *oligarchy*—rule by the few at the top.

The Nature of Bureaucracy

The most influential analysis of the nature of bureaucracy was written by the German sociologist Max Weber at the beginning of this century.[13] Weber saw the bureaucratic form as a specific example of the process of *rationalization*—the process by which logical, calculated rules and procedures are substituted for spontaneous, traditional, informal methods. Weber regarded rationalization as the dominant process in the modern industrial world, and he viewed it without enthusiasm. The world, he felt, was being "disenchanted," and in the process the finest human values were being subordinated to a quest for technical proficiency. Bureaucracy was a particularly disturbing form of rationalization because, unlike the rationalization of, say, industrial production, which is based on the calculated arrangement and organization of mere machinery, bureaucracy involves the rationalization of human beings, who are calculatedly and systematically subordinated to the technical requirements involved in meeting impersonal goals.

According to Weber, a bureaucracy is the most efficient possible means of coordinating people to achieve a given objective. The typical bureaucracy has the following basic characteristics:

1. There is a division of labor among the various officials. Each individual has specific, specialized duties to perform and has a strictly limited range of duties.

[13]Max Weber, *From Max Weber: Essays in Sociology*, trans. Hans H. Gerth and C. Wright Mills (New York: Oxford University Press, 1946).

2. There is a hierarchy of authority, pyramidal in shape. Each official takes orders from above and then supervises and is responsible for his immediate subordinates.
3. An elaborate system of rules, regulations, and procedures guides the day-to-day functioning of the organization. All decisions are based on these rules and on established precedents.
4. Officials treat people as "cases," not as individuals. They remain emotionally detached from these "cases," so that their rational judgment is not distorted by sympathy for particular people.
5. Employees tend to make a lifelong career of service in the organization. Promotion is supposedly based on merit or seniority or both, but not on favoritism or other criteria that might be used in an informal group.
6. Bureaucracies contain a specialized administrative staff, whose duties are to keep the entire organization functioning by maintaining files, records, accounts, and internal communications.

Weber saw the growth of modern bureaucracy as inevitable, indeed, as essential for the existence of democracy. Unless there is a system of rules, regulations, and carefully designed procedures to handle administration and redress public grievances, the rulers have a free rein to exercise a capricious authority. Favoritism and despotism can only be checked by laws and bureaucratic procedures which are inviolate and universally applicable. Yet Weber perceived an inescapable paradox: although bureaucracy is necessary for democracy, it also tends to subvert the democratic ideal. The very existence of bureaucracy means that the individual citizen has less and less control over his life; he or she is subject to more and more regulations and interference by organizations that assume an impetus of their own and are less and less accountable to the public. The pursuit of equality in society inevitably means the rise of great regulatory bureaucracies to regulate the economy and social services, but the freedom of the individual to do as he or she pleases often suffers in consequence.

Although Weber acknowledged the necessity of bureaucracy as a prerequisite for the attainment of democracy and equality, he also viewed the process with foreboding. He held out only one hope: the existence of the phenomenon he called *charisma*. To Weber, charisma is a specifically irrational force associated with people and movements, which sweeps through the established order. A charismatic leader, for example, owes his influence to the extraordinary characteristics that people attribute to him, not to his position of authority in some formal organization. Similarly a charismatic movement, such as the Hell's Angels or the Jesus Freaks, derives its appeal from its unusual qualities and not from any formal, rational organization or program. Weber believed that rationalization often has unintended consequences and tends to produce irrational outcomes that were never envisaged. For example, rational rules that are fair for general cases may be irrational and unjust in particular cases—as when a needy person is refused welfare because of failure to meet some trifling requirement of the established regulations. Weber believed that highly routinized, rationalized situations might produce, as an unanticipated outcome, irrational, charismatic reactions. The emergence of a youthful counterculture in the sixties can be seen as one such unforeseen charismatic reaction to a highly rationalized, bureaucratic society.

Dysfunctions of bureaucracy. Although bureaucracy is usually highly functional for the attainment of overall organizational goals, it also has many dysfunctions, particularly when bureaucrats are dealing with particular cases or with unanticipated problems. Officials tend to think in terms of rules and regulations and precedents, which are appropriate for standard situations but not for exceptional ones. When they encounter a novel situation, they are often unable to take any initiative other than "passing the buck" or referring the problem to some other official. The sociologist Thorstein Veblen caustically described this tendency as "trained incapacity"—the bureaucrat's training makes him unable to handle any irregular situations that do not fit his rulebook. A striking example of the ineptitude of the formal organization in the face of novel circumstances occurred in American colleges in the sixties, when university administrations were suddenly confronted by militant student movements. The response of the administrations was predictable and typical: to set up committees and subcommittees, to draft memos and commission reports, and to propose vague long-term modifications of the existing institutions. But these responses were quite inappropriate; rapid, flexible, and sensitive responses were needed. The reactions of the college administrations, although often made in good faith, were widely interpreted as stalling devices or attempts to deceive the militants and avoid change, and thus served to escalate rather than reduce confrontation.

Workers in bureaucracies are also very subject to alienation in their jobs. Because they have so little opportunity for taking initiatives or making innovations, and because their field of authority is so specialized and circumscribed, they are liable to perceive themselves as cogs in a machine and have little sense of making a significant contribution to the organization to which they are dedicating their working lives. Victor Thompson finds that bureaucrats suffer from lack of recognition of their talents and resent the apparent meaninglessness of work routines, such as filling in and filing endless triplicated forms.[14]

Bureaucracies, too, tend to become concerned with their own institutional preservation and to lose sight of their original goals. Several writers have made half-satirical references to the internal inefficiencies that seem intrinsic to the bureaucratic enterprise. C. Northcote Parkinson, for example, has enunciated "Parkinson's Law"—that in any formal organization, "work expands to fill the amount of time available for its

[14]Victor Thompson, *Modern Organization* (New York: Knopf, 1961).

A large organization always has a bureaucratic structure, with officials working at carefully defined tasks and with an extensive system of rules, procedures, and records. Bureaucracies achieve overall efficiency, but can be slow and inefficient in handling individual cases. (*George Gardner*)

completion."[15] A surprisingly high number of officials, he contends, perform tasks that are really redundant; many of them, for example, spend their working hours checking each other's work or producing trivial memos "for the record." Laurence Peter has outlined the "Peter Principle"—that in any formal organization, every employee tends to rise in the hierarchy "to his own level of incompetence."[16] Any employee who is performing his duties well, argues Peter, tends to be promoted steadily until he finally finds himself in a job that is beyond his capacities—where he remains. As a result, any official who is doing a job well tends to be promoted out of it, and officials who are performing badly tend to remain where they are. The entire organization is accordingly in a perennial state of inefficiency.

The Iron Law of Oligarchy

Why is it that organizations so often seem unresponsive to the interests of the public and of their own members? One answer was provided

[15]C. Northcote Parkinson, *Parkinson's Law* (Boston: Houghton Mifflin, 1957).
[16]Laurence J. Peter and Raymond Hull, *The Peter Principle: Why Things Always Go Wrong* (New York: Morrow, 1969).

by Robert Michels, another German sociologist and a friend of Max Weber. Writing soon after World War I, Michels came to the conclusion that any organization would inevitably become an oligarchy, that is, it would be ruled by the few at the top of the hierarchy. His thesis has come to be known as the "Iron Law of Oligarchy."

Michels was a socialist and had been deeply disturbed to find that the new socialist parties in Europe, which had supposedly democratic structures designed to give the mass membership control over party affairs, seemed to be dominated by their leaders no less than the older, aristocratic parties. In both cases, it seemed, authority was exercised almost exclusively by the leaders, and the constitutional arrangements of the socialist parties permitting participation by the mass membership did not make the slightest difference. Michels came to the conclusion that democracy and large-scale organization were inherently incompatible:

> It is organization that gives birth to the domination of the elected over the electors, of the mandatories over the mandators, of the delegates over the delegators. Who says organization says oligarchy.[17]

Why should this necessarily be so? Michels points out that if a social group is to have any realistic hope of achieving its objectives over any length of time, it must be organized. The sheer problems of administration of the group and its activities necessitate some kind of bureaucracy, which in turn must be hierarchically organized because immediate, day-to-day decisions cannot be made by large numbers of people. Some power must be delegated to the officials at the top of the hierarchy. Hence the dilemma of modern man: the very organizations on which his society depends can function effectively only if power resides in the hands of the few people who control them.

There are, contends Michels, several reasons why the mass membership cannot exercise effective control over the organization. He points out that the leaders achieve their position precisely because they have superior talents for persuasion, organization, public speaking, and manipulating opinion. They are people who are adept at getting their own way and winning support for their views. Once they are in leadership positions, their capacity to influence others is naturally enhanced; they have access to information and facilities that are not available to people lower down in the hierarchy. The leaders also tend to promote junior officials who share their views in preference to those who do not, so that the oligarchy tends to become a self-perpetuating one. The leaders are strongly motivated to retain their positions and promote the policies they believe in, and utilize all their power and influence for these purposes. The masses, on the other hand, tend to revere and trust the leaders, and place far more credence in what they say than in

[17]Robert Michels, *Political Parties* (New York: Free Press, 1962), p. 365.

statements from lesser officials. The mass membership is much less sophisticated and is prepared to allow the leaders to exercise their own judgment on most matters. Moreover, in contrast to the full-time leaders, the ordinary members have only a part-time commitment to the organization and have neither the time nor the knowledge to keep a close check on leadership initiatives. Michels did not see the leaders as necessarily evil, power-hungry, or dishonest men. They might be people of the very highest ideals, shaping the organization and its policies in a selfless way for what they believe to be the best interests of the people. But the very structure of organizations implies that, whether the leaders are right or wrong, the masses can have little influence on their decisions.

Michels' thesis has disturbed many social scientists for decades. His "iron law" should not be too uncritically accepted, however, for there are certain checks on the abuse of authority which he overlooked. In most organizations there are competing oligarchies, such as the different factions in American political parties. If the dominant oligarchy becomes out of touch with popular sentiment, another may take advantage of the situation and displace the established leadership, as happened when the McGovern forces seized the Democratic presidential nomination from the party establishment in 1972. Furthermore, if the leaders depart too far from the wishes of their subordinates, there may be mass defections from the organization as members switch their allegiance to some other competing organization or interest. It must also be remembered that organization has its positive aspects: without organization, many desired social objectives could not possibly be achieved. It does seem clear, however, that the very structure of organizations limits the possibility of popular control over their affairs, whether it is control of corporations by stockholders or of government bureaucracies by voters.

THE MULTINATIONAL CORPORATION

One of the most important developments in the world of the giant private organizations is the emergence of multinational corporations: vast business enterprises whose assets, manufacturing facilities, stockholders, and management are spread over many nations. The global impact of these corporations is immense; they now account for nearly a quarter of total world production, and their share will rise to over a half by the end of the century.[18] Many of the corporations are far more wealthy than the countries in which they operate, and their direct investment of capital in foreign countries has replaced trade as the single most significant element in international economics.[19] Most of the mul-

[18]Ronald Segal, "Everywhere at Home, Home Nowhere," *Center Magazine*, vol. 6, no. 3 (May–June 1973), pp. 8–9.
[19]Frank Church, "Will They Usher in a New World Order?" *Center Magazine*, vol. 6, no. 3 (May–June 1973), p. 15.

tinational corporations are based in the United States, and the estimated value of their foreign output was $130 billion at the end of the last decade. In fact, United States-controlled industry abroad is the third largest economy in the world after the United States and the Soviet Union.[20]

The multinational corporation is as controversial as it is large. Some observers take a favorable view of them and believe that they will create international peace and cooperation where political organizations have failed. Samuel Pisar, for example, argues:

> The world has become caught up in an unprecedented and, in my opinion, wholesome quest for economic integration. Inexorably, mankind is groping toward unity . . . through the mundane, pragmatic, yet highly compelling processes of the marketplace.

> I see the economic instincts of man . . . reaching out across artificially created political and ideological boundaries to join in a common cause: the promotion of peaceful commerce and industry. This development has enormous potential for the welfare and well-being of humanity. Once peoples and governments have become inextricably tied to one another by economic self-interest, the specter of instability and war begins to recede.[21]

There can certainly be no question that the multinational corporations have played an important role in international economic development, founding new industries and spreading technological and managerial skills around the globe.

On the other hand, the multinational corporations are viewed with the greatest suspicion by many observers. The existence of these huge, powerful organizations—subject to the authority of no single nation, responsible only to the stockholders, dedicated to the pursuit of profit, unconcerned with social goals, and exercising an influence that is largely unscrutinized—is perceived as a major social problem. For example, Richard Barnet, Ronald Müller, and Joseph Collins have contended that:

> The rise of the planetary enterprise is producing an organizational revolution as profound in its implications for modern man as the industrial revolution and the rise of the nation-state itself. . . . The rise of the global corporation . . . has put the world economy under the substantial control of fewer than five hundred business enterprises which do not compete with one another according to the traditional rules of the market. . . . Power to influence the direction of national economies is now being concentrated in what are, legally and politically speaking, private hands. . . .

> The rise of the global corporation is producing new sets of loyalties which transcend and often conflict with national loyalties. . . . Be-

[20]Neil H. Jacoby, "The Multinational Corporation," *Center Magazine,* vol. 3, no. 3 (May 1970), pp. 37–55.
[21]Quoted in Church, "Will They Usher in a New World Order?" p. 16.

Multinational corporations conduct their business in several countries, and are already one of the most important factors in the international economy. Because they can escape the laws of many of the countries in which they operate, much of their activity is unscrutinized and unregulated. (*Ken Heyman*)

cause of their incentive and their ability to shift jobs and profits from one country to another, global corporations are exacerbating some fundamental conflicts. Tax-avoidance practices, currency transactions, pricing arrangements, and job-relocation policies that are optimal from the corporation's viewpoint have highly unfavorable effects on the majority of people who, unlike the corporations, cannot escape the territory in which they live. . . .

The most revolutionary aspect of the planetary enterprise is its political pretension. The managers of the global corporations are seeking a role in shaping the contemporary world. . . . What they are demanding in essence is the right to transcend the nation-state, and in the process, to transform it.[22]

One manifestation of this unregulated and largely unscrutinized power is the speculation in international currency in which the corporations often engage—speculation that can lead to national and international economic instability. In May 1971, for example, no less than a billion U.S. dollars were sold in the course of thirty-five minutes in order to

[22]Barnet, Müller, and Collins, "Global Corporations: Their Quest for Legitimacy," pp. 56–57.

buy German marks on the expectation that the mark would be revalued upward. United States-based multinationals were responsible for almost the entire sum.[23] The U.S. Tariff Commission has estimated that at the end of that year private institutions held no less than $268 billion in liquid (readily available) form, with most of this capital controlled by United States-based multinational corporations. The commission pointed out that this sum was "more than twice the total of all international reserves held by all central banks and international monetary institutions in the world at the same date. . . . It is clear that only a small fraction needs to move in order for a genuine crisis to develop."[24] That such power should rest in the hands of a few corporate executives who are subject to the laws of no one country and whose primary purpose is to maximize private profits is a matter for great concern.

The Abuse of Power: The ITT Case

Serious charges of the abuse of corporate power have been leveled against the International Telephone and Telegraph Company (ITT), a vast multinational conglomerate owning hundreds of companies in diversified industries all over the world. It is alleged that ITT not only attempted to corrupt the U.S. government, but also sought to bring down the democratically elected government of another country, Chile, in order to promote its own economic interests. The case has been carefully documented by Anthony Sampson in his book *The Sovereign State of ITT*.[25]

In 1968 Harold Geneen, the president of ITT, after having engineered an impressive series of corporate mergers, attempted to bring about the greatest merger in American history by taking over the Hartford Insurance Group, one of the largest insurance companies in the world. The directors of Hartford were considerably less enthusiastic about the merger than ITT, but after ITT had applied what Geneen himself described as "inexorable pressure" in the form of financial inducements, the Hartford representatives capitulated under pressure from their stockholders. But the proposed merger was vigorously resisted by Richard McLaren, the chief of the Justice Department's antitrust division, on the grounds that such a merger would reduce the economic competition necessary for effective free enterprise and would, therefore, not be in the public interest. A court case resulted, which the Justice Department was determined to take to the Supreme Court if necessary.

Suddenly, however, the Justice Department decided to drop the case against ITT. Coincidentally, Sheraton hotels, an ITT subsidiary, made a $400,000 pledge to the Republican National Convention in San Die-

[23]Segal, "Everywhere at Home, Home Nowhere," p. 9.
[24]Ibid., p. 10.
[25]Anthony Sampson, *The Sovereign State of ITT* (Greenwich, Conn.: Fawcett Crest, 1973).

go—the largest sum ever given by any corporation for such purposes. A clearer indication of the relationship between the two events emerged in February 1972, when muckraking Washington columnist Jack Anderson obtained and published a secret internal ITT memo written by the corporation's congressional lobbyist, Dita Beard. She wrote: "I am convinced . . . that our noble commitment has gone a long way toward our negotiations on the mergers coming out as [Geneen] wants them. Certainly the President has told Mitchell [then attorney-general] to see that things are worked out fairly. It is still only McLaren's mickey-mouse we are suffering. . . . Please destroy this, huh?" A storm of controversy broke in Washington, and senators demanded an immediate interview with Dita Beard, who promptly fell ill and was removed to Colorado for a prolonged convalescence. When seven U.S. senators traveled to her bedside to put their questions to her, she claimed to be too ill to answer them, but did designate the senators as "a bunch of little bums." Both ITT and the administration denied any collusion in the matter. When Richard Kleindienst, who as acting attorney general had finally ordered the court case dropped, was asked at his Senate confirmation hearings whether any pressure had been applied on him from the White House, he emphatically denied the accusation. This was an outright lie, as was discovered in 1974, when under court subpoena President Nixon surrendered White House tape recordings in which he specifically instructed Kleindienst to drop the case.

Meanwhile, columnist Jack Anderson obtained further copies of internal ITT memos which indicated that corporate executives were attempting to prevent the election of the left-wing Salvador Allende Gossens as president of Chile and if necessary to bring down his democratically elected government. One internal ITT memo to Harold Geneen suggested these tactics against Chile:

> (1) Banks should not renew credits or should delay doing so.
> (2) Companies should drag their feet in sending money, in making deliveries, in shipping spare parts, etc.
> (3) Savings and loan companies there are in trouble. If pressure were applied, they would have to shut their doors.[26]

Another memo, addressed to an ITT director who had previously headed the Central Intelligence Agency, recounted preliminary steps to bring about a military coup in Chile:

> Today I had lunch with our contact . . . and I summarize for you the results of our conversation. Approaches continue to be made to select members of the Armed Forces in an attempt to have them lead some sort of uprising—no success to date.[27]

---

[26]Quoted in "The Square Scourge of Washington," *Time* (April 3, 1972), p. 42.
[27]Ibid.

Another paper recorded a telephone message from a high ITT official to the administration:

> Mr. Geneen is willing to come to Washington to discuss ITT's interest and we are prepared to assist financially in sums up to seven figures.[28]

A final paper recorded that:

> Late Tuesday night Ambassador Edward Korry finally received a message from the State Department giving him the green light to move in the name of President Nixon. The message gave him maximum authority to do all possible . . . to keep Allende from taking power.[29]

Salvador Allende's government was eventually overthrown by a military coup in which Allende himself was murdered. The new Chilean regime quickly attracted international notoriety for its brutal suppression of civil liberties and systematic torture of political opponents. In 1974 a Senate investigation discovered that the U.S. Central Intelligence Agency had spent at least $8 million in an effort to bring down Allende; the money had been used for such purposes as financing opposition groups and bribing legislators to vote against Allende's programs. The facts of this sordid alliance between American government and corporations have done the United States immense damage throughout Latin America.

Sampson considers that the ITT case highlights the need for new forms of controls over the activities of the multinational corporations; they are not inherently good or evil, but have emerged so rapidly that there has been no time for the development of appropriate social regulation:

> Without need of much plotting, the multinationals have achieved over the last twenty years, with the opening up of world communications, a position of sudden dominance: they have found a vacuum and filled it. Their skills and technology have brought new benefits, and paved the way for others to follow; but they have also produced a serious imbalance between their centralized drive and the fragmented and confused state of the countries and communities with which they deal. This imbalance should be gradually rectified, as the nations catch up with the new state of the world, and begin to come together to form their own communications and controls. But in the meantime the multinationals must open themselves up, and allow themselves to be inspected and questioned, if they are not to find themselves in a bitter conflict with their hosts.[30]

[28]Ibid.
[29]Ibid.
[30]Sampson, *The Sovereign State of ITT*, pp. 312–313.

IS THERE A "POWER ELITE"?

To what extent are major decisions in America made by a small elite of influential citizens? The issue was raised by the radical sociologist C. Wright Mills in his book *The Power Elite*, published in 1956, and has been debated by sociologists ever since. Mills argues that corporate capitalism requires long-range, highly coordinated decision-making. It cooperates to this end with other institutions, primarily governmental, that can guarantee the stable conditions in which corporate interests will be maximized. The "power elite" is not really a conspiracy, and the individuals within it have not necessarily sought to attain power and influence; they simply happen to be at the top of the great organizations which dominate society:

> The power elite is composed of men whose positions enable them to transcend the ordinary environments of ordinary men and women; they are in a position to make decisions having major consequences. . . . They are in command of the major hierarchies and organizations of modern society. They rule the big organizations. They run the machinery of the state and claim its prerogatives. They direct the military establishment. They occupy the strategic command posts of the social structure, in which are now centered the effective means of the power and the wealth and the celebrity which they enjoy.[31]

This power elite, according to Mills, is composed of men of very similar background. They are mostly native-born Americans of American parents; they are from urban areas; and except for the politicians, they are mostly from the East. Most are Protestant and a high proportion have attended Ivy League colleges. The members of the power elite tend to share the same attitudes and values and to know one another on a personal basis. They sit together on corporation boards and government commissions, forming an informal "interlocking directorate." At this level, decisions made in one area tend to affect interests in other areas, and there is a strong incentive for a coordination of activities and policies to reflect this community of interest.

Mills contends that there are three distinct levels of power and influence in American society. At the top of the hierarchy is the power elite, which operates invisibly but makes informal decisions on the most vital matters of public policy. The second level consists of a diversified plurality of interest groups which operate visibly but make decisions of lesser importance, primarily through the lobbying and legislative process in Congress. At the third and lowest level is the mass society, consisting of almost powerless individual citizens who have little direct influence over decisions and who often are unaware that decisions are being made at all.

[31]C. Wright Mills, *The Power Elite* (New York: Oxford University Press, 1956), pp. 3–4.

Other sociologists have challenged Mills's thesis. David Riesman, for example, acknowledges that power is unequally shared in American society, but strongly denies that there is any coordinated power elite.[32] He suggests instead that there are two levels of power in American society. The upper level consists of a balanced plurality of "veto groups" — strong interest groups that protect themselves by blocking efforts of other groups that encroach on their interests. No one group determines policy; in fact, the locus of influence shifts from issue to issue, and in the long run no one group is favored over the others. At the second level is the unorganized public, which Riesman believes is not so much dominated by the groups as it is sought as an ally in their campaigns. The difference between the two views, then, lies in Riesman's denial of the existence of a *coordinated elite* that exercises a largely unrestrained power in its own interests.

But whichever view one accepts, it does seem that major decisions are not in the hands of the ordinary citizen, but rather in those of organized groups. Many of these groups have been highly successful in achieving their aims, which they press in Congress through the use of professional lobbyists — experts in persuasion who deluge congressmen with propaganda, favors, proposed legislation, or organized letter campaigns. One interest group whose congressional lobbying has been markedly successful is the oil industry, which has succeeded in preventing a tax reform that would eliminate the "oil depletion allowance," a tax loophole that results in oil companies paying only about 8 percent of their income in taxes compared to about 40 percent for other corporations. The American Rifle Association has been successful in preventing several attempts at gun control legislation, which it has fought with funds derived largely from weapons manufacturers. The American Medical Association, representing the country's physicians, has prevented the introduction of socialized medicine through strenuous campaigns that have included successful efforts to unseat legislators favorable to the proposal. These campaigns of concerted lobbying are not the only techniques that have been used by large organizations to influence the political process. Although most organized interests adhere strictly to legal means of promoting their objectives, the Watergate scandal uncovered at least two dozen cases in which leading American corporations had made illegal campaign donations — often to candidates of both parties — presumably in the hope of achieving political favors.

Whether or not one accepts the contention that there is a "power elite," there can be little doubt that the oligarchies of major interest groups exercise a disproportionate power in American society. G. William Domhoff suggests that this power is likely to be exercised primarily in the interests of those who wield it:

> However much the power elite may try to take us into account . . . they have — like all of us — biases, implicit assumptions, and nar-

[32]David Riesman, *The Lonely Crowd* (New Haven, Conn.: Yale University Press, 1969).

rowed outlooks based upon their upbringings and their occupations.
. . . The power elite set priorities . . . and the wealth and well-being statistics suggest that they set them for the corporate rich.[33]

Yet it should not be forgotten that, in the long term, the power in a democracy resides ultimately in the electorate. This knowledge serves, to a great extent, to inhibit the gross abuse of power and influence by privileged groups.

THE MILITARY–INDUSTRIAL COMPLEX

One of the areas in which the interrelationship between government and corporations has been most closely studied is that of the military-industrial complex, the interlocking network of politicians, Pentagon officials, military chiefs, and executives of corporations that supply military hardware. The military-industrial complex has been severely criticized by liberals who believe that funds are often wastefully channeled into corporate coffers by officials shielded from public accountability and by conservatives who charge that the complex has systematically violated the free enterprise system in the United States.

The term "military-industrial complex" is not a coinage of any radical critic of the American system. It was first used by President Dwight Eisenhower, a conservative and former general of the U.S. Army. In his farewell presidential address to the nation, Eisenhower issued a grave warning to the American people:

> Until the latest world conflicts, the United States had no armaments industry. American makers of ploughshares could, with time and as required, make swords as well. But now we can no longer risk emergency improvisation of national defense; we have been compelled to create a permanent armaments industry of vast proportions. . . .
>
> The conjunction of an immense Military Establishment and a large arms industry is new to the American experience. The total influence — economic, political, even spiritual — is felt in every statehouse, every office of the Federal Government. We recognize the imperative need for this development. Yet we must not fail to comprehend its grave implications. Our toil, resources, and livelihood are all involved; so is the very structure of our society. In the councils of government we must guard against the unwarranted influence, whether sought or unsought, by the military-industrial complex. The potential for a disastrous rise of misplaced power exists and will persist.[34]

[33]G. William Domhoff, "How the Power Elite Sets National Goals," in *The Triple Revolution Emerging: Social Problems in Depth*, 2d ed., Robert Perrucci and Marc Pilisuk (Boston: Little, Brown, 1971), pp. 218–219.

[34]Quoted in Seymour Melman, *Pentagon Capitalism: The Political Economy of War* (New York: McGraw-Hill, 1970), p. 235.

The Pentagon and Industry

Eisenhower's warning has been widely quoted, but his advice has been largely neglected. Half the total annual expenditure of the federal government is devoted to defense, and if defense-related expenditures are included, the proportion rises to nearly 70 percent.[35] The Department of Defense is located in the Pentagon, the largest office building in the world, and employs some 1.3 million civilians, over a third of all federal employees. The Pentagon owns more property than any other organization in the world and has assets worth over $200 billion. The influence of the Pentagon extends throughout the economy: 3.8 million industrial workers owe their jobs directly to defense contracts, and one of every nine jobs in America is dependent on the military establishment. Some 350 American communities have at least one defense plant or factory, and in many it is the dominant industry or largest employer. Defense money flows into more than three-quarters of the nation's congressional districts.[36]

The military-industrial complex described by Eisenhower is an informal system of integrated institutions and officials acting to further common objectives. In recent years a series of industries have emerged that depend for their very existence on winning contracts for sophisticated defense equipment. The top one hundred corporations in the United States monopolize three-quarters of these contracts, and more than 80 percent of them are awarded without competition. Defense contracts are especially appealing to large corporations because profits are so high and the Pentagon permits massive cost "overruns" beyond the original contracted price of the products. Numbers of projects have been abandoned, often because the products did not meet design specifications when finally manufactured, but the Pentagon still pays the manufacturers handsomely. The nuclear ANP aircraft was abandoned after $511.6 million had been invested in its development; the Seamaster aircraft was scrapped after an investment of $330.4 million; the Navaho missile after an investment of $679.8 million, and the Dyna-soar ordnance after an investment of $405 million.[37] The reason for the Pentagon's tolerance of incompetence among the corporate suppliers of its weaponry is that it has become not merely a customer, but also a captive of these industries—if they should collapse into bankruptcy, the Pentagon would have no suppliers at all, since only a few companies have the capacity to produce sophisticated defense equipment. Admiral Hyman Rickover, a high-ranking military official who is critical of the incompetence of the corporations, declares:

> Large defense contractors can let costs come out where they will, and count on getting relief from the Department of Defense. . . .

[35]*U.S. News & World Report* (February 11, 1974), p. 22.
[36]Donald McDonald, "Militarism in America," *Center Magazine*, vol. 3, no. 1 (January–February 1970), pp. 14–15.
[37]Melman, *Pentagon Capitalism*, pp. 177–179.

The military-industrial complex consists of interrelated individuals holding important positions in private corporations and in government departments, particularly the Pentagon. These individuals and the organizations they represent coordinate policies to serve common goals. (*Ken Heyman*)

Wasteful subcontracting practices, inadequate cost controls, shop loafing, and production errors mean little to these contractors, since they will make their money whether their product is good or bad; whether the price is fair or higher than it should be; whether delivery is on time or late. Such matters are inconsequential to the management of most large defense contractors, since, as with other regulated industries, they are able to conceal the real facts concerning their management ineptitude from the public and from their stockholders, until they stumble finally into the arms of the government for their salvation.[38]

An additional cause of concern derives from the fact that major corporations in the defense industry, such as Lockheed and General Dynamics, obtain nearly all their income from federal defense contracts. Accordingly, they have a strong interest in persuading the Pentagon and Congress to spend ever larger sums on defense. These corpora-

[38]Quoted in Ernest Fitzgerald, "The Pentagon as the Enemy of Capitalism," *World* (February 27, 1973), p. 21.

tions maintain numbers of lobbyists in Washington who attempt to persuade both Pentagon officials and congressmen of the necessity for new weapons, and they make great efforts to maintain intimate ties with the Pentagon establishment. By the end of the sixties, the top one hundred military contractors employed some 2,072 retired military officers with the rank of colonel or above. The ten largest contractors employed 1,100 of these men, many of whom presumably retained influence with their former colleagues at the Pentagon. There is almost a revolving door for personnel of the large corporations and the Pentagon. President Eisenhower's secretary of defense, for example, was Charles E. Wilson, formerly president of General Motors (noted for his observation that "What's good for General Motors is good for the United States"). President Johnson's secretary of defense was Robert McNamara, formerly president of Ford Motors. President Nixon's undersecretary of defense was David Packard, founder of the Hewlett-Packard company, a major defense contractor in which he owned $3.4 million of stock, and to which he returned after his time at the Pentagon.

Many critics have contended that much of the impetus behind the arms race comes from the pressures of contract-seeking corporations rather than genuine strategic needs. Ralph Lapp argues:

> The word "parity" rubs raw the nerves of Americans who reckon strength in preatomic measures. They prefer superiority, for it connotes the ability to win. . . . Superiority is translated into outproducing an enemy in weapons—in building more and more powerful arms. Thus America . . . overreacted to the threat of foreign competition and escalated its arms spending. Part of this overreaction—and it will remain for historians to dig out the facts, if they can—was due to the self-interest of the military-industrial complex. Once the defense plants were built they could be abandoned only at great political risk . . . the Congress was not equipped to do battle with the Pentagon. Furthermore, the economic impact of defense expenditures on the various states grew greater with each passing year. . . .
>
> When a state has a considerable fraction of its manufacturing labor force working on defense or other federal contracts, the danger exists that a temporary contractual arrangement will harden into a permanent feature of its economy. Here we find the cruelest expression of the weapons culture—its perpetuation for reasons other than national security.[39]

Yet this seems to be what has happened; the economy is so geared to military production that it would be severely dislocated if weapons manufacture were significantly reduced. When Lockheed, a major military contractor, found itself on the brink of bankruptcy in 1971 after an

[39]Ralph Lapp, *The Weapons Culture* (New York: W. W. Norton, 1968), pp. 11–30.

ill-advised investment in a civilian aircraft, the federal government came to its aid with a loan of $250 million—a remarkable step in a society priding itself on a free enterprise system in which government does not aid or interfere with the free operation of the marketplace. Secretary of the Treasury John Connally explained the loan:

> What do we care whether they perform? We are guaranteeing them basically a two hundred and fifty million dollar loan. Why for? Basically, so they can hopefully minimize their losses, so they can provide employment for thirty-one thousand people throughout the country at a time when we desperately need that type of employment. That is basically the rationale and justification.[40]

At the time that it received the federal loan, Lockheed employed over two hundred high-ranking ex-military officers. The Pentagon fully supported Lockheed's request for the loan, and Pentagon lobbyists joined forces with Lockheed's representatives in persuading congressmen to approve the measure. The Pentagon maintains the largest professional lobby in Washington: some 339 lobbyists, or one for every two members of Congress. In all, the Pentagon spends over $30 million each year on public relations—in effect, using public tax money to persuade the public to spend more tax money on Pentagon programs.

A Case Study: The F-111

One of the most widely criticized defense contracts is that granted to General Dynamics to build the F-111, an all-purpose supersonic fighter-bomber. It has been charged that the contract was awarded for economic and political reasons to the wrong company, that cost overruns reached intolerable limits, and that the finished product falls far short of design specifications. Although the F-111 is an extremely sophisticated plane, it has continued to be plagued with economic and mechanical problems.

When the Pentagon originally decided to develop the aircraft in the early sixties, two corporations, Boeing and General Dynamics, submitted tenders for the contract. A panel of military experts was unanimous in recommending that the contract be given to Boeing, which appeared to have better facilities for developing the aircraft and offered what seemed to be a more realistic costing. Instead, the contract was awarded to General Dynamics. There is very strong evidence that the decision was based on the fact that General Dynamics (under the presidency of Frank Pace, formerly secretary of the navy) had lost $400 million in the preceding years as a result of earlier mistakes, and needed a major defense contract to stave off financial collapse. The decision to award the contract to General Dynamics was made after the personal intervention of Secretary of the Navy Fred Korth, who had been presi-

[40]Quoted in Fitzgerald, "The Pentagon as the Enemy of Capitalism," p. 18.

dent of a Texas bank that loaned money to General Dynamics to keep it solvent.

The original price of the aircraft was to be $2.4 million each, and the Pentagon placed an order for 1,700 planes. When the first planes were produced, they did not meet basic design specifications; indeed, they were so much heavier than specified that they could not carry some of the sophisticated equipment that had been specially manufactured for them. More disturbingly, the plane displayed an alarming propensity to crash; in particular, wings cracked and several planes failed to come out of dives on training flights. The first contingent of F-111s sent to Vietnam either crashed or were shot down so readily that the planes were all ordered grounded within a few weeks. Foreign governments canceled orders for the F-111, costing the United States hundreds of millions of dollars in anticipated export earnings. Meanwhile, the cost of the F-111 had escalated to $8 million apiece by the end of the sixties, at which point the Pentagon canceled the original contract and paid General Dynamics compensation of $215.5 million. General Dynamics is now offering a modified version of the F-111, which still does not meet the original design specifications, at a price of $13 million apiece, and the Pentagon is still buying them, though in more limited numbers. When attempts were made in a hostile Congress to impose controls on the escalating cost of the F-111, the Pentagon official in charge of the program, Major General "Zeke" Zoeckler, retorted that "inefficiency is national policy" and that the money should be spent on the F-111 for "social goals"[41] — presumably to avoid the massive economic dislocation that would follow a cut in the defense budget.

Commenting on this billion-dollar bungle, I. F. Stone states:

> It shows the diminishing relationship between military procurement and genuine considerations of defense. It demonstrates the growing extent to which procurement is determined by military-bureaucratic and industrial considerations. The prime determinants were to save the largest company in the military-industrial complex financially and to appease the bomber generals, who simply will not admit that their expensive toys have grown obsolete. Billions which could do much for poverty are squandered to maintain these Pentagon clients of the military relief rolls in the lush style to which they have become accustomed.[42]

The F-111 has also been severely criticized in Congress on the grounds that the aircraft was obsolete before it was built and was never needed in the first place. The chairman of the Senate Appropriations Committee, Senator Richard B. Russell of Georgia, expressed the dominant view when questioning General John P. McConnell, the Air Force Chief of Staff:

[41]Ibid.

[42]I. F. Stone, "Nixon and the Arms Race: The Bomber Boondoggle," *New York Review of Books*, vol. 11, no. 12 (January 2, 1969), p. 6.

SENATOR RUSSELL: Would it be a very serious matter if one of these planes were recovered by any potential enemy in a reasonably good condition?

GENERAL McCONNELL: Yes, we have quite a few things in it that we would not want the enemy to get.

SENATOR RUSSELL: That is mainly electronic devices.

GENERAL McCONNELL: That is true of practically all the aircraft we have.

SENATOR RUSSELL: Of course the Russians got a B-29 when they were one of our allies. They fabricated a great many of them as nearly comparable to the B-29's as they could. I was hoping if they got a F-111 they would fabricate some of them as near ours as they could and see if they had as much trouble as we did. It would put their Air Force out of business.[43]

The implications of the Pentagon's massive support of failing or incompetent corporations is a serious one, for it undermines the free enterprise system at the very highest levels of government. Ernest Fitzgerald contends:

The principal threat to American capitalism as we have known it comes not from anti-capitalism ideologists but from government support of inefficient and incompetent practices that are the antithesis of a free economy. It is difficult, if not impossible, to maintain an open economic system in which efficiency and excellence are basic determinants when the largest single complex in it is arbitrary to the point of being quixotic, and wasteful to the point of being massively irrational. How ironic that the one institution most intimately identified with the preservation of the American business system—the Pentagon—should turn out to be its enemy. . . .

Regardless of their performance, the bumbling giants demand that the tax-payers furnish whatever money they say they need. Worse, the national administration seems always to end up supporting their demands. . . . In the end, the Pentagon and its supporting cast of contractors unite to pick the public pocket.[44]

In fact, the relationship between the Pentagon and the leading corporate suppliers of military equipment is barely distinguishable from the relationship between government and industry under socialism—except that in the American case, corporations can make vast profits.

Since the Vietnam war, congressional criticism of the Pentagon has mounted. But the Pentagon has unique characteristics that make it resistant to reform: much of its activity is classified as secret; few outsiders have the technical knowledge to make informed judgments of its plans; and opposition to the Pentagon's programs has been easily mis-

[43]Senate Appropriations Committee Hearings on the 1969 Defense Department Budget, quoted in Ibid., p. 5.

[44]Fitzgerald, "The Pentagon as the Enemy of Capitalism," p. 18.

The F-111: Did We Need It?

We now have three major ways of destroying the Soviet Union. One is the ICBM, the intercontinental ballistic missile. The second is the submarine-launched nuclear missile, the Polaris. The third is the intercontinental bomber force of the Strategic Air Command. Any one of these three forces can itself deliver much more than the 400 megatons which . . . would destroy three-fourths of the Soviet Union's industrial capacity and 64 million people or one-third its population.

The bomber fleet is an expensive luxury, a toy on which the bomber generals dote, and which the aircraft industry is only too happy to supply. High-flying bombers cannot get through the Soviet's radar and SAM (surface-to-air) missile defenses. So the F-111 is designed to duck low under Soviet radar defenses, drop nuclear bombs, and make a high fast getaway, all at supersonic speeds. The basic argument against the F-111 is that if we ever want to hit major targets in the Soviet Union, we would do so with missiles which can reach their targets in thirty minutes with fifteen-minute warning time instead of planes whose flight and warning time would be measured in hours. If we tried to use bombers first, they would only warn the enemy and provide plenty of time for retaliatory missile strikes against our cities. If these bombers were to be used for a second strike after a Russian attack on us, the bombers (if any were left) would arrive hours after the missiles, and there would be little if anything left to destroy anyway. The intercontinental bomber is a surplus and obsolete deterrent. . . .

But this is not the end of this expensive nonsense. The military always assumes that the enemy will do what we do, that anything we produce they will produce. This is sometimes but not always true. The geographical and strategic situation of the Soviet Union is not the same as that of the United States; this dictates differences in weapons systems. In addition—no small consideration—the country which is poorer and has fewer resources to waste will be more careful in its expenditures. But we always estimate that the enemy will spend as prodigally as we do. This is how the bomber and missile gap scares originated. So we are spending billions to "keep ahead" of Soviet bombers and bomber defenses. We are also assuming that the Soviets will be as silly as we are and also build a fleet of F-111's to "get under" our radar defenses. So Congress has already embarked on another multi-billion-dollar program of building new radar "fences" and new types of interceptor planes to deal with these hypothetical Soviet F-111's.

SOURCE: I. F. Stone, "Nixon and the Arms Race: The Bomber Boondoggle," *The New York Review of Books* (January 2, 1969).

interpreted as lack of patriotism. As a result, the Pentagon is relatively immune from scrutiny as it—and indirectly the corporate suppliers of military equipment—consumes the lion's share of taxes from the American people.

THE SURVEILLANCE OF THE CITIZEN

One respect in which individuals seem almost helpless before the big organizations is that of surveillance over their private lives. Government agencies, private corporations, credit bureaus, and other giant organizations maintain millions of files on American citizens, and there are few of us who do not appear in one or more of these records. Thanks to modern computer technology, organizations are equipped to gather and collate this information with an efficiency that was impossible a few decades ago. Modern computers can hold millions of separate items of information, and these can be kept up-to-date and added to by the use of input terminals that can be located almost anywhere in the United States. Similarly, information can be extracted in a few seconds from a computer storage file thousands of miles away. As more and more agencies integrate the material in their files, more and more private information—much of it inevitably inaccurate and possibly damaging—becomes available to government officials and private investigators.

An investigation of one credit agency, the Retail Credit Company, found that it had six thousand full-time "inspectors," operating out of 1,500 offices in every state and the Canadian provinces, and maintaining offices in Mexico and Europe. The company's inspectors conducted ninety thousand investigations every working day, checking people's credit for merchants, their general background for potential employers, and their credentials for insurance companies and banks. They also maintained files on no less than 42 million American citizens, drawing their information from past investigations, newspaper clippings, and public records.[45] This organization is only one of several such credit agencies operating at the national level; there are also thousands of local agencies that gather evidence—sometimes hearsay material from neighbors—and exchange this information among themselves. Many citizens have had the experience of being denied credit or even a job as a result of an unfavorable report from these agencies, even when the report is based on inaccurate information. A computer error in the accounting department of a large corporation can easily result in an individual being listed as a bad credit risk; this information may go uncorrected and be disseminated from agency to agency for years afterward. Under the Fair Credit Reporting Act, individuals are entitled to demand the name of the credit agency which supplies information

---

[45]Vance Packard, *The Naked Society* (New York: McKay, 1964), p. 9.

on the basis of which credit has been refused, but they have no right to demand the source of the incorrect information.

The surveillance by government agencies is no less extensive. As one writer observes:

> Federal investigators have access to 264 million police records, 323 million medical histories, 279 million psychiatric reports and 100 million credit files. The Treasury Department is allowed to share information received from banks with other government agencies. . . . The information on the FBI network is available to 40,000 federal, state, and local law enforcement agencies.[46]

The U.S. Armed Forces have maintained thousands of files on private citizens whose views—left-wing and right-wing—were deemed suspect. The Defense Department also keeps files on a variety of other people, such as scientists working on defense contracts, and it conducts security investigations of many thousands of individuals each year. The U.S. Civil Service Commission maintains a dossier on nearly everyone who has applied for federal employment since World War II. And the FBI and other law enforcement agencies keep files on millions of Americans, including many who have never been charged or convicted of any offense.

As newer and bigger computers from various agencies are linked together, the possibility of invasion of the citizen's privacy increases. It has even been suggested that at some point in the future, all available information will be stored in central computerized files, so that a very full profile of any American can be obtained by authorized officials at the push of a button.

PROSPECTS FOR THE FUTURE

With the present trend to increased concentration of economic power in the hands of a small number of corporations, and with the steady growth in size and number of government bureaucracies, the prospects for a radically changed relationship between citizen and formal organization might seem gloomy. But, paradoxically, there are hopeful signs, if only because the social problem posed by the government and corporations has become so serious that citizens are finally bestirring themselves into action.

Citizen groups. One of the most promising developments in recent years has been the emergence of citizen groups that act as watchdogs over government and corporations. The best known of these are the various bodies established by consumer advocate Ralph Nader— bodies such as the Center for Auto Safety, the Center for the Study of

[46]Frank R. Scarpitti, *Social Problems* (New York: Holt, Rinehart & Winston, 1974), p. 506.

Ralph Nader on Corporations

Corporate fraud and other economic crimes . . . escape the normative perception that would be applied, for example, to a pickpocket by most people. From educational to media systems, people are not afforded adequate opportunities to learn about and ethically evaluate price-fixing, adulterated citrus juices, hams and poultry, deliberately fragile bumpers, unperformed but billed-for services, suppression of life-giving innovations and many other crimes which bilk the consumer of some $200 billion yearly. . . . These depredations are part of a raging corporate radicalism which generates technological violence, undermines the integrity of government, breaks laws, blocks needed reforms and repudiates a quality-competitive system with substantial consumer sovereignty. If radicalism is defined as a force against basic value systems of a society, then the corporate state is the chief protagonist.

SOURCE: Quoted in Morton Mintz and Jerry S. Cohen, *America Inc.* (New York: Dell, 1973).

Responsive Law, Nader's Raiders, and the Public Interest Research Groups. Nader's work provides an outstanding example of the impact that even a single dedicated citizen can make; his success in forcing corporations to respond to the public interest has lent enormous prestige and confidence to the consumer movement, and a 1974 opinion poll showed that his efforts were approved by a massive 80 percent of the American public.

Nader first came to public attention in the sixties when he wrote a book, *Unsafe at Any Speed*,[47] in which he accused General Motors of putting profits before auto safety. General Motors responded by setting private investigators after Nader in the hope of uncovering information that could be used to discredit him. Nader sued GM for invasion of privacy and was granted damages of $280,000, all of which he devoted to his work. Many of his investigations have resulted in legislation to correct abuses that he uncovered. His findings that our meat supply is "often diseased or putrescent, contaminated by rodent hairs and other assorted debris," resulted in the Wholesome Meat Act of 1967. After his report on slack conditions at the Federal Trade Commission—where officials spent hours "working" in bars while others never came to work at all—the federal government thoroughly reorganized the agency. When his researchers compiled damning evidence about the Food and Drug Administration's continued approval of cyclamates as artificial sweeteners, despite having known for some years that the chemi-

[47]Ralph Nader, *Unsafe at Any Speed* (New York: Grossman, 1965).

cal might cause cancer and genetic mutations, the FDA rapidly banned the chemical and rejected protests from the corporate manufacturers. Other Nader-inspired legislation includes the Gas Pipeline Safety Act of 1968, the Radiation Control for Health and Safety Act of 1968, the Coal Mine Health and Safety Act of 1969, and the Comprehensive Occupational Safety and Health Act of 1970. More recently he has charged that the mid-seventies oil shortage was partly an artificial creation of the major oil companies, designed to force up the price of gasoline. Nader does not consider himself a radical: he is not seeking to bring down the capitalist system, but merely to make it function better by eliminating deceit, corruption, and inefficiency.

Another important new citizen group is Common Cause, founded by former Secretary of Health, Education, and Welfare John Gardiner. The group also intends to change the system from within, and attempts to confront corruption in government and wastage of public money by federal bureaucracies. Common Cause attracted a large membership and has also received sufficient grants from foundations to provide it with a multimillion-dollar budget. The group has already been credited with some legislative changes, such as the federal election law requiring full disclosure of major political campaign contributions. Common Cause intends in the future to force the federal administration, through the courts if necessary, to abide by its own laws and regulations on such matters as antitrust policy. Many other smaller citizen groups have scored notable successes, particularly environmental protection groups that have brought cases against big corporate polluters and even forced government agencies, such as the Atomic Energy Commission, to file reports on the environmental effects of their activities, which they often, and illegally, have neglected to do. One important area in which citizen groups might initiate new legislation is that of the surveillance of the citizen by private and public organizations; the right to privacy from commercial or governmental spying deserves to be better protected by the law.

Scrutinizing the large organizations. It will be necessary in the future to develop more effective means of scrutinizing large private and public organizations. Multinational corporations, for example, have become so significant in the international economy that their continuing freedom from regulation and enforced social responsibility is unlikely to be tolerated much longer. Individual nation-states will have to create new and coordinated policies that take account of the advantages the multinational corporation offers by way of economic development, but prevent these organizations from pursuing their own interests to the exclusion of those of their host countries or to the detriment of international relations.

The inefficiencies of government bureaucracies also need closer scrutiny. At present there is one federal agency, the General Accounting Office (GAO), which acts as a watchdog on the affairs of other government departments; it claims to save the taxpayer some $300 million a year by reducing waste and inefficiency elsewhere in the federal bureaucracy. The GAO has also extended its activities into other fields; for example, it has found that the 1972 wheat sales to the Soviet Union by the Department of Agriculture were mismanaged, that military equipment held by U.S. troops in Europe for emergency use was not even combat-ready, and that the Justice Department failed to carry through investigations into campaign-law infractions. The GAO scrutinizes only a tiny fraction of federal bureaucratic activity, however, and most wastage and abuses probably go unchallenged. Unlike many other federal regulatory bodies, the GAO has retained some independence and has not become a mere adjunct of the organizations it is supposed to be investigating – as some critics charge has happened with the Federal Communications Commission, the Food and Drug Administration, and many other agencies.

One of the most difficult areas to scrutinize is that of the military-industrial complex, because much of its activity is conducted in secret for national security reasons. But the declining prestige of the military, due to the Vietnam war and the détente in East – West relations in the seventies, has created a climate in which it may be possible to subject the military and its corporate weapons suppliers to a more aggressive congressional scrutiny than has been possible in the past. The Pentagon itself has recently subjected contracts to much closer study than before, and has discovered in some cases huge profit markups concealed by tricks of accountancy, such as subcontracting work to another division of the same company and thus doubling the profit margin. In 1974, when the Pentagon signed a contract with General Dynamics for the single most expensive item it has ever purchased, a submarine costing $285.4 million, special safeguards against cost overruns were written into the agreement at the Pentagon's insistence. Congress, too, is becoming less willing to hand out public money to the armaments manufacturers. In the same year, the Senate voted down by 53 votes to 35 an appeal from Grumman, a major weapons supplier, for a loan of $100 million to ensure the continuing solvency of the company. Senators were particularly irritated to learn that Grumman had already received a massive loan from the navy to meet operating expenses, but had instead invested the money in short-term, high-dividend securities which yielded a net profit of $3 million for the company.[48]

Changing public attitudes and values. If abuses of corporate and bureaucratic power are to be prevented, the most effective means will probably be a climate of opinion in which the public reacts to these abuses with anger rather than apathy. The distaste of many young people for the formalism of corporate and bureaucratic life has already been noted; the present younger generation seems likely to be much

[48]*Time* (August 26, 1974), p. 69.

Government and Corporations: A Theoretical Review

The social problem of government and corporations represents the gap between a *social ideal* of governmental and corporate institutions that are responsive, efficient, and dedicated to serving public interests, and the *social reality* of unresponsive, impersonal organizations that are more concerned with their institutional interests than with those of the people. Government and corporations have assumed immense power and influence, and their lack of social accountability is increasingly regarded as a social problem.

The *social-disorganization* perspective offers a fruitful way of analyzing the problem posed by government and corporations. Viewed from this perspective, the problem stems from rapid social changes that have led to the emergence of huge formal organizations. The development of these organizations has not been accompanied, however, by any real development in our capacities to exercise social control over them. Government bureaucracies in the United States have grown over the course of this century in response to public demands for more and more government services and in response to the need for agencies to regulate an increasingly complex economy. But although these organizations have been functional for some purposes, they have also had unanticipated dysfunctions. They have grown so large and impersonal that they cannot respond quickly to changing conditions or to individual needs, and citizens have very little control over the very organizations that were designed to serve them. Some government organizations, notably the Pentagon, have become so large and engage in such technically complex activities that even Congress can no longer effectively scrutinize them: congressmen simply do not have the time or the specialized knowledge to do so. Large corporations, too, have grown at a rapid rate. Mergers and takeovers have been so common in the past that many areas of the national economy are now dominated by a handful of powerful firms. These corporations have so much influence on the economy that the traditional free-enterprise system is severely threatened. Ownership of these corporations is concentrated in the hands of a few individuals and corporate stockholders, with the result that the most important areas of the economy are under the control of a few professional businessmen who are not formally accountable to the public at all. A number of these corporations have now become multinational and extend their operations over many different countries. They exert great influence in these countries and indeed often have much larger budgets than the governments of the nations in which they operate. Yet the multinational corporations are not fully responsible to any one government and so are able to escape many of their social obligations. The growth of these large corporations is in many respects functional, both for raising profits and stimulating economic development, but it has had unanticipated dysfunctions, particularly in limiting social control over the economy.

Another problem is that governmental and corporate elites may tend to collaborate in order to preserve and enhance their own objectives; some sociologists believe that a "power elite" has emerged in the United States as a result. The military-industrial complex provides one example of this close and largely unregulated collaboration between government and corporate institutions, and there are many others. Society may be considered disorganized in that a great many important decisions are made by unelected officials of large governmental and corporate bureaucracies, often without due reference to public wishes. A strong element of oligarchy has been introduced into our democratic system, primarily because we have not had time to develop means of social control over the huge organizations.

The *value-conflict* perspective is useful in focusing attention on the conflicts of interests and values between the large organizations and other areas of society. The interests of the organizations and the interests of those who have less social power and influence very often conflict: ordinary citizens may feel that they are being exploited by commercial corporations or that government departments are needlessly interfering with and complicating their lives. Conservatives often resent the manner in which the large corporations have disrupted the traditional free-enterprise system; they may also be highly critical of the extension of government control into many hitherto private areas of life; and they may consider the immense budgets of some government departments to be a gross waste of public money. Liberals are more inclined to resent the large corporations for their monopolistic and exploitative practices, to be critical of the unresponsive and often arrogant behavior of government departments and officials, and to consider certain government expenditures (notably on defense) to be a misallocation of economic resources. Deep value conflicts are a recurrent feature of this social problem.

The *deviance* perspective is of limited use in the analysis of the problem, but it should be noted that those who engage in corporate or other institutional malpractice are likely to be considered deviant as public awareness of the social problem develops.

more critical of remote and unresponsive organizations than their elders have been. If social norms and values come to reflect a much stronger disapproval of corruption, inefficiency, and arrogance in the great organizations that dominate our society, these characteristics will tend to be regarded as deviant rather than inevitable and in consequence are likely to be less common. Ultimately, even the richest corporation or mightiest government is a creature of society, subject to modification in terms of prevailing social values.

FURTHER READING

Blau, Peter M., *Bureaucracy in Modern Society*, 1956. Peter Blau, probably the foremost sociologist in the field of formal organizations, presents a short but comprehensive analysis of the functions, disfunctions, workings, and social impact of the bureaucracy.

Goodman, Paul, *People or Personnel*, 1965. How can the individual survive the effects of all-powerful organizations? Special critic Paul Goodman attempts to answer this question.

Michels, Robert, *Political Parties*, 1962. Although first published after World War I, this book remains a classic and still relevant to the problem—the difficulty of regaining democratic control over large organizations. The book contains a clear account of Michels's famous "Iron Law of Oligarchy."

Mintz, Morton and Jerry Cohen, *America, Inc.: Who Owns and Operates the United States*, 1973. A well-documented account of the immense economic and political power of two hundred leading corporations in the United States. The book is an exposé of the interrelationship between economic and political power in America.

Parkinson, C. Northcote, *Parkinson's Law*, 1957. A satirical account of the inefficiencies of large organizations and an explanation of the notorious "Parkinson's Law."

Peter, Laurence J. and Raymond Hull, *The Peter Principle: Why Things Always Go Wrong*, 1969. A short and sardonic book explaining bureaucratic inefficiency in terms of "The Peter Principle"—which states that in any large organization, each individual is promoted to his or her level of incompetence.

Roszak, Theodore, *The Making of a Counter Culture*, 1969. Roszak argues that many young people are refusing to surrender their spontaneity and humanity to a dehumanizing, technological, and bureaucratic society; he believes that this refusal led to the birth of the "counterculture" of the 1960s.

Sampson, Anthony, *The Sovereign State of ITT*, 1973. A carefully documented and highly readable account of the abuse of power by the International Telephone and Telegraph Company. Sampson provides a critical analysis of the potential for good and evil that such huge multinational corporations possess.

Townsend, Robert, *Up the Organization*, 1970. Townsend, himself a top corporate executive, presents a brief and witty critique of formal organization. He speculates on alternative, nonbureaucratic forms of organization.

8

Poverty

THE NATURE AND SCOPE OF THE PROBLEM

By many standards, the United States is the most fabulously wealthy society in history. But over 25 million of our citizens are living below the officially determined poverty line – on incomes acknowledged by the government to be inadequate to meet basic requirements of food, clothing, and shelter. And these are not the only poor in America – there are millions more, living just above the poverty line, whose plight is not much better. In 1974 there were 37 million Americans who were so poor that they were entitled to food stamps, although the publicity and distribution system for the food-stamp program is so inefficient that only 35 percent of those eligible for aid were actually receiving it.[1] Despite our celebrated affluence, we have some of the worst slums in the industrialized world, some of the most inadequate social services, and an apparently callous attitude to the old, the sick, and the poor. The United States is one of the very few remaining countries in the modern world that does not have a socialized medical service available, either free or at nominal charge, to all its citizens. Our TB rates are higher than in the less affluent countries of Western Europe, and in the prevention of infant mortality, the wealthy United States is in eighteenth place among the nations of the world.[2]

Poverty in America

Poverty in America does not simply mean that the poor do not live quite as well as other citizens. Poverty often means families of eight or

[1]*New York Times* (June 20, 1974).
[2]John J. Chandler, "Perspectives on Poverty, 5: An International Comparison," *Monthly Labor Review*, vol. 92, no. 2 (February 1969), pp. 55–62.

ten people living in one- or two-room shacks. It means severe malnutrition for hundreds of thousands of children, and old people eating pet food to stay alive. Poverty means greater susceptibility to disease, to alcoholism, and to mental disorders. It often means unstable marriages, poor housing, illiteracy, ignorance, victimization by criminals, inadequate medical facilities, and shortened life expectancy. Poverty can mean low self-esteem, despair, and the stunting of human potential.

To make matters worse, poverty is often "escape proof." The employment opportunities open to the poor typically offer none of the stability and fringe benefits of the jobs available to the more affluent and better educated. Migrant workers are locked into a cycle of seasonal work; the urban poor can often obtain only nonunion jobs and have no security against sudden periods of unemployment; the rural poor often can find no jobs at all. And the poor are exposed to the rigors of a competitive job market without the protection that the rich can provide for their own offspring. As William Goode writes:

> In the so-called achievement societies—the most conspicuous being traditional China and the industrial West—the norm of free competition has been accepted for other people's sons, but most parents have believed that their own sons deserved somewhat better than that.[3]

Although most people might feel their children to be more deserving, only the better off have the resources—in terms of money and connections—to translate this wish into tangible advantage.

The poor also profit less from the educational system. A recent study found that only 7.5 percent of all lower-class males complete college, whereas upper-class males were six times more likely to do so.[4] There is strong evidence that lower-class children are channeled into vocational curricula rather than academic studies, so that their chances of attending college are restricted. Because education is increasingly important as a pathway into higher-paying jobs, the inequalities in educational opportunity stemming from differences in wealth and income threaten to lock significant numbers of the poor into permanent poverty.

The numbers of the poor in the United States are declining, but the plight of the remaining poor seems to be worsening. In testimony before the Senate Select Committee on Nutrition and Human Needs in 1969, physician Robert Coles reported:

> We had seen . . . not only extreme poverty, but gross, clinical evidence of chronic hunger and malnutrition—evidence that we as doctors found it hard to deal with ourselves, let alone talk about,

[3]William J. Goode, "The Protection of the Inept," *American Sociological Review*, 32 (February 1967), p. 9.

[4]William Sewell and Vimal P. Shah, "Socioeconomic Status, Intelligence, and the Attainment of Higher Education," *Sociology of Education*, 40 (Winter 1967), p. 9.

because we had been unprepared by our own medical training for what we saw. Today's American physicians are simply not prepared by their education to find in this nation severe vitamin deficiency diseases, widespread parasitism, and among infants, a mortality rate that is comparable, say, to the underdeveloped nations of Asia or Africa. . . .

I saw. . . malnourished children, children who are not getting the right amount and kinds of food, who suffer from several diseases and see no physician, who indeed were born in shacks without the help of a doctor and under conditions that are primitive, to say the least. . . . Why . . . must these children go hungry, still be sick? Why must families essentially without money be asked to pay for food stamps with money they don't have? Why do American children get born without the help of a doctor, and never, never see a doctor in their lives? It is awful, it is humiliating for all of us that these questions still have to be asked in a nation like this, the strongest and richest nation that ever was. . . .

I do not understand why these things have to persist and why we have to talk about this again and again and again, and people like me have to come and repeat all these findings.[5]

That statement was made in 1969. In June 1974, the same Senate Select Committee heard evidence, based on studies of over a hundred specialists, that the poor in the United States were hungrier and needier than they had been at the end of the sixties.[6]

The Emergence of Poverty as a Social Problem

Even though the United States has always had an impoverished "underclass," the existence of poverty has not always been regarded as a significant social problem. Unemployment and its attendant poverty were certainly seen as a major social problem during the depression years of the thirties, but World War II changed the focus of public attention to other issues. In the relatively prosperous postwar years, new issues aroused public concern — anxieties about the cold war, communism, and America's new global involvement. The topic of poverty was almost nonexistent in sociological literature. Of the eleven most widely used social problems textbooks published in the United States between 1956 and 1964, eight did not mention poverty at all, and only one — published in 1964 — gave the topic serious treatment.[7] It was only in the sixties that poverty reemerged as a major social problem, perceived once more as a condition that represented a glaring gap between American ideals and American reality.

[5]Robert Coles, Testimony Before the Select Committee on Nutrition and Human Needs of the United States Senate, February 1969.
[6]*New York Times* (June 20, 1974).
[7]Jack L. Roach and Janet K. Roach, eds., *Poverty: Selected Readings* (Baltimore: Penguin Books, 1972), p. 9.

Why did the problem of poverty recede from public consciousness for so long? John Kenneth Galbraith has argued that the poverty which afflicted millions in the thirties was regarded primarily as a problem of unemployment.[8] Once the New Deal and World War II provided new job opportunities it was somehow assumed that poverty had also been eliminated. The economy boomed, and a very large section of the population that had previously experienced poverty enjoyed more secure and affluent circumstances. But some people were left behind and forgotten. The newly prosperous middle classes left the city centers and insulated themselves from the poor in the expanding suburbs. The poor gradually became invisible — confined to city ghettos, trapped in the more remote rural areas, sitting in isolation and despair in rented rooms and old-age homes. And they were not only invisible, but also economically and politically impotent; even those who were able to find jobs were usually employed in occupations that the unions had not yet organized. No organizations or powerful lobbies pressed their case, and it went unheard.

In 1962 a single, powerful book riveted attention on the existence of poverty in the midst of an affluent society. Michael Harrington declared in *The Other America* that as many as a quarter of the American people lived in poverty,[9] and provided startling evidence of the continued existence of severe deprivation and malnutrition in America. His work stimulated a large number of studies of poverty, the media took up the issue, and public interest in the problem increased rapidly. On March 3, 1964, President Lyndon Johnson delivered a special message to Congress in which he declared a War on Poverty — a major, wide-ranging campaign that made the elimination of poverty one of the highest priorities of the nation. Numerous programs were generated by the War on Poverty — VISTA, Head Start, Neighborhood Youth Corps, Job Corps, Neighborhood Legal Services, the Community Action Program. The problem of poverty was publicly recognized, government intervention was accepted as an appropriate instrument for its solution, and Johnson was determined to make the elimination of poverty the great achievement of his administration — comparable to Roosevelt's New Deal in the thirties. America stood poised to become the first nation in history to abolish poverty. But instead, the United States became embroiled in a long, costly, unwinnable war in Southeast Asia, which distracted public and congressional attention, diverted national resources from the poverty programs, and finally drove Johnson from office. Public awareness of the problem had increased, but little had been done.

Poverty in the Midst of Wealth

The problem of poverty in the United States is aggravated because it occurs in a society in which the overall distribution of wealth and in-

---

[8]John K. Galbraith, *The Affluent Society* (New York: Houghton Mifflin, 1958), pp. 100–102.
[9]Michael Harrington, *The Other America* (Baltimore: Penguin Books, 1962), p. 9.

come is extremely unequal. While over 25 million citizens are living below an officially determined poverty line, 1 percent of the population controls over a third of the country's wealth, and 2 percent of private stockholders own about two-thirds of all stocks held by individuals.[10] Much of this wealth is not earned by its possessors, but instead is passed on within families through inheritance: Edwin Kuh has found that among persons earning more than $100,000 per year, inherited wealth accounts for 57 percent of total assets.[11] John Paul Getty, born a millionaire, has accumulated an estimated net worth of between $700 million and $1 billion. The distribution of income is also grossly unequal. The poorest fifth of the families in the United States receives only 5.4 percent of the nation's annual income, and the next poorest fifth, only 11.9 percent, but the richest fifth receives 41.4 percent of the annual income.[12] The richest tenth of the population receives over 20 percent of the national income.[13] There are over 200,000 millionaires, and about 3,000 families have an annual income of over $1 million. John Paul Getty receives $300,000 every day.[14]

Percent of Income Received by Each Fifth of Families, 1947–1972

INCOME RANK	1947	1950	1960	1966	1972
Total families	100.0	100.0	100.0	100.0	100.0
Lowest fifth	5.1	4.5	4.8	5.6	5.4
Second fifth	11.8	11.9	12.2	12.4	11.9
Third fifth	16.7	17.4	17.8	17.8	17.5
Fourth fifth	23.2	23.6	24.0	23.8	23.9
Highest fifth	43.3	42.7	41.3	40.5	41.4
Top 5 percent	17.5	17.3	15.9	15.6	15.9

SOURCE: *Economic Report of the President* (Washington, D.C.: U.S. Government Printing Office, 1974).

To make matters worse, the poor have a heavier tax burden than the rich. Income tax is meant to be progressive, that is, to take away progressively more in tax as income increases. But the wealthy and their accountants are able to manipulate and take advantage of a taxation system that Philip Stern has termed "Uncle Sam's welfare program for the rich." Stern has investigated tax data over several years and has found, for example, that in 1968 some 381 people with incomes of over $100,000 per year (21 of whom had incomes of over $1 million per year) paid no taxes whatever—quite legally.[15] In 1970, he found, 112 persons with an income in excess of $200,000 per year managed to pay no taxes at all. President Kennedy was reportedly shocked to discover that, dur-

[10]Herbert J. Gans, "The New Egalitarianism," *Saturday Review* (May 6, 1972), p. 43.

[11]Edwin Kuh, "The Robin Hood Syndrome," *New York Times* (March 5, 1973).

[12]*Economic Report of the President* (Washington, D.C.: U.S. Government Printing Office, 1974), p. 140.

[13]Gans, "The New Egalitarianism," p. 43.

[14]Philip M. Stern, "Uncle Sam's Welfare Program—for the Rich," *New York Times Magazine* (April 16, 1972), p. 28.

[15]Philip M. Stern, "How 381 Super-Rich Americans Managed Not to Pay a Cent in Taxes Last Year," *New York Times Magazine* (April 13, 1969), p. 30.

This Texan oil millionaire is one of the few super-rich Americans. The super-rich, particularly those in the oil industry, are enabled to escape much of their tax liability through loopholes in the tax laws. (H. Kubota/Magnum)

ing the early sixties, John Paul Getty paid only a few thousand dollars in income tax. Under the tax rates supposedly applicable to all citizens he should have paid approximately $70 million each year. Thanks to tax loopholes, he kept his millions and paid about as much as the average man. Other forms of taxation, such as the sales tax, hit the poor proportionately harder than the rich; both pay the same tax on a consumer item, but it represents a much greater percentage of the income of a poor person than a rich person. As a result, poor people pay a greater share of their incomes in taxes than any other group. Those earning less than $2,000 per annum pay fully half of their incomes in direct and indirect taxes, compared with those earning $50,000 per year or more, who pay only 45 percent of their income in taxes.[16] The wealthy may also enjoy other benefits provided by their companies, such as cars, credit cards, expense accounts, medical care, or vacations disguised as business trips. Gabriel Kolko found that 80 percent of the checks at the most expensive restaurants and over a third of Broadway theater tickets were covered by expense accounts.[17] None of these benefits is taxed.

[16]Gans, "The New Egalitarianism," p. 43.
[17]Gabriel Kolko, *Wealth and Power in America: An Analysis of Social Class and Income Distribution* (New York: Praeger, 1962), p. 19.

Because the United States does not have the obvious class divisions that many other industrialized countries have, we tend to think of equality as the norm in our society. But in fact, the United States is extremely unequal in many respects. The wealthy not only have financial resources, but they also have political influence out of proportion to their numbers. One indication of the existence of this influence is the failure of Congress to plug the loopholes in a supposedly progressive tax system, which in practice places a disproportionate share of the nation's tax burden on the poor rather than on the rich.

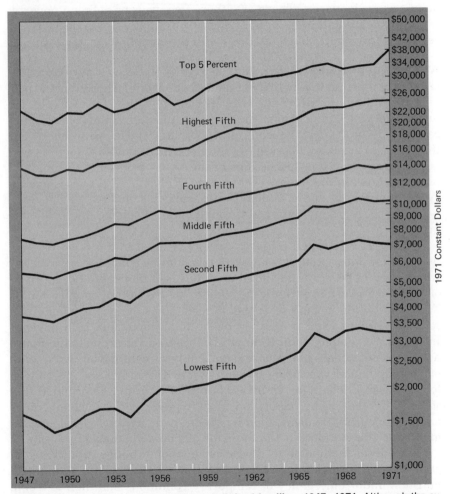

Average family income received by each fifth of families, 1947–1971. Although the average income of American families has risen substantially over the past two decades, inequalities in the distribution of wealth have remained almost constant throughout the period. (SOURCE: Executive Office of the President: Office of Management and Budget, *Social Indicators, 1973* [Washington, D.C.: U.S. Government Printing Office, 1973], p. 159.)

APPROACHING THE PROBLEM

When Is Someone Poor?

Defining poverty is not easy. We might consider some people poor, for example, because they are literally starving and without shelter, that is, without the basic necessities of life. Or we might consider some people poor because, although they have these basic necessities, their share of society's wealth is so small that they cannot maintain the living standards customary in their society, so that they suffer a loss of social opportunity and self-respect, even though their physical health may not be in serious jeopardy. There are, then, two ways of defining poverty: in terms of absolute deprivation—lack of basic needs—or in terms of relative deprivation—in comparison with the surrounding standards.

Absolute deprivation. A definition of poverty in terms of absolute deprivation centers on the inability of an individual or of a household to provide even the basic necessities of life. Gabriel Kolko, for example, defines poverty as "the economic inability to maintain standards of medical care, nourishment, housing, and clothing."[18] The poor, then, are those who are lacking necessities that money can buy. It should be noted, however, that the "necessities of life" vary from time to time and place to place; in some parts of the world, a change of clothes is a luxury, not a necessity. In the United States, concepts of what is a "necessity" have been greatly enlarged through cultural change and economic growth.

Poverty in the United States is usually defined in terms of absolute deprivation. Most analysts simply determine an annual income below which they believe an individual or family will inevitably be deprived of what are considered basic necessities of life in our country today. The point on the income scale that is selected as the poverty line naturally determines what proportion of the total population is in poverty. In 1958, for example, John Kenneth Galbraith arbitrarily set the figure at a thousand dollars per year and on that basis considered that a tenth of the population was poor. In 1962, Leon Keyserling set the limit at four thousand dollars for an urban family of four and determined that some 23 percent of the population were in poverty.[19] A more ingenious and less arbitrary determination has been made by the federal government, and this standard is the basis for official definitions of poverty.

The federal method is to devise an economy budget specifying in great detail the weekly quantities of food needed to maintain adequate nutrition under emergency or temporary conditions and then to treble this cost to allow for all other expenditures. The standard is adjusted for differences in family size, sex of family head, place of residence,

[18]Ibid., p. 70.
[19]Leon Keyserling, *The Prevalent Monetary Policy and Its Consequences* (Washington. D.C.: U.S. Government Printing Office, 1964), pp. 6, 39.

and several other variables. The federal poverty line is revised annually to take into account inflation, and the cutoff point has risen from
$2,973 in 1959 to $4,540 in 1973 for a nonfarm family of four.[20]

The sum is scarcely a princely one, and there is no guarantee that
families living at the poverty line will in fact achieve adequate nutrition.
Not all households are equally skilled in shopping habits, and some
might need more income to support a nutritionally satisfactory diet.
Unexpected expenditures may wreak havoc with the family budget.
There is also strong evidence that the poor tend to pay more for inferior
quality goods. As David Caplovitz notes:

> They tend to lack the information and training needed to be effec-
> tive consumers in a bureaucratic society. Partly because of their
> limited education and partly because they are unfamiliar with ur-
> ban culture, they are not apt to follow the announcements of sales
> in newspapers, to engage in comparative shopping, to know their
> way around the major department stores and bargain centers, to
> know how to evaluate the advice of salesmen—practices necessary
> for some degree of sophistication in the realm of consumption. The
> institution of credit introduces special complex requirements for
> intelligent consumption. Because of the diverse and frequently mis-
> leading ways in which charges for credit are stated, even the highly
> educated consumer has difficulty knowing which set of terms is
> most economical.[21]

The poor, too, are encouraged to purchase items that might be considered frivolous by the federal budget analysts, such as cars or TV sets.
Caplovitz refers to these purchases as "compensatory consumption"—
an attempt to share some small part of the American dream, even
though the purchase in fact increases real deprivation by diverting the
family's already scarce budgetary resources. The federal government's
method of measuring absolute poverty also has the disadvantage that
annual adjustments do not take into account rising expectations—only
rising prices. But the method does provide us with a means of establishing with some precision the number of Americans who are unquestionably without the economic means to provide themselves with basic
necessities.

Relative deprivation. One problem with an absolute definition of poverty is that it is narrowly conceived. It does not take into account the
relative position of the poor as compared to the more wealthy. People
are poor not only in relation to their needs, but also in relation to other
people who are not poor. This fact is most apparent at the international
level, as economist Kenneth Boulding notes:

> In the twentieth century, the per capita income of the richest coun-
> try is at least forty times that of the poorest . . . and the gulf widens

---

[20]U.S. Bureau of the Census, *Current Population Reports*, series p–60, no. 94 (Washington, D.C.: U.S.
Government Printing Office, 1974), p. 1.
[21]David Caplovitz, *The Poor Pay More* (New York: Free Press, 1963), p. 14.

between them all the time. It is this gulf which constitutes the main problem of poverty today. Persons regarded by a rich society as very poor would be regarded as relatively rich in a poor society. We see this illustrated in the fact that to the American, the migrant laborer is the poorest of the poor and constitutes in his mind a serious problem. To the Mexican villager, joining the ranks of our migrant workers is seen as a road to riches and as a way to lift the grinding burden of the poverty under which he labors. And yet Mexico is one of the richer of the poor countries. To hundreds of millions of Asians and Africans, the standard of life of the Mexican laborer would seem almost luxurious.[22]

The same principle applies at the national level. The poor in America can see the affluent all around them, and they evaluate their poverty not only in relation to their needs (which may be desperate), but also in relation to the surfeit of wealth in the surrounding society. As Herman Miller writes:

The essential fallacy of a fixed poverty line is that it fails to recognize the relative nature of "needs." The poor will not be satisfied with a given level of living year after year when the levels of those around them are going up at the rate of about 2.5 per cent per year. Old-timers may harken back to the "good old days" when people were happy without electricity, flush toilets, automobiles, and television sets; but they also realize that, once it becomes possible for all to have these "luxuries," they will be demanded and will quickly assume the status of "needs." For these reasons, it is unrealistic in an expanding economy to think in terms of a fixed poverty line.[23]

A definition of poverty in terms of relative deprivation centers on the economical inability of people to maintain the standards of living that are considered normal in the society in which they live. Under such a conception of poverty, the poor are arbitrarily defined as some proportion of the lowest income earners in the society, say, the bottom tenth or the bottom fifth. Improvement in the status of the poor is then measured by the degree to which the income of the poor rises in relation to the rest of the population. The data for the United States show no such trend: the proportion of income received by the lowest fifth has remained fairly stable since the end of World War II, and the very richest group has not experienced any appreciable decline in its share of the national income since the turn of the century.[24] This definition of poverty, then, focuses more on relative inequality than actual deprivation, although, of course, some of those who are defined as relatively poor may be poor in an absolute sense. Under a relative definition,

[22]Kenneth E. Boulding, "Reflections on Poverty," in *The Social Welfare Forum: 1961* (New York: Columbia University Press, 1961), pp. 45–58.
[23]Herman Miller, "Changes in the Number and Composition of the Poor," in *Inequality and Poverty*, ed. Edward C. Budd (New York: Norton, 1968), p. 165.
[24]Ibid., p. 163.

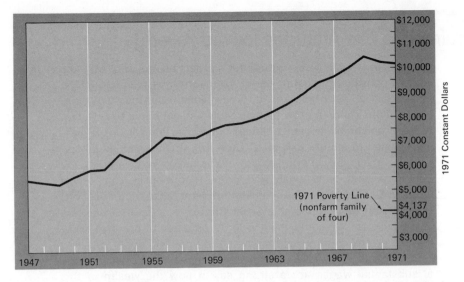

Median family income, 1947–1971. The median family income is the point at which families can be divided into two equal income groups, with 50 percent of the families receiving an income above the median and 50 percent below. The discrepancy between the median income and the poverty line is a substantial one and indicates the relative deprivation of poor families as compared to others. (SOURCE: Executive Office of the President: Office of Management and Budget, *Social Indicators, 1973* [Washington, D.C.: U.S. Government Printing Office, 1973], p. 152.)

poverty can never be completely eliminated while there is significant inequality in society.

The choice of whether to use absolute or relative criteria in defining poverty is largely a matter of the judgment of the individual analyst concerned. If we assume that a reasonable standard of nutrition and shelter is the significant criterion, then a fixed, absolute standard is appropriate. If we assume that disparities between the rich and the poor should be the significant criterion, then a proportionate, relative standard is appropriate. Definitions of poverty are not simply a technical matter; they are influenced by the values and attitudes of the analyst concerned.

Attitudes, Values, and the American Welfare System

The 1970 census showed that 25.5 million Americans were living below the federally determined poverty line. It has been calculated that to raise the income of all families above that line would require 14 billion dollars a year,[25] a sum representing less than a fifth of our annual expenditure on defense and less than 2 percent of our gross national product. The elimination of poverty, then, is well within our means. Yet

[25]U.S. Bureau of the Census, *Current Population Reports*, series p–60, no. 77 (Washington, D.C.: U.S. Government Printing Office, 1971), p. 60.

Confronting Our Attitudes Toward Poverty

To examine some . . . "structural" problems, to ask why the world's richest and most powerful nation chooses to spend 70 billion dollars a year on its armed forces, while thousands and thousands of our children grow up malnourished, get bitten by rats, suffer lead poisoning because certain buildings, thousands of them, are allowed to stand — to look at such awful paradoxes is unnerving. . . . We could, of course, look at this nation very carefully. We could ask who owns what, who profits enormously from whose labor. We could, that is, ask the kind of blunt, unsparing questions that a Ralph Nader does or a Cesar Chavez or a Saul Alinsky or a Jesse Jackson. We could, if we wish the sanction of our own history, take up the southern and midwestern populist cause: that is to say, we could emphasize the rights all men have — for decent work at substantial wages, for a strong say in how the wealth of this country is divided up; and it is wealth that was made over the years by the labor of millions of men and women, many of them penniless slaves. But . . . we are likely to find it painful to look at such matters. The closer we get to looking, the more probable it is that we will be confronted with — ourselves. True . . . we want all sorts of changes, and are proud to enumerate them and declare openly our hopes and dissatisfactions. There are limits, though; and especially when "they" begin pressing too hard, and even start calling us condescending or self-centered or bossy — then we stand up in all our pride and impatience and self-righteousness and let it be known who is where on this nation's various ladders and scales. Not that we are the kind to be rednecks or members of some "silent majority." Well-educated, articulate, determined to be known as compassionate and fair-minded, we shun nasty or abusive language and instead simply reach for the labels: they are this or that, they need help — of a kind that takes years to give, and even then the outcome is in doubt.

Meanwhile, every day thousands of bright, intelligent, resourceful children fight hard in our ghettos to live, to find their "deal," to outwit "the man," to come to terms with odds the rest of us never have faced and never will know.

SOURCE: Robert Coles, "Blaming the Victim," *American Journal of Sociology* (September 1972).

we make little attempt to achieve this objective; in fact, the United States spends less than half as much of its national income on welfare as do the less affluent countries of Western Europe — about 6.5 percent compared to an average of 14 percent.[26] Why do we deplore the very existence of poverty in our society and yet do so little to improve the living standards of the poor?

The answer lies, very largely, in traditional American attitudes and values. In colonial America, the poor were believed to be responsible for their own plight. Poverty was seen almost as a sign of disgrace, and unemployment as an indication of laziness. American values have historically been predicated on the ethics of work and profit, and those who seek public assistance have been regarded as shiftless, immoral, and idle. As A. Dale Tussing observes:

> The legitimacy of one's income and, especially, of one's position in the overall distribution of income, are central preoccupations in America. No welfare programs are inherently legitimate in the United States, where the dominant ideology of individualism still appears to reject the welfare state in principle. . . . In the view of many people, job-holders are members of and contributors to society; non job-holders are not. Job-holding legitimates one's political role, as well. In local, state and national politics, more is heard today about "taxpayers" than about "citizens."[27]

Many Americans regard welfare recipients as chiselers and freeloaders—people who are too lazy to work, rather than people who are victims of circumstance. (Interestingly, the same charge is not made as often against the idle rich who have inherited their fortunes; the fact that their ancestors once worked for the money seems to legitimize its enjoyment by the offspring.) In 1964, when the War on Poverty was declared and when public awareness of the problem was at its height, a Gallup poll asked, "In your opinion, which is more often to blame if a person is poor—lack of effort on his own part, or circumstances beyond his control?" Of the respondents, 33 percent felt that lack of effort was responsible, 29 percent felt that circumstances were responsible, 32 percent felt that both factors had equal influence, and 6 percent voiced no opinion. More recently, in 1972, a Harris poll asked a somewhat similar question and found that nearly nine out of ten Americans favored the idea of "making people on welfare go to work." Yet these attitudes bear no relation to the reality of the American welfare system: the welfare rolls are overwhelmingly composed of children, retired and disabled people, and others who cannot work for a living at all. The Department of Health, Education, and Welfare estimates that less than 1 percent of welfare recipients are able-bodied unemployed males, and they are required to sign up for work or training in order to retain welfare payments.[28] Welfare fraud does exist, but public conceptions of the welfare system and its workings are often very inaccurate.

[26]Robert L. Heilbroner, "Benign Neglect in the United States," *Trans-action,* 7 (October 1970), pp. 15–22.
[27]A. Dale Tussing, "The Dual Welfare System," *Society,* vol. 11, no. 2 (January–February 1974), p. 50.
[28]U.S. Department of Health, Education, and Welfare, *Welfare: Myths vs. Facts* (Washington, D.C.: U.S. Government Printing Office, 1972).

This welfare mother of six children lives in a home without water or electricity. Yet her welfare payments are dismally low—largely because of the American attitude that incentives must be provided for the poor to go out to work. *(Arthur Tress/Photo Researchers Inc.)*

Americans have been reluctant to aid the impoverished. Up to 1935 private charities and some local and state governments assumed the responsibility for welfare. In the depression years these haphazard arrangements broke down completely under the burden of some 40 million poor people, and, in the face of bitter opposition, the social security system was established. But the system was and is based on one overriding principle: relief is intentionally designed to fall short of adequate assistance in order not to undermine the cherished motive to work. No attempt is made to ameliorate poverty by placing an income floor under those who are unable to earn enough, that is, to supplement low wages so as to bring all earnings up to a suitable minimum income. Instead, those who work and do not earn enough to make a decent living are left in poverty; those who do not work are treated as if they were lazy, but would work if given the proper incentives. President Nixon expressed the dominant attitude well when, speaking of welfare, he declared, "I advocate a system that will encourage people to take work, and that means whatever work is available. If a job puts bread on the table, if it gives you the satisfaction of providing for your children and lets you look everyone else in the eye, I don't think that it is menial."[29] So strong are the traditional attitudes against welfare "handouts" to the poor that those who receive them suffer an immedi-

[29]Remarks of the President at the Republican Governors' Conference, Office of the White House Press Secretary, Washington, D.C., April 19, 1971.

ate loss of social status and often of personal pride. Americans tend to esteem the rich because of their wealth (even if they have not earned it), but to look down on the poor (even if they are not responsible for their poverty). Attempts to provide adequate federal assistance to the poor always run into opposition from critics who assert that increased benefits will undermine the work ethic; one proposed federal family-assistance plan was entitled "workfare" by its advocates in an attempt to make it seem more palatable to its opponents. Opposition does not come only from the middle and upper-middle classes in American society, it comes also from working-class citizens who are managing, often with great effort, to remain a few income dollars away from the welfare rolls and who deeply resent the use of their taxes to support supposed chiselers who choose not to work.

WHO ARE THE POOR IN AMERICA?

The poor are not randomly distributed throughout the population. Data from the 1970 census show that poverty is concentrated in specific population groups and geographic areas. Of the 5.2 million American families that are defined by the federal government as living in poverty, nearly 2 million are headed by women. The proportion of poor families headed by women is actually increasing—from 23 percent in 1959 to 37 percent in 1970 to 40 percent in 1971[30] and to 43 percent in 1972.[31] Because the mothers often have to remain at home to rear their children, they are unable to work, and they have to rely on public assistance in the form of Aid to Families with Dependent Children (AFDC). In a great many cases they have no other source of income, and existence on welfare is the only way of life they know. Poor families are also concentrated in certain geographic regions: about 2.3 million poor families live on small farms that are unable to compete with large-scale, mechanized agriculture; and about 20 percent of all families in the South are in poverty. The largest single group of the poor is children under eighteen. Children are particularly prone to poverty if they are members of large families: about 44 percent of all poor children are to be found in families with five children or more. Some 16 percent of America's children live in poverty.

Minority groups suffer a disproportionately high incidence of poverty. Although blacks constitute only 11 percent of the American population, they represent 28.9 percent of the poor. There are twice as many whites as blacks below the poverty line, but the chances of being poor are considerably greater if one is black: about one white in ten is poor, compared with nearly one black in three. The black population as a whole averages a smaller annual income than the white population.

[30]U.S. Bureau of the Census, *Current Population Reports*, series p–60, no. 86 (Washington, D. C.: U.S. Government Printing Office, 1972), p. 3.
[31]*Economic Report of the President*, p. 163.

Blacks generally earn substantially less than whites with similar qualifications, and the income gap between blacks and whites, which narrowed in the sixties, is now widening again. Poverty in black families correlates highly with the sex of the family head. A fifth of black families headed by a man are poor, but more than half of those headed by women are poor, partly because black women suffer a double discrimination in the job market on grounds of both race and sex. In a controversial report, *The Negro Family: The Case for National Action*,[32] Daniel Patrick Moynihan argued that poverty among blacks was not due only to discrimination and lack of opportunity, but also to social disorganization in the black community, which made female-headed families much more common than in the white community. Other critics rejected Moynihan's conclusions and argued instead that it was not so much family structure that generated the poverty, as racial and sexual discrimination that made a particular family structure especially vulnerable.

The reasons for the high incidence of poverty among blacks are complex, but there is no doubt that racial discrimination is at the root of the problem. Since their abduction from Africa and their arrival on our shores as slaves, blacks have been denied freedom of opportunity in education and employment. They are traditionally the last hired and first fired, and their jobs are vulnerable to fluctuations in the economy. They have also suffered as a result of other social changes: the mechanization of agriculture in the South has cut job opportunities, and the automation of manufacturing has eliminated many semiskilled openings that they used to fill. Poor education in segregated schools has also left many blacks ill-equipped for the challenge of better paid jobs that might provide an escape route from poverty.

Another minority group that suffers disproportionate poverty is the 600,000 native Americans, about two-thirds of whom live as wards of the government on more than three hundred Indian reservations.[33] Over half of the native American population is living below the poverty line. The average income of all native Americans—not just those below the poverty line—is about $1,500. Their living conditions are often desolate: about 80 percent of their dwellings are substandard. Only 70 percent of the native Americans finish school; only 1 percent attend college, and of these 60 percent drop out. Again, a long history of discrimination, prejudice, and exclusion from the benefits of the affluent society is responsible for their current plight. Yet another minority that suffers a high incidence of poverty is the Mexican-Americans, particularly those who work as migrant laborers at seasonal jobs in agriculture.

Another significant group among the poor is the elderly. Some 4,300,000 Americans aged sixty-four or over are poor, and they constitute over a fifth of their age group and nearly a quarter of the poor. A great

[32]U.S. Department of Labor, Office of Policy Planning and Research, *The Negro Family: The Case for National Action* (Washington, D.C.: U.S. Government Printing Office, 1965).
[33]Alan Batchelder, *The Economics of Poverty* (New York: Wiley, 1966), p. 133.

many more live just above the poverty line; thus the number suffering deprivation is substantially higher. Poverty in the aged is often associated, too, with isolation and loneliness: 42 percent of those who live alone or with unrelated individuals are in poverty. One out of ten people over sixty-four is poor and has no family to live with, and 83 percent of these isolated poor people are women.[34]

The elderly poor have few resources and consequently little hope of changing their situation. Many depend primarily on social security or other public assistance, or else rely on their savings, which can easily be wiped out by medical or other unanticipated expenses. The old are often ignorant of such public assistance as is available to them: in New York City in 1974, only 70,000 old people received Supplementary Security Income, although 275,000 of the city's aged were eligible under the program. Yet the elderly in New York have a higher poverty rate than any other group: more than 100,000 of them live on less than $1,000 a year, and half that sum is spent on rent.[35] The elderly are discriminated against in the job market, often being forced into retirement although they remain physically healthy, and the sudden transformation from being a responsible breadwinner to a dependent on welfare is often traumatic. The situation of the elderly poor is made worse by the fact that our society, unlike other more traditional societies, accords no honored place or useful social role to the aged. As Michael Harrington writes:

> The image of a querulous, nagging, meandering old age is not a description of an eternal condition of human nature. It is, in part, the impression of what society has done to people by giving them meaningless years in which to live. . . . Loneliness, isolation, and sickness are the afflictions of the aged in every economic class. But for those who are poor, there is an intensification of each of these tragedies: they are more lonely, more isolated, sicker.[36]

Where, then, are the welfare cheaters? An analysis of 1970 census data by the U.S. Office of Economic Opportunity suggests that they scarcely exist.[37] Some 63.9 percent of the unemployed were unable to seek work or hold employment. Children under fourteen represented 34.4 percent of this group; the elderly over 64 represented 18.2 percent; the ill and disabled represented 4.7 percent; and those in school represented 6.6 percent. Of the remaining 36.1 percent who were in theory able to work, 23.8 percent did some work, and the remaining 12.3 percent did none. So of the entire possible work force among the poor, only 12.3 percent did not work. But even this is not the whole story. The 12.3 percent represented a male component of 1.4 percent and

[34]U.S. Bureau of the Census, *Current Population Reports,* no. 86, pp. 4–5.
[35]*New York Post* (May 29, 1974).
[36]Harrington, *The Other America,* p. 103.
[37]U.S. Office of Economic Opportunity, *The Poor in 1970: A Chartbook* (Washington, D.C.: U.S. Government Printing Office, 1970), p. 30.

a female component of 10.9 percent, many or most of them mothers who had to stay at home to rear their children. Given that the very small remaining proportion of able-bodied poor who do not work must include people who lack employable skills or who live in impoverished areas without job opportunities, the number of welfare freeloaders seems relatively miniscule. Yet—such are our values and attitudes as a nation—our welfare system remains based on the notion that the poor must not be given so much assistance that they will have no incentive to work, and so all of the poor are penalized, irrespective of their circumstances. There is, of course, some welfare cheating, but there is no evidence that it is remotely as common as is often supposed. Despite vigorous checks by welfare inspectors, less than half of 1 percent of welfare cases are referred for prosecution for fraud.[38] There is, however, cheating by the states themselves. The federal Department of Health, Education, and Welfare has charged that thirteen states have been trimming their budgets by underpaying their welfare recipients in defiance of federal welfare guidelines.[39] And millions of the poor fail to claim benefits to which they are entitled, presumably because they remain ignorant of the existence of the programs.

WHY DOES POVERTY PERSIST?

Why is there poverty in America? Many other societies face the inevitability of poverty, because they lack the resources which, even if equally shared, might lift their peoples beyond deprivation. But the United States has quite enough wealth to ensure that no one is poor, at least in the sense of absolute deprivation. Lack of resources, then, is not the cause of poverty in our society. How, then, can we account for its persistence? There can be no simple answer to such a question. The poor are not a homogeneous group and there are many factors that can push an individual or a family into poverty, such as unwise management of credit, illness, or unemployment. But while these factors may be satisfactory explanations for particular cases of poverty, they do not account for the persistence of poverty as a general feature of our society. The causes of poverty lie much deeper—in imbalances of the economy, in cultural values and attitudes, and in the political realities of contemporary America.

Economic Factors

If poverty were caused solely by racial discrimination in the job market, we would expect to find it concentrated in the ethnic ghettos. But more than two-thirds of the poor are white. If poverty were caused solely by low intelligence or physical disability, we would expect to find

[38]U.S. Department of Health, Education, and Welfare, *Welfare: Myths vs. Facts,* p. 2.
[39]"Welfare—The Shame of a Nation," *Newsweek* (February 8, 1971), p. 25.

Social Blindness Toward Poverty

There are mighty historical and economic forces that keep the poor down; and there are human beings who help out in this grim business, many of them unwittingly. There are sociological and political reasons why poverty is not seen; and there are misconceptions and prejudices that literally blind the eyes. The latter must be understood if anyone is to make the necessary act of intellect and will so that the poor can be noticed.

Here is the most familiar version of social blindness: "The poor are that way because they are afraid of work. And anyway they all have big cars. If they were like me (or my father or my grandfather), they could pay their own way. But they prefer to live on the dole and cheat the taxpayers."

This theory, usually thought of as a virtuous and moral statement, is one of the means of making it impossible for the poor ever to pay their way. There are, one must assume, citizens of the other America who choose impoverishment out of fear of work (though, writing it down, I really do not believe it). But the real explanation of why the poor are where they are is that they made the mistake of being born to the wrong parents, in the wrong section of the country, in the wrong industry, or in the wrong racial or ethnic group. Once that mistake has been made they could have been paragons of will and morality, but most of them would never even have had a chance to get out of the other America.

SOURCE: Michael Harrington, *The Other America* (Baltimore, Md.: Penguin Books, 1962).

it spread more or less at random throughout the population. But poverty is concentrated in certain geographical areas of the country, especially the South and the adjacent states, where nearly half of America's poor families are to be found. Closer examination of these and other "pockets" of poverty indicates that high unemployment rates are usually responsible for the low average incomes of the poor people concerned. Persistent, localized unemployment of this kind is known as *structural unemployment*, because unlike other forms of unemployment (such as that occurring in a temporary recession), it is built into the very structure of the economy and is extremely difficult to correct.

Structural unemployment is usually the result of dislocations resulting from economic change. The history of the mining industry in Appalachia, now one of the most impoverished areas of the country, illustrates this process of change. When the extraction of coal from the region started in earnest at the beginning of the century, much of the work was carried out by hand. Thousands of agricultural workers, black and white, were lured off the cotton plantations and the farms by the relatively attractive wages offered by the mines. The industry grew rapidly and became the dominant employer in the area. The workers formed unions and gained significant wage increases. But in the years after World War II, the industry began to install labor-saving machines that required fewer workers and consequently reduced production costs. Large-scale automation threw thousands of miners out of work. Today, about 140,000 miners dig more coal than 700,000 were able to dig sixty years ago.[40] The region now has a persistent high rate of structural unemployment, and one of the lowest average incomes in the nation. As Harry Caudill records:

> Hoping against hope that expansion of other industries would eventually absorb the displaced miners, government agencies waited. When the stranded miner had exhausted his unemployment insurance benefits and his savings, when he had come to the ragged edge of starvation and was cloaked in bewilderment and frustration, government came to his rescue with the dole. It arranged to give him a bag of cheese, rice, cornmeal, beef, butter, and dried milk solids at intervals, and in most instances to send him a small check. Having thus contrived to keep the miner and his family alive, the government lost interest in him. Appropriations were made from time to time for his sustenance, but little thought was given to his spirit, his character, his manhood. He was left to dry-rot in the vast paleface reservation created for his perpetuation in his native hills.[41]

Structural unemployment of this kind has followed in the wake of automation in many parts of the economy. Small farmers and agricultural laborers have been displaced by the introduction of tractors, threshers, mechanical pickers, and numerous other technological devices which now make it possible for food to move from field to supermarket virtually untouched by human hand. One result of these innovations is that American agriculture has become the most productive in the world. But another result is that the farm labor force has declined rapidly, from 12 percent of the nation's workers in 1950 to 4 percent in 1970. Automation in these and other parts of the economy does not only throw people out of work, it also tends to reduce the number of unskilled jobs available, and there are many workers who are not equipped for any other jobs. The days of the self-made man who starts as an unskilled laborer and works his way to the top of the firm are almost over; education is the route for advancement, and the poorly educated are employable only in the dwindling number of unskilled

---

[40]U.S. Department of Health, Education, and Welfare, *Welfare: Myths vs. Facts,* p. 2.
[41]Harry Caudill, "The Permanent Poor: The Lesson of Eastern Kentucky," *Atlantic Monthly,* vol. 213, no. 6 (June 1964), pp. 50–51.

or semiskilled occupations that remain. Automation, of course, opens up new jobs, but the jobs typically require a higher level of skill than was required by the repetitive tasks the machine has replaced, so retraining is often necessary. In some cases, displaced workers can migrate from one part of the country to another where employment opportunities are better. But people may be understandably reluctant to make the move, which is often to more expensive and inferior urban housing, away from relatives, friends, churches, and a traditional way of life.

Automation has not proceeded so rapidly in the less skilled service occupations, such as domestic cleaners, hospital attendants, dishwashers, janitors, and watchmen. The prospect of these jobs—which require little education or training—has lured many displaced rural workers to the cities. But unskilled service jobs usually pay very low wages and usually offer little security and no fringe benefits. Employment opportunities of this kind offer no solution to the problem of poverty; indeed, the 1970 census showed that over half of the heads of the families officially defined as poor were employed. Some 20 percent of all poor families were headed by a person who worked all year round, but still failed to bring home enough wages to raise the family living standard above the poverty line. And another 33 percent of the poor-family breadwinners were able to find work only in part-time occupations or in seasonal jobs such as fruit-picking. The economy is structured so that these low-prestige, low-skill service jobs are very poorly paid, and this provides a further basis for continuing poverty in America.

The cumulative effect of these changes in the structure of the economy is to trap an "underclass" of unemployed or unemployable people at the bottom of American society. S. M. Miller has argued that the United States is increasingly moving into a "dual economy," in which the main economy is characterized by high standards of living and stable employment, while the marginal economy is characterized by low standards of living and unstable employment. The marginal economy is centered on low-level service trades and occupations, many of them offering only part-time or temporary work. The workers in the marginal economy are often drawn from minority groups and remain unemployed for long periods. The children of these workers tend to receive inferior educations and so find it more difficult to break out of the marginal economy into the more affluent main economy.[42]

Much of the poverty in the United States, then, is rooted in dislocations caused by economic change and in the very institutional design of the economy. Stimulating growth and creating more jobs would not necessarily provide an effective remedy because many of the poor cannot readily be absorbed into new occupations. And it must be remembered that the occupational structure determines only the *demand*

[42]S. M. Miller, "Poverty, Race, and Politics," in *The New Sociology: Essays in Social Science Theory in Honor of C. Wright Mills*, ed. Irving L. Horowitz (New York: Oxford University Press, 1964), pp. 298–299.

for certain kinds of labor; the *supply* of particular types of labor is influenced by other factors. Economic influences, therefore, are only a partial explanation for the persistence of poverty in the United States.

Cultural Factors

Are the poor significantly different in their attitudes and values from the rest of society? And if so, is this a reason for the persistence of poverty? A number of observers have noted a tendency for poverty to be transmitted from one generation to the next. City welfare rolls all over the United States are registering the adult sons and daughters of welfare parents, which indicates that the poor are in some sense passing on their dependent status to their offspring. Many social scientists have argued that it is not only welfare status that is passed on, but also a wide range of other values that reinforce the difficulty of the poor in entering the mainstream economy. Some analysts have suggested that the poor are members of a distinctive subculture in society—a subculture which, like all cultures, has its own values, norms, and roles. Children born into this subculture, it is argued, are socialized into an acceptance of the subculture and its limited expectations, and they are, therefore, unlikely to break out of poverty and into the larger national culture.

The anthropologist Oscar Lewis is the most widely known proponent of the notion of a *culture of poverty.* Drawing on his field studies of poor neighborhoods in different parts of the world, he asserts that there exists a distinct culture or life style that transcends ethnic divisions, national boundaries, or regional differences:

> The culture of poverty is not just a matter of deprivation or disorganization, a term signifying the absence of something. It is a culture in the traditional anthropological sense in that it provides human beings with a design for living, with a ready-made set of solutions for human problems, and so serves a significant adaptive function. . . . Wherever it occurs, its practitioners exhibit remarkable similarity in the structure of their families, in interpersonal relations, in spending habits, in their value systems, and in their orientation to time.[43]

Lewis found, for example, that marriage and family patterns of the poor typically differ from those of the middle class. Even though the poor view legal marriage as the ideal, many never marry but instead live together in an informal or "consensual" union. This loose bond appeals to men who have little or no property to pass on, who have no stable jobs or expectations of economic security, and who are not disposed to plan for the future. It also appeals to women who realize that they have a stronger claim on their children if the father is not the legal

[43]Oscar Lewis, "The Culture of Poverty," *Scientific American,* vol. 215, no. 4 (October 1966), pp. 19–25.

Is this child being reared in a "culture of poverty?" Many social scientists believe that the children of the chronically poor internalize attitudes of resignation and hopelessness which make it even more difficult for them to escape from poverty. *(Paul Fusco/Magnum)*

parent and that they retain the legal right to what little property they might own. These consensual unions are typically unstable, and the family therefore tends to be matriarchal. Lewis' findings suggest that female-dominated families are not a trait peculiar to black American society, but appear in poor communities throughout the world.

Those who live in the culture of poverty also tend to be socially isolated. They have few organized ties to a group larger than their own family, in marked contrast to middle-class citizens, who participate in a wide range of voluntary organizations and social contacts. The poor, Lewis believes, are disengaged from the major institutions of society: they make little use of banks, hospitals, department stores, libraries, museums. In fact, they are hostile to those institutions that they perceive as belonging to the dominant classes. In particular, they fear and dislike the police and mistrust the government and all officials. The general outlook of the poor is provincial and narrow. They have little sense of their own history and know only the way of life of themselves and their neighbors. They lack the knowledge and the political ideas that might enable them to see similarities between their own problems and those of their counterparts elsewhere. Their very isolation prevents them from perceiving their private troubles as part of a social problem that is amenable to collective solution.

Lewis argues that this culture, like any other, fosters the development of a distinctive set of psychological and personality traits:

> The individual who grows up in this culture has a strong feeling of fatalism, helplessness, dependence and inferiority. . . . Other traits include a high incidence of weak ego structure, orality and confusion of sexual identification, all reflecting maternal deprivation; a strong present-time orientation with relatively little disposition to defer gratification and plan for the future, and a high tolerance for psychological pathology of all kinds. There is a widespread belief in male superiority and among men a strong preoccupation with *machismo*, their masculinity.[44]

Lewis believes that the culture of poverty, with its distinctive values and personality traits, is not simply the consequence of low incomes. Many so-called primitive peoples have low incomes, but do not display these cultural characteristics. The culture of poverty, Lewis contends, emerges only after long periods of deprivation in highly stratified, capitalist societies, where the poor are trapped into attitudes of despair. They evolve a culture of poverty that continues to have an existence independent of the economic situation that created it, and their own norms, values, and expectations serve to limit their options and prevent their escape.

A number of social scientists have criticized Lewis' belief that the poor participate in a distinct culture that reinforces their poverty and transmits it from one generation to another. Instead, they see the distinctive values and behavior of the poor as conditions imposed on them by society—a consequence and not a cause of continuing poverty. Hylan Lewis, for example, has suggested that "it is probably more fruitful to think of lower-class families reacting in various ways to the facts of their position and to a relative isolation rather than to the imperatives of a lower-class culture."[45] Similarly, Richard Cloward and Lloyd Ohlin take the view that the characteristics and attitudes of the poor are simply realistic and predictable responses to their existing situation. They argue that the behavior of the poor is an adaptive response—often an unsuccessful one—to the surrounding society, and not the creation of a particular culture. The poor have to abandon the attitudes, values, and expectations of the middle class, because middle-class culture is irrelevant to their situation. Another criticism of the "culture of poverty" theory is that it focuses attention on the faults of the poor, instead of laying the blame for their poverty on the social system as a whole.

Whether the "culture of poverty" is regarded as a cause or a conse-

---

[44]Ibid., p. 23.
[45]Hylan Lewis, "Culture, Class and the Behavior of Low Income Families," mimeographed (Paper delivered at the Conference on Views of the Lower Class Culture, New York City, June 27–29, 1963), p. 43.

quence of poverty, or even as a combination of the two, with the cultural values reinforcing poverty and being reinforced by them, it does seem that the poor are socialized into a particular set of roles, values, and expectations that severely limit their horizons and social mobility and so compound the problem of poverty. The culture of the poor should not be judged by ethnocentric standards, however, for like any other culture it has its own worth and validity. To take but one example, the most important indigenous modes of musical expression in America—the blues, jazz, and country music—are the products of impoverished individuals and communities.[46]

There is one other way in which cultural factors contribute to continuing poverty in the United States, and that is through the attitudes and values of the dominant culture. As we have seen, these values prize hard work, thrift, and the accumulation of wealth. The possibility of upward mobility is held out even to those at the bottom of the social hierarchy. According to the doctrine of "self-help," anybody can achieve success, provided he or she works hard enough. Consequently, those who remain poor are regarded as being to some extent personally responsible for their situation, and it is felt that they ought to be discouraged from expecting handouts from those citizens who work for a living. One consequence of this attitude is that all welfare claims are subjected to a thorough investigation for possible fraud, whereas income tax returns (which involve far more fraud) are subjected only to occasional spot checks. Only one tax return in 75 is audited by tax investigators. The traditional attitude takes no account of the extent to which advantages of birth and education influence subsequent social status and income, nor does it take into account the fact that the overwhelming majority of the poor are in poverty not because they refuse to work, but because they are unemployable or underpaid. Yet the dominant American attitude has contributed to a widespread absolute poverty that could have been avoided if all our citizens were guaranteed a basic minimum income.

Political Factors

One reason for the persistence of poverty in the United States is that our society is an inegalitarian one, and there are many political pressures to keep it that way. As Robert Dentler points out, we do not have poverty in America because of scarcity, but because it is a condition of institutional design.[47] The persistence of poverty in the United States requires the acquiescence of our political institutions, which in turn are under pressure from many interest groups to resist changes which might lead to a redistribution of wealth and income in favor of the poor.

As Herbert Gans has pointed out, poverty is useful and functional to our society in several respects. The existence of an underprivileged, im-

[46]Robert Dentler, *Major Social Problems* (New York: Rand McNally, 1967), p. 124.
[47]Ibid., p. 118.

poverished section of the community functions to maintain the stability of the rest of society and the privileges of the other classes. According to Gans, some of these functions are:

1. *Poverty ensures that "dirty" work will get done.* If there were no poor people willing to scrub floors and clean bedpans, "dirty" work would have to be rewarded with incomes superior to that of "clean" work before anyone would touch it.
2. *Poverty creates jobs for some of the nonpoor.* A substantial part of the population derives employment from jobs that involve "servicing" the poor — police, social workers, welfare investigators, pawnbrokers, and the like.
3. *Poverty facilitates the life style of the affluent.* The existence of poverty guarantees a supply of gardeners, cooks, domestic cleaners, and other workers who perform various chores and thus free the upper classes to pursue other activities, including frivolous ones.
4. *Poverty provides a market for inferior goods and services.* Poor people buy the goods and services that others do not want: day-old bread, secondhand autos, deteriorating housing, or the advice of incompetent doctors and lawyers.
5. *Poverty guarantees the status of the nonpoor.* In a hierarchical society someone has to be at the bottom, and the existence of an underprivileged class confirms the superior status of those above. Just as poverty makes the poor feel relatively deprived, so it makes the nonpoor feel relatively advantaged.
6. *Poverty legitimizes American values.* The poor, by their very existence, confirm the desirability of the qualities they are supposed to lack. As Gans points out, "to justify the desirability of hard work, thrift, honesty and monogamy, for example, the defenders of these norms must be able to find people who can be accused of being lazy, spendthrift, dishonest, and promiscuous."
7. *Poverty provides a group that can be made to absorb the political and economic costs of change.* The poor, for example, bear the brunt of the unemployment that results from automation; or when new highways have to be constructed, these highways are routed through and devastate the neighborhoods of the poor rather than those of the wealthy.[48]

The very existence of poverty, then, lends stability to the norms and institutional arrangements of the entire society. If poverty were to be eliminated, various other interest groups would suffer. Gans stresses, however, that many of the contemporary functions of poverty are not socially necessary, even if they are socially convenient in some respects, and many of the functions could be fulfilled in other ways that would not involve the existence of poverty. He also points out that pov-

[48]Herbert J. Gans, "The Uses of Poverty: The Poor Pay All," *Social Policy*, vol. 2, no. 2 (July–August 1971), pp. 21–23.

erty is dysfunctional as well; it is highly dysfunctional to the poor, and it creates a potential conflict in society and provides a drain on many social resources that could be productively used in other ways.

Many political and economic interests oppose measures that might improve the position of the poor through income redistribution. The objectives of these pressure groups include the maintenance of the existing system of corporate capitalism and of the various tax and subsidy benefits that are available to private enterprise, theoretically as incentives to increase production and profit. Organized business interests have always been able to modify or even rebuff measures that run counter to their interests. Private enterprise, for example, accepts no responsibility for those who are made unemployed by its technological advances: these people are regarded instead as the responsibility of the government and ultimately of the taxpayer. (Similarly, private enterprise attempts to evade responsibility for the pollution generated by its technological advances; again, the government and ultimately the taxpayer is expected to assume the responsibility for cleaning up the environment.) Moreover, business enterprises have been successful in attracting federal subsidies and grants in support of programs that indirectly generate unemployment, but neither government nor business has been keen to support programs to aid the workers who are thus impoverished. An example is the billions of dollars in federal subsidies that are paid to rich individual and corporate farmers to enable them to mechanize their production. As a result of these subsidies, production in the fields has increased twice as fast as in the factories, but millions of rural workers have become economically superfluous. At present, federal subsidies to private enterprise, designed to help them increase their profits, total over $30 billion per year. This figure includes only direct payments; if indirect payments, exemptions, and other advantages were included, the figure would be very much higher.[49] The lobbying of organized interest groups has also been instrumental in preventing any substantial changes in the distribution of wealth and income in the United States; this has been achieved mainly through the system of tax loopholes that offer benefits to corporations and wealthy individuals which are not available to the ordinary worker. Government willingness to subsidize private enterprise lavishly while keeping welfare payments to a minimum reflects the political priorities of contemporary America.

Several writers have argued that the government in fact hands out vast sums in "welfare" to the rich, but because the handouts are not termed "welfare," these huge subsidies pass almost unnoticed. Philip Stern points out that if the tax relief obtained by those with incomes of over a million dollars a year were renamed "welfare," there would be an outcry; for the savings amount to an average of $720,000 for each of these super-rich Americans, or a total of $2.2 billion per year. Stern suggests that it makes little difference whether the sum is termed "wel-

[49]Thomas Bodenheimer, "The Poverty of the State," *Monthly Review*, 24 (November 1972), p. 14.

"If We Could Only Have an Acre..."

Mrs. Moore, although she is articulate and vigorous, is typically trapped in that cycle of poverty, fed by racism . . . making even the skies on a sunny day, as we rode from dwelling to dwelling, exude a curious atmosphere of bleakness.

Past the lush fields of beans and cotton on the wealthy plantations. Past the green and red cotton pickers and other machinery which, though lying idle for the moment, are said to pick 17,000 pounds of cotton a day, compared with the average 250 pounds per day picked by the men they have replaced. Past the acres and acres of fertile land that lie vacant—turned to weeds—to keep the prices of cotton and other crops jacked up for the wealthy farmers—while people are starving within a stone's throw for lack of a plot of ground to plant some greens and corn. "Look at all the land," said our guide sadly. "If we could only have an acre—half an acre." But the plantation owners won't rent it because they receive more money from the government for keeping it barren.

SOURCE: *Nutrition and Human Needs: Hearings before the Select Committee on Nutrition and Human Needs of the U.S. Senate,* Testimony by National Council of Negro Women (October 1968).

fare" or "tax relief"; in either case, the U.S. Treasury is $2.2 billion poorer, and the rest of the taxpayers have to pay an added $2.2 billion to make up the difference. Stern contrasts the fact that the average tax relief for the poorest section of the community—those earning under $3,000 per year—is $16.[50]

A similar view is expressed by A. Dale Tussing, who contends:

Two welfare systems exist simultaneously in this country. One is well known. It is explicit, poorly funded, stigmatized and stigmatizing, and is directed at the poor. The other, practically unknown, is implicit, literally invisible, is nonstigmatized and nonstigmatizing, and provides vast but unacknowledged benefits for the non-poor. . . . Our welfare systems do not distribute benefits on the basis of need. Rather, they distribute benefits on the basis of legitimacy. Poor people are viewed as less legitimate than non-poor people. . . .

By and large, welfare programs for the poor are obvious, open and clearly labeled, and those for the non-poor are either concealed (as in tax laws, for instance) and ill understood, or are clothed in protective language. . . . Whether or not a person is poor can often be determined by the names of his welfare programs. If his programs

[50]Stern, "Uncle Sam's Welfare Program—for the Rich."

are called "relief," "welfare," "assistance," "charity" or the like, he is surely poor; but if they are called "parity," "insurance," "compensation" or "compulsory saving," he is surely a member of the large majority of non-poor persons who do not even think of themselves as receiving welfare payments.[51]

As an example of the "welfare" payments to the nonpoor, Tussing cites the deductibility of interest on home mortgages and property taxes. These two items cost the federal government $2.4 billion and $2.7 billion respectively in 1971. In effect, they are a "rent supplement" to home owners. If they were acknowledged as such, they would represent by far the largest housing program in the federal budget—more than four times the amount spent on all housing programs for the poor. According to U.S. Treasury figures, some 85 percent of the benefits from this "rent supplement" goes to the taxpayers with incomes of over $10,000, while less than .01 percent goes to those with incomes of $3,000 or less. The same pattern of concealed preferential benefits to the wealthy recurs in many other areas of government budgets.

The bias in our economic and political system is against the poor, who are both a small minority and an inadequately organized one. Herbert Gans points out that the poor are rendered politically impotent not only by the power of the corporations and the wealthy few, but also by the logic of majority rule:

> Although every citizen is urged to be active in the affairs of the community and the nation, in actual practice these rules mean that political participation is carried out by two kinds of groups, fairly permanent organized pressure groups or lobbies who want something from government, and transitory groups who are unhappy about a specific governmental action or inaction and may organize only to protest. . . . As a result, legislation in America tends to favor the interests of the businessman, not the consumers, even though the latter are a vast majority; of landlords, not tenants; of doctors, not patients. Only organized interest groups have the specific concerns and the time, staff, and money to bring their demands before government officials. . . .
>
> The poor are powerless because they are a minority of the population, are not organized politically, are often difficult to organize, and are not even a homogeneous group with similar interests that could be organized into a single pressure group. . . . Given the antagonism toward them on the part of many Americans, any programs that would provide them with significant gains are likely to be voted down by a majority. Legislative proposals for a massive anti-poverty effort . . . have always run into concerted and united opposition in Washington. . . . Since the poor . . . will probably always be outvoted by a majority, they are thus doomed to be *permanently outvoted minorities.*[52]

[51]Tussing, "The Dual Welfare System," pp. 50, 53.
[52]Herbert J. Gans, *More Equality* (New York: Pantheon, 1968), pp. 133–135.

PROSPECTS FOR THE FUTURE

There is no single cause of poverty in the United States, and similarly there is no single solution to the problem. As we have seen, people may be poor for a variety of reasons: discrimination, ill health, old age, lack of education and skills, or residence in depressed areas. Efforts to alleviate and perhaps ultimately eliminate poverty can therefore be made on a number of different fronts.

Eliminating discrimination. Discrimination against ethnic minorities, women, and older people underlies much of the poverty in America today. Discriminatory beliefs and practices are pervasive in our society, and they will be eradicated only with great difficulty and over a long period of time. Nevertheless, there is an "equality revolution" abroad in the United States, with blacks, women, consumers, students, native Americans, Mexican-Americans, and others demanding an end to established hierarchies, old prejudices, and artificially limited opportunities. Governments cannot legislate directly for changes in attitudes and values, but they can prohibit the translation of discriminatory beliefs into practice. Public attitudes tend to follow changes in the law, however, so the legal initiatives may indirectly influence attitudes as well as practices. Already, federal and state governments have enacted many statutes to protect the interests of groups that have suffered discrimination in the past, but in every case it has taken strong pressure from organized groups to bring about government action.

Creating job opportunities. The relationship between poverty and economic change is complex, but properly directed economic growth can bring about an expansion of jobs and a reduction in poverty. A situation of full employment, in which there is a high demand for labor, is a powerful solvent of discriminatory barriers. Groups that are impoverished largely as a result of discrimination, such as women or blacks, are especially benefited in an expanding economy, just as they are particularly penalized in times of recession. Job opportunities can be expanded in various ways. One method is to cut taxes, which gives people more money to spend, raises demand, and so stimulates production. Another method is to cut interest rates, which encourages borrowing and thus allows people to spend more on goods and services. Measures such as these can be highly effective; President Kennedy's tax cuts in the early sixties stimulated a period of great prosperity. But the measures are extremely complex and can also be dangerous; increased demand for goods and services can force prices up and generate inflation. Economic change therefore has to be very carefully guided if it is to avoid the twin perils of unemployment and inflation.

Stimulating an economy does not necessarily create more jobs, however. If business invests its money in more sophisticated equipment rather than a larger work force, economic advance might not be ac-

Many of the poor are locked into poverty because they are old, handicapped, live in depressed rural areas, or are members of minority groups that are subject to job discrimination. *(Ken Heyman)*

companied by a corresponding increase in jobs. Moreover, economic change may bypass those regions, such as Appalachia, that are permanently depressed. For these impoverished areas, more specific programs are needed. One measure originally designed to aid such areas was the Area Redevelopment Administration (ARA). Founded in 1961, this federal agency was supposed to supply long-term loans to attract private industry to depressed areas and thereby create jobs. But the ARA's useful years were few; it quickly became a "pork barrel," raided by many congressmen to aid their own not-so-depressed areas and thus win favor with local voters. Many other countries confront the problem of depressed areas by offering tax incentives to industries to locate themselves in these areas and by establishing government-supported enterprises in persistent pockets of poverty.

Training and education. In an industrial society in which jobs are increasingly specialized, there is less and less opportunity for the unskilled laborer, and lack of education and training severely restricts occupational mobility. The poorly educated citizen who lacks specific job training is at a very severe disadvantage in the United States and is likely to join the ranks of the impoverished. One strategy that can be used to combat poverty is intensive training designed to upgrade the skills of people who might otherwise be unemployable. Congress has already enacted a number of programs to provide financial support for training of this kind, notably the Manpower Retraining and Development Act, the Economic Opportunity Act, and the Work Incentive Program. There has been considerable criticism of these programs, however, on the grounds that they are poorly funded, do not offer training in a sufficiently wide range of skills, and fail to reach many of those citizens who would most benefit from them.

There is also a need for major effort to improve the educational opportunities available to the children of the poor. Unlike many other countries, the United States finances education on the basis of local taxes, so that affluent areas have well-funded, well-equipped schools, while impoverished areas are unable to afford decent educational facilities. Yet the children in these areas are the ones most in need of a good education. Since education is a major route to economic success in America, the children of the poor start out with an added handicap in addition to all the others their poverty imposes on them.

Reform of the welfare system. The American welfare system is at present cumbersome, inefficient, and inconsistently applied. The amount of welfare payments given to an individual or family often depends not on need, but on the particular state in which the recipient resides or the particular program under which he or she falls. Some needy people may be denied benefits simply because they are arbitrarily defined as ineligible for each of several programs. Others receive far less than they might simply because they are defined as falling under one program rather than another. An example of these inconsistencies is provided by the Aid to Families with Dependent Children (AFDC) program. Poor women with children find it hard to take a job because child-care centers are often not available. A direct cash subsidy is a necessity in these cases and is available through the AFDC program. But grants under the program are available only to broken families; if the husband is present, the family is ineligible, even if the husband is ill or unemployed. To guard against "welfare chiselers" who secretly live with men (including their husbands) but draw AFDC allowances for their families, investigators in many states have been directed to observe homes at random hours of the day and night to see if any men are present. Many critics of the AFDC program have urged its abolition and the substitution of a system of unconditional family allowances. Daniel Moynihan writes:

> The United States is the only industrial democracy in the world without a system of automatic income supplements for people living with their children. It is the simplest and possibly most effective of

all social welfare arrangements. . . . It was past time we came to our senses and stopped penalizing families with a father in the home.[53]

Numerous other inconsistencies exist in the present welfare system. A thorough overhaul of the system is necessary to integrate the various programs, to eliminate unnecessary hardships, and to ensure that the amount of benefits is determined by the need of the recipients rather than by such fortuitous circumstances as the particular program or state authority under which the claimants fall.

Redistribution of wealth. Poverty cannot be eliminated simply by the use of programs designed to alleviate its symptoms. Poverty is an inevitable consequence of the inequality in American society and is likely to persist until there is some significant redistribution of wealth in the United States. The more radical socialist proposals for the takeover of large corporations and the appropriation of large personal fortunes are unlikely to find much favor in the United States because of our deeply ingrained belief in the virtues of free enterprise. But there are a number of intermediate measures that could reduce some of the poverty stemming from our institutionalized inequality. Tax reform could plug many of the loopholes by which the wealthy are enabled to escape the payment of millions of dollars each year—vast sums that mean increased taxation for the rest of the community in order to make up the loss to the treasury. Another measure would be to increase the amount of direct welfare payments and to allocate a much greater proportion of tax money to services for the poor: low-cost housing, job retraining, medical clinics, education, school lunches, food stamps, and the like. The continuing existence of poverty in the midst of material abundance seems morally unjustifiable and is a poor international advertisement for the American system. The problem can only be solved by some redistribution of national income and resources.

Negative income tax. An idea which has been widely debated in recent years is that of the "negative income tax." The proposal is a simple one: persons earning above a certain fixed amount would pay income tax, but persons earning below the amount would receive a grant—the negative tax—to bring their income up to the fixed level. The level would be reviewed from time to time, but would always be enough to sustain an individual or family at a level somewhat above the poverty line. The main advantage of the system is that it directly aids all of the poor, irrespective of the occupational, regional, age, or other category they belong to. The system could replace virtually all the existing programs—AFDC, old-age benefits, minimum wage laws, and others—and would also apply to those of the poor who are not covered

---

[53]Daniel P. Moynihan, "The President and the Negro: The Moment Lost," *Commentary*, vol. 43, no. 2 (February 1967), p. 36.

Poverty: A Theoretical Review

The social problem of poverty represents the gap between a *social ideal* of a society free from want and deprivation, and the *social reality* of the United States as an affluent society containing many millions of citizens whose incomes are inadequate to meet the basic requirement of food, clothing, and shelter, or whose share of the national income is so small that they cannot maintain the living standards that are normal in our society. Poverty may be defined either in absolute terms—as a lack of basic needs—or in relative terms—as compared with the surrounding standards of living.

The *social-disorganization* perspective offers valuable insights into the problem of poverty. Wealth is very unequally distributed in our society, and many social factors operate to maintain this inequality. The wealthy, for example, pay a significantly smaller percentage of their income in taxes than the poor, and the very wealthy are sometimes able to use tax loopholes so effectively that they pay little or no tax at all. Moreover, the wealthy are able to provide various advantages for their children—such as good education or inheritances—so that their offspring have much greater opportunities in life than the children of the poor. Inequalities in wealth are thus perpetuated from generation to generation, and the poor often find their poverty "escape-proof."

Society is further disorganized when there is an inconsistency between the American value of free competition and equal opportunity and the reality of discrimination against some groups, notably racial and ethnic minorities, old people, and women. These groups are often prevented on arbitrary grounds from gaining the same economic advantages that are more freely available to other groups. Certain structural features of the American economy are also dysfunctional in that they serve to perpetuate poverty among certain groups and in certain areas: automation, for example, has thrown many low-skilled workers out of their jobs, and they find it difficult to obtain new jobs or jobs that pay adequate wages. Migrant agricultural workers, too, are locked into a seasonal cycle of poorly paid work. The existence of poverty is in some respects functional for most nonpoor members of society: for example, it ensures that "dirty" work will get done and guarantees the superior status of the nonpoor; but it is, of course, highly dysfunctional for the poor themselves. In a society as affluent as the United States, poverty could be reduced or eliminated by making significant changes in society: poverty exists not because it is unavoidable, but because American society is so organized that poverty is inevitable. The persistence of poverty may thus be regarded as a consequence of social disorganization.

The *value-conflict* perspective highlights the fact that there are many basic conflicts of values and interests between the poor and the nonpoor in American society. Many Americans believe that the poor are responsible for their own poverty and as a result are unwilling to take steps to help them. It is widely believed that people on the welfare rolls are too lazy to go to work and deliberately choose to live on welfare handouts; and there is a strong belief that the work ethic would be undermined if welfare payments were adequate to maintain a decent standard of living. Largely for these reasons, the payments are kept to a bare minimum. The poor, however, take a very different view of the origins of their poverty, and believe that the various reasons given for the treatment they receive from the rest of society merely mask the unwillingness of people to share their wealth with others, however deserving.

It is clear that there is a considerable conflict of interest between those who have wealth and those who do not. Any attempt to reduce or eliminate poverty in America would have to be paid for from the tax money of the more wealthy, and the nonpoor are as reluctant to be taxed for this purpose as the poor are eager to receive additional aid. In fact, the more affluent actually receive more funds in disguised "handouts"—such as tax rebates on mortgage payments—than the poor; and they would inevitably lose some of their benefits if funds were channeled to the less privileged groups in society. This conflict of interest is reflected in a conflict of values, with the wealthy believing that they are fully entitled to retain the advantages they have earned, and the poor believing that society, whose very structure has created their poverty in the first place, owes them greater assistance to make the most of their opportunities.

The *deviance* perspective has sometimes been employed in the analysis of the problem of poverty, although it is less commonly used today. In the past, the poor were often seen as deviants from basic social norms, particularly the norm specifying the work ethic as a basic belief of the dutiful citizen. The poor were considered to be shiftless, immoral people who had failed to internalize or who had rejected basic norms of responsible citizenship. Few sociologists still take this view, although there is some evidence that the poor in general do not adhere to many basic middle-class norms, probably because these norms are irrelevant to their situation.

by any of these programs. Naturally, the system would involve many administrative problems, but it would probably be more efficient and less expensive to operate than the variety of measures now in existence. The main obstacle to a guaranteed minimum income of this kind is, of course, public resistance to such sweeping handouts of something for nothing. There is also scope for disagreement as to how much the minimum income should be.

Organizing for change. An important development in the battle against poverty has been the creation of the National Welfare Rights Organization (NWRO). The organization was founded in 1966 with an objective which seemed hardly radical: to make welfare agencies abide by their own rules and regulations. Half the eligible poor are not on the welfare rolls at all, and many are getting fewer benefits than they are entitled to. As Frances Piven and Richard Cloward point out:

> Welfare practice has everywhere become more restrictive than welfare statute; much of the time it verges on lawlessness. Thus, public welfare systems try to keep their budgets down and their rolls low by failing to inform people of the rights available to them; by intimidating and shaming them to the degree that they are reluctant either to apply or to press claims, and by arbitrarily denying benefits to those who are eligible.[54]

With the rules, regulations, and law on its side, the NWRO has won many court cases, including a Supreme Court ruling upholding the privacy of welfare recipients against arbitrary inspection of their homes by officials. For the first time, the poor are being represented by an organization devoted to their interests—a prerequisite for any measure of political influence. The NWRO now has 125,000 members, challenging existing regulations and seeking to change the attitudes and values that characterize the dominant American attitude toward the poor. The assumption behind the NWRO's work is that improvements in the living conditions of the poor will not happen automatically; they must be made to happen.

Of all the countries of the world, the United States has the best chance to utterly eradicate absolute poverty. The resources exist; only the will and the effort are lacking.

[54]Francis Fox Piven and Richard Cloward, "A Strategy to End Poverty," *The Nation*, vol. 202, no. 18 (May 2, 1966), p. 510.

FURTHER READING

Caplovitz, David, *The Poor Pay More: Consumer Practices of Low Income Families*, 1963. An important book documenting the fact that the poor pay more for inferior goods and services. The poor, indeed, are the ignorant and often helpless victims of unethical or even illegal business practices.

Galbraith, John Kenneth, *The Affluent Society*, 1958. A classic work in which a well-known economist explains the workings of the American economy in nontechnical language. Galbraith argues that the United States is marked by "private affluence" and "public poverty" — that is, expenditure of national capital is devoted disproportionately to private consumption rather than public need.

Gans, Herbert J., *More Equality*, 1973. Gans takes a hard look at the American belief that all citizens are, if not born equal, at least given equal opportunity to advance in our society. His examination of the many difficulties that stand in the way of more equality helps distinguish practical possibility from the utopian dream.

Harrington, Michael, *The Other America*, 1962. A powerful book that was the first to draw attention to continuing poverty in America; it still remains readable and relevant today. Harrington contends that the existence of poverty in a society as wealthy as the United States is unnecessary and shameful.

Leacock, Eleanor B., ed., *The Culture of Poverty: A Critique*, 1971. A collection of essays offering a wide range of viewpoints on the concept of the culture of poverty. Most of the contributors reject the concept and find other explanations for the persistence of poverty.

Lewis, Oscar, *La Vida*, 1966. The anthropologist outlines his controversial "culture of poverty" theory, using evidence drawn from the Puerto Rican communities of San Juan and New York City. The use of an anecdotal style makes the treatment of the problem particularly interesting.

Piven, Francis Fox and Richard A. Cloward, *Regulating the Poor: The Functions of Public Relief*, 1971. Presents the provocative argument that the public welfare system in the United States is designed not to help the poor, so much as to regulate them — by preventing them from overt violence and by labeling the poor as nonparticipants in normal social life.

Ryan, William, *Blaming the Victim*, 1970. A forceful argument that the blame for poverty is placed on the poor rather than on the social institutions that create poverty. Ryan systematically dissects and debunks many of the popular myths concerning the poor.

Stern, Phillip, *The Rape of the Taxpayer*, 1973. A lengthy, racy, and indignant account of how super-rich Americans manage to dodge taxes by the use of legal loopholes. Stern shows how political considerations contribute to the retention of these loopholes, which cost ordinary citizens billions of dollars each year.

Will, Robert E. and Harold G. Vatter, *Poverty in Affluence: The Social, Political, and Economic Dimensions of Poverty in the United States*, 2d ed., 1970. A very useful collection of articles on many aspects of the social problem of poverty.

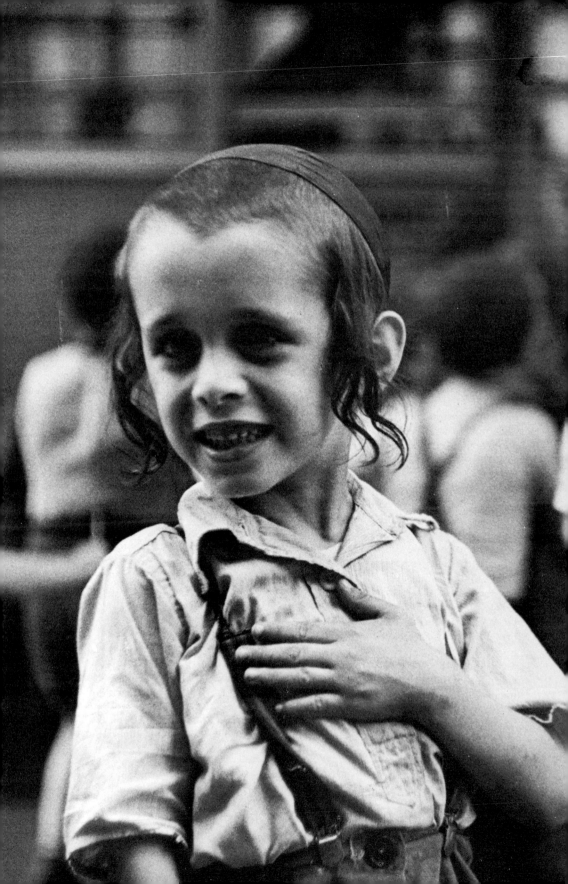

9

Race and Ethnic Relations

THE NATURE AND SCOPE OF THE PROBLEM

Unlike most other peoples, we are primarily a nation of immigrants. Our citizens or their ancestors were drawn from many parts of the globe—some coming as refugees from religious and political persecution, some as adventurers from the Old World seeking a better life in the New, some as captives brought to our shores against their will to be sold into slavery. Though we all share a common American culture, our nation contains many racial and ethnic subcultures with their own distinctive characteristics. And these differences, however trivial or irrelevant they may seem to outside observers, have contributed to intergroup conflicts that have been a recurring theme in our history and a persistent problem to our society.

The nation was explicitly founded on the principle of human equality, but in practice we have fallen far short of that ideal. Our society is a stratified one, with power, wealth, and status unequally distributed among our citizens. This unequal distribution is not simply a matter of distinctions between social classes: it tends to follow racial and ethnic lines as well, with the result that class divisions often parallel racial divisions. The first settlers from "Anglo-Saxon" Northern Europe quickly assumed control of economic assets and political power in the United States; and they have maintained this control, to a greater or lesser degree, ever since. Successive waves of immigrants from other parts of Europe and elsewhere in the world have had to struggle long and hard to become assimilated into the mainstream of American life. Some have succeeded and have shared in the American dream; others—notably those whose ethnic or racial characteristics differ most markedly from those of the dominant group—have been systematically excluded by formal and informal barriers from full participation in American life. The result of this discrimination has been a severe and continuing racial tension in the United States that has periodically erupted into outright violence. The most recent outbreak of violence—the ghetto riots of the sixties—profoundly affected American society and made race and ethnic relations a major preoccupation of social scientists, politicians, and the general public.

The Nature of Race and Ethnicity

The 3.8 billion people in the world today display a bewildering variety of skin colors, hair types, and other distinctive physical features. All humans, of course, belong to the same species—that is, they can interbreed with one another—and there is no evidence that different groups inherit different psychological characteristics, such as intelligence, musical ability, or aggressiveness. There is a vast range of different human cultures, however, and these cultures usually, although not always, are based on racial or ethnic communities. Different peoples are socialized into very different cultural patterns, attitudes, and values, and so the immense variety of physical types is complemented by a veritable kaleidoscope of different cultural forms.

Confronted with this great range of human characteristics, social scientists have attempted to create some kind of conceptual order by classifying people into very broad racial categories. Most humans can be roughly grouped into one of three main types: Negroid, Caucasoid, or Mongoloid. But there are some peoples, such as the dark-skinned but often fair-haired aborigines of Australia, who do not fit into this classification at all. In addition, there are many populations, such as the South Pacific islanders, that are almost impossible to classify with certainty because of their intermediate position between other racial categories; and there are millions of individuals whose ancestry is so mixed that they cannot possibly be assigned to any one category.

Race refers to physical characteristics, but the concept of ethnicity refers only to cultural distinctions. A Polish American, for example, may be physically indistinguishable from an Irish American, but each may participate to some extent in a distinctive subculture based on the traditional ethnic background of the group in question. Because ethnic differences are not as immediately apparent as racial differences, it is more difficult to use them as a basis for discrimination, and so antagonism between ethnic groups is usually much less intense than between racial groups.

Race, then, is simply a biological fact. But the sociologist is interested in racial differences as *social* facts, because these differences acquire significance only through the meanings that society attaches to them. The difference between people with long noses and those with short noses is also a biological fact, but because society attaches no particular significance to this difference, it has no social consequences and is of no interest to the sociologist. To the sociologist, therefore, a racial group is not so much a biological unity as it is any collection of people who, in their interactions with other groups, regard themselves or are regarded as a distinct race. Any group may distinguish itself from other groups, attribute virtues to its own group and undesirable characteristics to other groups, and act on that basis—and problems of race relations result.

Racism

Most groups that believe themselves to be a racial or an ethnic unity tend to be *ethnocentric:* that is, they automatically assume that their own culture and characteristics are superior to those of other groups and that their own religion, attitudes, values, and norms are right and proper, while those of other peoples are quaint, bizarre, immoral, or even savage. In extreme cases, these ethnocentric views from the basis for oppressive treatment of other groups—a phenomenon termed *racism.* Sociologist Robert Blauner defines the phenomenon:

> Racism is a principle of domination by which a group seen as inferior or different in terms of alleged biological differences is exploited, controlled, and oppressed socially and psychically by a superordinate group.[1]

For centuries racist attitudes were respectable in the Western world. The European colonial powers believed that their technological civilization was a sign of their own racial superiority over the "primitive" peoples they colonized. It was even argued that God had divided the human species into different races with the intention of clearly differentiating the superior from the inferior. The institution of slavery was closely linked to this attitude: by defining slaves as innately inferior, or even subhuman, it was possible to treat them in ways that would otherwise have seemed morally distasteful to a supposedly Christian people.

Racist attitudes, however, are by no means restricted to the whites of Europe and North America; they are to be found all over the world. In many parts of the Sahara, Arabs and black Africans are currently slaughtering one another for no other reason than the racial and cultural differences that exist between them. In parts of East Africa, especially Uganda, black Africans display racist attitudes toward Asiatic minorities and have been systematically expelling them from countries in which they have lived for generations. In many parts of South America, the dominant Spanish-speaking population tends to adopt racist attitudes toward the indigenous Indians, and even in the seventies some South American governments have been accused of outright genocide

[1]Robert Blauner, "Internal Colonialism and Ghetto Revolt," *Social Problems*, vol. 16, no. 4 (Spring 1969), p. 396.

of Indian tribes. Tensions between ethnic groups are also found all over the world, especially where ethnic differences coincide with differences in religious belief. The Soviet Union discriminates against Jews; Nigeria recently suffered a devastating civil war between its component ethnic groups; and the Indian subcontinent has had to be partitioned into separate nations because of the apparent inability of Hindus and Muslims to live together peaceably.

But although racism is still widespread in the modern world, as a doctrine it is no longer respectable. It was made utterly and permanently disreputable by Adolf Hitler, who carried ethnocentric and racist notions to unprecedented limits:

> All the human culture, all the results of art, science and technology that we see before us today, are almost exclusively the product of the Aryan [blond, blue-eyed race]. . . . He is the Prometheus of mankind from whose singing brow the divine spark of genius has sprung at all times. . . . It is no accident that the first cultures arose in places where the Aryan, in his encounters with lower peoples, subjugated them, and bent them to his will.[2]

Theories such as these led to concentration camps and the gas chambers, to a global war and the slaughter of millions of human beings. Since that time, racist theories have been utterly discredited; although racist attitudes and even racist policies still exist in some parts of the world, no governments — except for those of the white minority regimes in South Africa and Rhodesia — dare to openly endorse a racist attitude.

It is by no means inevitable that different racial or ethnic groups should live in conflict. There are many plural societies around the world in which the different groups live in great harmony. Tanzania, for example, has excellent race relations between its black, white, Arabic, and Asiatic populations. The Netherlands has assimilated without difficulty large numbers of immigrants from its former colonies in Indonesia. The German, French, and Italian populations in Switzerland coexist in harmony, as do the white, Chinese, Japanese, and native inhabitants of Hawaii. There is nothing innate in the nature of humanity that makes us react favorably or unfavorably toward other groups: race relations, be they good or bad, are a purely social product, and can be worsened or improved by social forces.

The United States: A "Melting Pot"?

It is a cherished American belief that our society serves as a "melting pot" for various peoples. The idea of America as a great crucible in which diverse races and cultures are blended has a long history; its essence was captured in the play *The Melting Pot*, a popular Broadway success in 1908. One of the actors expresses the "melting pot" credo:

[2]Adolf Hitler, *Mein Kampf*, trans. Ralph Manheim (Boston: Houghton Mifflin, 1948), pp. 290, 295.

America is God's crucible, the great Melting Pot, where all the races of Europe are melting and re-forming! Here you stand, good folk, think I, when I see them at Ellis Island, here you stand in your fifty groups, with your fifty languages and histories, and your fifty blood hatreds and rivalries. But you won't long be like that, brothers, for these are the fires of God you've come to—these are the fires of God. A fig for your feuds and vendettas! Germans and Frenchmen, Irishmen and Englishmen, Jews and Russians—into the Crucible with you all! God is making the American.[3]

The truth, however, is that the United States is and always has been a very heterogeneous society. Although there has been a good deal of assimilation of new immigrants into the American mainstream, the process has been a long and arduous one, largely restricted to those groups—such as Germans and Scandinavians—who were ethnically and culturally akin to the dominant Anglo-Saxon group. Other immigrant groups, such as the Mexican Americans and the Chinese, have proved an unassimilable element in the melting pot.

Racial and ethnic conflict has marked the entire history of the United States. When the first European settlers arrived in America, there were about 1,500,000 Indians in the country. They were promptly branded as savage, treacherous, and almost subhuman; settlers stripped them of their lands, almost exterminated the buffalo on which many tribes depended for their existence, and slaughtered tens of thousands of the native Americans during the westward migration. Even today the American Indian population consists of only 800,000 people, concentrated largely on the 300 reservations that are all that is left to them of the country that was once their own.

The first Africans were brought to the United States in 1619. Within a few decades the demand for their cheap labor had led to a massive slave trade, which ultimately brought some 400,000 Africans to North America. Captured in their native villages, the blacks were shipped in wretched and crowded conditions to the Caribbean and then to the east coast of the United States, where they were sold like cattle at auctions. The Northern states began to outlaw slavery after 1780, but the Southern states, in which black slaves had become the mainstay of the economy, maintained the institution of slavery until it was ended by the Civil War and Lincoln's emancipation of all slaves in 1863. Racial segregation, often imposed by law, continued to be practiced until the 1960s, and even today there are many informal barriers to black advancement in our society.

The Mexican Americans, or Chicanos, became U.S. citizens involuntarily when parts of the Southwest were ceded to the United States in 1848 after the Mexican War. These areas had been inhabited by dark-skinned peoples of mixed Spanish and Indian origins for over four hundred years. Their numbers have been greatly increased in the course of this century by legal and illegal immigration of Mexican migrant

[3]Israel Zangwill, *The Melting Pot* (New York: Macmillan, 1930), p. 33.

workers. Today there are 5 million Chicanos in the United States, most of them concentrated in the Southwest. Traditionally, they have taken poorly paid jobs, such as seasonal agricultural work.

The island of Puerto Rico has been an American possession since the Spanish-American War, and Puerto Ricans have been citizens of the United States since 1917. They are a people of mixed Spanish, Indian, and Negroid descent and have migrated in increasing numbers from their island to the better job opportunities available in the continental United States. Three-quarters of the continental population of one million live in New York, usually in conditions of poverty in Puerto Rican ghetto areas.

At the time of the 1820 census, virtually all the white inhabitants of the United States were of Anglo-Saxon Protestant background. From that point on, however, successive waves of immigrants of different European nationalities arrived in the United States. The first group, arriving soon after 1820, was the Irish. Other immigrants from Catholic areas of Northern Europe followed soon after. The established population deeply resented the new arrivals; there were virulent anti-Irish and anti-Catholic riots in several major American cities during the mid-nineteenth century. Between 1860 and 1890 there was another major influx of immigrants, this time from Scandinavia and Germany; in fact, the Germans were the largest immigrant group ever to come to America, and were perhaps the most readily assimilated. The final wave of European immigration took place between 1880 and 1914, this time from two main areas, Italy and Eastern Europe. Over 4 million Italians left their native land to come to the United States, and millions of other immigrants, many of them Jewish, arrived from such countries as Hungary, Poland, the Balkan states, and Russia. Some of these groups were more easily assimilated than others; but all were initially resented by the groups that had preceded them. Those groups that settled in the large Eastern cities, however, were assisted by the local Democratic Party machines, which effectively traded economic benefits for the votes of the newcomers; even to this day, the "white ethnic" groups remain overwhelmingly Democratic in their political allegiance.

The United States also has a substantial Asiatic minority. Between 1850 and 1880, over 300,000 Chinese had settled in America—mostly in California, where they worked in mining and railroad construction. Their presence aroused violent anti-Chinese feelings, and there were many lynchings of Chinese immigrants in California and even a wholesale massacre of twenty-nine Chinese in Wyoming in 1885. Fears of the "yellow peril" led to the Chinese Exclusion Act of 1882, which specifically restricted the number of Chinese entrants to the United States, and from 1902 to World War II the immigration of Chinese laborers was totally prohibited.

The Japanese began immigrating to the United States—mainly to Hawaii—somewhat later than the Chinese; several anti-Japanese organizations campaigned to prevent their continuing entry. During World

War II, the entire Japanese population, including Nisei (second generation Japanese—U. S. citizens), was removed by military decree from
the cities of the West Coast and interned in security camps in the desert
and the Rocky Mountains, allegedly because they might be disloyal to
the United States. These Japanese Americans suffered the loss of some
$250 million as a result of this unprecedented invasion of civil liberties.
Although they have been better assimilated than the Chinese, who still
live in their own ghettos (except in Hawaii, where they are fully assimilated), the Japanese continue to be widely regarded as intruders into
American life.

The idea of the "melting pot," then, is something of a myth. The more
dissimilar a group has been in terms of race, ethnicity, religion, and
values from the dominant "Anglo-Saxon" culture, the more difficult has
been its incorporation into the mainstream. The United States is, in
fact, a plural society containing many different racial and ethnic subcultures whose mutual relationships are often antagonistic.

APPROACHING THE PROBLEM

The problem of race and ethnic relations in the United States may be
analyzed from the perspectives of both social disorganization and value
conflict.

From the social disorganization perspective, problems of race and
ethnic relations result in part from structural inequalities built into
American society; racial discrimination limits the opportunities of some
groups and prevents them from achieving social, economic, political,
and personal goals. Moreover, the formal values of American society,
which strongly endorse the principle of human equality, are not applied in reality; the socialization process of many Americans is such
that they internalize derogatory concepts of other groups and act toward them in prejudiced and discriminatory ways. Although racial
discrimination may be functional to those who benefit from it, it is
highly dysfunctional to those groups that are discriminated against.
Moreover, discrimination is dysfunctional to society as a whole, because
it generates conflict and places artificial barriers against the potential
contributions of millions of citizens. If society were better organized, so
that social practice conformed to the official social values of human dignity and equality of opportunity, the problem of race and ethnic relations
would tend to disappear.

From the value-conflict perspective, the problem of race and ethnic
relations arises because different groups in society have different values and different interests to maintain; it suits some groups to feel superior to and to exploit others, and they develop elaborate rationales to
justify their attitudes and actions. The subordinate groups, who hold
values contradictory to those of the dominant groups, develop feelings
of oppression and resentment and may come into sharp conflict with

the dominant groups. Social conflict theorists often see conflict as potentially valuable to society because it may serve as a mechanism for change. They point to the fact that black Americans were successfully discriminated against for perhaps thirteen or fourteen generations, and usually accepted their plight with relative passivity; but as soon as they openly challenged the social order and created severe conflict in America, national attention was focused on their problems, a series of civil rights acts was passed, overt discrimination declined abruptly, and blacks made many economic gains. Conflict theorists predict that similar gains will be made by other groups when they take action to bring about change, as American Indians and Mexican Americans are now beginning to do.

Prejudice and Discrimination

Any discussion of race and ethnic relations centers around the concepts of prejudice and discrimination. *Prejudice* refers to "prejudged" *attitudes* toward other people or objects, whereas *discrimination* refers to *actions* directed against another group on the grounds of supposed group characteristics. Prejudice and discrimination are the opposite sides of the same coin, but they should not be confused. It is possible, for example, to be prejudiced against a group, but not to discriminate against them in practice; and it is also possible to discriminate against a group—perhaps because one's job demands it—without feeling any personal prejudice against its members. The distinction between prejudice and discrimination was first made evident in a classic study conducted in 1934. A Chinese couple was sent on an extended tour of the United States, during which they stopped at some 250 hotels and restaurants. In only one case were they refused service: that is, they were discriminated against. The researchers then sent letters to each of the 250 establishments inquiring whether they would serve "members of the Chinese race." Half of the hotels and restaurants ignored the query, but over 90 percent of those that replied indicated that they would not accept Chinese: that is, they were prejudiced against them. When they were presented with real-life Chinese, however, they had failed to translate their prejudice into discrimination.[4]

Sociologist Robert K. Merton has devised a model containing four different types of persons and their characteristic prejudice or discrimination responses to other groups:

The unprejudiced nondiscriminator adheres to the formal values of American democracy and upholds American ideals of freedom and equality in both belief and practice. He or she is a champion of the underdog and takes traditional American principles seriously.

The unprejudiced discriminator is not personally prejudiced but may sometimes discriminate when it is expedient to do so because he or she

[4]Richard T. LaPierre, "Attitudes Versus Action," *Social Forces*, 13 (December 1934), pp. 230–237.

may suffer loss of status or financial disadvantage by failing to discriminate.

The prejudiced nondiscriminator feels hostile to other groups, but recognizes that law and social pressures are opposed to overt discrimination. Reluctantly, he or she does not translate prejudice into action.

The prejudiced discriminator discriminates against other groups in both word and deed. He or she does not believe in the values of freedom and equality and consistently acts on the basis of prejudiced feelings.[5]

The nature of prejudice. Social scientists have devoted a good deal of attention to the phenomenon of prejudice. Essentially, the prejudiced person is someone who maintains a rigid mental image of a group and applies it indiscriminately to all members of that group. This rigid image is termed a *stereotype*. A prejudiced person may, for example, harbor a stereotype of the "inscrutable" Chinese, or of the "miserly" Jews, or of the "lazy" blacks. The stereotype is not easily altered by the presentation of evidence that contradicts it. If the prejudiced person believes that some group has a particular characteristic and encounters a member of the group who obviously does not share the characteristic, this evidence is simply taken as "the exception that proves the rule." Stereotyped thinking, combined with a consistent refusal to test the stereotype against reality, are fundamental to prejudiced thinking.

Many studies have shown that prejudiced people make little attempt to check their mental stereotypes against social reality. One of the most dramatic experiments illustrating this fact was conducted by Eugene Hartley, who gave his subjects a long list of races and nationalities and asked for their reactions. Prejudiced people responded negatively not only to Jews and blacks, but also to the Danireans, the Wallonians, and the Pireneans. They recommended discriminatory acts against these last three peoples, such as refusing them admission to the United States or even expelling all those presently living here. In fact, the Danireans, the Wallonians, and Pireneans do not even exist; they were dreamed up by Hartley to see if people prejudiced against existing groups would also be prejudiced against nonexisting ones. His experiment showed that over three-quarters of the people who were prejudiced against Jews and blacks proved to be prejudiced against fictitious people whom they could never have met or heard anything about. Clearly, then, prejudiced attitudes are learned through contact with prejudiced people, rather than through contact with the people toward whom prejudice is directed.[6]

Other studies have indicated that the thinking of prejudiced people is often confused and inconsistent: they tend to believe any statement

[5]Robert K. Merton, "Discrimination and the American Creed," in *Discrimination and National Welfare*, ed. Robert M. MacIver (New York: Harper & Bros., 1949).
[6]Eugene Hartley, *Problems in Prejudice* (New York: King's Crown Press, 1946).

that feeds their prejudice, even if several of these statements contradict each other. In a test designed to measure attitudes toward Jews, Gordon W. Allport deliberately inserted unfavorable propositions that were mutually inconsistent. He included, for example, pairs of items that dealt with the "seclusiveness" and "intrusiveness" of Jews—two mutually contradictory characteristics. Here are two such pairs:

> —Much resentment against Jews stems from their tending to keep apart and exclude gentiles from Jewish social life.
> —The Jews should not pry too much into Christian activities and organizations nor seek so much recognition and prestige from Christians.

and:

> —Jews tend to remain a foreign element in American society, to preserve their old social standards and resist the American way of life.
> —Jews go too far in hiding their Jewishness, especially such extremes as changing their names, straightening their noses, and imitating Christian manners and customs.

Allport found that nearly three-quarters of those who dislike Jews for being "intrusive" also dislike them for being "seclusive." Similarly, those who dislike them for being capitalistic and controlling business also dislike them for being communistic and subversive; those who dislike them for begging from others also dislike them for having too much money, and so on. Clearly, genuine group characteristics are not at issue; prejudiced people are simply seeking any justification for their attitudes.[7]

The nature of discrimination. Discrimination may take many forms, but discriminatory practices can be conveniently divided into two main types: legal discrimination and institutional discrimination.

Legal discrimination refers to discriminatory acts and policies that are encoded in the law of the land. Throughout most of American history, racial discrimination was written into our statutes. The laws prohibiting Chinese immigration are one example; the series of laws enforcing segregation in the South provides another. These laws resulted from existing feelings of prejudice and served to legalize existing patterns of discrimination, but they had the further effect of reinforcing prejudicial attitudes by restricting intergroup contact and making segregation seem natural and respectable. Laws that discriminate between the various racial groups in the United States have been repealed or struck down by the Supreme Court since the middle of the present century, and are now considered unconstitutional.

---

[7]Gordon W. Allport, *The Nature of Prejudice* (Garden City, N.Y.: Anchor Books, 1958).

Institutional discrimination refers to discriminatory acts and policies that are not officially practiced or legally endorsed, but are nonetheless pervasive in the major institutions of society such as the economy, political life, education, or the legal system. Institutional discrimination is based on traditional patterns of behavior and is very difficult to eradicate; it is usually impossible to prove, for example, that a person was refused employment on the grounds of race, and it is therefore difficult to apply corrective action. The removal of legal discrimination against racial minorities in the United States has not eliminated institutional discrimination, as many indices ranging from housing patterns to average-income levels confirm. (American women are currently discovering that the same is true in their case: laws that discriminate against them are being repealed, but they are still vulnerable to institutional discrimination in many areas of society.)

The causes of prejudice and discrimination. Why should one group be prejudiced against another, even to the point where it applies discrimination? Ideas about the superiority of any one race or ethnic group have no scientific standing whatever, but they are believed in and used as a basis for attitudes and actions that sour race and ethnic relations and have many undesirable social consequences. Why should this be? Several theories have been proposed, and it is probable that elements of all of them can help to account for prejudice and discrimination in the contemporary United States.

Historical factors. If two racial groups have a history of hostility between them, prejudice and discrimination are likely to become institutionalized in their relationships. American whites and American Indians, for example, were extremely antagonistic toward each other from a very early point in our history. Each group developed negative stereotypes about the other, and these attitudes have persisted to this day. Similarly, American blacks were kept as slaves for generations and had to be defined as childlike, undisciplined, and inferior—one could hardly make a slave of someone whom one defined as one's equal. These attitudes have become deeply embedded and have persisted long after the abolition of slavery.

Economic factors. When groups of people compete for the same economic goals, hostility often arises between them. The strong feelings that established Americans showed against Chinese immigration in California or European immigration in the cities of the East Coast seems to have stemmed largely from a fear of economic competition. Some social scientists believe that much contemporary anti-black prejudice among white workers derives from a feeling that blacks, no longer willing to do only the lowest-paid work, represent an economic threat.

Cultural factors. As we have seen, most groups tend to take an ethnocentric attitude toward other groups and to believe that their own culture, religion, habits, values, and norms are superior to those of others. When the less privileged groups have long been denied access to equal housing, education, or employment opportunities, they will inevitably appear inferior in many respects to more privileged groups, thus confirming the latter groups' contemptuous view of them. The "superior" group may forget that the characteristics of the "inferior" group are the product of environmental factors and may believe they are inevitable attributes of the group in question, so that prejudice against them seems well-founded.

Political factors. It often suits one group to maintain political control over another — especially if, as in the case of slavery in the old South, it derives economic benefits from this control. Some groups have always found it politically expedient to encourage negative stereotypes of other groups. The political objective of fulfilling America's "manifest destiny" of expansion to the West Coast required that the possessors of the land in question — Indians and Mexicans — be negatively defined. Similarly, white supremacists, whose interests would be undermined if blacks had full voting rights, introduced many discriminatory laws to prevent blacks from exercising their franchise.

Psychological factors. Research evidence suggests that some people tend to have an "authoritarian personality": they are intolerant, insecure, highly conformist, submissive to their superiors and bullying to those they consider socially inferior, and are apt to think in categorical, stereotyped terms.[8] People who have these personality traits are disproportionately likely to be prejudiced against groups other than their own. Another psychological mechanism that may lead to prejudice and discrimination is "scapegoating" — placing the blame for one's troubles on some group that is incapable of offering resistance. The most outstanding historical example of scapegoating was the Nazi treatment of the Jews, who were conveniently blamed for Germany's economic misfortunes.

All of these factors may reinforce one another, until prejudice and discrimination are deeply rooted in society and very difficult to combat, especially in the short term.

MINORITIES IN CONTEMPORARY AMERICA

In the broadest sense, there are an infinite number of minorities in the United States, ranging from red-haired people to vegetarians. Sociologists, however, use the word "minority" in a special sense to refer to a group that is considered "different" and suffers in consequence. Louis Wirth defines a minority as:

[8]Theodore W. Adorno, et al., *The Authoritarian Personality* (New York: W. W. Norton, 1950).

a group of people who, because of their physical or cultural characteristics, are singled out from the others in the society in which they live for differential and unequal treatment, and who therefore regard themselves as objects of collective discrimination. The existence of a minority in a society implies the existence of a corresponding dominant group with higher social status and greater privileges. Minority status carries with it the exclusion from full participation in the life of the society.[9]

In effect, then, any group other than the dominant, white Anglo-Saxon Protestant ("WASP") majority is a "minority" group in American society. Let us look more closely at those minorities whose problems have attracted the most public attention in recent years—the blacks, the Indians, the Chicanos, and the "white ethnics."

Blacks

The largest minority group in the United States is the blacks, who number over 24 million or about 12 percent of the population. Throughout most of their history in America, the blacks have been concentrated in the South and have served as agricultural laborers or menial domestic servants. During the course of this century, however, there has been a massive migration of blacks to the cities of the North and a corresponding urbanization of blacks in the South; today, half of the black population live in the North and some 70 percent of all blacks live in metropolitan areas. The movement from the traditional rural environment to the more heterogeneous urban context has tended to enhance black consciousness of their oppression and has contributed to the increasing militancy that blacks have shown throughout this century.

The history of the black American has been one of sustained oppression, discrimination, and denial of basic civil rights and human dignity. Brought to this country as slaves, blacks were kept in servitude for generations. The myth of their racial inferiority—their irresponsibility, promiscuity, laziness, and lower intelligence—was assiduously propagated as a justification for their continued subjugation. The whip or even the lynch mob served as a means of asserting social control over those slaves who challenged the established order.

Even after the emancipation of slaves in 1863, wholesale discrimination was practiced against black Americans. Many states passed segregation laws designed to keep the races apart in schools, housing, restaurants, and other public facilities, and institutionalized discrimination kept blacks in the lowest-paid jobs. A variety of methods, such as rigged "literacy" tests, were used to keep them off the voters' rolls and thus to prevent them from exercising their democratic rights. Discriminatory laws continued to be enacted in Southern states until the middle of the present century.

[9]Quoted in George Eaton Simpson and J. Milton Yinger, *Racial and Cultural Minorities: An Analysis of Prejudice and Discrimination,* 3d ed. (New York: Harper & Row, 1965), p. 16.

Many black Americans are reaffirming their ties to African culture and emphasizing the distinctive contributions Afro-Americans can make to American life. This pride in cultural heritage has served as a stimulating example for many other minority groups. *(Charles Moore/Black Star)*

As the Swedish sociologist Gunnar Myrdal pointed out in his classic work *An American Dilemma*,[10] the treatment of black Americans was totally at variance with the American creed of human equality and with the deep concern for civil rights that is written into the Constitution. Myrdal predicted that the tension between egalitarian values and discriminatory practices would eventually grow intolerable. He was eventually proved right.

Changes were at first slow. Earlier in this century black organizations, such as the National Association for the Advancement of Colored People (NAACP), were remarkably compromising and tolerant in their approach to the situation: they presented petitions, tried to negotiate improvements in the economic and social status of blacks, or used legal channels to challenge the validity of existing discriminatory statutes. In fact, the most significant advances were made by the United States Supreme Court, which after World War II began to whittle away at the structure of racial segregation in America. The most important decision of the court was in the case of *Brown v. Board of Education*, in which the court ruled that "separate educational facilities are inherently unequal";[11] and a year later the court ordered schools to be desegregated

[10]Gunnar Myrdal, *An American Dilemma* (New York: Harper & Bros., 1944).
[11]*Brown v. Board of Education*, 347 U.S. 483 (1954).

"with all deliberate speed,"[12] although for another fifteen years little was done to implement this decision. This new doctrine—that separate facilities are necessarily unequal—was gradually extended by the court to a number of other public facilities, ranging from golf courses to beaches. The court progressively struck down a series of legal pretexts that had been used to deny blacks their voting rights, as well as various segregation laws, such as those banning interracial marriage. But a great deal of legal discrimination remained on the statute books, and institutionalized discrimination remained the American norm.

By the late fifties black Americans would no longer tolerate discrimination. Young blacks, often aided by radical white students, began to "sit in" at segregated restaurants, demanding service. Protesters went on "freedom rides" to desegregate buses and terminals. Massive campaigns for voter registration were mounted in a climate of growing violence; dozens of young volunteer campaigners were murdered and hundreds were injured. But the mood for change was irresistible and by the start of the sixties a major civil rights movement had arisen. In 1963 over 20,000 protesters were arrested in Southern states, and in one civil rights demonstration 200,000 marchers converged on Washington. The federal government responded. President John F. Kennedy ordered school desegregation in the South, and Attorney General Robert F. Kennedy sent federal marshals to Southern schools to enforce the order. President Kennedy also presented to Congress a sweeping civil rights bill, which empowered federal agencies to deny funds to localities and institutions that practiced discrimination in accommodations, employment, and other areas; the bill was enacted the following year.

The changes, however, came too late to prevent violence. In 1964 riots erupted in the streets of New York, Chicago, and Philadelphia. The following year there was a major riot in the Watts area of Los Angeles; the disturbance continued for several days at a cost of thirty-four lives, hundreds of injuries, and $35 million in destroyed property. In 1966 there were some forty-three outbreaks of rioting, with particularly serious episodes in Chicago and Cleveland, and in 1967 there were eight major riots. The following year Dr. Martin Luther King, the leader of the civil rights movement, was shot down by a white assassin. The murder touched off a coast-to-coast wave of the most violent rioting yet seen; in Washington the flames could be seen from the Capitol and the White House. Within a week, Congress enacted a new civil rights bill—one which had been pending for the previous two years—in order to end discrimination in housing.

The rioting finally subsided, but it left a new mood among black Americans. Feelings of pride replaced feelings of inferiority; slogans declared that "black is beautiful"; and the black community showed signs of unprecedented self-confidence. Equally important, many black

---

[12]*Brown v. Board of Education,* 389 U.S. 294 (1955).

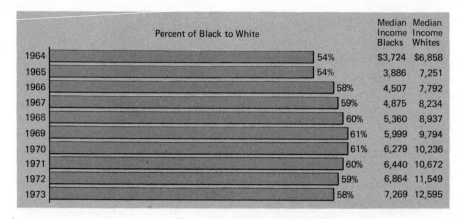

Percent of Black to White		Median Income Blacks	Median Income Whites
1964	54%	$3,724	$6,858
1965	54%	3,886	7,251
1966	58%	4,507	7,792
1967	59%	4,875	8,234
1968	60%	5,360	8,937
1969	61%	5,999	9,794
1970	61%	6,279	10,236
1971	60%	6,440	10,672
1972	59%	6,864	11,549
1973	58%	7,269	12,595

The income gap. During the 1960s blacks made remarkable economic advances. In the early 1970s, however, the income gap between the median income of black families and white families has grown wider. The gains of the sixties appear to have slowed down and in some cases have reversed. (SOURCE: U.S. Bureau of the Census, in *The New York Times* [July 24, 1974].)

leaders began to ask whether full integration into the American mainstream ought really to be the goal of the black minority—or whether blacks ought not to coexist with other groups in a plural society containing heterogeneous and distinctive communities living in mutual respect.

The elimination of legal barriers to black advancement has been a major gain for the black minority, but institutionalized discrimination is still rife in the United States. Housing is still segregated to a very large extent; for example, the 1970 census revealed that of the 2,159 census tracts in New York City, over two-thirds were more than 90 percent white or 90 percent black.[13] This pattern is repeated in city after city across America. Schools remain largely segregated in practice, and because the black communities are among the most economically depressed in the nation and therefore the least able to support educational facilities, the quality of schooling is relatively poor. Although blacks represent 12 percent of the population, only 8.3 percent of college graduates are black. Institutional discrimination, reinforced by poor educational opportunities, has kept the median black income in 1973 to only 58 percent of the median white income; in fact, the income gap between the two groups is currently widening.[14]

Race relations between black and white still leave much to be desired. A Harris poll found in 1971 that 81 percent of all blacks believe that "whites feel that blacks are inferior"; 79 percent believe that "whites give blacks a break only when forced to"; and 70 percent believe that "whites are really sorry slavery for blacks was abolished."

[13]*New York Times* (March 6, 1972).
[14]*New York Times* (July 24, 1974).

Blacks felt that most institutions — such as churches, the federal government, state governments, police forces, and corporations — "really don't care" about blacks achieving full equality; only the Supreme Court and television are thought to have a concern for the status of blacks.

Many whites still harbor negative stereotypes about blacks. A 1971 Harris poll showed that 40 percent of whites believe that "blacks have lower morals than whites"; 39 percent, that "blacks want to live off the hand-out"; 37 percent, that "blacks have less native intelligence"; 27 percent, that "blacks breed crime"; and 22 percent, that "blacks are inferior to whites."[15] Another Harris poll in 1973 found that although 89 percent of whites want to see "equality for blacks," some 57 percent believe that "blacks are asking for more than they are ready for" and 52 percent believe blacks are "trying to move too fast in their push for equality." Although these views are a considerable improvement on those revealed in polls a decade earlier, it is clear that black Americans are not yet accepted as equals by many of their white fellow citizens.

American Indians

The 600,000 Indians, or native Americans, have been so effectively segregated from our national life that their problems were virtually unknown to other citizens until the emergence of a "Red Power" movement in the late sixties. Few minority groups have been as consistently denigrated or treated in terms of such absurdly false stereotypes as the American Indians.

When the early colonists and pioneers found the Indians standing in the way of their westward advance, they adopted a policy which in many cases came very close to deliberate extermination. "The only good Indian," it was said, "is a dead one." The advancing whites rapidly developed ethnocentric attitudes toward the Indians: they thought of themselves, for example, as "pioneers" rather than "invaders," and viewed the Indians' resistance as the product of cruel savagery rather than stubborn nationalism. These early stereotypes have become deeply embedded in our historical consciousness. The American Indian scholar Alvin M. Josephy, Jr., points out:

> The relating of American history by white historians has reflected their own Western-civilization-based point of view, as well might have been expected, but what they wrote has also been self-serving. The frontier Indian, resisting white expansion and exploitation, *had* to be a skulking savage. To the seeker of his land, he *had* to be an aimless nomad. To the civilizer, he *had* to be lazy. Even the romantic, the poet, and the philosopher had to give the Indian a false image: to them he was the noble child of nature. To almost no one could he be real.[16]

[15]Louis Harris, *The Anguish of Change* (New York: W. W. Norton, 1973), pp. 233–237.
[16]Alvin M. Josephy, Jr., "Indians in History," *Atlantic Monthly,* 225 (June 1970), p. 69.

Inspired by the success of the black civil rights movement, American Indians have begun a militant campaign for political autonomy. After years of enduring discrimination, Indians are demanding respect for the dignity of their culture. *(Gary Renaud/Magnum)*

Once the culture of the Indians had been almost destroyed and the bulk of their lands taken from them, the federal government was left with the problem of how to deal with the shattered tribes that remained. After the Civil War, government reservations were established for the Indians, and in 1871 Congress determined that no Indian tribe would ever be recognized as an independent entity again. All Indians were made wards of the federal government, without any rights of citizenship. A government report of 1890 reveals the contemporary attitude toward the Indians and their future. Indians, the report noted, are "cowards in warfare," "treacherous," "the embodiment of cruelty," "filled with insatiable greed," "low in instincts," and lacking in "reasoning powers." The report pointed out:

> Being the original occupant and owner of the lands, the Indian can not see why he should give way, go to the wall, or move to parts unknown. He cannot understand the profit to him and his by being despoiled first and absorbed afterward. . . . In all future dealings with the reservation Indians, . . . teach the Indian that it pays to be clean, to be industrious, to have but one wife . . . and teach him to follow the best habits of the white people. Show him that it is to his interest to be like other men.[17]

Not until 1924 was the right of American citizenship extended to the Indians — the original inhabitants of the land.

[17] *Indians Taxed and Indians Not Taxed in the United States at the 11th Census: 1890* (Washington, D.C.: n.p., 1894), p. 63.

The social and economic conditions of the Indians in the United States are probably worse than those of any other minority group. The average Indian has only five years of schooling. The average family income is only $1,500 a year. The unemployment rate is a staggering 45 percent.[18] The suicide rate is far above the national average. The average Indian life expectancy is 44 years—more than 25 years below the national average. Indians have by far the highest infant mortality rate of any minority group in the United States (among Alaskan Eskimos, one child in four dies before his or her first birthday). Many reservation Indians live in unheated log houses, tarpaper shacks, old tents, and even old automobile bodies.[19] Their problems are compounded by the stereotyped images that most other Americans—reared on a media diet of Western movies—continue to apply to them. Sociologist Pierre van den Berghe has caustically charged that the Indian reservations have been reduced "to the status of human zoos for the amusement of tourists and the delight of anthropologists."[20]

Since the sixties a militant Indian movement has arisen, inspired by the success of the civil rights campaign. Indians have founded intertribal organizations and demanded "Red Power." Alcatraz Island was seized and "reclaimed" for the Indians, and the American Indian Movement (AIM) attracted international publicity by "capturing" the South Dakota town of Wounded Knee, scene of the historic defeat of the plains Indians. Like the black Americans, the Indians are now demanding not assimilation but respect for their own culture, not full integration but the right to control their own institutions.

Chicanos

The 5 million Chicanos, or Mexican Americans, are primarily Catholic, Spanish-speaking people in a predominantly Protestant, English-speaking country. For many years they have been regarded as aliens on American soil, although their ancestors had occupied the territories of the Southwest for over four centuries. It is only in recent years that they have slowly come to be regarded as a genuinely American minority, or what one writer refers to as "Americans on parole."[21]

The Chicanos, like most minority groups in the United States, are predominantly lower class. The average family income is about $6,000 per year, and some 3 million are living in poverty.[22] Urban Chicanos are concentrated in "barrios" (ghettos), while many of the rural population work as migrant farm laborers. The Chicanos' low earnings and restricted job opportunities result partly from institutionalized discrimination and prejudice against them, but also from poor education and

---

[18]Peter I. Rose, *They and We: Racial and Ethnic Relations in the United States,* 2d ed. (New York: Random House, 1974), p. 25.
[19]Robert Burnette, *The Tortured Americans* (Englewood Cliffs, N.J.: Prentice-Hall, 1971), p. 22.
[20]Quoted in Rose, *They and We,* p. 22.
[21]John Womack, Jr., "The Chicanos," *New York Review of Books,* vol. 19, no. 3 (August 31, 1972), p. 13.
[22]Ibid., p. 14.

The "Dirty" Language

You know it almost from the beginning; speaking Spanish makes you different. Your mother, father, brothers, sisters, and friends all speak Spanish. But the bus driver, the teacher, the policeman, the store clerk, the man who comes to collect the rent—all the people who are doing important things—do not. Then the day comes when your teacher—who has taught you the importance of many things—tells you that speaking Spanish is wrong. You go home, kiss your mother, and say a few words to her in Spanish. You go to the window and look out and your mother asks you what's the matter?

Nada, mama, you answer because you don't know what is wrong.

Howard A. Glickstein, then Acting Staff Director of the Commission, asked witness Edgar Lozano, a San Antonio high-school student, whether he has ever been punished for speaking Spanish at school. "Yes, in grammar, in junior high, and in senior high schools," he answers.

"I mean, how would you like for somebody to come up to you and tell you what you speak is a dirty language? You know, what your mother speaks is a dirty language. You know, that is the only thing I ever heard at home.

"A teacher comes up to you and tells you, 'No, no. You know that is a filthy language, nothing but bad words and bad thoughts in that language.'

"I mean, they are telling you that your language is bad. . . . Your mother and father speak a bad language, you speak a bad language. I mean, you communicate with dirty words, and nasty ideas."

Edgar, like many Mexican-Americans before him, had been scarred with the insults of an Anglo world which rejects everything except carbon copies of what it has decreed to be "American." You start being different and you end up being labeled as un-American.

SOURCE: Ruben Salazar, "Stranger in One's Land," U.S. Commission on Civil Rights, *Clearinghouse* (May 1970).

their generally limited facility in the English language. At home many Mexican American families use Spanish exclusively, and the children have little chance to learn English before entering school. The lack of fluency in English serves as a barrier to subsequent educational and employment opportunities.[23]

[23]Ellwyn R. Stoddard, *Mexican Americans* (New York: Random House, 1963), p. 161.

The economic exploitation of Chicano farm workers has been an explosive issue in California and parts of the Southwest ever since Cesar Chavez unionized migrant workers, brought them out on strike, and organized nationwide boycotts of fruit picked by underpaid workers. Powerful economic interests have deeply resented the work of Chavez, and there have been a number of violent attempts to break strikes that he has organized. Inevitably, Chavez's campaign has taken on political overtones, and since the late sixties Chicanos have organized themselves to run candidates in local elections; they have even founded the Raza Unida (united people) party. But the Chicanos' political attempts to improve their conditions have met with little success so far. Because Chicanos are often regarded as Mexican rather than American — as sojourners in the United States who can "go back home" if they are dissatisfied — other Americans have paid relatively little attention to their grievances. John Womack comments:

> Most galling to the [leaders], who expected to take off like the blacks, has been their manifest failure to touch many white consciences. As ignorant of the East as the East has been of them, they did not understand . . . that the special reservoirs of white guilt that the blacks could tap would never open to them . . . Only slowly have they learned that they can make gains only by their muscle.[24]

The Chicanos, like blacks and American Indians, are developing a fierce sense of group pride. This is particularly evident among the young; in 1968, for example, 15,000 Chicano schoolchildren in Los Angeles marched out of their high schools, demanding revised curricula that would detail Mexican contributions to their country, the end of punishments for the offense of speaking Spanish, and the transfer of racist teachers. A high school girl expresses the new consciousness:

> I am a Mexican-American. I was not always one. Once upon a time I was just a human being who had happened to be born in the United States. Sometime during the process of receiving my education I became a Mexican-American. Perhaps it was during my primary years when a teacher with blue eyes told me, "Wash your hands . . . *you people* always manage to be filthy . . ." or maybe it was the teacher who told me, "We don't want to hear you speaking *that language* here again. . . ." Somewhere along the road I learned that "*you* people" meant Mexican-American and "*that* language" meant Spanish. . . . They taught me many things and they taught other Mexicans, too. We learned our lessons well. Some of us majored in Hatred, which we stored up in our hearts until the day we could use it. Others took up Bitterness, which we engraved upon ourselves in forms of distrust against any Anglos. . . . I am a Mexican-American. I want my people to have their rights . . . I want to become more than a second-class citizen. I want to be proud of what I am.[25]

[24]Womack, "The Chicanos," p. 15.
[25]Quoted in Stoddard, *Mexican Americans*, p. 205.

Race relations between Chicanos and the "Anglos" of the Southwest remain poor, with many members of each group harboring highly negative stereotypes of the other. One study found that Chicanos generally view white Americans as conceited, inconstant, insincere, mercenary, exploitative, and unkind.[26] Many whites, for their part, hold the entire Mexican-American culture in contempt and resent the attempts of Chicanos to better their living conditions through strikes, boycotts, and political action.

White Ethnics

When the various ethnic groups came to the United States from Europe, they attempted as far as possible to become assimilated into American life: but they always retained some traditional ethnic loyalties and a sense of ethnic community. The seventies have been marked by an entirely unanticipated revival of ethnic sentiment in America — a revival that seems closely related to the emergence of militancy among racial minorities in the previous decade.

Although upper-class ethnics have tended to be absorbed fairly readily by the dominant WASP culture, the working-class ethnic groups have tended to live together in closely knit communities, particularly in the big cities. Irving M. Levine and Judith Herman note:

> In most of the cities where the white working class is ethnic — in the Northeast and Midwest particularly — common origin is reflected in distinctive neighborhoods. People tend to live near one another according to ethnic background, even "unto the fourth generation." For some, the choice is a conscious one, influenced by the presence of such institutions as the church. For others, the ethnic neighborhood is a convenience, maintaining some features of the extended family, lost (but yearned for) in more heterogeneous neighborhoods.[27]

These ethnic loyalties are strong, and they are often complemented by a resentment against the dominant "WASP" culture, whose members seem to have easy access to the heights of political, economic, and social power in the United States. Michael Novak, an American of Slavic ancestry, writes of the experience of growing up in America as a member of an ethnic minority:

> Growing up in America has been an assault upon my sense of worthiness. . . . All my life, I have been made to feel a slight uneasiness when I must say my name. Under challenge in grammer school concerning my nationality, I had been instructed by my father to announce proudly, "American." When my family moved

---

[26]Ozzie G. Simmons, "The Mutual Images and Expectations of Anglo Americans and Mexican Americans," *Daedalus,* vol. 90, no. 2 (Spring 1961), pp. 286–299.

[27]Irving M. Levine and Judith Herman, "The Life of the White Ethnics," *Dissent,* 19 (Winter 1972), p. 290.

White-ethnic America has found its voice and is insisting that it too be heard. "Irish Power," "Polish Power," and "Italian Power" indicate that the ethnic minorities will no longer be silent. *(Bob Adelman/Magnum)*

from the Slovak ghetto . . . to the WASP suburb on the hill, my mother impressed upon us how well we must be dressed, and show good manners, and behave—people think of us as "different" and we mustn't give them any cause. . . .

Nowhere in my schooling do I recall an attempt to put me in touch with my own history. The strategy was clearly to make an American of me. English literature, American literature; and even the history books, as I recall them, were peopled mainly by Anglo-Saxons. . . . I don't remember feeling envy or regret: a feeling, perhaps, of unimportance, of remoteness, of not having heft enough to count.

We did not feel this country belonged to us. We felt fierce pride in it, more loyalty than anyone could know. But we felt blocked at every turn.[28]

Like all other minority groups, then, the ethnic minorities have been made to feel "different," and have to some extent accepted the relatively unfavorable image that the dominant culture has of them.

The new racial consciousness of black Americans has had a profound impact on the ethnic groups. Black consciousness has legitimated

[28]Michael Novak, "White Ethnic," *Harper's,* 243 (September 1971), pp. 4–5.

A Burning Silence

I am born of PIGS—those Poles, Italians, Greeks, and Slavs, non-English-speaking immigrants, numbered so heavily among the workingmen of this nation. Not particularly liberal, nor radical, born into a history not white Anglo-Saxon and not Jewish—born outside what in America is considered the intellectual mainstream. And thus privy to neither power nor status nor intellectual voice.

Those Poles of Buffalo and Milwaukee—so notoriously taciturn, sullen, nearly speechless. Who has ever understood them? It is not that Poles do not feel emotion: what is their history if not dark passion, romanticism, betrayal, courage, blood? But where in America is there anywhere a language for voicing what a Christian Pole in this nation feels? He has no Polish culture left him, no Polish tongue. Yet Polish feelings do not go easily into the idiom of happy America, the America of the Anglo-Saxons and, yes, in the arts, the Jews. (The Jews have long been a culture of the word, accustomed to exile, skilled in scholarship and in reflection. The Christian Poles are largely of peasant origin, free men for hardly more than a hundred years.) Of what shall the man of Buffalo think, on his way to work in the mills, departing from his relatively dreary home and street? What roots does he have? What language of the heart is available to him?

The PIGS are not silent willingly. The silence burns like hidden coals in the chest.

SOURCE: Michael Novak, "White Ethnic," *Harper's* (September 1971).

cultural pluralism in America: for the first time, a minority group has asserted its right to be different, instead of attempting to minimize its differences. The example has not been lost on the white ethnics, who have rapidly come to regard their ethnicity as a source of potential pride not only in their community, but also in the wider society.

But there is a deeper reason for the surge of white ethnic sentiment—a strong resentment against the WASP majority for appearing to favor black Americans over other working-class groups, and a resentment at the blacks themselves for breaking the "rules of the game" and not "waiting in line" for their turn to rise in the American social hierarchy as other groups have done before them. Novak speaks of his regret that the educated WASP does not feel for the ethnic groups

that same sympathy that the educated find so easy to conjure up for black culture, Chicano culture, Indian culture, and other cultures of the poor. . . . Why do the educated classes find it so difficult to want to understand the man who drives a beer truck, or the fellow with a helmet working on a site across the street with plumbers and electricians, while their sensitivities race easily to Mississippi or even Bedford-Stuyvesant?[29]

Sociologist Peter Rose describes how white ethnic feeling has grown in the seventies as a backlash reaction to the supposed success of the blacks in breaking the rules of the game and extorting benefits from guilt-ridden WASP policy makers. The ethnics, Rose suggests, take the view that

The earlier immigrants faced great difficulties and obstacles, but they accepted the challenges and internalized the values of the wider society, values that were quite often alien to their own heritages. . . . They knew what it meant to be helped by others in similar straits and how to use certain public institutions to advantage — especially the schools, political machines, and, eventually, the civil service. But what they also knew, and this is perhaps the most persistent theme, was that one could not ask for special favors because of background or by pleading "special conditions."

Given these sentiments, it is not surprising that many white ethnics reacted with astonishment at the seeming capitulation being made to demands by blacks and other nonwhites for group rights and privileges. "Nobody ever gave us that kind of treatment," they began saying. "Who in the hell do they think they are?" . . . A growing resolve to get their own share arose. A sense of righteous indignation at being put down by those above them to satisfy the demands from below became more and more apparent. . . . Many argued that they were loyal, decent, hard-working, God-fearing and patriotic Americans who had had nothing to do with slavery or with segregation but were being forced to pay for the sins of other peoples' fathers.[30]

Black power, then, is indirectly responsible for pluralism having become more respectable, legitimate, and even institutionalized than ever before in American history. Many Americans are no longer criticizing our society because it fails to serve as a "melting pot"; instead, they are questioning the very desirability of a "melted," homogeneous nation. Good race relations, it is argued, are quite compatible with a plural society — provided the various groups interact on the basis of equality and mutual respect.

THE SOCIAL COSTS OF PREJUDICE AND DISCRIMINATION

Prejudice and discrimination against racial or ethnic groups exact many social costs in contemporary America.

[29]·Ibid., p. 5.
[30]Rose, *They and We*, pp. 226–227.

Economic costs. Any society that erects artificial barriers against full participation by a substantial number of its citizens invites economic losses. In the United States many forms of institutional discrimination deny minority group members the opportunity to contribute to their society and to exploit their talents to the full; and the entire nation suffers in consequence. Moreover, federal and local agencies have to invest additional sums in controlling or treating the many personal problems and pathologies — such as riots, crime, alcoholism, or poverty — that result in part from discrimination.

Political costs. Discrimination and prejudice generate poor race relations and lead to tension and antagonism between the groups in question. The hostility between groups poisons interpersonal relations and can culminate in open conflict, including rioting and other forms of civil strife. The attention of government and administrative agencies is diverted from other pressing national problems while race-relations problems create a persistent climate of political instability.

Psychological costs. Discrimination and prejudice can have severe psychological effects on minority group members — particularly when the group collectively internalizes and accepts the derogatory stereotypes that others apply to it. People who are persistently denied full human dignity may have diminished feelings of self-worth. Studies conducted in the sixties, for example, indicated that black children had a clear preference for white dolls or playmates; white children, however, prefered their own group. The implication is that the black children had much lower self-esteem.[31]

Personal costs. For minority group members the personal costs of prejudice and discrimination are multiple. There is a strong relationship between membership in a minority group, educational attainment, and income level. The minority group member is likely to be poorly educated, and so tends to earn less and to rear his or her children in a depressed neighborhood with low-quality schools — and so the cycle repeats itself in the next generation. Institutionalized discrimination makes it difficult to break out of the cycle: in the 1970 census, for example, it was found that the unemployment rate for all males was 6 percent, and among minority males aged between sixteen and twenty-four the rate was much higher: for Chicanos, 14.3 percent; for blacks, 20.1 percent; and for Puerto Ricans, 25.4 percent. Lack of job opportunities traps minority group members in the lower stratum of society, where life expectancy is shorter, crime rates higher, drug addiction more common, and marital breakdown much more frequent. None of these personal problems is directly linked to the race of the individual; they are simply consequences of the social environment in which that particular group habitually lives.

[31]Kenneth J. Moreland, "Race Awareness Among American and Hong Kong, Chinese Children," *American Journal of Sociology*, 2 (November 1969), pp. 360–374.

International costs. Few Americans realize the extent to which the international reputation of the United States is damaged by our continuing intergroup tensions and institutionalized discrimination. The United States seeks to win support around the globe for values of liberty and equality, yet continues to tolerate a system of stratification in which the boundaries of racial or ethnic groups are tied to those of social class. Indeed, foreign diplomats in the United States frequently complain of being mistaken for, and hence treated like, members of American minority groups. Understandably, the nations of the world—most are nonwhite—look askance at our domestic race relations.

PROSPECTS FOR THE FUTURE

What are the prospects for improved race relations in the United States, and what patterns of intergroup relations are likely to emerge in the future?

Prospects for Improved Race Relations

Most indications are that American race relations, despite—or perhaps because of—the turmoil of the sixties, are slowly but perceptibly improving. Opinion polls show a very marked shift in white attitudes toward tolerance of other groups. In 1942 only 35 percent of whites would not have objected to a black neighbor; by 1956, 51 percent would not object; and by 1968, some 65 percent were willing to have a black neighbor.[32] The number of whites who feel that blacks are inferior to whites has dropped from 31 percent in 1963 to 22 percent in 1971. The overwhelming majority of whites now declare that they believe in racial equality.[33] A majority of blacks—52 percent—believe that they are making "progress" in American society, and blacks now profess to favor nonviolence over violence by a margin of 75 percent to 6 percent. Faith in the federal government as a source of assistance has dropped sharply, however: some 72 percent of blacks relied on the federal government for improvements during Kennedy's presidency, but their numbers dropped to a scant 3 percent under the Nixon administration.[34]

Blacks have made considerable economic and political progress since the early sixties. In 1961, 13 percent of blacks earned over $10,000 per year, but by 1971 their number had risen to 30 percent. Many blacks, however, remain in poverty; about 5 million collect some form of welfare payment.[35] Blacks have been elected to the mayorships of many American cities, including Los Angeles, Cleveland, Newark, Cincinnati, and Washington. In 1974 they held nearly three thousand elective offices in the United States—well over double the number held at

---

[32]Jerome H. Skolnick, *The Politics of Protest* (New York: Simon & Schuster, 1969), p. 181.
[33]Harris, *The Anguish of Change*, pp. 230–236.
[34]Ibid., pp. 231–233.
[35]"America's Rising Black Middle Class," *Time* (June 17, 1974).

The ideal of cultural assimilation has a long history in the United States—but the reality is very different. Those groups who shared the racial, cultural, and religious characteristics of the dominant group were readily assimilated; but those groups that differed in significant respects have never been fully accepted. *(Dennis Stock/Magnum)*

the start of the decade—yet only one of these elected public officials was a senator and only fifteen were representatives. Demographic trends, however, are placing blacks in a position to hold the balance of political power in many Northern communities, and their power in the South will continue to increase.

The American Indians' demands are being taken seriously by the federal government, and the most likely future trend will be toward increasing Indian self-government. The federal Bureau of Indian Affairs is currently making contracts with Indian tribes in terms of which the Indians assume management and control over their reservations. In due course all the reservations are likely to be controlled entirely by the Indians who live on them, and not by the distant federal government. The old stereotype of the Indian as a "savage redskin" will die hard, but already Western movies are portraying Indians in a much more accurate and sympathetic light.

There is a growing feeling among Chicanos that they should resist attempts to "Americanize" them at the expense of their own language and distinctive culture. But they will also have to attract more national attention to their plight, which policy makers have so far tended to ignore. It is scarcely conceivable that the federal government or any state government would allow 5 million WASP Americans to endure the wages and other conditions that the Chicanos suffer, and Chicano militants will have to concentrate on alerting public concern to the deprivation suffered by their people if significant changes are to be made. Like the other racial and ethnic groups, Chicanos may be expected to insist on changes in school curricula, particularly history. A sense of group pride inevitably rests to a great extent on an awareness of historical background and cultural achievements — especially when current conditions are depressing and humiliating.

The prejudice and discrimination that still exist in the United States cannot be banished immediately, by law or any other means. Laws are important, however; as Dr. Martin Luther King once observed:

> The law may not make a man love me, but it can restrain him from lynching me, and I think that's pretty important.[36]

And laws are important not only for their immediate practical effects; they also tend to shape public opinion in the long run even when they initially lack strong popular support.

A more controversial method of combating prejudice and institutionalized discrimination is the busing of children from segregated schools, both to improve the standard of minority children's education and to encourage the more tolerant racial attitudes that are known to develop if different groups are in daily contact with one another. (The busing controversy is discussed in more detail in the chapter on education.) Education in tolerant attitudes — primarily through the schools and the media — is a vital tool in combating prejudice, for prejudice is simply an attitude that is learned through the socialization process.

"Affirmative action" programs are another controversial method of ending employment discrimination and opening up opportunities for minority group members. The programs usually involve establishing quotas in order to ensure that a minimum number of minority group applicants receive appointments to jobs or admissions to educational institutions. The federal government is empowered to withhold funds from certain public institutions and programs that do not practice affirmative action policies. Ethnic minorities, who, unlike racial minorities, are not eligible for the programs, tend to resent the advantages that affirmative action offers to the racial minorities. Some employers and colleges, too, are reluctant to appoint applicants or admit students on the ground of minority group membership rather than strictly according to merit. The issue is a delicate one, but no other means has been found to prevent subtle discrimination against racial minorities in hiring and admission procedures.

Future Patterns of Race and Ethnic Relations

The resurgence of group pride among so many American minorities during the last decade has severely shaken many American assumptions about the desirability of assimilation and integration.

[36]Quoted in Rose, *They and We*, p. 103.

Race and Ethnic Relations: A Theoretical Review

The social problem of race and ethnic relations represents the gap between a *social ideal* of a nation free of racial and ethnic prejudice, discrimination, and strife, and the *social reality* of a society marked by continuing hostile relations and even outright conflict between its component groups. Hostile relationships between the various groups in America have been a continuing social problem in our society—a problem which remains to this day and of which the end is not yet in sight.

The *social-disorganization* perspective provides a valuable insight into the nature of our problem of race and ethnic relations. Our society is severely disorganized in that there is a striking inconsistency between our official commitment to human dignity and equality and our continuing practice of institutionalized discrimination against minority groups. Although the popular myth has it that the United States serves as a melting pot for different racial and ethnic groups, the fact of the matter is that new arrivals have been assimilated only to the degree that they already shared the cultural, racial, and religious attributes of the dominant white, Anglo-Saxon, Protestant majority. The earliest European immigrants were almost entirely composed of members of this "WASP" group, and they quickly took control of social, political, and economic power in the United States—power which they have managed to retain ever since. The United States is now organized as a stratified society, with the boundaries of social class often superimposed on the boundaries of race. Racial minorities often suffer low socio-economic status in addition to prejudice, and they have to fight the many disadvantages of poverty as well as the institutionalized discrimination that limits their opportunities. Although racial and ethnic discrimination may be functional to those who benefit by it—for example, by eliminating possible economic competitors from minority groups—it is, of course, highly dysfunctional for the groups that are discriminated against, and is also dysfunctional for society as a whole. Any arbitrary barrier against the fulfillment of human potential can only result in costs to the entire society.

Social disorganization contributes to the problems of racial and ethnic relations, but poor race relations also contribute to further social disorganization. Bad race relations generate tension and conflict; they cause economic losses through the underutilization of talent; they divert social resources that might be applied to other pressing problems; they undermine the self-esteem of millions of citizens and generate a multitude of personal problems.

The *value-conflict* perspective is also useful in the analysis of race and ethnic relations. It is clear that many people have very different value orientations to the problem. Most groups tend to be rather ethnocentric and to assume that their own group is somehow superior to others; they often socialize the next generation into antagonistic attitudes toward any group other than their own. In some cases, ethnocentric feelings are exaggerated into outright racism, the deliberate oppressive treatment of other groups or members of these groups. Some racial or ethnic groups may exploit others, and may develop elaborate justifications for doing so—usually by defining the other groups as basically inferior. The exploited group naturally reacts with hostility and resentment, and develops antagonistic stereotypes of the dominant group. Conflicts of interests and values underlie any situation of racial and ethnic tension. It remains to be seen whether the current tendency toward cultural pluralism and the emphasis on group identity will worsen race relations by making people even more conscious of their group loyalty, or whether it will improve race relations by making the different groups more likely to respect one another.

Conflict theorists, who often believe that conflict may be valuable to society if it is kept within reasonable limits, may take the view that the heightened racial conflict of recent years will eventually have beneficial results. Black Americans suffered discrimination for generations until they created civil disturbances in the sixties; since that time, they have made significant advances. Conflict theorists predict that similar gains will be made by other racial and ethnic groups if they take action to bring about change, rather than waiting for their problems to resolve themselves.

The *deviance* perspective is of limited use in the analysis of racial and ethnic problems. It should be noted, however, that racist attitudes were quite respectable until fairly recently, and those who did not share them were often considered deviants and stigmatized, particularly in some areas of the country. These attitudes tended to reinforce prejudice and discrimination, and so contributed to the problem. Today it is the outright racist who is more likely to be considered deviant, and this labeling probably reduces the amount of overt racism in our society.

Sociologist Milton M. Gordon has suggested that there are three possible patterns of intergroup relations that may be followed in the future: Anglo-conformity, melting pot, and cultural pluralism.[37]

Anglo-conformity is a broad term used to cover a variety of viewpoints about assimilation, but all assume the desirability of maintaining modified English institutions, language, and culture as the dominant standard in American life. In practice, "assimilation" in America has always meant Anglo-conformity, and the groups that have been most readily assimilated have been those that are ethnically and culturally most similar to the Anglo-Saxon group.

The melting pot is, strictly speaking, a rather different concept, which views the future American society not as a slightly modified England but rather as a totally new blend, both culturally and biologically, of all the various groups that inhabit the United States. In practice, the melting pot has been of only limited significance in the American experience.

Cultural pluralism refers to a series of coexisting groups, each preserving its own tradition and culture, but each loyal to an overarching American nation. Although the cultural enclaves of some immigrant groups, such as the Germans, have declined in importance in the past, many other groups, such as the Italians, have retained a strong sense of ethnic identity and have resisted both Anglo-conformity and inclusion in the melting pot.

Current trends indicate that, for the foreseeable future at least, cultural pluralism is likely to be the dominant pattern in the United States. In the long run, our society may become a true "melting pot," or it may eventually tend toward Anglo-conformity; at present, however, most minorities are finding a source of pride and identity in their own histories and cultural backgrounds. But it should be remembered that the three possible patterns are not mutually exclusive, all-or-nothing possibilities. A group like the Jews, for example, may be Anglo conformist in dress, may be assimilated into the economy, and yet may be pluralist in its religious or marital preferences. It is likely that members of various groups will experience many problems of role conflict as they attempt to determine their identities and sort out their lives into Anglo-conformist, assimilated, and pluralist elements. The general trend, however, seems to be toward pluralism. But whether an openly pluralist society will enjoy better race relations than our present society remains to be seen.

[37]Milton M. Gordon, "Assimilation in America: Theory and Reality," *Daedalus*, vol. 90, no. 2 (Spring 1961), pp. 363–365.

FURTHER READING

Allport, Gordon W., *The Nature of Prejudice,* 1954. A classic work on the mechanics of prejudice, containing a full account of the role of stereotyping and irrationality in prejudiced attitudes.

Brown, Dee, *Bury My Heart at Wounded Knee,* 1971. A moving history of the American West told from the American Indian's point of view. A series of photographs recaptures the vigor and pride of Indian life before the Indians were conquered and confined to reservations. The book is an admirable corrective to the myths about Indians that have been propagated in Western movies for decades.

Clark, Kenneth B., *Dark Ghetto: Dilemmas of Social Power,* 1965. A black social scientist's account of life in an urban ghetto.

Fanon, Frantz, *The Wretched of the Earth,* 1965. A passionate indictment, by a black African, of white racism around the world.

Greeley, Andrew M., *Why Can't They Be Like Us: America's White Ethnic Groups,* 1971. A former Roman Catholic priest presents a strong argument for the perpetuation of ethnic differences in American society. Greeley believes that ethnicity provides a necessary identity for ethnic group members and cultural enrichment for society as a whole.

Knowles, Louis and Kenneth Prewitt, eds., *Institutional Racism in America,* 1969. An important collection of essays on the many forms of discrimination that are built into various American institutions.

Marden, Charles F. and Gladys Meyer, *Minorities in American Society,* 1973. Provides an up-to-date and comprehensive treatment, chapter by chapter, of the history and problems of all the American minority groups.

Rex, John, *Race Relations and Sociological Theory,* 1971. An account of race and ethnic relations from a sociological perspective. Rex shows how minorities are systematically kept at the lowest socioeconomic levels of any society.

Rose, Peter, *They and We: Racial and Ethnic Relations in the United States,* 2d ed., 1974. A brief and readable review of intergroup relations in the United States. Includes material on the history, life style, and problems of each group.

Simpson, George E. and J. Milton Yinger, *Racial and Cultural Minorities,* 3d ed., 1965. An excellent introductory text on the sociology of race relations, covering both fact and theory.

10

Education

THE NATURE AND SCOPE OF THE PROBLEM

Education in America has probably never been more controversial than it is today. In recent years our schools have been deeply embroiled in issues of social and racial equality, and so have become a battleground for conflicting groups and interests. It is a fundamental part of the American creed that all our citizens should have equality of opportunity in life. The schools are generally believed to be one of the most important determinants of an individual's subsequent social and economic status in our society, but the quality of education they offer varies widely—and varies in such a way that those who are most in need of a good education are concentrated in the schools with the worst facilities and lowest paid teachers. The educational system, it has been charged, is serving to maintain the stratified nature of American society by channeling the less privileged into the most menial occupational roles while further reinforcing the advantages that the more privileged already possess. It is alleged that instead of serving as an avenue to social mobility, the schools are helping to perpetuate the economic and racial divisions in the United States. These are serious failings, and serious efforts have been made to confront the problem. But the attempts to change our educational system have aroused deep antagonisms and even outright violence.

Education in America

The school has always occupied a special place in American life. In most other cultures throughout most of history, formal education and literacy have been reserved for the elite; citizens of lower status either did not attend school at all, or else received only a vocational training.[1] But in the United States the concept of universal public education took hold very early. The nation was explicitly founded on the ideal of democracy and human equality, and early American statesmen strongly advocated the education of all citizens in the basic intellectual skills which they believed would encourage the development of an informed and freedom-loving citizenry. By the time of the Civil War, most of the states supported free public elementary schools—a development which took place long before the advent of similar institutions in most parts of Europe. From about 1850, the states also began to supply free secondary education, and early in the nineteenth century publicly supported colleges began to flourish. Today, with some 65,000 public elementary schools, over 25,000 secondary schools, and more than 1,000 public colleges and universities,[2] we have a far more extensive national educational system than any other country.

On the face of it, our educational system seems to be the best in the world. Even in industrialized Europe, only about 20 percent of all sixteen- and seventeen-year-olds attend school, whereas in the United States over 80 percent of the population in this age group do so. Only 10 percent of European children who complete high school go on to some form of higher education, compared with well over 50 percent in the United States. We take it for granted that every child is entitled to twelve years or more of free public education, yet in many other countries a majority of children do not attend school at all. We expect a doctor, lawyer, or other professional to spend perhaps twenty years of his or her life in formal education—a period equal to half or more of the average life expectancy in some developing nations. Each year we spend an average of over $1,000 for each public school pupil, or a total outlay of more than $50 billion.[3] A further $5.4 billion is spent on private schools and $32.5 billion on higher education.[4]

Yet despite this massive expenditure on education, our schools seem to be failing in even their most basic tasks. Statistics for six of the nation's largest cities indicate that almost three-quarters of their elementary schoolchildren are reading below grade level.[5] In the late sixties, one man in four failed the Armed Forces qualifying tests through lack of basic literacy.[6] At the beginning of the present decade, over 1 million Americans over the age of fourteen could not read at all.[7] And the

---

[1]Gerald L. Gutek, *A History of the Western Educational Experience* (New York: Random House, 1972).

[2]U.S. Bureau of the Census, *Statistical Abstract of the United States, 1973* (Washington, D.C.: U.S. Department of Commerce, 1973), Table 157, p. 104.

[3]Ibid., Table 201, p. 128.

[4]Ibid., Table 162, p. 108.

[5]Leonard Butler, "Pupils Here Show Gain in Reading," *New York Times* (February 15, 1974).

[6]John R. Coyne, Jr., "The Voucher System: Slates and Hamsters," *National Review* (March 23, 1971), pp. 309–311.

[7]U.S. Bureau of the Census, *Statistical Abstract*, Table 179, p. 116.

overwhelming majority of these educationally disadvantaged Americans are members of our lower class.

Critics have made charges of inadequate performance against the schools for many years. But recently another complaint has been heard: that the schools are an important element in the maintenance of racial and social inequality in America. Despite the egalitarian rhetoric of our society, there are disturbing gaps between the educational attainment of whites as compared with many minority groups, and between the middle class as compared with the lower class. In 1972, for example, only 43.7 percent of blacks over age twenty had received four years of high school, compared with 63.6 percent of whites,[8] and the median years of schooling completed by black adults was almost two years less than whites.[9] Similarly, whites from lower-income families leave school in much greater proportions than those from the middle class,[10] with the result that white lower-class children receive about 1.5 years less schooling than their middle-class counterparts.[11]

The gap is even more evident at the college level. In 1972 almost 24 percent of all whites in the 18–24 age group were enrolled in college, compared with only 18.3 percent of blacks, two-thirds of whom were in predominantly black schools.[12] In the same year 12.6 percent of all whites aged twenty-five or older had completed college, but only 5.1 percent of all blacks had done so.[13] The disparity between high-income and low-income groups is even more marked. Only 20 percent of high school graduates from families with incomes below $3,000 went on to college, compared with 87 percent of those from families with incomes of $15,000 or more.[14] These discrepancies do not necessarily result from differences in the intellectual abilities of the students concerned: less than 10 percent of students with high incomes and high abilities fail to enter college, whereas a quarter of low-income students with comparable abilities do not continue their education.[15]

Since intelligence is presumably distributed randomly throughout the population, there should be no significant difference in the educational attainment of different economic or racial groups unless some other influences are at work. The fact that major differences exist strongly suggests that the various groups do not have equal opportunity for educational attainment. In a society in which education seems to be increasingly important as the principal avenue to success, the unneces-

[8]Executive Office of the President, Office of Management and Budget, *Social Indicators, 1973* (Washington, D.C.: U.S. Government Printing Office, 1974), Table 3/2, p. 100.
[9]U.S. Bureau of the Census, *Statistical Abstract,* Table 175, p. 115.
[10]Christopher Jencks, et al., *Inequality: A Reassessment of the Effect of Family and Schooling in America* (New York: Harper Colophon Books, 1973), p. 19.
[11]Ibid., p. 24.
[12]Executive Office of the President, Office of Management and Budget, *Social Indicators,* Table 3/13, p. 105.
[13]U.S. Bureau of the Census, *Statistical Abstract,* Table 175, p. 115.
[14]Jencks, *Inequality,* pp. 19–20.
[15]Executive Office of the President, Office of Management and Budget, *Social Indicators,* Table 3/14, p. 106.

sarily depressed achievement of lower-class children in general and minority-group children in particular represents a gross wastage of talent, a source of tension and discontent, and a serious social problem.

APPROACHING THE PROBLEM

The social problem posed by inequality in American education may be analyzed from the social-disorganization perspective or the value-conflict perspective.

From the social-disorganization perspective, the problem arises because American society is so structured that education tends to reinforce rather than reduce social inequality. There is an inconsistency between the American ideal of equality of opportunity and the institutional reality of a school system which is to a great extent racially segregated and which accords superior facilities to those groups that are already advantaged. The education system, which is one of our most important social institutions, is failing in some of the tasks that society expects it to perform. The existing system tends to be dysfunctional in its effects, both because it generates discontent and conflict and because it deprives society of the full realization and expression of the potential talents of many of its members.

From the value-conflict perspective, the problem arises because competing groups in society have their own interests, values, and even prejudices to defend. Because the existing system favors those who are more privileged, they in turn tend to favor the system. On the other hand, those groups who find that their existing disadvantages are compounded by poor educational facilities and unequal opportunity are highly critical of the schools and seek major changes in the system. The issue is complicated by the fact that some of these changes would involve racial desegregation of schools and the transfer of some resources that are currently being concentrated on the education of the privileged; and many citizens are reluctant to see full integration or the reallocation of resources which chiefly benefit them or their children. Social conflict is therefore inevitable, but in the view of many conflict theorists it may ultimately have the beneficial effect of bringing about needed changes in the system.

The Social Function of the Schools

Unlike most other animal species, human beings do not come into the world with their behavior patterns already programmed by their genetic inheritance. Most human behavior is learned, and new arrivals into human society are socialized in the norms of their society by those who came before them.

In small preliterate communities this process takes place in a fairly informal way, and the education of the young does not require special-

One of the most important functions of the schools is the transmission of culture from one generation to the next. Using both formal and informal methods, the schools encourage a loyalty to the dominant social values. *(Paolo Koch/Rapho Guillumette)*

ized institutions. The total body of cultural knowledge in these societies is relatively small, and every adult shares in this knowledge to much the same degree. The culture of these traditional societies changes comparatively slowly, and the children acquire basic knowledge and internalize social norms simply through everyday contact with their parents and other members of their community. But when a society grows more complex, change and innovation become a permanent feature of existence. Knowledge expands rapidly, especially in the areas of science and technology. Social and occupational roles become highly specialized, and people require lengthy and specialized training if they are to fill these roles effectively. Inevitably, formal institutions are created to provide the education that the parents are no longer able to offer.

Emile Durkheim, a French sociologist working around the turn of the century, was the first social scientist to analyze systematically the social functions of the schools. He concluded that education serves primarily as a means for "the methodical socialization of the young."[16] The schools, he contended, serve to transmit the values, norms, and intellectual heritage of the culture to each new generation, thereby ensuring the solidarity and survival of the entire society. But the schools, Durkheim contended, are inevitably conservative: because they transmit the values and norms of the older generation, they will always tend to reflect

[16]Emile Durkheim, *Education and Sociology* (Glencoe, Ill.: Free Press, 1950), p. 71.

society rather than change it. Sociologists still debate this point: some take the view that education can be used to transform society by changing peoples' attitudes, values, and skills; others take the view that the educational system must necessarily reflect society (as ours seems to do in America today) and that society itself must be changed before the schools can change. The controversy has considerable relevance in the contemporary United States, where many efforts are being made to use the schools as a tool for social engineering in the hope that the inegalitarian structure of society can be modified.

The functions of the schools can be regarded as falling into two basic categories—the *manifest* (obvious or intended) functions and the *latent* (concealed or unintended) functions.

The most manifest function of the school is to provide children with the basic literacy and skills that they will need in a modern industrial society. This task is what we usually have in mind when we speak of "education," and parents tend to judge schools in terms of their success in achieving this objective. The school serves as a sorter of people: it teaches them specific subjects, tests and awards them certain qualifications, and so allocates them to different roles and statuses in society.

The school functions as an important socializing agent in society; for it teaches not only knowledge, but also values and attitudes. Schools perform this manifest function with the approval of the parents; when a Gallup poll asked parents in 1972 what they particularly wanted their children to learn in school, some of the most frequent answers were "How to get along better with others" and "Respect for law and authority." To the extent that the schools transmit much the same cultural heritage to all pupils, they also function to create a relatively homogeneous society with shared values and assumptions. For this reason, the schools have always been considered to have an important function in the American "melting pot" process—although clearly this is a function that they have fulfilled to only a limited degree. Yet another manifest function of the schools, especially at the level of higher education, is the development of new knowledge through research.

The latent functions of the school are also many and varied. One function of the schools is that they serve as agents of social control. We have generally been conscious of this control function in totalitarian societies, but have only recently begun to realize that our own schools also have this function, although it is not so explicit. Children in our schools learn a strong loyalty to their nation, the governmental system, and the dominant ideology. The very structure of the school—itself a miniature social system—prepares children for the subsequent experience of life in an industrial society. They learn, for example, to divide time rigidly between work and recreation, to perform uninteresting routine tasks, to compete against their fellows, and to take orders from those above them in the hierarchy of authority—all of them necessary qualities for the adult American worker. Charles Silberman, a prominent critic of our schools, illustrates one aspect of this control function:

In lecturing the students on the need for and virtues of absolute silence, an elementary school principal expostulates on the wonders of a school for the "deaf and dumb" he had recently visited. The silence was just wonderful, he tells the assembly; the children could get all their work done because of the total silence. The goal is explicit: to turn normal children into youngsters behaving as though they were missing two of their faculties.[17]

Another latent function of the schools may be to solidify and perpetuate the racial and class divisions in our society. Paul Lauter and Florence Howe, after referring to the repeated failure of our schools to educate the lower-class child for middle-class achievement, suggest that these failings "can be better understood as contradictions between the professed objectives of educators . . . and the real social and economic forces to which the educational system was in fact responding."[18] The economy, Lauter and Howe argue, needs lower-class workers in its factories, and so lower-class children are educated to be industrial workers, regardless of stated ideals. The schools adapt to the structure and needs of our society because it would be difficult to fill menial jobs with high school graduates who had been educated in middle-class skills and expectations.

The educational system also has several other unintended latent functions. One of these is the development of a distinctive youth culture as a result of the removal of the young from their homes and their segregation from the rest of society. Another latent function, especially at college level, is that of facilitating the process of courtship and mate selection. A further latent function is that the very process of education may develop critical abilities that can be directed back against society. The educational philosopher John Dewey, who strongly believed that the schools could change society, recognized this latent function.

If we once start thinking, no one can guarantee what will be the outcome, except that many objects, ends, and institutions will surely be doomed. Every thinker puts some portion of an apparently stable world in peril, and no one can wholly predict what will emerge in its place.[19]

It is possible, therefore, for a wide discrepancy to exist between the declared goals of education and the actual functions that it performs. At present, it is a stated social goal to use the schools to enhance equality of opportunity between middle-class and lower-class children, and between white children and minority-group children. But will the

---

[17]Charles Silberman, *Crisis in the Classroom: The Remaking of American Education* (New York: Random House, 1971), p. 128.

[18]Paul Lauter and Florence Howe, "How the School System is Rigged for Failure," in *Crisis in American Institutions*, 2d ed., eds. Jerome Skolnick and Elliott Currie (Boston: Little, Brown, 1973), p. 322.

[19]Quoted in Donald McDonald, "Culture and Personality," *Center Magazine*, vol. 6, no. 1 (January–February 1973), p. 2.

The Cardinal Sin

There was one heady moment when I was able to excite the class by an idea: I had put on the blackboard Browning's "A man's reach should exceed his grasp, or what's a heaven for?" and we got involved in a spirited discussion of aspiration vs. reality. Is it wise, I asked, to aim higher than one's capacity? Does it not doom one to failure? No, no, some said, that's ambition and progress! No, no, others cried, that's frustration and defeat! What about hope? What about despair?—You've got to be practical!—You've got to have a dream! They said this in their own words, you understand, startled into discovery. To the young, clichés seem freshly minted. Hitch your wagon to a star! Shoemaker, stick to your last! And when the dismissal bell rang, they paid me the highest compliment: they groaned! They crowded in the doorway, chirping like agitated sparrows, pecking at the seeds I had strewn—when who should appear but [Mr. McHabe, the administrative assistant to the principal].

"What's the meaning of this noise?"
"It's the sound of thinking, Mr. McHabe," I said.

In my letter box that afternoon was a note from him, with copies to my principal and chairman (and—who knows?—perhaps a sealed indictment dispatched to the Board?) which read:

"I have observed that in your class the class entering your room is held up because the pupils exiting from your room are exiting in a disorganized fashion, blocking the doorway unnecessarily and *talking*. An orderly flow of traffic is the responsibility of the teacher whose class is exiting from the room."

The cardinal sin, strange as it may seem in an institution of learning, is talking.

SOURCE: Bel Kaufman, *Up the Down Staircase* (Englewood Cliffs, N.J.: Prentice-Hall, 1964).

schools be able to perform this function—or will they continue to reflect and reinforce the divisions in society?

EDUCATION AND SOCIAL CLASS

Long before the current concern about the relationship between educational achievement and social class, teachers knew that lower-class children in general did less well in school than their middle- and upper-class peers. Today, a wealth of research evidence has established that social class influences school performance so strongly that it is the single most important determinant of educational success. The average higher-status child stays in school longer, and does better at all levels while there, than his lower-status counterpart. Since there is no reason to suppose that the children of lower-class parents are born with innately inferior intelligence, this differential — which has so many profound effects on society and on the lives of the children concerned — is likely to be the product of cultural factors or of unequal opportunity to benefit from the educational experience.[20] The sources of this inequality of opportunity are located both within the social environment of lower-class children and in the schools themselves.

Effects of Social Environment

Children do not wait until the age of five or six before they begin to learn. By the time a child enters kindergarten, he or she has already laid the foundations for subsequent intellectual development, internalized a basic set of values, acquired a distinctive way of perceiving the world, and developed some personal image of self. And all these characteristics are deeply influenced by the environment into which the child is born, and this environment varies immensely depending on the socioeconomic status of the parents.

Psychologist Robert Coles makes this point by drawing attention to an extreme situation, the early learning environment that a slum child might experience:

> Mothers who live in broken-down tenements, who never know when the next few dollars will come, have little energy left for their children. Life is grim and hard, and the child has to learn that. He learns it and learns it and learns it — how to survive all sorts of threats and dangers, why his parents have given up on school, why they have fallen on their faces. He learns about racial hatred; . . . he learns whether he is an insider or an outsider; whether storekeepers and property owners and policemen treat his family with kindness and respect or with suspicion and even out-and-out contempt.[21]

Unlike the middle-class family, the lower-class family is likely to have few books and little money to spend on travel and other enriching experiences. The home is likely to be overcrowded and noisy because lower-class families tend to be larger and to live in smaller homes than middle-class families. The domestic environment may fail to provide the encouragement and opportunities for learning that are so freely available in middle-class homes. And to compound the problem, chil-

---

[20]See Irwin Katz, "Academic Motivation and Equality of Educational Opportunity," *Harvard Educational Review*, 38 (Winter 1968), pp. 57–65.

[21]Robert Coles, "What Can You Expect?" *The New Yorker* (April 19, 1969), p. 170.

dren who are reared in impoverished surroundings face serious physical obstacles to educational success. Poor health care can adversely affect their energy and concentration, while sustained malnutrition, particularly in infancy and the early years of childhood, can have irreversible effects on subsequent intellectual growth by stunting the development of the brain.

Researchers believe, however, that the material environment of the parental home may not be the crucial element in the lower-class child's educational failure, important though this factor is. The parents' attitudes and values, particularly toward education, seem to be even more significant. Their ambitions and expectations for themselves and their children may be substantially lower than those of middle-class parents; they may see less value in schooling, may take less interest in their children's progress, and may be content for the child to leave school early.

Some social scientists have suggested that this relative difference in attitudes toward formal education stems from a much deeper difference in the value systems of the lower and middle classes. Florence Kluckhohn and Fred Strodtbeck argue that any social group forms its attitudes toward aspects of the world on the basis of a general "value orientation." The content of this orientation is determined by the group's assessment of social realities and of the opportunities realistically available to its members. The American middle-class orientation, for example, reflects a sense of mastery and optimism that is derived in turn from the middle-class experience of the world. This value orientation stresses the importance of doing rather than being, of the future as more important than the present or the past, of the desirability of achievement, and of the virtues of deferred gratification—a willingness to put off present enjoyment for the sake of some future benefit. Attitudes such as these are obviously important to success in school, and so middle-class children are equipped to do well. But lower-class children—who may not have these attitudes, who may be more fatalistic, and who may see little value in deferred gratification—are ill-prepared for the demands of formal education.[22] Moreover, it is even possible for people to regard a value as good but not see it as relevant to themselves. A lower-class child may believe that hard work and deferral of gratification are not going to mean higher status and better job prospects for him, though they may for his middle-class schoolmate; consequently he may perceive these values as irrelevant to his own future and see no reason to work for a good education.[23] The recent upsurge in race and ethnic pride among minority groups may, however, result in significantly changed value-orientations and ambitions for their members.

Another possible factor behind depressed lower-class achievement is language. Sociologist Basil Bernstein points out that educational suc-

[22]Florence Kluckhohn and Fred L. Strodtbeck, *Variation in Value Orientations* (Westport, Conn: Greenwood Press, 1973).
[23]Ralph H. Turner, *The Social Context of Ambition* (San Francisco: Chandler, 1964).

cess is largely dependent on linguistic skill. Through language the child can organize his or her ideas and experiences, think in terms of options and possibilities, and manipulate a problem mentally while attempting to solve it. Bernstein's research indicates not only that lower-class children hear and learn quantitatively less speech in childhood, but also that the speech they hear and learn is of a qualitatively different kind. The difference is not simply a matter of pronunciation or bad grammar. Lower-class language, Bernstein finds, is based on short, gramatically simple sentences, includes many set phrases, and has a high percentage of concrete, descriptive terms. Middle-class language, on the other hand, is complex, subtle, and individualistic; it contains more concepts and abstractions, it has more complex sentence structures, and it stresses the interrelationship of ideas, concrete objects, and possibilities. In the course of learning language, each child therefore learns a way of perceiving and thinking about the world. The middle-class child discovers a world that is ordered and potentially comprehensible, with logical relationships between its parts and demonstrable connections between past and future. The lower-class child, on the other hand, discovers a more arbitrary world, focused on the here-and-now, in which objects are more easily described than understood or related to one another. Consequently, Bernstein argues, the middle-class child arrives at school already prepared for the educational tasks that await him; but the linguistic background of the lower-class child serves to deprive him of the basic intellectual skills he needs for academic success.[24] Bernstein's theory has yet to be fully tested, but a number of studies have already shown a close correlation between linguistic competence and general academic achievement.[25]

Moreover, minority group children may be penalized for a poor command of standard American English. Chicano children, for example, typically speak Spanish at home, and may have difficulty in understanding the language of the school or in expressing themselves in oral and written work. Black children face a somewhat different problem: a great many of them speak black English—a perfectly correct, regular, and grammatical dialect of the English language, comparable to the many other dialects that are found throughout the English-speaking world. But many teachers mistakenly regard black English as "ungrammatical" or "wrong" and penalize pupils for not conforming to the standard American dialect of the language.

Effects of School Environment

For many years it was assumed that the domestic environment of the lower-class child was an adequate explanation for poor school perfor-

[24]Basil Bernstein, *Class, Codes and Control*, vol. 1 (London: Routledge and Kegan Paul, 1971).
[25]See John Nisbet, "Family Environment and Intelligence," in *Education, Economy, and Society*, eds. A. H. Halsey, et al. (Glencoe, Ill.: Free Press, 1961), pp. 273–287; Denis Lawton, *Social Class, Language and Education* (New York: Schocken Books, 1968).

mance. Only recently have sociologists realized that the schools themselves may often channel lower-class children further into failure.

Lower-class children live in lower-class areas, and these areas tend to have the worst schools in the nation. The reason is that in the United States more than half the receipts of the public schools are from local funds, more than 80 percent of which are raised through property taxes.[26] When taxable property per pupil is measured, some districts may have up to ten thousand times the fiscal capacity of others.[27] Consequently, a wealthy middle-class neighborhood can afford excellent facilities and high-salaried teachers, while schools in lower-class neighborhoods, where the children are already deprived, have markedly inferior facilities. Vast disparities exist in the amount of money spent in different areas on the education of a child. In one recent year, Alabama, with its high concentration of poor people, could afford only $489 per pupil, while Alaska spent $1,429 per pupil. The variation in individual districts was even wider, ranging from a scant $175 per pupil in the lowest district in South Dakota to a spectacular $14,554 per pupil in a district in neighboring Wyoming.[28] Moreover, a dollar spent on schools in a depressed urban area usually buys less education than one spent in a neighboring surburb. In Newark, for example, the schools have to spend $26 per pupil each year merely to guard the buildings against vandals,[29] and the National Education Finance Project estimates that it would cost New York City more than a third as much per pupil to offer an education equivalent to that in the nearby suburban system.[30]

But poor facilities are only one of the problems lower-class children must face in school. Another is the fact that the educational system is founded on middle-class values and assumptions, and is staffed largely by middle-class teachers. There is evidence to suggest that children tend to fail or succeed in school according to the teachers' expectations of them, and not simply according to their own ability. It seems that middle-class teachers may underrate children who do not behave or speak in the approved middle-class fashion. Lower-class children are apt to be assigned to the slow tracks early in their school years, and then held to a slow pace and to a low level of final achievement. The whole process may then become a self-fulfilling prophecy: believing that certain children will fail, school authorities react in such a way that the children do fail, and thus the prophecy appears to be justified by the result.

In fact, the prophecy may well be the cause of the final result, as a much-publicized experiment conducted by Robert Rosenthal and Le-

[26]Robert D. Reischauer, Robert W. Hartman, and Daniel J. Sullivan, *Reforming School Finances* (Washington, D.C.: Brookings Institution, 1973), p. 5.

[27]Ibid., p. 67.

[28]"A Profile of the U.S. Public Education System," *Congressional Digest*, vol. 51, no. 8–9 (August–September 1972).

[29]Reischauer, Hartman, and Sullivan, *Reforming School Finances*, p. 62.

[30]Ibid., p. 65.

Many American children enjoy excellent educational facilities. But because our schools are funded primarily from local property taxes, the finest facilities are concentrated in the wealthiest areas. The poorest children, who are most in need of a good education, are rarely educated in an environment such as this. *(George Zimbel/Monkmeyer)*

nore Jacobson has suggested.[31] In their study they administered a "Harvard Test of Inflected Acquisition" to pupils in a West Coast school. The researchers indicated to the teachers in the school that this newly designed test was able to predict precisely which children were likely to experience a sudden spurt in learning abilities during the following year. The teachers were given the names of the children and asked to watch their progress, but were told not to reveal their expectations to the children or to the children's parents.

In fact, there is no such thing as the "Harvard Test of Inflected Acquisition." The test the researchers used had no predictive value whatever: Rosenthal and Jacobson selected the names of the "spurters" quite arbitrarily from among both good and poor students. The only characteristic that distinguished these children from their classmates, then, was the teachers' expectation that their work would improve markedly. The children were given no special instruction or help; they were simply watched. The results of the experiment startled even the researchers. In some grades, a disproportionate number of the "spurters" made significant gains over the next year. Pupils in the first and second grades showed the most dramatic changes: about one in five of the non-"spurters" gained up to twenty I.Q. points, but nearly one in two of the "spurters" made similar gains. The greatest gains of all were by Chicano children, supposedly the most "disadvantaged" group in the school. It seemed that the teachers' attitude toward the children had changed in subtle ways, and the children in turn had responded to

[31]Robert Rosenthal and Lenore Jacobson, *Pygmalion in the Classroom* (New York: Harper & Row, 1969).

The Failure of the Schools

A black student does poorly in a Northern high school for three years. When he expresses interest in college, his guidance counselor assures him that he is not "college material." Through the intercession of some white friends, and over the objection of the guidance counselor, he is admitted into the federally financed Upward Bound Program at a nearby college, which provides an intensive remedial program during the summer, and special tutoring during his senior year. His grades shoot up so rapidly that the Upward Bound officials recommend him for a special Transitional Year program at Yale University, designed to give "underachieving students" with high potential the academic skills and the self-confidence they need to realize their potential. The counselor begrudgingly supplies the necessary transcripts, after remarking to the boy, "What, you at Yale? Don't make me laugh."

But when the student is admitted — one of sixty selected, out of 500 applicants — the school system's public relations apparatus springs into action. The boy's picture appears in the local newspaper in an article reporting the high school's success story; the superintendent of schools introduces him to the public at an open meeting of the board of education; and when a group of local black leaders meet with school officials to press some of their complaints about the system, they are told that the boy's admission to the Yale program shows how well the school is serving black students.

SOURCE: Charles E. Silberman, *Crisis in the Classroom: The Remaking of American Education* (New York: Vintage Books, 1971).

the school's expectations of them. Rosenthal and Jacobson hypothesize that a similar situation exists in other schools: teachers expect better results from middle-class children, and the children duly yield them. The findings of this study are controversial, however. Some subsequent studies have drawn very similar conclusions, but others have not detected the "self-fulfilling prophecy" effect.[32] More research is needed to determine by what mechanisms and under what conditions, if any, the phenomenon occurs.

[32]See, for example, Ray C. Rist, "Student Social Class and Teacher Expectations: The Self-Fulfilling Prophecy in Ghetto Education," *Harvard Educational Review,* vol. 40, no. 3 (August 1970), pp. 411–451; Robert L. Thorndike, "Review of *Pygmalion in the Classroom*," *American Educational Research Journal,* vol. 5, no. 4 (November 1968), pp. 708–711; Robert Rosenthal, "Empirical Versus Decreed Validation of Clocks and Tests," *American Educational Research Journal,* vol. 6, no. 4 (November 1969), pp. 689–691; William J. Gephart, "Will the Real Pygmalion Please Stand Up?" *American Educational Research Journal,* vol. 7, no. 3 (May 1970), pp. 473–474; and Theodore Barber, et al., "Five Attempts to Replicate the Experimenter Bias Effect," *Journal of Consulting and Clinical Psychology,* vol. 3, no. 1 (February 1969), pp. 1–6.

EDUCATION AND RACE

In the United States today, issues of race are inextricably linked with issues of social class. Minority groups such as the blacks, the American Indians, the Puerto Ricans, and the Chicanos are vastly overrepresented among the numbers of the poor. Prejudice, institutionalized discrimination, and poor education all serve to keep millions of minority-group members in poverty. It was inevitable that the movement for racial equality in the United States would eventually focus on education, partly because the schools provide a context in which children can learn mutual tolerance, and partly because education is an important avenue to social and economic advancement in America. Accordingly, the civil rights movement always regarded school integration as one of its main objectives.

But progress has been slow. When in 1954 the Supreme Court ruled in the historic case of *Brown v. Board of Education* that segregated school systems were inherently unequal and therefore unconstitutional, civil rights advocates thought that the battle had been won. Yet by the early seventies nearly 50 percent of black schoolchildren in America were still attending schools that were more than 90 percent black,[33] and only a very small minority were in schools that were predominantly white. At the time of the 1954 Supreme Court decision, school segregation was regarded as a largely Southern problem that could be solved by the passage of laws and the enforcement of constitutional guarantees. We have since learned that the problem is a good deal more complicated.

The Northern parts of the United States have never practiced *de jure* segregation, that is, segregation formally required by law. But they have practiced, and continue to practice, *de facto* segregation, the kind that "just happens" as a result of the dispersal of different groups into different neighborhoods, the unwritten understandings of the various communities, and the political maneuverings of local interest groups. So long as the black population of the North was fairly small, the de facto school segregation could be ignored; but when large numbers of blacks started migrating North after World War II, the situation began to change. By the fifties the North was in the midst of a "race problem" — and de facto segregation has persistently proved more difficult to eradicate than the de jure kind. In fact, the record of school integration in the South is today better than that of any other part of the country. Less than a quarter of Southern black children still attend schools that are almost all black. This degree of integration has been achieved in spite of the fact that originally the South had rigidly enforced school segregation, and in spite of the fact that blacks form a much higher percentage of the school population in the South — about 25 percent of all pupils, compared with 15 percent in the North.

---

[33]*New York Times* (May 12, 1974).

What do we know about the effects of segregated schooling? In the early sixties the federal government asked sociologist James Coleman to survey the subject. His findings, published in 1966 as *Equality of Educational Opportunity*[34] ("the Coleman Report"), are an important source of information on race and education in America. Coleman and his team measured the actual educational achievement of both black and white pupils, and found that blacks consistently scored lower than whites at all levels; moreover, this gap widened as the pupils advanced to higher grades. Coleman's data indicated that the quality of school facilities was a relatively unimportant factor behind the difference in achievement. The most significant influences, he found, were the family background of the child, the cultural influence of the child's neighborhood, and the social-class "atmosphere" of the school as determined by its ratio of lower-class to middle-class pupils. Lower-class blacks in schools with middle-class "atmospheres," for example, did better than lower-class blacks in schools with lower-class "atmospheres." Coleman urges that we should modify our concept of equal education: we should focus less exclusively on equality of *input* (facilities and resources) and instead should concentrate on achieving equality of *output* (academic results). Coleman acknowledges that there would still be great *individual* variation in academic results in a situation of equality of output, but there would no longer be identifiable *groups* that were consistently underachieving.

A few years later David Cohen and Thomas Pettigrew reexamined Coleman's data and uncovered an additional fact: the level of interracial harmony in a school was very important in improving the achievement of black children. Desegregation in an atmosphere of hostility and tension had no beneficial effects on minority pupils.[35] The effects of school integration and segregation still require much more research, but a few conclusions are now generally accepted: black pupils tend to achieve more success in integrated schools than in segregated ones because integrated schools have a more middle-class "atmosphere"; integration alone does not close the black-white achievement gap and must be complemented by a supportive atmosphere; white achievement does not seem to be affected by school integration; and integration works best for all groups if it takes place in the early years of schooling.[36]

Programs for Equal Education

Two main approaches have been used to confront the problem of unequal schooling: compensatory education and busing.

[34]James Coleman, *U.S. National Center for Educational Statistics: Equality of Educational Opportunity* (Washington, D.C.: U.S. Government Printing Office, 1966).
[35]U.S. Commission on Civil Rights, *Racial Isolation in the Public Schools* (Washington, D.C.: U.S. Government Printing Office, 1967).
[36]See Frederick Mosteller and Daniel Patrick Moynihan, *On Equality of Educational Opportunity* (New York: Random House, 1972).

Compensatory education. The idea behind compensatory education is that children in lower-class neighborhoods with inferior schools should be compensated for this environment. Many different forms of compensatory education have been attempted; the best known was Headstart, a government program directed at preschool children of lower-income families. Children enrolled in Headstart programs were given a year or more of wide-ranging nursery-school activity in order to compensate for the presumed cultural deprivation of their home and neighborhood environments. Educators hoped the children would thus be better able to compete with middle-class children when they entered school. But Headstart was not particularly successful: although many of the children did show considerable initial gains in I.Q., these gains did not hold in subsequent schooling—probably because the schools failed to build on the early Headstart foundation and because the home and neighborhood environments remained unchanged. By the second or third grade, most Headstart children were performing no better than their lower-class peers. The early optimism about compensatory education has not been justified, but some new programs are now focusing on even earlier years of childhood and are centering on the home rather than the school in the hope that different strategies will yield better results.

Busing. Since the mid-fifties, the degree of residential segregation of Northern blacks and whites has increased. White citizens have been moving in growing numbers to the suburbs, leaving the city centers disproportionately black. In Washington, D.C., for example, whites have left the city center in such numbers that by 1974 a total school population of 140,000 included fewer than 5,000 whites. As a consequence of this trend, the Northern schools have become progressively more segregated, and the discrepancy has steadily widened in the quality of facilities between the poor city centers and the affluent suburbs. The busing of students from one neighborhood to another—primarily of black students to white schools—is seen by many educators and social scientists as the only effective means of correcting the racial imbalance.

The issue, however, has become an explosive one. Although a 1972 Gallup poll found that 65 percent of the public favored school integration while only 25 percent opposed it, the poll also found that only 20 percent approved of busing and that 69 percent were against it. Bills have been introduced into Congress to ban or limit long-distance busing for the purpose of racial balance, and there have even been proposals for a constitutional amendment to prohibit the practice. Many suburban parents strongly resent the importation of lower-class children into their schools because they fear that educational standards might suffer; and they resolutely oppose any suggestion that their own children be bused into the ghettos in order to correct racial imbalance in the central cities. Attempts at court-enforced busing have some-

The busing of schoolchildren seems to be the only method by which racial segregation in our schools can be ended. But busing has provoked such strong reactions from some white communities that the children have to be taken to and from school under police escort. *(Wide World Photos)*

times met with violent responses in white neighborhoods, even in such traditionally liberal cities as Boston. The resentments and antagonisms that busing has aroused in some areas may inhibit any beneficial effects of school integration; but unless children are physically transported from one neighborhood to another, school segregation with all its attendant problems will become a permanent feature in many Northern states—perhaps creating even more hostilities in the long run.

The Race and I.Q. Debate

It is generally accepted by social scientists that intelligence is the product of an interaction between innate and environmental factors, although there is still considerable debate as to how significant the contribution of each set of factors is in the final determination of any individual's intellectual powers. In the United States educational system, intelligence is usually assessed by the I.Q. (intelligence quotient) test, which measures the performance of an individual as compared with the rest of his age group. The I.Q. test is misnamed, for it is not really a test of intelligence, but rather a measurement of performance. The tests actually ignore many intellectual abilities—such as the capacity to compose music, write poetry, or create other art forms—and focus almost exclusively on those skills that are demanded by the standard school curriculum. The tests have been highly valued in American schools in the past because they have a good predictive value: children who do well on them in the early years of schooling tend to do well later on. Now that we are more aware of the dangers of the self-fulfilling prophecy, I.Q. tests have become more suspect. It may be, for example, that a child who does badly on an early test will be placed in a lower track, given less skilled teachers, made to consider himself less bright than his classmates, and may thereafter perform in accordance with these personal and professional low expectations.

The whole issue of I.Q. testing has become much more controversial since 1969, when psychologist Arthur Jensen published an article in which he argued that blacks were innately inferior to whites in intelligence as measured by I.Q. tests.[37] On the average, blacks, like other lower-class groups, do score somewhat lower on I.Q. tests than average whites, but Jensen argued that this lower score had a hereditary basis. His view was inevitably seized upon by those interests that oppose racial integration of the schools or the channeling of more funds into compensatory education. Blacks, it was argued, could not really benefit from these programs, so why bother?

In fact, there are very sound reasons why blacks and other minority groups do not do as well as middle-class whites on I.Q. tests, and there is no need to hypothesize genetic factors as an explanation of the phenomenon. As we have seen, children reared in lower-class environments have a diminished scholastic aptitude as a result of the cultural deprivation they experience in infancy and childhood. Moreover, the I.Q. tests tend to be "culture-bound"—that is, they contain implicit assumptions and information that are more likely to be shared by one group than another. For example, an I.Q. test may require the subject to "choose the odd one" out of a group of four different animals. A middle-class child, who may have seen these animals in his books if not on a visit to the zoo, will have no difficulty in performing the task. But a ghetto child may be entirely unfamiliar with the animals and so may be unable to answer the item correctly. Clearly, what is being tested is not intelligence but, rather, cultural knowledge, which is a very different thing. This point was made in 1914, in fact, by Wilhelm Stern, the developer of the concept of I.Q.:

> No series of tests, however skillfully selected it may be, does reach the innate intellectual endowment, stripped of all complications, but rather [it assesses] this endowment in conjunction with all other influences to which the examinee has been subjected up to the moment of testing. And it is just these external influences that are different in the lower social classes.[38]

[37]Arthur Jensen, "How Much Can We Boost I.Q. and Scholastic Achievement?" *Harvard Educational Review*, vol. 39, no. 2 (1969), pp. 273–274.

[38]Quoted in Lillian Zach, "The I.Q. Debate," *Today's Education*, vol. 61, no. 6 (September 1972), p. 40.

Moreover, there is very strong evidence that blacks find the testing situation much more stressful than do whites, probably because they do not expect to do well. Several studies have shown, for example, that if blacks are tested by a black tester, they do better than if tested by whites; if they are told that their results will be compared with those of other blacks, they do better than if told the results will be compared with those of whites; if they are told that the test is part of a black graduate student's research project, they do better than if told that the test is for the state board of education. The average difference in I.Q. score between these more and less stressful situations is eight points, so that this stress factor alone is enough to account for about half the difference between average scores of blacks and whites.[39]

Of course, there is a great range in intelligence among individual blacks, and in fact middle-class blacks in the North have a higher average I.Q. than lower-class whites in the South. The evidence is overwhelming that cultural factors account for the relatively lower average I.Q. of blacks and other minority groups, and very few social scientists believe that genetic factors play any role in the discrepancy.

PROSPECTS FOR THE FUTURE

Although most Americans declare that they favor equality of educational opportunity, the social and economic costs of making that equality a reality are so inconvenient and dislocating that many powerful interests are simply not prepared to bear them. The problem of unequal education is therefore not one that will be easily or quickly solved, but various strategies have been proposed, or are being implemented experimentally, with the objective of improving the educational opportunities of the disadvantaged groups in our society.

Community control. Many minority-group neighborhoods are seeking decentralization of the control of their schools. Residents of these neighborhoods often claim that the urban or regional education authority that administers their schools is remote, unsympathetic, and preoccupied with the interests of the white middle class. Several cities, such as New York, have already decentralized control to some extent, so that black or other minority-group districts are able to develop the curricula and methods that the local community feels is most appropriate to the needs of its children. Community control has some advantages but presents two problems: local communities lack the financial resources to develop facilities and programs to levels comparable to other schools; and decentralization may reduce contact among various groups and so may solidify the segregated pattern of education.

[39]See Peter Watson, "Can Racial Discrimination Affect I.Q.?" in *Race and Intelligence*, eds. Ken Richardson and David Spears (Baltimore: Penguin Books, 1972), pp. 56–67.

Redistribution of revenue. The quality of educational facilities in lower-class areas would be much improved if the United States, like most other countries, financed education on a regional or national basis rather than a local one, so that per capita pupil expenditures would be much the same irrespective of the area in which the child happened to live. The tradition of local financing of the school is probably too entrenched in the United States for the system to be changed in the foreseeable future, but it might be possible for the states or the federal government to allocate more funds to the existing equalizing programs that gear grants to local needs. At the very least, some minimal nationwide level of educational expenditure per pupil could be established, and a district too poor to finance this minimum could receive subsidies.

Education vouchers. One interesting proposal is for every parent to be given an education "voucher" for each child of schoolgoing age. The child could attend any school in a wide area, and would give the voucher to the school that was selected for attendance. The voucher would then be redeemable by the school from the state or federal government for a specified sum, so that the school's budget would depend on the number of students who enrolled—and if lower-class children's vouchers were worth more, it would also depend on the school's success in attracting lower-class children. Schools might then compete in making special efforts to cater to the educational needs of these children, and schools in which there was a high concentration of lower-class pupils would have higher budgets than other schools.

College quotas. One controversial method of providing specific advantages to minority-group students is to guarantee them a specified proportion of the places at colleges. In effect, this is "reverse discrimination," because in some cases a minority-group student might occupy a place that would otherwise have gone to a somewhat better qualified white middle-class applicant. Some critics have contended that this system, which is now being widely practiced in the United States, might even be unconstitutional and in any case is unjust; but supporters of the programs argue that there is so much prior discrimination against minority-group members, as a result of cultural deprivation and racial prejudice, that the quota system merely redresses the balance, if only to a limited extent.

"Deschooling society." Another proposal, worth mentioning perhaps more for the attention it has aroused than for the likelihood of its being applied, is that we change fundamentally our attitudes toward the entire institution of formal education. Ivan Illich, the most celebrated proponent of the "deschooling society" approach, contends that our current concern with narrow, time-consuming, formalized education is becoming farcical. Formal education, he contends, has become little more than a profitable commodity that can be processed and packaged,

Education: A Theoretical Review

The social problem of educational inequality represents the gap between a *social ideal* of equal educational opportunities for all and the *social reality* of a school system that offers superior facilities and opportunities to those who are already advantaged, and inferior facilities and opportunities to those who are the most disadvantaged. Education serves many functions in society, and in the United States the schools are often regarded as the main avenue to subsequent economic and social success. Our segregated and unequal facilities are therefore widely believed to have the effect of solidifying the existing racial and class divisions in our society.

The *social-disorganization* perspective offers a particularly fruitful way of looking at the problem of educational equality. From this perspective, society may be regarded as disorganized in that a major social institution is not fulfilling some of the important functions that are required of it; in fact, the schools may be having some dysfunctional effects. Society may also be regarded as disorganized in that there is a striking inconsistency between a value strongly held in the United States, that of equal opportunity, and the reality of a school system which denies equal opportunity to millions of its citizens.

Two particularly significant functions are expected of education in the United States: the schools should serve as a means of social mobility, and they should fulfill a "melting pot" function by providing a shared socialization experience for children from diverse racial, ethnic, and socioeconomic backgrounds. But these functions are disrupted by two main factors: the racial segregation that persists in the educational system, and the method that we use for funding the schools. Although the old system of de jure segregation has been abolished by the Supreme Court and by the laws of the land, a system of de facto segregation still remains. The massive migration of black Americans to the Northern cities since World War II has led to substantial concentrations of blacks in segregated neighborhoods; and the degree of segregation has been further increased by the flight of white middle-class citizens to the suburbs. In consequence, the schools in the Northern cities tend to be predominantly black or predominantly white. The pattern of school segregation that results is very difficult to eradicate, and the "melting pot" function of our educational system is seriously impaired. An indirect result of segregated education may be that racial tensions are maintained in our society: research has indicated that racial hostility is greater between groups that have little contact than between groups whose members interact.

The problem of unequal education is compounded by the fact that the schools in the United States are financed primarily on the basis of local property taxes. As a result, affluent areas are able to support well-equipped schools with highly paid teachers, while depressed areas tend to have some of the worst schools in the nation. The question of how far school facilities influence achievement is a controversial one, but many social scientists believe that unequal schooling may severely depress the scholastic achievement of lower-class children, and may also have adverse effects on other aspects of personality development. The educational system may contribute to the continuing stratification and inequality in American society by channeling the less privileged into menial occupational roles, and by enhancing the advantages that the more privileged already possess. Society is thus disorganized in that many citizens are denied the opportunity to achieve their goals or to make full use of their talents.

The *value-conflict* perspective also provides a useful way of analyzing the social problem of educational inequality. Different groups in society have very different interests to defend in the field of education. Those groups whose interests are favored by the existing system tend to support it, while those groups who suffer from unequal schools and unequal opportunity are naturally highly critical of the system. Proposals for change naturally generate conflicts. The suburban middle class, for example, may be reluctant to see its tax money used to help the children of inner-city residents, while inhabitants of depressed areas may believe that a redistribution of resources would represent a fair and just compensation for the many educational disadvantages that they suffer. The problem is complicated by the fact that the schools are embroiled in issues of racial integration. Many prejudiced people do not wish to see the schools of their neighborhood integrated, and even some nonprejudiced middle-class citizens resist integration because they believe it would lead to a lowering of academic standards. Social conflict over equality of educational opportunity is inevitable, but many theorists believe that this conflict may ultimately be beneficial in that it will lead to necessary changes.

The *deviance* perspective is of little relevance to the problem of educational inequality.

bought and sold, and kept in the form of a certificate for the possessor's own advantage. Such a system, Illich contends, inevitably supports social inequality, and should simply be dismantled.[40] A similar approach is taken by John Holt, who believes that we should turn schools into learning centers with facilities open to anyone who wishes to use them; degrees and diplomas would be abolished and education would be pursued for its own intrinsic or humanistic ends rather than for its economic value.[41]

Focus on other institutions. Some social scientists despair of using the schools as a means of ending inequality in society, and suggest that efforts at reform be focused elsewhere. One such critic is Christopher Jencks, whose book *Inequality* aroused great controversy through its contention that education has very little effect on the economic position of Americans. Other social factors, Jencks contends, are responsible, and we should focus on more fundamental changes involving the elimination of gross disparities in income between rich and poor. Jencks points out that economic opportunities are often related more to the state of the economy and the labor market than to the educational attainment of individuals—if there are more qualified people than there are jobs for them to fill, their level of education becomes almost irrelevant. Jencks sees education as only one of several variables affecting economic success. Many social scientists believe, however, that Jencks may have underestimated the importance of education, and even if he is correct in his view that education is not very relevant to the job prospects of lower-class groups, there still remain many other reasons why these people should enjoy a rich and nonsegregated educational experience. Jencks is probably correct, however, when he contends that changes in the school system alone will have only a limited impact on racial and economic inequality; the changes would have to be supported by changes in attitudes, values, and other institutions.

If Emile Durkheim was correct in his belief that schools can only conserve and never change a social order, then inequality in education will be with us for as long as our society is unequal. It is possible that Durkheim was wrong and that the schools can be a highly effective agent of change—but if we are ever to find this out, we will have to make a far more serious effort to change society through the schools.

---

[40]Ivan Illich, *Deschooling Society* (New York: Harper & Row, 1971).
[41]John Holt, *Freedom and Beyond* (New York: Dutton, 1972).

Banks, Olive, *The Sociology of Education,* 1972. A good and comprehensive introduction to the sociology of education. Includes material on the functions of education and on the influence of social class and family background on educational achievement.

Coleman, James F., et al., U.S. National Center for Educational Statistics: *Equality of Educational Opportunity,* 1966. A special report on educational opportunity done for the U.S. Department of Health, Education, and Welfare. Includes Coleman's surprising finding that the quality of school facilities is less important than the atmosphere of the school. Coleman offers a series of proposals designed to ensure equal educational opportunity for all children.

Illich, Ivan, *Deschooling Society,* 1972. A provocative argument for abandoning our existing system of education, which turns education into a commodity and leaves people greatly overeducated for their ultimate jobs. Illich contends that schooling stifles personal development and imagination and suggests some alternatives.

Jencks, Christopher, et al., *Inequality: A Reassessment of the Effect of Family and Schooling in America,* 1973. A controversial book in which the authors contend that schooling is not a significant factor in the maintenance of inequality in our society.

Kozol, Jonathan, *Death at an Early Age,* 1967. A young teacher's personal account of life in a Boston ghetto school. Kozol claims that an obsessive and unnecessary concern with discipline and school regulations diverts the attention of teachers and administrators from the educational task.

Rosenthal, Robert and Lenore Jacobson, *Pygmalion in the Classroom,* 1969. The findings of a controversial experiment on the "self-fulfilling prophecy" in education.

Spears, David, et al., eds., *Race and Intelligence,* 1972. A useful collection of articles by psychologists, sociologists, geneticists, and anthropologists on the subject of race and I.Q. The contributors unanimously reject the view that some racial groups are inherently less intelligent than others and produce formidable evidence to support their opinions.

U.S. Commission on Civil Rights, *Racial Isolation in the Public Schools,* 1967. An important evaluation of the data on equality of educational opportunity. The authors present evidence suggesting that interracial harmony within the school is essential if desegregation is to be effective in enhancing equal opportunity.

11

Sex Roles

THE NATURE AND SCOPE OF THE PROBLEM

In the mid-sixties a few American women began to demand liberation. Their movement was regarded by some men as a joke. The leaders were widely scorned; many men derided the motives and objectives of the liberationists, and many women seemed vaguely threatened and embarrassed by the new campaign. Yet sex roles have rapidly come to be regarded as a major problem in American society, and already an amendment to the U.S. Constitution prohibiting sex discrimination has been passed by Congress and awaits ratification by the states.

As we have seen, a social problem exists when a significant number of people or a number of significant people perceive an undesirable difference between social ideals and social realities, and believe that this difference can be eliminated by collective action. In the case of sex roles, the social problem has arisen not because of a deteriorating social reality, but rather because of a rapid change in social ideals. For centuries a sex-based division of labor and hierarchy of power have been regarded as part of the natural order, biologically and perhaps even divinely ordained. But in recent years these social arrangements have come to be regarded as artificial, cultural products — created by society, and therefore, in principle, capable of being modified by society.

Betty Friedan, one of the earliest leaders of the women's liberation movement, wrote in 1963 of the dawning perception of sex roles as a social problem:

The problem lay buried, unspoken, for many years in the minds of American women. It was a strange stirring, a sense of dissatisfaction, a yearning that women suffered in the middle of the twentieth century in the United States. Each suburban wife struggled with it alone. As she made the beds, shopped for groceries, matched slip-cover material, ate peanut butter sandwiches with her children, chauffeured Cub Scouts and Brownies, lay beside her husband at night—she was afraid to ask even of herself the silent question—"Is this all?" . . .

If a woman had a problem in the 1950's and 1960's, she knew that something must be wrong with her marriage, or with herself. Other women were satisfied with their lives, she thought. What kind of woman was she if she did not feel this mysterious fulfillment waxing the kitchen floor? She was so ashamed to admit her dissatisfaction that she never knew how many other women shared it. If she tried to tell her husband, he didn't understand what she was talking about. She did not really understand it herself. . . .

But on an April morning in 1959, I heard a mother of four, having coffee with four other mothers . . . say in a tone of quiet desperation, "the problem." And the others knew, without words, that she was not talking about a problem with her husband, or her children, or her home. Suddenly they realized they all shared the same problem.[1]

Today, millions of people have changed their ideas about the "natural" basis of established sex roles, and find our existing social reality an affront to their new ideals. What was once unthinkingly accepted as an unalterable fact of life is now seen as a profoundly oppressive system that condemns one-half of the population to permanent inferiority and frustration of potential, and the other half to the rigid demands of life-long competitiveness, insensitivity, and aggressiveness.

Sex Roles in America

What exactly is a sex role? The sociological concept of a "role" is analogous to the role of the actor or actress in the theater, where a person takes on the behaviors and attitudes appropriate for someone in his or her particular social situation. A role is a socially determined set of expectations that specify how a person in a particular situation should behave and be treated by others. Sex roles are sets of expectations that define the ways in which members of each sex in a given society should think and act. During the socialization process, each individual internalizes the content of these roles and plays his or her part accordingly.

At birth, every individual in every society is classified on the basis of physiological characteristics into one of two categories, male or female. But each society also elaborates these basic biological differences be-

---

[1]Betty Friedan, *The Feminine Mystique* (New York: Dell, 1963), pp. 11–15.

The "Natural" Inferiority of Subordinate Groups

Woman has lived, almost always, as the subordinate member of the species, defined as biologically and physically limited—to be given, at best, a place of protection or of benign neglect. This relationship of women to men has been readily accepted by civilization after civilization as one whose inherent justice has been decreed, not by the rough approximations of the laws of man, but rather by the profounder exactitude of the laws of nature; a relationship having nothing, really, to do with the evolutionary dictates of political or cultural decisions, but rather to do with the fulfillment of a logic determined by the cosmological order of things.

The perception of the categorical inferiority of one group of humans by another group of humans is as old as recorded time, and in each instance of its occurrence it is described as "natural," as being in accordance with the cosmic will of things. The ancients said it was "natural" for slaves to be slaves and for free citizens to be free citizens. The nobility of the middle ages claimed "natural" or divine right for the rule of royalty and the subsequently subhuman status of serfs. In modern times white men have claimed that the subjugation of blacks is merely proof that whites rule by virtue of their "natural" superiority. And, unfailingly, in each and every instance, when those who occupy the inferior space on the board begin the long push upward toward the announcement of their full humanity, the hue and cry ensuing from those in the position of thoughtless and essentially unearned superiority is that the "natural" order of things is being challenged—and surely the earth must open and the heavens will fall if things are permitted to go on much longer like this.

SOURCE: Vivian Gornick and Barbara K. Moran, eds., *Woman in Sexist Society: Studies in Power and Powerlessness* (New York: Basic Books, 1971).

tween male and female into secondary, nonbiological differences—cultural notions of "masculine" and "feminine." Masculinity and femininity refer to social and psychological differences, not physiological ones: differences in such characteristics as clothing, prestige, occupational role, and temperament. Each society, however, tends to regard its concepts of masculinity and femininity as representing as much a part of the natural order as do the basic biological differences between male and female; and it is precisely this notion that is under such strong assault in America today.

American sex roles, however, are markedly less rigid than those of most societies. Unlike women in some parts of the world, the American wife does not expect to be beaten if she displeases her husband, and it is possible, though difficult, for an American woman to achieve independence and even eminence in what is essentially a man's world. But this flexibility in roles is only relative. Clearly defined sex roles still exist in America, and are reflected in the behavior, personality, status, and economic functions of American men and women.

Sex-linked personality characteristics. The woman is traditionally supposed to be conformist, passive, affectionate, sensitive, intuitive, dependent, self-sacrificing for her family, and primarily concerned with domestic trivia. She is supposed to be ignorant of sports, politics, and economics, but deeply concerned about her personal appearance and her routine domestic duties. She should not appear ambitious or too obviously intelligent, or she risks being regarded as "unfeminine." In her relationships with men she should not take the initiative, but should be expressive, emotional, tender, and appreciative.

The American man, on the other hand, is traditionally supposed to be fearless, tough, self-reliant, logical, competent, independent, and aggressive. He should display little emotion, and in particular must never cry. (Edmund Muskie, front-runner for the Democratic presidential nomination in 1972, severely damaged his political standing by crying in public after a slur had been made on his wife; even *The New York Times* dismissed Muskie with the tart comment that he "shows himself to be a man who . . . tends toward emotional outbursts under pressure."[2]) The American male should have definite opinions on the major issues of the day, should be capable of making authoritative decisions in the home and on the job, and should be the breadwinner for the family. He takes the initiative in relationships with women, and expects to dominate them in virtually every sphere of life.

Paradoxically, however, the masculinity of the American boy seems to be regarded as potentially fragile, and far more care is taken to maintain it than the femininity of the girl. The boy has a terror of appearing in any way "effeminate," and parents are far more disturbed by indications that their son is a "sissy" than that their daughter is a "tomboy." The social reaction against boys who violate "masculine" norms is very strong. The fashion of long hair on males had to be imported to America from Europe, and was met with an intensely negative reaction: the very right of a boy to choose his own hair length in school or at work has had to be won piecemeal in court battles across the nation, and even now is often considered unacceptable for a self-respecting male. It is very unlikely that if girls chose to wear their hair short they would encounter the same outraged response. As Una Stannard points out, the women's liberation movement has focused so much attention on the training of girls for their roles that the much more restrictive training of boys has passed largely unnoticed:

---

[2]*New York Times* (March 9, 1972), p. 32.

Young American males are socialized into roles that demand aggression, competitiveness, toughness,
and control of the emotions. Boys
who deviate from these norms may
arouse anxiety in parents, teachers,
and psychiatrists. *(Leif Skoogfors/
Woodfin Camp)*

The narrowness and severity of this training is far greater than
comparable "training" for the femininity in girls. Girls can be tom-
boys, wear jeans and other men's clothing, fight, climb trees, play
sports, ride bikes. Their mothers may become somewhat anxious
about them, but this behavior will not be cause for great alarm, nor
will it be forbidden or cruelly ridiculed. Similarly, they will be considered "strange" or "unfeminine" if they continue to be active, to
succeed academically or professionally; however, many women do
so nonetheless, without feeling a fundamental challenge to their
identity. The training and subsequent behavior of boys is not so flexible. It would be unheard of for boys to wear dresses; if they want
to cook or are afraid to fight, this is a cause for panic by parents,
educators, and psychologists. And in fact, boys do conform closely
to the male goals and behavior required of them. They learn early
not to exhibit feminine personality traits – to hide emotions and pre-
tend even to themselves that they do not have them, to be independent participants in activities rather than be personally involved
with friends. Later, as men, they are careful never to choose wom-
en's careers unless they are prepared to bear enormous stigma.[3]

[3]Una Stannard, "Being and Doing: A Cross-Cultural Examination of the Socialization of Males and
Females," in *Women in Sexist Society: Studies in Power and Powerlessness*, eds. Vivian Gornick and
Barbara K. Moran (New York: Basic Books, 1971), p. 277.

These features of the socialization process stem from the fundamental inequality of the sexes in our society: the little girl who aspires to the higher status and acts in a boyish way is at least behaving in a way that is comprehensible, but the little boy who behaves in a girlish way is regarded as seriously maladjusted.

Sex-based division of labor. The division of labor in America reflects a belief in the superior abilities of the male. The woman's place is in the home, and housework is considered a very menial job indeed—when domestic servants are paid to do it, their wages are among the lowest in the nation. Men work outside the home, usually in more highly paid and prestigious jobs than women, and they tend to be promoted to much higher positions. Interestingly, the personality characteristics attributed to each sex are very selectively interpreted in the division of labor. Women are supposed to have deft fingers—but only for sewing, not for brain surgery. Women are supposed to be understanding and intuitive—but only as mothers, not as clergy or psychiatrists. Women are supposed to be caring and nurturant—but only as nurses, not as doctors. Thus it is that women represent only 32 percent of American writers, artists, and entertainers, 28 percent of college teachers, 20 percent of accountants, 9 percent of physicians, and 1 percent of engineers. On the other hand, they represent 70 percent of teachers (mostly in elementary schools), 83 percent of librarians, 87 percent of cashiers, 96 percent of nurses, typists, and child-care workers, and, unsurprisingly, 99 percent of all secretaries.[4]

Women earn far less than men, partly because they are paid less for doing the same work, partly because they are concentrated in the lower-paying jobs. The average working white woman earns less than the average working black man, and the black woman, subject to double discrimination, earns least of all. Of the 3.5 million families in America that are headed by a woman, nearly 2 million live below the poverty line. The median income of women is actually shrinking in relation to that of men. In 1955 it was 63.9 percent of the male income; in 1969 it was 60.5 percent; and in 1970, only 59.4 percent. By the end of the last decade some 28 percent of American men earned over $10,000 per year, but only 2.9 percent of American working women achieved this income level.

This sex-based division of labor, with its discrepant economic rewards, is fundamental to the maintenance of existing sex roles in America because it institutionalizes the role of the male as family breadwinner and ensures the economic and hence status dependency of the female. Major changes in American sex roles are unlikely to come about unless there are significant changes in the distribution of jobs and incomes between men and women. At present the man who is supported by his wife, or who earns less than she does, is likely to experience feelings of

[4]"The Drive to Open Up More Careers for Women," *U.S. News & World Report* (January 14, 1974), pp. 69–70.

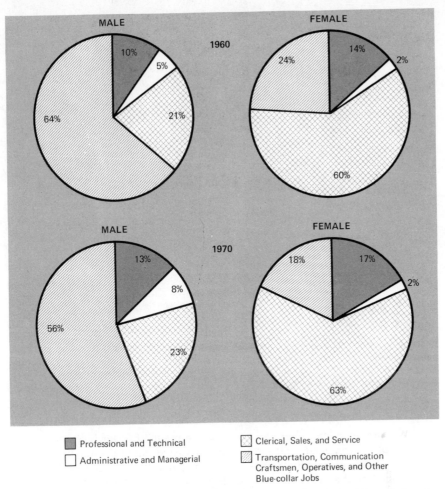

MALE   1960   FEMALE

MALE   1970   FEMALE

■ Professional and Technical

☐ Administrative and Managerial

▦ Clerical, Sales, and Service

▨ Transportation, Communication
Craftsmen, Operatives, and Other
Blue-collar Jobs

Percent of males and females in various occupations, 1960–1970. Although females comprise 40 percent of the labor force, their jobs tend to be very different from those of males. Sixty-three percent of the females employed in 1970 held clerical, sales, and service jobs, whereas, only 23 percent of the males were engaged in this type of work. Even the relatively high proportion of females in professional and technical occupations is misleading because females are concentrated in the lower-level professions, such as teaching, nursing, and social work. (SOURCE: Judith Blake, "The Changing Status of Women in Developed Countries," *Scientific American* [September 1974].)

inadequacy and even shame; and there are strong social sanctions against the wife who makes a success of her career in a "man's world," as though there were somehow something "wrong" with the professional businesswoman.

The nature of sexism. Writers have coined a new word, "sexism," to describe the institutionalized discrimination against women. Vivian Gornick and Barbara Moran explain the concept:

In many countries, females perform work that we have traditionally regarded as being appropriate only for males. American attitudes and values are changing rapidly. It is now possible for females to do many "male" jobs, but there is still a stigma attached to males who do "female" work. *(Fred Mayer/Woodfin Camp)*

Woman's condition, here and now, is the result of a slowly formed, deeply entrenched, extraordinarily pervasive cultural (and therefore political) decision that—even in a generation when man has landed on the moon—woman shall remain a person defined not by the struggling development of her brain or her will or her spirit, but rather by her childbearing properties and her status as companion to men who make, and do, and rule the earth. Though she is a cherished object in her society, she shall remain as an object rather than becoming a subject. . . . She may use wealth but cannot make it; she may learn about independence only so that she can instill it in her male children, urge it forward in her husband. . . . Her sense of these characteristics of adult life is sharply and distinctly *once removed*. . . . Everything in her existence, from early childhood on, is bent on convincing her that the reality of her being lies in bearing children and creating an atmosphere of support and nurturance for those who aggress upon the world with the intent of asserting the self, grasping power, taking responsibility—in other words, those who are living life as it has always been defined by human principle.

This is the substance of sexism. This is the creation of thousands of years of thought and reinforced patterns of behavior so deeply imprinted, so utterly subscribed to by the great body of Western conviction, that they are taken for "natural" or "instinctive." Sexism has made of women a race of children, a class of human beings utterly deprived of self-hood, of autonomy, of confidence—worst of all, it has *made the false come true.* Women have so long shared acquiescently in society's patriarchal definition of them . . . that they have become the very thing itself.[5]

Sexism is thus conceived as a form of institutionalized discrimination analogous to racism and other forms of deeply entrenched prejudice against underprivileged groups.

APPROACHING THE PROBLEM

The problem of sex roles in America is usually analyzed either from the social-disorganization perspective or from the value-conflict perspective.

From the social-disorganization perspective, problems relating to sex roles stem from the fact that society is organized in such a way that women, who constitute a majority of the members of the society, are artificially deprived of the opportunity to achieve many socially valued goals. The current disorganization is the product of changes in attitudes and values: so long as both men and women accepted their respective roles, the roles were to some extent functional for the overall balance of the social system. Many citizens now reject these roles, but the system has shown itself slow to adapt to changing attitudes and values. The existing sex roles are creating discontent and are becoming dysfunctional.

From the value-conflict perspective, problems relating to sex roles stem from the fact that men and women have different interests to defend. Women are deprived of the opportunities for self-fulfillment that are available to men, and are making rightful demands to rectify the situation. Inevitably, they will meet with considerable resistance, for not only are basic norms and values slow to change, but these very changes are threatening to many males. The occupational and social advancement of women represents threats to the self-identification and professional status of many men. Conflict, such as that brought about by the women's liberation movement, is regarded as inevitable and may also be considered desirable to the extent that it brings about social change.

In analyzing the problem of sex roles, sociologists make use of the findings of research in the fields of biology, anthropology, and social psychology. These findings yield important information on the extent to which social roles for the sexes can be constructed independently of physiological differences between them.

[5]Vivian Gornick and Barbara K. Moran, eds., *Women in Sexist Society: Studies in Power and Powerlessness* (New York: Basic Books, 1971), pp. ix–xx.

Innate Sex Differences: Biological Evidence

That there are certain innate, unlearned differences between the sexes is not in dispute. The problems that confront researchers are to determine which differences, if any, provide a basis for our existing sex roles, and which differences are innate and which are learned through the socialization process.

There are obvious sexual and reproductive differences between males and females, and these differences are normally reflected in some of the cultural arrangements governing sexual behavior and kinship structure. Women, for example, bear and suckle children, and so the care of young infants almost inevitably falls to them.

Apart from these basic differences, there is clear evidence that women are physically healthier than men in all societies. The male fetus inherits a greater number of sex-linked weaknesses resulting from the chromosomal characteristics of the male genes. Over thirty disorders, such as hemophilia, webbing of the toes, and certain forms of color blindness, are found exclusively in the male for this reason. The rate of fetal and infant mortality is significantly higher for males than for females, and women are less susceptible to most diseases and tend to live substantially longer than men. Women's rate of physical maturation is also faster than that of men in every respect except muscular development.

Some differences between the sexes can be observed soon after birth. Female babies, for example, tend to be more content and less physically active than boys and are also more sensitive to a number of physical stimuli—warmth, cold, pain, touch, and sound. It seems likely that these differences are innate, although some social scientists have argued that they may be the product of early social influences: even from the time of birth, parents often react differently to boy or girl babies, influencing their behavior in accordance with parental expectations.

Greater differences between the sexes emerge as the children grow older, but it is almost impossible to determine the origins, learned or innate, of many of these differences. Girls become more passive, docile, and dependent than boys. They also learn to talk and read at an earlier age and seem more intellectually mature: remedial education classes in elementary and junior high schools are filled with boys, not girls. Girls are superior to boys at numerical computation and tasks involving verbal facility, but boys are somewhat better than girls at tasks based on mechanical, spatial, and analytic ability. These intellectual differences are maintained throughout the school years, and I.Q. tests are carefully designed to balance subtests on which boys do better than girls and vice versa, in order to yield uniform scores. These differences might be innate, but they might also be the product of cultural conditioning. Girls may be better at language and reading than boys, for example, simply because they are encouraged to spend more time in the company of adults; and they may escape remedial classes simply because they are socialized to be more attentive and docile in school and so present fewer discipline problems than boys and learn more readily.

Some of the most significant research on sex-linked behavior concerns studies of children who have been mistakenly assigned to the wrong sex at birth. If a child is biologically male but reared as a female, what happens? A biologically determinist view would predict that the child would resist socialization as a female, and grow up with "masculine" characteristics as a result of his innate genetic predispositions. In fact, however, children can be readily socialized into the "wrong" sex role. John Money and his associates studied clinical evidence from a number of cases in which babies had been mistakenly classified at birth as belonging to the opposite sex. They found that the misassigned children adopted the sex roles into which they had been socialized, and unless the mistake was discovered and corrected before the age of three or four, the children strongly resisted attempts to change them and had great difficulty making the new role identification. The researchers concluded that sex role is in fact quite independent of physiological sex, and that the human species is "psychosexually neuter at birth."[6]

On the basis of the evidence available, it seems that males and females may be biologically predisposed to tentative gender orientations, but that these predispositions can easily be modified, and perhaps overridden, by the socialization process.

Other Cultures: Anthropological Evidence

Humans are reared by other humans, and it is therefore very difficult to separate the learned from the unlearned components of behavior. Historical and cross-cultural evidence can be helpful in this respect, however. If all cultures reveal much the same pattern in their sex roles, then the case for an absolute, biological basis for these roles is strengthened; but if there are wide cultural variations in the sex roles, the biological basis must be much less important.

In fact, sex roles vary a great deal across cultures and through history. Although every society institutionalizes at least some sex-role differences, the content of the roles and the mutual relationships of the sexes are subject to considerable variation. Even within our Western culture there have been many historical variations. At present we consider a concern with cosmetics and jewelry to be a primarily a feminine characteristic, but not so long ago it was the European male who wore silks, wigs, stockings, and perfume. Long hair on males has been normal throughout most of Western European history, although it has been considered "effeminate" for most of this century. (Short hair was fashionable during the time of World War I, because troops in the

---

[6]John Money, Joan Hampson, and John Hampson, "Imprinting and the Establishment of Gender Role," *Archives of Neurology and Psychiatry*, vol. 77, no. 3 (March 1967), pp. 333–336.

trenches had to shave their heads to rid themselves of crawling lice.) In several parts of Europe, men have worn skirts; the Scottish kilt and the monk's frock are among the few surviving examples.

Studies of other cultures around the world have consistently shown a fairly clearly defined division of labor between the sexes. The origin of this division of labor appears to be the biological fact that women bear and suckle children. The young human requires a very long period of dependence on adults, a requirement which stems from the evolutionary increase in the size of the human brain. If the infant were born more fully developed, the head could not pass through the mother's birth canal. Consequently the human infant, unlike the offspring of most other animals, is helpless and in need of attention for a period of several years after birth. The adult who bears and suckles the child is likely to continue the task of rearing the child after weaning, and so is unable to devote much time to other activities, particularly those taking place at a distance from the home. Since women are usually allocated the task of child-rearing, they commonly assume responsibility for other domestic duties, such as home care, food preparation, clothes manufacture, and light agriculture. Men, on the other hand, are physically more powerful and can leave their offspring for long periods, and so tend to become engaged in activities such as hunting, fighting, heavy agriculture, and the care of wandering livestock.

In an analysis of the division of labor by sex in some 224 societies, George P. Murdock found some quite sharp differences in the types of activities assigned to members of each sex. It is noteworthy that the allocation of duties does not necessarily correspond to our own notions of what constitutes man's or woman's work. Many areas in the United States have local laws restricting the weights that a working woman may lift, but in most cultures the carrying of heavy burdens is considered to be a woman's job.[7]

The family and kinship patterns of other cultures also reveal a tendency toward male dominance. In another survey of 565 societies, Murdock found that 376 were predominantly patrilocal (married couples living near the husband's parents), and only 84 were matrilocal. About three-quarters of the societies transmitted rights and property patrilineally (through the father) and only a quarter matrilineally. Murdock found some 431 societies that permit polygamous marriage; but of these, 427 permit the husband to have more than one wife, while only 4 permit a wife to have more than one husband.[8]

Other cross-cultural studies have shown that most societies accord men greater power than women in the family. Wives are usually expected to show deference to their husbands; a rare exception to this general rule was medieval chivalry, which institutionalized an elabo-

[7]George P. Murdock, "Comparative Data on the Division of Labor by Sex," *Social Forces*, 15 (May 1935), pp. 551–553.
[8]George P. Murdock, "World Ethnographic Sample," *American Anthropologist*, 59 (August 1957), pp. 664–687.

Division of Labor in 224 Societies by Sex

ACTIVITY	NUMBER OF SOCIETIES IN WHICH ACTIVITY IS PERFORMED BY				
	Males Always	Males Usually	Either Sex Equally	Females Usually	Females Always
Pursuit of sea mammals	34	1	0	0	0
Hunting	166	13	0	0	0
Trapping small animals	128	13	4	1	2
Herding	38	8	4	0	5
Fishing	98	34	19	3	4
Clearing land for agriculture	73	22	17	5	13
Dairy operations	17	4	3	1	13
Preparing and planting soil	31	23	33	20	37
Erecting and dismantling shelter	14	2	5	6	22
Tending fowl and small animals	21	4	8	1	39
Tending and harvesting crops	10	15	35	39	44
Gathering shellfish	9	4	8	7	35
Making and tending fires	18	6	25	22	62
Bearing burdens	12	6	35	20	57
Preparing drinks and narcotics	20	1	13	8	57
Gathering fruits, berries, nuts	12	3	15	13	63
Gathering fuel	22	1	10	19	89
Preservation of meat and fish	8	2	10	14	74
Gathering herbs, roots, seeds	8	1	11	7	74
Cooking	5	1	9	28	158
Carrying water	7	0	5	7	119
Grinding grain	2	4	5	13	114

SOURCE: Adapted from George P. Murdock, "Comparative Data on the Division of Labor by Sex." *Social Forces* (May 1935).

rate courtesy on the part of the male to the female. Traces of this chivalry still remain today: it is considered polite for a man to open a door for a woman or to rise when a woman enters a room, but it would be entirely inappropriate for a woman to raise her hat for a man. There are a few societies, such as the Berber in North Africa, in which the female appears to exercise more authority in the family than the male, but there are no societies in which men are not politically dominant.

In an extensive cross-cultural study of human sexual behavior, Clellan S. Ford and Frank Beach found a consistent tendency to male sexual dominance and privilege. In most societies, it is believed that men should take the initiative in sexual matters, although there are some societies, such as the Maoris and the Trobrianders, in which the women are expected to do so. The sexual behavior of unmarried girls is much more rigidly controlled than that of unmarried boys in nearly all societies, and married women are usually subject to much stricter sanctions for extramarital sex than married men. There are a few societies in which both sexes go nude, but far more societies require a woman to cover her genitals than a man, and there is no society in which men are obliged to cover their genitals while women are not.[9]

Are there recurrent similarities in the temperament and personality

[9]Clellan S. Ford and Frank Beach, *Patterns of Sexual Behavior* (New York: Ace Books, 1951).

of the sexes in different cultures? After a study of the evidence available, anthropologist Roy G. D'Andrade concludes:

> The cross-cultural mode is that males are sexually more active, more deferred to, more aggressive, less responsible, less nurturant, and less emotionally expressive than females. The extent of these differences varies by culture. And in some cultures some of these differences do not exist (and occasionally the trend is actually reversed).[10]

The fact that some societies succeed in reversing the "normal" personality characteristics associated with each sex is of great significance, because it shows how the content of sex roles can be radically altered by an appropriate cultural environment. One of the most influential studies of sex roles differing from our own was conducted by anthropologist Margaret Mead. She studied three tribes in New Guinea and found that one required both males and females to behave in a way we would consider "feminine"; the second required both sexes to behave in a way we would consider "masculine"; and the third reversed the personality types we would consider "normal" for the two sexes. Mead concluded:

> If those temperamental attitudes which we have traditionally regarded as feminine—such as passivity, responsiveness, and a willingness to cherish children—can so easily be set up as the masculine pattern in one tribe, and in another to be outlawed for the majority of men, we no longer have any basis for regarding such aspects of behavior as sex-linked.

> We are forced to conclude that human nature is almost unbelievably malleable, responding accurately and contrastingly to contrasting cultural conditions. . . . Standardized personality differences between the sexes are . . . cultural creations to which each generation, male or female, is trained to conform.[11]

The question still remains, however, of why most societies institutionalize male supremacy and the different personality types and occupational roles that support it. The answer probably lies in two related facts. First, a society functions more efficiently if there is a division of labor and if members are socialized into the roles appropriate for these tasks. Second, men are physically more powerful than women, and so tend to assume dominance in society. A division of labor along sex lines is functional and convenient for a traditional society, and since men are the dominant partners in this arrangement, their roles and personality characteristics are more highly regarded. But although a rigid division

---

[10]Roy G. D'Andrade, "Sex Differences and Cultural Institutions," in *The Development of Sex Differences,* ed. Eleanor Maccoby (Stanford: Stanford University Press, 1966), p. 201.
[11]Margaret Mead, *Sex and Temperament in Three Primitive Societies* (New York: William Morrow. 1935), pp. 190–191.

of labor and stereotyping of personality differences might be functional for a traditional community, it makes little sense in a sophisticated and diversified modern society, where the daily activities of men and women are far removed from any traditional functional division of labor.

Acquiring Sex Roles: Social Psychological Evidence

Psychologists have devoted considerable attention to the process through which the developing child comes to acquire his or her sex role. Three main accounts have been put forward: the psychoanalytic, the behaviorist, and the cognitive-developmental.

Psychoanalytic theory. Sigmund Freud, the founder of the psycho-analytic tradition, believed that society, primarily through the agency of the family, shapes the basically plastic nature of the individual; but he also assigned some importance to innate drives, notably the drive for sexual expression.

Freud believed that both male and female infants initially identify with the mother, because they are reared by her and perceive the father as more remote and less nurturant. This situation poses a particular problem for the growing boy, who has to break his identification with the mother and identify instead with his father if he is to develop into a normal male adult. Freud believed that the male child develops a strong sexual love for the mother and deeply resents the father, who has prior rights over the mother. Freud termed this phenomenon the "Oedipus complex," after the mythical Greek hero who unwittingly killed his father and married his mother. The boy experiences intense conflict, sometimes even fearing that the father will castrate him, and also real-izing that his love for the mother is inappropriate. This conflict is finally resolved when the boy represses his love of the mother and identifies instead with the father, and is thus enabled to internalize masculine norms of behavior. Freud also toyed with the idea of a parallel process for the girl: although her sex role is already established through her identification with the mother, she still needs to loosen this bond to some extent in order to develop an independent sense of self. He therefore hypothesized a "penis envy" on the part of the small girl which leads her to identify to some extent with her father; once she realizes the futil-ity of the envy, she is free to develop her own independent female sex role.

Freud's theories have intrigued social scientists and the general public for decades. The theories are not really capable of empirical proof, since the processes of identification are said to be unconscious, and many social scientists today reject the specifics of Freud's ideas on sex-role acquisition as being merely fanciful speculation. But one element in his theory remains accepted: the notion that sex-role acquisition is a complex process depending very much on the early experiences of the child in his or her familial and social environment.

Behaviorist theory. Some psychologists believe that all human behavior, attitudes, and values are learned through a process of rewards and punishments. The child who touches a hot stove is punished by the experience of pain, and so learns not to repeat the act; the child who conforms to his or her sex role is rewarded for doing so, and the behavior is repeated and extended. Deviance from the appropriate sex-role behavior, such as that of the little boy who plays with girls' dolls, is punished, if only by ridicule, and so the behavior is discouraged.

Some of these learning experiences are deliberately offered by parents and others: they provide opportunities for the girl to learn to sew, but not the boy; they provide the boy with a baseball, but not the girl. Other conditioning occurs more randomly as the children attempt various behaviors for themselves, and find that some are rewarded while others elicit a negative social response. Gradually, the children are conditioned through this complex process of rewards and punishments into an acceptance of whatever sex-role behaviors are considered appropriate in their society, and they regard any deviation from these roles, in themselves or in others, as being somehow "wrong."

Cognitive-developmental theory. This newer approach, as outlined by Lawrence Kohlberg, differs from behaviorist theory in an important respect. Kohlberg acknowledges the importance of social learning, but places much more emphasis on the individual, who he believes actively constructs his or her own sex role, rather than being passively conditioned into it. Kohlberg regards sex-role acquisition as a consequence of cognitive — that is, intellectual — development. The child, he believes, makes a basic intellectual judgment early in life that he or she is a boy or girl, and then actively selects those activities and values that conform to this self-image. Children define themselves as belonging to one category or another; they develop a strong preference for the category that includes themselves, and construct their experience to conform to this preference.

Kohlberg succinctly explains the difference between the behaviorist approach and his own theory. In the former, the child says, "I want rewards; I am rewarded for doing boy things, therefore I am a boy." In the latter, the child says, "I am a boy, therefore I want to do boy things, therefore the opportunity to do boy things is rewarding to me." The difference between the two approaches lies in the role of the individual: in behaviorist theory, the child is passively conditioned by society; in cognitive-developmental theory, the child takes his cues from the surrounding society but actively constructs his or her own sex role. Both theories acknowledge, however, the importance of socialization as the prime agency through which the individual acquires a sex role.[12]

[12]Lawrence Kohlberg, "A Cognitive-Developmental Analysis of Children's Sex-Role Concepts and Attitudes," in *The Development of Sex Differences*, ed. Maccoby, pp. 82–173.

SEX-ROLE SOCIALIZATION IN AMERICA

Socialization, then, is the process by which an individual becomes a member of his or her society. Humans can survive under an extraordinary range of conditions precisely because, unlike other animals, they lack rigidly patterned responses; they are highly adaptable and almost all their behavior is learned. The growing individual internalizes social norms into his or her personality, and accepts them as defining the "natural" way to behave. Like all social norms, those surrounding sex roles tend to be conservative and resistant to change, which tends to bring about temporary instability and confusion. Deviance from sex-role norms is rare and, as the early women's liberationists discovered, can be strongly penalized.

The learning of sex roles in America takes place largely through three important agencies of socialization: the family, the schools, and the media. Throughout the process, moreover, the peer group plays an important role in monitoring and reinforcing sex-appropriate behavior.

The Role of the Family

Socialization into appropriate sex roles starts early in America, almost at the time of birth. Babies are dressed in sex-related colors and given sex-related toys; the girls are cooed over and the boys are bounced on the parental knee. By the time they are eighteen months old, the children are already behaving according to expectations; the few who attempt to deviate from these expectations thereafter are subject to strong family and peer-group pressure to conform.

In fact, children are so effectively socialized into their sex roles by their parents that they have a clear sense of their own sex and identify with others of like sex long before they are aware of the physiological basis of sex differences. Allan Katcher has found that when children up to the age of four or five are asked to assemble segments of dolls in such a way that the segment containing the genitals matches other parts of the body and clothing style, most children reveal themselves to be confused or entirely ignorant of the genital basis of sex differences.[13] Yet they are quite satisfied that the categories of "boy" and "girl" exist, and identify strongly with their own personal category.

Throughout the childhood years, parents, often unknowingly, take great care to induce sex-appropriate behavior in their children. As Ruth Hartley notes:

> There is little in the girl's training to emphasize instrumental competence or achievement in the mastery of the impersonal aspects of the environment. From infancy, small females are valued in terms

[13]Allan Katcher, "The Discrimination of Sex Differences by Young Children," *Journal of Genetic Psychology*, 87 (September 1955), pp. 131–143.

Boys and girls are socialized into separate attitudes and interests. Parents contribute to this differential socialization in many ways, for example, by giving children sex-related toys and encouraging sex-specific activities. *(Ken Heyman; Joel Gordon/Taurus)*

of the attractiveness of their persons and the appropriateness of their interpersonal responses. They are directed toward the manipulation of persons as a means of obtaining gratification. Little is demanded of them in the way of competitive or autonomous achievement. The stress is not on proving one's prowess, but rather on avoiding the objectionable. Girls gain approval . . . by doing the rather undemanding things that are expected of them. . . . A girl need not be bright as long as she is docile and attractive. Brightness is often regarded as a hazard, and girls are made to feel they should disguise such unseemly tendencies. This kind of treatment is likely to produce rather timid, unventuresome, unoriginal, conformist types.[14]

The early socialization of boys, however, is entirely different:

Almost from birth the boy has more problems to solve autonomously. In addition, he is required to limit his interests at a very early age to sex-appropriate objects and activities, while girls are permitted to amble their way to a similar status at a more gradual and natural pace. . . . He is challenged to discover what he should do by being told what he should *not* do, as in the most frequently employed negative sanction, "Don't be a sissy!" . . . Interest in girlish things is generally forbidden and anxiety-provoking in American boyhood. . . . The boy is constantly open to a challenge to prove his masculinity. He must perform, adequately and publicly, a variety of physical feats that will have very little utility in most cases in adulthood. He is constantly under pressure to demonstrate mastery over the environment, and, concomitantly, to suppress expression of emotion.[15]

By encouraging some behavior and discouraging other behavior, the parents ensure that the early experience of their children will equip them with a strong preference for particular sex-role orientations.

The Role of the School

The school reinforces sex roles in many ways. Often, there is a sex-based segregation of many curricular activities: girls are channeled into sewing and cooking classes, and boys into woodworking and printing classes. The girl who tries to enter a mechanics class may still face ridicule and even a tough battle to register for the course, and so may the boy who tries to register for a sewing or ballet class. The school discourages boys in particular from pursuing "feminine" interests: they may find deviance from the female role in the direction of the male role just tolerable, but reverse deviance is shameful and incomprehensible.

[14]Ruth E. Hartley, "American Core Culture: Changes and Continuities," in *Sex Roles in Changing Society,* eds. Georgene H. Seward and Robert C. Williamson (New York: Random House, 1970), pp. 140–141.
[15]Ibid., p. 141.

Although girls are academically more advanced than boys of the same age during the early school years, they gradually lose this advantage. They do progressively less well compared with the boys, fewer of them go on to college, and fewer still to graduate school. Many factors underlie this wastage of female talent, but one of them is probably the fact that many schools do not encourage academic success in girls to the same extent as in boys. The girls, perhaps lacking confidence in their ability to achieve in such subjects as science, are given little encouragement to tackle "masculine" courses. As Elizabeth Janeway points out:

> "Why should I bother to study this science or tackle that technical subject?" an intelligent girl may still ask herself. She is encouraged by the very situation in which she finds herself to let inertia take hold and say, "I needn't bother learning that, I'm only a girl."[16]

Children's schoolbooks also encourage sex-typed attitudes. Several studies have shown how the literature for children, in both its stories and illustrations, presents sex-typed images of how children should behave in later years. One study focused on the children's picture books that are supposed to be the very best available—those that have won the Caldecott medal of the American Library Association for the best children's books of the year. These books are widely used in preschool education, but in close to a third of the books in the sample there was no female character at all; and when females were present, they usually had an insignificant or inconspicuous role. Since women represent 51 percent of the population, it might have been expected that about half the characters would be female, but in fact males outnumbered females in the books by a ratio of 11 to 1. In the case of the other animals with obvious sex identities, the ratio was even higher: 95 to 1. The ratio of titles featuring males and females was 8 to 3. As for the general content of the books, the researchers concluded:

> In the world of picture books, boys are active and girls are passive. Not only are boys presented in more exciting and venturesome roles, but they engage in more varied pursuits and demand more independence. . . . In contrast, most of the girls in the picture books are passive and immobile. Some are restricted by their clothing—skirts and dresses are soiled easily and prohibit more adventurous activities.[17]

School textbooks follow a similar pattern. One study by Marjorie U'Ren found that many books devote only 15 percent of their illustrations to women, and concluded, "the significance of this imbalance is

[16]Elizabeth Janeway, *Man's World, Woman's Place: A Study in Social Mythology* (New York: Dell, 1971), p. 101.
[17]Lenore J. Weitzman, et al., "Sex Role Socialization in Picture Books for Preschool Children," *American Journal of Sociology*, vol. 77, no. 6 (May 1972), pp. 1125–1149.

obvious. We tend to forget the simple fact that the female sex is half the species, that women are not merely a ladies' auxiliary to the human race."[18] Florence Howe points out that in an annotated catalog of books distributed to teachers through the National Council of Teachers of English, titles are listed separately under "especially for boys" and "especially for girls." Howe's own analysis of school readers that are intended for both sexes concluded:

> Primers used in the first three grades offer children a view of a "typical" American family: a mother who does not work, a father who does, two children—a brother who is always older than a sister—and two pets—a dog and sometimes a cat—whose ages and sexes mirror those of the brother and sister. In these books, boys build or paint things; they also pull girls in wagons and push merry-go-rounds. Girls carry purses when they go shopping; they help mother cook or pretend that they are cooking; and they play with their dolls. . . . Plots in which girls are involved usually depend on their inability to do something—to manage their own roller skates or to ride a pony.[19]

These images, Howe points out, may contribute significantly to children's sense of their own identity and potential.

There is some evidence that girls are afraid of academic success because of its "unfeminine" connotations. One researcher, Matina Horner, administered a simple test to groups of male and female students. The male students had to make up a story based on the cue: "After first term exams, John finds himself at the top of his medical school class." The girls had to make up a story based on the same cue, but with the name "Anne" substituted for "John." When male students made up a story, over 90 percent of them showed strongly positive feelings to the cue. A typical story, for example, included comments such as:

> John is a conscientious young man who always worked hard. He is pleased with himself. John always wanted to go into medicine and is very dedicated. . . . He continues to work hard and eventually graduates top of his class.

When female students made up a story, however, some 65 percent of them were troubled, disconcerted, or confused by the cue. The academic achievement of "Anne" was clearly associated with loss of femininity and prestige. Most of the responses indicated negative consequences for "Anne": "Anne will deliberately lower her academic standing next term, while she does all she subtly can to help Carl. . . . His grades come up and Anne soon drops out of medical school. They marry and he goes on in school while she raises their family." And: "Aggres-

---

[18]Marjorie B. U'Ren, "The Image of Women in Textbooks," in *Women in Sexist Society,* eds. Gornick and Moran, p. 326.
[19]Florence Howe, "Sexual Stereotypes Start Early," *Saturday Review* (October 16, 1971), p. 82.

sive, unmarried, wearing Oxford shoes and hair pulled back in a bun, she wears glasses and is terribly bright." Male students also react negatively if the name of "Anne" is substituted for "John" in their cue. Their responses are overwhelmingly along the following lines: "Anne is paralyzed from the waist down. She sits in a wheelchair and studies for medical school." Or: "Anne is not a woman. She is really a computer, the best in a new line of machines."[20] The informal attitudes and values reflected in these comments are an important element in an academic and peer-group environment which discourages female ambition and success.

The Role of the Media

The media, and particularly media advertisements, are an important influence on sex-role socialization. Lucy Komisar draws attention to this function of advertising:

> Advertising is an insidious propaganda machine . . . it spews out images of women as sex mates, housekeepers, mothers and menial workers—images that perhaps reflect the true status of women in society, but which also make it increasingly difficult for women to break out of the sexist stereotypes that imprison them. . . . Advertising . . . legitimizes the ideal, stereotyped roles of woman as temptress, wife, mother and sex object, and portrays women as less intelligent and more dependent than men. It makes women believe that their chief role is to please men and that their fulfillment will be as wives, mothers, and homemakers. It makes women feel unfeminine if they are not pretty enough and guilty if they do not spend most of their time in desperate attempts to imitate gourmet cooks. . . . It makes women believe that their own lives, talents, and interests ought to be secondary to the needs of their husbands. . . . Advertising also reinforces men's concepts about women's place and women's role—and about their own roles. . . . Why is it masculine for men to wash cars, but a sign of "henpecking" for them to wash dishes?[21]

Media advertisements, particularly TV commercials, are often alleged not only to reflect false stereotypes, but also to exploit the sexuality of women and to demean their intelligence. Germaine Greer makes this point with considerable force:

> Every survey ever held has shown that the image of an attractive woman is the most effective advertising gimmick. She may sit a-

[20]Vivian Gornick, "Why Women Fear Success," *New York Times Magazine* (December 20, 1971).
[21]Lucy Komisar, "The Image of Women in Advertising," in *Women in Sexist Society,* eds. Gornick and Moran, pp. 304–311.

stride the mudguard of a new car, or step into it ablaze with jewels; she may lie at a man's feet stroking his new socks; she . . . may dance through woodland glades in slow motion in all the glory of a new shampoo; whatever she does her image sells. . . . Her glossy lips and mat complexion, her unfocused eyes and flawless fingers, her extraordinary hair all floating and shining, curling and gleaming, reveal the inhuman triumph of cosmetics, lighting, focusing and printing, cropping and composition. She sleeps unruffled, her lips red and juicy and closed, her eyes as crisp and black as if new painted, and her false lashes immaculately curled. Even when she washes her face with a new and creamy toilet soap her expression is as tranquil and vacant and her paint as flawless as ever. If ever she should appear tousled and troubled, her features are miraculously smoothed to their proper veneer by a new washing powder or a bouillon cube. For she is a doll: weeping, pouting or smiling, running or reclining, she is a doll. . . .

So the image of woman appears plastered on every surface imaginable, smiling interminably. An apple pie evokes a glance of tender beatitude, a washing machine causes hilarity, a cheap box of chocolates brings forth meltingly joyous gratitude . . . even a new stick-on bandage is saluted by a smirk of satisfaction.[22]

Advertising copywriters do not seem to have a high regard for the intelligence of their female audience. The following is a profile of the typical housewife, printed in *Ad Age,* a magazine for professional advertisers:

She does not enjoy reading a great deal. . . . She finds her satisfaction within a rather small world and the center of this world is her home. She has little interest or skill to explore, to probe into things for herself. Her energy is largely consumed in day-to-day living. She is very much open to suggestion and amenable to guidance.

She tends to have a negative or anti-conceptual way of thinking. Mental activity is arduous for her. Her ability for inference particularly in unfamiliar areas is limited. And she tends to experience discomfort and confusion when faced with ambiguity or too many alternatives. . . . She is a person who wants to have things she can believe in with certainty, rather than things she has to think about.[23]

As a result of these attitudes, TV ads show women rapturously caressing newly polished tables, or going into ecstasies over the dazzling whiteness of their wash. Advertising directed to a male audience also exploits the stereotype of the unintelligent woman. Parker pens used

---

[22]Germaine Greer, *The Female Eunuch* (New York: Bantam Books, 1971), p. 57.
[23]Quoted in Komisar, "The Image of Women in Advertising," p. 312.

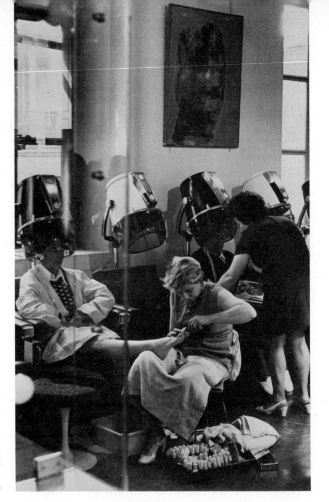

American females learn to place great value on their physical attractiveness and their youth. Mass media advertising encourages these attitudes, and a multi-billion dollar cosmetics industry exploits them. *(Martine Frank, VIVA/Woodfin Camp)*

this advertisement: "You might as well give her a gorgeous pen to keep her checkbook unbalanced with. A sleek and shining pen will make her feel prettier. Which is more important to any girl than solving mathematical mysteries."[24] IBM has a telling advertisement for a new typewriter: "If she makes a mistake, she types right over it. If her boss makes a revision, she types just the revision." Secretaries, it seems, make "mistakes," but bosses make only "revisions."[25] A Dictaphone corporation advertisement shows a calculator being presented to an attractive secretary, with the caption, "Our new line of calculators goes through its final ordeal. The dumb blonde test."[26]

These images are part of our culture, both reflecting and reinforcing existing sex roles. No individual reared in our society is entirely immune from them, and most of us are unconsciously but profoundly affected by them.

[24]Ibid., p. 306.
[25]Ibid., p. 308.
[26]Ibid., p. 309.

THE SOCIAL COSTS OF CONTEMPORARY SEX ROLES

Our existing sex-role arrangements exact considerable personal and social costs – partly through the economic and cultural loss to society resulting from the underutilization of the talents of half the population, and partly through the psychological stresses that adherence to rigid sex roles can cause in both males and females.

The United States makes poor use of the potential talents of women. Since the defining aspects of success in America – dominance, aggressiveness, competitiveness – are all ascribed to the male in our society, women tend to be relegated to a subordinate status, and valued for their personal appearance and nurturant support rather than for their talents and abilities. Women are not expected to become writers, rock guitarists, engineers, or nuclear physicists, and this expectation becomes a self-fulfilling prophecy: many women internalize the low image that society has of them and do not seriously consider a "male" career.

The unemployment rate for women is about a third higher than that for men, and the median income is lower even in the same occupations. Among professional workers, women earn only two-thirds of the salary of similarly employed men; among sales workers, they earn only 40 percent of the wages of men. The socialization process prepares women to aspire primarily to menial, low-paid positions – eternally the organization's secretary, never its president.

Women Earn Less in All Types of Employment

Type of Employment	MEDIAN ANNUAL EARNINGS OF FULL-TIME WORKERS	
	Male	Female
Professional, technical	$12,518	$8,312
Schoolteachers	9,913	8,126
Managerial	12,721	6,738
Clerks	9,124	5,696
Salesmen	10,650	4,485
Craftsmen	9,627	5,425
Factory hands	7,915	4,789
Laborers	6,866	4,548
Service workers	7,111	4,159

SOURCE: "Sex Equality: Impact of a Key Decision," *U.S. News & World Report* (May 28, 1973).

Women have little influence in public life. In the mid-seventies, they held less than two dozen seats in the House of Representatives, no seats in the Senate, and no mayorships of large cities. They headed no government departments, regulatory agencies, large corporations, or major universities. The relatively low educational attainment of women compounds their difficulties in aspiring to positions of eminence in other areas of life. At the end of the last decade, women represented 42 percent of those taking a bachelor's degree, 37 percent of those taking a master's degree, and only 13 percent of those taking a Ph.D. or its equivalent.[27]

In addition to the economic, cultural, and educational barriers that women face, they also have to contend with legislation that is often based on the notion of a woman as a person incapable of handling her own affairs. Although many of these laws are being repealed, and most will become unconstitutional when the new Equal Rights Amendment is ratified, there are still restrictions on a married woman owning property, acquiring credit cards, or entering contracts without her husband's signed consent. A federal commission reported in 1970 that

> At the state level there are numerous laws regulating marriage, guardianship, dependents, property ownership, dower rights and domicile, which clearly discriminate against women as autonomous, mature persons.[28]

Traditional sex roles pose difficult psychological problems for many women. Germaine Greer argues that these role requirements turn women into "female eunuchs" rather than females: "the characteristics that are praised and rewarded are those of the castrate — timidity, plumpness, languor, delicacy, preciosity." Modern women, she maintains, are not so much women as "female impersonators," impersonating an impossible and absurd notion of femininity as endorsed by a male-dominated society and encouraged by a thriving cosmetics industry. If they accept this stereotype, women must relinquish all possibility of fully exploring their human potential and talents; if they reject it, they face problems of role conflict and personal identity, and risk being regarded as "unfeminine." The psychological costs are particularly severe when the woman approaches middle age: socialized into believing that her main asset is her physical attractiveness and her main function the rearing of a family, she often watches with feelings of desolation as both her children and her youth leave her.

Although much has been written of the psychological costs to women of contemporary roles, the psychological costs to men have been largely neglected. The American male is often unable to show emotion; in particular, he is prohibited from exhibiting signs of distress or from expressing the same degree of affection to other males that American females may express to one another. Although we are now an urbanized, sophisticated society, the image of the tough, self-reliant frontiersman still lingers in America; the dullest corporate bureaucrat seems to feel that inside him there is a John Wayne struggling to leap out. The American horror of "effeminacy" affects even the gentler modern youths: unlike their counterparts in Paris or London who sport lace,

---

[27]U.S. Bureau of the Census, *Statistical Abstract of the United States, 1971* (Washington, D.C.: U.S. Department of Commerce, 1971), p. 13.

[28]Report of the President's Task Force on Women's Rights and Responsibilities, *A Matter of Simple Justice* (Washington, D.C.: U.S. Government Printing Office, 1970), p. 5.

The Female Eunuch

I'm sick of the masquerade. I'm sick of pretending eternal youth. I'm sick of belying my own intelligence, my own will, my own sex. I'm sick of peering at the world through false eyelashes, so everything I see is mixed with a shadow of bought hairs; I'm sick of weighting my head with a dead mane, unable to move my neck freely, terrified of rain, of wind, of dancing too vigorously in case I sweat into my lacquered curls. I'm sick of the Powder Room. I'm sick of pretending that some fatuous male's self-important pronouncements are the objects of my undivided attention, I'm sick of going to films and plays when someone else wants to, and sick of having no opinions of my own about either. I'm sick of being a transvestite. I refuse to be a female impersonator. I am a woman, not a castrate.

SOURCE: Germaine Greer, *The Female Eunuch* (New York: McGraw-Hill, 1971).

velvet, and even earrings without feeling their masculinity undermined, these young Americans still prefer rough jeans and army jackets. Ruth Hartley argues that the sex-role socialization process for males inevitably destines them to personal conflicts in later years:

> The boy is not adequately socialized for adulthood. Many of the demands made on him are inconsistent with the requirements of adulthood. Intellectual performance is subordinated to physical prowess in childhood and adolescence; increasingly complex technology demands more and more intensive training in abstract concepts in adulthood. The boy is conditioned to live in an all-masculine society, defining his own self-image by rejecting whatever smacks of femininity. In adulthood he will have to adjust to a heterosexual work world, perhaps even take orders from a female, a species he has been taught to despise as inferior. Finally, the emphasis on repression of the emotions, the high value of stoicism, leaves the boy wholly unprepared for the emotional closeness and intimate personal interaction now more and more expected of a lover and a spouse.[29]

American men are also subject to some legal restrictions or obligations that do not apply to women: to fight in time of war, for example. A husband is legally obliged to provide financial support for his family, and failure to provide this support can constitute grounds for desertion or divorce by the wife. A separated husband who wishes to rear his own children may also find himself facing a divorce court that tends to view women as being uniquely equipped, regardless of their personal characteristics, to bring up children; in disputes over custody of chil-

[29]Hartley, "American Core Culture: Changes and Continuities," p. 142.

dren, legal agencies look much more favorably on the claims of the mother.

The traditional male role in our society is a very demanding and stressful one. Men are five times more likely than women to commit suicide, and it is noteworthy that the suicide rate among husbands rises much more sharply than among wives after the breakup of a marriage. Men suffering from severe mental disorders outnumber women by three to one. Alcoholics and narcotics addicts are overwhelmingly male. Men are also far more prone to criminal activity and to deviant behavior of almost every kind. They also have a disproportionately high rate of stress-related illnesses, such as ulcers, hypertension, and heart disease.

Each sex role has its advantages and disadvantages. To some extent the roles are mutually derogatory, but because they permit men and women to feel superior to one another in some ways and inferior in others, they encourage a feeling of mutual dependence and so are functional to some extent. The problem is that many of our sex-role attributes are relics of a past age, serve no particular function, and in fact exact unnecessary social and personal costs.

PROSPECTS FOR THE FUTURE

American sex roles are changing rapidly, primarily under the impact of the women's liberation movement. The double standard of sexual morality, which tolerated a degree of sexual promiscuity on the part of males but required females to be virginal before marriage and faithful thereafter, is fast disappearing. The rights of women to achieve high occupational status are at least formally recognized, and many corporations, colleges, and other organizations are making deliberate efforts to hire women in preference to similarly qualified men. The need for extended day-care facilities which might release women from the home is becoming recognized, and these facilities are being provided to an unprecedented, if still inadequate, extent. Several states have enacted legislation to make abortions easier to obtain, and this legislation has been held constitutional by the Supreme Court (although many people reject the view that abortion is a "women's lib" issue and see it as a purely ethical one). Women who demand equal rights with men are no longer considered neurotics or deviants. But there still remain major barriers to further changes in sex roles.

One of these barriers is the attitudes of women themselves, who have been somewhat conservative and slow to assert their rights—a phenomenon found in all subordinate groups in the initial stages of the awakening consciousness of their disadvantaged situation. In a 1970 Gallup poll, some 65 percent of American women agreed that "women get as good a break in this country as men." In 1971 a Gallup poll showed that a plurality of women (42 percent to 40 percent, with the rest undecided) were opposed to "efforts to strengthen and change women's place in society." The following year, however, views had changed: such efforts were supported by a small plurality of women (42 percent to 38 percent). Most women still remained unsympathetic to radical liberationist efforts to improve their position, however, and opposed the women's liberation movement by 49 percent to 35 percent. But three-quarters of women believed in 1972 that a woman in public office could act "as rationally as a man."[30] It is likely that women's support for changes in the female sex role will increase in future years, as an idea of equality that once seemed far-fetched and unnatural becomes an accepted part of social reality.

A second barrier, however, is likely to be the male population. Already discomforted to some extent by the new demands of women, men are likely to have to face a campaign for "men's liberation" at some point in the future, and since male sex roles are both more advantageous and more deeply entrenched, change is likely to be slow. But if women are enabled to occupy the more highly paid jobs, the basis for the male's domination of the family will be substantially eroded as he is deprived of his sex-linked economic importance; and some adjustment in the patterns of authority and deference between husband and wife will inevitably follow. Already, too, many males find it much easier to be gentle, emotional, and expressive than they did even a few years ago.

But full equality will involve extensive structural changes in American society. Equal wages will have to be paid for equal work, and more important, women will have to be paid reasonable wages for the work that has traditionally been reserved for them. Socialization patterns as mediated through the schools, movies, TV, radio, and newspapers will have to be altered. Many powerful interests, such as the advertising industry or the giant $3 billion per year cosmetics industry, will not readily sacrifice the profits to be gleaned from stressing traditional sex-role stereotypes. Many of these structural changes may come about through the application of the new Equal Rights Amendment to the Constitution, which states unambiguously: "Equality of rights under the law shall not be denied or abridged by the United States or by any State on account of sex."

At the moment there is no clarity as to exactly what the sex roles of a future American society will be like. Sexual equality does not necessarily mean sexual similarity, and there is no reason to suppose that a "unisex" society will ultimately emerge. Similarly, sexual equality does not necessarily mean that women will have to adopt the existing attributes of men, nor that men and women will have to converge on some happy medium between the two present roles. What is important is that we realize that human beings can, in principle, be socialized into whatever kind of sex role is desired: what is to be hoped for is that the

[30]Judy Klemesrud, "Do Women Want Equality? A Poll Says Most Do Now," *New York Times* (March 24, 1972), p. 35.

Sex Roles: A Theoretical Review

The social problem of sex roles represents the gap between a *social ideal* of full equality between the sexes with the elimination of rigid, sex-based roles, and the *social reality* of a society in which women are subordinated to men and in which each sex is expected to adhere to an arbitrary and stereotyped role. The social problem is in a sense a "new" one: although it was latent (concealed) for generations, it is only within the last decade or so that there has been a wide realization that the characteristics we term "masculine" and "feminine" are social products, and are not necessarily related to the biological characteristics of "male" and "female."

The *social-disorganization* perspective provides a useful framework for the analysis of the social problem of sex roles. In the past, the allocation of different roles to each sex served certain functional purposes. In a traditional hunting and gathering community, it was useful to have women rear children and take care of the home while men engaged in more strenuous activities further afield. This basic division of labor has some biological basis: a woman who is pregnant or suckling cannot go hunting or foraging at a distance from the home; and men, who are better adapted physically for short-term feats of endurance, tended to undertake functions that called for these qualities. The superior strength of the male, combined with his role as family provider, guaranteed him a dominant role over the female, and it seems that these early arrangements have become institutionalized in most societies—lingering even when they are no longer relevant or appropriate.

Our modern industrial society still has a sex-based division of labor, but, although a division of labor is itself functional to a society, a division on such arbitrary grounds as sex is dysfunctional. It deprives society of the full use of the talents of half of the population, and has many other effects as well—notably the continued subordination of the female as a result of her relatively low earnings. Sex roles and the personality characteristics that come with them have become so deeply ingrained in our culture that many people regard them as "natural" rather than as a social product. This phenomenon is common in other cases of prolonged definition of one group as inferior to another: slave-owning societies have always regarded slaves as "naturally" inferior, and the same is true of the attitudes of racist majorities toward subordinate racial minorities.

The social problem has become increasingly visible because of the rapid changes in attitudes and values of the past few years. As long as women shared the view that they were biologically destined to be subordinate to men, their position was at least tolerable, but now that our sex-role arrangements are seen as an unjust violation of basic norms of social equality, women feel increased frustration. Men, too, are becoming aware that the stresses of the male role are not inevitable. The inconsistency between social norms specifying human equality and equality of opportunity, on the one hand, and, our sexist practices, on the other hand, is a symptom of an underlying social disorganization.

The *value-conflict* perspective also offers a useful way of looking at the problem. Men and women have different interests in our society as it is presently structured, and some value conflicts between them are inevitable. Women are deprived of many of the opportunities open to men, and meet a good deal of resistance when they attempt to rectify the situation. Many males have been socialized into a belief in their natural superiority, and they find the new demands of women threatening to their own sense of identity and, in some cases, to their economic security. Significant changes in the economic and social status of women will tend to undermine the authority of the husband in the home, and to many men such a development would be extremely disturbing. In addition, there is considerable scope for conflict between those men and women who are willing to reject traditional roles and those men and women who still prefer and adhere to the traditional roles. Many value-conflict theorists regard the conflict surrounding the problem of sex roles as essentially beneficial; if there were no conflict the issues involved might not attract public attention, and the traditional sex roles might be maintained indefinitely.

The *deviance* perspective is also helpful in the analysis of the problem of sex roles. All the important agencies of socialization in our society—family, media, peer group, and schools—have traditionally reinforced the old sex-role stereotypes, and to a very large extent they continue to do so. Those who fail to internalize or who reject the established sex roles are often regarded as deviant, and this labeling process serves to restrain deviance from the existing roles. The early spokeswomen of the women's liberation movement were often stigmatized for what appeared at the time to be highly deviant behavior, but women are now permitted a much wider range of deviance from the traditional roles than before—although there are still limits. Deviance in men, however, remains highly stigmatized, and "feminine" behavior of any kind is met with ridicule. Our existing sex roles will continue to be reinforced for as long as those who reject them are labeled as deviants.

roles will be functional for the maintenance of society and the dignity of all its members. As Janet Chafetz observes:

> We need to develop some alternatives: a utopia. This cannot consist merely of concrete suggestions like "equal pay for equal work" and more day care centers, important as such things are. We need a vision of what it would mean to be a society not of feminine and masculine creatures, but comprised of humans. The truth of the matter is that we have no real notion of what it means to be human, divorced from notions of masculinity and femininity. Traditionally, human has largely meant masculine; all too often today we make the same error, and, for many, women's liberation becomes merely a question of how females can acquire the prerogatives traditionally allocated to males. I for one do not wish to trade the disadvantages of the feminine sex role simply to be burdened with those of the masculine role.[31]

---

[31]Janet Saltzman Chafetz, *Masculine/Feminine or Human?* (New York: Peacock Publishers, 1974), p. 201.

FURTHER READING

Brenton, Myron, *The American Male: A Penetrating Look at the Masculinity Crisis*, 1966. A readable account of the inconsistencies and tensions inherent in the stereotypical male role. Brenton contends that our contemporary conflict about masculinity has undesirable effects on both males and females. The book is written for the general public but is based on social science research.

Cade, Toni, ed., *The Black Woman*, 1970. An anthology of fiction and scholarly essays on the problems of being a black woman in America and, therefore, subject to double discrimination.

Chafetz, Janet Saltzman, *Masculine/Feminine or Human?* 1974. A comprehensive introductory text on sex roles. Chafetz strongly argues the need to develop new sex roles and not simply to make women more like men.

Ford, Clellan S. and Frank Beach, *Patterns of Sexual Behavior,* 1951. A modern classic on sex roles and sexual behavior, drawing together and comparing data from many cultures around the world. The book is essential reading for anyone who wishes to see American sex roles in broader perspective.

Friedan, Betty, *The Feminine Mystique,* 1963. The book that launched the women's liberation movement. A movingly written account of the subordinate role of women in contemporary America.

Gornick, Vivian and Barbara K. Moran, eds., *Women in Sexist Society: Studies in Power and Powerlessness,* 1971. An outstanding collection of eminent writings. The contributions cover a variety of topics, including the sex-role socialization provided by the school and the media.

Greer, Germaine, *The Female Eunuch,* 1971. A best seller, probably the most widely read and eminent book of its kind in recent years. Greer writes in a warm, humorous, and pungent style that provides penetrating insights into the way women are socialized into adopting certain attitudes toward their bodies, themselves, and men.

Maccoby, Eleanor, ed., *The Development of Sex Differences,* 1966. A collection of very sophisticated articles on the acquisition of sex roles. The book includes essays on the cognitive-development and the social-learning theories of sex-role acquisition, as well as cross-cultural material and an extensive bibliography.

Mead, Margaret, *Male and Female,* 1968. A distinguished anthropologist, who has studied sex roles in the United States, analyzes our notions of masculinity and femininity in a cross-cultural context.

Report of the President's Task Force on Women's Rights and Responsibilities, American society. Contains a wealth of data and information on the many ways in which women continue to suffer from discrimination in the United States.

part four

Private Troubles and Public Issues

ne of the most important sociological insights is into the intimate connection between the problems of the individual and the nature of the social environment. However private a person's troubles may seem, they are often ultimately traceable to the features of the society in which he or she lives. The American sociologist C. Wright Mills believed that the capability to see this relationship between "private troubles" and "public issues" is a major element in the sociological imagination. This sociological imagination has profoundly affected our understanding of many social problems.

In the past many apparently private troubles—such as suicide or alcoholism—were analyzed in terms of individual biology or psychology. Today purely individual explanations are no longer adequate. We recognize that we must take into account the social context in which a person determines to take his life or become an alcoholic.

In this section we explore a number of social problems that may seem at first sight to originate in the behavior of the individual. For example, a family problem such as divorce is often regarded as a private trouble; but sociological analysis reveals that the divorce rate varies from one society to another and that the United States has the highest divorce rate in the industrialized world. Certain social forces, therefore, make it more likely that an American marriage will end in the personal misfortune of divorce.

The human life cycle may seem, at first, to be a biological process of no particular concern to the sociologist. A closer analysis shows that the nature, length, and content of the life cycle is influenced by the social context in which it is lived—some social groups, for example, have a much shorter life expectancy than others. Even the content of the phases of the life cycle depends on social forces; the troubled phase of adolescence is unknown in most parts of the world, as is the loneliness that many of the aged experience in American society.

Crime, too, cannot be fully analyzed on the level of an individual crime and an individual victim; different types of crime are found in different social contexts, and members of some social groups are more likely to engage in criminal acts than members of other social groups. Indeed, the very decision to make some acts (such as smoking marijuana) a crime is a social decision. The nature and incidence of crime is thus influenced by social forces.

Mental disorders have usually been regarded as a private trouble. Historically, those with mental disorders were considered the victims of their own heredity or even of evil spirits. Today we realize that there is no absolute dividing line between the sane and the insane. The definition depends on socially relative judgments, and we realize that the incidence of mental disorder varies from society to society. Some social contexts, therefore, seem more likely than others to promote emotional disturbance. Again, the nature and frequency of a personal trouble is seen to be intimately linked to the society in which it is found.

Variant sexual behavior has been traditionally seen in purely personal terms, with deviance being explained by an individual's biology, heredity, or even morality. But sociological analysis shows that definitions of sexual normality vary from situation to situation, as does the degree of variance that is socially permissible. The incidence of many forms of sexual variance is culturally relative, as is the social response to the variance.

Drug abuse is an individual act that often leads to personal tragedy. A high rate of drug abuse in a society depends on such factors as the availability of drugs, subcultural norms that tolerate or encourage drug consumption, and social pressure that may drive individuals or groups to abuse drugs. Even the decision as to what constitutes a drug is a socially variable one; one task of the sociologist is to discover why some dangerous drugs are freely available in our society while other less dangerous ones are illegal.

12

The Family

THE NATURE AND SCOPE OF THE PROBLEM

Nearly one American marriage in every four ends in the divorce courts, and the average marriage lasts only seven years.[1] Of those marriages that still survive, many are merely "empty shell" arrangements, in which the partners continue to live in loveless apathy through sheer habit, or in which they attempt to suppress their mutual antagonism "for the sake of the children." There is no shortage of critics who assert that the family as we know it is doomed—the victim either of moral decay or of irresistible social forces. Throughout the seventies, a stream of books and articles has lamented—and sometimes welcomed—the imminent demise of the American family.[2]

There is certainly a good deal of evidence to support the view that something is seriously amiss with our family system. The divorce rate has doubled since the early sixties and is still rising; moreover, the social stigma attached to divorce is no longer as strong as it was even a few years ago. Illegitimacy rates have soared, and they would probably be a good deal higher if abortions and contraceptive devices were not so freely available. Teen-agers are running away from home in unprecedented numbers. The aged are being cast adrift from the family in increasing numbers, and many of them live alone or with unrelated people. Homosexuality and bisexuality are being openly advo-

[1]Paul C. Glick and Arthur J. Norton, "Perspectives on the Recent Upturn in Divorce and Remarriage," *Demography*, vol. 10, no. 3 (August 1973), pp. 301–314.
[2]See, for example, Gordon F. Streib, ed., *The Changing Family: Adaptation and Diversity* (Reading, Mass.: Addison-Wesley, 1973); Gwen B. Carr, *Marriage and Family in a Decade of Change* (Reading, Mass.: Addison-Wesley, 1972); Frank D. Cox, ed., *American Marriage* (Dubuque, Iowa: William C. Brown, 1972); and John F. Crosby, *Illusion and Disillusion: The Self in Love and Marriage* (Belmont, Calif.: Wadsworth, 1973).

cated as alternative life styles, and a number of churches have performed homosexual marriages. The "sexual revolution," with its sanctioning of sexual intercourse outside marriage and its tolerance of group sex or "swinging," seems to be undermining the sexual basis of the marital institution. The women's liberation movement has put new strain on the traditional family by asserting the right of the wife to full equality, and some feminists have even condemned the entire institution as inherently oppressive. Experimental alternatives to the family abound—group "marriage," "open" marriage, "free love" communes, and semipermanent cohabitation between partners who do not intend to marry. The family is also the site of a great deal of intergenerational and interpersonal conflict, and it often seems ill adapted to handle the many problems—such as mental disorders, alcoholism, or juvenile delinquency— that may profoundly affect the home.

Although most sociologists recognize that the family institution is currently in a state of some disorganization, they do not usually share in these gloomy predictions. Fears about the disintegration of the family and the consequent disruption of society are as old as history; ancient manuscripts from dozens of cultures contain long catalogs of complaints that might be very familiar to modern Americans. And although the United States has had the highest divorce rate in the Western world for over twenty years, there are other societies—notably in the Middle East—that have experienced much higher rates without a collapse of their family or social systems. The family, it is true, has contributed to a good deal of human grief over the centuries, but it has also had such positive personal and social value that it still remains a basic social unit in every culture. Sociologists, therefore, take the view that the family is not so much dying as changing. The changes may be drastic, they may take forms that we cannot yet foresee, and the future family may fulfill functions rather different from those of our present institution, but there will still be families of some kind. Before we examine some of the problems of the family, let us take a closer look at the institution itself.

The Nature of the Family

We all assume that we know what a "family" is, but in fact the institution is not easily defined. Are illegitimate children, for example, members of a family? Is a second cousin's brother-in-law a member of the family? Are separated but undivorced partners still in the same family? As sociologist Arlene Skolnick points out:

> The family has proved to be an elusive concept, in spite of our conviction that we know what families are all about. Trying to pin down the meaning of the term is not just an intellectual game. There is . . . genuine doubt among those who have thought about the matter just what it is that distinguishes families from non-families, and

whether there is a single definition of family that applies to all times and places.[3]

One sociologist, Lucile Duberman, defines a family as any institution that provides a child with a legitimate place in society and provides the nurturance that will enable the child to function as a fully developed member of the community.[4] Ira Reiss believes that any institution that performs the function of caring for the young is a family — even if it is a social unit in which the roles of "parent" as we traditionally understand them do not exist.[5] Morris Zelditch, on the other hand, argues that a family only exists if it is legitimated by the presence of someone fulfilling the role of father.[6] In general, however, the American family is usually thought of as an independent unit consisting of a married couple and their dependent children.

The consequences of this conception of the family can be very important. It may lead, for example, to many arbitrary distinctions. A divorced father may spend a great deal more time visiting his children than does a married father who, because he is a seaman or traveling salesman, sees his children much less frequently. Yet the former family is considered disrupted while the latter is regarded as intact. Moreover, as soon as people accept some standard definition of a family, they tend to regard this particular form as the "ideal" family, and to believe that it is natural and good, if not God-given and immutable. Potential alternative structures are consequently belittled because they seem to violate the natural order. Those who defy the marital conventions are apt to be regarded as escapist, immoral, neurotic, immature, or irresponsible. Family units that differ from the "ideal" form are usually treated as deviant and undesirable patterns, rather than as viable alternatives in their own right.

Family patterns in other cultures. One of the reasons why social scientists are so confident that the American family is unlikely to disappear is that no society has ever existed without the institution. As sociologist William Goode observes:

> The family still looms large as a major kind of social arrangement in all societies, not just in our own. Many societies do not have formal organizations for making war. A goodly number of societies do not have markets as we know them; many have economic systems that are not at all separated from the family patterns. But all societies, however primitive or industrialized, have family patterns.[7]

Many of these family patterns, however, are very unlike our own. An-

[3]Arlene Skolnick, *The Intimate Environment* (Boston: Little, Brown, 1973), p. 5.
[4]Lucile Duberman, *Marriage and Its Alternatives* (New York: Praeger, 1974).
[5]Ira L. Reiss, *The Family System in America* (New York: Holt, Rinehart & Winston, 1971).
[6]Morris Zelditch, "Family, Marriage, and Kinship," in *Handbook of Modern Sociology*, ed. R. E. L. Faris (Chicago: Rand-McNally, 1964), pp. 680–733.
[7]William J. Goode, *The Contemporary American Family* (Chicago: Quadrangle Books, 1971), p. 5.

thropologists have found societies in which lineage is traced through the mother, not the father. They have found societies in which young children are sent to live permanently in other households. They have found societies in which husband and wife separate for several years after the birth of each child, and they have even found societies in which husband and wife are expected to live in separate dwellings. There are some societies in which the biological father is not considered to be the real father at all, and plays no part in the children's upbringing; in these societies the mother's brother is usually responsible for raising the children. In many parts of the world the "arranged marriage" is the norm, and parents select prospective partners for their children, who may not see their future spouses before the wedding day. In Muslim countries husbands have traditionally been able to divorce their wives by the simple expedient of saying "I divorce thee" three times. In many societies husbands may take more than one wife, although there are very few societies in which wives may take more than one husband. In many parts of Africa an intending husband cannot acquire a wife without paying a specified number of cattle to his prospective father-in-law. And in a great many societies romantic love is not considered a necessary basis for marriage. All these societies, of course, regard their own family patterns as perfectly natural, if not divinely ordained.

Extended and nuclear family systems. All family systems may be roughly, divided into two basic types: the *extended family* and *nuclear family*.

The *extended family* has been the dominant form in most societies throughout history, and remains to this day the usual pattern in small-scale or agrarian societies. In the extended family, several generations live in close proximity, and the parent-child relationship is embedded in a much wider context of aunts, uncles, grandparents, and perhaps in-laws and cousins. The system has many advantages, notably its capacity for providing considerable material or emotional support to any individual member who needs it. The extended family usually serves as a complete self-contained economic unit, and the potential it offers for a familial division of labor makes it highly functional in traditional societies.

The *nuclear family* is always to be found embedded within the extended family, but its existence as an independent unit is a relatively recent historical phenomenon. It consists of a single married couple and their dependent children, living away from their relatives. The nuclear family system has rapidly become the norm in all the industrialized societies of the world, largely because of the greater social mobility made possible by a complex economy and the greater geographical mobility resulting from technological innovations in transport

The modern American family is typically a nuclear one, consisting of a married couple and their dependent children. The absence of other relatives in the home and in daily activities emphasizes the personal bonds between family members, but it also means that stresses and strains are concentrated on a very few individuals. *(Ron Sherman/ Nancy Palmer)*

and communications. The nuclear family is the established family form in America; few newlyweds expect to continue to live with their parents, or even to spend their entire married lives in close proximity to the parental home. The nuclear family is more functional than the extended family in the complex modern society because its reduced size and potential mobility enable it to adapt more easily to changing conditions; but it pays the price of having to bear many stresses and strains that might once have been diffused throughout an extended kin.

The functions of the family. If the family is a universal phenomenon, it must serve some universal and very important social functions that no other institution can fulfill. Social scientists have identified several major, interrelated functions of the family system.[8]

Replacement of members. No society can survive unless it has some system for replacing its members. The family provides a convenient,

[8]See George Peter Murdock, *Social Structure* (New York: Free Press, 1949); William J. Goode, "The Sociology of the Family," in *Sociology Today*, eds. Robert K. Merton, Leonard Broom, and Leonard J. Cottrell (New York: Basic Books, 1959); and Duberman, *Marriage and Its Alternatives*.

institutionalized means for this replacement to take place in a regularized and predictable way. The biological capacity to reproduce is thus placed in a stable social context, in which the mutual rights and obligations of the reproductive partners are clearly defined and protected.

Regulation of sexual behavior. Every society must somehow regulate the sexual behavior of its members. Failure to provide this regulation would result in the birth of large numbers of infants for whom no specific fathers could be held responsible. A totally permissive society would tend to be a society with numerous unwanted children, and there would be no social unit to which they could be specifically attached.

Care of the young. Unlike the young of most other animals, human offspring are virtually helpless for several years after birth, and require care and protection until at least the age of puberty. The family provides an institution that can take full responsibility for the care and upbringing of the young. This function cannot easily be fulfilled by the mother alone because pregnancy, childbirth, and the need to suckle and tend new infants may incapacitate her economically.

Socialization of new members. To become a full member of society, the infant has to be socialized into an acceptance of the norms of his or her culture. The child is expected to acquire language, to internalize social values, and to dress, behave, and otherwise perform like any normal member of the society. In other societies the extended family served as the main agent of socialization at least until adolescence, and often beyond. Today the nuclear family still assumes responsibility for the primary socialization of new members of society, but other institutions play their part in a further socialization process. The schools, for example, teach technical skills and impart the intellectual heritage of the culture, while the mass media and the peer group provide other influences—many of them at variance with those offered in the family environment.

APPROACHING THE PROBLEM

Sociologists usually analyze the problems of the family from the social-disorganization perspective, although some sociologists view them as problems of value conflict or deviance.

From the social-disorganization perspective, the problems of the family result from rapid social changes that have placed tremendous stresses on the family system. Industrialization, accompanied by many changes in social values, has imposed many extra burdens on the nuclear family system. A variety of changes in the structure and the norms of society—such as the growing economic independence of women and the spread of permissive attitudes toward sexuality—have generated confusion and uncertainty about the family and its role. Sociologists who take this perspective believe that the American family has failed in some respects to adapt to the rapid changes in our society, and social and familial disorganization have resulted.

From the value-conflict perspective, the problems of the family result from competing ideas about the place and nature of the family as an institution. Some people, including many religious leaders, wish to retain what they believe to be the traditional virtues of the American family; others, including many feminist leaders, regard what they believe to be the conservative, oppressive nature of the family as a problem. Different individuals and groups have very different hopes and fears about the family.

From a deviance perspective, the problems of the family stem from the fact that many people have failed to internalize or have rejected the dominant social norms governing appropriate marital behavior. The deviants—or those who are labeled "deviant"—no longer conform to established norms requiring marital fidelity or specifying divorce as undesirable. If people conformed to the dominant norms, family problems would tend to be reduced.

Marriage in America

Most American families begin with marriage, and most American marriages follow from romantic love. We take it for granted that romantic love is a prerequisite for marriage, although this belief is not one that many other societies share. Let us look more closely at the concept.

Romantic love. It comes as a surprise to Americans, who look with horror on marriages based on anything other than love, that there are actually rather few societies in which romantic love is regarded as the normal and most desirable basis for marriage. In most societies in the world, far more pragmatic considerations than "flights of the heart" are used to determine which man shall marry which woman. Most—though not all—societies recognize the existence of romantic love, but many cultures consider it an inconvenience that is apt to interfere with the ordinary, rational, practical process of mate selection. This attitude persisted in middle- and upper-class Western culture until fairly recently: parents were quite satisfied if their daughter married "well"—that is, to a male who was eligible by reason of his social status and economic assets. A standard dramatic theme of novels of the last century concerns the havoc wrought by the daughter who falls in love with someone beneath her station in life, and even today middle-class parents are apt to look askance at dating between their daughter and a lower-class male. But as sociologist Ira Reiss has pointed out, romantic

Most Americans regard romantic love as a necessary basis for a successful marriage. Although two people rarely live "happily ever after," romantic love may serve to perpetuate a relationship. Certainly our society places a higher value on "falling in love" than most other societies. *(Christopher G. Knight/Photo Researchers)*

love is usually regarded by Americans as a necessary basis for a successful marriage.[9]

From a very early age Americans learn of the glories of romantic love. Children's stories are filled with tales of breathtaking romance. Comic books, when not extolling violence, provide endless "happy ending" romantic adventures. Books, movies, and TV programs all serve to convince us that every normal person eventually falls in love and gets married. As psychoanalyst Ernest Van Den Haag notes:

> Movies, songs, TV, romance magazines, all intensify the belief that love alone makes life worthwhile, is perpetual, conquers all the world's evils, and is fulfilled and certified by marriage. "Science" hastens to confirm as much. Doesn't popular psychology . . . tell us, in effect, that any male who stays single is selfish or homosexual or mother-dominated and generally neurotic? And any female frustrated . . . ? A normal person, we are told, must love and thereupon marry.[10]

[9]Ira L. Reiss, *Family System in America* (New York: Holt, Rinehart & Winston, 1971), Chapter 7; see also William J. Goode, "The Theoretical Importance of Love," *American Sociological Review,* 24 (February 1959), pp. 38–47.

[10]Ernest Van Den Haag, "Love or Marriage?" *Harper's* Magazine, 224 (May 1962), p. 44.

Accordingly, much of our emotional energy, particularly in our teens and twenties, is devoted to finding somebody to love – that special person with whom we want to spend the rest of our lives.

Sociologist Sidney Greenfield has summed up the "culture trait" of American romantic love in five steps:

1. Two . . . rational adolescents of the opposite sex meet, most probably by accident, and find each other to be personally and physically attractive.

2. They soon come to realize that they are "right for each other."

3. They fall victims to forces beyond their control, and fall in love.

4. They then begin – at least for a short time – to behave in a flighty, irrational manner that is at variance with the way they normally conduct themselves.

5. Finally, believing that love is a panacea and that the future holds only goodness for them, they marry and form a new nuclear family.[11]

The implication is that, once married, the couple will "live happily ever after," and that love will solve whatever problems may arise as they discover differences in their basic values, needs, interests, and desires. Love, too, is expected to compensate for any deficiencies in role performance – if, for example, the husband is a poor provider, or the wife a poor housekeeper, or if they are unable to have children.

It is perhaps significant that we use one set of terms – bride and groom – to describe people at the climactic moment of the romantic-love relationship, and another set of terms – husband and wife – to describe their subsequent life together. The change in terminology almost seems to be a tacit recognition of the fact that romantic love does not, after all, solve all difficulties, and that more prosaic and rational considerations must enter into the lifelong mutual commitment of two people.

The American married-life ideal is somewhat different from the romantic-love ideal. The married-life ideal focuses more on familial and social roles, and contains a definite economic element. There is usually a fairly clear sex-role differentiation, despite the changes wrought by the women's liberation movement: the husband is usually the breadwinner and the wife is usually the homemaker. The couple are expected to raise children, and the greater part of the wife's time and interest is devoted to their care. The economic position of the family is expected to improve over the years as a result of the husband's progressive advancement in his job. The family hopes ultimately to acquire ownership of its own home. The children should do well at school and ideally should go to college. Over the years the couple's enjoyment and appreciation of each other's company is expected to become deeper and more secure.

[11]Sidney M. Greenfield, "Love and Marriage in Modern America: A Functional Analysis," *The Sociological Quarterly*, 6 (Autumn 1965), pp. 361–377; see also Reiss, *Family System in America*, p. 90.

Clearly, this ideal is not always fulfilled in practice. But unrealistic as it may be in many cases, there is a certain beauty about the ideal: it suggests harmony, peace, and fulfillment—all of them values worth seeking. Yet this married-life ideal does not really require romantic love for its foundation: one can imagine such a family being built—as stable and fulfilling families were often built in the past and as they are still built in many parts of the world today—on the basis of a rational, coolheaded choice of partners by both sides. There is even some reason to suppose that nonromantic considerations do, in fact, carry more weight in the mate selection process than we usually like to admit. Why, then, do Americans place such value on romantic love?

Functions of romantic love. William Goode believes that our society assigns such immense importance to romantic love because it is highly functional in maintaining the institution of the nuclear family.[12] Conversely, a high degree of romantic love between married partners would tend to be dysfunctional in an extended family system, and so is often discouraged by societies practicing the system.

One function of romantic love is that it helps young couples to sever the bonds that bind them to their original families, a step which is a necessity if the nuclear family is to be successfully established. When the couple become totally absorbed in each other as required by the romantic ideal, it is easier for them to leave their parental families and found a new family.

Another function of romantic love is that it serves to tide the couple over in hard times and to maintain their mutual loyalty in stressful circumstances. In the extended family system, this mutual love would not be so vital, as many other relatives would be available to lend emotional support. In fact, strong romantic love between any two members of an extended family might be dysfunctional, as it could distract the couple from their wider obligations to the rest of their kin.

A third possible function of romantic love has been suggested, perhaps a little cynically, by Greenfield,[13] who contends that nuclear marriage holds so many disadvantages for the partners—such as support obligations by the male and overdependence on the part of the female—that romantic love serves as an emotional bait to lure them into making a commitment to marriage. The inhabitant of a modern society has more choice than the inhabitant of a traditional society as to whether to marry or not, and so some additional enticement is necessary.

There may be still other reasons, which sociologists have not yet identified, to account for the high value that our society places on romantic love. But the fact that Americans regard this love as a normal prerequisite to marriage, whereas many inhabitants of other societies do not even expect ever to "fall in love," is clearly a product of social and not just individual factors.

[12]Goode, "The Theoretical Importance of Love."
[13]Greenfield, "Love and Marriage in Modern America."

The choice of marital partners. What factors influence the choice of marital partners? At present, social scientists understand very little about the significance of personality characteristics in the choice of a spouse. It may be that "birds of a feather flock together" and people choose partners whose personalities seem like their own; or it may be that "opposites attract" and people select mates who complement rather than replicate their own personalities; or — more likely — the process may be much more complex and dependent on the quirks of the individual.[14] If there is a general pattern to the psychology of choosing a marital partner, it has not yet been discovered.

The sociological characteristics of mate selection have been extensively studied, however, and a number of factors that influence mate selection have been clearly established. Generally speaking, people tend to marry people whose social characteristics are similar to their own. Several of these factors have been isolated.

Relative age. Married couples are usually of roughly the same age. Most husbands are older than their wives, but usually by less than five years. The difference in age, however, is gradually declining.[15]

Proximity. Two people have a greater chance of marrying if they live near each other — not only because they have more opportunity to meet, but also because they are more likely to be similar in other respects as a result of their common environment.

Social class. People tend to marry within or close to their own social class, as measured by income level and occupational status. When interclass marriages occur, there is no clear tendency for either husband or wife to be from the higher class.[16] Among college students, however, interclass marriages are more common.[17]

Education. The number of years of schooling a person receives is closely correlated with his or her income and social class, and it is therefore difficult to evaluate this factor in isolation; but there is a strong tendency for husbands and wives to be on a similar educational level. This tendency is particularly true of the college-educated, although this fact may imply merely that college is a good place for males and females to meet.

Race background. Even today, interracial marriage is very much the exception, especially between blacks and whites.[18] These marriages are commonest, however, in areas that are not residentially segregated and between partners who share the same socioeconomic status.

[14]See Robert F. Winch, *Mate Selection* (New York: Harper & Bros., 1958).
[15]Robert Parke, Jr. and Paul C. Glick, "Prospective Changes in Marriage and the Family," *Journal of Marriage and the Family*, 29 (May 1967), pp. 249–256.
[16]J. Richard Udry, *The Social Context of Marriage*, 2d ed. (Philadelphia: Lippincott, 1971), p. 187.
[17]Gerald R. Leslie and Arthur H. Richardson, "Family Versus Campus Influence in Relation to Mate Selection," *Social Problems*, 4 (October 1956), pp. 117–121.
[18]Duberman, *Marriage and Its Alternatives*, pp. 85–87.

Ethnic background. Americans are more likely to marry within their own ethnic group than outside it, although with the decline of large-scale immigration and the "Americanization" of immigrant groups this tendency is declining. It is not clear whether the trend will be checked by the recent resurgence of ethnic consciousness.

Religion. If only the major categories of Protestant, Roman Catholic, and Jewish are considered, the great majority of marriage partners share the same religion. But if denominations such as Baptist or Congregationalist are considered, interreligious marriages are very common. It should also be remembered, however, that in many cases one partner converts to the religion of the other for the sake of the marriage.

Physical characteristics. Surprisingly, numerous studies have shown a tendency for marriage partners to be physically similar, not only in height and weight but also in hair color, general health, and even basal metabolism.[19]

Some Causes of Family Disorganization

Let us look more closely at some of the factors that are thought to contribute to the disorganization of the American family. These factors are complex and interrelated, but it is possible to identify several of them.

Women's liberation. The changing status of women in the United States has inevitably had repercussions on a family system that has traditionally assigned to the wife a subordinate role as housekeeper, child-rearer, and nurturant supporter of her economically active husband. As social scientist Andrew Hacker observes:

> The major change in the family in recent years, and the problems of the future, are both summed up in one word: women. In the past and until very recently, wives were simply supplementary to their husbands, and not expected to be full human beings . . . The trouble comes from the fact that the institution we call marriage can't hold two full human beings—it was only designed for one and a half.[20]

The changes in the attitudes and expectations of women have been accompanied by a gradual increase in female economic independence. Some 40 percent of American women are currently employed, and although on the average they still earn substantially less than men, they are no longer as heavily reliant on their husbands for economic support as they were a few decades ago. It is now possible for a wife to have her own professional career—and even to earn more than her husband, whom, if it were not for the likely social reaction, she might rea-

[19]Ernest W. Burgess and Paul Wallin, *Engagement and Marriage* (Philadelphia: Lippincott, 1973).
[20]Quoted in "The American Family: Future Uncertain," *Time* (December 28, 1970).

sonably expect to stay at home and do the housework in order to maximize the economic benefit to the family. But the family institution has been slow to adapt to these changes, and in consequence is undergoing pressure.

The aftermath of romantic love. Because Americans are so thoroughly socialized into an almost impossible ideal of lifelong romantic love with their chosen partners, they often experience severe disappointment when their married life turns out to fall short of their hopes. Romantic love is built on fantasy, mystery, spontaneity, bursting emotion, and surprise. It is meant to "sweep you off your feet," to make you "lose your senses," to make you "blind to all else." When these expectations are confronted with the garbage can, the dishpan, and the diapers, they tend to shrivel. And when they do, millions of Americans assume that because the "thrill is gone" from their relationship with their spouses, the partnership must have failed. This is not necessarily true, for love takes many forms. Married love grows and changes as the partners grow and change; it is a love that may be mature, reasonable, realistic, and deeply fulfilling—but Americans are not socialized to expect it, to recognize it, or to appreciate it.

Thus, as long as the passions of romantic love continue to be extolled as the only viable grounds for a successful marriage, and as long as the fading of romance is considered to herald the fading of a marriage, the American family will have problems as millions of disillusioned couples discover that their dreams about their "one true love" are slowly disappearing in a pile of laundry, work pressures, and routine predictability.

Sexual permissiveness. The formal morality of American society has always restricted sexual intercourse to marital partners. But we are rapidly becoming an openly permissive and eroticized culture, and the marital institution, which is theoretically so firmly grounded in strict, monogamous fidelity, is inevitably affected by this development.

Many social factors have contributed to the new permissiveness. In the past, the amount of nonmarital sexuality was limited by religious scruples, feelings of guilt, lack of opportunity and mobility, the immense value placed on virginity in women, and fear of pregnancy. But the development of convenient and effective contraceptives has served to separate two major functions of sexual relations, procreation and recreation. Before the advent of modern contraceptives, it was necessary for society to promote the virtues of marital sex and inhibit the practice of nonmarital sex in order to prevent the birth of large numbers of dependent, illegitimate children. Many of the old attitudes are now changing as the social norms that sanction them are losing their force.

With sexual satisfaction as highly valued as it is in the United States, and with society becoming increasingly permissive, it is scarcely surprising that many people look outside their marriages for sexual pleasure, or, if unmarried, see no reason why those who are single should be deprived of sexual experience. Premarital sexual intercourse is now the norm for the majority of Americans, and most of those who are married have had extramarital sexual experience. Substantial numbers of otherwise respectable middle-class Americans engage periodically in "swinging," or consensual exchange of marital partners; it has been estimated that hundreds of thousands of Americans have participated in these activities.[21] All these trends serve to some extent to undermine the institution of marriage as it has traditionally been conceived.

The impact of industrialism. As we have seen, modern industrialism has shattered the extended family system and reduced the family's practical usefulness to both its members and the community. William Goode identifies several points of pressure on the family that are specifically related to industrialism:

> 1. It calls for physical movement from one locality to another, thus decreasing the frequency and intimacy of contact among members of a kin network. . . .
>
> 2. Industrialization creates class . . . mobility. That is . . . one or more persons may move rapidly upward while others do not, thus creating discrepancies in styles of life, taste, income, etc., and making contact somewhat less easy and pleasant.
>
> 3. Urban and industrial systems of agencies, facilities, procedures, and organizations have undermined large . . . kin groupings, since they now handle the problems that were solved within the kin network before industrialization: political protection, pooling funds to educate bright youngsters, defending a locality, lending money, etc.
>
> 4. Industrialization creates a value structure that recognizes achievement more than birth; consequently, the kin have less to offer an individual in exchange for his submission. He has to make his *own* way.[22]

All these changes have profoundly affected the family. Many of its functions—such as education, recreation, and socialization—have been lost in varying degrees to commerce, industry, schools, and government agencies. Yet, paradoxically, the nuclear family has had additional burdens imposed on it. In the extended family system, the individual could turn to many relatives for advice, comfort, reassurance, approval, admiration, and help. In today's isolated nuclear family there are far fewer resources of this kind. The members of the small modern family must rely very heavily on one another for understanding and emotional support, and sometimes the qualities demanded are more than these

[21]Gilbert Bartell, "Group Sex Among the Middle Americans," in *Beyond Monogamy*, eds. James R. Smith and Lynn G. Smith (Baltimore: Johns Hopkins Press, 1974), pp. 185–201; see also Duane Denfield and Michael Gordon, "The Sociology of Mate Swapping: Or the Family that Swings Together Clings Together," in *Beyond Monogamy*, eds. Smith and Smith.

[22]William J. Goode, *World Revolution and Family Patterns* (New York: Free Press, 1963), pp. 369–370.

few members can provide. The problem is aggravated when one family member is suffering some severe disability. The extended family could absorb an alcoholic, delinquent, or mentally disordered member with relatively little disruption, but the small nuclear family becomes severely disorganized if it has to confront these difficulties in one of its members.

Changing attitudes and values. Most societies are suspicious of change, but Americans tend to welcome it and to lack the strong predisposition of other societies to assume that the old ways and values are better. Our attitudes toward aspects of our basic institutions may change rapidly: divorce, for example, was highly stigmatized until relatively recently, but today it is regarded more as a personal misfortune than a public disgrace.

One of the most important changes in our attitudes and values during this century has been the growth of individualism. We are far more aware than our ancestors of the individual person—of his or her wants, needs, rights and potential. This individualist attitude is expressed in many ways, some of them perhaps difficult to reconcile with the maintenance of the traditional family system. The women's liberation movement, for example, draws much of its inspiration from a concern for the dignity of the individual woman rather than any concern for the family as a traditional institution. William Goode comments on some implications of our belief in individualism:

> It is not possible to state the basic "causes" of this change in attitude. It is merely one facet of a broader set of changes in Western society called "secularization": patterns that were once weighted by strong moral norms have come to be evaluated by instrumental norms. Instead of asking, "Is this moral?" the individual is more likely to ask, "Is this a more useful or better procedure for my needs?" Sometimes the term "individualism" is applied to the change. Instead of asking whether his church or his community approves of divorce, the individual asks, "Is it the right thing for *me* to do?"[23]

Modern individualism, then, has signaled the breakdown of many traditional institutional ties and loyalties, and the family has inevitably been affected.

DIVORCE

One of the most obvious manifestations of the mounting pressures on the American family is the incidence of divorce. Although intact families may suffer from painful conflicts, tensions, and dissatisfactions, the official declaration that the unit is dissolved represents a final admission of failure by the marital partners.

[23]Robert Merton and Robert Nisbet, *Contemporary Social Problems* (New York: Harcourt, Brace & World, 1966), p. 488.

Although they are usually founded on romantic love, American marriages have much interpersonal discord. The average marriage lasts only seven years, and a large number of reported assaults involves marital partners. *(Mimi Forsyth/Monkmeyer)*

Divorce presents a series of problems to those involved. In a couple-oriented society, the divorced person is to some extent excluded from the normal patterns of social life, although this is less true today than it was a few decades ago when the divorcee was stigmatized. The emotional effects can also be severe, for divorce can represent a disruption of the individual's personal universe. Research has also indicated that men are more likely to be fired from their jobs, or to perform their jobs less well, during or shortly after a divorce.[24] Even the death rates for divorced persons are higher than for other people, at nearly all age levels.[25] In addition, the one-parent family faces many difficulties: the functions that the nuclear family performs assume a particular structure, and if that structure is fractured the family's capacity to carry out its social and personal functions may be diminished.[26] If, as is usually the case, the children remain with the mother, the family may experience severe economic problems as a result of the lower earning capaci-

[24]William J. Goode, *After Divorce* (New York: Free Press, 1956).
[25]Alexander A. Plateris, *Increases in Divorces: United States—1967* (Washington, D.C.: U.S. Department of Health, Education, and Welfare, 1970), Table 5, p. 14.
[26]Paul Glasser and Elizabeth Navarre, "Structural Problems of the One-Parent Family," *Journal of Social Issues,* 21 (January 1965), pp. 98–109.

ty of females in our society. If the mother is also black, and thus subject to double discrimination, the economic problem is compounded.

But divorce may be a partial solution as well as a problem. In the past, divorce was seen as a personal catastrophe to be avoided at any cost, but today there is a growing recognition that some marriages are better ended than continued. Divorce may sometimes be more con-structive than an attempt to preserve a marriage in which severe con-flict is an everyday occurrence, and many couples are now prepared to make a break and start again, for their children's sake as well as their own.

The incidence of divorce. How many marriages will end up in the di-vorce courts? There are several ways of arriving at an assessment of the divorce rate, but the statistics can be misleading.

One method, for example, is to compare the number of marriages in a given year with the number of divorces in the same year. If we use this method, the rise in the rate of divorce seems a dramatic one. In 1920 there was one divorce for every seven marriages, in 1940 one for every six, in 1960 one for every four, and in 1972 one for every three.[27] The total number of divorces in 1972 involved some 1,674,000 adults and a substantial number of children.[28] In fact, in recent years the rate of increase in divorce has outstripped that of both marriage and popula-tion growth: in the decade from 1962 to 1972, the annual number of marriages rose by 44 percent, while divorces rose by 103 percent.[29]

The problem with these figures is that the population that is eligible for divorce is far larger than the population that is eligible for marriage. Anyone who is currently married is a potential candidate for divorce, but the potential candidates for first marriage come from a much smaller group—primarily the unmarried population aged eighteen to thirty. It is hardly surprising, therefore, that the divorce rate looks high compared with the marriage rate in any one year. Moreover, the fac-tors that influence the decision to divorce vary over time, and they are not necessarily the same factors that influence the decision to marry. Divorce rates, for example, may be influenced by changes in the law affecting the ease of obtaining a divorce, or by the current employment opportunities for single women. Marriage rates, on the other hand, may be influenced by such factors as the number of people in the country who are aged eighteen to thirty, or by contempory attitudes toward al-ternatives to legal marriage.

Other methods of calculating divorce rates have also been devised. One method, for example, is to project the future divorce rate in terms of the number of divorces per 1,000 existing marriages; another is to

[27]U.S. Bureau of the Census, *Population of the United States,* Series P-23, no. 49 (Washington, D.C.: U.S. Department of Commerce, 1974), p. 70.
[28]Wayne King, "Demand for Divorce Brings Laws to Make It Easier and Cheaper," *New York Times* (January 5, 1974).
[29]"No Fault Divorces—They're Catching On," *U.S. News & World Report* (June 4, 1973), p. 41.

survey samples of all those married in the past few decades. The tentative conclusions drawn from these methods are that the rate of divorce has doubled in the United States in the decade up to 1974, and that at least one in three first marriages and a higher proportion of subsequent marriages end in divorce.

Divorce-prone marriages. Which marriages are more likely to end in divorce? Just as there are identifiable patterns that predict the likelihood of marriage, so also are there certain patterns discernible in those marriages that break up. Again, attempts to establish consistent personality characteristics among partners whose marriages end in divorce have been inconclusive, but sociological characteristics have considerable predictive value. Sociologists have identified several such factors.

Age of partners. The largest single group of divorced partners are in their twenties at the time of divorce. The divorce rate declines as couples grow older.[30]

Duration of marriage. Most divorces per single year take place within two years after marriage. The longer a couple are married, the less the likelihood of their being divorced.[31]

Marriage order. People who have been married more than once are considerably more likely to be divorced than partners in a first marriage.[32]

Social class. Divorce is more common at the lower socioeconomic levels than among the more affluent. Class as such may not be responsible, however; it may be that unemployment and economic problems generate the marital instability.[33]

Education. The chances for a lasting marriage are better for those with more years of schooling. Divorce is more likely if the husband's educational level is below that of the wife than if the husband is the better-educated partner.[34]

Religion. Divorce rates are higher for interfaith marriages and for Protestant marriages than they are for Catholic or Jewish marriages. But the more religious the partners, the less likely they are to become divorced.[35]

Richard Udry, a sociologist who has studied the backgrounds of divorced couples, concludes:

---

[30]Udry, *The Social Context of Marriage*, p. 187.
[31]Ibid.
[32]Ibid.
[33]Goode, *After Divorce.*
[34]Paul C. Glick, *American Families* (New York: Wiley, 1957).
[35]Udry, *The Social Context of Marriage*, p. 187.

The larger the social differences between two people, the more social differences, and the more significant the social differences, the
more likely their marriage is to be a source of conflict between
them and other social groups (relatives, neighbors, friends, and social institutions). . . . *Those who are least likely to marry are, therefore, most likely to have trouble if they do.*[36]

Sociologist William Goode has also detailed a series of background
factors associated with greater or lesser proneness to divorce. According
to Goode, greater proneness is found among urban couples, among
those married at a very young age, among those who have had only a
short acquaintance or engagement before marriage, among those whose
parents had unhappy marriages, and among those whose relatives and
friends disapprove of the marriage.[37]

Divorce and the law. Divorce represents the formal dissolution of an
important social unit, and it can take place only with society's formal
approval, in a manner prescribed by law.

Because society has always discouraged the breakup of the family,
the divorce laws have historically been designed to make divorce difficult to obtain. Moreover, the divorce court has typically followed the
standard "adversary" judicial procedure, in which an aggrieved party
attempts to prove the "guilt" of an offending party. The case is heard
on the legal assumption that one party is innocent, while the other is
guilty of "cruelty," desertion, or some other offense. In many if not
most instances, of course, both partners have contributed to the breakdown of the marriage, but divorce under the adversary system is only
obtainable if they are prepared to maintain the fiction that one of them
is at fault. The great majority of divorces are uncontested: one partner agrees beforehand to accept the "blame" for some offense against
the other. Consequently, there is very little relationship between the
actual causes of marital breakdown and the legal grounds on which
the court allows a divorce.

The adversary system has one very undesirable effect: it pits the two
partners against each other, so that unpleasant, expensive, and psychologically damaging battles are more likely to result. Often one partner
will agree to an uncontested divorce only as part of a bargain involving
alimony payments or privileges to visit the children. As David Cantor
comments:

Because the defendant can always delay a divorce, and often defeat
it, the divorce itself becomes an object of trade. . . . The defendant
. . . negotiates by offering the plaintiff an uncontested hearing – for
a price. The price will normally be agreement to terms of alimony,
support, custody, visitation or division of joint assets which the

---

[36]Ibid., p. 301.
[37]Merton and Nisbet, *Contemporary Social Problems,* pp. 500–501.

plaintiff, if not under duress, would not accept. These issues then become determined not on the basis of objective fairness, but rather on the basis of the plaintiff's desperation.[38]

For these reasons, many states have now enacted "no fault" divorce laws, which eliminate the need to lay blame on one of the partners; the couple merely declare to the court that their marriage has broken down irreparably. But the old adversary process is usually still available to those who wish to make use of it.

The legal responsibility for alimony payments by one partner to the other, and for support payments by one partner to the partner who retains custody of the children, remains controversial. In most cases custody of the children is awarded to the mother, and the father is often ordered to pay both alimony and child-support payments. Former husbands, however, default on child-support payments more often than not. A 1973 federal survey found that 46.9 percent of all families that should have been receiving court-ordered support payments were not receiving any money at all, and from other studies it appears that only 13 percent of orders are complied with by the tenth year after the divorce.[39]

Changing sex roles have also led to the emergence of new problems. Many fathers now wish to retain custody of their children, and resent the apparent sexist bias of courts that assume that only women can adequately perform child-rearing tasks. And although alimony could be awarded only to the wife until recently, most states now make provision for the wife to be required to pay alimony to the husband—although few courts have yet made such orders.[40]

Divorce, then, can be a traumatic experience with multiple problematic consequences. But the experience of divorce does not seem to destroy the appetite for marriage. The marriage rate for divorcees at all ages is higher than that for widowed or single persons.[41] The old adage "Once burned, twice shy" does not seem to hold: the divorced seem still committed to the idea of marriage.

ILLEGITIMACY

An illegitimate child is variously defined as one born out of wedlock; as one conceived out of wedlock, even if born after marriage; or as one born to any woman, whether married or not, if fathered by someone other than her husband. Some people see illegitimacy as a problem because it appears to be a symptom of the breakdown of the family and

[38]David J. Cantor, "A Matter of Right," *The Humanist*, 30 (May–June 1970), p. 10.
[39]King, "Demand for Divorce Brings Laws to Make It Easier and Cheaper."
[40]Enid Nemy, "The Fathers Can Afford to Support Their Families, but They Don't," *New York Times* (April 2, 1974).
[41]Plateris, *Increases in Divorces*, Table J, p. 10.

of moral decay; others see it as a problem because illegitimate children and their mothers suffer considerable stigma and sometimes adverse economic consequences as a result of social attitudes toward illegitimacy.

The incidence of illegitimacy. The statistics on illegitimacy have to be treated with caution because, as in the case of all other forms of deviant behavior, reporting is uneven and probably inaccurate. Moreover, the illegitimacy statistics are affected by changes in other social factors, such as the size of the total population or the number of marriages and legitimate births. In any consideration of the statistics, it is particularly important to distinguish between the illegitimacy ratio and the illegitimacy rate. The *ratio* refers to the proportion of illegitimate births to all births; the *rate* refers to the proportion of illegitimate births to all unmarried females. Consequently, a population in which most of the females are unmarried could have a very high illegitimacy ratio but a relatively low illegitimacy rate. In fact, this was the case with the American teen-age population in the sixties, when relatively few girls had babies — a low rate — but a relatively high number of those who did have babies had them illegitimately — a high ratio. Failure to keep in mind the distinction between rate and ratio can result in a good deal of misplaced anxiety about the problem.

But there is no doubt that illegitimacy has increased over the past few decades, in ratio, in rate, and in absolute number of births. In one major study reported in the late sixties, Alice Clague and Stephanie Ventura found that the annual rate had increased over the previous fifteen years from 7.1 to 23.5 per thousand unmarried women of childbearing age.[42] The ratio had increased from 37.9 per thousand to 77.4 during the same period, and the absolute number of illegitimate births had soared from 89,500 to 291,200.[43]

The illegitimacy rate for nonwhite women is higher than for white women, but during the last decade the rate for white teen-agers rose by 50 percent, compared with an 8 percent increase for nonwhite teenagers.[44] The generally higher illegitimacy rate for nonwhites does not, however, necessarily mean that they are more likely to conceive illegitimate children; it may simply mean that they are less likely to obtain abortions or to marry the father before the birth of their children.

Social values and attitudes. Why does our society take such an unfavorable attitude toward the illegitimate child and its mother? At first glance, there would seem to be no rational reason why children born outside a family should be treated any differently than other children, and the stigmatization of thousands of guiltless individuals seems to be

---

[42]Alice J. Clague and Stephanie J. Ventura, *Trends in Illegitimacy: United States—1940–1965* (Washington, D.C.: U.S. Department of Health, Education, and Welfare, 1968).
[43]Ibid.
[44]*Teenagers: Marriages, Divorces, Parenthood, and Mortality* (Washington, D.C.: U.S. Department of Health, Education, and Welfare, 1973), p. 23.

a consequence of little more than middle-class self-righteousness. But in fact there are very sound sociological reasons for the dominant negative attitude toward illegitimacy. The legitimately constituted family provides a structure for the economic support and socialization of children, and in our society these functions are not easily fulfilled outside that structure. The stigmatization of illegitimacy is highly functional, for it helps to ensure that most births will take place within the context of the family, the social institution optimally designed to take care of the young. There are certainly some social groups in the United States in which illegitimate births are not stigmatized and in which an unwed woman may have a child through choice rather than by accident—but these are precisely the groups that display the least loyalty to the traditional family system. If illegitimacy attracted no social stigma whatever, marriage would tend to have fewer attractions and the institution of the nuclear family might be endangered.

VIOLENCE IN THE FAMILY

Most of the homicides and assaults that take place in the United States every year are perpetrated by one family member on another. As Suzanne Steinmetz and Murray Straus observe, "It would be hard to find a group or an institution in American society in which violence is more of an everyday occurrence than it is within the family."[45] Whenever one family member willfully inflicts pain and suffering on another, some measure of trust, loyalty, and affection is destroyed. Since these qualities are basic to the functioning of the family, violence is profoundly disruptive of the institution.

Explanations of family violence. Why should violence be so common in a social institution that is supposedly founded on love?

William Goode considers that force is a personal resource which can be acquired, bartered, and applied to gain advantage for the person who uses it.[46] This resource can be used in the family for many purposes—either directly, as when a brother pushes his sister from the room or when a parent physically punishes a child, or indirectly, as when the implicit threat of violence is enough to make a child obey its parent or a wife submit to an order from her husband. The critical question for sociologists, then, is: under what conditions does force, rather than respect and love, become the dominant resource for control and power in the family? The plausible answer, suggested by John O'Brien and others,[47] is that people resort to force as a resource when their other resources are exhausted, diminished, or nonexistent. Thus a man

---

[45]Suzanne K. Steinmetz and Murray A. Straus, *Violence in the Family* (New York: Dodd, Mead & Co., 1974), p. 3.

[46]Goode, *The Contemporary American Family.*

[47]John O'Brien, "Violence in Divorce Prone Families," *Journal of Marriage and the Family,* 33 (November 1971), pp. 692–698.

who feels he has lost the respect and affection of his family, perhaps because he cannot support them, may fall back on physical abuse as a final resource for the assertion of his authority.

Another explanation of family violence may lie in the connection that social scientists have observed between frustration and aggression. Steinmetz and Straus point out:

> In a society such as ours, in which aggression is defined as a normal response to frustration, we can expect that the more frustrating the familial and occupational roles, the greater the amount of violence.[48]

Violence as a response to frustration is by no means confined to the out-of-work father. A mother who has tended a houseful of children all day is almost expected to "blow her stack" by early evening; a child who fails again and again to complete a particular chore is almost expected to "throw a tantrum"; and an adolescent son who cannot make his parents understand his view of things is almost expected to "storm out of the house" in a fury. In lower-class culture, too, violence is often valued as an appropriate means of solving problems, perhaps because its members have less access to other resources than do middle-class citizens.

Child abuse. One aspect of family violence that has attracted a great deal of attention in recent years is child abuse. This practice does not refer to the spankings and other physical punishments typically meted out to American children by their parents; it focuses on much more serious acts, such as severe beatings, tying up children or locking them in closets for hours or days on end, burning children with cigarettes or on hot stoves, and even—in extreme cases—breaking bones, amputating limbs, or killing the children. David Gil, a social scientist who has conducted several studies of the subject, defines child abuse as follows:

> Physical abuse of children is the intentional, nonaccidental use of physical force, or intentional, nonaccidental acts of omission on the part of a parent or other caretaker, aimed at hurting, injuring, or destroying that child.[49]

On the basis of his research, Gil estimated at the end of the last decade that between 250,000 and 4 million children in America experience real abuse each year.[50]

Research on the characteristics of child abusers indicates that a disproportionately large number of them are poor. Many of the families

[48]Steinmetz and Straus, *Violence in the Family,* p. 9.

[49]David G. Gil, *Violence Against Children: Physical Child Abuse in the United States* (Cambridge, Mass.: Harvard University Press, 1970), p. 6.

[50]David G. Gil, "Incidence of Child Abuse and Demographic Characteristics of Persons Involved," in *The Battered Child,* eds. Ray E. Helfer and C. Henry Kempe (Chicago: University of Chicago Press, 1968), pp. 19–40.

involved have females as the head of the household; many others contain an adult male who is not the child's biological father; and most have relatively large numbers of children. The parents are usually under thirty and tend to be relatively poorly educated. The abusers frequently have a history of mental disorder, criminal conviction, or mental retardation. Significantly, abusive parents frequently have histories of abuse in their own childhoods. They often set unrealistically high standards of conduct for the children, and respond in an angry and uncontrolled way to behavior they perceive as misconduct. They frequently consider their disciplinary measures justified; and indeed, they are merely taking to extremes the socially sanctioned right of parents to apply physical punishment to their children.

Within the past few years public authorities have become aware of child abuse as a serious problem. Every state has now passed laws requiring or urging that known or suspected cases of child abuse be reported to the appropriate authorities. It is often difficult to prove abuse, however, because the parents are usually the only ones to testify about the events in question, and may assert that any injuries to the child were accidental. Child abuse, occurring in the privacy of the home and perpetrated against individuals so young that they are unlikely to complain to authorities, is extremely difficult to control.

PROSPECTS FOR THE FUTURE

With the weaknesses so glaringly apparent in the nuclear family form in America and with continuing changes taking place in social values, sex roles, and norms of sexual conduct, it is hardly surprising that many Americans are experimenting with a variety of new kinds of sexual relationships and family organization. To some people, these experiments represent sincere and needed efforts to create new, more satisfactory ways of meeting human needs; to other people, they seem utopian and unrealistic; and there are those who think of them as so many excuses for irresponsibility and immorality. Although there may be some truth in all these views, it is clear that the alternative forms represent something more profound than a mere carnival of fornication. It is not yet possible, however, to assess the long-term social significance of these developments.

The experimental alternatives to marriage in the United States today are so various and fluid that only the main ones can be outlined here. Some of them are simply a matter of sexual relations outside the context of formal marriage. Casual sexual encounters among college students and other unmarried young people seem to be fairly standard today, especially now that reliable methods of contraception have reduced the risk of unwanted pregnancy and peer group norms are more permissive. Cohabitation, or "living together," is also common; sometimes it serves as a prelude to marriage, and sometimes even as a

Many Americans have rejected the nuclear family system in favor of communal living. Communes vary in the degree of sexual freedom that their members enjoy, but usually all adults participate in domestic and child-raising duties. *(Dennis Stock/Magnum)*

permanent substitute, but more often it is simply a now-oriented relationship formed without any particular thought for the future. Within marriage, "swinging" may not be as common as the sensationalists would have us believe, but it is far from rare.

Communal and group "marriages" differ from these more casual alternatives to traditional marriage in that they imply not only a sharing of sexual life but also of economic and child-raising responsibilities.[51] In fact, the commune may not entail sexual communality at all. Communes range from highly organized establishments with strict membership requirements to amorphous, relaxed groups with shifting membership. Sexual practices vary: the true group marriage, in which all adults participate in sexual relations with one another, is quite rare; the complications involved in these multilateral arrangements are such that there are few instances of group marriages lasting more than a few months.[52] In most cases couples pair off to some extent, although without claiming exclusive right to each other. After infancy, children are generally regarded as being as much the responsibility of the group as that of their parents.

[51]See Larry L. Constantine and Joan M. Constantine, *Group Marriage* (New York: Macmillan, 1973).
[52]Albert Ellis, "Group Marriage: A Possible Alternative?" in *The Family in Search of a Future,* ed. Herbert A. Otto (New York: Appleton-Century-Crofts, 1970), pp. 85–97.

The Family: A Theoretical Review

The social problems associated with the American family represent the gap between a *social ideal* of a stable family system that provides the best opportunities for marital harmony and successful socialization of children, and the *social reality* of a family system that is rejected by a substantial number of Americans as oppressive or as unsuited to their needs. The family is a fundamentally important institution in society, and serves a number of crucial social functions. The fact that various social forces appear to be undermining the established family system, and particularly the institution of marriage, is regarded by many Americans as a major social problem.

The *social-disorganization* perspective offers a valuable way of looking at the problems of the family. From this perspective, the established family system may be regarded as falling victim to various forces that have been created by rapid social change. It may be that the family as we know it is not capable of adapting to these changes; or it may be that if the family does adapt, it may ultimately be so transformed as to be quite unlike the existing institution.

The modern nuclear family, usually consisting of a married couple and their dependent children, is itself a product of rapid social change. In traditional societies the typical family form is the extended system in which several generations live together. The rise of industrialism has shattered the extended family system because it was dysfunctional in a society that prized individualism and rapid mobility. The new nuclear form is much more functional in some respects, but it also suffers from some disadvantages. In particular, the smaller nuclear family must now bear many strains that might once have been diffused throughout an extended kin. The extended family, for example, could relatively easily absorb a single member who was delinquent or mentally disordered, but the presence of such a person in the nuclear family is usually very disrupting.

Rapid changes in attitudes and values have also had a disruptive effect on the institutions of marriage and the family. The growing economic independence of women and the rise of a women's liberation movement have created a good deal of change within these institutions. The spread of permissive attitudes toward premarital and extramarital sexuality have often appeared to undermine the institution of marriage, as has the greater social tolerance of divorce. The increased freedom that our society extends to teen-age children has also loosened their bonds to the family; young people expect to engage in far more extrafamilial activities than would have been the case in the past. The social norms that once upheld the sanctity of marriage and the family have lost a good deal of their force, and the entire family system is to some extent disorganized in consequence.

The *value-conflict* perspective also provides a useful means of analyzing the problems of the family. There are many competing ideas in our society about the desirability of the nuclear system and about the value of the marital institution. Some people believe very strongly that our traditional institutions should be maintained, and often see the issue as a moral as well as a practical one; others believe that our existing institutions are becoming outmoded and serve to restrict rather than enhance human potential. The many experimental alternatives to marriage that abound in the contemporary United States are one symptom of this underlying value conflict. But there are many other value conflicts associated with the family—for example, over what the domestic or professional status of the wife should be, or over how our society should react to illegitimacy, or over the question of what forms of nonmarital sexual behavior, if any, should be considered acceptable in our society.

The *deviance* perspective is also of use in the analysis of the problem of the family. From this perspective, many of the problems arise because numbers of people have failed to internalize or have rejected the social norms governing appropriate marital or familial behavior; if these deviants adhered to the traditional social norms the dimensions of the problem would be much reduced. Deviance from the traditional norms is becoming more widespread, however, as the old values lose their force; and indeed many kinds of behavior that might once have been considered deviant are becoming increasingly respectable. The divorcee, for example, was considered deviant and was stigmatized in our society until relatively recently. This social reaction probably had the effect of limiting the number of divorces, but the current attitude of tolerance toward divorce probably contributes to the growing incidence of marital breakups.

A number of other marital or familial problems may also be analyzed from the deviance perspective. For example, family violence and child abuse may be regarded as a form of learned deviant behavior.

Family of the Future?

The most obviously upsetting force likely to strike the family in the decades immediately ahead will be the impact of the new birth technology. The ability to pre-set the sex of one's baby, or even to "program" its IQ, looks and personality traits, must now be regarded as a real possibility. Embryo implants, babies grown *in vitro,* the ability to swallow a pill and guarantee oneself twins or triplets, or, even more, the ability to walk into a "babytorium" and actually purchase embryos—all this reaches so far beyond any previous human experience that one needs to look at the future through the eyes of the poet or painter, rather than those of the sociologist or conventional philosopher.

It is regarded as somehow unscholarly, even frivolous, to discuss these matters. Yet advances in science and technology, or in reproductive biology alone, could, within a short time, smash all orthodox ideas about the family and its responsibilities. When babies can be grown in a laboratory jar, what happens to the very notion of maternity? And what happens to the self-image of the female in societies which, since the very beginnings of man, have taught her that her primary mission is the propagation of and nurture of the race?

SOURCE: Alvin Toffler, *Future Shock* (New York: Random House, 1970).

What form is the typical American family likely to take in the future? Given the amount of change and disorganization in our family system today, it would be foolhardy to attempt any precise forecasts, but it seems safe to predict continuing change. The divorce rate, the number of unsatisfied couples, and the number of people looking for alternatives are all likely to increase. But this does not necessarily mean that the family, or even the nuclear family, will disappear. However, we may find ourselves in the unique position of supporting, for the first time in history, more than one form of family within the same society. Although no society has yet existed that has sanctioned multiple family forms, it is also true that no society has yet existed that has offered the technological and life-style opportunities for alternatives that are available in modern America.

The fact remains, however, that at present no less than 94 percent of Americans enter into a traditional marriage at some time during their lives. The family is in a state of profound change, but it will remain a central institution in our society. As anthropologist Margaret Mead has remarked, the family "is the only institution we have that doesn't have a hope of disappearing."

FURTHER READING

Bartell, Gilbert, *Group Sex: A Scientist's Eyewitness Report on Swinging in the Suburbs,* 1971. An anthropologist's study of "swinging" in Middle America.

Constantine, Larry L. and Joan M. Constantine, *Group Marriage,* 1973. The best book on group marriage and its many problems.

Duberman, Lucile, *Marriage and Its Alternatives,* 1973. A sociologist's critical discussion of the American family and some alternatives to it.

Goode, William J., *The Family,* 1964. A short text providing a world-wide perspective of the family and its problems.

Gordon, Michael, ed., *The Nuclear Family in Crisis: The Search for an Alternative,* 1972. An interesting collection of essays on alternatives to the nuclear family, including group marriage.

Hedgepeth, William and Dennis Stock, *The Alternative,* 1970. An excellent and well-written study of contemporary American communes of every description.

Helfer, Ray E. and C. Henry Kempe, eds., *The Battered Child,* 1968. An important collection of articles on child abuse; contains particularly valuable information on the background of parents who abuse their children.

Reiss, Ira L., *The Family System in America,* 1971. An outstanding and wide-ranging treatment of various aspects of the American family. It includes discussion of many contemporary problems, such as the "new morality" and divorce.

Skolnick, Arlene S. and Jerome H. Skolnick, *The Family in Transition: Rethinking Marriage, Sexuality, Child Rearing, and Family Organization,* 1971. Presents some radical criticisms of the family. The Skolnicks propose that the nuclear family is itself a social problem and should be studied in that light.

13

Life Cycle

THE NATURE AND SCOPE OF THE PROBLEM

Barring premature death, every human being proceeds through a predictable course of biological development—leading from infancy to childhood, on to adolescence and youth, then to adulthood and middle age, and finally to old age and ultimate extinction. But this developmental sequence is not simply a biological one; it is also a social process, because the nature of the life cycle—its length, its stages, its problems, its rewards—varies in accordance with the historical and social location of each individual and generation.

In some traditional societies, the process of the life cycle presents relatively few problems. In these communities, roles and statuses are ascribed by age and sex in a fairly rigid pattern; there are few significant options open to the individual as he or she proceeds through the life cycle, and the comparatively static nature of the culture provides stability in the roles and mutual interactions of the generations. A notable feature of these traditional societies is that they usually accord a respectable and an honored place to the old who, because of their years of experience, are the repository of the knowledge and wisdom of the community.

The United States presents a very different picture. We are a vast, heterogeneous, rapidly changing society. Different generations are socialized into very dissimilar worlds, and their attitudes and values often differ markedly. In addition, the individual in America is presented with an almost infinite range of options at every stage in the life cycle, and so always risks problems of uncertain identity. Moreover, we are a fundamentally youth-oriented society. Americans do not grow old gracefully; we try to maintain the appearance of youth even as it vanishes, and we offer the aged no honorable, useful, or even clearly defined role in society.

Social Influences on the Life Cycle

At first sight it might seem that the process of maturation and aging is a purely physiological one, but in fact social and biological influences interact in ways that profoundly shape the content and course of the life cycle.

One of the most obvious social influences is the extent of medical knowledge and services available in any society. Our average life span in America today is twice that of our ancestors a few generations ago. In 1900 the infant mortality rate was 162 per 1,000 live births; today it has been reduced to slightly over 20 deaths per 1,000. The ailments that once claimed most human life were communicable diseases such as tuberculosis, pneumonia, or smallpox, which usually struck in the early stages of the life cycle. Today, degenerative diseases such as heart ailments, strokes, and cancer have become the main cause of death, and they usually affect individuals in the later part of the life cycle. In consequence, our life cycles are very much extended, a fact which has important social effects. As Matilda Riley and Anne Foner observe:

> The later stages of the life cycle become increasingly significant as man becomes increasingly likely to live them out. A man born in the middle of the past century was engrossed with the activities of the first four decades of life, the span through which, on the average, he was then likely to live. Today, a man born in the United States can look forward, on the average, to living well into his sixties; a woman can look forward, on the average, to living well into her seventies.[1]

We now have a far higher proportion of elderly people in our society than ever before, and we have come to regard death as an event occurring primarily in old age rather than in infancy and childhood. The social impact of this change is considerable, as Michael Totten points out:

> As degenerative diseases account for more and more deaths, aging and dying tend to become synonymous, and in a society bent on forgetting death the elderly have been cordoned off from the mainstream of American life. The devaluation of the elderly parallels the premium placed on vitality, vigor, mobility, freshness. . . . A clear set of dichotomies—between young and old, productive and useless, mobile and immobile, important and unimportant, living and dying—has pervaded our social structure.[2]

[1]Matilda W. Riley and Anne Foner, eds., *Aging and Society: A Sociology of Age Stratification*, vol. 3 (New York: Russell Sage Foundation, 1969), p. 1.
[2]Michael Totten, "Death, Dying, and Society," in *The Study of Society* (Guilford, Conn.: Dushkin Publishing Group, 1974), p. 324.

A second social influence on the life cycle derives from the fact that the "stages" of the life cycle are as much a matter of social interpretation and definition as they are of biological maturation. The developmental sequence must be seen not only in chronological and physiological terms, but in social and cultural terms as well. The category of "adolescence," for example, has emerged only relatively recently, and is not recognized at all in many cultures. This was the case in preindustrial Europe: paintings of the period, for example, invariably show children and adolescents as miniature adults in both dress and facial features.[3] Even in the United States at the turn of the present century, the natural stages of the human life cycle were considered to be infancy, childhood, young adulthood, mature adulthood, and old age. The word "adolescent" was first popularized in 1904 by the psychologist G. Stanley Hall,[4] who used the term to refer to a new age group that was emerging in industrialized societies—young people who had attained puberty but were denied any adult responsibilities. The need for a period of formal education to prepare the young for their roles in a technologically advanced society was the main factor behind the emergence of this "new" stage of life, which we now take for granted as a "natural" part of the cycle. We still tend to think of the transition to and from adolescence as a relatively slow process, but in many traditional communities the change in status from child to adult is an abrupt one, usually marked—at least in the case of males—by an abrupt and often painful initiation ceremony. Interestingly, we still retain vestiges of initiation ceremonies in our own society—such as the high school graduation, the twenty-first birthday celebration, or the Jewish bar mitzvah.

Another important social influence on the development of the individual life cycle is the ascriptive status into which each person is born. Certain statuses are ascribed to us at birth by reason of our sex, race, or the socioeconomic level of our parents. These ascriptions can profoundly affect the entire subsequent course and even the duration of the life cycle. Women, for example, have far fewer opportunities for self-fulfillment than men, and members of each sex have certain arbitrary social limitations imposed on the life options that they can explore. Similarly, an individual who is born a member of a minority group in the United States, or who is born into the lower socioeconomic stratum of our society, faces numerous handicaps. Some of these handicaps are psychological and manifest themselves in characteristic personal crises. Other handicaps result from the impact of social influences on physiological development: the minority-group member or the poor person is likely to be less healthy and to die significantly earlier than members of other groups in society.

Many of the problems of the life cycle, then, are not simply the result of the process of human growth and aging. They are also *social* prob-

[3]J. H. Plumb, "The Great Change in Children," *Horizon*, vol. 13, no. 1 (Winter 1971), pp. 4–13.
[4]G. Stanley Hall, *Adolescence: Its Psychology and Its Relations to Physiology, Anthropology, Sociology, Sex, Crime, Religion, and Education* (New York: D. Appleton, 1904).

The Ages of Man

All the world's a stage,
And all the men and women merely players;
They have their exits and their entrances;
And one man in his time plays many parts,
His acts being seven ages. At first the infant,
Mewling and puking in the nurse's arms;
Then the whining school-boy, with his satchel
And shining morning face, creeping like snail
Unwillingly to school. And then the lover,
Sighing like furnace, with a woeful ballad
Made to his mistress' eyebrow. Then a soldier,
Full of strange oaths, and bearded like the pard,
Jealous in honour, sudden and quick in quarrel,
Seeking the bubble reputation,
Even in the cannon's mouth. And then the justice,
In fair round belly with good capon lin'd,
With eyes severe and beard of formal cut,
Full of wise saws and modern instances;
And so he plays his part. The sixth age shifts
Into the lean and slipper'd pantaloon,
With spectacles on nose and pouch on side;
His youthful hose, well sav'd, a world too wide
For his shrunk shank; and his big manly voice,
Turning again toward childish treble, pipes
And whistles in his sound. Last scene of all,
That ends this strange eventful history,
Is second childishness and mere oblivion;
Sans teeth, sans eyes, sans taste, sans everything.

SOURCE: William Shakespeare, *As You Like It*, Act II, Scene VII.

lems, because their nature and the points in the life cycle at which they occur are profoundly influenced by social forces that vary from society to society, and from group to group within a society.

APPROACHING THE PROBLEM

The problems of the life cycle are so varied and so changing that they cannot be comprehended through any single perspective. Specific problems may be analyzed as appropriate from either the social-disorganization, the value-conflict, or the deviance perspective, or through some combination of these.

From the social-disorganization perspective, many of the current problems of the life cycle derive from the rapid social change that is a permanent characteristic of an advanced industrial society. Social change introduces uncertainty and instability into traditional norms, roles, and statuses, and so continually creates new potentials for characteristic problems and crises at different points of the life cycle. For example, the socialization experiences of the younger and the older generations in the United States are so different that the younger generation has not internalized, and indeed has rejected, many significant norms of their elders; in consequence, society is to some extent disorganized and generational conflict ensues. Another example is the status of the aged: changes in medical science have made possible the extension of the life cycle, so that the United States has a steadily increasing proportion of elderly people. But society is disorganized in that there have been few accompanying changes that might assure the aged of a useful and fulfilling role in society.

From the value-conflict perspective, some problems of the life cycle stem from an incompatibility of interests between different age groups in society. Each age group has unique characteristics because of the particular experiences it has shared and the particular knowledge and attitudes it has acquired. Moreover, each age group is at a different point in the life cycle and, therefore, has different privileges, obligations, and expectations. In American society, for example, the middle-aged differ from the young in that the former are less educated, more affluent, more conservative, and more influential in political and economic life. Problems such as the "generation gap" may be readily analyzed from the value-conflict perspective.

The deviance perspective has sometimes been applied to life-cycle problems, particularly in the analysis of youth cultures. The "hippie" movement and the student radical movement of the sixties have been analyzed as forms of deviance from the dominant social norms, attitudes, and values; similarly, many types of adolescent behavior that violate social norms are classified as juvenile delinquency and analyzed as forms of deviance. To some sociologists, the deviance of the hippie or radical is a quality of the individual concerned; to other sociologists who adhere to the labeling theory of deviance, the "deviant" is simply someone who has been successfully labeled as such by the dominant majority, in this case the older members of society. Suicide—the deliberate termination of one's own life cycle—may also be analyzed as a deviant act.

Erikson's Stages of Life

The most influential modern account of the stages of the life cycle is that of the psychologist Erik Erikson. Originally trained as a Freudian psychoanalyst, Erikson became progressively more dissatisfied with Freud's theories as he tried to apply them to his patients. According to

Freudian theory, most of the neurotic symptoms of the patients should have been caused by repressed sexual problems. But Erikson found that a great many of his patients seemed to be suffering from problems of *identity* — personal crises that came at various points in the life cycle and seemed to be related more to the social environment than to sexual difficulties. The patients seemed to have lost the sense of who and what they were and what their ultimate goals in life should be. The main problem, it seemed to Erikson, was one of identity confusion, not sexual neurosis.

Erikson accordingly developed a new theory. He proposed that the life cycle consists of a series of psychosocial stages as well as physiological stages. At each of these psychosocial stages the individual has to establish new orientations to himself and the world, and failure to do so at any stage can disrupt development in the subsequent stages. There are, Erikson argues, eight psychosocial stages in the life cycle, each of which has both a positive and a negative component. The well-adjusted individual is able to orient himself or herself toward the positive component at each step, and thus build a foundation for subsequent development.

Erikson's stages do not represent some absolute description of a rigid and inevitable pattern; he proposes them as merely one possible way of viewing the life cycle. His stages are as follows:

1. *Trust versus mistrust.* This stage covers the first year of life, and involves the two extremes of trust and mistrust. The infant whose needs are met in a warm, consistent fashion will develop a trusting view of the world, while the infant who is rejected and whose needs are neglected may come to mistrust her or his environment and other people.
2. *Autonomy versus doubt.* In this stage, which runs from age two to three, the child attempts to develop a sense of personal autonomy. This sense of autonomy is confirmed if the child succeeds in his or her efforts, but if the child is treated in a critical or overprotective way by parents, feelings of personal doubt may arise instead.
3. *Initiative versus guilt.* Between the ages of four and five the child begins to initiate his or her own activities. If the initiatives are encouraged and rewarded, the child feels confident and competent; if the child is punished or ridiculed for these efforts, a sense of guilt may emerge instead.
4. *Industry versus inferiority.* From age six to age eleven the child is extremely active and industrious, constantly creating ideas, objects, and situations. If these activities are rewarded, a sense of creativity and industry is enhanced; if they are regarded as a nuisance and derogated, feelings of inferiority may result. At this stage in the life cycle, the parents cease to be the almost exclusive agency of socialization, and other agencies, particularly the schools and the peer group, begin to play their roles.

5. *Identity versus role confusion.* This important period covers the teen-age years, when the individual discovers many new and highly personalized ways of looking at the world. He or she is able, in particular, to conceive of ideals and contrast them with social realities. If the adolescent has successfully passed through the earlier stages, he or she can now call on resources of trust, autonomy, initiative, and industry, and so may arrive at a meaningful and appropriate self-concept or identity. But if the young person is entering adolescence with feelings of mistrust, doubt, guilt, and inferiority, role confusion may result. Social influences are important in the establishment of an enduring identity: in a stable, traditional society, there are fewer options and possibilities to explore and the force of social norms is very strong; but in the United States the adolescent risks being overwhelmed by potential alternatives and experiences, and frequently cannot rely on unquestioned social norms for guidance.

6. *Intimacy versus isolation.* This period covers young adulthood. Intimacy refers to the capacity to share oneself with another person. But some people may be incapable of such intimacy, feeling they will lose themselves in the process. Inability to form intimate bonds with others may leave the individual isolated, alone in the world without anyone with whom to share feelings and existence.

7. *Generativity versus self-absorption.* This stage covers middle age. Generativity refers to the important capacity to develop a concern for others besides oneself—for the social world, perhaps, or for the future of one's children. Those who fail to achieve a sense of generativity may relapse into a self-absorbed state, a condition in which their prime concern is for their own needs rather than the welfare of others.

8. *Integrity versus despair.* This stage covers the last years in the life cycle. As death approaches, the individual who can look back on his or her life's achievement with satisfaction senses a feeling of personal integrity; but despair is the fate of those who can only regret their mistakes and think of what might have been.[5]

The personal characteristics of which Erikson writes appear at first to be psychological and individual in nature. But as Erikson stresses, even the most private and individual aspects of life are influenced by the social context in which they originate and by which they are modified. In some cultures or subcultures the prospects for an individual's achieving the positive components of the eight stages might be very favorable, whereas in another culture or subculture, social forces might encourage such negative characteristics as role confusion in adolescence, isolation in young adulthood, self-absorption in middle age, or despair among the elderly.

[5]Erik H. Erikson, *Childhood and Society,* rev. ed. (New York: W. W. Norton, 1964).

Let us now look more closely at some of the more problematic points in the American life cycle: adolescence and youth, the middle years, old age, and death.

ADOLESCENCE AND YOUTH

As we have seen, the stage of life that we term *adolescence* is a fairly recent one, the product of a developing industrial society that requires personnel with relatively highly developed and specialized skills. Prolonged education has become an economic necessity in our society; indeed, Americans receive far more years of education than any other people in history. Since 1900 the amount of education received by the average American has increased by more than six years; at the turn of the century only 6.4 percent of Americans completed high school, compared with over 80 percent who do so today. In traditional societies, individuals typically move directly from childhood to adult status at the time of puberty, but in industrialized societies adolescents are relegated to marginal, ambiguous roles: for example, they are physically capable of reproduction, but sexual experience is officially forbidden to them and marriage is strongly discouraged until very late in adolescence. Adolescents are excluded from the labor force, segregated from other age groups, and concentrated together in schools under conditions of intimate peer-group interaction. Inevitably, they tend to develop norms, values, and attitudes which are in some respects markedly different from those predominating in the society from which they have been segregated and in which they lack many privileges.

The concept of *youth* as a stage of the life cycle is of even more recent origin; the term was proposed by Kenneth Keniston at the end of the sixties to designate a specific "new" stage intervening between adolescence and adulthood. Keniston contended that:

> Millions of young people are in a stage of life that lacks even a name. Unprecedented prolongation of education has opened up opportunities for a new extension of psychological development, creating a "new" stage of life.[6]

Youth, Keniston argues, is an emergent stage in the life cycle in our society: it is still optional and many people may still pass straight from adolescence to adulthood. The stage of youth runs roughly from age eighteen to thirty and comprises the many young people who refuse to "settle down" and accept those attitudes, life styles, and responsibilities that our society regards as the defining characteristics of mature adulthood. Essentially, the individuals who are in this period are attempting to prolong the advantages of adolescence far beyond the point at which they would normally have had to abandon them. People in this stage

[6]Kenneth Keniston, "Youth: A New Stage of Life," *American Scholar*, vol. 39, no. 4 (Autumn 1970), pp. 631–654.

share in much of the culture of late adolescence; their attitudes, values, tastes, and life-style preferences are markedly at odds with those of the established adult culture.

The period between childhood and adulthood in the United States is, according to Erikson, a time for the trial of emergent identities, for the exploration of possibilities and the exercise of personal freedom. Erikson believes that this period is essentially a "moratorium," a psychosocial interlude in which there are few responsibilities and in which emergent identities can be explored and consolidated. But the emergence of this new period in the life cycle has occurred at a point in history when an unprecedented range of new options, problems, and challenges abound, so that the possibilities for role confusion and personal crises are immense.

Adolescent and Youth Cultures

One of the most publicized problems of the life cycle in the United States has been the existence since the early sixties of a highly distinctive culture of the young. There is nothing new about a discontinuity in the values and cultural styles of the generations, but the contemporary cleavage between the generations in the United States—and in much of the Western world, where young people followed the example of their American counterparts—is generally agreed by social scientists to be almost without precedent. So different did the culture of the young seem when it first emerged that it has become known as the "counterculture."

The early manifestations of the counterculture were so strikingly at variance with the established norms of our society that the older generation responded with horrified incredulity; as sociologist Theodore Roszak observed, the young had created

> a culture so radically disaffiliated from the mainstream assumptions of our society that it scarcely looks to many as a culture at all, but takes on the appearance of a barbaric invasion.[7]

The new counterculture comprised two related elements. One was a radical, activist political wing, consisting mostly of students who challenged established authority in the colleges and national policies at home and abroad, particularly in relation to the Vietnam war and the civil rights of American minority groups. The second element in the counterculture reacted against American culture rather than American policies, and adopted new styles of dress, new forms of drug usage, and new values that were radically at variance with those of the older generation. Competition, aggressiveness, deferral of gratification, restrictive sexuality, and the rational-scientific world view were all rejected in favor of their polar opposites. Both wings of the new counterculture,

[7]Theodore Roszak, *The Making of a Counter Culture* (Garden City, N. Y.: Anchor Books, 1969), p. 42.

however, derived most of their recruits from the white middle class – in other words, from those young people who were exempted from more mundane economic concerns and who had the time, affluence, and security to challenge established social institutions and to explore experimental life styles.

Why did this distinctive culture of the young suddenly emerge? The *basis* for the counterculture was already present at the end of the fifties: young people were segregated from society in growing numbers as a result of the postwar "baby boom"; society itself was becoming increasingly affluent; and the young were developing a strong sense of characteristic generational identity – an identity much reinforced through the medium of rock music, which provided culture heroes and transmitted anti-establishment messages specifically directed at a young audience. But the actual *content* of the counterculture seems to have been the result of a failure of the American socialization process: many of the young were reluctant to assume their adult roles and engaged instead in an "anticipatory rejection" of the goals and futures that their society offered them. As Keniston has pointed out, youth and adulthood present very conflicting images to the maturing adolescent. Society requires of the adolescent that he or she abandon a relatively carefree and hedonistic life style for the rigid separation of work and leisure, the deferral of gratification, and the other restrictive patterns that define responsible adulthood. Not surprisingly, there is a reluctance to relinquish the existing life style for one that seems to offer few attractive compensations.[8] Herbert Marcuse has similarly pointed out that each growing individual has experienced a paradise of play, pleasure, and instant gratification in childhood, and thus retains the memory of an implicit utopia against which the economic and social demands of adulthood are measured. The adolescent may easily feel a strong tension between these competing images.[9] To Theodore Roszak, the growth of the counterculture is to be explained in terms of youth's reassertion of spontaneity, individuality, and hedonism in the face of a society that is increasingly impersonal, artificial, and dehumanized by large organizations and technology.[10] John A. Clausen draws attention to the importance of young people's perception that the values into which they are socialized by the older generation are often not practiced; countercultural forms represent a reaction to parental hypocrisy and an attempt to put into effect the ideals that the older generation teaches but does not apply.[11] Each of these theorists focuses on slightly different factors in the creation of a counterculture, but their explanations all imply a failure of the socialization process in preparing the young for a smooth transition to adult status.

[8]Kenneth Keniston, *Youth and Dissent: The Rise of a New Opposition* (New York: Harcourt Brace Jovanovich, 1971).
[9]Herbert Marcuse, *Eros and Civilization* (Boston: Beacon Press, 1956).
[10]Roszak, *The Making of a Counter Culture.*
[11]John A. Clausen, "The Life Course of Individuals," in *Aging and Society,* eds. Riley and Foner, pp. 457–513.

The period of youth is a "new" stage of life in American society, and it is unknown in most other parts of the world. Many young post-adolescents are slow to accept full adult responsibilities and continue to experiment with different life styles and identities. *(Harvey Stein)*

The seventies, however, have seen a marked change in the counter-culture: many of the "dropouts" have dropped back in, the radical activism of the sixties has been replaced by a pervasive apathy toward the political system, the earlier idealism has given way to a degree of cynicism, and the more extravagant variations in dress and behavior that marked the sixties are less in evidence. One of the original spokesmen of the counterculture, James S. Kunen, has since looked back on the early days of the movement:

> We had concluded, correctly, that we were living in a rotten, corrupt, morally bankrupt, brutally exploitative system, failing to apprehend only that this meant that the world was clicking along as usual.[12]

The culture of the young no longer seems so radically at odds with the rest of society. One reason is that the young today are considerably more conformist, probably because of the pressures of an uncertain economy. A second reason is that many of the distinguishing features of the counterculture—such as hair length, dress styles, musical tastes, and in modified form, some values—have been absorbed into the dominant culture. But the differences between today's culture of the young and that of the sixties should not obscure the fact that countercultural influ-

[12]James S. Kunen, "The Rebels of 1970," *New York Times Magazine* (October 28, 1973), p. 78.

ences still linger, and there are still very marked differences in the attitudes, values, and interests of the young and the old in our society. The young are by no means indistinguishable from their parents in many important respects, and the potentials for intergenerational value conflicts, and for significant social change when the present younger generation assumes political power, remain considerable.

Irrespective of the fate of the contemporary culture of the young, it seems inevitable that a society such as ours will continue to give rise to distinctive cultural forms in the younger generation. Indeed, these youth cultures may be functional for society, as sociologist Talcott Parsons has pointed out: they provide a transitional period of adjustment between the very different roles of child and adult.[13]

THE MIDDLE YEARS

The personal problems that occur in the middle years of life have long been neglected by social scientists, and it is only recently that researchers have focused attention on the "mid-life crisis" faced by many people, usually in their forties. The mid-life period is marked by relatively high rates of depression, alcoholism, and suicide; a sudden rise in the divorce rate also takes place at this stage of life. Many social scientists believe that these phenomena are related to the personal crises that men and women experience, in somewhat different ways, as they come to the realization that their lives are more than half over.

In the early thirties, husband and wife are in the process of settling down, raising a family, and developing the attitudes that will cement and give meaning to their lives together. There is still room for idealistic speculation about the future that awaits them. But by their forties, they can have no more illusions; typically, the pattern of their lives has become settled and predictable. Both partners face the inevitable signs of aging; they lose the sense of growing up and realize they are beginning to grow old. The change in orientation from time-since-birth to time-left-to-live can be traumatic, but the precise age at which people experience these feelings and the degree to which they are disturbed by them varies immensely, as John A. Clausen points out:

> Some men and women are acutely aware of aging at a period of life when others feel they are at their prime. Chronic poor health and loss of youthful looks are obvious cues that vigor and beauty are on the decline, but there may be more subtle cues as well. Declining response from members of the opposite sex can be devastating to the erstwhile Don Juan or his female counterpart. . . . The athletic individual who took great pride in his ability to perform physical feats may experience a measure of despair when his manifest strength and endurance begin to drop off noticeably, even though

[13]Talcott Parsons, "Age and Sex in the Social Structure of the United States," in *Essays in Sociological Theory*, ed. Talcott Parsons (New York: Glencoe, 1949).

he may surpass most people in their prime. One man takes pleasure in seeing his son's powers surpass his own; another strongly contests his son because the son's ascendance can only mean his own decline.[14]

The individual in the middle years of life also begins the gradual process of coming to terms with the inevitability of his or her own death, an event which earlier had seemed impossibly distant. Gail Sheehy, who has made an extensive study of the mid-life crisis, comments that this is the time when people begin to feel perishable. Suddenly headaches are believed to be the first sign of a brain tumor, any lump is suspected of being cancerous. The middle-aged watch as their parents and friends die; and these deaths, which might seem removed from the twenty-five-year-old, are to the forty-year-old a sign of his or her own mortality. The feeling that "I'm next" becomes a warning sign to make the most of life while there is still time.[15]

One researcher, Daniel Levinson, believes that the ten-year period from thirty-five to forty-five is crucially important for men. The period covers the end of early adulthood to the start of middle age, and no individual, he argues, can pass through it unchanged. The man experiences discontinuity in his life as he copes with the unmistakable signs of aging and the dawning realization of just how much further he is likely to advance in his career and what his ultimate achievements in life are likely to be.[16] Sheehy notes that as a man approaches forty, he faces the disconcerting fact that he has arrived at the middle of his life and the middle of his career. At thirty, anything seemed possible; his choice of career as well as his success were still open to hopeful speculation. At forty, he realizes "where he has placed in life's professional battles";[17] and he senses that even if he has been successful, he must attempt to avoid stagnation. But if he has failed to achieve his youthful expectations of himself, he faces the difficult task of coming to terms with that reality without experiencing undue bitterness or disappointment.

For the woman in our society the mid-life crisis may take a rather different form. Every woman must face the clearly demarcated and predictable changes involved in menopause, although the actual timing and psychological impact of the event are variable. The woman usually does not have a professional career, and so does not experience directly some of the concerns that affect her husband. But if she has devoted most of her married life to the care and upbringing of her children, their departure from home may come as a traumatic event to her. This "empty nest" situation may be particularly disturbing to the wife who

[14]Clausen, "The Life Course of Individuals," p. 493.
[15]Gail Sheehy, "Catch-30 and Other Predictable Crises of Growing Up Adult," *New York* Magazine (February 18, 1974), p. 36.
[16]See Maggie Scarf, "Husbands in Crisis," *McCall's*, vol. 99, no. 9 (June 1972), pp. 76–77, 120, 122, 124–125.
[17]Sheehy, "Catch-30 and Other Predictable Crises of Growing Up Adult, p. 44.

has lavished her attention on her children partly to distract her from an unsatisfactory marriage, and she may experience feelings of loneliness, isolation, and futility. Deprived of what had become almost the main reason for her existence and realizing that much of her life has been devoted to her family rather than to any enhancement of personal talents and abilities, a woman at this point in life may come to resent her subordinate status and may wish to seek fulfillment outside the home — to the consternation of her husband. Sheehy describes this situation in one couple that she studied:

> She is ready to strike out, get a job, go back to school, kick up her heels; just as he is drawing back, gasping for breath, feeling futile about where he has been and uncertain about simply keeping his balance on the job and in bed. How is he likely to react to her sudden surge toward independence?[18]

Many marital difficulties ensue at this stage of the life cycle as the husband and wife—frequently under no romantic illusions about each other and experiencing few mutual sensual delights—face the remainder of life without the company of their children and with the prospect of a significantly lower standard of living once the husband has retired.

OLD AGE

The number of the aged—defined by the Bureau of the Census as those citizens over sixty-five years of age—is steadily increasing. In 1900 only 4 percent of the population survived for sixty-five years or more, but today the aged comprise some 10 percent of the nation, or more than 20 million people.[19] The aged face many problems in our society: the loss of physical health, isolation and loneliness, poverty, discrimination, and the fact that they survive beyond the age at which they are offered or are able to perform meaningful social roles.

In time, the burden of the years affects even the healthiest individual. Aging is accompanied by physiological changes that are not necessarily the result of any disease: apart from the more obvious manifestations of age—such as baldness, wrinkling of the skin, changes in body form, and stiffness of limbs—there is a general process of cellular atrophy and progressive degeneration. Over three-quarters of those citizens who are over sixty-five suffer from some chronic health condition.[20] There may be considerable discrepancy, however, between biological and chronological age, resulting in a great degree of variation in the rate of physiological aging. Some people seem relatively young at

---

[18]Gail Sheehy, "Why Mid-Life is a Crisis Time for Couples," *New York Magazine* (April 29, 1974), p. 33.
[19]E. J. Kahn, Jr., *The American People* (New York: Weybright and Talley, 1974), p. 305.
[20]See Leonard Z. Breen, "The Aging Individual," in *Handbook of Social Gerontology,* ed. Clark Tibbitts (Chicago: University of Chicago Press, 1960), p. 147.

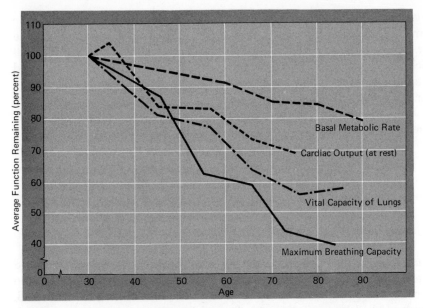

Estimates of physiological aging after thirty. Aging is accompanied by a general decline in the organism's capacity to resist environmental pressures. This process of progressive physiological deterioration accelerates after the age of thirty and eventually results in death. However, rates of physiological aging are not constant, and there may be a considerable variation between a person's chronological and biological age. (SOURCE: Adapted from N. W. Shock, "The Physiology of Aging," *Scientific American,* 206 [1962]; as cited in *Aging and Society,* vol. 1, eds. M. W. Riley and A. Foner [New York: Russell Sage Foundation, 1968].)

seventy, and some men even father children at eighty; other people, however, show noticeable signs of aging as early as fifty. In general, however, chronic ill health becomes more common with advancing age.

As we have seen, traditional societies usually accord a well-defined role and a fulfilling status to the old. One major study of a number of traditional societies found that, almost without exception, these communities offered such a satisfactory role to the elderly that many people looked forward to old age rather than fearing it.[21] In traditional societies the old person is often the dominant member of the family group; and especially where there is no system of writing to transmit cultural knowledge, the old serve as the main source of information on a variety of subjects ranging from religion to medicine. Old men typically wield considerable political power, and the aged of both sexes are usually expected to remain active in the community and to perform some forms of light labor until advanced old age.

In our society, in contrast, the aged are deprived of the roles and statuses they traditionally enjoyed in preindustrial society, and are poorly

[21]Leo W. Simmons, *The Role of the Aged in Primitive Societies* (New Haven, Conn.: Yale University Press, 1945).

integrated into the social structure. They can no longer lay automatic claim on their kin for support and social participation, and any advice they give is likely to be considered irrelevant in a changing world about which their descendants are probably much better informed. The aged have little function in our society, which provides no new roles for them after retirement from economic activity. To retain some sense of identity, the aged person has to try to retain preexisting roles, or may become preoccupied with a review of the past.[22] As Clausen notes:

> In the later years, the life review serves to preserve an identity that can no longer be validated in the present. Lacking roles that bring respect and admiration, and lacking goals toward which he can strive, the very old person invokes the past to remind himself and his listeners that his life was meaningful and his identity worthy of respect.[23]

An urban, industrialized society such as the United States is oriented toward youth, mobility, and activity. It has little place for the aged, who are often required to retire at or around the age of sixty-five; indeed, retirement has become almost a formal transition to the status of "elderly." The implications of retirement can be profound, because the transition is not simply one from work to leisure. It may also be one from relative affluence to relative economic hardship; the old person is no longer able to maintain his or her place in the economy, and if living with mature children, automatically becomes a dependent in his or her own household. Moreover, work signifies far more than income. It provides a goal for energy, it gives a status and a role, it provides a sense of identity, it prevents boredom, and it is a source of friends and social contacts. Deprived of all these and cast into a role that is at best ambiguous, the elderly person may experience problems of adjustment.

Some writers have likened the aged to other minority groups that encounter discrimination on the basis of some arbitrary characteristic. The term "age-ism" — analogous to racism and sexism — has been used to refer to the manner in which the aged are informally but systematically excluded from participation in society, politics, and the economy, so that their contribution is far less significant than it might be in terms of their numbers.[24] The discrimination against the aged can readily be measured in dollars and cents: for example, less than 1 percent of the federal mental health budget goes to research on the aged, although old people represent 25 percent of mental hospital admissions.[25]

Like other minorities that lack real political power, the aged are disproportionately poor. The 1970 census found that the median income for all heads of families was $9,867, but for heads of families aged sixty-

---

[22]Robert N. Butler, "The Life Review: An Interpretation of Reminiscence in the Aged," *Psychiatry*, vol. 26, no. 1 (February 1963), pp. 65–76.
[23]Clausen, "The Life Course of Individuals," p. 498.
[24]See Milton I. Barron, *The Aging American* (New York: Thomas Y. Crowell, 1961).
[25]Bernice L. Neugarten, "The Old and the Young in Modern Societies," *American Behavioral Scientist*, vol. 14, no. 1 (September–October 1970), pp. 13–14.

In a supportive social environment, old age can be a time of satisfaction and fulfillment. All too often, however, our society accords no useful or respected role to its older citizens. *(Hella Hammid/Rapho Guillumette)*

five or over it was only $5,035. Some 27.1 percent of the aged are living below the poverty line, and for those who are living on their own the figure rises to 48.5 percent[26] — a fact which is a shameful reflection on the attitudes toward the aged in the most affluent society in the world. Most of those who live alone are women, because men tend to die rather younger; in fact, there are four times as many widows as widowers in the United States.[27]

The treatment of the aged in America is a product not of design but of neglect; it is a symptom of severe social disorganization, involving a discrepancy between American ideals and practices, as well as the systematic if unintended denial to millions of citizens of opportunities to find a fulfilling role in the last years of the life cycle.

DEATH

American culture has often been termed "death-defying." The inhabitants of traditional societies are more accustomed to the idea of death than we are; they are familiar with it from childhood and are better equipped to deal with it, both emotionally and practically. As anthropologist Margaret Mead observes:

[26]Kahn, *The American People*, p. 306.
[27]Ibid., p. 311.

> In peasant communities where things didn't change and where people died in the beds they were born in, grandparents taught the young what the end of life was going to be. So you looked at your mother, if you were a girl, and you learned what it was like to be a bride, a young mother. Then you looked at your grandmother and knew what it was like to be old. Children learned what it was to age and die while they were very small. They were prepared for the end of life at the beginning.[28]

Americans, however, have made death almost a taboo subject—one rarely to be discussed, and almost never to be mentioned to someone who is actually dying. We have even institutionalized death: more than two-thirds of all deaths occur in the setting of the hospital or geriatric institution, with professional personnel in attendance. Death has been effectively removed from the context of everyday life, but there is growing controversy over whether an institutionalized death—in the context of a general conspiracy of friends, relatives, and doctors to deny its existence—really does provide the most dignified and painless passing. Although the hospital provides all the advantages of modern medical facilities, it also creates an environment that may be psychologically stressful to the dying and to their relatives.

Barney Glaser and Anselm Strauss have conducted intensive research on the situation of terminally ill patients and find that the patient is usually kept in a *closed awareness* context: that is, he or she is prevented from learning of impending death. Initially, at least, this attempt to hide the facts is successful: patients are medically incompetent to interpret their own symptoms, the hospital is able to hide the medical diagnosis from the patient, and medical personnel and family collude in maintaining the illusion that the patient will get well. Commonly, however, the patient begins to suspect the truth, but different patients react to those around them in different ways: some maintain the pretense, while others confront doctors and family and demand the opportunity to talk about their impending fate. The research of Glaser and Strauss strongly supports the view that the patient should be told the truth: that is, that there should be an *open awareness* context. The patient is thus enabled to act toward self and others in a more honest and realistic way, which markedly eases the acceptance of death.[29]

The fact of approaching death is not at first readily accepted by the patient, however. Elisabeth Kübler-Ross has identified five stages through which the terminally ill patient typically proceeds after being told the truth. The first stage is *denial*, usually expressed in disbelief— "It can't happen to me." The second stage is *anger* and resentment—

---

[28]Margaret Mead, "Dealing With the Aged: A New Style of Aging," *Current*, no. 136 (January 1972), p. 44.

[29]Barney G. Glaser and Anselm L. Strauss, *Awareness of Dying* (Chicago: Aldine Press, 1965); *Time for Dying* (Chicago: Aldine Press, 1968); and "Patterns of Dying," in *The Dying Patient*, eds. Orville G. Brim, et al. (New York: Russell Sage Foundation, 1970), pp. 129–155. See also Robert Kastenbaum, "The Kingdom Where Nobody Dies," *Saturday Review of Science*, vol. 55, no. 2 (January 1973), pp. 33–38; and Thomas Powers, "Learning to Die," *Harper's*, 242 (June 1971), pp. 72–80.

"Why me?" The third stage is *bargaining*—an implicit agreement with God or fate to go quietly if one can just live long enough to participate in or witness some important event, such as the arrival of spring or a family wedding. The fourth stage is *depression,* which is marked by anxiety over the loss of self and the loss to one's family. The final stage is *acceptance,* in which the dying individual accepts his or her fate and approaches death with true peace of mind.[30] Kübler-Ross stresses the importance to the patient of open and honest interaction between the dying patient and others:

> After the first shock, numbness, and need to deny the reality of the situation, the patient begins to send out cues that he is ready to "talk about it." If *we,* at that point, need to deny the reality of the situation, the patient will often feel deserted, isolated, and lonely and unable to communicate with another human being what he needs so desperately to share. . . .
>
> To such patients, we should never say, "Come on now, cheer up." We should allow them to grieve. . . . If the patient expresses his grief, he will feel more comfortable, and he will usually go through the stage of depression much more rapidly than he will if he has to suppress it. . . . Only through this kind of behavior on our part are our patients able to reach the stage of acceptance. . . . The patient now shows no more fear, bitterness, anguish, or concern over unfinished business. People who have been able to sit through this stage with patients and who have experienced the beautiful feeling of inner and outer peace that they show will soon appreciate that working with terminally ill patients is not a morbid, depressing job but can be an inspiring experience.
>
> The tragedy is that in our death-defying society, people grow uncomfortable in the presence of a dying patient, unable to talk to the terminally ill and at a loss for words when they face a grieving person.[31]

Kübler-Ross's view is typical of the arguments of a growing number of sociologists and medical practitioners who believe that our societal attitudes toward death and dying are in need of a major change if the ultimate point in the life cycle is to become a less harrowing experience for all concerned.

Suicide

The deliberate attempt to terminate one's own life cycle is surprisingly frequent in the United States: it is believed that at least 125,000 and perhaps as many as 225,000 citizens attempt suicide each year.[32] The

[30]Elisabeth Kübler-Ross, *On Dying and Society* (New York: Macmillan, 1969).

[31]Elisabeth Kübler-Ross, "Facing Up to Death," *Today's Education* (January 1972), pp. 30–32.

[32]Marshall B. Clinard, *Sociology of Deviant Behavior* (New York: Holt, Rinehart & Winston, 1968), p. 501; Ronald W. Maris, *Social Forces in Urban Suicide* (Homewood, Ill.: Dorsey, 1969), pp. 5–6.

number who actually succeed, however, is far smaller. Suicide statistics are notoriously unreliable — whenever there is any doubt as to the manner of death there is usually strong pressure from relatives to have the death certified as accidental rather than deliberate.[33] The number of suicides officially recorded is about 25,000 per year, although the true figure may be very much higher.

Suicide seems to be a highly individual act, but the rate of suicide varies from one social context to another, a fact which demonstrates yet again the immense importance of social forces on individual psychology and behavior. The French sociologist Emile Durkheim was the first researcher to draw attention to the relationship between social context and suicide.[34] He found that the suicide rate varies in a consistent fashion over the years from one region or population group to another. Suicide is more common, for example, among urban residents than among rural dwellers; it is more common among Protestants than Catholics, and it is more common in times of economic change than in times of economic stability. Durkheim believed that the likelihood of suicide was intimately connected to the degree that the individual was integrated into society, and he made a famous distinction between two ways in which the force of social norms, or the lack of force of such norms, could impel an individual to take his or her own life. In the case of *anomic suicide,* the individual's behavior is no longer regulated by social norms — including those that prohibit self-destruction. For a variety of reasons, the individual may find no meaning in life and so may resort to suicide. The anomic form of suicide is particularly common in the modern world. In the case of *altruistic suicide,* however, the individual takes his or her own life precisely because he or she is fully integrated into social norms that specify suicide as an appropriate act under certain conditions. In India, for example, wives were traditionally expected to commit ritual suicide after their husbands' deaths; ancient Romans were expected to kill themselves in times of personal dishonor; and a similar tradition persisted in Japan for centuries. In general, the altruistic form of suicide is more common in traditional societies. In the first case, then, poor integration into social norms may lead to suicide; in the second, full integration may have the same effect and a person may willingly die simply because society expects it. A highly individual act is thus closely linked to social forces.

The suicide rate in the United States is rather high — it represents nearly twice the number of deaths resulting from murder and nearly half the number resulting from auto fatalities. The rate fluctuates noticeably, however, in times of economic change, perhaps because people who suddenly experience relative poverty or relative affluence are thrust into an anomic state in which the norms to which they have adhered for a lifetime no longer seem appropriate for their changed con-

---

[33]Jack D. Douglas, *The Social Meaning of Suicide* (Princeton, N.J.: Princeton University Press, 1967).
[34]Emile Durkheim, *Suicide* (Glencoe, Ill.: Free Press, 1964).

dition. At the time of the Depression, for example, the suicide rate among white males was double that of the preceding years.[35]

The rates of suicide and attempted suicide are higher for some social groups than for others. One large study revealed that those who typically attempt suicide are white females, who commonly take an overdose of barbiturate drugs. Those who successfully complete the attempt, however, are typically white males, who commit suicide by hanging, exposure to auto exhaust fumes, or shooting.[36] The significantly higher success rate for males may imply that they are more serious about the attempt and less inclined to use an apparent suicide attempt as a means of attracting the attention of others to their problems.

What are the immediate causes of a suicide attempt, successful or otherwise? Ernest Mowrer has proposed that there are two types of contexts: situational suicides and escapist suicides. The *situational suicide* is impulsive and unpremeditated and is a reaction to sudden psychological stress that the individual is unable to tolerate, such as a rupture in the relationship with a loved one. The *escapist suicide* is less impulsive and often occurs after a much longer period of unhappiness; it frequently involves the attempt to escape from moral or social responsibilities that the individual feels unable to bear.[37]

PROSPECTS FOR THE FUTURE

The life cycle in America will continue to present many problems to individuals at every stage; some of the problems will be enduring ones, such as value conflict between generations, while others will be novel problems created by social change in the future. It may eventually be possible, for example, to extend the human life span many decades by intervening in the biochemical processes that are responsible for cellular atrophy and aging. The impact of such technological developments would be incalculable.[38]

The socialization experiences of each new generation will continue to differ for as long as society continues to change at a rapid pace, with the result that there will always be a potential for identity confusion in adolescence and youth and for conflict between the generations. Margaret Mead points out that in a traditional society the young have merely to be socialized into the attitudes and norms of their elders: culture is relatively static and the old, by virtue of their greater experience, know more than the young. But the current pace of technological change is such that important aspects of the social environment may

[35]George Allen and Edward Ellis, *The Traitor Within* (Garden City, N.Y.: Doubleday, 1961), pp. 20–30.
[36]Edward S. Schneidman and Norman L. Farberow, *The Cry for Help* (New York: McGraw-Hill, 1961), pp. 22–46.
[37]Ernest R. Mowrer, *Disorganization: Personal and Social* (Philadelphia: Lippincott, 1942), pp. 357–365.
[38]Bernard L. Strehler, "A New Age for Aging," *Natural History*. 82 (February 1973), pp. 8–18, 82–85; Albert Rosenfeld, "The Longevity Seekers," *Saturday Review of Science*, vol. 1, no. 2 (February 24, 1973), pp. 46–51.

Life Cycle: A Theoretical Review

The social problems associated with the human life cycle represent the gap between a *social ideal* of a relatively untroubled developmental process offering lifelong opportunities for satisfaction and fulfillment, and the *social reality* of life cycles disrupted by unnecessary tensions and crises stemming from an unfavorable social environment. Although the course of the life cycle might at first seem to be a purely biological process, it is in fact also a social one. The length, nature, stages, and problems of the life cycle depend very much on the social context in which each generation lives and dies.

The *social-disorganization* perspective is very relevant to some of the problems of the life cycle. Many of the typical crises and problems faced by modern Americans during their life cycles can be traced to social disorganization resulting from rapid social change. There is a marked contrast in this respect between our society and traditional societies, in which roles and statuses are assigned to people on the basis of their age and sex and in which people have few significant options as to who or what they will become or how they will conduct their lives. In these societies, for example, the transition from childhood to adulthood is typically a smooth one, often marked by a short initiation ceremony; and the aged have a clearly defined and respected role in the community. But in a modern, heterogeneous society such as the United States, the individual is presented with a great range of options at nearly every stage in the life cycle and so always risks problems of uncertain identity. Traditional norms, roles, and statuses tend to lose their validity and stability in a rapidly changing society, for they do not change at the same pace as other elements in the social system. The low status of the aged in our society is directly linked to social and scientific changes that have increased the span of life, but have left old people with no useful role. Rapid social change also has the effect of creating conflicts between generations, for the reason that each generation is socialized into rather different worlds and so adheres to rather different norms. In addition, the structure of society ensures that different social groups have different opportunities for personal fulfillment during the life cycle: our society may be considered disorganized to the extent that women, blacks, or the poor are denied many chances for fulfillment on purely arbitrary grounds. Some social groups even have a shorter average life span than others: in general, the lower a person's socioeconomic status, the more likely he or she is to die at an earlier age. Continuing changes in technology and society inevitably disorganize the existing norms governing appropriate behavior and expectations at different points in the life cycle, and so the nature of the problems and crises faced by each generation is constantly changing as well.

The *value-conflict* perspective is also useful in the analysis of some problems of the life cycle. There is often a conflict of interests between different generations in society, because each generation has its own unique characteristics as a result of the distinctive experiences shared by its members. Each age group is at a different point in the life cycle and, therefore, has different expectations and different obligations in relation to all other age groups. The conflict between the younger and older generations in our society is relatively severe compared with intergenerational conflicts in other societies or in our own past, and probably results in part from the very different socialization experiences that the generations have undergone. The young in the United States often hold values that are significantly different from their parents, and these differences in values inevitably lead to conflicts. The very old, too, have interests that differ from those of most of the rest of society: they suffer from a form of discrimination that has been termed "age-ism" and are increasingly coming into conflict with younger citizens over the roles and rights of the elderly. Value conflicts such as these are evident not only at the societal level; they also translate into personal problems and crises for the individual.

The *deviance* perspective also provides a useful focus for some problems of the life cycle. Society has certain expectations of individuals at every point in the life cycle, and those who for one reason or another depart from significant norms are readily regarded as deviants. In a heterogeneous society such as the United States, opportunities for deviance abound; indeed, behavior that might be considered highly deviant by members of one generation may become so common in the next generation that it is regarded as perfectly normal. Perhaps because the older members of society are the ones who have the most power to label others as deviant, it is the young rather than the old to whom this label is most commonly applied. Drop-outs, delinquents, and others who do not fulfill the role expectations that the rest of society has for people of their age are readily defined as deviants and treated accordingly.

change many times during the life cycle of a single individual. The young are growing up in a world of which their parents may have little knowledge; for the first time in history, the young may have more relevant information to impart to the old than vice versa. In a sense, argues Mead, the rate of change is so great that the parents have no children and the children no parents. Under such circumstances, cultural differences between the generations seem inevitable; and the younger generation, deriving few relevant and firm guidelines for thought and action from the socialization process offered by their predecessors, risk many problems of confusion and uncertainty.[39]

One area in which major changes are most likely to occur is in the role of the elderly and in public policy related to their needs. Already the elderly are beginning to form activist organizations, such as the American Association of Retired Persons and the Gray Panthers. The former organization has some 5 million members, all of them fifty-five years of age or over, and runs an impressive series of programs, ranging from congressional lobbying to efforts to keep old people intellectually and socially active. The Gray Panther movement, which is open to anyone regardless of age, is considerably more radical and enjoys a good deal of support from its youthful members, many of whom recognize that if current attitudes toward the old persist, the young of today will be denied a meaningful future role in society.[40] Changes in the demographic structure of the United States are likely to have an important impact on the status of the old and on the proportion of national resources allocated to their needs in the future. At present we are a very young society, with a median age of only 27.9. The main factor contributing to the relatively large number of young people in our society was the postwar "baby boom." But since the years immediately after World War II, the birth rate has steadily declined, so that there will be fewer young people in the United States in the future. Meanwhile, the "baby boom" generation will continue to grow older—with the consequence that within a few decades our society will be "top heavy" with old people rather than weighted with younger citizens as at present. By the year 2000 there will be some 30 million people of sixty-five years of age or over; indeed, more than 12 million of them will be over seventy-five. The median age of the nation will rise sharply to 37.2 years.[41] The political and cultural influence of the old is likely to increase substantially, perhaps with a comparable reduction in the influence of the youth. Changes like these—demographic and otherwise—will tend to keep the nature of the life cycle and its problems in a constant state of flux.

[39]Margaret Mead, *Culture and Commitment* (Garden City, N.Y.: Natural History Press, 1970).
[40]Carole Offir, "Old People's Revolt—At 65, Work Becomes a Four-Letter Word," *Psychology Today,* vol. 7, no. 10 (March 1974), p. 40.
[41]Kahn, *The American People,* p. 315.

FURTHER READING

Alvarez, A., *The Savage God*, 1972. A discussion from many angles of the problem of suicide. The book includes a summary and evaluation of several theories of suicide.

Barron, Milton I., *The Aging American*, 1961. An account of the problems of the aged in American society and, particularly, of the institutionalized discrimination that they face.

Brin, Orville G., et al., eds., *The Dying Patient*, 1970. A very useful collection of essays on the psychological problems of the dying patient and his or her relatives; it includes much recent social science research.

Erikson, Erik H., *Childhood and Society*, 1964. A modern classic by a famous contemporary psychoanalyst. Erikson presents his theory of personal development through a life cycle of eight stages and deals in detail with the problems of personal identity in modern society.

Keniston, Kenneth, *Youth and Dissent*, 1971. An important collection of writings by America's leading scholar on trends in the youth culture. The book includes essays outlining Keniston's concept of "youth" as a "new" stage of life.

Mead, Margaret, *Culture and Commitment*, 1970. An anthropologist's lucid analysis of the problems that rapid social and technological change can cause in the human life cycle. The old, Mead contends, were socialized into a world that has almost passed out of existence and so are cast adrift in modern society. The young, on the other hand, cannot turn with confidence to their elders for guidance, as they could in the past, because the middle-aged are not able to experience youth's own distinctive problems.

Riley, Matilda W. and Anne Foner, eds., *Aging and Society: A Sociology of Age Stratification*, 3 vols., 1969. An important collection of articles on the human life cycle. This is probably the best resource for easily accessible information on the subject.

Roszak, Theodore, *The Making of a Counter Culture*, 1969. A sociological analysis of the sixties counterculture, which Roszak sees as a product of a youthful refusal to accept the adult roles offered by American society.

14

Crime and Justice

THE NATURE AND SCOPE OF THE PROBLEM

Crime has been perceived with startling rapidity as a major social problem in America. In 1963 a Harris poll found that only 2 percent of Americans regarded crime as a serious issue. But by 1968, only five years later, attitudes had changed dramatically: no less than 65 percent regarded crime as the most important problem facing the nation. And by 1971 some 70 percent of those surveyed expressed the view that "law and order have broken down in the country."[1]

The nation's crime statistics certainly give cause for concern. Every 13 seconds someone breaks into a building somewhere in the United States in order to rob it. Every 36 seconds a car is stolen. Every 38 seconds someone is either robbed, raped, violently assaulted, or murdered.[2] These serious crimes alone cost Americans over a billion dollars a year.

Statistics like these have brought fear into the lives of the American people. Opinion polls showed that by the end of the sixties, more than half the population openly admitted that they kept a gun in their homes and that they were afraid to walk on their own streets.[3] In a fairly typi-

[1]Louis Harris, *The Anguish of Change* (New York: W. W. Norton, 1973). p. 169.
[2]Federal Bureau of Investigation, *Crime in the United States: Uniform Crime Reports, 1972* (Washington, D.C.: U.S. Government Printing Office, 1973), p. 30.
[3]Harris, *The Anguish of Change*, p. 74.

cal Eastern city, Baltimore, polls revealed that one person in five found himself "watching out of the window for suspicious strangers"; one in four slept with a protective weapon nearby; half talked to callers through the door instead of opening it; and half deliberately "stayed at home in the evening rather than going out."[4]

The rising concern about crime has been accompanied by an increasing scrutiny of the entire system of justice: police, courts, and corrections. The integrity of the police has been challenged as never before. Their role in the campus confrontations and antiwar demonstrations of the sixties led to repeated allegations, particularly by young people and minority groups, of "police brutality." In New York the Knapp Commission uncovered widespread corruption in the city police, sometimes involving every single detective in an entire precinct. And the nationwide publicity that the commission's report generated led many Americans to wonder if the New York City police were an exception, or whether corruption was common in other police forces as well. Even the efficiency of the police has been doubted: although some $12 billion is spent every year on crime control, only one-fifth of all serious crimes result in an arrest.[5] The courts, too, have been criticized, both for their interminable delays in bringing cases to a final conclusion and for their sentencing practices. Critics have been quick to point out the discrepancy between the stiff sentences meted out to "ordinary" criminals in contrast to the light fines imposed on "white-collar" criminals such as industrial polluters, corporate price-fixers, or wealthy tax-evaders, whose crimes often have greater economic impact on the lives of all our citizens. This issue was highlighted during the Watergate scandal, in which high officials managed to plea-bargain and escape with light sentences, while lesser officials received stiffer sentences. Earlier, former Vice-President Agnew was able to escape a prison sentence by pleading "no contest" to a minor tax evasion charge, instead of having to answer to the more serious charge that the income on which he had failed to pay taxes was in the form of bribes. At the same time, prisons in America were filled with many thousands of people convicted for thefts of sums far smaller than those in question in the Agnew case.

The prisons have also become a focus of public attention, especially after the riots, often quelled by bloody shootings, at Attica, San Quentin, and several other penal institutions. The prisons are clearly failing in what Americans believe to be their prime function: the rehabilitation of their inmates. The rate of recidivism—that is, return to prison—is disturbingly high. In 1972, for example, some 65 percent of those arrested had been arrested at least once before in the previous five years; in fact, the average was four arrests within the five-year period.[6] A poll in the early seventies revealed that 64 percent of Americans believe that

[4]Ibid., p. 168.
[5]Federal Bureau of Investigation, *Crime in the United States*, p. 31.
[6]Ibid., p. 36

Robbery	77%
Forgery	74%
Auto theft	73%
Burglary	71%
Fraud	69%
Assault	68%
Gambling	65%
Weapons	62%
Larceny	61%
Narcotics	60%
Embezzlement	34%
All Others	66%
Total	65%

Percent repeaters by type of crime. How successful is the criminal justice system in deterring convicted individuals from further criminal acts? In a study of 228,032 offenders arrested between 1970 and 1972, it was found that 65 percent had been arrested before. The rates for repeating criminal acts were particularly high for crimes such as robbery: of the people arrested for robbery in this two-year period, 77 percent were repeaters. (SOURCE: Federal Bureau of Investigation, *Crime in the United States: Uniform Crime Reports, 1972* [Washington, D.C.: U.S. Government Printing Office, 1973], p. 37.)

"jails are the real breeders of crime"[7] — a damning public indictment of a penal system whose stated goal is the reduction of crime through rehabilitation of prisoners.

What Is Crime?

A crime is an act prohibited by law. All crime, in a sense, is political, because it takes an act of political authority — that is, the making of a law — to define what conduct is punishable by the state. Generally speaking, the state designates as criminal certain forms of conduct that violate strongly held values and norms. The laws simply serve to make the process of societal reaction to these violations more orderly, by defining the specific offense, the class of persons to which the law will be applied, and the kind of punishment that will be meted out.

However, not all forms of conduct that violate important norms are

[7]Harris, *The Anguish of Change*, p. 178.

¹mp.

prohibited by laws. In some cases the regulation of such conduct is left
to the informal process of public disapproval. In other cases the law is
worded in such a way that some violations of norms are perhaps unintentionally excluded; many state vice laws, for example, make mention
only of female prostitutes, so that male prostitutes are technically entitled to operate with impunity. And just as there are violations that are
not covered by laws, there are laws covering forms of conduct that,
because of changing norms, are no longer seen as violations by the society. These obsolete laws, such as the Massachusetts law prohibiting
card-playing on Sundays, often remain on the statute book but tend not
to be applied. Without the sentiment of a community behind it, a law
loses its moral and practical force, as the American experiment with
Prohibition so effectively demonstrated.

Some acts are regarded as criminal in virtually every human society.
These acts, such as murder, involve conduct that no society can tolerate and still preserve social order. Other acts, however, are not universally regarded as evil, and laws prohibiting them are simply a reflection
of the values of a particular society at a particular point in time. These
offenses may seem trivial or even laughable to outsiders. In medieval
Iceland, for example, it was a criminal offense to write verses about a
person—even verses of praise—beyond a certain length.[8] In many
Arab countries the use of marijuana is acceptable, while the use of alcohol is prohibited by law, but in our country precisely the opposite is
true. In short, laws are relative to the societies that create them.

A distinction is often made between crimes that have victims and
crimes that have none. A crime of the former type, such as murder,
robbery, or rape, has an identifiable victim who suffers in a definable
way as a result of the criminal act. But in the case of crimes without
victims, such as prostitution, gambling, and drug abuse, there is no one
who suffers directly from the act, except perhaps the person who
commits it. The problem of whether these victimless crimes should be
punished by criminal sanctions is being increasingly debated in American society, with many people arguing that the state does not have the
right to prescribe and enforce moral norms for the private lives of its
citizens.

Who Are the Offenders?

The incidence of arrests for criminal activity is not uniformly distributed throughout the population. The person arrested for a crime is likely
to be young, male, and a city-dweller.

The most likely age for arrest is sixteen.[9] Forty-four percent of all
serious crimes are committed by persons under the age of eighteen,
and almost 20 percent are committed by youths under fifteen. How-

[8]Edwin H. Sutherland and Donald R. Cressey, *Principles of Criminology,* 7th ed. (New York: Lippincott, 1966), p. 16.
[9]Federal Bureau of Investigation, *Crime in the United States,* p. 126.

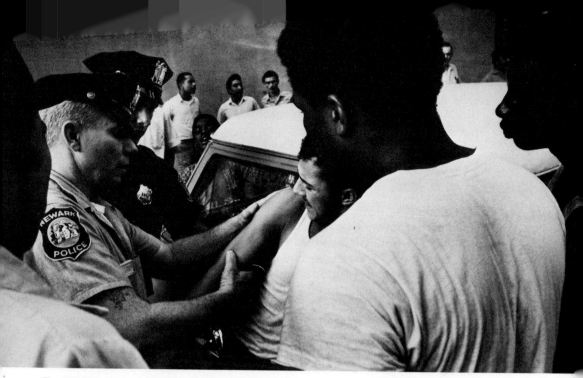

The likelihood of arrest and conviction is far greater for lower-class than for upper-class people, even though many studies have shown that the actual crime rate is similar for both groups. (*Ken Heyman*)

ever, juvenile offenders are more likely than others to commit certain categories of crime: they are much more likely than their elders to be arrested for vehicle theft and much less likely to be arrested for murder. Many of these young people are arrested with depressing frequency: 43 percent of those juveniles arrested between 1970 and 1972 had been arrested before, at an average rate of once every three months.[10] Convicted juvenile offenders are far more likely than other juveniles to become adult offenders.

Young or old, the offender is likely to be male. Males are arrested about six times more often than females; only in juvenile runaway cases do female offenders feature in the statistics as often as their male peers. There are probably two reasons for this differential arrest rate. First is the greater aggressiveness that our society encourages in males in contrast to the passivity and conformity that is encouraged in females. Second is the tendency of law enforcement agencies to deal more leniently with female offenders. But crime among females is increasing at a much faster rate than among males: between 1967 and 1972 the male arrest rate rose by 18 percent, but the female arrest rate rose four times as fast.[11]

Both crime rate and arrest rate increase with the size of the community. Over 50 percent of all serious crimes against the person take place

[10]Ibid., p. 36.
[11]Ibid., p. 34.

in 26 major cities, containing only 18 percent of the population.[12] Cities with more than 250,000 inhabitants have twice the arrest rate of suburbs and three times the arrest rate of rural areas.[13] Within the city, however, crime tends to be concentrated in particular areas. Those parts of the city that are changing rapidly have much higher crime rates than more stable areas. The fact that the American population is growing steadily more urban and steadily younger probably accounts for much of the increase in the crime rate, but it does not provide a full explanation, since the crime rate is increasing even faster than these two forces.

One other group that is disproportionately vulnerable to arrest is the black population. Black adults are arrested five times as often as white adults.[14] One reason for this high arrest rate is that the black community is also a poor one, and there is a high correlation between poverty and the arrest rate for crime. Another reason may be prejudice against minority and lower-class groups; numerous studies have shown that the likelihood of arrest and imprisonment for an offense decreases as the social status of the offender rises. Judges are not immune to such prejudice. In one experiment, some three dozen judges were given fact sheets on hypothetical cases and asked to determine an appropriate sentence. The sheets contained the following basic information:

> "Joe Cut," 27, pleaded guilty to battery. He slashed his common-law wife on the arms with a switchblade. His record showed convictions for disturbing the peace, drunkenness, and hit-run driving. He told a probation officer that he acted in self-defense after his wife attacked him with a broom handle. The prosecutor recommended not more than five days in jail or a $100 fine.[15]

On half the sheets, however, "Joe Cut" was identified as white and on the other half as black. The judges who thought he was white gave him a jail sentence of three to ten days, but the judges who thought he was black gave him a sentence of five to thirty days.

How Accurate Are Crime Statistics?

The crime statistics give a profile of the "typical" criminal: young, male, urban, perhaps black. But in fact the statistics give us only a very partial view of who the offenders really are. The basic source for crime statistics is the Uniform Crime Report (UCR), issued each year by the FBI. Naturally, the crime report covers only those people who get caught and whose crimes are reported. Furthermore, it deals with only certain types of crime. The UCR presents data on a total of twenty-nine

---

[12]President's Commission on Law Enforcement and Administration of Justice, *The Challenge of Crime in a Free Society* (Washington, D.C.: U.S. Government Printing Office, 1967), p. 28.
[13]Federal Bureau of Investigation, *Crime in the United States*, p. 120.
[14]President's Commission on Law Enforcement and Administration of Justice, *The Challenge of Crime in a Free Society*, p. 44.
[15]Donald Jackson, "Justice for None," *New Times* (January 11, 1974), p. 51.

Who Are the Criminals?

The discovery that crime and delinquency do not vary significantly from one social group to another, whereas the vast majority of inmates of correctional institutions are lower class, has led criminologists to take a closer look at the way in which offenders are selected for arrest, prosecution and punishment.

It is common knowledge among most students of crime and delinquency that the officially designated criminal is the final product of a long process of selection. Those caught up in the system are overwhelmingly the poor, the lower class, members of minority groups, immigrants, foreigners, persons of low intelligence and others who are in some way at a disadvantage. Those who have a good chance of escaping the system are the affluent criminals, corporate criminals, organized criminals and intelligent criminals. In general, the most successful criminals (i.e., those realizing the greatest economic gain) escape the system while the less successful are caught.

If, as hidden-crime studies have indicated, only a small proportion of persons who commit crimes are eventually caught and punished and if these are usually the least successful, then the criminal justice system expends most of its resources on a small group of individuals whose offenses are relatively less significant. This very selective bias in the legal system means that most studies of crime take as their starting point a stereotype of the "criminal" that is a social and legal artifact.

SOURCE: Eugene Doleschal and Nora Klapmuts, *Toward a New Criminology* (Hackensack, N.J.: National Council on Crime and Delinquency, 1973).

categories of crime, from arson to violations of curfew, and it concentrates on seven serious crimes: murder, rape, robbery, aggravated assault, burglary, larceny of $50 and over, and auto theft. The report thus omits a great number of other crimes, mostly those committed by upper-class individuals. It does not include, for example, data on executives caught at price-fixing, presidential aides found to have perjured themselves in sworn testimony, industrialists charged with polluting water and air, or corporation heads engaged in unfair labor practices. The inclusion of these individuals in the statistics would significantly alter the profile of the "typical" criminal.

More important, however, is the fact that the UCR excludes the successful criminal, the one who escapes arrest—and that includes most of us. According to research by the National Council on Crime and Delinquency, "a large number of self-report studies conclude that close to 100 percent of all persons have committed some kind of offense, although few have been arrested."[16] Even among juveniles, a delinquent episode is the norm rather than the exception. In a national survey of thirteen- to sixteen-year-olds, 86 percent reported delinquent acts, but examination of police records showed that of these only 9 percent had had so much as a brush with the law, and only 4 percent had criminal records.[17] Another study of 1,700 persons turned up no less than 91 percent who admitted to at least one crime sufficiently serious to have put them under risk of imprisonment if detected. Another study has indicated that about 75 percent of insurance claims are fraudulent.[18]

Many of these crimes are missing not only from the arrest statistics, but also from the crime statistics: data on many white-collar offenses are not even collected, and many of these crimes go unreported in any case. For example, employers who discover a case of minor embezzlement may think twice, not only about the family and the career of the employee in question but also about their own distaste for trial publicity, before going to the police. The National Crime Panel of the federal government recently commissioned the Census Bureau to interview 22,000 residents and 2,000 businessmen in thirteen cities about their experience of crime and found that 80 percent of discovered larcenies under $50 went entirely unreported. The actual crime rate, it seemed, was at least twice as high as the statistics indicated.[19] Findings such as these have brought into serious question the traditional distinction between the criminal and the noncriminal. The "typical" criminal is in reality merely the criminal who typically gets caught. And he is usually the young male who commits an offense, such as auto theft, that society chooses to define as somehow more serious than other offenses, such as corporate price-fixing, even though the latter may have a much greater social cost.

One other factor distorts crime statistics: the manipulation of the data by the police. Politicians and police are under great public pressure to keep the crime rate low, and one way to do this is to include serious crimes in different, less serious categories. In Philadelphia, where the mayor was the ex-Commissioner of Police, the National Crime Panel found that the actual crime rate was five times as high as the official statistics indicated. A striking example of how reporting procedures can influence the apparent crime rate was the remarkable rise in Chicago's crime rate between 1928 and 1931, after the Chicago Crime Commission, believing that the true incidence of crime was being obscured by police reporting methods, insisted on a change in reporting

[16]Eugene Doleschal and Nora Klapmuts, *Toward a New Criminology* (Hackensack, N.J.: National Council on Crime and Delinquency, 1973), p. 4.
[17]Ibid., pp. 15–16.
[18]"Living With Crime, USA," *Newsweek* (December 18, 1972).
[19]David Burnham, "New York is Found Safest of 13 Cities in Crime Studies," *New York Times* (April 15, 1974), p. 51; and "Unreported Crime Twice as High," *LEAA Newsletter*, vol. 3, no. 11 (March 1974), pp. 1, 9, 11.

Crime Victimization Rates in Thirteen Selected Cities

	CRIME VICTIMIZATION PER 1,000 RESIDENTS 12 AND OVER				HOUSEHOLD VICTIMIZATION PER 1,000 HOUSEHOLDS			COMMERCIAL VICTIMIZATION PER 1,000 BUSINESSES		
	Crimes of Violence	Rape and Attempted Rape	Robbery	Assault	Burglary	Household Larceny	Auto Theft	Burglary	Robbery	Ratio of Unreported Crime to Reported Crime
Detroit	68	3	32	33	174	106	49	615	179	2.7 to 1
Denver	67	3	17	46	158	168	44	443	54	2.9 to 1
Philadelphia	63	1	28	34	109	87	42	390	116	5.1 to 1
Portland, Ore.	59	3	17	40	151	149	34	355	39	2.6 to 1
Baltimore	56	1	26	28	116	100	35	578	135	2.2 to 1
Chicago	56	3	26	27	118	77	36	317	77	2.8 to 1
Cleveland	54	2	24	28	124	80	76	367	77	2.4 to 1
Los Angeles	53	2	16	35	148	131	42	311	47	2.9 to 1
Atlanta	48	2	16	30	161	102	29	741	157	2.3 to 1
Dallas	43	2	10	31	147	147	24	355	48	2.6 to 1
Newark	42	1	29	12	123	44	37	631	98	1.4 to 1
St. Louis	42	1	16	25	125	81	47	531	94	1.5 to 1
New York	36	1	24	11	68	33	26	328	103	2.1 to 1

SOURCE: National Crime Panel Surveys, Law Enforcement Assistance Administration, in *New York Times* (April 15, 1974).

procedures. In three years the robbery rate increased from 1,263 to 14,544 per year, and the burglary rate soared from 879 to a spectacular 18,689 per year.[20]

APPROACHING THE PROBLEM

Why do some people become criminals? The question has been answered in many ways over the centuries. Traditionally, the criminal has been regarded as innately wicked, his criminality being the result of some inherited and ineradicable vice. The culmination of this tradition was the work of Cesare Lombroso, who attempted around the beginning of this century to establish physical criteria that could be used to distinguish criminals from noncriminals. After extensive studies of the inmates of prisons, Lombroso claimed to have identified as the signs of the born criminal such "stigmata" as a long lower jaw, a flattened nose, and insensitivity to pain.

The problem with these traditional theories, of course, is that they do not take into account the relative nature of crime, that is, that each society defines criminality differently and that a crime in one society may be a virtue in another. Supposed inborn characteristics of an absolute nature are thus useless as an explanation of a culturally relative

[20]Donald R. Cressey, "The State of Criminal Statistics," *National Probation and Parole Journal*, 3 (July 1957), p. 232.

phenomenon. Social scientists today accept the tenet that criminal behavior is learned behavior, that the criminal is simply someone who has failed to internalize or who rejects the prevailing social norms expressed in the criminal law and in the values and attitudes that the law reflects.

Sociological Theories of Crime

The sociological study of crime is usually conducted within the framework of the theoretical perspective of deviance: the criminal is seen as a deviant who violates social norms that are encoded in legal statutes. The question that interests sociologists is why certain individuals rather than others become deviants, and three main theories have been developed to account for the process: labeling, differential association, and anomie.

The criminal as product of labeling. The labeling theory of deviance, as outlined by sociologists such as Howard S. Becker, views deviance, including many forms of crime, as a social process rather than as a characteristic of the deviant. The deviant, Becker argues, is simply someone to whom the label of deviant has been successfully applied by society.[21]

Labeling theorists point out that many people engage in deviant, criminal behavior, such as tax avoidance, but that because they are not discovered and labeled as criminals, they do not regard themselves as criminals and are not regarded as such by society. Most individuals engage at some time or another in criminal activity—particularly minor forms of juvenile delinquency. Generally this behavior is not maintained for any length of time; it is often merely an exploratory adventure in the process of growing up and usually passes unnoticed. But if significant people such as parents, friends, or even the police notice the behavior, they react by labeling the individual as a "delinquent" and begin to treat him accordingly. Then, gradually, the individual begins to accept this definition of himself as a deviant and to construct his choices in accordance with this self-image. The original label thus becomes a prophetic one, and the deviant behavior eventually becomes the "normal" behavior for that person.

Many radical sociologists, combining the labeling perspective with the value-conflict perspective, point out that the labeling process frequently involves differing interests and values on the part of the labelers and the labeled. To understand why some acts are defined as crimes and why some crimes are defined as more serious than others, we have to look not at the criminals but at the people who define the nature of criminality and label others in terms of this definition. For example, the reason that minor larcenies of the lower class are often regarded as more serious than white-collar crimes of the middle class involving

---

[21]Howard S. Becker, *Outsiders: Studies in the Sociology of Deviance* (New York: Free Press, 1963).

greater sums may be that laws and courts reflect middle-class rather than lower-class interests. In the same way, the fact that consumption of alcohol is permitted in the United States while use of marijuana is prohibited may be explained on the grounds that alcohol, although addictive and dangerous, is the favored drug of the powerful and privileged in society, whereas marijuana is the favored drug of the powerless young. If those who have the power to define criminality suddenly began to favor marijuana, the laws would probably be changed to reflect this preference.

Labeling theorists do not insist that all crime is relative; they concede that such deviant acts as murder or robbery are intolerable to any society. But the perspective does usefully focus attention on the way in which different groups in the community can influence or suffer from social definitions of what constitutes a crime and of who is a criminal.

The criminal as product of differential association. Another influential theory to account for criminal deviance is that of Edwin Sutherland, who argues that people may become criminals if their socialization process provides instruction in criminal techniques or encourages a defiant attitude toward prevailing social norms and laws. Just as one youth might learn conformist, nondelinquent behavior from his intimate associates, such as family and friends, so might another youth learn deviant, delinquent behavior by growing up among people who are contemptuous of the law.

Sutherland's theory is essentially a sophisticated version of the old "bad companions" formula; as he put it, "a person becomes delinquent because of an excess of definitions favorable to violation of the law over definitions unfavorable to violation of the law."[22] The number of contacts is not the only important factor in determining whether an individual will tend toward delinquency; the intensity, duration, and frequency of the contacts are also relevant, along with the age at which the contacts are experienced. Thus prolonged contact at an early age with law-abiding people may see an individual safely through an adolescence surrounded by delinquent peers, but a less favorable early environment followed by further socialization in a delinquent subculture might predispose an individual to criminal behavior.

The theory of differential association lends strong support to the view that commitment to a penal institution may have counterproductive effects, particularly on juveniles. Separated from society and thrown into the company of experienced criminals, the young person encounters "an excess of definitions favorable to violation of the law" and is quite likely to learn new ways to burgle, rob, defraud, or pick locks. From the perspective of the differential-association theory, recidivism can be explained in the sense that the ex-inmate may return to crime simply because he has returned to the associations which steered him toward crime in the first place. Research may help to clarify the extent

[22]Sutherland and Cressey, *Principles of Criminology*, p. 81.

to which differential association is a factor in both initial and recidivist crime, but unfortunately the theory does not lend itself readily to empirical measurement. How does one analyze in practice such concepts as duration, frequency, and intensity, and which gets the most weight? However, despite the difficulties of applying the theory to empirical research, differential association remains an influential account of the origins of criminal deviance.

The criminal as product of anomie. The theory of *anomie* as an explanation of deviance was developed by Robert K. Merton, and is an attempt to link the deviance perspective with the perspective of social disorganization.

Anomie is essentially a state of normlessness: the anomic individual is one who has failed to internalize or who has rejected important social norms and whose behavior is therefore unregulated by them. Anomie arises from a form of social disorganization in which there is a discrepancy between social goals and the social opportunities available to achieve them. The United States, for example, is a materialistic society in which a high value is placed on the goal of acquiring wealth, but the social opportunities for becoming rich are restricted and unequally distributed. Although the society holds out the myth that great rewards are available to anyone who works hard, the fact is that the social structure puts some people at a distinct disadvantage in the competition for success. People who still accept the goal but lack the means to achieve it may fall into an anomic state in which they reject the norms specifying the appropriate methods for achieving success. They resort instead to other methods, including ones that are contrary to the law.

Deviance is therefore intimately linked to the norms and values of society as a whole. If a society prizes material goods but denies people equal access to them, it invites theft. If a society prizes sexual experience but restricts sexual relations to the married, it invites prostitution. If a society prizes novelty and entertainment but markets them only to those who can pay for them, it invites delinquency among penniless juveniles in search of kicks. As Merton explains:

> It is only when a system of cultural values extols, virtually above all else, certain *common* success-goals for the population at large while the social structure restricts or completely closes access to approved modes of reaching these goals for a considerable part of the same population, that deviant behavior ensues on a large scale.[23]

The theory of anomie is particularly useful in explaining the disproportionate number of lower-class and black criminals who crowd our courts and jails, for they are precisely the people who are often denied access to legitimate means of achieving the goals that are held out to all Americans.

[23]Robert K. Merton, *Social Theory and Social Structure*, 2d ed. (Glencoe, Ill.: Free Press, 1957), p. 146.

THE FORMS OF CRIME IN AMERICA

Crime is not a single phenomenon; it takes many diverse forms. As the President's Commission on Law Enforcement and Administration of Justice points out:

> A skid-row drunk lying in the gutter is crime. So is the killing of an unfaithful wife. A Cosa Nostra conspiracy to bribe public officials is a crime. So is a strong-arm robbery by a 15-year-old-boy. The embezzlement of a corporation's funds by an executive is a crime. So is the possession of marihuana cigarettes by a student. . . . Thinking of "crime" as a whole is futile.[24]

Let us examine some of the major forms of crime in America.

Juvenile Delinquency

Juvenile delinquency is of great concern to both the public and sociologists. The concern arises partly from the fact that juveniles account for such a high proportion of all arrests and partly from a concern for the juveniles themselves, simply because they are young. Social policy has to be carefully designed not only to protect the public from acts of juvenile delinquency, but also to treat the delinquents in such a way that their chances of acquiring a criminal record and becoming persistent offenders are minimized.

Most research on juvenile delinquency has focused on gang members in lower-class urban neighborhoods. For example, Albert Cohen,[25] who has analyzed juvenile delinquency in terms of Merton's theory of anomie, sees delinquency as a reaction to the discrepancy between goals and opportunities in the lives of lower-class juveniles. Lower-class boys are not socialized in such a way as to become successful in the middle-class world and may experience "status frustration." The dominant society expects them to be ambitious, responsible, achievement-oriented, respectful of property, self-disciplined, and willing to plan ahead and defer gratification. Unable to meet these requirements, the young people end up rejecting them by behaving in a way exactly opposite to that prescribed by the dominant norms: they consider an act appropriate precisely to the degree that it violates the norms of the larger culture. Status in the gang is achieved by "hell-raising," behavior which, according to Cohen, is nonutilitarian, malicious, and negative, but which provides the opportunities for prestige that are unattainable by legitimate means.

It seems likely, however, that the range of alternative behavior is wider than Cohen implies: not all delinquents express their "status frustration" in the same "hell-raising" way. Just as access to legitimate

---

[24]President's Commission on Law Enforcement and Administration of Justice, *The Challenge of Crime in a Free Society*, p. 3.
[25]Albert Cohen, *Delinquent Boys: The Culture of the Gang* (Glencoe, Ill.: Free Press, 1955).

In the past, sociologists concentrated on the gang as the breeding ground for juvenile delinquency. Recent research, however, indicates that middle-class juveniles commit at least as many crimes as gang members, but the gang is more visible and attracts more police attention. (*Paul Conklin/Monkmeyer*)

channels to success is blocked for some, so too are opportunities for illegitimate conduct unevenly distributed. This point has been made by Richard Cloward and Lloyd Ohlin, who suggest that there are three distinct delinquent subcultures, all of which result from an anomic reaction to the discrepancy between socially approved goals and the lower-class juvenile's opportunities for achieving them. The first type of subculture, the criminal subculture, is organized for the purpose of material gain through systematic theft, extortion, robbery, and fraud. The criminal subculture often has links with adult crime and sometimes serves as an avenue into a criminal career. The second type of subculture, the conflict-oriented subculture, usually involves tension and battles between rival gangs engaged in territorial disputes. The gang member does not aspire, however, to adult forms of violence or to adult forms of criminality. The third type of subculture, the retreatist subculture, is made up of those who cannot succeed in or are denied access to the other subcultures. They retreat into a private world and seek solace in drugs, alcohol, or other forms of "kicks" that are less publicly visible than the activities of the other two subcultures. Cloward and

Ohlin also found that boys who become members of delinquent gangs explicitly attribute their failure in the wider society to the shortcomings of the social order rather than to any inadequacies of their own. They are highly critical of society and consider themselves entirely justified in rejecting the dominant social norms and values.[26] The formulation of Cloward and Ohlin is useful in highlighting the fact that juvenile gangs may take more than one basic form, although it is probable that many gangs include characteristics of more than one of the three types outlined and are not so highly specialized as these two sociologists claim.

Other sociologists have contested the view that lower-class juveniles become delinquent through a frustrated desire to achieve the goals of the dominant culture. Instead, it is argued, the lower-class culture itself generates delinquent behavior, since mere adherence to some lower-class values can lead an individual into trouble with the law. A leading proponent of this approach is Walter Miller, who identifies certain "focal concerns" of lower-class culture. *Trouble* is a major concern, whether one gets into it or stays out of it; ideally, one walks the line between doing what one wants and becoming entangled with middle-class institutions such as the law or welfare agencies. Other focal concerns are *toughness,* what we might today call male chauvinism or machismo, an emphasis on physical strength and endurance and a disdain for anything "effeminate"; *smartness,* the capacity to be streetwise, to hold one's own in the world; *excitement,* perhaps in the form of fighting or gambling, to relieve the dismal routine of working without ever "getting ahead"; *autonomy,* the desire to be free of external social controls and authority; and *fate,* the sense that the ups and downs of life are beyond one's control. Miller argues that the gang provides an environment in which basic lower-class values can be expressed, for the gang is also preoccupied with such focal concerns as smartness, toughness, trouble, and autonomy. The gang provides security, stability, and support for juveniles who have internalized norms prevalent in their community. Miller acknowledges that not all lower-class youths are prone to delinquency, particularly because some will identify with middle-class rather than with lower-class values. The delinquent, however, is the one who embraces the lower-class values.[27] Miller's approach thus focuses on the lower-class culture as being in itself a cause of delinquency, rather than on the juvenile's inability to achieve middle-class goals.

Sociologist David Matza has challenged all the theories that emphasize the delinquent subculture as a starting point of analysis. He believes that the distinction between delinquents and nondelinquents is at best a tenuous one and that most juveniles behave conventionally a great deal of the time, with only sporadic lapses into misbehavior:

[26]Richard S. Cloward and Lloyd E. Ohlin, *Delinquency and Opportunity: A Theory of Delinquent Gangs* (Glencoe, Ill.: Free Press, 1960).
[27]Walter B. Miller, "Lower Class Culture as a Generating Milieu of Gang Delinquency," *Journal of Social Interest,* 14 (1958), pp. 5–19.

> Commitment to delinquency is a misconception . . . Delinquency
> consists of precepts and customs that are delicately balanced be-
> tween convention and crime.[28]

Matza describes this state of balance between delinquency and crime
as *drift*.

Matza's view has received a good deal of support from recent research, which seems to be undermining the notion that gangs provide
the basic environment for juvenile delinquency. Self-report studies
within the last few years indicate that delinquent acts are frequently
committed by juveniles acting on their own, and not in groups.[29] In one
study of California high school students, solitary acts of delinquency
outnumbered those in which two or more people were involved.[30] More
important, research is casting severe doubt on whether delinquency is
even found primarily among lower-class juveniles. The juveniles in the
arrest statistics are overwhelmingly from the lower class, but this does
not mean that they commit the most delinquent acts, only that they are
more often arrested. One national self-report survey of teen-agers
found little relationship between delinquency and social class, except
that higher-status boys were slightly more delinquent than lower-status
boys. The high-status boys committed more thefts and even more assaults than the lower-status boys.[31] A careful study by William J. Chambliss of two teen-age gangs, the middle-class Saints and the lower-class
Roughnecks, turned up a far greater number of delinquent acts on the
part of the Saints. Yet the Roughnecks were the ones in constant trouble and were universally considered to be delinquent, while the behavior of the Saints, on the rare occasions when it was noticed, was more
apt to be considered as youthful high spirits:

> The local police saw the Saints as good boys who were among the
> leaders of the youth in the community. Rarely, the boys might be
> stopped in town for speeding or for running a stop sign. When this
> happened the boys were always polite, contrite, and pled for mercy.
> As in school, they received the mercy they asked for. None ever
> received a ticket or was taken into the precinct by the local police.
> . . . Townspeople never perceived the Saints' high level of delin-
> quency. The Saints were good boys who just went in for an occa-
> sional prank. . . . The Roughnecks were a different story. . . .
> Everyone agreed that the not-so-well-dressed, not-so-well-man-
> nered, not-so-rich boys were heading for trouble. . . . From the
> community's viewpoint, the real indication that these kids were in
> for trouble was that they were constantly involved with the police.
> . . . There was a high level of mutual distrust and dislike between

[28]David Matza, *Delinquency and Drift* (New York: Wiley, 1964), pp. 59, 28.
[29]Maynard L. Erickson, "Group Violations, Socioeconomic Status and Official Delinquency," *Social Forces*, vol. 52, no. 1 (September 1973), p. 51; and "The Group Context of Delinquent Behavior," *Social Problems*, vol. 19, no. 1 (Summer 1971), pp. 114–129.
[30]Michael J. Hindelang, "The Social Versus Solitary Nature of Delinquent Involvement," *British Journal of Criminology*, vol. 11, no. 2 (April 1971), pp. 167–175.
[31]Doleschal and Klapmuts, "We Need Criminals," p. 16.

the Roughnecks and the police. The boys felt very strongly that the police were unfair and corrupt.[32]

Why, if the Saints were more delinquent than the Roughnecks, did the police, school, and community hold a distorted impression of the behavior of the two gangs? Chambliss believes that a labeling process was responsible:

> Differential treatment of the two gangs resulted in part because one gang was infinitely more visible than the other. This differential visibility was a direct function of the economic standing of the families. The Saints had access to automobiles and were able to remove themselves from the sight of the community. . . . Through necessity the Roughnecks congregated in a crowded area where everyone in the community passed frequently, including teachers and law enforcement officers. They could easily see the Roughnecks hanging around the drugstore. . . .

> To the notion of visibility must be added the difference in the responses of group members. . . . If one of the Saints was confronted with an accusing policeman . . . his demeanor was apologetic and penitent. A Roughneck's attitude was almost the polar opposite . . . the Roughneck's hostility and disdain were clearly observable. . . .

> Selective perception and labeling—finding, processing and punishing some kinds of criminality and not others—means that visible, poor, nonmobile, outspoken, undiplomatic "tough" kids will be noticed, whether their acts are seriously delinquent or not. Other kids . . . disciplined and involved in respectable activities, who are mobile and monied, will be invisible when they deviate from sanctioned activities. They'll sow their wild oats—perhaps even wider and thicker than their lower-class cohorts—but they won't be noticed.[33]

Crimes Without Victims

The United States invests enormous resources in controlling victimless crime. Of the 8.7 million arrests recorded in the FBI Uniform Crime Report for 1972, over half involved crimes without victims. More than 3 million arrests were made for offenses involving liquor and for disorderly conduct, which is often alcohol-induced. Over 400,000 juveniles were arrested for running away from home or for violating a town curfew. There were 525,000 drug arrests, of which 292,000 were for possession of marijuana. Prostitution accounted for 51,600 arrests and gambling for 78,000 arrests.[34]

---

[32]William J. Chambliss, "The Saints and the Roughnecks," *Society* (November–December 1973), pp. 26, 27.
[33]Ibid., pp. 29, 30, 31.
[34]Federal Bureau of Investigation, *Crime in the United States,* pp. 119, 122, 128.

The criminalization of some acts that have no victims stems from the fact that society regards these acts as morally repugnant and wishes to restrain individuals from engaging in them. Many of those arrested for victimless crimes are never prosecuted: arrest and overnight lock-up are used simply as a means of exerting social control over the drunk or prostitute without going to the bothersome lengths of creating a convincing prosecution case against the offenders. Habitual drunks may build up formidable "criminal" records through being repeatedly arrested even though they may never have harmed anyone, except possibly themselves.[35] One study found that two-thirds of repeatedly arrested alcoholics had been charged with nothing more than public intoxication and related offenses, such as vagrancy, throughout their long "criminal" careers.[36]

The people who are affected by these laws, however, may not regard themselves as engaging in morally reprehensible behavior and may deeply resent the attempts of other groups to impose the dominant morality upon them. They perceive no genuine moral force in the laws that criminalize their conduct, and consequently their attitude to the law is simply pragmatic. The college student who smokes marijuana or the businessman who gambles feels no guilt at violating the law; his only concern is with escaping detection. If enough people adopt this attitude of moral indifference to a law, it gradually falls into disuse, as has happened, for example, with laws against adultery or Sunday sports events. In such cases the law is often not repealed. Attempts to repeal it would evoke outcries from interest groups that still support the law, and so controversy is avoided by simply not enforcing it. Very occasionally, the police explicitly indicate that they will no longer enforce a particular law: the New York Commissioner of Police, for example, stated publicly in 1970 that his officers would make no further arrests under the city's Sunday Closing Law. In times of rapid social change, however, groups that are considered deviant are often reluctant to wait in anticipation that the laws affecting them will gradually cease to be applied, and instead resort to open protest. But in the meantime, there are millions of convictions each year as the police and the courts continue to apply laws against such groups as homosexuals, drug users, prostitutes, gamblers, and pornography sellers — laws that large sections of the community do not recognize as legitimate and simply refuse to obey.[37]

Laws against victimless crimes are largely responsible for the existence of organized crime in the United States. Organized crime makes its money by satisfying consumer demands for goods and services that have been made illegal in the supposed interests of the moral regulation of society. Prohibition is the outstanding historical example of this

[35]Wayne R. La Fave, *Arrest: The Decision to Take a Suspect into Custody* (Boston: Little, Brown and the American Bar Foundation, 1965), p. 439.

[36]David Pittman, as cited in Stephan Landsman, "Massachusetts' Comprehensive Alcoholism Law — Its History and Future," *Massachusetts Law Quarterly,* vol. 58, no. 3 (Fall 1973), p. 288.

[37]Alexander B. Smith and Harriet Pollack, "Crimes Without Victims," *Saturday Review* (December 4, 1971), pp. 27–29.

process: the attempt to ban alcohol resulted in a massive criminal network which supplied alcohol at inflated prices. Likewise, a good deal of the gambling facilities, drug supply, and prostitution in the United States today is controlled by organized crime.

An additional problem with victimless crimes is that most corruption of police and courts is associated with these offenses. Few police are willing to accept bribes from murderers, burglars, or other criminals whose acts are patently harmful and have identifiable victims. However, many policemen tend to feel that victimless crime is not particularly serious and that, in any case, it is impossible to eradicate. Hence organized crime is often readily able to buy police protection for its activities. The Knapp Commission's report on the New York City police found corruption of this kind to be nearly universal in the precincts it investigated; some policemen were reported to have trimmed their Christmas trees with $100 bills — protection money from brothel keepers, drug pushers, pornography shops, and gambling dens.

Most police violations of the civil liberties of suspects take place during the course of attempts to obtain evidence against criminals who have no victims. Prostitutes and drug pushers, for example, are frequently victims of police entrapment, for the simple reason that there often is no other means by which the police can obtain evidence to secure a conviction. As Alexander B. Smith and Harriet Pollak point out:

> The prostitute's client has not been forcibly seduced; the housewife who bets a quarter on the numbers has not been robbed; the dope user has harmed only himself. Because there are no victims available to testify for the state, the burden of producing enough evidence for the prosecution rests entirely on the police. It is this need for evidence to make morals offense violations "stick" that traditionally has produced the greatest number of civil liberties violations by the police. . . . If their customers cannot testify, who besides the plainclothesman can? And what better way of establishing a case than by offering an obviously willing girl a little "encouragement"? Official police records indicate that an incredible number of gamblers and drug pushers "drop" gambling slips and narcotics at the mere approach of a policeman. This so-called dropsie evidence is frequently a euphemism for an illegal search. . . .[38]

Because so many problems are connected with the enforcement of laws against victimless crimes and because enforcement takes up so much time and money that police and courts could be devoting to the reduction of more serious crime, there has recently been increasing support for the repeal of at least some of these laws. As Smith and Pollak note:

> For every murderer arrested and prosecuted, literally dozens of gamblers, prostitutes, dope pushers and derelicts crowd our courts'

[38]Ibid., pp. 28–29.

dockets. If we took the numbers runners, the kids smoking pot, and winos out of the criminal justice system, we would substantially reduce the burden on the courts and the police. . . . Moral laws that do not reflect contemporary mores or that cannot be enforced should be removed from the penal code through legislative action because, at best, they undermine respect for the law.[39]

White-Collar Crime

As we have seen, the usual profile of the "typical" criminal is of someone who is young, male, probably poor, and disproportionately likely to be black. But recent studies have suggested that a great deal of the crime in society—and perhaps most of the crime—is actually perpetrated by respectable middle-class and upper-middle-class citizens in the course of their business activities. This type of criminal activity is known as "white-collar crime."

The term was first used by Edwin Sutherland in an address to the American Sociological Association in 1939. "White-collar crime," he declared, "may be defined approximately as a crime committed by a person of respectability and high status in the course of his occupation."[40] Sutherland documented the existence of this form of crime with a study of the checkered careers of 70 large, reputable corporations, which together had amassed 980 violations of the criminal law, or an average of 14 convictions apiece. Behind the offenses of false advertising, unfair labor practices, restraint of trade, price-fixing agreements, stock manipulation, copyright infringement, and outright swindles were perfectly respectable middle-class executives.

As Sutherland pointed out, the full extent of white-collar crime is difficult to assess. Many corporate malpractices go undetected, and many wealthy people are able to evade taxes for years without being found out. More important, white-collar crimes are usually regarded as somehow less serious than the crimes of the lower class, and there is often strong pressure on police and courts not to prosecute at all in these cases—to take account of the offender's "standing in the community" and to settle the matter out of court. A company that finds its safe has been burgled in the night will immediately summon the police, but may be more circumspect if it finds that one of its executives has embezzled a sum of money. To avoid unwelcome publicity, the company officials may simply allow the offender to resign after making an arrangement for him to pay back what he can.

On the whole, American society is remarkably tolerant of white-collar crime. A petty thief who steals $100 may well go to prison, but imprisonment of a person evading payment of a similar sum in taxes is almost unheard of; indeed, tax evasion has to reach massive proportions before the Internal Revenue Service refers the matter to the FBI

---

[39]Ibid., pp. 27–28.
[40]Edwin Sutherland, *White Collar Crime* (New York: Dryden, 1949), p. 9.

rather than settling it privately. In commercial activity as well, we accept a certain amount of deception as the norm; the most striking examples of this tacit tolerance of deceit may be found in the field of advertising. As Edwin Shur points out:

> Modern mass advertising at its heart represents a kind of institutionalization of deception and misrepresentation. . . . The cumulative effect of advertising is to nurture a disposition both to engage in and to succumb to fraudulent practices . . . at all social levels of our society. . . . Mass advertising promotes a philosophy of behavior and of man's nature which cannot help but exert indirect influence on the value patterns and dominant activities of our society.[41]

Because most white-collar crime is unrecorded, its total economic impact is difficult to ascertain. Even when it is detected, the cost is difficult to measure. How do we evaluate the social cost of illegal pollution of air and water, of the inclusion of illegal additives in food, of the marketing of insufficiently tested new drugs, of the use of false advertising, or of a major stock swindle? We do have some indications, however, of just how great the economic impact of some white-collar crime can be. The President's Commission on Law Enforcement and the Administration of Justice compared the annual cost of four categories of white-collar crime — embezzlement, forgery, tax evasion, and fraud — with the annual cost of four categories of property crime — auto theft, robbery, burglary, and larceny of sums exceeding $50. The total cost of the white-collar crimes, $1,730,000,000, was almost three times that of the property crimes, $614,000,000.[42]

These facts raise serious questions about our traditional conceptions of crime and criminals. So long as the typical criminal is considered to be a member of the depressed lower class, it is possible to regard criminality as stemming from personal pathology, disorganized surroundings, or discrepancies between goals and opportunities. But if, as is possible, the typical criminal is a middle-class businessman who does not even regard himself as a criminal, our theories of the origin of criminal activity may seem inadequate. Sutherland, however, believes that white-collar crime arises through the same process of differential association that generates lower-class crime: since the businessman or professional associates with others who regard white-collar crimes as normal, defensible practices, he is likely to begin conforming to these illegal norms.

Theorists who regard a good deal of criminal deviance as the result of a labeling process rather than as a characteristic of the so-called deviants have been quick to point out the implications of white-collar crime. A single price-fixing arrangement may present consumers with

---

[41]Edwin M. Schur, *Our Criminal Society* (Englewood Cliffs, N.J.: Prentice-Hall, 1969), pp. 168–170.
[42]"White Collar Crime: Huge Economic and Moral Drain," *Congressional Quarterly* (May 7, 1971), p. 1048.

a bigger bill than thousands of burglaries. Why then does the burglar receive the stigma and the severe penalities while the offending businessman receives only mild disapproval and a nominal fine—often not in his own name, but in the name of his company? The answer, labeling theorists assert, is to be found in the power structure of society; the offenses that are labeled serious are those that damage the interests of the dominant group.

Violence

Violence is the form of crime that people fear most: the stealthy footstep, the jab of the knife, the scream of the ambulance on its way to the hospital. The likelihood of an American's falling victim to a violent crime—that is, murder, forcible rape, assault, and robbery (defined as theft involving threats)—increased 149 percent between 1960 and 1972.[43]

Although violent crime preoccupies public attention, it actually constitutes only 14 percent of all serious crime and represents an even lower proportion of all crime. Of every 100,000 Americans who were victimized by criminals in 1972, about 2,800 were victims of serious crime, but only 400 suffered crimes of violence, and only 9 were murdered. In fact, three times as many people die from auto accidents as from murder. The risk of murder is much greater, however, in large cities; in urban areas with more than a quarter of a million inhabitants, 20 citizens out of every 100,000 were slain.[44] The risk of robbery is also much greater in urban areas. Two-thirds of all robberies occur in cities of more than a quarter of a million inhabitants; and more than half of these big-city robberies are street muggings,[45] a fact that has contributed greatly to public perception of crime as a serious social problem. Rape is also more common in the cities. About 40 women out of every 100,000 were victims of rape or attempted rape in 1972, but the rate was 92 per 100,000 in cities. However, since rape is the most underreported of violent crimes—many victims being unwilling to undergo the ordeal of a harrowing police investigation and a public trial—the risk of rape is probably much higher than the statistics suggest. About 30 percent of rapes involve additional brutal treatment by the rapist, and the chances of being murdered in the course of a rape are about 1 percent.[46]

Part of the fear of street violence stems from a dread of being attacked by a total stranger, but in fact most persons who are murdered, assaulted, or raped have at least a passing acquaintance with their assailant. Most murders and most assaults arise in the course of family arguments or romantic entanglements. In three-quarters of all homicides, the murderer and victim are acquainted, and at least two-thirds

---

[43]Federal Bureau of Investigation, *Crime in the United States*, p. 2.
[44]Maggie Scarf, "The Anatomy of Fear," *New York Times Magazine* (June 16, 1974), p. 10. The rate for murder was 8.9 in 1972; the rate for auto fatalities was 27.2.
[45]Federal Bureau of Investigation, *Crime in the United States*, p. 15.
[46]Don C. Gibbons, *Society, Crime, and Criminal Careers* (Englewood Cliffs, N.J.: Prentice-Hall, 1968), p. 388.

of all rape victims know their assailants at least casually.[47] Street crime is also relatively unlikely to result in serious injury: only 3 percent of the victims are detained in the hospital overnight or longer.[48] Curiously, people are more likely to get hurt during an unarmed robbery than during an armed one, probably because they are less inclined to resist the robber if he is armed.[49] Less than one-half of one percent of all robberies culminate in murder.[50]

As measured in these numerical terms, violent crimes are probably less common than most people assume. But this is no consolation to the victims of the crimes, nor is it a persuasive advertisement for the quality of the American way of life. Violent crime in the United States is common enough to seem almost intolerable in a civilized society. The United States ranks fourteenth out of eighty-four countries in frequency of violent crimes and has a homicide rate more comparable to those of socially disorganized developing societies than to those of other modern industrialized nations.

The problem of violence in America is compounded by the fact that some violent crimes, ranging from ambushing of the police to bank robbery, kidnapping, and hijacking, are committed by people who consider that they are engaged not in crime but in legitimate guerrilla warfare. Most of the suspects on the FBI's list of the most-wanted fugitives are not typical criminals; they are people who are charged with politically motivated violence. Although these militant individuals are fringe elements with virtually no public support, their activities attract considerable publicity and have contributed to the public perception of violence as a critical element in the social problem of crime in America.

Another factor contributing to the increased anxiety about violence in America was the riots of the sixties. Violent rioting as a form of protest has a long history in the United States, and unlike specific acts of politically motivated violence, it often wins a large measure of support from the particular community to which the rioters belong. The violent campus confrontations in the sixties were often endorsed by majorities of the student bodies, and even in 1974, when conditions were considerably calmer, a Gallup poll showed that nearly 4 students in 10 believed that violence was sometimes justified to bring about social change.[51] The ghetto riots of the sixties, too, won wide support from black people; a nationwide survey of blacks conducted after the riots showed that while most of those surveyed claimed that they would not have participated personally, 60 percent believed the rioting was justified[52] as a means of protesting against racial discrimination, forcing social attention on their grievances, and creating a sense of group cohe-

[47]Menachim Amir, "Forcible Rape," *Federal Probation*, 31 (March 1967), pp. 51–58.
[48]"Unreported Crime Twice as High," p. 11.
[49]President's Commission on Law Enforcement and Administration of Justice, *The Challenge of Crime in a Free Society*, p. 19.
[50]Ibid.
[51]*New York Times* (May 14, 1974).
[52]Nathan S. Caplan and Jeffrey M. Paige, "A Study of Ghetto Rioters," *Scientific American*, vol. 219, no. 15 (August 1968), pp. 12, 15–21.

siveness and political power.[53] Furthermore, participation in the riots was not confined to a small percentage of those living in riot areas. Some 45 percent of the inhabitants of the neighborhoods involved in the Newark riots of 1967 said they had taken part, and since many people may have been reluctant to make this admission, the true percentage is probably even higher. Moreover, surveys found that rioters were generally similar to nonrioters in education, income, employment, and personal stability.

Why is there so much violence in American society? In the past, many philosophers have held that man is innately aggressive and have contended that it is not the existence of violence but rather the existence of peace that needs explaining. Although a few social scientists still adhere to this view, most psychologists and sociologists believe that violent behavior is learned rather than innate. If violence were innate in the nature of man, we would expect to find it throughout history in all societies, but in fact there are many small communities and tribes in which violence plays little or no part in social life. The Tasaday, a recently discovered Stone Age tribe in the Philippines, do not even have any words in their language to express hostility or aggression.

Some social scientists believe that violence has its origins in frustration.[54] An individual's desires are thwarted, and so he or she lashes out, either verbally or physically, in sheer frustration. Violence is thus seen as an expressive reaction, a form of release of tension, that results from some frustrating situation — poverty, discrimination, or perhaps just the heat of the summer. It remains to be determined, however, why frustration should lead to aggression only in some people and in some situations.

Other social scientists take the view that violence is learned through the socialization process. Some cultures and subcultures encourage violent or aggressive behavior; such behavior is considered more appropriate, for example, in lower-class than in middle-class families in America. American society as a whole, however, tolerates more aggression in the male than virtually any other modern nation. The United States is probably the only industrial society in which the word "aggressive" can be used in a favorable sense. (In some job advertisements, companies often specify that they want an "aggressive" salesman or executive.) The United States has a long history of domestic conflict, starting with the subjugation of the American Indian and continuing through the nineteenth century in the vigilante violence of the Old West and in the immense sufferings of the Civil War, and through the twentieth century in the bloody conflicts of the labor movement and in the urban riots of the sixties. A recent Harris poll found that a substantial majority of Americans agree with such statements as "justice

[53]Thomas E. Bittker, "The Choice of Collective Violence in Intergroup Conflict," in *Violence and the Struggle for Existence*, eds. David N. Daniels, Marshall F. Gilula, and Frank M. Ochberg (Boston: Little, Brown, 1970), pp. 165–191.

[54]See John Dollard, et al., *Frustration and Aggression* (New Haven: Yale University Press, 1939).

may have been a little rough and ready in the days of the Old West, but things worked better than they do today with all the legal red tape"; "human nature being what it is, there will always be wars and conflict"; and "when a boy is growing up, it is important he have a few fist fights."[55] Our mass media, too, often present violence as an approved method of solving problems.

It is probable, however, that there is no single explanation for all forms of violence. The question should rather be under what conditions human beings tend to wreak violence on others. Once we have answers to this question, we can begin to solve the problem by modifying the conditions. But even when solutions seem obvious, implementation is not always, or even often, an easy matter. After violent events that have been traumatic for the entire nation, such as the assassinations of John Kennedy, Robert Kennedy, and Martin Luther King in the sixties, support has always risen for gun control legislation, but so far Americans have balked at taking the crucial step of prohibiting or even seriously restricting the private possession of firearms. The argument against this step—an argument widely championed by firearms manufacturers—is that it would leave law-abiding citizens unarmed while criminals remained in possession of their weapons. Interestingly, the British reverse this argument: British police, who do not carry guns, have always resisted any suggestion that they be armed, on the grounds that this would encourage criminals to carry arms as well. At present, Britain, with a population of over 55 million, has fewer homicides each year than the city of Philadelphia, with a population of just over 2 million. The British start with the advantage, however, that they have always had stringent gun control, so that weapons are not readily available to criminals in the first place.

Organized Crime

Founded upon the provision of illegal goods and services, recruiting from delinquent gangs, and employing violence as a fundamental method of operation, organized crime is one of America's largest industries. The gross income of organized crime is estimated to be twice that of all other kinds of illegal activity;[56] the income from gambling receipts alone is put at $30 billion per year.[57] The existence of organized criminal syndicates with ramifications in many parts of the American economy is a serious problem in America, not least because it seems unlikely that organized crime on this scale could persist without some measure of tolerance by highly placed public officials.

Strictly speaking, any group of cooperating criminals may be called

[55]Harris, *The Anguish of Change*, p. 169.

[56]President's Commission on Law Enforcement and Administration of Justice, *The Challenge of Crime in a Free Society*, p. 32.

[57]Robert W. Ogren, "The Ineffectiveness of the Criminal Sanction in Fraud and Corruption Cases: Losing the Battle Against White-Collar Crime," *American Criminal Law Review*, vol. 11, no. 4 (Summer 1973), p. 973.

"organized crime." But the term is usually restricted to large-scale organizations — complete with bureaucracies and specialized officers —
which operate in much the same way as any other commercial organization, except that the goods and services that they sell and the methods
by which they conduct business are illegal. Unlike most other forms of
crime, organized crime does not necessarily steal from or defraud the
public: indeed, it offers goods and services for which there is obviously
a wide public demand. The existence of organized crime therefore
depends on two social factors: the criminalization of certain activities,
such as gambling and prostitution, and the willingness of very large
numbers of citizens to pay for these services even if they are illegal.

The very existence of organized crime has been debated; for many
years J. Edgar Hoover, longtime head of the FBI, denied that there was
such a thing in the United States. More recent investigations, however,
have proved beyond doubt the existence of syndicated crime, organized around the Mafia, or Cosa Nostra. Criminologist Donald Cressey
describes the Mafia not as an international syndicate of Sicilian crooks,
but as a loose network of American regional syndicates, coordinated by
a "commission" composed of the heads of the most powerful crime
"families."[58] There are 24 of these families, ranging in size from 20 to
700 members and each having a similar basic organization. At the head
of every family is the boss *(don)*, who has absolute authority over his
family unless overruled by the commission. He is assisted by an under-
boss *(sottocapo)* and a counselor *(consigliere)*. Next in the hierarchy
are the "lieutenants" *(capidecina)*, each of whom supervises a group of
"soldiers" *(soldati)*, who in their turn take the responsibility for specific illegal enterprises. The leadership of the Mafia is Italian-American,
but lower ranks may be drawn from all ethnic groups. The Mafia
seems to have developed during the Prohibition era, when criminal
groups were organized to supply illegal alcohol. When Prohibition was
ended, the groups invested their vast profits in other forms of crime,
primarily gambling. Always tailoring their activities to popular demand,
organized crime has more recently become deeply involved in the supply of narcotic drugs.

The organizational chart of the Mafia leaves out one important participant: the public official who is corrupted by organized crime. By paying off police, prosecutors, judges, and politicians, the Mafia is able to
ensure minimal interference from the law. The American public is well
aware of this fact: a 1971 Harris poll showed that 80 percent of the population believe that "organized crime has corrupted and controls many
politicians in this country."[59] The continuing relative impunity with
which the Mafia is able to operate in the United States inevitably undermines public confidence in the integrity of the entire law enforcement system.

[58] Donald R. Cressey, *Theft of the Nation: The Structure and Operations of Organized Crime in America* (New York: Harper & Row, 1969), p. 6.
[59] Harris, *The Anguish of Change*, p. 179.

Sociologist Donald Cressey suggests that social changes are likely to bring about changes in the form and activities of organized crime:

> With the rationalization and absorption of some illicit activities into the structure of the economy, the passing of an older generation that had established a hegemony over crime, the general rise of minority groups . . . and the break-up of the urban boss system, the pattern of crime . . . is passing as well. Crime, of course, remains as long as passion and the desire for gain remain. But big, organized city crime, as we have known it for the past seventy-five years, was based on more than these universal motives. It was based on certain characteristics of the American economy, American ethnic groups, and American politics. The changes in all these areas means that it, too, in the form we have known it, is at an end.[60]

Cressey also anticipates other changes. He sees the Mafia as retaining its hold on gambling but widening its sphere of activities into legitimate businesses through its control of enormous reserves of capital and its ruthless use of force. In some businesses, organized crime already has a monopoly and is reaping monopoly profits. However, moving into legitimate activities has not changed the structure or methods of organized crime, and so it is likely to pose an even greater threat to society as it extends its operations and sphere of influence.

THE POLICE

Our society places an enormous burden on its 400,000 policemen. The police are the link between the public and those who make the law, and within limits they have considerable discretion in determining whether or not the law should be applied. Not everyone who commits an offense within a policeman's sight will be arrested. The number of laws is immense — 30,000 local, state, and federal statutes, most of them containing numerous clauses and subclauses specifying various categories of offenses. Many of these laws are ambiguous, many directly contradict one another, and many are hopelessly outdated. The decision to act upon or ignore an offense is therefore often in the hands of the individual policeman on the beat.

Despite criticisms that the police tend to be both corrupt and brutal, most Americans take a very favorable view of their police. A Harris poll shows that two-thirds of the public give state and local police positive ratings on the job they do. Only 11 percent regard the police as "not too bright"; only 9 percent consider them "corrupt"; and only 6 percent believe that they are "violent." Only among blacks and the young is there widespread criticism of the police; polls indicate that pluralities of both groups charge the police with "excessive brutality."[61]

[60]Quoted in Daniel Bell, "Crime as an American Way of Life," *The Antioch Review*, vol. 13, no. 2 (June 1953), p. 154.
[61]Harris, *The Anguish of Change*, p. 176.

The question of how the police can be made more effective in the maintenance of "law and order" has been debated in many communities as the incidence of crime has risen. One common demand is for more policemen. Surprisingly, however, the evidence indicates that the number of policemen does not significantly affect the crime or arrest rate; the President's Commission on Law Enforcement and the Administration of Justice reported that

> There appears to be no correlation between the differing concentrations of police and the amount of crime committed or the percentage of known crimes solved in the various cities.[62]

This statement refers to the number of police on duty, not to the number who are on patrol. Actually, the number on patrol is often only a small proportion of policemen on duty; New York, for example, employs 31,000 police, but only 1,000 are on patrol at any given time. (One reason for this is that it takes almost ten hours of an officer's time to process an arrested suspect through the courts.)[63] The evidence on whether high visibility of police has any effect on crime is mixed. When uniformed policemen were stationed in every subway train in New York City, the number of subway crimes dropped by 36.1 percent.[64] In Kansas City, however, the police were taken off patrol in some areas for an entire year without any significant increase in the crime rates in these areas.[65] Preliminary evidence suggests that police patrols probably do more to make people feel safe than to ensure their safety.

Another and more divisive question is whether police should be given increased powers, even if this means limiting the various procedural requirements that are designed to safeguard the civil rights of accused suspects. In their desire for protection, sections of the public often demand that "the handcuffs be taken off the police." The "handcuffs" in this case are rulings of the Supreme Court concerning the procedural rights of the accused. In *Mapp v. Ohio*, the court dismissed the case, ruling that evidence illegally obtained was inadmissible, and in *Miranda v. Arizona*, the court set free a confessed child rapist because the police had not advised him of his right to counsel during police interrogation. Thus in recent years the police have had to take considerable care not to infringe the civil liberties of suspects.

If these restrictions annoy some members of the public, they are widely resented by the police. But the restrictions are imposed for a reason: to balance the concern for maintenance of law and order with a due respect for the rights of a suspect who may well be innocent. As

[62]President's Commission on Law Enforcement and Administration of Justice, *The Challenge of Crime in a Free Society*, p. 106.

[63]"Study on Police: Some Things Just Never Change," *New York Times* (February 24, 1974). p. 5.

[64]President's Commission on Law Enforcement and Administration of Justice, *The Challenge of Crime in a Free Society*, p. 95.

[65]Patrick J. Murphy, "Courts, Police and Individuals," *Philanthropy in a Changing Society: Proceedings of the 16th Annual Conference of the National Council on Philanthropy* (New York: National Council on Philanthropy, 1974), p. 36.

Jerome Skolnick points out, the special nature of the policeman's job is such that excessive authority in procedural matters would almost inevitably lead to abuses:

> The combination of *danger* and *authority* found in the task of the policemen unavoidably combine to frustrate procedural regularity. If it were possible to structure social roles with specific qualities, it would be wise to propose that these two should never, for the sake of the rule of law, be permitted to co-exist. Danger typically yields self-defensive conduct. . . . Authority under such conditions becomes a resource to reduce perceived threats. . . . As a result, procedural requirements take on a "frilly" character, or at least tend to be reduced to a secondary position.[66]

The experience of numerous countries in which the rule of law has been undermined through the granting of undue authority to the police serves as a strong reminder of the virtues of a balance between the power of the police and the rights of the citizen.

THE COURTS

Above the entrance to the Supreme Court building in Washington are inscribed the words "Equal Justice under the Law." The motto reflects a high ideal, but the reality of the American judicial system is different. In theory, the defendant has every possible safeguard: privilege against self-incrimination and rights to pretrial bail, to counsel for his defense, to a jury trial, to appeal in higher courts. But in practice, many suspects cannot afford bail and so end up spending days, weeks, or even months in jail awaiting trial. If they cannot afford to hire their own lawyers and have to settle for the more perfunctory services of an overworked court-appointed lawyer, they are put under strong pressure to plead guilty. (Over 95 percent of the people who appear in lower courts plead guilty and are sentenced on the spot.) Those who do insist on a jury trial and are eventually convicted receive on the average heavier sentences than those who forego the trial; they are punished, in effect, for wasting the court's time by insisting on their right to a trial. And although the length of a sentence depends in great part on the discretion of one fallible individual, the judge, there is usually no right of appeal against the sentence itself; only the actual conviction may be appealed.

Only a privileged few are able to take advantage of the formal system of "adversary" justice in which the truth about the alleged offense is supposed to emerge, in the style of "Perry Mason," from the formalized courtroom clash of prosecution and defense. This process, with all its procedural protections for the accused, is the exception, not the rule. In the lower courts, where nearly every defendant pleads guilty, a

---

[66]Jerome Skolnick, *Justice Without Trial* (New York: Wiley, 1966), p. 67.

single judge may hear two hundred to four hundred cases a day.[67] Even the right to a lawyer, guaranteed in more serious matters by the Supreme Court in 1963, was not extended until 1973 to people charged with misdemeanors. Thus a defendant who could not afford a lawyer but who still wanted to contest a misdemeanor charge against him was obliged to enter the lists on his own behalf against a prosecutor trained in law and experienced in courtroom procedure. Even in federal courts, where crimes are serious and penalties severe, only 10 percent of all cases actually go to trial. The rest of the accused plead guilty, partly to escape a heavier sentence and partly to avoid the expense of a lawyer's fee.

The process of pleading guilty is facilitated by the practice of plea-bargaining, a judicial procedure found virtually nowhere else in the world. In plea-bargaining, the prosecutor, in return for a plea of guilty from the defendant, agrees to lighten the sentence by reducing the charges against the defendant or by recommending leniency to the judge. Plea-bargaining is an informal procedure, however, and has no official recognition in law or in court rules. In consequence, a corrupt prosecutor can extort money in return for modifying the charges, and an overzealous one can even double-cross the defendant in court and ask for a harsher penalty than the one agreed upon. Also, by pleading guilty, the defendant deprives himself of the opportunity to have the handling of his case by the police and the prosecutor reviewed by the court. Those who insist on trial run the risk of far heavier sentences, a circumstance which seems to represent a deliberate encouragement on the part of the courts for defendants to plead guilty.[68]

American judges have wider latitude in fixing sentences than judges in any other Western nation. As a result of this freedom—and also perhaps as a result of the fact that sentences are seldom open to review—there are extremely wide variations in sentences for similar offenses. The race and the social status of the defendant is one factor that often makes a difference.[69] Another is pretrial imprisonment; prisoners who are not released on bail before the trial are more likely to be convicted and more likely to receive heavier sentences. The poor are very much at a disadvantage in this respect; in New York City, for example, a study showed that 25 percent of those arrested could not come up with the $25 in cash that would have enabled them to be set free on bail before trial.[70] The severity of sentence may also be dependent on the tendencies of the particular judge who hears the case: one judge may give

---

[67]Edward J. Barrett, Jr., "Mass Production," in *Law and the Lawless*, eds. Gresham Sykes and Thomas Drabek (New York: Random House, 1969), p. 341.

[68]See Skolnick, *Justice Without Trial*, Chapter 1; and Abraham S. Blumberg, *Criminal Justice* (Chicago: Quadrangle, 1967), Chapter 8.

[69]Whitney North Seymour, Jr., "Social and Ethical Considerations in Assessing White Collar Crime," *American Criminal Law Review*, vol. 11, no. 4 (Summer 1973), pp. 821–834.

[70]President's Commission on Law Enforcement and Administration of Justice, *The Challenge of Crime in a Free Society*, p. 131.

The formal adversary process of the courtroom—often portrayed on TV—is familiar to most Americans. But in practice the full-scale trial is available only to the affluent, and the vast majority of offenders plead guilty and are sentenced on the spot. (*Ken Heyman*)

probation less than 10 percent of the time, while another judge in the same system gives probation 40 percent of the time.[71] One federal judge has never given a sentence of more than seven years during his thirty-seven years on the bench; others believe in stiff punitive and deterrent measures and hand out maximum sentences regularly. Judge John Sirica, the federal judge who heard so many of the Watergate cases, is known in legal circles as "Maximum John."

Sometimes the length of the sentence is not determined by the judge at all. In some states a judge may give an indeterminate sentence—that is, he puts the decision as to the length of the sentence into the hands of a parole board which periodically reviews the progress of the prison inmates. The original intention of the indeterminate sentence was to allow the early release of prisoners who appeared motivated to rehabilitate themselves. In practice, however, the system has actually lengthened sentences by subjecting prisoners to the whims of parole board members and of public opinion. In California, a state which pioneered the system of indeterminate sentences, the median term served by felons up to the point of their first release rose from 24 months in 1960 to

[71]Sutherland and Cressey, *Principles of Criminology*, p. 438.

36 months in 1970. One former inmate pleaded: "Don't give us steak and eggs . . . Free us from the tyranny of the indeterminate sentence."[72] As with so many other aspects of the judicial process, the reality falls far short of the ideal.

CORRECTIONS

The term "corrections" refers to the various means by which society handles convicted offenders: means such as imprisonment, probation, and parole. The objectives of the corrections process are many, and include *punishment* for the crime, *deterrence* of others through the example of punishment, *incapacitation* of the offender by excluding him from society, and *rehabilitation* of the offender by giving him the attitudes and skills that will enable him to become a law-abiding member of society.

Over a hundred years ago, the nation's leading prison officials met in Cincinnati and declared that "Reformation, not vindictive suffering, should be the purpose of the penal treatment of prisoners."[73] That remains the ideal to this day. Polls show that 78 percent of the American public believe that rehabilitation, rather than punishment, deterrence, or incapacitation, should be the basic aim of the prisons.[74] But the prisons are failing in that task. Forty percent of released prisoners are reimprisoned within five years.[75] We spend over a billion dollars a year to produce this high failure rate, but most of the money does not go for rehabilitation. Out of every dollar spent in the entire corrections system, approximately some 95 cents goes toward feeding, clothing, housing, and guarding prisoners, while only 5 cents is spent on rehabilitation.[76] In many states, prisons offer no suitable job training for prisoners, partly because unions and local businesses have lobbied against the development of prison industries that might compete in the marketplace and hold down wages and profits.

The United States has about 5,000 local and county jails and 400 state and federal prisons. On an average day, about 1.3 million offenders are confined in these institutions.[77] Of those incarcerated in the jails, over half have not been convicted of any crime, and of these, four out of five are eligible for bail but cannot raise the cash.[78] The very nature of the prison as an institution makes it difficult for much attention to be devoted to rehabilitation; the chronic problem of control takes priority over all else. The result is that the prison is organized as what sociologist

[72]Jessica Mitford, *Kind and Unusual Punishment* (New York: Knopf, 1973), pp. 86–87.
[73]"Shame of the Prisons," *Time* (January 18, 1971), p. 51.
[74]Harris, *The Anguish of Change,* p. 183.
[75]"Shame of the Prisons," p. 51.
[76]James P. Campbell, et al., "A Survey of American Corrections," in *Justice, Punishment, Treatment: The Correctional Process,* ed. Leonard Orlando (New York: Free Press, 1973), p. 139.
[77]Daniel L. Goldfarb, "American Prisons: Self-Defeating Concrete," *Psychology Today,* vol. 7, no. 8 (January 1974), p. 20.
[78]"Shame of the Prisons," p. 50.

The prison is a "total institution" in which inmates are stripped of their individuality, segregated from the outside world, and subjected to control of every aspect of their lives. Is rehabilitation possible in such an environment? (*Danny Lyon/Magnum*)

Erving Goffman terms a "total institution,"[79] a place of residence and work where the inmates are in a similar situation, are cut off from the wider society, and lead an enclosed, formally administered life. (Other examples of "total institutions" are mental hospitals, boarding schools, and army camps.) The inmate, kept under the absolute control of the administrative authorities, is deprived of liberty, possessions, heterosexual outlets, and personal autonomy. The psychological effects of prolonged imprisonment under these conditions can be devastating, and there is evidence that some long-term inmates become incapable of readjusting to the responsibilities of life in society. Despite the psychological stresses of imprisonment and despite the fact that many prisoners have severely disturbed personalities, there are only fifty full-time psychiatrists in the entire American prison system, and fifteen of them are in the federal institutions, which account for only 4 percent of prisoners.[80]

[79]Erving Goffman, *Asylums: Essays on the Social Situation of Mental Patients and Other Inmates* (Garden City, N.Y.: Anchor Books, 1961).
[80]"Shame of the Prisons," p. 53.

A frightening experiment conducted by social psychologist Philip G. Zimbardo gives some insights into the nature of the prison as a "total institution." In an attempt to investigate the psychological experience of imprisonment, Zimbardo created a simulated prison and selected two dozen college-educated, emotionally stable young volunteers to participate in the experiment. He divided them at random into "prisoners" and "guards" and paid them to participate in the study, which he anticipated would last for two weeks. Zimbardo arranged for the "prisoners" to be picked up at their homes by a city policeman in a squad car; they were then searched, handcuffed, fingerprinted, and taken blindfolded to the "jail." There they were stripped, deloused, put into uniform, given a number, and incarcerated. The "guards," meanwhile, were equipped with uniforms, wrap-around reflective sunglasses, whistles, clubs, and handcuffs. They were put on eight-hour shifts and were allowed to improvise rules for the maintenance of order and of respect for authority. The results of the experiment were very disturbing:

> At the end of only six days we had to close down our mock prison because what we saw was frightening. It was no longer apparent to most of the subjects . . . where reality ended and their roles began. The majority had indeed become prisoners or guards, no longer able to clearly differentiate between role-playing and self. There were dramatic changes in virtually every aspect of their behavior, thinking, and feeling. In less than a week the experience of imprisonment undid (temporarily) a lifetime of learning; human values were suspended, self-concepts were challenged and the ugliest, most base, pathological side of human nature surfaced. We were horrified because we saw some boys (guards) treat others as if they were despicable animals, taking pleasure in cruelty, while other boys (prisoners) became servile, dehumanized robots who thought only of escape, of their own individual survival and of their mounting hatred for the guards.
>
> We had to release three prisoners in the first four days because they had such acute situational traumatic reactions as hysterical crying, confusion in thinking and severe depression. Others begged to be paroled, and all but three were willing to forfeit all the money they had earned if they could be paroled. . . .
>
> About a third of the guards became tyrannical in their arbitrary use of power, in enjoying their control over other people. They were corrupted by the power of their roles and became quite inventive in their techniques of breaking the spirit of the prisoners and making them feel they were worthless. Some of the guards merely did their job as tough but fair correctional officers. . . . However, no good guard ever interfered with a command by any of the bad guards; they never intervened on the side of the prisoners, they never told the others to ease off because it was only an experiment.[81]

[81]Philip G. Zimbardo, "Pathology of Imprisonment," *Society,* 9 (April 1972), pp. 4–8.

A Letter from a Prisoner

I was recently released from solitary confinement after being held therein for 37 months (months!). A silent system was imposed upon me and to even whisper to the man in the next cell resulted in being beaten by guards, sprayed with chemical mace, blackjacked, stomped and thrown into a strip-cell naked to sleep on a concrete floor without bedding, covering, wash basin or even a toilet. The floor served as toilet and bed, and even there the silent system was enforced. To let a moan escape your lips because of the pain and discomfort . . . resulted in another beating. I spent not days, but months there during my 37 months in solitary. . . . I have filed every writ possible against the administrative acts of brutality. The state courts have all denied the petitions. Because of my refusal to let the things die down and forget all that happened during my 37 months in solitary . . . I am the most hated prisoner in (this) penitentiary, and called a "hard-core incorrigible."

Maybe I am an incorrigible, but if true, it's because I would rather die than to accept being treated as less than a human being. I have never complained of my prison sentence as being unjustified except through legal means of appeals. I know that thieves must be punished and I don't justify stealing, even though I am a thief myself. But now I don't think I will be a thief when I am released. No, I'm not rehabilitated. It's just that I no longer think of becoming wealthy by stealing. I now think only of killing—killing those who have beaten me and treated me as if I were a dog. I hope and pray for the sake of my own soul and future life of freedom that I am able to overcome the bitterness and hatred which eats daily at my soul, but I know to overcome it will not be easy.

SOURCE: Philip G. Zimbardo, "Pathology of Imprisonment," *Society* (April 1972).

Zimbardo concludes that the prisons are breeding grounds for hatred of society and argues that the prison experience contributes to the high rate of recidivism by hardening the inmates rather than rehabilitating them.

Some prisoners may be so dangerous, so unreformable, that imprisonment may be the only way in which society can deal with them. But for many other criminals, imprisonment may be of little positive value, either to themselves or to society in the long run. For decades we have ignored the conditions in our prisons, and it is likely that this long neglect of the prisons has compounded the social problem of crime in the United States.

Probation and Parole

Although prisons get the lion's share of whatever public attention and resources we devote to corrections, two-thirds of convicted offenders serve all or part of their sentences outside prison under the supervision of a probation or parole officer. In theory these officers give counsel to their charges, help them through difficult periods, and generally work with them toward their rehabilitation. In practice, however, the probation and parole officers are so burdened with cases that they can devote very little time to any individual: two-thirds of all felons and three-quarters of all misdemeanants report to parole or probation officers with a caseload of one hundred or more. Juvenile offenders receive somewhat more attention, but nearly 90 percent of them report to officers with a caseload of fifty or more.[82] Typically, officers see the offenders assigned to them only once a month for a brief ritual visit. There is little evidence that supervision by a probation or parole officer has any effect on the rehabilitation of offenders. One large-scale federal study did not find a single individual, even among those receiving intensive supervision, who attributed any effect to the officers. Instead, credit for keeping the offender out of trouble was given to family, friends, and the offender's own personal efforts.[83]

PROSPECTS FOR THE FUTURE

The prospects for reducing crime in the United States in the future are uncertain, largely because we do not know enough about why people engage in criminal activity or how to rehabilitate them once they do. Although appeals for law and order often include demands for stiffer penalties, there is no conclusive evidence relating severity of sentence either to the incidence of crime or to the amount of recidivism among former convicts.

White-collar crime is likely to receive more attention in the future. The Watergate scandals—in which many high-ranking members of an administration pledged to "law and order" were accused of such abuses as extortion, bribery, illegal wiretapping, conspiracy to violate civil rights, conspiracy to pervert the course of justice, perjury, destruction of evidence, tax fraud, and misappropriation of campaign funds—focused public attention on the issue of white-collar crime as never before. The discrepancies between the sentences received by these criminals and the much stiffer sentences meted out to ordinary thieves and burglars aroused comment, and the pardoning of former President Nixon, who faced a number of possible criminal charges, excited a major controversy. The existence of white-collar crime, especially if it goes largely unpunished, undermines public respect for those in

---

[82]President's Commission on Law Enforcement and Administration of Justice, *The Challenge of Crime in a Free Society*, p. 169.
[83]Richard F. Sparks, "The Effectiveness of Probation: A Review," in *The Criminal in Confinement*, vol. 3, *Crime and Criminal Justice*, eds. Leon Radzinowicz and Marvin E. Wolfgang (New York: Basic Books, 1971), p. 214.

positions of economic and political influence and creates a climate in which all violations of the law seem less reprehensible. As the Mafia comes more and more to resemble white-collar crime in its operations, demands for effective control of white-collar crime are likely to increase.

Variations in sentences received by different criminals for the same crime will also require attention. If justice is to be equal for all, then the race, sex, and economic status of the defendant ought not to influence the sentence received. One way to confront the problem of differentials in sentencing would be to make sentences subject to appeal. This would vastly increase the amount of court time spent on appeal cases, but if we are to take our commitment to equal justice seriously, the inconvenience is one we may have to accept. Legislative changes could also make sentences more uniform by reducing some of the latitude given to judges in this matter.

We can anticipate continuing controversy over the existence of laws governing crimes without victims. Some groups, such as the gay liberation movement, regard the campaign to repeal some of these laws as nothing less than a moral crusade, while other groups, such as marijuana smokers, now violate the laws on such a large scale that in many areas the laws seem to be falling into disuse as a result of police failure to apply them. Prostitution is legal in only one state, Nevada, but many other countries allow prostitutes to ply their trade without criminal sanctions so long as they do not create a public nuisance by importuning customers in the streets. Current changes in American attitudes toward sexual activity may create a climate in which laws regulating prostitution will be reviewed. Gambling laws, too, are likely to change in the future: these laws do not seem to have widespread public sentiment behind them, and already several cities and states have set up legal gambling activities, such as lotteries. With public institutions engaged in the gambling business, it seems unlikely that private groups can be severely restricted for much longer.

Most of the innovations in the future, however, are likely to take place in the corrections system. The public is clearly aware that the system is consistently failing to meet the important objective of rehabilitation, often with undesirable social consequences. Of the various reforms that have been proposed, one is the use of behavior modification techniques to reform prisoners. These techniques are based on the assumption that criminal behavior is learned through positive rewards to the criminal, and therefore can be unlearned—by giving him negative sanctions for undesirable behavior and positive rewards for desirable behavior. Patuxent Institution in Maryland is one prison that has pioneered these methods: by improved behavior, prisoners work their way up from one tier of rewards to the next, receiving on the various levels such positive reinforcements as vocational training, picnics with their families, and parole. Although most of the prisoners in Patuxent are hardened cases, recidivism is lower than average.[84]

[84]Goldfarb, "American Prisons," p. 85.

Crime and Justice: A Theoretical Review

The social problem of crime and justice represents the gap between a *social ideal* of a society free of crime and violence, practicing equal justice for all, and the *social reality* of a society plagued by a rising crime rate and characterized by an inconsistent application of the laws and of the penalties for breaking them. The crime rate has risen so rapidly in the United States during recent years that a great many citizens regard crime as the most serious social problem facing the nation.

The *social-disorganization* perspective has some relevance to the problem of crime and justice, but perhaps not as much relevance as sociologists used to believe. Because the incidence of arrests for crime is much higher in socially disorganized neighborhoods such as slums, sociologists considered that the disorganization led directly to crime. More recent research, however, has indicated that the arrest rate does not necessarily correspond to the crime rate: lower-class people are just more likely to be arrested. In fact, the great majority of Americans have committed crimes of some sort. Social disorganization may account for particular forms of crime found among lower-class criminals, but the same explanation cannot be applied to white-collar crime. It may be, however, that the general rise in the crime rate in recent years is related to the breakdown of established moral norms. Rapid technological change and urbanization have weakened the force of many traditional norms and social disorganization may therefore be indirectly involved in the rising crime rate.

The *value-conflict* perspective is also useful in the analysis of some aspects of the social problem of crime and justice. It is perhaps most relevant to the issue of crimes without victims, an area in which there is a genuine conflict of interest and values between the criminals and the rest of society. Many of these criminals—gamblers, homosexuals, or marijuana smokers—are otherwise quite law-abiding, and violate particular laws because they do not regard their acts as criminal and see no moral force in the laws. There is considerable value conflict, therefore, over whether socially disapproved acts that have no victims should continue to be illegal. Another area to which the value-conflict perspective is relevant is that of sentencing and corrections. Some Americans believe that harsh penalties are the answer to the rising crime rate. Other Americans believe that our present sentencing procedures are basically unfair and that our corrections system may contribute to the crime rate because of the attitudes it breeds in prisoners. Some citizens contend that the police should be given more power to obtain evidence from suspects; other citizens are more concerned about the civil liberties of arrested people. Citizens are by no means agreed on which acts should be criminalized or on how to proceed once offenders have been caught.

The *deviance* perspective is particularly useful for the analysis of the problem, and most research has been conducted within the framework of this perspective. The criminal is regarded as someone who has violated social norms that are encoded in laws.

Theorists who regard deviance as the product of a labeling process acknowledge that there are some crimes, such as murder or robbery, that would be regarded as crimes in virtually any society. They contend, however, that many other criminals are simply people to whom the label of "criminal" has been successfully attached. The great majority of citizens, they point out, have committed one or more crimes at some point in their lives (such as acts of juvenile delinquency or minor tax fraud), but because they are not caught they do not regard themselves as criminals and are not regarded as criminals by others. If they are labeled as criminals by peers, relatives, or the police, however, they may come to accept this definition of themselves and behave accordingly. Some labeling theorists argue that the reason white-collar crime attracts much less attention and much lighter sentences than lower-class crime is that the middle class, not the lower class, has the power to label—and it labels the criminal acts of other groups rather than its own as the most serious.

Theorists who see criminal deviance as the product of differential association believe that criminal behavior is learned through contact with other people who reject social norms governing crime. Prolonged contact with such people—whether they be fellow juveniles or fellow white-collar businessmen—creates a disrespect for law and provides opportunities to learn how to commit criminal acts.

Theorists who regard criminal deviance as the result of anomie believe that criminals have internalized certain social goals—such as the desirability of becoming rich—but do not have access to socially approved means of achieving the goal. This is why they resort to criminal behavior. This perspective may be combined with the social-disorganization perspective: if society is so organized that large numbers of people are deprived of the opportunity to achieve valued goals, the incidence of criminal behavior caused by anomie will be much increased.

Other proposals for rehabilitation involve transitional programs such as short-term furloughs, work-release, and halfway houses. These programs are designed to ease adjustment problems and to permit families to stay together to some extent. The furlough system allows the prisoner to make short visits to his home. Although it is objected that furloughs facilitate escape, Michigan and Mississippi, the two states making the most use of furloughs, report that only 1 percent of prisoners escape while on home leave.[85] Work-release programs use the resources of the community to free prisoners from the suffocating boredom and idleness of prison. In the program those who can go back to the jobs they held before imprisonment are permitted to do so; others are given training and sent out to new jobs. Most states still do not have work-release programs, however, and even in those that do, most of the prison population is considered ineligible. Halfway houses are residential institutions that allow prisoners a certain degree of freedom, while providing a structured environment in which rehabilitation can take place. They are designed to provide a transition between prison and complete release; however, if the prisoner misbehaves while in the halfway house, he may be returned to prison. In some cases, particularly those involving juvenile delinquents, the halfway house can also be used as an alternative, rather than a supplement, to incarceration: the delinquent is simply sentenced to a period in a halfway house instead of a reformatory.

While many of these reforms seem promising, the very concept of the prison, reformed or not, is likely to be challenged in the future. Many people are adopting the view that imprisonment is counterproductive and inappropriate for a majority of offenders. California, in an effort to find an alternative to confinement, is currently experimenting with a program for nonresidential community treatment for juvenile offenders. The delinquents are required to come at regular intervals to community centers, where their progress is followed and where support, therapy, and training are available. Preliminary results show a significantly lower rate of recidivism among these delinquents than among those who are institutionalized.[86] Other states, such as Massachusetts,[87] Iowa,[88] and Wisconsin,[89] have been transferring juvenile and adult offenders from penal institutions to community rehabilitation centers, and they too report encouraging results. It seems likely that in the future our corrections system will come to rely more and more on combinations of different types of facilities rather than on a uniform policy of incarceration for those who violate our criminal code.

[85]President's Commission on Law Enforcement and Administration of Justice, *The Challenge of Crime in a Free Society*, pp. 176–177.
[86]"Special Community Programs," in *Justice, Punishment, Treatment: The Correctional Process*, ed. Orlando, p. 213.
[87]The Citizen's Study Committee on Offender Rehabilitation, *Final Report to the Governor* (Madison: The Wisconsin Council on Criminal Justice, 1972), p. 8.
[88]Judy Klemesrud, "Should These Criminals Go to Prison? Iowa Doesn't Think So," *New York Times* (April 15, 1974), p. 36.
[89]The Citizen's Study Committee on Offender Rehabilitation, *Final Report to the Governor*, p. 7.

FURTHER READING

Blumberg, Abraham S., *Criminal Justice,* 1967. A probe of the American judicial system, with particular attention devoted to the plea-bargaining process by which defendants can avoid being prosecuted for major offenses by pleading guilty to minor ones.

Cloward, Richard A. and Lloyd E. Ohlin, *Delinquency and Opportunity: A Theory of Delinquent Gangs,* 1960. An important analysis of juvenile delinquency in terms of the relative opportunity that boys from different backgrounds have—both for entering "normal" society and for becoming delinquent.

Cressey, Donald R., *Theft of the Nation: The Structure and Operations of Organized Crime in America,* 1969. A sociologist's fascinating account of the mafia and its operations.

Geis, Gilbert, ed., *White Collar Criminal: The Offender in Business and the Professions,* 1968. A collection of essays on the problem of white-collar crime in American society.

Merton, Robert K., *Social Theory and Social Structure,* 1968. Contains Merton's theory of anomie which, ever since its original publication in 1938, has been of major significance in the sociological analysis of deviance.

Orlando, Leonard O., ed., *Justice, Punishment, Treatment: The Correctional Process,* 1973. A useful and comprehensive collection of essays on every aspect of the American correctional system.

President's Commission on Law Enforcement and Administration of Justice, *The Challenge of Crime in a Free Society,* 1967. An authoritative federal report on crime in America, written in nontechnical language and containing a mass of information on the nature of criminal behavior in our society. The report includes many suggestions for reforms.

Schur, Edwin M., *Crimes Without Victims—Deviant Behavior and Public Policy,* 1965. A lawyer turned sociologist analyzes various crimes that have no victims and argues for a change in social policy toward these crimes.

Sutherland, Edwin H. and Donald R. Cressey, *Principles of Criminology,* 8th ed., 1970. An important introductory text on criminology that utilizes Sutherland's theory of differential association.

15

Mental Disorders

THE NATURE AND SCOPE OF THE PROBLEM

About one in every twelve Americans will spend some part of his or her life in a mental institution. On any given day of the year, nearly 500,000 Americans are in confinement in the mental wards of hospitals; in fact, nearly half of all the hospital beds in the United States are occupied by people suffering from mental disorders. Of the nation's children some 10 percent are considered to be seriously maladjusted, and of these about half a million are treated each year for mental disturbances. One American in eight will suffer depression serious enough to require psychiatric treatment during his or her lifetime; about 125,000 citizens are hospitalized each year with depression, 200,000 more are treated privately, and an estimated 4 to 8 million more are in need of treatment but do not seek it.[1] Of the 50,000 to 70,000 suicides that take place each year in the United States, about half are committed by persons suffering from severe depression. Mental disorders are one of our three major health problems; cancer and heart disease are the other two.

The statistics do not tell the whole story. Only a small proportion of mental disorders are actually treated. Many Americans, including some who have severe symptoms, do not know they need help or refuse to seek it or cannot find the help they seek. Millions more suffer from serious but less acute mental disorders, such as anxiety and tension, but these difficulties do not show up in the official figures. Such people may

[1]"Coping with Depression," *Newsweek*, vol. 81, no. 2 (January 8, 1973), pp. 51–54.

Recovering from Schizophrenia

It was only when she was returning to her room in the afternoon that the world hurt. Young and rustling, loud with charm-bracelets and giggling, the high school and young college girls would overwhelm the buses, and she would once again find herself peering into the world of the elaborately vain, mirror-mad, fearing and predatory young girls—a world where she had failed, a world that she knew looked much better than it really was, but to the eyes of its outcasts, a world that glowed with mysterious brilliance. She looked down at her own school skirt and sweater. She looked the way they did, but she was still a stranger, the imitation of a young schoolgirl. . . .

That evening at the church, Deborah invited her hymnbook mate out for a soda. The girl blanched and stammered so badly that Deborah became frightened that those who had seen might think she had said something indecent. She saw a momentary picture of the ancient fear, as Onward Christian Soldiers marched onward against the little girl of the past. Slipping back to invisibility she sang on through choir practice about Compassion.

SOURCE: Hannah Green, *I Never Promised You a Rose Garden* (New York: Holt, Rinehart and Winston, 1964).

expend immense energy in trying to preserve a façade of happiness and normality despite their underlying turmoil, and this effort involves a further toll in job inefficiency, personal anguish, and problems with family and friends.

The plight of the mentally disordered person is complicated by a factor that is not present in the case of ordinary physical illnesses. Our society attaches a stigma to the mentally disordered, even when they have been pronounced cured. One reason for this stigmatization is that mental disorder is often confused with a totally different condition, mental retardation—the incurable condition of people such as idiots and imbeciles, who suffer, usually from birth, from organic brain defects. (There are currently 200,000 such individuals in public institutions in the United States.) A second reason is that public stereotypes of the mentally disordered tend to emphasize bizarre behavior patterns—violent outbursts, foaming at the mouth, would-be Napoleons, and so forth. The mentally disordered are regarded not merely as ill, but also as deviants. Although most patients are returned to their communities within a matter of months or even weeks, treatment for mental disorder—like imprisonment for crime—carries with it a label. The label may remain for years afterward, affecting the way the individual is viewed by his employers, friends, and even family. Readjustment to social life is thus made more difficult; Erving Goffman has said that the victims of mental disorder have a "spoiled identity."[2]

An example of this stigmatization occurred when Senator Thomas Eagleton was selected as the Democratic vice-presidential candidate by George McGovern in 1972. The choice was warmly received until it was revealed that earlier in his career the senator had undergone treatment for acute depression. Public reaction was so severe that Senator Eagleton was forced to withdraw from the ticket; McGovern's personal judgment was called into question, and his entire campaign suffered a setback from which it never recovered. There was, of course, no way of knowing if Thomas Eagleton's mental health at the time of the conventions was any better or worse than that of the other candidates, such as George McGovern, Richard Nixon, or Spiro Agnew: it was the label from Eagleton's past, rather than his current behavior, that damned him in the eyes of many. Interestingly, one U. S. President was almost certainly a sufferer from an acute manic-depressive syndrome, but because he was not treated, his condition did not arouse any public concern. The president was Abraham Lincoln, whose depression was so severe his friends feared he might commit suicide. In 1841 Lincoln wrote: "If what I feel were equally distributed to the whole human family, there would not be one cheerful face on earth."[3]

What is Mental Disorder?

A person may be said to be mentally disordered if he or she is psychologically incapable of coping realistically and effectively with the ordinary challenges and tasks of daily life. But this definition is a very general one. How can we apply it to particular cases to determine if someone is suffering from a mental disorder? How, for example, do we tell if someone is "mad"?

There is no easy answer to that question, because "madness" is a matter of definition, not an objective fact. It is extremely difficult to draw a fine line between sanity and insanity. Behavior which would be normal in a large city may seem antisocial or eccentric in a rural village. In the seventeenth century, religious leaders who burned heretics at the stake were considered to be well-adjusted members of the community, an example of righteousness and sanity for all to follow, but any religious leader who attempted to burn heretics today would be committed to an institution as an obvious psychopath. If we find a friend praying to God, his behavior is comprehensible to us, but if we find him talking to spirits—which is not so very different—we think his behavior very odd indeed. In making determinations of whether or not someone is men-

---

[2]Erving Goffman, *Stigma: Notes on the Management of a Spoiled Identity* (Englewood Cliffs, N.J.: Prentice-Hall, 1963).
[3]Rona Cherry and Laurence Cherry, "Depression, the Common Cold of Mental Ailments," *New York Times Magazine* (November 25, 1973), p. 38.

tally disordered, there is always a subjective judgmental component, because what is considered bizarre or irrational depends on the standards of the culture, of the subculture, and of the individual observer. This problem is illustrated often in the criminal courts, where, after studying the same evidence, expert psychiatrists regularly give conflicting judgments as to the sanity of the accused.

In fact, there is no real consensus on how to classify mental disorders. For years psychiatrists in different countries have used a variety of terms to describe a wide range of different mental disorders they believed they had diagnosed, but there was little general agreement on the terms appropriate for particular symptoms. Since 1968 there has been a formal agreement on an International Classification of Diseases, but there is still little consistency in diagnosis from country to country and from psychiatrist to psychiatrist in each country.

In the United States and Western Europe mental disorders are generally grouped into two broad categories, *neuroses* and *psychoses*. Neuroses are less serious and usually do not require hospitalization, whereas the psychoses typically involve a severe break with reality. It is not always possible in practice, however, to establish a borderline between normality and neurosis or between neurosis and psychosis.

Neuroses. A neurosis is generally considered a personality disturbance rather than a disease. The chief characteristic of the neurotic is an anxiety, which is believed in most cases to have its origins in childhood experiences. Despite this anxiety, the individual still has a firm grasp on reality and is able on the whole to function in life: the impairment is often limited to a particular area, and the neurotic may be normal in all other respects. The neurotic often knows that he has a problem, although he may not know its cause; and he usually wishes to overcome his disability. There are several subtypes of neurosis, of which the most common are:

Anxiety reaction: The individual feels a deep, generalized anxiety about life, but has no conscious awareness of the reasons for the anxiety.

Neurotic depression: The individual feels deeply depressed, often for long periods; in extreme cases the depression can lead to suicide.

Hypochondria: The individual believes himself to be physically ill, although in fact he is quite healthy.

Obsessive neurosis: The individual has a compulsion to behave in a particular way without any rational explanation; he may wash his hands many times a day, for example.

Phobia: The individual has an unreasonable fear. Some of these fears are very common, such as acrophobia (the fear of heights) and claustrophobia (the fear of enclosed spaces). But even butterflies can bring terror to some phobic neurotics.

Psychosomatic illness: The individual has psychological problems which appear as physical ailments — headache, backache, rashes, ulcers, or even, in extreme cases, blindness or paralysis. He does not realize that his illness is due to emotional stress.

Psychoses. The essential difference between the neurotic and psychotic is that the psychotic experiences a sharp break with reality. He may not recognize that he is mentally disordered; in fact, he may strongly deny it. His mental processes are more grossly deranged, and he is unable to evaluate external reality; he is out of touch with his own situation and does not attempt to adapt to the world. There are two main types of psychosis. *Organic psychoses* are those with an identifiable physiological basis and result from damage to the brain tissues by physical injury, senility, alcoholism, advanced syphilis, brain tumors, or other causes. *Functional psychoses* are those that have no clearly defined physical basis and whose origin is presumed to be partly or wholly psychological. These are the most severe mental disorders, and patients suffering from them constitute about 80 percent of first admissions to mental hospitals. There are three main subtypes of functional psychosis:

Paranoia: This is a relatively rare form of disorder, which is characterized by persistent delusions of persecution or grandeur — the individual may believe, for example, that the Martians wish to kidnap him. Paranoid delusions are often organized into logical systems focused on a few areas and are impervious to rational arguments. Other intellectual and emotional functions are not impaired, and there are usually no hallucinations or other abnormal behavior patterns.

Affective psychosis: This term covers a wide category of disorders characterized by extremes of mood rather than by bizarre behavior, although in some cases there may be hallucinations and delusions. In the *manic* form, the individual may be highly excitable and occasionally violent; in the *depressive* form, he may be depressed and withdrawn, even suicidal. Sufferers who fluctuate between these extremes are termed manic-depressive; their cycles of moods vary in length and regularity, but the depressive phase of the cycle usually predominates over the manic phase.

Schizophrenia: This is the most common form of functional psychosis. The term means "split personality" — not, as is commonly thought, in the sense that the individual has two different personalities, but in the sense that his intellectual and emotional functions are separated. Thus schizophrenics may laugh or cry at inappropriate moments, speak to inanimate objects, or talk in an incoherent fashion. They may suffer delusions, feelings of persecution, and visual and auditory hallucinations. There are several types of schizophrenia, of which the most common are: *simple schizophrenia,* characterized by general with-

Mental Knots

There must be something the matter with him
    because he would not be acting as he does unless there was
    therefore he is acting as he is
    because there is something the matter with him

He does not think there is anything the matter with him because
    one of the things that is
    the matter with him
    is that he does not think that there is anything
    the matter with him

therefore
    we have to help him realize that,
    the fact that he does not think there is anything
    the matter with him
    is one of the things that is
    the matter with him

SOURCE: R. D. Laing, *Knots* (New York: Pantheon Books, 1970).

drawal from reality into a closed world; *hebephrenic schizophrenia*, characterized by giggling, infantilism, hallucinations, and seclusion; *catatonic schizophrenia*, characterized by episodes of stupor and immobility which may persist for hours or even decades; and *chronic undifferentiated schizophrenia*, a residual category used when the individual's symptoms are not clear and he cannot otherwise be categorized.

The diagnoses are based on major aspects of the symptoms displayed by the patients, but they tend to be very unreliable in the long run, as particular individuals may simultaneously or sequentially exhibit symptoms from several different diagnostic categories. Psychiatrists often do not reach very convincing agreement on questions of diagnosis, even on the crucial question of whether someone is psychotic or not. In one study, psychiatrists disagreed as to whether people were psychotic in 20 percent of the cases they were asked to judge. On the question of specific diagnosis of exactly what form of psychosis an individual is suffering from, agreement among psychiatrists rarely exceeds 50 percent.[4] As one psychiatrist, D. L. Rosenhan, observes:

> Whenever the ratio of what is known to what needs to be known approaches zero, we tend to invent "knowledge" and assume that we understand more than we actually do. We seem unable to ac-

[4]Myron G. Sandifer, Charles Pettus, and Dana Quade, "A Study of Psychiatric Diagnosis," *Journal of Nervous Mental Disease*, 139 (October 1964), pp. 350–356.

knowledge that we simply don't know. The needs for diagnosis and remediation of behavioral and emotional problems are enormous. But rather than acknowledge that we are just embarking on understanding, we continue to label patients . . . as if in those words we had captured the essence of understanding. The facts of the matter are that we have known for a long time that diagnoses are not useful or reliable. . . .[5]

This state of uncertainty has far-reaching implications. For as we shall see, some critics of our current approaches to mental disorders have argued that mental illness is simply a social definition, not a pathological state — and that schizophrenia, for example, is simply a variant state of consciousness (like dreaming, transcendental meditation, religious ecstasy, or a psychedelic trip), and not really a disease at all.

The Treatment of Mental Disorders

Historical attitudes. Attitudes toward mental disorders have varied a great deal through history. Some preliterate communities have regarded the mentally disordered with awe and have interpreted their disjointed statements as messages from the supernatural. More commonly, the behavior of the mentally disordered has been attributed to the presence of some evil spirit that has taken up abode within the body. One of the earliest types of surgery of which we have evidence is called trephining: used by the ancient Egyptians four thousand years ago, this operation consisted of chipping a hole in the skull to allow the evil spirit to escape. In medieval Europe, the church began to define the mentally disordered as heretics and witches: it was reasoned that if an evil spirit was visiting the body, it must have been invited there through a pact with the devil. Flogging and starvation were used to make the body a less habitable place; and in many cases the mentally disordered were hanged or burned at the stake. Elaborate rituals of exorcism were used to drive out the spirits. This attitude persisted for centuries; several mentally disordered women were condemned and executed in the 1692 witchcraft trials in Salem, Massachusetts. Up to the late eighteenth century, the mentally disordered were held to be at least partly responsible for their condition, which was associated with moral degeneracy. Considered dangerous to society, they were kept chained and shackled in cells. Large institutions gradually developed for the control of "madmen." One of the earliest was St. Mary of Bethlehem Hospital in London — "Bedlam" for short. Conditions were such that to this day the word "bedlam" signifies noise, disorder, and turmoil. The hospital even sold tickets to the public so that they could view the more violent inmates through the bars of their cells. The less violent were allowed out to beg on the streets.

[5]David L. Rosenhan, "On Being Sane in Insane Places," *Science,* 179 (January 19, 1973), pp. 250–258.

The "crib" was a device used in the United States at the end of the last century for the purpose of restraining and punishing mental patients. Its use reveals how far the hospitals had departed from their initial purpose of providing care and asylum for the mentally disordered. *(The Bettmann Archive)*

The first great change in attitudes toward the mentally disordered came during the French Revolution, when the physician Phillippe Pinel was placed in charge of the Paris institution for the insane. Pinel was a humane reformer, and his first act was to cut the chains from the inmates. By treating them with kindness and concern, he demonstrated that they were not necessarily incurable and would respond to treatment. His approach became known as "moral treatment" and led to movements to create safe, humane places of refuge — "asylums" — for mentally disordered persons.

In colonial America no special facilities were offered to the mentally disordered until the time of the War of Independence, when private organizations began establishing asylums. These were followed, some decades later, by state institutions. But the demand for places far exceeded the supply, and gradually the original aim of the asylum — to provide a place of refuge and moral treatment — was lost. The asylums faced many problems. The mentally disordered did not always respond to treatment, the institutions were overcrowded, many patients were unruly, and the staffs were overworked. As a result, the asylums eventually assumed a custodial function: they became little more than large institutions to which the mentally disordered could be committed, often involuntarily and often for life, as a means of ridding society of their troublesome presence. The term "snake pit" was widely used as late as the 1950s to describe conditions in the state mental hospitals. The number of patients in these institutions grew rapidly throughout the first half of this century, until by 1955 it peaked at a total of 559,000. Since that time there have been consistent efforts to find alternatives to mental institutions. Among these are the treatment of the mentally disordered in general hospitals and outpatient clinics or through private psychiatrists, and today there are more psychiatric admissions to general hospitals than to the state mental hospitals. Another alternative was created by the Community Mental Health Centers Act of 1963, which provided for a system of centers in which the mentally disordered could be treated in the context of their own community.

Contemporary treatment. The contemporary treatment of mental disorders, both inside and outside the state mental hospitals, is usually based on one or more of three broad approaches: psychotherapy, somatic therapy, and chemotherapy.

Psychotherapy: There are many variant forms of psychotherapy, but most are based to some extent on the Freudian hypothesis that mental disorders are unconsciously motivated strategies or defense mechanisms which are adopted to avoid emotional pain, although the strategies may cause more pain than the problems they were meant to solve. It is usually assumed that the individual is the victim of unconscious conflicts that influence his behavior and interpretation of reality, but which remain outside his conscious control. The intention of psychotherapy is to bring the patient to understand the reasons for the condition, in the hope that this understanding will enable the patient to modify the behavior. Psychotherapy is often highly successful, particularly with neurotics, but the overall recovery rate of those who have been treated with psychotherapy is not significantly higher than the rate for those who have received no treatment at all. Psychotherapy is also an expensive and time-consuming form of treatment.

Somatic therapy: This method refers to all treatment administered directly to the body. One such technique is psychosurgery, which involves the severing or removal of apparently healthy tissue for the purpose of inducing changes in the patient's behavior. The most controversial form of psychosurgery is lobotomy, an operation in which nerves in the frontal lobes of the brain are severed. During the fifties about 50,000 lobotomies were performed, mostly on violent patients. The operation subdues them—but in some cases it also turns them into little more than living vegetables. The use of lobotomies has been much restricted since that time, but even so, about five hundred lobotomies are still performed each year.[6] Another form of somatic therapy is electroshock treatment, a method originally introduced in the thirties. At that time the patient was given electric shocks while fully conscious, and a team of attendants was needed to hold him down so that he would not break his limbs or spine during his writhings and convulsions. Despite these precautions, fractures were frequent and deaths not uncommon. Patients often needed a dose of strychnine to get them breathing again after the treatment. Today an injection containing a mixture of anesthetic and muscle relaxant is given to the patients to

[6]David Krech, et al., *Elements of Psychology*, 3d ed. (New York: Knopf, 1974), p. 637.

render them unconscious and reduce the convulsions. Electrodes are placed on either side of the head and a bolt of electric current of about 150–170 volts is sent into the patient's brain for a period of a second or less. The patient wakes up a few minutes later. The treatment is particularly effective for cases of depression, which can usually be cured after six or eight sessions, and is sometimes helpful in treating schizophrenia. The use of electroshock treatment is very controversial, however. Patients often hate and fear the method and complain that it causes confusion and loss of memory. No one knows how electric shock treatment works or what temporary or permanent effects it has in the depths of the brain.

Chemotherapy: The use of drugs has revolutionized the treatment of mental disorders since 1954, when tranquilizers were first introduced into mental hospitals. Chemotherapy has been a major factor in reducing the number of mental patients in hospitals in recent years; many patients who might have spent their lives in institutions have been released, and many others have been made more amenable to psychotherapeutic treatment. There are two main types of drug: tranquilizers, which calm excitable or violent patients, and antidepressants, which relieve extreme depressive symptoms. About 20 million prescriptions for antidepressants are written each year; they appear to be effective in about 60 percent of cases. It is not known precisely how these drugs work, nor is it known why they work on some people but fail to have any effect on others who appear to have identical symptoms. Drugs do not cure mental disorders; they merely suppress the symptoms. For this reason their use is sometimes criticized as being merely a form of psychic first aid, alleviating the symptoms without getting to the underlying causes. But drugs do represent a hopeful advance in the treatment of mental disorders.

APPROACHING THE PROBLEM

The Medical Model

Mental disorders are treated in terms of a medical model, as though they were analogous to physical ailments. The disorders are referred to as mental "illness"; the sufferers become "patients" in "hospitals" where they are given "treatment" by "doctors." This attitude stems from a belief that, to a greater or lesser extent, mental disorder has some organic basis, either in heredity or in the chemistry of the brain. If in fact mental disorders are simply a form of physical illness, then the medical model is probably appropriate. If, however, mental disorders have some quite different origin, then rigid adherence to the medical model may be a waste of effort. How valid is the medical model for the treatment of mental disorders?

The evidence that at least some mental disorders may have a hereditary, genetic basis is persuasive. Children of schizophrenics have a greater risk of becoming schizophrenic themselves. About 10 percent of children who have one schizophrenic parent and nearly half the children who have two schizophrenic parents become schizophrenic themselves. This finding in itself does not prove that the schizophrenia was genetically transmitted; the children might have become schizophrenic through being raised by schizophrenic parents. But other evidence is more persuasive. Children who are removed from schizophrenic mothers at birth are more likely to develop schizophrenia than children taken from normal mothers at birth.[7] Another study has shown that the same is true of children whose mother is normal but whose father is schizophrenic.[8] Studies of identical twins show that if one twin suffers from schizophrenia, the chances are 69 percent that the other twin will also be affected. The likelihood of this happening in nontwin siblings is 11 percent.[9] These findings seem to indicate that heredity may predispose individuals to schizophrenia. But it cannot be concluded that heredity is an absolute determinant; if it were, we should expect that any pair of identical twins would be either both normal or both schizophrenic, since they have identical heredity.

There is also persuasive evidence that chemical factors may underlie some mental disorders. Ever since the discovery of the "flight and fear" hormone, adrenaline, it has been known that specific chemical compounds can introduce marked changes in mood and behavior. Considerable emotional changes take place in women, for example, at the time of the hormonal changes accompanying menstruation and menopause: indeed, one writer has referred to human females as "walking pharmacies." We also know that many chemicals, such as tranquilizers and even industrial pollutants, can affect the workings of the brain. Lead poisoning can cause severe and permanent changes in behavior; in our cities, lead intake is about ten thousand times normal, as a result of pollution from automobile emissions. Carbon monoxide in the atmosphere, mostly from the same source, can markedly diminish efficiency in many areas of cerebral functioning. Insecticides, now found in virtually everything we eat, can lead to mental disturbance if the concentration is sufficiently great.

The workings of the human brain are staggeringly complex. Within each of our brains are about 10 billion nerve cells, or neurons, each of which may be connected with a thousand or more other neurons. Brain activity, which forms the basis of our thinking and behavior, consists of chemical and electrical processes between these cells. Each cell acts as

[7]Leonard I. Heston, "Psychiatric Disorders of Foster-home-reared Children and Schizophrenic Mothers," *British Journal of Psychiatry*, 112 (August 1966), pp. 819–825.

[8]Paul H. Wender, David Rosenthal, and Seymour S. Kety, "A Psychiatric Assessment of the Adoptive Parents of Schizophrenics," in *The Transmission of Schizophrenia*, eds. David Rosenthal and Seymour S. Kety (London: Pergamon, 1968), pp. 235–250.

[9]Franz J. Kallman, "The Genetic Theory of Schizophrenia," *American Journal of Psychiatry*, 103 (November 1946), pp. 309–322.

a tiny computer, receiving, processing, and transmitting information through electrical impulses. The contact points between the cells, the synapses, are separated by minute gaps, and these have to be bridged by a chemical "transmitter" released by the neuron before an electrical impulse can hurtle along the neural pathway, across the synapse, and on to the next neuron—a process which takes less than a millionth of a second. Some theorists believe that our moods are governed by the abundance, or lack, of chemical "transmitter" substances in certain regions of the brain. It may be, they argue, that chemical imbalances inhibit the effective transmission and processing of electrical impulses and that disordered behavior is the result. The effectiveness of some drugs does lend support to the view that biochemical disturbances may underlie some mental disorders. So far, however, there seems to be no conclusive evidence of consistent biochemical differences between psychotics and normal people.

Criticisms of the medical model. The medical model may prove to be the most effective approach. But there are several points at which the analogy between mental and physical disorders breaks down. In physical disorders, such as measles or a broken leg, there is general agreement on the symptoms and diagnosis. As we have seen, this is not so in the case of mental disorders. In physical disorders, there is general agreement on the appropriate methods for treatment, and there is usually an understanding of how the treatment works. In the case of mental disorders, there is little agreement on appropriate treatment and little understanding of how methods such as electrotherapy or drugs actually operate. In physical illnesses, the symptoms are the same in all cultures—measles has identical symptoms wherever it appears. But in the case of mental disorders, the symptoms vary in accordance with the local stereotypes of how a mentally disordered person is supposed to behave. In parts of Malaysia, for example, a standard symptom is to "run amok" in a public place after formally announcing to an authority figure—father or village headman—that one intends to do so. Finally, the relationship between the physician and the patient is fundamentally different in the two cases. In the case of physical illness, the patient usually defines himself as ill; the doctor confirms the diagnosis and then treats the patient with the patient's consent, which may be withdrawn at any time. But in the case of mental disorders, the patient may define himself as healthy. The physician may define him as ill, and treat him against his will—perhaps drugging him, locking him up, giving him electric shocks, or even severing his brain tissues. It is not clear to whom the physician is responsible—perhaps to the family, perhaps to the state—but it is certainly not to the patient.

These difficulties have led some writers to attack the medical model very strongly. One of the most outspoken critics is Thomas Szasz, a psychiatrist who asserts:

I submit that the traditional definition of psychiatry, which is still in vogue, places it alongside such things as alchemy and astrology, and commits it to the category of a pseudo-science.[10]

In books with titles such as *The Myth of Mental Illness* and *The Manu-facture of Madness,* Szasz has insisted that there is no such thing as mental illness. He does not deny that the behavior labeled as "mental illness" exists, only that these behaviors are not illnesses, but merely deviations from accepted moral, legal, and social norms. Many other writers have suggested that the medical model is too narrowly con-ceived. Mental disorders, they argue, can only be fully understood in the social context in which the disorders emerge. These criticisms imply other, sociocultural models to account for the origin of mental disorders.

The Sociocultural Approach

Where the traditional medical model has focused on mental disorder as a function of individual pathology, the sociocultural approach takes into account the wider human context: both the social factors which might drive people "mad" and also the factors which might influence other individuals to define or label them as "mad." The most influential state-ments of this perspective have been those of Gregory Bateson, Thomas Scheff, Thomas Szasz, and R. D. Laing.

Bateson's theory. One of the earliest sociocultural approaches was that of Gregory Bateson, who elaborated a "double-bind" theory of schizophrenia.[11] Bateson believes that certain family interaction pat-terns have the effect of confusing and disturbing children to such an extent that, in extreme cases, they may become mentally disordered. The double-bind is a specific example of these "pathogenic communi-cations" in the family. In a double-bind situation, the individual re-ceives two contrary messages; if he obeys either, he has acted wrongly, but he cannot escape the situation. Thus the father may insist that he will only respect his son if he "acts like a man," but he will punish the son for standing up to him. The situation may be made worse if another member of the family is also involved in the situation and is uncon-sciously manipulating it for his or her own ends. If the family interac-tion patterns consistently take this form, argues Bateson, then the indi-vidual—intellectually confused but emotionally involved in the other family members—may become severely disturbed and adopt the ster-eotyped role of a "sick" person. The individual is thus released from his normal social relationships and is no longer held responsible for his behavior.

[10]Thomas S. Szasz, *The Myth of Mental Illness* (New York: Harper & Row, 1961), p. 1.
[11]Gregory Bateson, et al., "Toward a Theory of Schizophrenia," *Behavioral Science,* vol. 1, no. 4 (October 1956), pp. 251–264.

Scheff's theory. Another influential statement is that of Thomas Scheff, who argues that the mentally disordered are social deviants of a special type.[12] All societies have certain norms; if any person violates these norms he or she is considered a deviant and is labeled accordingly. Those who violate norms of property ownership, for example, may be labeled criminals; those who violate norms of drug usage may be labeled addicts. But there are, says Scheff, certain "residual norms" that are so much taken for granted that they appear to be almost a part of nature. One does not, for example, talk to someone who is not present. Violation of these residual norms is frightening to people; they consider that the violator has taken leave of his senses and label him as mentally ill. Thus, although the individual's initial violation of residual norms may have been simply a temporary deviance caused by his inability to deal with a particular social situation, he finds that as a result of this first offense he has been labeled. The individual may then, in an involuntary, unconscious manner, accept the label that has been applied to him and start to behave in ways that are considered appropriate for the sick role of a mentally disordered person. There are, says Scheff, certain behavioral rules in every culture which mentally disordered people follow; these rules are learned in childhood from a variety of sources—anecdotes, films, comics, books, TV. Accepting the label and following these rules gives the individual an opportunity to withdraw into a socially established sick role in which he can relinquish all personal responsibility for his actions. But once he has gone this far, it is hard to turn back; the label is not cast aside as easily as it was taken on. Scheff thus sees mental disorder as a form of learned behavior. But the condition remains, of course, a genuine and serious one.

Szasz's theory. Another critique is that of Thomas Szasz, who acknowledges that mental disorders exist, but claims that they are not illnesses: they are simply "a problem in living."[13] He sees mental disorders as defective strategies that people adopt in order to handle difficult or irresolvable situations. Human relations are fraught with tensions and problems, and "illness" is simply used at an unconscious level as an excuse for avoiding unpleasant reality. In all cultures, Szasz points out, there is a practice of making life easy, at least temporarily, for those who are ill. Those who become mentally "ill" do so because they do not have effective ways of handling their problems. Their disorder is nothing more than "the language of illness," a form of defective communication which is employed "either because another language has not been learned well enough, or because this language happens to be especially useful." The psychiatrist is not a physician in any real sense; he is merely an interpreter of social norms who unwittingly penalizes people whose strategies for interpersonal relations are defective.

[12]Thomas J. Scheff, *Being Mentally Ill: A Sociological Theory* (Chicago: Aldine, 1966).
[13]Szasz, *The Myth of Mental Illness.*

Laing's theory. A still more radical critique has been made by R. D. Laing. He has offered two distinct formulations, one earlier in his career and one more recently. In his early work, Laing acknowledges that the mentally disordered are "ill" and that it is the psychiatrist's function to readapt them to reality.[14] The problem with the mentally disordered, he suggests, is that they suffer from what he terms "ontological insecurity"—that is, insecurity in their very being. As a result of social pressures, both from the family and from an unsympathetic, competitive society, such people feel their basic selves to be divided and vulnerable, consisting of an inner, true, authentic self and an outer, false, social front. The boundaries between these selves are collapsing, and the individual feels his essential self to be in danger. Laing argues further that the behavior of schizophrenics makes sense if viewed in the social and familial context in which the disorder arose. The disconnected, rambling, and irrelevant speech of schizophrenics has inner meaning to anyone who takes the trouble to learn about their previous experience and then listen with an open mind to what they say.

In his more recent formulation, Laing adopts a much more radical approach[15]—so radical that many orthodox psychiatrists consider that Laing himself is insane. He now rejects entirely the concept of insanity; instead, he argues that there are differing forms of consciousness, each of them equally valid. What used to be called "insanity" he now calls "hypersanity," which is in his view no worse than our own distorted sanity. The statesmen of the world who boast that they have doomsday weapons, comments Laing, are as divorced from "reality" as the worst raving lunatic. Laing argues that the psychiatrist merely interferes with a natural healing process when he tries to "cure" the "mentally ill." The schizophrenic experience is in his view a voyage into hypersanity, and if the psychiatrist has any role at all, it should be as "priest," to escort the individual on this voyage:

> Can we not see that *this voyage is not what we need to be cured of, but that it is itself a natural way of healing our own appalling state of alienation called normality?*[16]

Laing does not argue, however, that "hypersanity" is a particularly blissful state. Because it has its origins in our "normal" reality, it is in a sense as "sick" as our normality is "sick":

> From the alienated starting point of our pseudo-sanity, everything is equivocal. Our sanity is not "true" sanity. Their madness is not "true" madness. The madness of our patients is an artifact of the destruction wreaked on them by us and by them on themselves. . . .
> The madness that we encounter in "patients" is a gross travesty,

[14]R. D. Laing, *The Divided Self* (New York: Pantheon, 1969).
[15]R. D. Laing, *The Politics of Experience* (New York: Pantheon, 1967).
[16]Ibid., p. 116.

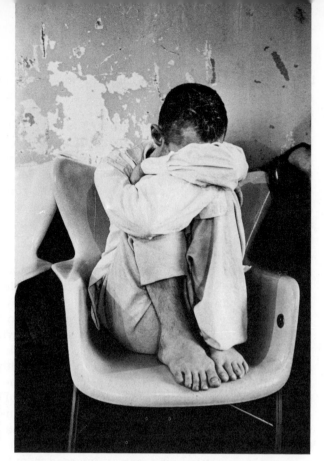

Is this mental patient immersed in some other, private reality— or is he simply disordered? The work of radical psychiatrists such as R. D. Laing has made the issue a highly controversial one. *(Bill Stanton/Magnum)*

a mockery, a grotesque caricature of what the natural healing of that estranged integration we call sanity might be.[17]

On the basis of studies he and his colleagues have made of schizophrenic subjects, Laing concludes that their behavior is a meaningful strategy that they have unconsciously adopted as the only one open to them — with tragic results for themselves:

> It seems to us that *without exception* the experience that gets labeled schizophrenic is a *special strategy that a person invents in order to live in an unlivable situation.* In his life situation the person has come to feel he is in an untenable position. He cannot make a move, or make no move, without being beset by contradictory and paradoxical pressures and demands, pushes and pulls, both internally from himself, and externally from those around him. . . . There is no such "condition" as schizophrenia, but the label is a social fact. . . . The person labeled is inaugurated not only into a role, but into a career of patient. . . . The "committed" person labeled as patient, and specifically as "schizophrenic," is degraded from full existential and legal status as a human agent. . . . After being sub-

[17]Ibid., p. 101.

jected to a degradation ceremonial known as a psychiatric examination, he is bereft of his civil liberties in being imprisoned in a total institution known as a "mental" hospital.[18]

Evaluation. Laing's views have attracted much attention, but they are emphatically rejected by most orthodox psychiatrists. However compelling his views and those of other sociocultural theorists are, it should be remembered that they constitute only a critique of the medical model, not a total refutation of it. Rather, their views provide a complementary perspective. It may be that at some point in the future a physical basis will be found for all mental disorders. All psychological states must have some neurochemical basis, and in principle at least it ought to be possible to intervene chemically and modify behavior. But the sociocultural approach implies that the *ultimate* causes of mental disorders may lie in social context, not in brain chemistry; that is, the emotional state of the individual may influence his brain chemistry, which may in turn influence his behavior. Because of our present knowledge, it is probably better to combine the two approaches into a broader, sociomedical perspective: some people may be genetically or neurochemically vulnerable to mental disorders, but social influences are extremely important in determining which individuals will actually be affected and how they react. As John Clausen observes:

> Certainly the most tenable hypothesis as to the etiology of schizophrenia at this time is that various combinations of hereditary vulnerability and environmental stress (either in early childhood or in later life) may lead to overt manifestation of the disorder. . . . This formulation is conjectural, but it is in keeping with the evidence available. . . .[19]

THE INCIDENCE OF MENTAL DISORDERS IN SOCIETY

Are any particular groups in a population particularly vulnerable to mental disorders? Is any social class especially affected? Are people in cities at greater risk than people in rural areas? What do we know about the social circumstances that give rise to a high incidence of mental disorders?

Methodological problems. At first sight these questions might seem easily answerable; a researcher would simply have to find the figures for the incidence of mental disorder and then correlate them with particular variables such as class, density of population, and so on. In fact,

---

[18]Ibid., pp. 78–79, 83–84.
[19]John A. Clausen, "Mental Disorders," in *Contemporary Social Problems,* 3d ed., eds. Robert K. Merton and Robert Nisbet (New York: Harcourt Brace Jovanovich, 1971), p. 60.

however, there are very severe methodological problems. How do we determine, for example, the incidence of schizophrenia? Mental hospital statistics alone are misleading. Different hospitals have different criteria for admission, and different psychiatrists have different criteria for diagnosis. It may also be that members of one social class are more likely to seek treatment than members of another social class, and this would bias the data. Moreover, there is evidence that people are more likely to be hospitalized if there is a mental hospital in their vicinity, so that the location of these institutions will influence the number of recorded cases in particular regions. Statistics on patients in private nursing homes or outpatient clinics are often difficult to obtain, and it is even more difficult to get facts and figures on people who are being treated privately, not to mention the people who have mental disorders but are not being treated at all.

Mental disorders and social class. One of the earliest investigations into the social correlates of mental disorder was conducted in Chicago in the thirties by sociologists Robert Faris and Warren Dunham.[20] They obtained information on all the patients in both private and public mental hospitals in Chicago and then plotted the residential distribution of the patients. The results made it quite plain that mental disorders were not randomly distributed throughout the area. Instead, the highest rates were found in the city center, in areas of high population density and poor socioeconomic conditions. Much lower rates of incidence were encountered in the more affluent suburbs. The figures were influenced by the fact that many "skid row" alcoholics and others suffering from organic psychoses had congregated in the inner city, but even allowing for their presence, there was a strong indication that mental disorder was linked to place of residence and social class. Faris and Dunham attributed this fact to the social disorganization of the city center, with its high crime rates, lack of employment, social instability, and crowded living conditions.

Another revealing study was conducted by A. B. Hollingshead and F. Redlich in New Haven, Connecticut, in the late fifties.[21] They were able to secure data not only from the public and private hospitals in the area, but also from private psychiatrists. They found that the prevalence of schizophrenia was eleven times greater for the lower class than for the upper class if measured in terms of hospitalization rates; this difference was largely due to the fact that persons of lower social status were more likely to be kept in the institutions for a longer period of time. For private treatment, however, the upper class had a much higher rate than the lower strata. It seemed that upper-class persons

---

[20]Robert E. L. Faris and H. Warren Dunham, *Mental Disorders in Urban Areas* (Chicago: University of Chicago Press, 1939).

[21]August B. Hollingshead and Frederick Redlich, *Social Class and Mental Disorder* (New York: Wiley, 1958).

were much more likely to define their problems in psychological terms and to seek treatment. Both the nature and duration of treatment varied with social class. Upper-class patients were more likely to be treated with psychotherapy and to be institutionalized only for brief periods; lower-class patients were more likely to be treated with drugs or electrotherapy, and they took longer to recover. Some 52 percent of the lower-class patients were referred for treatment by courts, and a further 20 percent were referred by welfare agencies; on the other hand, some 70 percent of the upper-class patients were referred by their families or by themselves.

A more ambitious study was conducted by Leo Srole and his associates in midtown Manhattan in the sixties.[22] They decided not to work with information from hospitals and psychiatrists, as this would provide data only on people who were being treated; instead, they investigated a random cross section of the entire population of the area. Extensive interviews were conducted with nearly seventeen hundred people in midtown Manhattan. The subjects were interviewed to determine if they had ever had a nervous breakdown, sought psychotherapy, or displayed psychosomatic or other neurotic symptoms. The information was then given to a team of psychiatrists who were asked to rate each case as to the degree of psychiatric impairment. The findings were surprising and disturbing. Over 23 percent of the population was considered to be "significantly" impaired in mental functioning, and only 18 percent were considered to be fully healthy. The degree of mental health correlated very closely with social class. In the lowest stratum, nearly one person in every two was considered psychologically impaired, but the rate fell to one in eight for the highest stratum. The upper class also tended to seek early treatment. A fifth of the upper-class individuals who were rated as impaired were receiving therapy at the time, and over half had received psychiatric treatment at one time or another—usually as outpatients. But only 1 percent of the lower-status group was receiving therapy at the time, and only 20 percent of them had ever had psychiatric treatment—almost always inside mental hospitals. Thus the lowest socioeconomic group was the one most in need of attention—and the one receiving the least attention.

The poor and the deprived, then, seem more prone to mental disorders than those who are better off. The reasons are presumably linked to their social status, which influences their attitudes, values, education, personality development, job satisfaction, economic well-being, and sense of personal autonomy. The poor are much less likely to seek treatment, which means that their condition may well deteriorate before they receive attention; and they are more likely to become institutionalized and receive less individualized attention than upper-class people.

[22]Leo Srole, et al., *Mental Health in the Metropolis* (New York: McGraw-Hill, 1962).

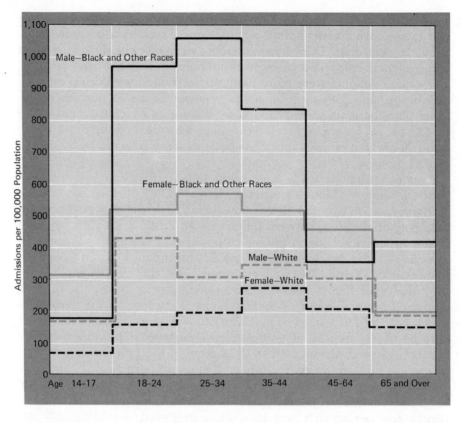

Admission rates to mental hospitals by age, race, and sex, 1970. The breakdown of statistics on admissions to state and county mental hospitals by race and sex confirms the evidence that mental disorder and hospitalization are linked to socioeconomic factors. In the age group of twenty-five to thirty-four years, approximately three and one half times as many black males as white males enter mental hospitals. The admission rate for black females in this same age group is three times more than the rate for white females. (SOURCE: Executive Office of the President: Office of Management and Budget, *Social Indicators, 1973* [Washington, D.C.: U.S. Government Printing Office, 1973] p. 13.)

Other correlates of mental disorders. Although social status seems to be a crucial variable, other factors can also be important. The aged, for example, are much more liable to mental disorders, particularly the organic psychoses. Degeneration of brain cells is one reason for this, but it is also likely that the sick role that is commonly offered to the old in our society has its effect. Since we have no rewarding role to offer the elderly, they are often left with a sense of isolation and meaninglessness. Upward or downward social mobility is also associated with mental disorder (and with suicide); this may be because people find it difficult to adjust to radically changed social and economic circumstances. And for reasons that are not fully understood, men are three times as vulnerable to psychosis as women, but women are four times as vulnerable to neurosis as men. Men, too, are five times more likely to commit suicide than women. Research findings consistently show that mental disorders are not randomly distributed. They recur in particular social contexts among particular social groups — presumably those that are most subject to stress. This finding lends support to a sociocultural view of the origins of at least some forms of mental disorder.

MENTAL DISORDER AND SOCIAL CONTROL

Society has always sought to exercise at least minimal control over persons defined as mentally disordered. The reasons are obvious — some disordered persons may be a danger to themselves and others, and some may be incapable of taking care of themselves. But there are critics who contend that the social control of people labeled as mentally disordered has taken on more sinister implications.

In the Soviet Union, many dissenters in recent years have been sent, not to concentration camps in Siberia, but to insane asylums. The list of poets, writers, and intellectuals who have been defined as "mentally ill" rather than criminal by the Soviet authorities is a lengthy one, and includes people who would be highly respected in the West. Soviet psychiatrists may not be as cynical as we might think; given that their "reality" is a Marxist–Leninist one, it may seem obvious to many of them that people who are not adapted to that reality are psychologically impaired. But whether they are fully aware of the political implications of their diagnoses or not, these Soviet psychiatrists are clearly using the label of mental illness as a method of social control.

The Labeling of Nonconformists

Does anything similar happen in the United States? We certainly do not have an officially sponsored system for labeling political dissenters as mad. But can it be that the label of mental illness is used, perhaps unintentionally, as a means of social control over individuals who do not conform to social expectations? As we have seen, Thomas Szasz argues that this form of social control is a major function of modern psychiatry:

> I have long maintained that the psychiatrist impersonates a medical role; actually, he is an interpreter of moral rules and an enforcer of social laws and expectations.[23]

Certain violations of established moral and legal norms, says Szasz, are liable to be defined as "sick"; the officials who make the definitions assume that their own standards are somehow natural and healthy. Thus, earlier in this century, masturbation was considered a symptom

[23]Thomas S. Szasz, "The Psychiatrist as Double Agent," *Trans–action*, vol. 4, no. 10 (October 1967), p. 16.

of mental disorder, and it was only in 1974 that the American Psychiatric Association removed homosexuality from its official list of mental disorders. To make his point, Szasz quotes from a handbook for college psychiatrists written by Dana L. Farnsworth, a Harvard psychiatrist who is probably the foremost authority in the United States on college psychiatric services:

> Library vandalism, cheating and plagiarism, stealing in the college or community stores or in the dormitories, unacceptable or anti-social sexual practices (overt homosexuality, exhibitionism, promiscuity), and the unwise and unregulated use of harmful drugs, are examples of behavior that suggest the presence of emotionally unstable persons. . . .[24]

Such a view of deviant behavior, Szasz suggests, has no medical basis whatsoever. What is involved is simply the violation of certain established social norms. Criminal penalties seem inappropriate because the violators are young and often privileged, so the label of "emotionally unstable" is used instead. Szasz believes that just as the church once labeled some deviants as "heretics," so the psychiatrist now labels them as "mentally ill." The clergyman or the psychiatrist may not fully understand his own role, but what he is doing in effect is to exert social control and ensure conformity to the norms of society. The existence of the label serves as an implied threat and thus restrains deviance; or, if deviance does take place, the label serves to define the deviant as being outside the "normal" community. The right to apply these definitions to others depends very largely on the power and influence of the people concerned:

> Administrators and faculty members have the privilege of incriminating students as mentally ill; students have the privilege of incriminating their fellow students as mentally ill; but students do not have the privilege of incriminating administration and faculty members as mentally ill.[25]

A similar view has been taken by psychiatrist Robert Coles, who in the early days of the civil rights movement in the South obtained firsthand experience of how black "troublemakers," whom he considered quite normal, could be regarded as mentally disordered. The courts, he found, would:

> summon all the authority of medicine and science to the task of defending the status quo — which meant putting firmly in their place (a hospital or clinic) those who choose to wage a struggle against the status quo.[26]

---

[24]Quoted from Dana L. Farnsworth, *Psychiatry, Education, and the Young Adult,* in Szasz, "The Psychiatrist as Double Agent," p. 17.
[25]Szasz, "The Psychiatrist as Double Agent," p. 16.
[26]Robert Coles, "A Fashionable Kind of Slander," *Atlantic,* vol. 226, no. 5 (November 1970) p. 54.

Sanity or Madness?

The condition of alienation, of being asleep, of being unconscious, of being out of one's mind, is the condition of the normal man.

Society highly values its normal man. It educates children to lose themselves and to become absurd, and thus to be normal.

Normal men have killed perhaps 100,000,000 of their fellow normal men in the last fifty years.

SOURCE: R. D. Laing, *The Politics of Experience* (New York: Ballantine Books, 1967).

Coles detects the same type of attitude in the reaction to student dissenters in the late sixties and early seventies. Instead of considering the demands of the students and evaluating their criticisms of society, people in positions of power assume that there is something wrong with the students rather than society. There is supposed to be something amiss with the psychological state of the students: since there is nothing to protest about, the students must be "immature," or "out of touch with reality," or have "exhibitionist tendencies," or suffer from "authority problems." They are described as "acting out their fantasies" or having "poor ego controls," which make them "rebel against parent surrogates" and issue "unrealistic" statements. Coles notes that terms such as these are not used indiscriminately against anyone who exhibits antisocial or aggressive tendencies; they are only applied to those who challenge the existing order:

> What are we to say, for instance, about the "early childhood" or "mental state" of political leaders or business leaders or labor leaders who lie or cheat or order thousands to go off to fight and kill? What kind of "psychological conflict" enables a man to be an agent of the Central Intelligence Agency, or a pilot who drops napalm bombs? . . . Moreover, if students are out to kill their "parent surrogates", what indeed of our desires as grown-ups to squelch the young, subtly and not so subtly degrade them, be rid of them — because they inspire envy in us; because they confront us with all the chances we forsook, all the opportunities we have lost, all the tricks and compromises and duplicities we have long since *rationalized* or *repressed* or *projected*?[27]

The definitions of mental normality, Coles argues, are socially constructed by those who hold positions of authority in society:

> What indeed is mental health? Who indeed is normal? Were slave holders normal? . . . If a man tells me he is going to kill himself, I

[27]Ibid., p. 55.

call him "suicidal" and want to hospitalize him. If a man in Vietnam runs into a burst of machine gun fire, urging his comrades to do likewise, I call him a hero. If a man wants to kill someone, he is homicidal and needs confinement. If a man drops a bomb on people he doesn't even see or know, he is doing his duty. . . . Such ironies and vexing discrepancies ought to make us all at the very least aware that psychiatric judgements about what is or is not "appropriate" are not rendered in some scientific vacuum, but are made at a particular moment of history and in a given society by men who are distinctly part of that society — namely, its upper middle class.[28]

Involuntary Commitment to Institutions

In 1971, five inmates were released from an Ohio mental institution for the criminally insane. They had never been convicted of any crime; in fact they had been sent there only for observation — yet they had remained in the institution for periods of from twenty-two to forty-one years. They were released only because one psychiatrist had noticed them, considered them fit to be released, and taken up their case. He estimated at the time that there were over one hundred other patients in the institution who were in a similar position.[29] How could this happen?

Many of our state mental hospitals include people who have committed only trivial misdemeanors or who have not been convicted of any crime at all but have been sent there for "observation." The police and courts may refer individuals whose behavior appears odd for psychiatric examination, and if the person is found to be "insane" he can be confined in a mental hospital against his will for long periods — in some cases, for life. Daniel Oran, a lawyer who has taken a particular interest in such cases, has succeeded in intervening many times to obtain the discharge of patients who might otherwise have been kept indefinitely in institutions. Oran points out that there is no consistency in the way the patients are diagnosed as insane:

> In some states, such as California, this decision must be made within a few days. In some states, such as Georgia, [the patient] would have all the safeguards of the adversary process normally given to a criminal defendant, such as a court-appointed lawyer, the right to call and cross-examine witnesses, and a jury trial. In many others, not even a lawyer is provided, and the purpose of the hearing is often concealed from the patient. (This is especially unfortunate because most state mental hospitals are filled with poor people who have nobody to turn to.) In some states, a judge's decision to commit must be reviewed every six months. In others, it is good for a lifetime's incarceration. The only conclusion that can safely be drawn . . . is that the 50 states have 50 different combinations of commitment laws and lengths of time a mental patient can be held against his will. There are "one physician emergency commitments," "two

---

[28]Ibid., p. 54.
[29]*Los Angeles Times* (April 24, 1971), p. 6

physician evaluatory commitments," "temporary judicial commitments," and even "peace officer commitments." Connecticut alone has a dozen different laws to put people away.[30]

Oran concludes that " 'mental health' has become our polite, scientific euphemism for conformity."

It may be that much of the case against psychiatry as a form of social control is overstated. But the situation is serious enough for the American Psychological Association, representing over thirty thousand psychologists, to have made an official statement on the subject in 1972. The association declared that it

> condemns the practice, wherever it may occur, of suppressing or neutralizing political dissenters by diagnosing them as mentally ill and committing them to mental hospitals. We consider it the responsibility of individual psychologists to oppose such practices within the organization in which they are employed and, if they do not succeed in changing the practices, to dissociate themselves from personal complicity in them.[31]

THE MENTAL HOSPITALS

As we have seen, American mental hospitals were originally intended as a place of quiet refuge, but instead became custodial centers whose public image was that of the "snake pit." Many efforts have been made to reform the mental hospitals since the mid-fifties, yet the criticisms have continued. But the focus of criticism has changed from an earlier concern as to what went on inside the mental hospitals to a new concern as to whether mental hospitals can deal appropriately with mental disorders at all.

The main objection to the mental hospitals is that, however benign their intentions, they tend to adapt individuals to the needs of the system rather than the other way around. Isolation from the community seems a poor preparation for inmates who, on release, will have to continue their lives in the communities from which they have been separated. The architecture of the hospitals, most of which are old, is usually gloomy and forbidding: there are long corridors, dormitories without privacy, day rooms monitored by administrators boxed off in glass observation cubicles, and factory-type rather than residential lighting fixtures. Most hospitals currently hold about a quarter more patients than they were designed for, and because a small minority may attempt to escape, doors and windows are commonly barred and bolted. These physical conditions inevitably influence the atmosphere of the institutions.

[30]Daniel Oran, "Judges and Psychiatrists Lock Up Too Many People," *Psychology Today*, vol. 7, no. 3 (August 1973), p. 27.
[31]*American Psychological Association Monitor*, 4 (1973), p. 1.

Many social scientists and medical practitioners are concerned that incarceration in mental hospitals may worsen rather than improve the condition of some patients. A prolonged stay in one of these institutions could prove a depressing and depersonalizing experience. *(Paul Fusco/Magnum)*

Close control must be maintained over at least some inmates who might be prone to violence or suicide, and so everyone tends to come under surveillance. The staff find their jobs easier if there are straightforward rules and regulations applicable to everyone, and it enforces these by a system of punishments and rewards (such as granting or withholding permission to see films). A great deal of attention is devoted to record-keeping, food preparation, the administration of drugs, the restraining of difficult patients, and the scheduling of daily activities; there is relatively little time left for interpersonal contact or therapy. The patients have little contact with psychiatrists. Most of their contact is with the hospital aides, more than half of whom have not completed high school and most of whom have no prior training in mental health care; these aides control the wards and the access of patients to clinical staff. The atmosphere of the hospitals, with their gloomy regimentation and their forlorn population, would be depressing enough for a normal person who was required to spend even a day or so within the walls. The effect on someone who is already disturbed and who is forcibly committed, perhaps for months or years, could be the very opposite of therapeutic.

The Mental Hospital as a "Total Institution"

One of the most influential studies of mental hospitals is that of Erving Goffman.[32] He conducted his research while working for a year as an aide in a mental hospital, where he was able to move freely among the patients, talking to them and noting down his impressions. Goffman analyzes mental hospitals in terms of his concept of the *total institution*. A total institution is a place of work and residence in which a number of individuals in a similar situation are cut off from the wider society and lead an enclosed, formally administered life. Other examples of total institutions are army camps, boarding schools, naval vessels, and prisons. In the total institution there is an absolute cleavage between the inmates and the administrators. A hierarchy of officials has total control over the inmates, whose activity is scheduled and monitored from above. Entry into a total institution is a process of transition, in which the individual gives up his former, self-determining role and takes on the role of inmate. On entry the inmates are identified, examined, and coded; their personal possessions and clothes are taken from them and uniforms are substituted. All experience of the institution impresses on the inmates their sense of personal inadequacy: behavior is controlled by rewards and punishments and there is a total dependency on the institution for all physical needs. In order to be successful in such an institution, the inmate has to learn to play by the rules: the mental patient or prisoner who makes trouble is immediately defined as being unfit for release.

Goffman found that mental patients tended to be treated in terms of the institution's expectations of them: if they behaved normally, this was not considered significant and was not entered on their records, but a single episode of abnormal behavior was immediately noted. The individual patients, he found, tended to adopt one of three strategies: they would withdraw into themselves and ignore the institutional setting; or they would openly challenge the system and "make trouble"; or they would conform to the rules and surrender their personal autonomy.

Goffman concluded, and many social scientists and psychiatrists agree with him, that many patients are suffering not so much from the original condition for which they were admitted as from the depersonalizing effects of the mental hospitals themselves. The atmosphere of the institutions aggravates their condition, and they learn the "sick" role from other inmates around them. A study by Morton Kramer[33] has revealed that once a person has been inside an institution continuously for more than two years, his chances of being released are very small indeed. Those who are released at all are usually released within the

---

[32]Erving Goffman, *Asylums: Essays on the Social Situation of Mental Patients and Other Inmates* (Garden City, N.Y.: Anchor Books, 1961).

[33]Morton Kramer, et al., "A Historical Study of the Disposition of First Admissions to a State Mental Hospital," *Public Health Monographs*, no. 32 (Washington, D.C.: U.S. Government Printing Office, 1955).

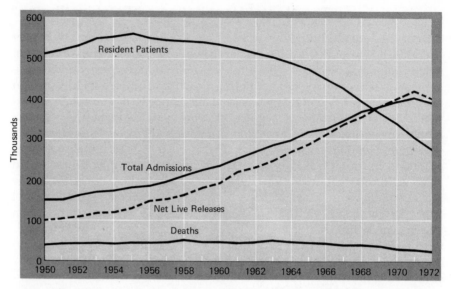

Number of patients in mental hospitals, 1950–1972. The graph illustrates the dramatic increase in the number of admissions to state and county mental hospitals since 1950. While admissions have doubled since 1955, the resident population in the hospitals has been cut in half during the same period. (SOURCE: Executive Office of the President: Office of Management and Budget, *Social Indicators, 1973* [Washington, D.C.: U.S. Government Printing Office, 1973], p. 12.)

first six months. The danger is particularly acute for young schizophrenics. If they are not discharged quickly they are apt to remain in the institutions for very long periods and are more likely to suffer periodic recurrences even if they are released. The problem of the long-term effects of hospitalization is now widely recognized, and in most hospitals every effort is made to release new patients before they suffer a loss of hope and personal responsibility. Since 1955 there has been a steady decline in the number of resident patients, even though the number of admissions has been rising; this is because the newly admitted patients do not stay as long as they commonly used to.

"Pseudopatients" in the Mental Hospital

In 1973 a study of mental hospitals was published which attracted national attention. A California psychiatrist, D. L. Rosenhan, had long been skeptical of the manner in which people were categorized as mentally ill, and he decided to find out what would happen if perfectly sane people attempted to gain admission to mental hospitals. He reasoned that if the imposters were detected, there would be strong evidence that the sane could be distinguished from the insane; but if they were not detected, this would raise serious questions about traditional modes of diagnosis. If the staff were competent and if the patient behaved normally but was still diagnosed as mentally disordered, this finding would reveal a great deal about mental hospitals.[34]

Rosenhan arranged for eight of his associates, none of whom had any previous history of mental disorder, to present themselves at twelve different mental hospitals in five states on the East and West coasts. The hospitals were carefully selected and included some of the most prestigious institutions in the United States. On arriving at the hospitals the pseudopatients told interviewers that they had one symptom: they heard a voice saying a single word (such as "thud," "empty," "hollow"). Apart from giving this information and falsifying their names and vocations, all other statements they made were true. They gave completely accurate life histories.

Without exception, the pseudopatients were diagnosed as schizophrenics and admitted to the mental hospitals. Once inside, they behaved completely normally and no longer claimed to hear voices. In no case was their normality detected by a single staff member—although many of the inmates approached the pseudopatients and accused them of being perfectly sane: they were thought to be journalists or academics "checking up on the place." The pseudopatients were held for an average of nineteen days—the shortest stay was a week and the longest was fifty-two days—and they were released not as cured, but as schizophrenics "in remission." All the behavior of the pseudopatients was interpreted on the basis of their prior diagnosis, rather than the other way around. For example, when a pseudopatient took notes of his experiences, this fact was inscribed in his record as "engages in note-taking behavior" and treated as a pathological symptom—by an attendant who was herself taking notes of the note-taking. Details of the pseudopatients' life histories were evaluated in the light of the false diagnosis and were interpreted as reasons for their subsequent schizophrenic condition. The staff tended to treat the patients as though they were scarcely present. They avoided eye contact and personal conversation:

> A nurse unbuttoned her uniform to adjust her brassiere in the presence of an entire ward of viewing men. One did not have the sense that she was being seductive. Rather, she didn't notice us. A group of staff members might point to a patient in the day room and discuss him animatedly, as if he were not there.[35]

The problem was not that the staff were inefficient or unkind; on the contrary, they usually seemed dedicated and concerned. But the mental hospitals were simply not organized to deal adequately with the problems of the patients:

> Powerlessness was evident everywhere. The patient is deprived of many of his legal rights by dint of his psychiatric commitment. He is

[34]Rosenhan, "On Being Sane in Insane Places."
[35]Ibid., p. 256.

> shorn of credibility by virture of a psychiatric label. His freedom of
> movement is restricted. He cannot initiate contact with the staff, but
> may only respond to such overtures as they make. Personal privacy
> is minimal. Patient quarters and possessions can be entered and
> examined by any staff member, for whatever reason. His personal
> history and anguish is available to any staff member who chooses to
> read his folder, regardless of their therapeutic relationship to him.
> His personal hygiene and waste evacuation are monitored. . . .
> Psychological categorization of mental illness is useless at best and
> downright harmful, misleading and pejorative at worst. . . . How
> many are wrongly thought to be mentally ill? How many have been
> stigmatized by well-intentioned, if erroneous, diagnoses?[36]

Few would deny that mental hospitals have their uses and that in many cases they may offer the most appropriate treatment that is available. But the shortcomings of mental hospitals are also being recognized, and it is accepted that for many patients hospitalization may create problems as well as solve them. Mental hospitals are increasingly being regarded as a last resort, to be used only if all else fails. There is a growing awareness of the civil rights of patients, and the goal is to admit all patients voluntarily if possible; committing agencies have to show why the patient cannot be better dealt with in an ordinary hospital, in an outpatient ward, or under the care of a private psychiatrist. The population of mental hospitals has dropped from a peak of over 559,000 in the mid-fifties to less than 300,000 today.

PROSPECTS FOR THE FUTURE

Mental disorders constitute a complex social problem for which there are no easy solutions. Our existing methods of diagnosis and treatment are being carefully examined, and social policy on mental disorders is now seen to have ramifications beyond the field of medicine and into such areas as politics and civil rights. How are we likely to confront the problem of mental illness in the future?

Improved drug therapy. One significant trend is the increasingly sophisticated use of drugs. Although drugs are sometimes criticized as a "chemical strait jacket" to control the mentally disordered person while the "real" problem is avoided, they have had dramatic effects on the lives of millions of neurotic and psychotic people, and they have greatly eased the burden on the staffs in mental institutions. But drug therapy cannot as yet cure mental disorders, it can simply repress the symptoms and thus make possible the use of other therapies. For example, drugs can be used to relieve depression to the point where the depressive becomes amenable to psychotherapeutic techniques which might

[36]Ibid., pp. 251, 256–257.

cure his condition. Research is proceeding on the pharmacological aspects of mental disorder, with three objectives in mind. First, we need to know exactly how the existing drugs work and why they work on some people but not on others. Second, we need to develop new and more effective drugs—ideally, drugs that will actually cure mental disorders rather than simply alleviate their symptoms. And third, we need to know much more about the chemical functioning of the brain and whether there is in fact a purely chemical basis for all types of mental disorder. If this is the case, then in theory at least we should be able to combat any neurosis or functional psychosis with the appropriate chemical treatment.

The therapeutic community. Another important development is that of the "therapeutic community," an innovation now being widely used in mental hospitals. Under the traditional system, staff could spend very little time in therapy with patients; an hour a day would be considered generous. But if the entire community of the institution is mutually involved in therapy, a more supportive and constructive environment is created. Group therapy is not just an economy measure: it encourages the development of interpersonal relationships by giving patients the opportunity to take an interest in one another, and it helps them to see their own problems more clearly. This development is symptomatic of the general change taking place in the climate of the mental hospitals.

Behavior modification. A technique which is being used with some success in many cases is that of behavior modification, a form of treatment based on the application of fundamental learning principles. The assumption behind the technique is that abnormal behavior, unless it has an organic origin, is learned and can therefore be unlearned. Accordingly, appropriate behavior is rewarded and inappropriate behavior mildly punished. The nature of the rewards and punishments varies from individual to individual but might include the granting or withholding of social approval or small luxuries. There has been some criticism of behavior modification, however, on the grounds that although it may eliminate inappropriate behavior, it does nothing to eliminate the original causes of the mental disorder.

Community mental health centers. Another development, which in the long run could constitute a revolution in our treatment of and attitudes toward mental disorder, is the community mental health center. In the fifties a movement arose to remove as many patients as possible from the state mental hospitals and to treat them in the community from which they came—if possible, without actual hospitalization. The movement won strong support, and in 1963 Congress passed the Community Mental Health Centers Act, establishing a system of matching federal grants with local and state grants to provide for the construction and staffing of these centers. The objective is to offer mental health and so-

Mental Disorders: A Theoretical Review

The social problem of mental disorders represents the gap between a *social ideal* of a society free from socially caused mental disorders, and the *social reality* of a society in which social pressures of various kinds are translated into severe psychological strains and mental disorders in many of its citizens. Mental disorders are a major health problem in the United States, but because the origins of many of these disorders are believed to lie in the social environment, the issue is regarded as an important social problem as well as a medical one.

The *social-disorganization* perspective provides a useful means of looking at the problem of mental disorders. Research has indicated that the incidence of mental disorders is not randomly distributed throughout society: mental disorders are particularly common in certain neighborhoods and among certain social groups and appear to be related to various forms of social disorganization. Mental disorders are more common in disorganized, densely populated, rapidly changing areas—particularly deteriorating urban slums. There is strong evidence that some social groups—primarily among the lower class—are subjected to more personal and psychological stress than others. Moreover, they are less likely to obtain early and adequate treatment. The structure of our society, then, appears to be such that some groups are made particularly vulnerable to mental disorders.

The social-disorganization perspective may also be used to explain the fact that there is a relatively high incidence of mental disorders in American society as a whole. Widespread mental disorder may be regarded as a consequence of the greater degree of social disorganization that characterizes the United States in contrast to the more homogeneous and slowly changing cultures of other parts of the world.

The *value-conflict* perspective is also of use in the analysis of the social problem of mental disorders. There is considerable controversy over the nature, causes, and treatment of mental disorders. Orthodox psychiatrists, for example, often adhere primarily to the medical model for their understanding and treatment of mental disorders, but more radical critics contend that the medical model is to a greater or lesser extent irrelevant, and even harmful in its effects. They feel that a rigid adherence to this model may actually worsen the plight of the disordered and argue that a full understanding and effective treatment of mental disorders must be based on a sociocultural view of the problem. There are also value conflicts between those who believe that the label of mental disorder is sometimes used as an instrument for social control over some political and other nonconformists and those who believe that these nonconformists are genuinely disordered. There are further conflicts over the role of the mental hospitals and over the question of the civil rights of mental patients. There are even value conflicts over the very concept of madness, with a small but growing number of critics taking the position that the concept is a basically unsatisfactory one: indeed, some psychiatrists hold the opinion that the state that we term "mad" is simply a variant form of consciousness and should be regarded and even respected as such.

The *deviance* perspective is especially useful in the analysis of the problem of mental disorders, and most sociological studies of the problem have been conducted within this framework. The mentally disordered person is regarded as one who has deviated from basic social norms relating to the very nature of reality.

Labeling theorists have probably made the greatest contribution to our understanding of mental disorders. They point out that the mentally disordered person in our society is regarded not only as "sick," but also as a deviant. The label of deviance carries with it a stigma, even when the disordered person has been pronounced cured, and people may continue to react to a former mental patient on the basis of a past label. Social reactions may, in fact, make it difficult for the former patient to readjust to society and may serve to encourage the development of further mental disorder.

Some theorists believe that mental disorders are a form of learned behavior that are reinforced by the labeling process. An individual may temporarily violate certain basic norms of behavior by, for example, "taking leave of his senses" during a period of stress. Other people may observe this behavior and label the person as mentally ill. The person may, at an unconscious, involuntary level, accept this definition and continue to behave on that basis. Often, the adoption of the role of a mentally ill person may be useful to an individual who is under stress. Our society excuses the sick person from many normal social responsibilities and obligations, and by adopting this role a person who is in a difficult social situation may find that he or she is able to escape responsibility for his or her actions. Once the label has been applied, however, the role of "mentally ill" is not as easily cast off as it was taken on.

cial services in an integrated fashion, so that a wide range of resources is made available to the troubled individual. The intention is that schools, hospitals, labor organizations, courts, police, welfare agencies, and interested citizens can participate in a variety of programs which emphasize the prevention of mental disorders or their cure through rapid community intervention. It is also hoped that, in addition to providing facilities for the mentally disordered, the centers will offer other services, such as marriage counseling; in this way, the stigma of attending the centers may be diminished. The centers are to be located in "catchment areas" of between 75,000 and 200,000 persons and are required to be "comprehensive," that is, they must offer inpatient care, outpatient care, day hospitalization, twenty-four hour emergency care, and "consultation and education." Over three hundred of these centers are now in operation, and it is hoped that by 1980 there will be a center for every 100,000 members of the population. The centers have encountered numerous initial difficulties, ranging from shortages of funds to involvement in community political issues, but their very flexibility gives them the potential to develop new and effective ways of confronting the problems of mental disorder.

Changing attitudes and values. Yet these new approaches will have relatively little effect unless there are accompanying changes in public attitudes and values. We need to acknowledge how very little we know about mental disorders. We need to recognize that we should not allow old assumptions to stand in the way of progress, nor should we accept too uncritically novel approaches which, however appealing, may lead nowhere. We need to remove the stigma from mental disorder because this stigma makes people reluctant to seek help and, if they have treatment, makes their readjustment to society much more difficult. Finally, we must have the courage to ask what it is about the very structure and nature of our society that gives us such a high incidence of mental disorders compared to other nations. Are we prepared to identify and change those aspects of our society and our relationships with one another that can drive people to that state labeled as madness?

FURTHER READING

Agel, Jerome, ed., *The Radical Therapist*, 1971. An important collection of essays on psychiatric therapies and their social and personal implications. The "radical therapist" is one who works to change the social system, rather than to readapt patients to fit into it once more.

Chesler, Phyllis, *Women and Madness*, 1972. A radical book in which the writer contends that psychiatric diagnosis and practice are influenced by our cultural heritage of sexism. She relates various forms of alleged mental disorder in women to sexual inequality in our society.

Goffman, Erving, *Asylums*, 1961. A sensitive account of life in a mental hospital, written by an acute participant-observer. Goffman suggests that the routines of life in a "total institution," such as a mental hospital, can worsen rather than improve the condition of the inmates.

———, *Stigma*, 1963. Goffman explores the concept of stigma and its meaning for those who are regarded as abnormal by other members of society. He includes several fascinating biographical sketches of stigmatized people.

Laing, R. D., *The Politics of Experience*, 1967. A powerful and often poetic book in which Laing presents his controversial argument that "insanity" is simply another form of consciousness — and that "sane" behavior is in reality dehumanizing and alienating.

Scheff, Thomas J., *Being Mentally Ill: A Sociological Theory*, 1966. Scheff analyzes mental illness in terms of a labeling theory of development and argues that certain people become "boxed in" to a socially defined role as a "sick" person.

Szasz, Thomas, *The Manufacture of Madness*, 1970; *The Myth of Mental Illness*, 1961. Hard-hitting books in which Szasz, a radical critic of contemporary psychiatry, outlines his arguments that mental disorder is not an illness and that the psychiatrist is simply an agent of social control.

16

Sexual Variance

THE NATURE AND SCOPE OF THE PROBLEM

All over America, there are people who perceive variant forms of sexual behavior as a social problem. Public authorities were so disturbed at the amount of pornographic material circulating in the United States in the late sixties that the president established a special national commission to investigate its spread and effects. Cities are constantly embarking on campaigns aimed at eliminating open prostitution in their downtown areas, but after decades of effort they seem no nearer to success. Homosexual or "gay" liberation movements have arisen, demanding that homosexuals be allowed to pursue their life style as a moral right, and their campaigns have excited strong reactions; in some states, for example, governors and state legislatures have threatened to cut off all funds to colleges whose student bodies recognize gay student societies.

The very nature of the problem of sexual variance is changing. For generations it has been taken for granted in America that variant forms of sexual conduct are depraved, engaged in by a small minority of citizens who are in a profound sense abnormal. Recently, however, this traditional view has been vociferously challenged. Many individuals and groups have charged that the problem of sexual variance lies not in the behavior itself but in society's reaction to it. They question whether it is legitimate to penalize individuals for purely private acts which have no identifiable victims or adverse social consequences. While some citizens urge the tightening of the laws against variant sexual conduct in order to preserve the "moral fiber" of the nation, others are calling for the repeal of laws that stigmatize individuals for behavior which, it is alleged, falls within the potential range of normal and harmless human behavior.

In this chapter we will not be concerned with those sexually variant acts that have victims, such as rape or child molestation. Acts of this kind are covered in the chapter on crime, and there is a general social consensus that criminal sanctions should be applied against those who commit them. Nor will we be concerned with forms of sexual variance that are not penalized by law and that affect such a relatively small proportion of the population that they are not usually considered social problems, such as sado-masochism or transsexualism. Instead, we will focus on the three most widespread and visible forms of variance: homosexuality, prostitution, and pornography.

Sexual Behavior in America

American sexual behavior, like other forms of social behavior, is governed by social norms whose content is learned by each individual in the course of the socialization process. The norms relating to sexual behavior are well-known, explicit, and often encoded in law. These norms derive from a particular interpretation of the ancient Judeo-Christian sexual morality, which designates only one form of sexual behavior as morally legitimate: genital heterosexual intercourse, limited to the context of marriage. Deviations from this pattern are considered to be depraved and sometimes sinful, and are often illegal as well.

To a greater extent than any other Western society, the United States has attempted to legislate the sexual morality of its citizens. Traces of the predominant morality are to be found on the statute books of every state in the Union. Adultery, for example, is still a criminal offense in forty-one states. Cohabitation—repeated sexual intercourse between unmarried partners—is illegal in twenty-six states. Fornication—a single act of intercourse between unmarried partners—is illegal in twenty-three states, and carries penalties of up to five years' imprisonment. Oral-genital contacts are prohibited by law in forty-one states, in six of which offenders are liable to up to twenty years' imprisonment. Anal intercourse is against the law in forty-five states, and in nine of these this act carries a sentence of up to twenty years' imprisonment. Prostitution is illegal in every state except Nevada. Homosexual acts were illegal in every state until recently, but several states have repealed or are in the process of repealing these statutes. Many of these laws, of course, have fallen into almost complete disuse, but prosecutions under some of them are still by no means uncommon.[1]

These, then, are the official norms into which most Americans are thoroughly socialized through the family, the school, and other agen-

---

[1]Ian Robertson, "Sex Roles," in *The Study of Society* (Guilford, Conn.: Dushkin Publishing Group, 1974), p. 301.

cies of socialization. These are the norms that most Americans assert they believe in: in a 1966 Gallup poll, for example, 68 percent of Americans expressed the view that premarital sexual relations were "wrong." But actual research into the sexual practices of Americans has demonstrated consistently and conclusively that there is a wide discrepancy between the moral norms specifying how Americans *ought* to behave, and the statistical norms revealing how they *actually* behave. In fact, the great majority of Americans have violated one or more of the traditional sexual norms of our society.

Research into the sex lives of Americans is at best sketchy; like other citizens, social scientists have been affected by the taboos surrounding the subject. The first major study of sexual behavior was published by Alfred C. Kinsey and his associates in the late forties and early fifties, and their work remains the most comprehensive source of data on the topic that we have. When Kinsey published his massive volumes *Sexual Behavior in the Human Male* and *Sexual Behavior in the Human Female*,[2] they evoked an uproar. *The New York Times* refused to carry publisher's advertisements for the books on the grounds that Kinsey's scrupulously scientific works were obscene. The general public was both shocked and fascinated to discover just how varied the sexual lives of Americans really were.

Kinsey found, for example, that nearly 70 percent of American men had frequented prostitutes. One man in six had as much homosexual as heterosexual experience. Some 85 percent of all men had experienced premarital intercourse, and 50 percent of married men had extramarital sexual experience. Kinsey found that 40 to 50 percent of the boys reared on farms had participated in sexual activities with animals. Some 92 percent of men had masturbated, and 59 percent had engaged in heterosexual oral-genital contacts. Of the women, 48 percent had engaged in premarital intercourse and 26 percent in extramarital intercourse. Some 58 percent of women had masturbated, 43 percent had engaged in oral-genital activity, and 28 percent had homosexual experience.

Caution must be exercised in comparing Kinsey's findings with those of later studies, because the various surveys do not all employ the same sampling techniques or ask precisely the same questions. The indications are, however, that there has been a substantial increase in many forms of variant sexual behavior, largely because of the more permissive attitudes adopted by younger Americans in the postwar years. In one recent study, Robert Sorensen found that 44 percent of all males between thirteen and fifteen have had sexual intercourse, with 36 percent of these experiencing their first episode by the age of twelve. By the age of nineteen, some 72 percent of boys and 57 percent of girls have experienced intercourse.[3] It has also been found that half the

[2]Alfred C. Kinsey, et al., *Sexual Behavior in the Human Male* (Philadelphia: W. B. Saunders, 1948); and Kinsey, *Sexual Behavior in the Human Female* (Philadelphia: W. B. Saunders, 1953).
[3]Robert Sorensen, *Adolescent Sexuality in Modern America: Personal Values and Sexual Behavior, Ages 13 to 19* (Cleveland: World Publishing, 1972).

teen-age girls who marry are pregnant at the time of the wedding ceremony.[4] Another study, reported in 1974, found that only a quarter of all men and women in a national sample considered anal intercourse "wrong," and nearly a quarter of married couples under the age of thirty-five have used the technique.[5] Even in conservative "middle America" there are signs of change. The practice of "swinging" – the consensual exchange of marital partners – is practiced by a substantial number of Americans, most of them middle-aged suburban residents. A 1970 study of "swingers" found that they were overwhelmingly antiblack and antihippie, and more than 40 percent of them were Wallace voters.[6]

If so many Americans violate basic norms of sexual behavior, why are some variant forms, such as homosexuality, pornography, and prostitution, more severely stigmatized and penalized than others? The reasons are not clear, but one factor does seem to be of particular importance. In the past, a society has had to ensure a very high birth rate in order to maintain its population, and it has had to maintain a stable family system in order to provide optimally for the care of children. Consequently, any sexual activity that was nonreproductive or incompatible with the family system would have proven highly dysfunctional: if it were sufficiently widespread, the society would collapse. The gratification of sexual desires through homosexuality is nonreproductive. Exclusive gratification through pornography is also nonreproductive, and many people feel that pornography encourages other nonreproductive forms of sexual experience. Extensive gratification through prostitution is largely incompatible with the family system. Another factor is that homosexuals, prostitutes, and pornography are publicly visible – in the first case because homosexuals form their own subculture, and in the latter two cases because prostitution and pornography are evident in the streets of our cities. Other outlets, such as heterosexual oral-genital contact, attract less public notice and social regulation because, although they are nonreproductive in themselves, they are not publicly visible. They can more readily be used as a supplement to marital intercourse; it is only when they are used as a substitute for normal intercourse that these acts are regarded as severely deviant. Although a high rate of reproduction is no longer functional in a world that is heavily overpopulated and in which advances in medicine have severely reduced the infant mortality rate, the old attitudes and values – endorsed for generations by religion and law – have been slow to change. Homosexuality continues to attract the greatest stigma because, unlike prostitution and pornography, it is considered impossible to reconcile with the family system that is so highly valued. Most

[4]Joseph Fletcher, "Ethics and Unmarried Sex: Morals Reexamined," in *The 99th Hour: The Population Crisis in the United States,* ed. Daniel O. Price (Chapel Hill, N.C.: University of North Carolina Press, 1967), pp. 97–112.
[5]Morton Hunt, *Sexual Behavior in the 1970s* (Chicago: Playboy Press, 1974), pp. 32, 204.
[6]Gilbert Bartell, "Group Sex Among the Mid-Americans," *Journal of Sex Research,* vol. 6, no. 2 (May 1970), pp. 113–130.

citizens, of course, are unaware of the original basis for our society's distaste toward these variant forms of sexual behavior, and instead merely internalize the dominant cultural attitude that these acts are perverted, unnatural, sinful, or repellent.

APPROACHING THE PROBLEM

Sociological analysis of sexual variance has traditionally been conducted within the framework of the theoretical perspective of deviance, although more recently some sociologists have sought to analyze the problem from a value-conflict perspective.

In the past, sexual variants have been regarded as innately perverse — the victims of their own genes or unnatural lusts. Sociologists no longer accept that traditional viewpoint, but instead view the sexual variant as someone who has failed to internalize or who for some reason has rejected the dominant social norms governing sexual behavior. One of the most fruitful ways in which sexual variance has been analyzed is through Robert Merton's concept of *anomie*, the term applied to the situation that may arise when there is a discrepancy in society between socially approved goals and the socially approved means for achieving them. In our society, for example, a very high value is placed on sexual experience, but the only approved means for achieving it is within marriage. Individuals who seek the goal of sexual fulfillment but lack the approved means of achieving it may be tempted by other non-approved methods, such as prostitution or the use of pornography. Similarly, the prostitute or seller of pornography may have internalized the social goal of "getting rich quick," but may lack the socially approved means of doing so. Prostitution or the sale of pornography offers a means of earning money — often considerable sums — and some individuals are tempted to enter these occupations even though they are socially disapproved.

Theorists who take a labeling perspective on deviance focus not so much on the sexual variants themselves as on the social process by which some people rather than others are labeled as deviants. Most citizens, they point out, deviate from social norms governing sexual behavior at one time or another. In fact, those who adhere throughout their lives exclusively to the norm of genital, heterosexual monogamy are a very small minority and are, statistically speaking, highly deviant. But they are not considered deviant because the citizens who endorse the dominant norms are those who hold the dominant positions in society and who have the power to label others. Labeling theorists see the various forms of sexual behavior as relative, with the determination of which practices are to be considered "normal" and which "deviant" depending on the social context in which the various behaviors take place. In ancient Greek society, for example, pornography was widespread and accepted; children's drinking vessels were sometimes decorated with portrayals of copulating couples. Homosexuality was highly valued and widely practiced; philosophers such as Plato and Socrates regarded it as nobler than heterosexual love. High-class prostitutes, the *hetaerae,* were highly regarded; they appeared in public with leading statesmen. Behavior that may be deviant in one context, then, may be considered quite normal in another. It is the dominant group in society that specifies one set of norms as appropriate and labels all others as deviant, thereby stigmatizing those who engage in variant acts.

From the value-conflict perspective, the social problem arises because various groups in society have their own interests and values to defend. Some citizens regard sexual variance with abhorrence and hope to restrict or eliminate it; others—including many who indulge in variant practices—regard some forms of sexual variance as legitimate and resent the attempts of one group to impose its own values on others. There are millions of Americans who are homosexual, and millions who visit prostitutes or use pornography, and there may be a fundamental conflict of values between these people and those who adhere to the traditional norms.

The Nature of Human Sexuality

As we have seen, individuals who are socialized in a particular society tend to regard the content of its culture as "natural" and to take its norms for granted. It often comes as something of a shock to find that some form of behavior that seems a part of "human nature" is in fact merely a social product, found in one society but absent in another. In few areas is this perspective so difficult for most people to accept as in that of sexual behavior. To most Americans it seems self-evident that males and females are biologically programed to mate with one another in a specific way. But research has unambiguously demonstrated that this is not the case. We are born with an innate "drive" for sexual expression—but the form it takes is entirely learned.

In the lower animals, mating behavior is instinctive. In many higher primates, however, it is learned. Harry F. Harlow's experiments with rhesus monkeys have revealed that if young monkeys are reared in isolation and prevented from observing adults mating, they are incapable of mating themselves in later years and it is almost impossible to teach them how to do so. The same is true of human beings. Kingsley Davis, a sociologist who has devoted much of his career to the study of marriage and family, observes: "Like other forms of behavior, sexual activity must be learned. Without socialization, human beings would not even know how to copulate."[7] The human sex drive can best be compared to the human hunger drive. Although we all have an innate tendency to feel hungry periodically, we have to learn through the socialization process what we may eat and what we may not eat. Some items

---

[7]Kingsley Davis, "Sexual Behavior," in *Contemporary Social Problems,* eds. Robert K. Merton and Robert Nisbet (New York: Harcourt Brace Jovanovich, 1971), p. 315.

are inedible, as the infant discovers when it bites a chair or a rock. Some are edible but taboo: Zulus learn not to eat fish, Jews learn not to eat pork, Americans learn not to eat snakes, dogs, or roaches. Unlike the inhabitants of some other societies, the well-socialized American who encounters a snake, dog, or roach does not for one moment perceive the creature as potential food—he has what he thinks is an "instinctive" aversion to the idea. The process by which we learn our sexual norms is similar: we start with a basic, undirected drive and learn through the socialization process to recognize some stimuli as being nonsexual, some as sexual, and some as sexual but taboo. The very fact that the human sex drive is so potentially flexible is one reason why every society makes its particular sex norms so explicit and rigid; there might otherwise be a far greater range of variance which would threaten reproduction and the family system.

The potential flexibility of the human sexual impulse is demonstrated by anthropological research on the sexual norms in other societies. These norms often differ radically from our own. Clellan S. Ford and Frank A. Beach conducted a major cross-cultural study of sexual behavior in 190 different societies and concluded:

> Men and women do not develop their individual patterns of sexual behavior simply as a result of biological heredity. Human sexual responses are not instinctive. . . . On the contrary, from the first years of life every child is taught about sex, either directly or indirectly. And most significant is the fact that different societies teach different lessons in this regard. In some cultural settings children learn that sex is a subject to be avoided and that any form of sexual expression during childhood is wrong. In other societies boys and girls are taught that certain sexual activities are permissible whereas others are not. As a result of such divergent experiences in early life, the adult members of different societies have quite different opinions as to what is proper or normal in sexual relations, and what is immoral or unnatural.[8]

Ford and Beach found immense cultural variations in sexual behavior. Most societies, they found, are permissive rather than restrictive in attitudes toward sex; of the 190 societies studied, only 10 wholly disapprove of both extramarital and premarital sexual intercourse. Even the approved position for intercourse varies from culture to culture, and the position considered "normal" in America is deviant or unknown in some other societies. Notions of personal beauty vary considerably: in some societies the eyes and mouth are significant determinants of attractiveness, but in others the shape of the ears is more important. In some societies men are aroused by the sight of female breasts, but in many others the breasts are not considered a sexual feature at all. Kissing is considered an erotic experience in many societies, but among some peoples, such as the Siriono of Micronesia, it is regarded as a

[8]Clellan S. Ford and Frank A. Beach, *Patterns of Sexual Behavior* (New York: Ace Books, 1951), p. 14.

uniquely disgusting act. Prostitution is relatively rare in the societies studied by Ford and Beach, probably because most of them are sexually permissive and other outlets are more readily available. Portrayals that might be considered pornographic in America are common in some other societies; many, for example, display public paintings or sculptures of the human penis as a symbol of fertility.

Attitudes toward homosexual behavior vary widely. In some of the societies in the Ford and Beach sample, homosexuality is punishable by ridicule, beatings, or even death. In 64 percent of the societies, however, homosexuality is regarded as acceptable either for some members of the community or for all members of the community at particular times. In a few societies homosexuals are accorded high social status, and some societies—such as the Lango of Uganda, the Koniag of Alaska, and the Tanala of Madagascar—make provision for a man to take another man as his "wife" along with his female wives. There are several societies—including the Siwans of Africa, the Aranda of Australia, and the Keraki of New Guinea—in which every male is expected to engage in homosexual activities as an exclusive outlet during adolescence. Among the Keraki, for example, the initiation ceremony for adolescents requires them to take the passive role in anal intercourse for a full year; thereafter they take the active role for the remainder of their adolescence until they enter heterosexual marriage. Nearly all cultures, however, institutionalize heterosexuality as the dominant norm even if they also accept homosexuality.[9] There are nonetheless a very small number of predominantly homosexual societies. The Etero people of New Guinea, for example, place a taboo on heterosexual intercourse for 295 days a year, but have considerable difficulty maintaining their population numbers. The neighboring Marindanim people, who are primarily homosexual and who segregate husbands from wives in separate sleeping quarters, have to kidnap children from surrounding tribes in order to maintain their own population.[10]

The evidence, then, points to the extremely flexible and exploratory nature of the human sexual impulse. Every society finds it necessary, in the interests of social cohesion and stability, to institutionalize certain norms to regulate the sexual behavior of its members, but every society is faced to a greater or lesser extent with the variations from those norms that will inevitably occur. Let us look more closely at those variations that are considered a social problem in the United States.

HOMOSEXUALITY

Homosexuality is the most stigmatized of the main forms of sexual variance in America. American attitudes toward male homosexuality are

[9]Ibid., pp. 132–141.
[10]Conrad Phillip Kottak, *Anthropology: Exploration of Human Diversity* (New York: Random House, 1974), pp. 287–288.

Sexual Variance: Value Conflict

New York Council Defeats Homosexual Rights Bill

The homosexual rights bill was defeated by the City Council yesterday, 22 to 19, while supporters in the balcony shouted "bigot" and shook their fists at the Councilmen below.

It was the opposition of the Roman Catholic Archdiocese of New York that most politicians cite as the key factor in the defeat of the measure, which would have banned discrimination in housing, jobs, or public accommodations because of "sexual orientation."

"This is a civil rights issue," argued Councilman Edward L. Sadowsky. "No democracy is safe unless it protects and guards zealously the rights of each minority."

"This is not a civil rights issue," retorted Councilman Angelo J. Arculeo. "It attempts to give legal identity to homosexual orientation and thereby mandate public acceptance."

Councilman Howard Golden quoted the Bible. Homosexuality, he said, "is an abomination." And Councilman Monroe Cohen said, "I cannot accept a homosexual life style for my three children."

Councilman Frederick Samuel said he had been told that support of the bill might mean political suicide. "As a black legislator," he asserted, "I say to you then that I will enter my political graveyard with a deep sense of pride."

But Councilman Archie Spigner, another black, said that he was worried about the effect on children of homosexual school teachers.

"We're there right now!" a man from the balcony shouted. "That might be the reason why my children are doing so poorly!" Mr. Spigner retorted, touching off an uproar that delayed the roll call for a moment or two.

The Reverend Louis Gigante, a Roman Catholic priest, said emotionally: "This bill simply says, 'Give them the right to live.' With all my Christian conscience, my priesthood, and as a human being, I emphatically vote 'yes.' "

The measure's main sponsor, Councilman Carter Burden, said after the vote that he intended to reintroduce the bill today.

SOURCE: Maurice Carroll, "Council Defeats Homosexual Bill by 22-to-19 Vote," *New York Times* (May 24, 1974).

reflected in laws against homosexual conduct that are among the most stringent in the world. Most of the countries of Western Europe permit homosexual acts between consenting adults; in fact, the closest parallel to American legislation in the modern world is found in the countries of the Soviet bloc, which also apply harsh penalties. Our laws probably reflect the attitudes of most citizens; a Harris poll in 1969 showed that over 60 percent of Americans regard homosexuality as "harmful to the American way of life." Lesbianism—female homosexuality—has generally escaped the attention of legislatures both in America and elsewhere in the modern world: lesbian acts are illegal only in Spain, Austria, and the state of Georgia. Lesbianism has also been largely neglected by social scientists, and research on the subject is very limited.

Public attitudes toward homosexuality are currently in a state of considerable flux, largely because of the renewed attention focused on the issue by the militant gay liberation movement that emerged at the end of the sixties. A few decades ago, homosexuals were considered depraved. This attitude was superseded by the view that they were psychologically "sick"—that homosexuality was a form of mental illness. The problem with this formulation, in the view of many social scientists, is that it is difficult to regard as "sick" someone who would be regarded as "healthy" in another society or context: a person with smallpox is indisputably sick wherever he may be, but there are many cultures and many points in history where homosexual behavior would be considered normal and even desirable. For many years, the American Psychiatric Association (APA) listed homosexuality in its official schedule of mental illnesses, but after extensive debates in 1973 all sixty-eight district branches of the APA resolved to remove homosexuality from the list. In a 1974 referendum, American psychiatrists voted by a large majority to eliminate homosexuality from the list of mental illnesses. Instead, the psychiatrists now recognize a "sexual-orientation disturbance"—stemming not from homosexuality itself, but from the societal reactions to it which may cause anxiety in some individuals.

Gay liberation spokesmen, with the backing of increasing numbers of social scientists, contend that homosexuality is simply a different "life style," not a "perversion" or "sickness." These arguments have met with a mixed reaction: some states, such as Illinois and Connecticut, have repealed antihomosexual legislation, and several cities, such as San Francisco and Seattle, have passed homosexual civil rights bills to prevent discrimination against homosexual teachers, police officers, and other city employees. Other states and cities, however, have emphatically rejected proposed reforms. The federal government continues to discriminate against homosexuals; for example, no homosexual is allowed to immigrate to the United States. One reason for the lack of clarity or consistency in public policy is the substantial ignorance about homosexuality that exists in America as the result of generations of treating the phenomenon as literally unmentionable.

Incidence

How common is homosexuality in America? The question is not easily answered—partly because surveys probably underestimate the number of homosexuals as a result of the unwillingness of some respondents to admit to homosexual inclinations, and partly because of the considerable difficulty of defining a "homosexual."

It is popularly supposed that the population falls into two neat categories, homosexual and heterosexual, but in fact most individuals fall on a continuum between the two. How do we categorize an individual who alternates between both forms of sexual behavior? Or someone who has a long heterosexual history but is currently practicing homosexuality? Or a married individual who has homosexual impulses but never expresses them? Or an individual who engages only in homosexual behavior, but fantasizes that his partner is of the opposite sex?

In his massive study of American sexual behavior, Kinsey found that 4 percent of males and about 2 to 3 percent of females were exclusively homosexual throughout their lives. He also found that a further 6 percent of males were primarily homosexual for at least three years between the ages of sixteen and fifty-five. Moreover, some 37 percent of American males and 13 percent of American females had, after adolescence, at least one homosexual experience resulting in orgasm, and 30 percent of all males had been brought to orgasm through oral stimula-

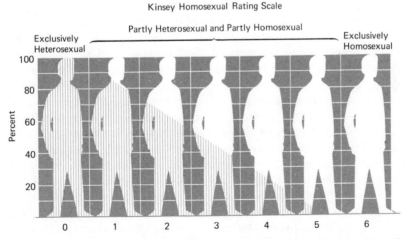

The Kinsey continuum of heterosexuality-homosexuality. Alfred Kinsey's research on human sexual behavior established that homosexuality and heterosexuality are not mutually exclusive categories: elements of both are found in most people in varying degrees. Kinsey's seven-point scale measures this balance, from the one extreme of exclusive heterosexual acts and/or feelings to the other extreme of exclusive homosexual acts and/or feelings. (SOURCE: Adapted from Alfred C. Kinsey, et al., *Sexual Behavior in the Human Male* [Philadelphia: W. B. Saunders, 1948], p. 638.)

tion by a member of their own sex. A further 13 percent of males reacted erotically to other males but had had no homosexual experience. Of those males who were predominantly homosexual, 80 percent had experienced heterosexual intercourse, and 10 percent were married. A more recent study conducted in 1970 found exactly the same figures as those in the Kinsey study of a quarter of a century earlier—4 percent of males were exclusively homosexual throughout their lives, and 37 percent had experienced at least one homosexual act.[11] The 1970 survey used very different sampling procedures, however, and the identical findings may be only coincidental. Kinsey himself was surprised at the high incidence of homosexual experience and rigorously checked his data; but he found the same pattern emerging from group after group in his sample. He rejected the notion that people can be divided into heterosexuals and homosexuals, and instead proposed a seven-point rating scale, with exclusive heterosexuality at one end and exclusive homosexuality at the other. Kinsey concluded:

> The world is not divided into sheep and goats. . . . Only the human mind invents categories and tries to force facts into separated pigeon holes. The living world is a continuum in each and every one of its aspects. The sooner we learn this concerning human sexual behavior the sooner we will reach a sound understanding of the realities of sex.[12]

Myths

Several myths surround the issue of homosexuality in America. One of the most common is that homosexuals suffer from gender confusion: that male homosexuals are typically "effeminate" and female homosexuals typically "masculine." Although a very small number of homosexuals may adopt the mannerisms associated with the public homosexual stereotype, the great majority are indistinguishable in manner and appearance from their heterosexual counterparts; there is no objective evidence that a "feminine" appearance in men is any more common among homosexuals than among heterosexuals, and the same is true of "masculine" women. The myth probably derives from a widespread confusion between homosexuality and transvestism—the wearing of the clothing of the opposite sex. A transvestite is sexually aroused by wearing these clothes, but many otherwise normal heterosexuals who have no homosexual impulses whatever engage in transvestite behavior; again, there is no evidence to suggest that transvestism is any more common among homosexuals than among heterosexuals. And although in our culture male homosexuality is commonly associated with effemi-

---

[11]Robert Athanasiou, Phillip Shaver, and Carol Tavris, "Sex," *Psychology Today*, vol. 4, no. 2 (July 1970), pp. 39–52.
[12]Kinsey, *Sexual Behavior in the Human Male*, p. 639.

nacy, historically it has frequently been associated with aggressive masculinity, as in the case of military commanders like Julius Caesar and Alexander the Great, or militarist groups such as the warrior Spartans and the Japanese Samurai swordsmen.

Another myth is that both male and female homosexuals typically play either an "active" or a "passive" role in their sexual relations. The evidence is, however, that most homosexuals take both roles. A further myth may be that homosexuals are more promiscuous and form less stable unions than heterosexuals. This might be true if the comparison were between the homosexual population in general and married heterosexuals, but there is no research evidence to suggest that it is true if the entire homosexual population is compared with the entire heterosexual population.

Another persistent myth is that homosexuals share a distinct and consistent personality type. In fact they are, like heterosexuals, a heterogeneous group who may have little in common other than their sexual orientation. In one study, Evelyn Hooker matched a selected group of homosexuals with a group of heterosexuals for age, I.Q., and educational attainment. She administered an extensive battery of personality and other psychological tests to both groups. The results of the tests were then evaluated by a panel of experienced clinical psychologists who did not know the sexual orientation of the subjects. The experts were unable to determine which of the subjects were homosexual, nor did the homosexuals score any better or worse than the heterosexuals in general personality adjustment. A wide range of personality types existed in both groups.[13]

Causes

Why do some individuals become predominantly homosexual in the face of powerful social norms specifying heterosexual conduct as the only legitimate expression of sexuality? The problem has vexed social scientists for decades, and no consensus has yet emerged, but several theories have been put forward.

Biological determinism. Some researchers have attempted to find a genetic or physiological basis for homosexuality. The evidence for any such basis is extremely limited, however. Studies of twins have shown that if one twin is homosexual, the chances are significantly greater than average that the other will be homosexual. But since twins are subjected to much more similar learning experiences than are other children, it is at least as likely that their common environment is responsible for their subsequent sexual orientation. Other attempts to find hormonal correlates of homosexuality have been at best inconclu-

[13]Evelyn Hooker, "The Adjustment of the Male Overt Homosexual," *Journal of Projective Techniques,* vol. 21, no. 1 (1957), pp. 18–31.

sive. Most social scientists now reject the biologically determinist view, for it cannot account for the changes in orientation that take place over an individual's lifetime, or the different incidence of homosexuality in different cultures at different times.

Early experiences. Some researchers believe that early childhood or adolescent experience of homosexuality may cause an individual to become predominantly homosexual later in life. This may be the case in some instances, but the problem still remains of explaining why some individuals and not others find the experience so pleasurable that they reject the heterosexual alternative that all the agencies of socialization are insistently urging on them. The great majority of American pre-adolescents and a substantial proportion of adolescents engage in homosexual activity, yet only a small minority of these become adult homosexuals. Others who have not had early homosexual experience also become homosexual later in life. The theory therefore cannot provide a comprehensive account for individual cases of homosexuality in adulthood.

Family environment. Psychoanalytic theorists have concentrated on the early environment of homosexuals and have attempted to isolate factors common to their home backgrounds. The main spokesman for this view is Irving Bieber, whose studies led him to believe that male homosexuals typically had cold, domineering mothers and ineffectual or hostile fathers.[14] Bieber's views have been much criticized, however, on the grounds that his research sample consisted entirely of subjects receiving psychiatric care. The sample was thus unlikely to be any more representative of the general homosexual population than heterosexuals receiving psychiatric care would be of the general heterosexual population. It is quite possible that a study of heterosexuals in psychiatric treatment would reveal a similar or equally disturbed home background — but such a finding could hardly be used to explain their heterosexuality. Other studies have failed to find any consistent differences in the parental background of homosexuals and heterosexuals, and it is clear that many homosexuals have home environments quite unlike those that Bieber described.[15]

Self-definition. A more plausible theory, which is attracting increased attention, is that homosexuals adopt their sexual orientation as a result of an early definition — often unconscious and involuntary — of themselves as homosexual. Some individuals may internalize the social belief that homosexuality and heterosexuality are mutually exclusive categories, but may fail to internalize fully the social prohibition on

[14]Irving Bieber, et al., *Homosexuality: A Psychoanalytic Study* (New York: Basic Books, 1962).
[15]Evelyn Hooker, "Parental Relations and Male Homosexuality in Patient and Nonpatient Samples," *Journal of Consulting and Clinical Psychology*, vol. 33, no. 2 (April 1969), pp. 140–142.

homosexual behavior. Consequently, when they engage in exploratory homosexual acts they may come to think of themselves as homosexuals, become trapped within their own definition, and structure their subsequent experiences in accordance with this view of themselves. If they are labeled as homosexuals by others, this definition of the self is further reinforced. As sociologist Edward Sagarin observes:

> It might be useful to start from a premise . . . that there is no such thing as *a homosexual*, for such a concept is . . . an artificially created entity that has no basis in reality. What exists are people with erotic desires for their own sex, or who engage in sexual activities with same-sex others, or both. The desires constitute feeling, the acts constitute doing, but neither is being. Emotions and actions are fluid and dynamic, learnable and unlearnable, exist to a given extent . . . but are constantly in a state of change, flux, development, and becoming.

> However, people become entrapped in a false consciousness of identifying themselves as *being* homosexuals. They believe that they discover what they are. . . . Learning their "identity," they become involved in it, boxed into their own biographies. . . . There is no road back because they believe there is none. . . .[16]

The Homosexual Community

The stresses on a homosexual in American society can be severe. Unless he or she is prepared to make an overt declaration of sexual preference and accept the adverse social reaction that follows, the homosexual must at all times be on guard against doing or saying anything that would give friends, employer, or others any reason to suspect his or her true sexual orientation. To these stresses may often be added feelings of guilt and shame, the constant embarrassments of leading a double life, and fear of the criminal penalties that could be applied to one's sexual acts.

The homosexual community provides an escape from these pressures and serves to socialize new entrants into the homosexual subculture and its norms and values. Homosexual communities are found primarily in large cities, where attitudes toward sexual variance are usually more tolerant than elsewhere. In most of these cities there are definable homosexual areas, in which whole streets are almost exclusively occupied by homosexuals and in which restaurants, shops, and other amenities cater primarily to homosexual customers. An important element in these communities is the "gay bar." Large cities, such as New York, San Francisco, and Los Angeles, have several hundred such bars. The bars often serve as an environment in which the individual

---

[16]Edward Sagarin, "The Good Guys, the Bad Guys, and the Gay Guys," *Contemporary Sociology*, vol. 2, no. 1 (January 1973), p. 10.

Several churches in the United States are now willing to marry homosexual couples, although these marriages have no force in law. Attitudes toward homosexuality are changing rapidly; nevertheless, a great deal of prejudice still remains. *(Mimi Forsyth/Monkmeyer)*

can accept his or her behavior as natural and as a source of pride. As Evelyn Hooker notes:

> The young man who may have had a few isolated homosexual experiences in adolescence, or indeed none at all, and who is taken to a "gay" bar by a group of friends whose homosexuality is only vaguely suspected or unknown to him, may find the excitement and opportunities for sexual gratification appealing and thus begin active participation in the community life. Very often, the debut, referred to by homosexuals as "coming out," of a person who believes himself to be homosexual but who has struggled against it, will occur in a bar when he, for the first time, identifies himself publicly as a homosexual in the presence of other homosexuals. . . . If he has thought of himself as unique, or has thought of homosexuals as a strange and unusual lot, he may be agreeably astonished to discover a large number of men who are physically attractive, personable, and "masculine"-appearing, so that his hesitancy in identifying himself as a homosexual is greatly reduced. Since he may meet a complete cross-section of occupational and socioeconomic levels at the bar, he becomes convinced that far from being a small minority, the

"gay" population is very extensive indeed. Once he has "come out," that is, identified himself as a homosexual to himself and to some others . . . they assist him in providing justifications for the homosexual way of life as legitimate.[17]

In a study of the "coming out" process, Barry M. Dank found that the gay community served the important function of giving the homosexual an acceptable view of himself and a feeling of normality. One of his subjects, for example, reported:

> I knew that there were homosexuals, queers and whatnot: I had read some books, and I was resigned to the fact that I was a foul, dirty person, but I wasn't actually calling myself a homosexual yet. . . . The time I really caught myself coming out is the time I walked into this bar and saw a whole crowd of groovy, groovy guys. And I said to myself, there was the realization, that not all gay men are dirty old men or idiots, silly queens, but there are some just normal-looking and acting people, as far as I could see. I saw gay society and I said, "Wow, I'm home."[18]

The impact of the gay liberation movement is likely to make the homosexual community and life style more visible in the future. Strong pressures will continue to be exerted to redefine the problem as being not homosexuality, but society's attitude toward it.

PROSTITUTION

Prostitution is the relatively indiscriminate exchange of sexual favors for economic gain. Termed "the world's oldest profession," prostitution is highly resistant to all attempts at elimination. Prostitution is illegal in nearly all American states, although the penalties of the law are usually applied only to the prostitute and not to her client — probably because the clients are much more likely to be respectable citizens of high status and because men, not women, make the laws. To many citizens, prostitution is a social problem simply because it is seen as immoral — it institutionalizes the use of sex for pleasure alone, rather than for expressive or reproductive ends. Other people are concerned by the social problems associated with prostitution — the spread of venereal disease, the existence of organized crime based on prostitution, and the robbery and blackmail to which clients are sometimes subjected. There is considerable debate, however, as to whether prostitution should continue to be illegal. Many people insist that the removal of criminal penalties would tend to legitimize prostitution in the eyes of the public, and so undermine moral standards. Others take the view that prostitution

[17]Evelyn Hooker, "The Homosexual Community," in *Proceedings of the XIV International Congress of Applied Psychology*, vol. 2, *Personality Research* (Copenhagen: Munksgaard, 1962), pp. 52–53.
[18]Barry M. Dank, "Coming Out in the Gay World," *Psychiatry*, 34 (May 1971), p. 187.

will continue to exist whether it is legal or illegal, but that many of the problems surrounding prostitution could be better solved if it was legally permitted but subjected to social regulation. It is also often argued that the state has no business interfering in the private lives of its citizens by making crimes of acts that have no victims.

Forms of Prostitution

Not all exchanges of sexual favors for rewards are considered to be prostitution: because they do not offer their sexual services in a relatively indiscriminate way, the woman who "marries for money" and the permanent "mistress" who is supported by a married man are not considered prostitutes. The true prostitute accepts a number of customers, feels no emotional tie to most or all of them, and uses prostitution as a major or sole source of income. Estimates of the number of prostitutes in the United States range from a quarter of a million to about half a million, but many of them practice their profession only intermittently or on a part-time basis.

Prostitution takes several main forms: the streetwalker, the housegirl, the call girl, and various types of male prostitute.

The streetwalker. The streetwalker has the lowest status and earnings among prostitutes. She solicits clients in public places, such as streets, bars, and the lobbies of cheap hotels, and her fee is often under $20. Some streetwalkers are young novices in the profession, but many others are older women who are no longer able to make a living in the higher-status forms of prostitution. The streetwalker is particularly subject to harassment by the police: uniformed officers may arrest her for loitering, and plainclothes vice officers may entrap her by posing as potential clients.

The housegirl. The housegirl has somewhat higher status. She works and sometimes lives in a brothel, an organized house of prostitution. The brothel is run by a "madam," usually an older retired prostitute who hires the women and supervises their activities. The madam takes a considerable percentage of the housegirl's fees, and quickly fires women who fail to attract clients. The housegirl is usually younger and more attractive than the streetwalker, for she cannot otherwise retain her job. Many brothels are disguised as "massage parlors" or "clubs," but the indications are that the number of brothels in the United States is rapidly declining. Urban "red light" districts containing dozens of brothels are a feature of the past.

The call girl. One reason for the decline of the brothel is the emergence of a new type of prostitute: the call girl, who has the highest status and earnings in the profession. The call girl works from her own room or apartment, is relatively selective in her choice of customers, and usually makes contact with them by telephone. Her clients consist largely of regular visitors who are introduced to her through the private recommendations of others. Many call girls occupy rooms in fashionable hotels and contact prospective clients through members of the hotel staff. Call girls may earn considerable sums; they sometimes charge several hundred dollars for one night's services. In some instances they may find wealthy clients who are prepared to maintain them in separate apartments as mistresses or even to marry them. Many call girls see their profession as a possible avenue to economic security and high social status.

The male prostitute. Male prostitution attracts very little attention in the United States, largely because most statutes against prostitution are directed only at females. Heterosexual male prostitution is very rare; even the "gigolo" usually serves only as a social companion to the wealthy woman who pays him. Homosexual prostitution, however, is common in large cities. The lowest status is accorded to the "hustler," who is usually adolescent and solicits customers on the streets of certain areas of the city. Many if not most of the hustlers consider themselves heterosexual and see their activities as a relatively temporary means of making money.[19] The "bar hustler" is somewhat older and solicits clients in certain gay bars. The "houseboy" works but rarely lives in a male house of prostitution, of which there are several in most large cities. The "call boy" has the highest status and earnings in the profession, and, like the call girl, operates out of his apartment or hotel room for a select group of clients. The call boy may also hope to become a "kept boy," the homosexual equivalent of the mistress maintained by a wealthy man.

Reasons for Prostitution

Why does prostitution exist in our society, and why is it so difficult to eradicate?

From the point of view of the prostitute, the occupation offers the opportunity for earnings far in excess of those available in most other occupations open to women. The successful prostitute can achieve a very substantial income; some are alleged to earn up to $100,000 per year.[20] To some women, the work of the prostitute may seem preferable to that of laboring for long hours as a factory machinist or keypunch operator for much lower rates of pay.

From the point of view of the client, prostitution offers the advantages of sexual variety free from the troublesome obligations of more

[19] Albert J. Reiss, Jr., "The Social Integration of Peers and Queers," *Social Problems,* 9 (Fall 1961), pp. 102–120.
[20] John M. Murtagh and Sarah Harris, *Cast the First Stone* (New York: McGraw-Hill, 1957), p. 2.

Despite endless campaigns to eliminate it, prostitution seems to be here to stay. There is growing a debate about whether the United States should continue to apply criminal sanctions to prostitutes or follow other industrial societies that have legalized its practice. *(Al Kaplan/DPI)*

socially acceptable relationships. For the older or physically handicapped man, prostitution provides perhaps the only opportunity for sexual experience with a young and attractive woman. For the man who is temporarily deprived of his normal sexual outlets — such as the traveler or the sailor — prostitution offers a convenient source of sexual gratification. The norms governing sexual expression in our society make no provision for men in these situations, and prostitution is highly functional in that it provides an alternative outlet for those dissatisfied with their existing opportunities. Kingsley Davis, who seems more concerned with the function of the prostitutes for men than with the effects of this service on the prostitutes themselves, observes:

> Enabling a small number of women to care for the needs of a large number of men, it is the most convenient sexual outlet for armies and for the legions of strangers . . . and physically repulsive in our midst. It performs a role which apparently no other institution fully performs.[21]

[21]Davis, "Sexual Behavior," p. 351.

Davis points out that prostitution could be eliminated only in a society that was totally permissive and in which sexual relations were freely available to all. Such a society would be impossible, he contends, because total permissiveness would be incompatible with the family system; without the family there might be no effective means of socializing children and the society would tend to collapse.

The increasing permissiveness of American society over the past few decades has unquestionably led to a decrease in the number of prostitutes and the number of men who use their services. In his 1948 survey, Kinsey found that 22 percent of college males had visited prostitutes; a 1968 study found that that only 4.2 percent had done so.[22] The decrease is presumably linked to the much greater availability of other sexual outlets to contemporary college males. A national survey in 1974 found a sharp decrease, as compared to Kinsey's figures, in the number of males who had experienced premarital intercourse with prostitutes and in the frequency with which they had such experiences.[23] The number of prostitutes also appears to be declining; a 1945 estimate put the total number of prostitutes at 1,200,000, more than twice as many as the current maximum estimates.[24]

Prostitution as a Profession

The limited studies that have been conducted on prostitution indicate that most of the women come from lower-class or lower-middle-class home backgrounds; they often have histories of considerable promiscuity in adolescence. One study of fifteen streetwalkers concluded that they were alienated from their parents and particularly their fathers.[25] Another study found that prostitutes tended to have histories of family instability, usually involving an alcoholic, violent, or absentee parent; more than half of the prostitutes had spent at least one year of their childhood in foster homes.[26] Another study of twenty-four call girls, all of them earning very high incomes, found that every one of them had suffered emotional deprivation in childhood; bonds of affection and love seemed to have been lacking in all their families.[27] The indications are that most prostitutes have disturbed backgrounds and relatively low self-esteem; indeed, it would be difficult to reconcile so stigmatized a profession as prostitution with high self-esteem.

[22]Vance Packard, *The Sexual Wilderness* (New York: McKay, 1968), p. 509.

[23]Hunt, *Sexual Behavior in the 1970s,* p. 144.

[24]"Vice, Regulation of," *The Encyclopedia Americana*, vol. 28 (New York: Americana Corp., 1945), p. 58.

[25]Norman R. Jackman, Richard O'Toole, and Gilbert Geis, "The Self-Image of the Prostitute," *The Sociological Quarterly*, 4 (April 1963), pp. 150–161.

[26]Nanette J. Davis, "The Prostitute: Developing a Deviant Identity," in *Studies in the Sociology of Sex*, ed. James M. Henslin (New York: Appleton-Century-Crofts, 1971), pp. 297–322.

[27]Harold Greenwald, *The Call Girl* (New York: Ballantine Books, 1958).

Clash of Life Styles

Open conflict breaks out on 49th Street. A busload of matrons from the suburbs is parked in front of the Eugene O'Neill Theater. The matinee is over and they are bored and hot. Across the street, in front of the Raymona Hotel, stands a lithe young prostitute. The bus driver swaggers over. . . .

"How much?"

"Twenty and ten."

"Twenty and ten!" (The ten is always for the room.)

It is Marsha from Minneapolis, the veteran street girl. . . . Marsha of the white elephant earrings and quick Polish temper.

The driver climbs back into the bus and the matrons are all agog. "How much?" "What does she charge?" They flutter to the windows gawking, giggling, pointing, transported by the raw street tawdriness of it all. One stout old dreadnought calls out: "Is that all you charge, *thirty dollars*?"

The most sensitive issue for a prostitute is respect. Now here was a busload of married women, natural poison to a prostitute, who had jarred a hooker's precarious sense of self-respect. When Marsha rocketed up the steps of their bus, I knew she was about to shove every word down their throats.

Prostitutes do, however, regard themselves as performing a valuable service. One prostitute comments:

We get 'em all. The kids who are studying to be doctors and lawyers and things, and men whose wives hate the thought of sex. And men whose wives are sick or have left them. What are such men going to do? Pick on married women . . . or run around after underage girls? They're better off with us. That's what we're for.[28]

Prostitutes also rationalize their own position by pointing to the immorality and hypocrisy of society at large. They may contend, for example, that the woman who marries an older man for money is not morally superior to a prostitute—and neither is the prostitute's "respectable" client. The prostitute can derive some self-esteem from the certainty that she is not a hypocrite; as one prostitute remarks:

We come into continual contact with upright, respected citizens whose voices are loudly raised against us in public, yet who visit us

[28]Quoted in John Gosling and Douglas Warner, *City of Vice* (New York: Hillman Books, 1961), p. 82.

"Listen, you got a lot of nerve to sit on this bus and mock me, when I got enough nerve to stand out here day and night to sell my body for money. Remember this about the thirty dollars I get. It comes out of your husband's paycheck once a week! And if it ain't in my pocket, it's in the next girl's pocket!" Aghast, the matrons fall back on platitudes about the evils of selling one's flesh.

"Honey, I'd rather sell it than lay up in the bed every day and worry about my bills being paid because my husband's taking thirty dollars out to pay a pross (prostitute). I know where my money's coming from. You don't!"

Whipped and beaten, the matrons drop weakly into their seats. But Marsha was like a dog with a slipper. Now she is up and down the aisle lecturing about the prostitute's social contribution, the plight of the American husband, the lack of class evidenced by the matrons' clothes. And one final blow:

"If you had any sense, you'd have done what I'm doing in your younger age. Right now your husbands might not be working some dumb job. They'd be laying up on your money, retired!"

SOURCE: Gail Sheehy, "The Landlords of Hell's Bedroom," *New York Magazine* (November 20, 1972).

in private. . . . If they are afraid at all . . . their fear is not that they are sinning against the laws of God or decency, or even so much that they may pass on to their wives and families whatever disease we may be suffering from . . . but rather that they will somehow be discovered consorting with us and lose thereby the respect of their fellows.[29]

Despite the stigma against their profession, there seems to be a reasonable degree of job satisfaction among prostitutes; a study by Wardell B. Pomeroy found that two-thirds of them expressed no regrets about their choice of occupation, although only one-fifth would advise others to enter it.[30]

Entry into prostitution typically appears to involve a slow transition rather than an abrupt decision. Most prostitutes drift into the profession, usually through contact with another prostitute who teaches them

[29]Quoted in Travis Hirschi, "The Professional Prostitute," *Berkeley Journal of Sociology*, vol. 7, no. 1 (Spring 1962), p. 45.
[30]Wardell Pomeroy, "Some Aspects of Prostitution," *Journal of Sex Research*, 1 (December 1965), pp. 177–187.

professional techniques — how to solicit in public, how to handle difficult customers, how to recognize plainclothesmen, and the like.[31] Others, however, are recruited by pimps. A pimp is a male who lives off the earning of one or more prostitutes, and a very high proportion of streetwalkers and call girls work for them. The prostitute may take pride in providing well for her pimp, whose ostentatious life style provides evidence of her own professional success. The pimp finds clients for the prostitute, arranges meetings, safeguards the prostitute against assault by customers, pays bail when she is arrested, and generally acts as her business manager. A successful pimp may "own" an entire "string," or "stable," of several prostitutes and may enjoy considerable affluence as a result of their efforts.

A good deal of prostitution, particularly that involving brothels, is under the control of organized crime. Criminal syndicates have the resources to pay off police and city authorities to ensure that the brothels do not receive undue attention from the vice officers; instead, the common streetwalker bears the brunt of official attention.

PORNOGRAPHY

Pornography — written or pictorial material designed to cause sexual excitement — is as old as civilization. There is general agreement that the amount of pornography circulating in the United States is increasing, and there have been many fears about its effect on American society in general and on young people in particular. Again, however, opinion is divided. As James McCary observes:

> The attitude of American men and women to pornography is varied indeed. Many consider it informative or entertaining; others believe that it leads to rape or moral breakdown, or that it improves the sexual relationship of married couples, or that it leads to innovation in a couple's coital techniques, or that it eventually becomes only boring, or that it causes men to lose respect for women, or that it serves to satisfy normal curiosity. More people than not report that the effects on themselves of erotica have been beneficial. Among those who feel that pornography has detrimental effects, the tendency is to see those bad effects as harming others — but not one's self or personal acquaintances.[32]

To many citizens, pornography is disgusting and fundamentally corrupting; they feel it presents a shameless and degrading view of human beings, contributes to the spread of sexual variance, and stimulates sex crimes. Others take the view that pornography is harmless, even if it is

---

[31] James H. Bryan, "Apprenticeship in Prostitution," *Social Problems*, 12 (Winter 1965), pp. 278–297.
[32] James Leslie McCary, *Human Sexuality*, 2d ed. (New York: Van Nostrand Reinhold, 1973), pp. 379–380.

Erotic displays are a commonplace feature of the downtown areas of all large cities. Many citizens consider these advertisements deeply offensive, while others eagerly patronize the establishments that display them. *(Ruth Block/Monkmeyer)*

distasteful, that it appeals only to people who are already predisposed to use it, and that it may reduce the number of sex crimes by serving as a substitute for criminal acts rather than as a stimulus to commit them.

The Problem of Censorship

The issue is further complicated by the question of censorship. Some Americans believe that the public must be protected from pornographic material, but others—including many who find the material offensive—are reluctant to accept censorship. They object that censorship deprives citizens of the right to make up their own minds, and thereby interferes with their personal liberty; moreover, censorship is easily abused. History is littered with attempts at censorship that seem ridiculous today: such works as *Huckleberry Finn, Alice in Wonderland, Robinson Crusoe, On the Origin of Species,* and even the Bible have run afoul of censors in the past, as have many paintings and sculptures by great artists. Pornography is very much in the eye of the beholder: to most Americans, William Shakespeare is a literary genius, but in some

American communities plays by Shakespeare have been banned from use in schools on the grounds that they are obscene. Any system of censorship lends itself to the imposition on the many of the prejudices of the few.

The courts in the United States have held that pornographic material is not protected by the First Amendment, which guarantees freedom of speech and expression. The courts have been confronted, however, with the problem of defining pornography. The guidelines laid down by the Supreme Court specify that material can be considered pornographic if "to the average person, applying contemporary community standards, the dominant theme of the material taken as a whole appeals to prurient interests . . . [and is] utterly without redeeming social importance." The difficulty of interpreting what the "contemporary community standards" actually are has been a severe one. In 1964 the Supreme Court ruled that "community standards" referred to national standards—a decision much resented by conservative local communities that did not share the more permissive attitudes of the nation as a whole. In 1973, however, the Court changed its decision, and ruled that local community standards would apply—a decision resented this time by those Americans who fear that genuine works of art may now be repressed in what they regard as the cultural backwaters of the nation. The way is now open for local communities to exercise much more censorship than they could in the past.

Findings of the Commission on Pornography

In 1967 Congress determined that the amount of pornography circulating in the United States was "a matter of national concern." The president appointed a National Commission on Obscenity and Pornography, consisting of nineteen experts on the subject. The commission investigated the problem for two years, and finally issued its report in 1970. Congress and most Americans expected that the report would recommend more stringent controls over pornography. Instead, the commission urged the relaxation of the laws; the only restrictions the commission recommended were those designed to prevent children from gaining access to pornographic material.[33]

The commission's report provided a great deal of evidence about pornography in the United States. More than 85 percent of adult men and 70 percent of adult women have been exposed to pornographic material, although only 3 percent have received it unsolicited through the mail. The main source of exposure is through people who show it to their friends. About 75 percent of those who have been exposed to pornography had their first exposure before the age of twenty-one. In general, the likelihood of exposure is greater for men than for women,

[33]*Report of the President's Commission on Obscenity and Pornography* (New York: Bantam Books, 1970).

for the young rather than for the old, and for the well-educated rather than the poorly educated. Young adults, the commission found, rarely patronize the bookstores that sell pornography; the typical customers are male, white, middle-class, middle-aged, and married. Between a fifth and a quarter of the adult male population has regular experience with pornographic material.

The commission found that a small majority of police chiefs believe that pornography plays a significant role in juvenile delinquency. On the other hand, a large majority of psychologists, psychiatrists, sex educators, and social workers believe that the materials are not harmful to either adolescents or others. The commission itself took the latter view:

> Research indicates that erotic materials do not contribute to the development of character defects, nor operate as a significant factor in antisocial behavior or in crime. In sum, there is no evidence that exposure to pornography operates as a cause of misconduct in either youths or adults.[34]

The commission also found, to the surprise of many, that "there is no evidence to suggest that exposure of youngsters to pornography has a detrimental impact upon moral character, sexual orientation, or attitudes."[35] The commission nonetheless recommended retention of legislation preventing the sale or distribution of pornographic materials to minors. This recommendation is perhaps inconsistent, but probably reflects the commission's awareness that American public opinion strongly favors retention of these laws. Whatever the findings of social science research, many people feel that their "common sense" is a better guide to action, and their intuition tells them, rightly or wrongly, that pornography is a corrupting influence. This attitude was adopted by President Nixon, who simply rejected out of hand the commission's entire report and conclusions. In fact, Nixon announced before the commission made its report, and before he had seen any of the evidence, that he would not accept any conclusion that favored relaxation of the law.

Pornography and Crime

One of the most serious worries about pornography is that it may encourage some individuals to commit sex crimes. Most psychologists take the opposite view, and contend that the use of pornography may actually provide sexual gratification to these individuals and so lessen the chances of their committing offenses against others. The president's commission took this view, largely on the basis of the existing research on the correlation between crime and the use of pornography. A sur-

[34]Ibid.
[35]Ibid.

vey of the major studies in this field shows that in most cases convicted sex offenders had significantly less exposure to pornography, and had been exposed to it at a much later age, than control groups of non-offenders.[36]

The experience of Denmark provides a further interesting insight into the relationship between sex crimes and the availability of pornography. In 1967 the Danes liberalized their laws on pornography. Within two years the number of reported sex crimes dropped by 40 percent. In 1969, largely as a result of this finding, the Danes abolished all remaining laws restricting the sale and distribution of pornography. Within a year there was a further 31 percent drop in the number of reported sex crimes: rape decreased by a small margin, but exhibitionism and child-molestation rates fell by very large margins.[37]

Whatever the findings of social science research, there is still a great deal of public concern about pornography. But it is becoming increasingly apparent that, as McCary notes, the chief objection to pornographic materials "must lie in their literary, theatrical or pictorial worthlessness, rather than their power to corrupt."[38]

PROSPECTS FOR THE FUTURE

Sexual variance is a permanent feature of the American scene; whether it will remain a social problem will depend very much on the attitudes and values of Americans in the years ahead. If Americans continue to regard variance from the traditional norms as a problem, and continue to treat variants in ways that make the lives of the variants problematic, the social problem will remain. If Americans become more tolerant of sexual variance, the laws regulating variant behaviors will tend to be repealed or to fall into disuse, and the issue may no longer be considered a serious social problem. In much the same way, the increasing tolerance of premarital sexual intercourse has made the issue seem much less of a problem than it did a few decades ago. But as long as our society continues to regard heterosexual monogamy as the ideal context for sexual behavior, other forms will continue to attract some measure of stigma and those who practice them will experience some personal difficulties in consequence.

Of the three main forms of variance discussed in this chapter, the most rapid and extensive changes are likely to take place in the attitudes toward the social status of the many million homosexuals in America. The gay liberation movement is presently encountering the same kind of opposition that the civil rights and women's liberation

---

[36]W. Cody Wilson, "Facts Versus Fears: Why Should We Worry About Pornography?" *Annals of the American Academy of Political and Social Science,* 397 (September 1971), pp. 105–117.
[37]Ibid.
[38]McCary, *Human Sexuality,* p. 387.

movements initially experienced, but there can be little doubt that legal restraints on homosexual behavior will be reduced and eliminated in the future. Many states are currently in the process of repealing their antihomosexuality legislation, and courts are striking down discriminatory regulations against homosexuals. Public attitudes and values will change more slowly, but as the climate becomes more tolerant and larger numbers of homosexuals declare themselves to friends, relatives, and employers, it will be increasingly difficult to discriminate against them. Changes in values and attitudes will be facilitated by the public availability, for the first time, of nonantagonistic and objective information about homosexuality; it is easy to forget that it is only a quarter of a century since no American newspaper would dare put the word "homosexual" in print.

The increasing permissiveness of American society is likely to lead to further decreases in the number of prostitutes and the number of men who utilize their services. There is no prospect of prostitution disappearing, however, because there will always be those who cannot conveniently find the gratification they seek in any other way, and there will always be those willing to provide the service for financial reward. It is likely that public policy will continue along its present lines for some time — with authorities ignoring the problem for the most part, but periodically conducting symbolic attempts to "clean up" prostitution. But there are likely to be some pressures to legalize prostitution. Nevada, like most Western European countries, has already taken this step, and now formally regulates the operations of the brothels in the state. The prostitutes are given regular medical checks against venereal disease, and the state reaps a large tax profit from the profession — a profit that formerly went to organized crime. An alternative method of decriminalizing prostitution was introduced in Britain in the sixties. Under British law, prostitution is not illegal, but it is illegal to solicit for the purposes of prostitution, and it is illegal for other parties — such as pimps — to live off the proceeds of prostitution. This law has the virtue of not interfering in the private affairs of citizens while at the same time seeking to prevent the public nuisance of open solicitation on the streets.

The great volume of pornography in the contemporary United States clearly meets a public demand, and that demand will not subside simply because action is taken against pornography. The civil libertarian tradition in the United States probably runs too deep for any major efforts to censor the reading and pictorial diets of Americans to be successful. The Supreme Court ruling that local community standards should apply in determining whether any material is pornographic or not is likely to lead to an increase in the amount of banned material and an increase in the number of court cases aimed at overturning the bans. Legislation in the future may be directed against unsolicited mailings or sidewalk displays that expose citizens to pornography

Sexual Variance: A Theoretical Review

The social problem of sexual variance represents the gap between a *social ideal* of a society in which there would be little or no disapproved sexual conduct, and the *social reality* of a society in which there are many stigmatized forms of sexual variance. It should be remembered, however, that the norms of sexual conduct in the United States are moral norms only; the statistical norms indicate that the great majority of Americans depart from the moral norms at some time in their lives. This does not necessarily imply hypocrisy, as people may feel deep guilt at departing from the moral norms and may want themselves and others to adhere to these norms in the future.

The *social-disorganization* perspective is of some use in the analysis of problems of sexual variance. Some sociologists consider that society is disorganized to the extent that the socialization process fails to ensure conformity to the prevalent norms, so that confused standards of conduct result. Many theorists also believe that sexual variance may actually contribute to social disorganization by undermining the family system and encouraging nonreproductive sexual activities, but this argument has lost some of its force in a world in which high birth rates are becoming severely dysfunctional.

The *value-conflict* perspective is being increasingly applied to the problem of sexual variance. It has often been assumed in the past that variant forms of sexual behavior are self-evidently immoral and abhorrent, but this traditional view is now being challenged. Many people believe that the social problem of sexual variance lies not in the variant behavior itself, but in society's attitude toward it, which creates severe personal and psychological problems for millions of our citizens. Many people are now questioning whether society really has the right to inferfere in the private lives of millions of citizens whose acts have no victims or identifiable adverse social consequences. Instead, they urge tolerance of variant forms of sexual behavior. There is clearly scope for considerable value conflict between those who believe that sexual variance is immoral, contagious, and damaging to society, and those—including many who engage in variant acts—who believe that sexual variance is not a moral issue and that people should mind their own business.

The *deviance* perspective has traditionally provided the framework for the analysis of the social problem of sexual variance. From this perspective, the sexual variant is seen as someone who has failed to internalize or who has rejected the dominant social norms governing sexual conduct in our society.

Many sociologists who believe that deviance is often caused by a state of anomie contend that sexual variance stems from the inability of some individuals to achieve valued social goals by socially approved methods. Our society places a very high value on sexual activity; the media, for example, extol the pleasures to be derived from sexual experience. But the official norms of our society sanction only one form of sexual experience: genital, heterosexual activity between married partners. Those individuals who do not have access to this means but who still desire the goal are therefore likely to seek other, socially disapproved means of sexual fulfillment, such as visiting a prostitute or using pornography. In the same way the prostitute or the seller of pornography may be a person who has internalized the valued social goal of getting rich quick, but who lacks an approved means of achieving this goal. An occupation such as prostitution or the selling of pornography offers an alternative means of achieving the social goal, even though the means is socially disapproved.

Theorists who regard deviance as the product of a labeling process, rather than as a characteristic of the deviants themselves, focus on the way in which some groups define others as deviant. They point out that the flexible nature of human sexuality is such that we are all capable of a very wide range of potential variance; every community, however, institutionalizes only a limited range of behavior and labels all others as deviant. But different communities institutionalize different ranges of conduct as "normal," and the determination of what is "normal" and what is "deviant" behavior therefore depends very much on who is making the definition. The dominant group in our society is committed to a particular view of what constitutes normal sexual behavior, and labels all other forms as deviant and undesirable. The deviant is therefore simply someone who has been defined as such. Many sociologists contend that the labeling process may box some individuals into a deviant career. Most Americans engage in an exploratory way in sexually variant acts at some time in their lives, usually in childhood or adolescence. If this behavior is discovered by others and the individual is labeled as a deviant, he or she may come to accept this definition, consider himself or herself deviant, and proceed to act on that basis in the future.

against their will, but there is also likely to be a relaxation of controls over the more private transactions of adults who wish to publish, sell, buy, and use pornography.

Social scientists themselves are likely to devote much more attention in the future to sex research, and colleges will offer more courses in human sexuality. The old taboos have long kept most citizens in a state of considerable ignorance about human sexual behavior, but the climate is now such that social science research can more fully illuminate this significant area of social and personal life and the problems that go with it.

FURTHER READING

Clor, Harry M., *Obscenity and Public Morality: Censorship in a Liberal Society,* 1969. A sophisticated discussion of the problem of censorship in a democratic society. Clor argues in favor of a very limited censorship.

Ford, Clellan S. and Frank A. Beach, *Patterns of Sexual Behavior,* 1951. A classic on sexual behavior by an anthropologist and a psychologist. The book is objective and easily readable and covers a tremendous range of anthropological, psychological, and even biological theory.

Gagnon, John and William Simon, eds., *Sexual Deviance,* 1967. The book covers several topics, including prostitution and male and female homosexuality. The writers suggest that, given the appropriate circumstances, we might all be sexual deviates.

Karlen, Arno, *Sexuality and Homosexuality: A New View,* 1971. A massive and well-researched volume, covering the historical, social, and psychological aspects of homosexuality.

Kinsey, Alfred C., et al., *Sexual Behavior in the Human Female,* 1953; *Sexual Behavior in the Human Male,* 1948. Classic studies of the sexual behavior of Americans that cover almost every aspect of the topic and include a wealth of statistical detail. Kinsey's work is still the most comprehensive research on the subject.

McCary, James L., *Human Sexuality,* 2d ed., 1973. A factual, well-written college textbook that covers most aspects of normal and variant sexual behavior.

Report of the President's Commission on Obscenity and Pornography, 1970. A comprehensive report on the problem of pornography by a group of experts from many different fields. The report includes summaries of social science research findings on the subject and concludes that there is no evidence that pornography has harmful effects on adults or even on children.

Schofield, Michael, *Sociological Aspects of Homosexuality,* 1966. An excellent sociological study of homosexuality; incorporates a good deal of social science research findings.

Storr, Anthony C., *Sexual Deviation,* 1964. A brief and readable book about problematic sexual behavior that includes chapters on most forms of sexual variance.

Winek, Charles and Paul M. Kinsie, *Lively Commerce: Prostitution in the United States,* 1971. A useful sociological analysis of prostitution. The book includes both historical material and contemporary information based on over 2,000 interviews.

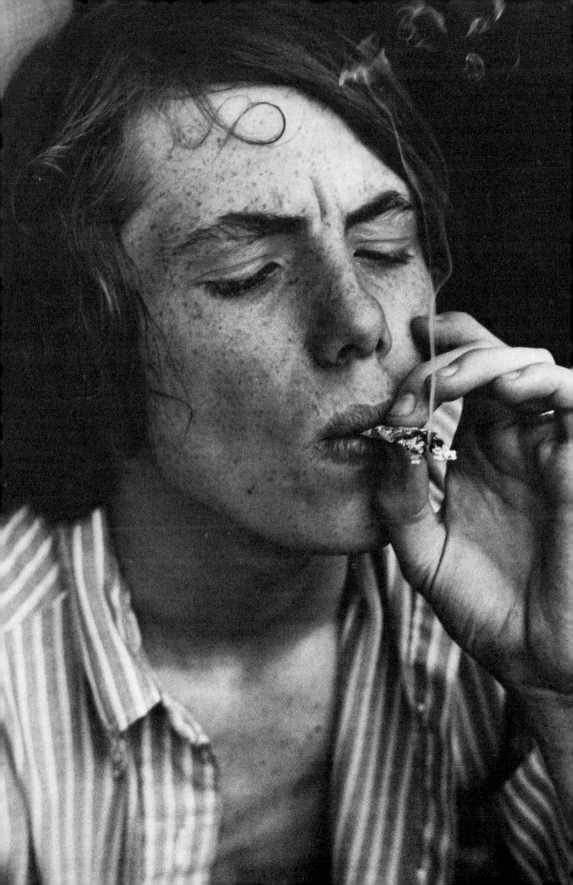

17

Drugs

THE NATURE AND SCOPE OF THE PROBLEM

The very word "drug" excites strong emotions in America. Although the United States has always been a drug-taking society, drug abuse is currently regarded as one of the most challenging social problems facing the nation. Opinion polls in the late sixties and early seventies have shown that the "drug problem" is perceived by most Americans as a major threat to our society, and particularly to its younger members.

What exactly is a drug? The term refers to any chemical that is psychoactive, or capable of modifying a person's behavior through its effect on emotions, thinking, or consciousness. Strictly speaking, many familiar substances such as aspirin or tea are drugs, but most Americans think only of outlawed substances such as heroin or LSD as drugs. A characteristic of many psychoactive chemicals is that they lead to *dependence*—the user develops a recurrent craving for them. Dependence may be psychological, physical, or both. In the first case, the user feels psychologically discomforted if supply of the drug is cut off, but in the case of physical dependence or *addiction*, severe bodily withdrawal symptoms may occur, taking many forms and ranging in severity from slight trembling to fatal convulsions. Users develop a *tolerance* for some drugs: that is, they have to take steadily increasing amounts to achieve the same effect.

Drug use is almost universal in human societies. The only peoples who do not use drugs belong to religious communities which prohibit the substances or to groups such as the Eskimo who live in places where the terrain is so bleak and barren that no drug-yielding plants can be cultivated. Because the use of a drug may have socially undesirable effects—through incapacitating the users, for example—each society regulates drug usage by social norms and often by law as well.

Every society regards some drug-taking as normal, but the content of norms varies a great deal from one society to another. Each society specifies which drugs are acceptable, who may legitimately consume them, and the circumstances under which drug use is appropriate. Failure to conform to these norms constitutes drug abuse in the society in question, although it may not be so regarded in another society or in the same society at a different time. In many parts of North Africa, for example, marijuana is acceptable, but alcohol is not. In India, opium is freely available in street bazaars, but alcohol consumption is prohibited by the constitution. In many parts of the world the use of cocaine carries severe penalties, but in parts of the Andes Mountains its use is nearly universal. No reliable global estimate of the number of marijuana smokers is currently available, but a United Nations survey in the fifties estimated that there were more than 200 million users in different parts of the world. In the modern industrialized states, alcohol, tobacco, and caffeine are the most commonly consumed drugs, and the use of synthetic chemicals, such as stimulants and sedatives, is also widespread.

The sociologist is interested in why some people abuse drugs, why they choose the drugs they do, and why particular societies permit some drugs but proscribe others—especially when the relevant norms or laws often bear little relationship to the actual hazards involved in the use of the various drugs themselves. The societal reaction to various forms of drug use is also of interest to the sociologist because it serves to define the role and status of the drug-taker.

The United States as a Drug-Taking Society

When the Pilgrims set sail for the New World, they took with them 14 tons of water—plus 42 tons of beer and 10,000 gallons of wine. The use and abuse of drugs in America has continued unabated ever since, although the issue has only been considered a serious problem at intermittent points in our history.

Widespread narcotics addiction was a feature of American society from the middle of the nineteenth century to the first decade of the twentieth. After the Civil War tens of thousands of men who had been treated with narcotics in order to relieve the pain of their wounds were left addicted to morphine. The narcotics addiction rate increased steadily until the turn of the present century, when about 1 percent of the population was addicted—a much higher rate than at any time since. One reason for this high rate of addiction was the general availability of opiates, such as heroin and morphine, for medical purposes. Grocery stores, pharmacies, and even mail-order houses did a flourishing sale in opiates, which were used to combat minor ailments, such as stomach pain, and to ease the distress of infants during teething.

The chewing of tobacco was common in the United States during early colonial times, but after 1870, when the drug was first widely smoked instead of chewed, the use of tobacco came to be regarded by many people as a social problem. It was variously claimed that smoking led to impotence, sexual deviance, and insanity, and that it was a "stepping stone" to the use of alcohol. The sale of tobacco was banned in fourteen states in the early part of the present century, but the ban proved ineffective and the laws were repealed after World War I. Now that we realize the serious hazards that it poses to the health of smokers, the use of tobacco is once more regarded as a social problem.

The smoking of marijuana has a long history in the United States. There were no laws prohibiting its use until this century, and marijuana was commonly smoked by artists and writers in the urban centers of the mid-nineteenth century. The drug became illegal only in the earlier part of the twentieth century when its use became associated in the public mind with unruly behavior among blacks and Mexican Americans; laws prohibiting the drug were quickly passed in some Southern and Southwestern states. The federal government did not act against marijuana until 1937, when a vigorous campaign against the drug was launched by Harry J. Anslinger, then head of the Federal Bureau of Narcotics. Marijuana had attracted little national attention up to that time, but Anslinger claimed that the drug was the "assassin of youth" and put forward a new version of the "stepping stone" theory. "The danger is this: over 50 percent of these young addicts started on marijuana. They started there and graduated to heroin; they took the needle when the thrill of marijuana was gone." The mass media took up the issue and printed many stories of "marijuana atrocities" — and so the stereotype of the crazed "drug fiend" was born. There is some evidence that Anslinger's sudden campaign against marijuana was motivated by the fact that his bureau's budget had been cut by 25 percent in the preceding four years; by finding a new drug issue he was able to ensure that fresh funds flowed to the bureau and that its continued existence as a major federal agency was assured.[1] As a result of this campaign, Congress enacted legislation against marijuana without any attempt whatever to form an objective opinion about its effects or addictive potential.

Within a few years after the Pilgrims landed, the governor of Massachusetts was complaining in his diaries of excessive drunkenness in the town of Plymouth. Since that time the abuse of alcohol has been recognized as a serious problem in this country. A strong temperance movement appeared in the early part of the nineteenth century, and after the middle of the last century a number of states began to pass legislation against alcoholic beverages; by the start of World War I about half the population lived in "dry" areas. In 1919 national prohibition was introduced when the Eighteenth Amendment to the Constitution was passed and ratified by every state except Rhode Island and Connecticut. Americans lived under Prohibition until 1933, when the amend-

[1]Donald Dickson, "Bureaucracy and Morality: An Organizational Perspective on a Moral Crusade," *Social Problems*, vol. 16, no. 2 (Fall 1968), pp. 146–156.

ment was repealed by a resounding majority. The experiment at Prohibition was a total failure; it did nothing to reduce alcohol consumption but it did help to create a vast network of organized crime—a system of criminal syndicates that have since moved into other fields and become so powerful that they now seem an ineradicable feature of American national life. The attempt at Prohibition convincingly demonstrated that legislative action is ineffectual in eliminating drug usage when it is endorsed by the norms of a substantial part of the community.

The use of drugs remains almost universal in American society. The great majority of Americans have at one time or another used psychoactive drugs. Each year we spend over a billion dollars on more than 225 million prescriptions for stimulants, sedatives, and tranquilizers. The alcohol industry sells over a billion gallons of spirits, wine, and beer each year, at a cost of $24 billion to some 100 million consumers. Despite the acknowledged link between tobacco consumption and such illnessess as lung cancer and heart disease, some 53 million adults smoke cigarettes. But patterns of drug use are shifting in one very important respect—from the legal to the illegal drugs. In the past, the use of illegal drugs was largely restricted to small subcultures, primarily among minority groups. Today, the use of illegal drugs has become a norm among a very substantial proportion of the younger generation. Marijuana is the most favored illegal drug of the young; studies have shown that it has been used by 8 percent of junior high school students, 25 percent of senior high school students, and 67 percent of college students. In 1972 it was estimated that a total of 26 million Americans have smoked marijuana, while approximately 7.6 million have taken a psychedelic drug, such as LSD or mescaline. In addition, there are several hundred thousand heroin users in the United States, many or most of whom are addicted to the drug.

Public concern about drug use has been increased by the common belief that there is a relationship between crime and the abuse of illegal drugs—either because the drugs cause people to commit crimes, or because users commit robberies and thefts to pay for the drugs. And the fact that the older generation has little experience or even accurate knowledge of the illegal drugs, as many surveys have shown, has made the problem more complex.[2]

APPROACHING THE PROBLEM

Sociologists may analyze drug problems from the theoretical perspectives of social disorganization, deviance, or value conflict; or they may use some combination of these perspectives.

---

[2]See Second Report of the National Commission on Marijuana and Drug Abuse, *Drug Use in America: Problem in Perspective* (Washington, D.C.: U.S. Government Printing Office, 1973); Michael R. McKee, "Main Street, USA: Fact and Fiction About Drug Abuse," *Journal of Drug Education*, vol. 3, no. 3 (Fall 1973), pp. 275–295.

From the social-disorganization perspective, the existence of widespread drug abuse is explained in terms of those features of the social system that may encourage people to abuse drugs or may enhance their opportunities for doing so. Theorists using this perspective have pointed, for example, to the fact that heroin addiction is primarily a phenomenon of the urban black ghetto. Where society is disorganized to the extent that many people are prevented—perhaps through discrimination—from realizing their goals, they may be "driven to drink" or may seek solace in drug experiences that provide the gratification society denies them.

Social-disorganization theorists may also regard society as disorganized to the extent that the behavior of many people is no longer regulated by the dominant social norms governing drug usage. In times of rapid social change these norms, like many others, may lose much of their validity. The emergence of a distinctive youth culture in the sixties was associated with the repudiation of many established norms. Illicit drug use became an established feature of the youth culture, and young people turned to new drugs whose existence was scarcely recognized, let alone regulated, by the dominant norms. Drug abuse is much more common in the heterogeneous, rapidly changing context of the cities than in traditional rural areas—a fact which suggests that the breakdown of the established norms governing drug usage is associated with the greater social disorganization of urban areas.

Social-disorganization theorists may also consider society disorganized to the extent that social control over drug abuse and over the supply of illicit drugs is inadequate. No effective means has yet been found of regulating drug abuse or of significantly curtailing the local manufacture or importation from abroad of illegal drugs.

From the deviance perspective, drug abuse is explained in terms of deviance from social norms. In the popular mind, drug abusers become deviants either because of their own irresponsibility, or because they are corrupted by peers or the malevolent "pusher." Most law enforcement officials take this view; they tend to see the spread of drug abuse as an "epidemic" analogous to the progress of a disease through a population—with the drug as the equivalent of the germ and the pusher as the equivalent of the carrier.

Most sociologists consider this view rather simplistic. Some regard the deviant drug user as one who has failed to internalize or has rejected the norms of the dominant culture regarding drug usage. The individual may, for example, be in a state of *anomie;* desiring the socially endorsed goals of happiness and fulfillment and unable to achieve them by socially approved means, he or she may believe that drugs provide an alternative, readily available route to personal satisfaction. Or the individual may have joined a subculture whose members reject certain norms of the dominant culture. The norms of the subculture may legitimize drug usage as a means of "escape" from the dominant society into novel forms of experience.

Drugs: An Unorthodox View

Most of the propagandists against drug abuse seek to justify certain repressive policies because of the alleged dangerousness of various drugs. . . .

To be sure, some drugs are more dangerous than others. It is easier to kill oneself with heroin than with aspirin. But it is also easier to kill oneself by jumping off a high building than a low one. In the case of drugs, we regard their potentiality for self-injury as justification for their prohibition; in the case of buildings we do not. . . .

Every individual is capable of injuring or killing himself. This potentiality is a fundamental expression of human freedom. Self-destructive behavior may be regarded as sinful and penalized by means of informal sanctions. But it should not be regarded as a crime or (mental) disease, justifying or warranting the use of the police powers of the state for its control.

Therefore, it is absurd to deprive an adult of a drug (or of anything else) because he might use it to kill himself. To do so is to treat everyone the way institutional psychiatrists treat the so-called suicidal mental patient: they not only imprison such a person but take everything away from him—shoelaces, belts, razor blades, eating utensils, and so forth—until the "patient" lies naked on a mattress in a padded cell—lest he kill himself. The result is degrading tyrannization. . . .

There are many things, from dynamite to guns, that are much more dangerous than narcotics (especially to others) but are not prohibited. As everyone knows, it is still possible in the United States to walk into a store and walk out with a shotgun. We enjoy this right not because we believe that guns are safe but because we believe even more strongly that civil liberties are precious. At the same time, it is not possible in the United States to walk into a store and walk out with a bottle of barbiturates, codeine, or other drugs.

I believe that just as we regard freedom of speech and religion as fundamental rights, so we should also regard freedom of self-medication as a fundamental right. Like most rights, the right of self-medication should apply only to adults; and it should not be an unqualified right.

SOURCE: Thomas S. Szasz, "The Ethics of Addiction," *Harper's* (April 1972).

Theorists who regard deviance as the result of a labeling process tend to take a relativistic view of drug usage. They point out that some drugs are stigmatized and some are not, and the decision as to which drug users are labeled deviant rests with those people who enjoy power and influence in society. Alcohol is the approved drug of those who have social power, so its use is regarded as normal and acceptable; marijuana, the approved drug of those who lack social power, is considered unacceptable and its users are labeled as deviants. Most experts agree that alcohol is a far more dangerous drug than marijuana. It seems, then, that the social response is not linked to the intrinsic qualities of the two drugs, but rather to the social status of those who use them. Labeling processes are also regarded as an important element in the creation of the individual deviant. A student, for example, may experiment with a particular illicit drug. Others observe this behavior and label the student as a drug user. The student accepts this label, comes to regard himself or herself as a deviant, and acts on that basis in the future.

From the value-conflict perspective, drug problems are linked to a clash of values between different groups in society. Some groups favor one drug; others favor another. The drugs that each group chooses are determined by the socialization of its members, since certain drugs are more available to some subcultures and more suitable for their life styles. The "drug problem" stems from a clash of interests and values between various groups, some of which seek to impose their own values on others. Value-conflict theorists sometimes regard this conflict as a potentially healthy one, for it might eventually lead to a situation in which social attitudes toward drugs and drug users become more equitable: continuing conflict over marijuana usage, for example, is likely to lead to a relaxation of disproportionately severe penalties for its use.

Attitudes and Values Toward Drugs

The societal reaction to particular forms of drug use can be fully understood only in terms of social attitudes and values toward drugs and the particular groups that use them. In certain cases, such as the abuse of alcohol or heroin, adverse social reaction is based largely on the universally acknowledged dangers of the drugs. But in many cases, there is no obvious connection between the dangers of the drugs and the degree of severity of social reaction to their use. The National Commission on Marijuana and Drug Abuse acknowledged this fact when it reported in 1973:

> It is no longer satisfactory to defend social disapproval of a particular drug on the ground that it is a "mind altering drug" or a "means of escape." For so are they all.[3]

[3]Second Report of the National Commission on Marijuana and Drug Abuse, *Drug Use in America,* p. 23.

The commission went on to point out that

> chemically induced mood alteration is taken for granted and gener-
> ally acceptable in contemporary America. The degree of acceptabil-
> ity, however, is defined by the source and type of substance taken
> as well as by certain characteristics of the individual, such as age
> and socio-economic status.
>
> This society is not opposed to all drug taking but only to certain
> forms of drug use by certain persons. Self-medication by a house-
> wife or a businessman with amphetamines or tranquilizers, for
> example, is generally viewed as a personal judgment of little con-
> cern to the larger community. On the other hand, use of such drugs
> by a college student or other young person to stay awake for study-
> ing or simply to experience the effect of such drugs is ordinarily
> considered a matter of intense community concern extending even
> to legal intervention.
>
> This variation in the acceptability of drug-using behavior is regard-
> ed by many young people as hypocritical. The Commission recog-
> nizes that contemporary social attitudes are indeed inconsistent,
> reflecting the special status which this society accords its youth. . . .[4]

Surveys conducted by the commission found a great deal of ignorance and even irrationality on the part of adults about the drugs used
by young people, particularly marijuana. The commission found, for
example, that 57 percent of adults believe that "if marijuana were legal,
it would lead to teen-agers becoming irresponsible and wild." Some 56
percent of adults consider that "many crimes are committed by persons
who are under the influence of marijuana." Although only 4 percent of
marijuana smokers have ever tried heroin, no less than 70 percent of
adults believe that "marijuana makes people want to try stronger drugs
like heroin." The belief that marijuana smokers can die from an overdose of the drug is held by 48 percent of adults, although in fact no such
death has ever been recorded. Only 9 percent of the population over
fifty years of age believe that "marijuana smokers lead a normal life."[5]
Moreover, only 39 percent of adults regard alcohol as a drug, and only
27 percent regard tobacco as a drug—but 80 percent regard marijuana
as a drug.[6] A majority of adults believe that even if marijuana were
legalized, its consumption would still constitute "drug abuse."[7] Since
there is a general consensus among medical experts that tobacco and
alcohol are far more dangerous drugs than marijuana, the attitudes
revealed by the commission's surveys seem to have little basis in reality. Yet these attitudes are very strongly held—so strongly, in fact, that

[4]Ibid., pp. 42–43.
[5]The Official Report of the National Commission on Marijuana and Drug Abuse, *Marijuana: A Signal
of Misunderstanding* (New York: New American Library, 1972).
[6]Second Report of the National Commission on Marijuana and Drug Abuse, *Drug Use in America*,
p. 10.
[7]Ibid., p. 13.

Many sociologists believe the social reaction to a particular drug depends less on the characteristics of the drug than on the social attitudes toward the people who use it. The public still associates marijuana and the hallucinogens with political and cultural radicalism among the young. *(E. Rice for WHO/ Monkmeyer)*

tens of thousands of young people have been jailed for experimenting with marijuana.

How can we account for these social attitudes? Many sociologists believe that the critical determinant of the societal response to a specific drug depends on social attitudes toward the group that chooses to use it. Throughout this century, narcotics addiction has been rife in urban black ghettos, but because it was largely invisible to the rest of society, and because society was little concerned about conditions in the ghettos, the problem was ignored. But in the sixties, when heroin spread to the white suburbs, it became a matter of intense public concern; President Nixon declared before Congress that heroin addiction was "public enemy number one."

The adverse social reaction to marijuana also seems to be connected with the fact that in the mid-sixties its use was associated with political radicalism and a burgeoning hippie "counterculture" that challenged established norms and values. Indeed, many adults felt that the use of marijuana actually caused young people to reject the values and life styles of their parents in favor of "dropping out" into a subculture that embraced hedonism, lack of motivation, and sexual liberation. There is no question that the use of marijuana was associated with an anti-establishment morality; a study by Edward Suchman found a strong correlation between marijuana use and the "hang-loose ethic" as defined by Jerry Simmons and Barry Winograd:

> One of the fundamental characteristics of the hang-loose ethic is that it is irreverent. It repudiates, or at least questions, such cornerstones of conventional society as Christianity, "my country right or wrong," the sanctity of marriage and premarital chastity, . . . the accumulation of wealth, the right and even competence of parents, the schools and the government to . . . make decisions for everyone—in sum, the establishment.[8]

There is, however, no evidence that marijuana usage causes these attitudes; people may develop the attitudes first and try marijuana as a consequence.

The Commission on Marijuana and Drug Abuse came to the conclusion that the reason society reacted so violently to marijuana use was that most adults saw it as a symbol of the rejection of cherished social values:

> Use of marijuana was, and still is, age-specific. It was youth-related at a time in American history when the adult society was alarmed by the implications of the youth "movement": defiance of the established order, the adoption of new life styles, the emergence of "street people," campus unrest, drug use, communal living, protest politics, and even political radicalism. In an age characterized by the so-called generation gap, marijuana symbolizes the cultural divide.[9]

Although in the seventies marijuana use is no longer so closely correlated with anti-establishment values, the old attitudes have lingered on and the marijuana smoker is still viewed as a threat to society and to self. For similar reasons, any drug that is associated with rebellious youth is still proscribed by our society, and even drugs that are tolerated when used by adults are disapproved of when used by young people for experiential or hedonistic purposes.

PATTERNS OF DRUG USE IN THE UNITED STATES

Patterns of drug use and abuse in the United States have shifted rapidly since the early sixties. As we have noted, one major shift has been from the use of legal to the use of illegal drugs, particularly among young people. But there are also continual shifts in the specific drugs that are favored—heroin, for example, was significantly more popular at the end of the sixties than it is in the seventies;[10] alcohol is far more commonly used by young people now than it was in the sixties;[11] and

---

[8]Quoted in Edward A. Suchman, "The Hang-loose Ethic and the Spirit of Drug Use," *Journal of Health and Social Behavior*, vol. 9, no. 2 (June 1968), pp. 146–155.
[9]The Official Report of the National Commission on Marijuana and Drug Abuse, *Marijuana*, p. 10.
[10]"Interview with the Administrator," *U.S. News & World Report* (April 1, 1974).
[11]Harold M. Schmeck, Jr., "Alcoholism Cost to Nation Put at $25-billion a Year," *New York Times* (June 11, 1974).

cocaine, a drug that was little used in the sixties, is much more widely used today.[12]

Moreover, the use or abuse of any drug can take many forms. The National Commission on Marijuana and Drug Abuse identified at least five distinct forms of usage in which the motivation and conduct of the user may differ:

Experimental use refers to short-term trial use of a drug: the individual uses it once or twice simply to experience its effects, and may never use the drug again.

Social-recreational use refers to occasional use among friends or acquaintances: the drug is taken as part of a shared experience to support and enhance social interaction among the group.

Circumstantial-situational use refers to use which is restricted to particular pressing circumstances: the drug may be used to keep a student alert for examinations, or an individual may feel pressured by his or her peer group into taking a drug.

Intensified use refers to long-term, patterned use of a drug: the individual habitually and regularly uses the drug over a long period of time.

Compulsive use refers to high-frequency use of the drug: the individual has great difficulty in facing life without the drug and becomes physiologically or psychologically dependent upon it.[13]

Social attitudes, and indeed the law, often fail to distinguish between these forms of drug use, and disapproval or legal penalties may be applied indiscriminately to all types of users, from the experimental to the compulsive.

The Role of Drug Subcultures

The fact that an individual uses or abuses drugs is often explained in psychological terms that focus on the individual's personal history, qualities of character, reactions to stress, or strength of will in the face of temptations to engage in illegal or dangerous conduct. Some psychologists have attempted to link particular personality types with particular patterns of drug usage—suggesting, for example, that the marijuana smoker has a mildly disturbed personality and the heroin user is severely maladjusted.[14]

Although sociologists acknowledge that psychological factors may predispose certain individuals to experiment with particular drugs, they find a purely psychological explanation of drug usage inadequate. Drug use does not take place in isolation from society: the drugs that

[12]Ann Crittenden and Michael Ruby, "Cocaine: The Champagne of Drugs," *New York Times Magazine* (September 1, 1974).

[13]Second Report of the National Commission on Marijuana and Drug Abuse, *Drug Use in America,* pp. 30–32, 93–98.

[14]See David P. Ausubel, "Causes and Types of Narcotics Addiction: A Psychosocial View," *Psychiatric Quarterly,* vol. 35, no. 3 (Fall 1961), pp. 523–531.

are used, the incidence of use of particular drugs, and the social definition of drug users all vary from place to place and from time to time. Particular social contexts may present opportunities for drug use, or they may present problems for which drug use appears as a potential solution. The fact that narcotics abuse is more common in urban than in rural areas, for example, does not necessarily mean that rural inhabitants are better adjusted psychologically than their urban counterparts: it may simply mean that people in cities are more likely to be exposed to narcotics and are therefore more likely to use them. Moreover, many sociologists are reluctant to accept that the users of illegal or even dangerous drugs are necessarily psychologically maladjusted: in many subcultures, the use of particular drugs is normal and the person who uses the drugs may be considered well-adjusted in terms of the subcultural norms in question. The mere fact that someone engages in dangerous behavior largely for the experience it offers is not in itself an indication of maladjustment – the charge is not made, for example, against mountaineers, stunt drivers, or astronauts. Some drug abusers, of course, may be highly disturbed individuals, but psychological factors cannot provide a comprehensive explanation of drug abuse.

The main agency for the socialization of individuals into a pattern of drug use or abuse is the drug subculture, usually composed of peers. Although a few addicts of alcohol or heroin may habitually take their drug alone, most drug-taking, particularly in the initial stages of use, takes place in the context of a social group that approves the use of the drug in question. This point was first made by sociologist Howard S. Becker in 1953 in a classic article, "Becoming a Marijuana User."[15] Becker found that the novice does not simply smoke marijuana and get "high"; he or she is introduced to the drug by a group, and learns to recognize the experience as a pleasant one through the reassurances of group members. Membership in the drug subculture serves to define the nature of the drug experience, to sustain drug use, and to influence further behavior. The new member, Becker argues, has to be partly resocialized by the group: he or she must learn to discard the established norms governing drug use, and to internalize the norms of the drug subculture.

Similar processes appear to take place in the initiation of individuals into the use of other types of drugs. A user of alcohol, for example, learns about the drug and its use in the presence of other alcohol users, where he or she internalizes the group norms governing the appropriate use of the drug. Similarly, the user of LSD is usually introduced to the drug by others who have experience with it; they explain its use and effects and define the nature of the experience for the new participant. Although it may be considered that the drug subculture has a decidedly negative impact on society through its function of providing opportunities for new individuals to engage in particular patterns of drug use, the subculture does serve an important positive function for

[15]Howard S. Becker, "Becoming a Marijuana User," *American Journal of Sociology,* 59 (November 1953), pp. 235–242.

the individual user. The subculture provides a stock of knowledge about the drug and a set of norms regulating its use; the common experience of the members allows them to determine the safety limits of dosages and any adverse effects of high-frequency use. The solitary individual who uses LSD or heroin for the first time runs much higher risks than the individual who first experiences the drug within the context of a subculture whose members know how to administer the drug and how to structure the subsequent drug experience.[16]

The Drugs That Americans Use

In analyzing the social problem of drug use, it is important to realize that the United States does not have a single drug problem but, rather, several separate problems. Each drug has a unique set of psychological and physiological effects, each draws users from a different segment of society, each has its own social, economic, and personal consequences, and each is viewed differently by society. The drugs whose use arouses most concern in America are alcohol, tobacco, narcotics, hallucinogens, marijuana, stimulants, and depressants. Let us look at each of these drugs in turn.

Alcohol. Medical and social scientists consider alcohol the most damaging drug in American society. The National Commission reported that "alcohol dependence is without question the most serious drug problem in this country today."[17] Most Americans, however, do not consider alcohol a problem; in one survey only 7 percent mentioned it as a serious social problem.[18]

Alcohol acts on the central nervous system as an anesthetic and as a depressant. The magnitude of these effects varies with the amount of alcohol that is in the bloodstream when it passes through the brain. The rate of absorption depends not only on the amount consumed, but also on the speed at which it is consumed, the weight of the drinker, and the presence or absence of food in the stomach. Generally, the effects become apparent when the concentration of alcohol in the blood of the drinker reaches .1 percent; extreme intoxication occurs when it reaches .2 percent; loss of consciousness results from concentrations of over .4 percent; and a concentration of over .7 percent causes death.

Alcohol affects behavior in two ways. First, it hinders task performance by impeding coordination, reaction time, and reasoning ability. Second, it serves as a psychological and emotional relaxant, and so is generally considered to have positive effects as a "social lubricant." The diminished capacity to perform tasks and the uninhibited behavior that alcohol produces may have highly undesirable social effects, however. About half of the 5 million arrests that take place in the United

[16]Jock Young, *The Drugtakers* (London: Paladin Books, 1971).
[17]Second Report of the National Commission on Marijuana and Drug Abuse, *Drug Use in America,* p. 143.
[18]Ibid., p. 144.

Alcohol is by far the most personally and socially damaging drug in America. There may be as many as 9 million alcoholics, and the drug is a major contributor to crime, marital breakdown, and highway fatalities. Ironically, most Americans do not consider alcohol a "drug" at all. *(Jim Anderson/Woodfin Camp)*

States every year are related to abuse of the drug. Moreover, about half of the homicides and a quarter of the suicides are alcohol-related. A survey of sex offenders revealed that alcohol was reported as a factor in 67 percent of sexual crimes against children and 39 percent of aggressive sexual acts against women.[19]

Most American adults are light drinkers, consuming up to five alcoholic beverages a week. About a fourth of the adult population are heavy drinkers, taking more than six drinks in seven days.[20] In addition, between 5 million and 9 million Americans are compulsive alcoholics.[21] Alcohol use begins earlier than other kinds of drug use, and continues longer. Some 40 percent of American youth report having tried alcohol before their eleventh birthday. The incidence of use rises rapidly from the middle teens to early adulthood, when 66 percent of those in the 22–25 age group use the drug. Throughout the remainder of the adult years use remains considerable, but it gradually tapers off until less than 40 percent of those over 50 continue to drink. Men are considerably more likely to use alcohol than women, and the better educated are

[19]Ibid., pp. 157–158.
[20]Ibid., p. 45.
[21]Edward M. Brecher, *Licit and Illicit Drugs: The Consumers Union Report on Narcotics, Stimulants, Depressants, Inhalants, Hallucinogens, and Marijuana—including Caffeine, Nicotine, and Alcohol* (Boston: Little, Brown, 1972), p. 260.

more likely to use it than are the less educated: 71 percent of those with college education drink, compared with only 38 percent of those with high school education. Urban residents are more likely to drink than rural residents. Among adults, alcohol use is highest in the Northeast, where 65 percent of adults use the drug, and lowest in the South, where only 37 percent do so. Use among young people is more evenly distributed across the nation.[22]

Alcoholism may be defined as the compulsive and excessive use of alcohol to the extent that it is harmful to the drinker's health, job performance, or interpersonal relations. Alcoholics are not necessarily physically addicted to the drug, although prolonged excessive use tends to lead to addiction. The addicted alcoholic has an insatiable desire for the drug, and if unable to obtain it, develops symptoms of physical withdrawal—rapid heartbeat, profuse sweating, uncontrollable trembling, and severe nausea. The time elapsing between the first experience of intoxication and ultimate alcohol addiction may be quite long, ranging from about seven to eighteen years. Prolonged use of alcohol may also cause irreversible damage to the liver and the brain. The combination of drinking and smoking increases enormously the risk of cancer of the mouth and throat—to fifteen times the rate for people who neither drink nor smoke. The total annual cost to the nation of alcohol abuse amounts to over $25 billion, most of it resulting from lost work, medical expenses, and motor vehicle accidents.[23]

There are strong indications that alcohol use and abuse are very much on the increase among young persons. A 1974 survey showed that 36 percent of high school students get drunk at least four times a year, and one high school male in seven gets drunk every week.[24] If this trend continues, the social problem of alcohol abuse and alcoholism is likely to become much more severe in the future.

Tobacco. Tobacco is probably the most physiologically damaging of all the drugs used in the United States. Cigarette smoking reduces life expectancy, can cause lung cancer and emphysema, and greatly increases the risk of heart disease. If a pregnant woman smokes, her child is likely to be born underweight and the chances of premature birth or miscarriage are doubled. Yet, in spite of these facts, millions of citizens persist in using the drug; some 38 percent of American adults and 17 percent of American youth smoke cigarettes. The extent of tobacco use among these smokers varies, but generally consumption tends to increase over time. Only 5 percent of youthful smokers use one pack a day or more, but 25 percent of adults have reached this level.[25] The incidence of tobacco usage increases with age until it

[22]Second Report of the National Commission on Marijuana and Drug Abuse, *Drug Use in America*, pp. 44–48.

[23]Schmeck, "Alcoholism Cost to Nation Put at $25-billion a Year."

[24]Ibid.

[25]Second Report of the National Commission on Marijuana and Drug Abuse, *Drug Use in America*, pp. 44–45.

reaches a peak in middle adulthood; nearly half of those in the 26–34 age group smoke. More men than women smoke, although among young smokers there are as many females as males. The incidence of smoking is highest in the South and in metropolitan areas, and is somewhat more common among nonwhites than whites.[26] There is also a pronounced relationship between smoking and other types of drug use; the person who smokes is much more likely than a nonsmoker to use alcohol, stimulants, sedatives, and marijuana.[27]

Tobacco is a highly addictive drug. The active ingredient is nicotine, a remarkable chemical that can act as a stimulant, a depressant, or a tranquilizer. Cigarette smokers rapidly develop a tolerance for nicotine, and increase consumption from an initial few cigarettes a day to one or more packs. Even a few trial experiments with cigarettes are enough to start a person on a smoking career, as one researcher, Hamilton Russell, points out:

> It requires no more than three or four casual cigarettes during adolescence virtually to ensure that a person will become a regular dependent smoker. . . . If we bear in mind that only 15 percent of adolescents who smoke more than one cigarette avoid becoming regular smokers and that only about 15 percent of smokers stop before the age of 60, it becomes apparent that of those who smoke more than one cigarette during adolescence, some 70 percent continue smoking for the next 40 years.[28]

Other studies have shown that even among those who have attended clinics and tried very seriously to stop smoking, more than 80 percent fail to do so.[29]

Why do many people, especially young people, take up cigarette smoking in the face of the widespread knowledge of its adverse effects? One reason is that tobacco is the subject of a barrage of advertisements designed to make use of the drug seem appealing. Cigarettes are subtly associated with sexual attractiveness, rugged manliness, or social sophistication, all in an endeavor to maintain and increase the profits of the large tobacco corporations. Another reason seems to be that young people simply do not appreciate quite how addictive tobacco is, and how very difficult the smoking habit is to break. In one study of teenage smokers, it was found that only 21 percent thought it was "very likely" that they would still be smoking five years later; the majority, with unwarranted optimism, confidently expected that they would stop within five years or less.[30]

---

[26]Ibid., p. 47.

[27]Ibid., pp. 44–47.

[28]M. A. Hamilton Russell, "Cigarette Smoking: Natural History of a Dependence Disorder," *British Journal of Medical Psychology*, 44 (1971), p. 9.

[29]William A. Hunt and Joseph D. Matarazzo, "Habit Mechanisms in Smoking," in *Learning Mechanisms in Smoking*, ed. William A. Hunt (Chicago: Aldine, 1970), p. 76.

[30]Lieberman Research Inc., "The Teenager Looks at Cigarette Smoking," survey conducted for the American Cancer Society, September 1969, table 108, p. 212.

Narcotics. There are many drugs that have a narcotic ("sleep-induc-ing") effect. The narcotics most commonly used in the United States are the opiates – opium, morphine, and heroin – which are all derived from the opium poppy. Opium, a drug renowned for centuries for its soothing, dreamlike effects, comes from the opium poppy plant; after the petals fall from the brilliant red flower, a milky substances oozes out from the seed pods that, when dried, is raw opium. Morphine is the main active ingredient of opium; the drug was first isolated in 1803 and has been used extensively as a painkiller ever since. Heroin is in turn derived from morphine, and is a still more potent drug. Opium may be taken orally, but it is usually smoked. Both morphine and heroin can be sniffed through the nose, or they can be injected into the skin, into a muscle, or – for maximum effect – directly into a vein ("mainlining"). Heroin is the most commonly abused opiate.

Narcotics act primarily on the central nervous system, and may pro-duce feelings of drowsiness, tranquillity, or even euphoria. An exces-sive dose, however, may result in a coma, or even in death by respir-atory failure. All the narcotics are highly addictive. Addiction develops after the user has taken the drug at regular intervals for a period of time. The length of the period depends on the particular narcotic, on the strength of the dosages, and the regularity of use, but addiction may occur within only a few weeks. The user rapidly develops a toler-ance for narcotics, so that he or she requires steadily increasing doses to achieve the original effect of the drug. If deprived of the drug, the addict may suffer unpleasant withdrawal symptoms, including sweat-ing, running of the nose, watering of the eyes, chills, cramps, and some-times acute nausea. An intense craving for the drug may recur inter-mittently for several months thereafter.

Addiction to narcotics is extremely difficult to break, particularly among young people. As the American Consumers Union noted in a report on drug use in America, the narcotic drug

> is one that most users continue to take even though they want to stop, decide to stop, try to stop, and actually succeed in stopping for days, weeks, months, or even years. It is a drug for which men and women will prostitute themselves. It is a drug to which most users return after treatment. . . . It is a drug which most users continue to use despite the threat of long-term imprisonment for its use – and to which they promptly return after experiencing long-term impris-onment.[31]

For reasons that are not clearly understood, it seems to be much more difficult for persons under thirty to break the heroin habit than for those in the mid-thirties and above. It appears that a majority of addicts do not continue to use the drug beyond their mid-thirties, but it is not certain

[31]Brecher, *Licit and Illicit Drugs*, p. 84.

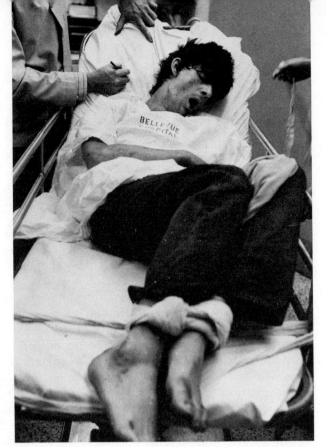

Heroin is probably the most dreaded drug in American society, although drugs like alcohol and barbiturates have far more addicts, contribute to far more deaths, and cause more severe withdrawal symptoms. *(Leonard Freed/Magnum)*

why they are successful in breaking a habit they could not break a few years previously.[32]

Most narcotics addicts are male, under thirty, poorly educated, and of low socioeconomic status, and the likelihood of addiction is significantly higher for blacks than for whites. Addiction is found primarily in large urban centers; about half of the nation's addicts are believed to be concentrated in New York City. Throughout most of the last few decades, heroin addiction was largely confined to urban black ghettos, but in the late sixties the drug spread to white middle-class suburbs and its abuse among the young was rapidly defined as a major social problem. The ready availability of cheap heroin in Southeast Asia contributed to considerable addiction among American soldiers in Vietnam, which further increased the size of the problem. At the end of the sixties, the number of heroin addicts in the United States was estimated up to 600,000. It seems certain the incidence of heroin addiction has dropped sharply since then; 1974 estimates put the number of addicts at a maximum of 300,000.[33]

Heroin abuse is nonetheless still regarded by many Americans as the gravest drug problem in the United States. This attitude bears very lit-

[32]See Lee N. Robins and G. E. Murphy, "Drug Use in a Normal Population of Young Negro Men," *American Journal of Public Health*, 57 (September 1967), pp. 1580–1596.
[33]"Interview with the Administrator."

tle relationship to the incidence of use of heroin or to its pharmacological effects. Heroin has by far the lowest rate of incidence of all the drugs mentioned in this chapter; the National Commission on Marijuana and Drug Abuse found that only 1.3 percent of adults and .6 percent of youths have tried the drug at least once. Of those who have never used the drug, only 1 percent expressed any interest in trying it, even if it were legal.[34]

If widespread abuse is not the basis for public concern about the drug, why does it excite such a strong social reaction? One important reason is the "dope fiend" mythology surrounding heroin, and the general belief that addicts commit violent crimes. The public is also alarmed by frequent reports of deaths due to heroin overdose, but there seems to be much less alarm over the number of fatalities linked to abuse of barbiturates, alcohol, and tobacco—although these drugs directly or indirectly claim hundreds of thousands of lives each year, in comparison with a few hundred heroin overdose deaths. The withdrawal symptoms associated with attempts to break addiction to heroin also receive unfavorable publicity, but these symptoms, though extremely unpleasant, are typically less severe than those experienced by chronic alcoholics or barbiturate addicts who are deprived of their drugs.

It is also commonly believed that narcotics addiction has adverse physical effects on the user, but in fact alcohol and tobacco are unquestionably more damaging to the human body than is heroin. So long as the heroin addict maintains a supply of the drug and avoids excess doses, there are no detectable ill-effects, and an addict may continue for decades without any signs of physical deterioration. Dr. Jerome Jaffe, former presidential advisor on drug problems, has noted:

> The addict who is able to obtain an adequate supply of drugs through legitimate channels and has adequate funds usually dresses properly, maintains his nutrition, and is able to discharge his social and occupational obligations with reasonable efficiency. He usually remains in good health, suffers little inconvenience, and is, in general, difficult to distinguish from other persons.[35]

In its report on drugs in America, the Consumers Union came to the conclusion that almost all of the undesirable effects usually attributed to the opiates are in fact the effects of the narcotics laws:

> By far the most deleterious effects of being a narcotics addict in the United States today are the risks of arrest and imprisonment, infectious disease, and impoverishment—all traceable to the narcotics laws, to vigorous enforcement of those laws, and to the resulting excessive black-market prices for narcotics.[36]

[34]Second Report of the National Commission on Marijuana and Drug Abuse, *Drug Use in America,* p. 69.

[35]Jerome H. Jaffe, quoted in Louis S. Goodman and Alfred Gilman, eds., *The Pharmacological Basis of Therapeutics,* 4th ed. (New York: Macmillan, 1970), p. 286.

[36]Brecher, *Licit and Illicit Drugs,* p. 22.

Because the possession of narcotics is illegal and severely penalized in the United States, the addict is by definition a criminal. The demand for illicit narcotics has inevitably led to the development of a black market in which the drugs, often diluted with dangerous impurities, are sold at grossly inflated prices. Organized crime has been attracted by the high profits in the narcotics trade and has become deeply involved in the smuggling and distribution of the drugs. The addicts, meanwhile, frequently have to resort to illegal means to finance their drug habits, and the constant search for a daily supply of the narcotic makes it extremely difficult for them to lead normal lives. Much of the problem of narcotics addiction in the United States stems from the social reaction to drug users rather than from any intrinsic quality of the drugs. The fact that society adopts an alarmed response to the commerce in heroin while tolerating or even encouraging the commerce in tobacco, alcohol, and barbiturates is a matter of considerable sociological interest. The rate of addiction and the physical dangers associated with the latter drugs are very much greater, yet many Americans scarcely regard them as drugs at all.

Hallucinogens. The three types of hallucinogens most commonly used in the United States are mescaline (peyote), psilocybin, and LSD. All are taken orally. Peyote, which is derived from a cactus plant, has been used in the Americas for centuries, and formed the basis for the "peyote cult" among American Indians in the late nineteenth century. Members of the Native American Church, a contemporary religious movement descended from the peyote cult, are still legally entitled to use peyote on ceremonial occasions. The synthetic form of peyote, mescaline, is illegally manufactured in the United States and is more commonly used than peyote. Psilocybin is derived from a small mushroom found in the Southwest of the United States; it too has a long history of use by American Indians. LSD was first synthesized in 1938, but researchers did not realize its hallucinogenic effects until one of them accidentally inhaled a dose in 1943. The researcher, Dr. Albert Hoffman, recorded in his notebook the extraordinary "illness" that overcame him:

> Last Friday . . . I had to interrupt my laboratory work in the middle of the afternoon and go home, because I was seized with a feeling of great restlessness and mild dizziness. At home, I lay down and sank into a not unpleasant delirium, which was characterized by extremely excited fantasies. In a semiconscious state, with my eyes closed (I felt the daylight to be unpleasantly dazzling), fantastic visions of extraordinary realness and with an intense kaleidoscopic play of colors assailed me.[37]

LSD is a colorless, tasteless substance of much higher potency than the other hallucinogens; a dose of 100 micrograms—an almost invisible

---

[37]Quoted in John Cashman, *The LSD Story* (Greenwich, Conn.: Fawcett, 1966), p. 31.

speck — will produce dramatic effects. The drug is relatively easy to manufacture and is the most readily available hallucinogen in the United States.

The effects of hallucinogenic drugs vary a great deal depending on the psychological state and expectations of the user and on the context in which the drug is taken. A typical trip lasts for about eight hours. Most users experience vivid hallucinations, and may "see" sounds as colors, experience heightened perception, and feel an enhanced awareness. In some cases, however, the user may have a "bad trip," involving panic, loss of self-control, or paranoid reactions. These negative effects are more likely to occur if the user is in a disturbed state at the time of taking the drug.

The hallucinogenic drugs are not addictive. Users rapidly develop a tolerance for hallucinogens, however, so that increased dosages have to be taken to experience the original effects. Tolerance develops so rapidly that sustained, high-frequency use of the drugs quickly produces virtually no effect whatever, however high the dose. No deaths directly due to the use of hallucinogens have ever been recorded, although there have been a very few highly publicized instances of indirect fatalities resulting, for example, from users' attempts to fly from upper-story windows. There are no confirmed long-term physical effects of the use of the drug; one experimenter suggested that LSD (like aspirin, caffeine, and many other drugs) might cause chromosome damage and perhaps lead to genetic defects, but other researchers have found contradictory evidence on this point. It has been established, however, that there is no relationship between parental exposure to LSD and birth defects in their offspring.[38]

There do appear, however, to be some long-term psychological effects of the use of hallucinogens. LSD in particular produces a "flashback" effect in a small minority of users — some of the reactions associated with an LSD experience recur days, weeks, or even months later. There is also evidence that prolonged high-frequency use of hallucinogens is followed by periods of depression in some people. It also seems that hallucinogenic drugs may have adverse long-term effects on people who are already psychologically disturbed.

Less than one American in twenty reports having used LSD or a similar hallucinogen,[39] and the incidence of use of these drugs has probably declined from a peak in the late sixties, when they were eulogized by rock stars and widely used in the "hippie" movement.

Marijuana. The hemp plant, *Cannabis sativa*, originated in central Asia but is now found in most parts of the world. The plant has long been cultivated in the United States; in the seventeenth century more than

---

[38]William H. McGlothlin, Robert S. Sparkes, and David O. Arnold, "Effects of LSD on Human Pregnancy," *Journal of the American Medical Association*, 212 (June 1, 1970), p. 1486.
[39]Second Report of the National Commission on Marijuana and Drug Abuse, *Drug Use in America*, p. 68.

half the winter clothing was made from hemp, and, after cotton, it was probably the most important cash crop in the South during the post-Revolutionary War period. Today, the main interest in the plant centers on its dried leaves — marijuana — and its dried resin — hashish. Both may be taken orally but are more commonly smoked. The resin is about six times more potent than the leaf.

Marijuana is widely used by Americans from a variety of backgrounds, but its use varies most significantly with age. The National Commission found that 55 percent of those in the 18–21 age bracket had used the drug, but experience with marijuana drops off rapidly among older groups. Men are more likely to use the drug than women, students are more likely to use it than any other occupational group, and the wealthy are more likely to use it than poorer groups. Geographically, marijuana use is disproportionately more common in metropolitan areas and in the West.[40]

The psychological effects of marijuana include relaxation, intensification of sensory stimulation, increase in self-confidence, and feelings of enhanced awareness and creativity. The drug has little observable effect on the performance of simple mental tasks, although more complex tasks such as driving may be somewhat impaired. The effects of the drug are heavily influenced by the user's mood, expectations, and the social context in which the drug is taken. Heavy dosages, particularly of hashish taken orally, can lead to psychotic episodes similar to a "bad trip," but this effect is rare.

The short-term physical effects of marijuana are minor: a slight rise in heart rate, a reddening of the eyes, and a dryness of the throat and mouth. The drug is not physically addictive, and even chronic users do not experience withdrawal symptoms when deprived of the drug. Nor does the marijuana user develop tolerance for the drug; there is no need for increasing dosages. Some researchers have suggested that there may be serious health hazards associated with long-term marijuana use — hazards involving brain damage, irritation of the bronchial tract and lungs, chromosome damage, and disruption of cell metabolism. These findings have not been corroborated by other researchers, however, and remain controversial.[41] A great deal more research must be done before it can be stated with confidence whether or not marijuana use represents a serious health hazard.

Although the use of marijuana has been seen by most Americans as a social problem, it is clear that growing numbers of citizens believe that the real problem lies in the laws against the use of the drug. The attempt to regulate marijuana usage has been described as a second "Prohibition,"[42] which is unlikely to be any more successful than the first, simply because a very substantial section of the population does

[40]Ibid., pp. 63–67.
[41]See Thomas H. Maugh, II, "Marijuana: The Grass May No Longer Be Greener," *Science,* 74 (August 23, 1974), pp. 683–685.
[42]John Kaplan, *Marijuana: A New Prohibition* (New York: World, 1970).

not regard the attempt to proscribe marijuana as legitimate. Laws that regulate crimes without victims are notoriously difficult to apply, especially when they criminalize the private acts of citizens who are otherwise law-abiding. In 1972 the national commission — like similar commissions established in Canada, Britain, Scandinavia — recommended that possession of marijuana for personal use should no longer be a criminal offense in the United States.

Stimulants. Many natural substances contain drugs that stimulate the central nervous system. Caffeine, which is found in coffee, tea, Coca-Cola, and cocoa, is a widely used stimulant in our society. It is even available in tablet form, such as No-Doz. Caffeine reduces fatigue, hunger, and boredom, and improves intellectual and motor activity. There is considerable evidence that the drug is addictive; many users find that they develop a tolerance for it and have to consume more and more coffee to achieve the same effects. When a person is accustomed to drinking large quantities of coffee each day, withdrawal symptoms — primarily depression — occur if caffeine use is stopped. When taken to excess, the drug may cause restlessness, disturbed sleep, and gastrointestinal irritation. In very large doses of ten grams or more, the drug can be fatal.

Since 91 percent of Americans drink either coffee or tea, caffeine is probably the most widely used of all psychoactive substances in the United States. Enough coffee is sold every year to provide over 180 billion doses of the drug to American consumers. Nevertheless, because coffee has the status of a "nondrug" in our society, coffee drinkers are not categorized as criminals, there is no black market for coffee, and no deviant subculture of coffee drinkers exists. Because coffee is legal, its price is reasonable and coffee drinkers are not tempted to adopt a life of crime to support their habit. Many sociologists believe that the experience of our society in dealing with the drug caffeine may have implications for our responses to other, currently illegal, drugs.

Cocaine is another natural stimulant. It is found in the leaves of a mountain shrub indigenous to the Andes mountain region of South America, where the inhabitants consider the drug to be a gift from the gods. Cocaine may be injected, but is more commonly sniffed through the nose. The drug stimulates the central nervous system and produces feelings of great confidence, well-being, and euphoria. It may also reduce pain and fatigue. But excessive dosages, particularly if they are injected, may lead to psychotic reactions involving impulsive and paranoid behavior. Cocaine is not physically addictive, but some users seem to become psychologically dependent on the drug and may become depressed if they are deprived of it. Although cocaine use is illegal in the United States, there are indications that the drug has become steadily more popular since the early seventies. The fact that it is illegal has inevitably led to the emergence of a black market in which vast profits are made; cocaine is probably the most expensive of the illegal

Coffee: A Dangerous Drug?

When we examine the behavioral effects of large doses of caffeine in animal experimentation, shocking findings must be noted. Several research teams have reported, for example, that rats fed massive doses of caffeine become aggressive and launch physical attacks against other rats. More remarkable still, a caffeine-crazed rat may bite and mutilate himself. Automutilation was so acute and intense in some rats that the animals died from hemorrhagic shock.

Some readers may here be moved to protest that the bizarre behavior of rats fed massive doses of caffeine is irrelevant to the problems of human coffee drinkers, who are not very likely to bite themselves to death. Let us promptly and wholeheartedly agree. There is a lesson to be learned, nevertheless, from these rat reports. If the drug producing this effect in rats were marijuana, or LSD, or amphetamine, the report would no doubt have made headlines throughout the country. One of the distorting effects of categorizing drugs as "good," "bad," and "nondrugs" is to protect the "nondrugs" such as caffeine from warranted criticism while subjecting the illicit drugs to widely publicized attacks—regardless of the relevance of the data to the human condition.

Thus we come to the coffee paradox—the question of how a drug so fraught with potential hazard can be consumed in the United States at the rate of more than a hundred billion doses a year without doing intolerable damage—and without arousing the kind of hostility, legal repression, and social condemnation aroused by the illicit drugs. The answer is quite simple. Coffee, tea, cocoa, and the cola drinks have been domesticated. Caffeine has been incorporated into our way of life in a manner that minimizes (though it does not altogether eliminate) the hazards inherent in caffeine use. Instead of its being classified as an illicit drug, thereby grossly amplifying caffeine's potential for harm, ways to make caffeine safer have been searched for and found.

SOURCE: Edward M. Brecher, *Licit and Illicit Drugs* (Boston: Little, Brown, 1972).

drugs and its habitual use is largely restricted to the more affluent in the United States.

The group of drugs called amphetamines ("speed") are synthetic stimulants. Their effects are similar to those of natural stimulants, but are longer lasting. Usually available as pills, the amphetamines increase alertness and improve physical skills; for these reasons they may be used by athletes, truckdrivers, students, astronauts, and others who feel they must maintain high levels of performance for relatively short periods of time. An amphetamine high, however, is followed by mental depression and fatigue. The drug rapidly produces tolerance; a user may eventually swallow an entire handful of tablets rather than one or two. But heavy use of amphetamines may produce serious psychoses.

Amphetamines may be taken legally only if they are issued on prescription, but many of the 30 million prescriptions that are written each year are used by people other than those for whom they are intended, and the drug is also illegally manufactured within the United States. One of the most destructive of all forms of drug abuse is the intravenous injection of large amounts of amphetamines. A "speed freak" may inject the drug several times a day, remaining awake for three to five days at a stretch and becoming progressively more tense, nervous, and paranoid. The speed freak typically loses his or her appetite, and may suffer insomnia and psychotic reactions for many weeks or months after breaking a pattern of long-term use of high doses of the drug. Many people experience amphetamines as psychologically addictive, and there is strong evidence that the drugs are physically addictive as well.

Depressants. The barbiturate drugs are commonly used to relieve insomnia and anxiety. There are over 2,500 different synthetic barbiturates, but the drugs may be divided into two basic categories. The "long-acting" barbiturates are primarily prescribed for nocturnal use to induce sleep, while the "short-acting" drugs are prescribed for daytime use to sedate anxious or tense patients. The use of barbiturates is illegal unless they are supplied through a physician's prescription.

The long-acting barbiturates are only moderately addictive, and are usually used only for therapeutic purposes. The short-acting barbiturates, on the other hand, are widely used for nontherapeutic purposes and are highly addictive; abuse of these drugs has been termed America's "hidden drug problem." Taken in sufficient doses, the short-acting barbiturates produce effects similar to those of alcohol. They remove inhibitions, with some users becoming calm and relaxed while others exhibit garrulous and hyperactive behavior. Regular use of barbiturate pills may lead to physical addiction, and withdrawal from the drug is accompanied by anxiety, profuse sweating, body tremors, fever, and hallucinations. In many cases fatal convulsions occur.

Barbiturates are particularly dangerous when taken with alcohol, because alcohol tends to increase the potency of the barbiturate and hence the likelihood that the user will take an overdose. Accidental deaths due to excessive doses are frequent, and deliberate overdose is a common means of suicide in America. One particularly dangerous method of abuse is the use of amphetamines with barbiturates, a combination which produces an alternating pattern of artificially induced "ups" and "downs."

Barbiturates are relatively easy to obtain, despite the laws prohibiting possession without a prescription. Over 3.5 billion doses of barbitu-

Facts About Drugs

(Question marks indicate conflict of opinion)

NAME	SLANG NAME	SOURCE	CLASSIFICATION	HOW TAKEN
Heroin	H., Horse, Scat, Junk, Smack, Scag, Stuff, Dope	Semi-synthetic (from morphine)	Narcotic	Injected or sniffed
Morphine	White Stuff, M.	Natural (from opium)	Narcotic	Swallowed or injected
Methadone	Dolly	Synthetic	Narcotic	Swallowed or injected
Cocaine	Coke, Corrine, Gold Dust, Bernice, Flake, Star Dust, Snow	Natural (from coca, not cocoa)	Stimulant, local anesthesia	Sniffed, injected, or swallowed
Marijuana	Pot, Grass, Hash, Tea, Dope, Joints, Reefers	Natural	Relaxant, euphoriant; in high doses, hallucinogen	Smoked, swallowed, or sniffed
Barbiturates	Barbs, Blue Devils, Reds, Yellow Jackets, Phennies, Downers, Blue Heavens	Synthetic	Sedative-hypnotic	Swallowed or injected
Amphetamines	Bennies, Dexies, Speed, Wake-Ups, Hearts, Pep Pills, Uppers	Synthetic	Sympatho-mimetic	Swallowed or injected
LSD	Acid, Sugar, Big D, Cubes, Trips	Semi-synthetic (from ergot alkaloids)	Hallucinogen	Swallowed
Mescaline	Mesc.	Natural (from peyote)	Hallucinogen	Swallowed
Psilocybin	Magic Mushroom	Natural (from psilocybe)	Hallucinogen	Swallowed
Alcohol	Booze, Juice, etc.	Natural (from grapes, grains, etc., via fermentation)	Sedative-hypnotic	Swallowed
Tobacco	Cancer Tube, Coffin Nail, etc.	Natural	Stimulant-sedative	Smoked, sniffed, chewed

*Persons who inject drugs under nonsterile conditions run a high risk of contracting hepatitis, abscesses, or circulatory disorders.

SOURCE: Adapted from *Today's Education: NEA Journal* (February 1971).

EFFECTS SOUGHT	LONG-TERM SYMPTOMS	PHYSICAL DEPENDENCE POTENTIAL	MENTAL DEPENDENCE POTENTIAL	ORGANIC DAMAGE POTENTIAL
Euphoria, prevent withdrawal discomfort	Addiction, constipation, loss of appetite	Yes	Yes	No*
Euphoria, prevent withdrawal discomfort	Addiction, constipation, loss of appetite	Yes	Yes	No*
Prevent withdrawal discomfort	Addiction, constipation, loss of appetite	Yes	Yes	No
Excitation, talkativeness	Depression, convulsions	No	Yes	Yes?
Relaxation; increased euphoria, perceptions, sociability	Usually none	No	Yes?	No
Anxiety reduction, euphoria	Addiction with severe withdrawal symptoms, possible convulsions, toxic psychosis	Yes	Yes	Yes
Alertness, activeness	Loss of appetite, delusions, hallucinations, toxic psychosis	Yes?	Yes	Yes
Insightful experiences, exhilaration, distortion of senses	May intensify existing psychosis, panic reactions	No	No?	No?
Insightful experiences, exhilaration, distortion of senses	?	No	No?	No?
Insightful experiences, exhilaration, distortion of senses	?	No	No?	No?
Sense alteration, anxiety reduction, sociability	Cirrhosis, toxic psychosis, neurologic damage, addiction	Yes	Yes	Yes
Calmness, sociability	Emphysema, lung cancer, mouth and throat cancer, cardiovascular damage, loss of appetite	Yes?	Yes	Yes

rates are manufactured in the United States every year, and many of them reach users through illegal channels. In the average year, about 11 percent of all adult Americans use barbiturates, legally or illegally; and 3 percent take them on a regular basis. The drugs are used by a wide cross-section of Americans, but use by young people for "kicks" tends to attract much more censure than use by other groups, such as businessmen and housewives who use the drugs to help them "cope" with their daily lives.

The Social Costs of Drug Use

Drug use and abuse in the United States exact a wide range of social costs—some obvious and measurable, some hidden and difficult to quantify.

Crime. There is a strong association between some forms of drug use and crime. The use of alcohol, for example, is highly correlated with violent crime; more than half of those committing murder and other violent assaults use alcohol immediately before the crime.[43] Heroin addiction, too, is related to crime, although not to violence. A heroin addict must find between $20 and $100 a day to support the habit, and most addicts find that they must steal in order to raise these sums.

Not all drugs, however, are related to crime. Contrary to what many Americans believe, marijuana is not associated with aggressive behavior of any kind; its calming effects are not conducive to violent acts, and because the drug is nonaddictive there is little motivation for the user to resort to theft to obtain it. Hallucinogens, too, have little or no relationship to violent or criminal behavior.

Organized crime is also involved in the use of illegal drugs. Because the user of these drugs cannot obtain a legal supply, he or she is obliged to rely directly or indirectly on criminal networks that manufacture, smuggle, and distribute the drugs. The profits to be reaped from this illicit commerce are vast, and there is strong evidence that the Mafia and other criminal syndicates have become deeply involved in the supply of heroin and, more recently, of cocaine.

Automobile accidents. Alcohol use is directly responsible for thousands of highway accidents and injuries; the drug is blamed for more than half of the annual total of traffic fatalities.[44] Some 60 percent of all drivers fatally injured in auto accidents have a blood alcohol concentration of over .05 percent, a level that the National Safety Council considers sufficient to impair driving ability, and over 35 percent have a concentration of over .15 percent, a level high enough to cause intoxication. The cost of property damage and medical expenses due to alcohol-related automobile accidents totals about $1 billion each year.

[43]Second Report of the National Commission on Marijuana and Drug Abuse, *Drug Use in America*, p. 157.
[44]"Rising Toll of Alcoholism: New Steps to Combat It," *U.S. News & World Report* (October 29, 1973).

There is little information on the effects of other drugs on highway accidents, but it is reasonable to suppose that most psychoactive substances, taken in sufficient doses, will impair driving ability. In simulated driving tests, marijuana has been found to affect performance by slowing down reaction time, reducing the driver's attention, and impairing his judgment.[45] Amphetamines, too, which are sometimes used by drivers to increase alertness, can reduce driving performance when fatigue sets in as the initial effect of the drug wears off.

Disrespect for the law. Existing statutes regulating drug usage define many millions of American citizens as criminals; a majority of American students, for example, have broken the laws relating to marijuana use. When laws are applied which many citizens regard as irrational, hypocritical, or outmoded, widespread disrespect for the legal system may result. Thousands of Americans have acquired criminal records and served jail sentences for acts that they do not believe should be regulated by the criminal code at all. For many young Americans, mere adherence to the norms of their peer group is sufficient to earn them the attention of law enforcement agencies: by the act of smoking marijuana they are categorized as deviants and are subject to prosecution. If young people perceive these laws as irrational and unworthy of respect, they may extend this attitude to other laws as well.

Economic losses. It is difficult to estimate the economic costs of drug use. As we have seen, the cost of alcohol abuse totals over $25 billion a year. There are also many compensatory costs that society must pay to support drug-dependent persons. The diversion of public welfare and law enforcement resources to the treatment and control of drug abuse represents a major drain on resources. About a third of all persons on welfare are reported to use alcohol excessively, and in New York City alone there are tens of thousands of narcotics addicts on welfare. By the mid-seventies, federal and state governments were spending over $1 billion per year on the treatment of various drug abusers. Another half billion dollars annually goes into processing alcoholics and other drug users through the criminal justice system;[46] well over half the arrests in the United States each year are for drug-related offenses. The economic losses resulting from criminal activities associated with drug use are enormous; it has been estimated that each heroin addict must steal property worth between $25,000 and $50,000 a year to support his or her habit.[47]

Effects on individuals. Drug dependence takes a heavy toll on personal health and safety. The heavy user of drugs is much more likely

[45]A. B. Dott, *Effect of Marijuana on Risk Acceptance in a Simulated Passing Test,* Public Health Service Publication (Washington, D.C.: U.S. Government Printing Office, 1972).
[46]President's Commission on Law Enforcement and the Administration of Justice, *Task Force Report: Drunkenness* (Washington, D.C.: U.S. Government Printing Office, 1967).
[47]Second Report of the National Commission on Marijuana and Drug Abuse, *Drug Use in America,* p. 175.

than a member of the general population to be killed or to take his or her own life, either deliberately or accidentally. Alcoholics, for example, have a death rate nearly three times higher than that of the general population; they represent a quarter of all suicides, and they are seven times more likely than non-alcoholics to suffer fatal accidents. Use of heroin increases one's chances of premature death through overdose, infectious diseases such as hepatitis and endocarditis, or suicide. Barbiturates also cause several thousand deaths in the United States every year. Many drugs have severe and sometimes irreversible effects on mental as well as physical health. Drug dependency, too, may affect many other areas of the individual's life—job employment, marital stability, or involvement in crime. The personal impact of drug abuse on the lives of the abusers and their associates is incalculable.

PROSPECTS FOR THE FUTURE

It is doubtful if the United States will ever be without a drug problem, but the nature of the problem and of the social responses to it is likely to change in the future. Patterns of drug usage will continue to change as a result partly of changing tastes, partly of changing attitudes, and partly of the continual introduction of new synthetic psychoactive agents.

Abuse of alcohol is likely to remain America's major drug problem in terms both of the number of addicts and also of the social and economic costs associated with the drug. If the present trend toward increased alcohol consumption among young Americans is maintained, the dimensions of the problem will become much more serious in the years ahead. The failure of Prohibition demonstrated that alcohol abuse cannot be legislated out of existence, and the problem is likely to remain an intractable one. The use of alcohol is currently regulated primarily through social norms that deprecate excessive consumption of the drug, but these norms clearly fail to govern the behavior of many millions of Americans. No fully effective method for the treatment of alcoholism has yet been found, but high success rates have been achieved by Alcoholics Anonymous, a voluntary association of some 400,000 ex-alcoholics who offer moral encouragement to heavy drinkers to break their habit. In 1970 a federal act was passed to establish a National Institute of Alcohol Abuse and Alcoholism and to provide for the expenditure of $300 million for research into the problem and treatment of alcoholics; it may be that the efforts of the institute will yield new methods for the treatment of alcoholism.

Tobacco will continue to ravage the health of millions of Americans. No society into which tobacco has been introduced has ever managed to rid itself of the drug, although many have imposed harsh penalties on smokers. The Sultan Murad of Constantinople even decreed the death penalty for smoking, but to no avail:

> Whenever the Sultan went on his travels or on a military expedition his haunting-places were always distinguished by a terrible increase in the number of executions. Even on the battlefield he was fond of surprising men in the act of smoking, whom he would punish by beheading, hanging, quartering, or crushing their hands and feet and leaving them helpless . . . Nevertheless, in spite of all the horrors of this persecution . . . the passion for smoking still persisted. . . . Even the fear of death was of no avail with the passionate devotees of the habit.[48]

The milder methods of dissuasion used in the United States are unlikely to be any more successful. It may be that some new means can be found to help smokers give up their habit—perhaps a chemical that eliminates the desire for nicotine but has no adverse effects itself. But future policy is likely to concentrate on dissuading young people from starting on a smoking career. An obvious target is the advertising of the tobacco industry; many Americans regard it as intolerable that the use of this dangerous drug should be publicly encouraged, particularly when young people are jailed for using other drugs that are far less harmful. TV advertising of cigarettes has been banned, and the restrictions may be extended to other media, although powerful economic interests will oppose any such measures.

Marijuana usage is almost certainly a permanent feature of American society. Attempts to suppress the drug are unlikely to be any more successful than Prohibition was in suppressing alcohol: too many people use the drug and regard the law as an unenforceable one. Unless strong evidence of severe adverse effects of marijuana is found—and this is possible—use of the drug will probably be legalized in the United States at some time in the future. Many states have already reduced penalties for possession or use of the drug, and in many areas the police tend to ignore the law and turn a blind eye to minor marijuana offenses, an indication that the law is falling into disuse. The enforcement of the marijuana laws diverts the time and efforts of police and courts from other more important problems, and unnecessarily criminalizes thousands of citizens every year. Increasing numbers of Americans believe that the laws against marijuana may present more of a problem than the drug itself.

The abuse of prescription drugs such as amphetamines and barbiturates will continue unless physicians themselves decline to prescribe the drugs as indiscriminately as they often appear to have done in the past. The overprescription of these drugs is a reflection of basic attitudes and values of American society: we are a nation of drug-takers, conditioned by advertising to believe that happiness, relief from pain or boredom, and various other desirable ends are obtainable by the simple expedient of taking the appropriate pill.

Narcotics addiction will probably continue to decline in the United

---

[48]Count Egon Caesar Corti alla Catene, *A History of Smoking*, trans. Paul England (London: George G. Harrap, 1931), pp. 138–139.

Drugs: A Theoretical Review

The social problem of drugs represents the gap between a *social ideal* of a society free of drug abuse and the *social reality* of the United States as a nation of drug-takers, many of whom abuse drugs that have damaging personal, physical, and psychological consequences. It should be remembered, however, that not all drug use constitutes abuse, and that the United States has not one but several drug problems.

The *social-disorganization* perspective provides a useful way of looking at the problem of drug abuse. A high incidence of abuse in any society or community strongly suggests the presence of social disorganization: people abuse drugs for a reason, and if social forces did not indirectly encourage the practice it would not be widespread. If, as may be the case in the United States, many people are unable to achieve personal goals, they may turn instead to drug abuse as a means of compensation or escape. Indeed, some of the worst forms of abuse—of alcohol and narcotics—are found disproportionately in depressed, lower-class communities. Society may also be considered disorganized to the extent that a large proportion of its members have failed to internalize or have rejected social norms governing drug abuse, because this tendency indicates a failure of the socialization process. In a heterogeneous society marked by significant differences in the values of the generations, some traditional social norms are readily abandoned. In addition, society may be considered disorganized to the extent that effective means of social control over the importation and manufacture of illicit drugs have not been developed; the social institutions charged with this responsibility are failing to fulfill their function.

The *value-conflict* perspective highlights the fact that there is a considerable conflict of values between different groups in society over the issue of drug use. Some groups favor some drugs, other groups favor other drugs, and these divisions are often linked to the age range of the groups in question. There is a wide measure of disagreement over the relative dangers of different drugs, and a further disagreement over which drugs, if any, ought to be regulated by the criminal law. Some conflict theorists regard these conflicts as potentially useful, since they focus attention on the issues, lead to public debate, and may result in needed changes in cases where social norms or laws are inconsistent with the actual characteristics or dangers of particular drugs.

The *deviance* perspective provides a particularly fruitful way of analyzing the problem of drug abuse, since those who use drugs that are disapproved by social norms or prohibited by law are usually regarded as social deviants. Although many people believe that deviant drug use is caused by psychological instability, irresponsibility, or other character defects, sociologists regard this view as simplistic and attempt to take into account the full social context in which drug abuse takes place.

Those sociologists who see the use of illicit drugs as the product of anomie believe that abusers may desire certain approved social goals, such as happiness and fulfillment, but may lack approved means of attaining those goals. They resort instead to socially disapproved means, believing that the use of drugs may provide an alternative route to personal satisfaction. Other sociologists emphasize the role of drug subcultures in the creation of the individual deviant. Few people enter on a drug-taking career in isolation; they are usually introduced to the drug in the presence of others who already have experience of the drug and an understanding of its effects. The norms of the drug subculture differ in significant respects from those of the rest of society, and the new participant is slowly resocialized into an acceptance of these norms, thereby becoming a deviant in the eyes of the dominant culture.

Sociologists who take a labeling perspective on deviance often believe that drug abuse is relative: the decision as to which forms of drug use are to be considered deviant depends on who has the power to make the decision. Those who enjoy power and influence in society, for example, are often consumers of alcohol and smokers of tobacco, and so these very dangerous drugs are freely available. On the other hand, those who sniff cocaine or smoke marijuana have relatively little power and influence in society, have no ability to label others, and find that their own drug preferences have been labeled as deviant. Many sociologists believe that those groups who have the power to determine social attitudes toward drugs often do so on the basis of their attitudes toward the groups that use particular drugs, rather than on the basis of scientific information about the drugs: the strong social reaction to marijuana, for example, seems to be related to the fact that its use was originally associated with youthful rebellion. Labeling theorists also believe that labeling is important in the process of becoming deviant: a person who experiments with drugs may be defined by others as a drug user, may accept this label, and may act on that basis in the future.

States in the future. The abrupt increase in the use of narcotics in the late sixties occurred at a time when old social norms and values were being widely challenged by young people; it was a period of considerable confusion and new norms regulating novel forms of drug behavior had not fully evolved. The use of heroin was not as negatively viewed by young people as it is today; experimentation with the narcotics was often a source of prestige with peers. Current norms of youth are much more unfavorable toward narcotics, and the use of the drugs among the young are likely to be less common in consequence.

The treatment of narcotics addicts will pose continuing problems. The traditional purely punitive approach is rapidly being replaced by a concern for rehabilitation, but there is considerable debate about how best to help heroin addicts. Some therapeutic communities, often staffed by former addicts, have claimed a fair degree of success in helping the addicts to break their habit. Another and more controversial method is the provision to addicts of the synthetic narcotic methadone as a legally available substitute for heroin. Methadone usually does not give the addict a "high," and so he or she can function normally in a social or work situation. The drug can be taken orally, helps to eliminate craving for other narcotics, and has few undesirable side effects if taken in moderate doses. Methadone is, however, an addictive drug, so its use constitutes merely the substitution of one addictive drug for another. A further problem with methadone is that supplies of the drug are entering the narcotics black market, with unfortunate effects: in 1974 the medical authorities of New York City found that, for the first time, narcotics deaths involving methadone were more common than those involving heroin.[49]

The use of hallucinogenic drugs will probably continue to be confined to a small minority of Americans who are attracted by the potential that the drugs are believed to offer for the exploration of human awareness. The widespread and somewhat indiscriminate use of the drugs that occurred in the turbulent sixties is unlikely to be repeated, however, largely because a good deal more is now known about the undesirable short- and long-term psychological effects that the drugs have in some cases.

A drug-free American is almost certainly an impossibility. Future policy will have to concentrate on honest and effective drug education to make the population, and particularly its younger members, fully aware of the dangers of certain drugs, particularly tobacco and alcohol. Drug use will have to be regulated in the future as in the past, but this will be more effectively done through rationally based and widely accepted social norms rather than primarily through the application of criminal sanctions to drug abusers. Ultimately, both the social norms and the laws will have to correspond much more closely to the intrinsic dangers of the drugs they regulate than they do at present.

[49]Cincinnati *Enquirer* (August 18, 1974).

FURTHER READING

Brecher, Edward and *Consumer Reports* Editors, *Licit and Illicit Drugs,* 1972. A report prepared for the Consumers Union of the United States. Written in a clear and interesting style, this book contains a great deal of information on all the drugs commonly used and abused in the United States. The report adopts a liberal attitude toward reform of the drug laws.

Fort, Joel, *Alcohol: Our Biggest Drug Problem,* 1973. Physician Joel Fort scrutinizes the use and abuse of alcohol in America. He presents recommendations for the prevention and treatment of alcoholism.

Goode, Erich, *Drugs in American Society,* 1972. A valuable and comprehensive sociological discussion of each of the main forms of drug abuse in the United States.

Grinspoon, Lester, *Marijuana Reconsidered,* 1971. A physician's thorough investigation of the social and medical implications of marijuana use.

McGrath, John H. and Frank R. Scarpitti, *Youth and Drugs: Perspectives on a Social Problem,* 1970. A collection of articles exploring various aspects of youthful experimentation with drugs.

National Commission on Marijuana and Drug Abuse, Official Report, *Marijuana: A Signal of Misunderstanding,* 1972; Second Report, *Drug Use in America,* 1973. Two important objective and wide-ranging federal reports on drug use in America. Written in clear nontechnical language, these authoritative reports contain surveys of research findings on drugs and offer recommendations for reform of the drug laws.

Yablonsky, Lewis, *The Tunnel Back: Synanon,* 1965. An account of the development of Synanon, a controversial drug rehabilitation center. The book details the problems involved in the rehabilitation of addicts.

Young, Jock, *The Drugtakers,* 1971. A sociologist's critical view of social attitudes toward drugs. Young argues strongly that the social reaction to drugs depends more on who uses them than the properties of the drugs themselves.

Acknowledgments

Chapter 2

From Otto Fredrich, "Population Explosion: Is Man Really Doomed? *Time,* September 13, 1971. Reprinted by permission from *Time,* The Weekly Newsmagazine; Copyright Time Inc.

Chart, "How Many People Have Lived on Earth?" *Population Bulletin* (February 1962). Population Reference Bureau, Inc., Washington, D.C. "World Population Data Sheet (1973)."

From Henry Borgstrom, "The Dual Challenge of Health and Hunger—A Global Crisis," *PRB Selection* no. 31 (Washington, D.C.: Population Reference Bureau, January 1970).

Reprinted with the permission of The Population Council from "World Population: Status Report 1974," by Bernard Berelson, *Reports on Population/Family Planning,* no. 15 (January 1974); pp. 37 and 47.

From Joni Mitchell, "Big Yellow Taxi," *Ladies of the Canyon.* Reprinted by permission.

From Paul Ehrlich, "Interview: Dr. Paul Ehrlich," *Playboy* Magazine (August 1970). Copyright © 1970 by *Playboy.* Reprinted by permission.

Frank W. Notestein, "The Population Crisis: Reasons for Hope"; excerpted by permission from *Foreign Affairs,* October 1967. Copyright 1967 by Council on Foriegn Relations, Inc.

Chapter 3

From Norman Cousins, "Affluence and Effluence," *Saturday Review,* May 2, 1970. © 1970 by Saturday Review, Inc. Reprinted by permission of Saturday Review/World.

Excerpted from *Moment in the Sun* by Robert Rienow and Leona Train Rienow. Copyright © 1967 by Robert Rienow and Leona Train Rienow. Used with permission of The Dial Press.

Charts, "The Biosphere" and "Biological Magnification of DDT." Reprinted with permission of Macmillan Publishing Co., Inc. from *World Facts and Trends* by John McHale. Copyright © 1972 by John McHale.

From *The New York Times,* February 27, 1972. © 1972 by The New York Times Company. Reprinted by permission.

From Edward Goldsmith, et al., "Blueprint for Survival," *The Ecologist* (January 1972). Reprinted by permission.

Chapter 4

Map, "Thirteen Major Megalopolises in the United States, courtesy of the Department of Commerce, Bureau of the Census.

From Louis Wirth, "Urbanism as a Way of Life," *American Journal of Sociology* (July 1938). © 1938 by The University of Chicago. All rights reserved. Reprinted by permission of The University of Chicago.

Table in Philip Hauser, "The Chaotic Society: Product of the Social Morphological Revolution," *American Sociological Review* (February 1959). Reprinted by permission of the American Sociological Association and Philip Hauser.

From Alvin Toffler, *Future Shock.* Copyright © 1970 by Alvin Toffler. Reprinted by permission of Random House, Inc.

Chapter 5

From the *Columbia Journalism Review* (May–June 1973) and (May–June 1974); Harold M. Evans, "Is the Press Too Powerful?" *Columbia Journalism Review* (January–February 1972). Reprinted by permission.

Charts, "Households with Television Sets: 1950–1972" and "Television Viewing by Sex and Age: November 1970," reprinted by permission of A. C. Nielsen Company.

From *The New York Times,* November 11, 1969; Pie Dufour, "Press v. President: It's an Old Story," *The New York Times,* November 30, 1969. © 1969 by The New York Times Company. Reprinted by permission.

From Harry S. Ashmore, "Journalism 1970: Uncertain Oracles" (November–December 1970); Sander Vanocur, "TV's Failed Promise" (November–December 1971). Reprinted with permission from *The Center Magazine,* a publication of the Center for the Study of Democratic Institutions.

Rudolf Klein, "Lords of the Press" (January 1973). Reprinted from *Commentary,* by permission; Copyright © 1973 by the American Jewish Committee.

Chapter 6

From Studs Terkel, *Working: People Talk About What They Do All Day and How They Feel About What They Do.* Copyright © 1972, 1974 by Studs Terkel. Reprinted by permission of Pantheon Books, a Division of Random House, Inc.

Chart, "Daily Use of Time: 1966, By Sex and Occupation," as it appeared in Executive Office of the President: Office of Management and Budget, *Social Indicators, 1973* (Washington, D.C.: U.S. Government Printing Office, 1973), p. 214. Data in chart come from John P. Robinson and Philip E. Converse, *Social Change Reflected in the Use of Time: The Human Meaning of Social Change.* Angus Campbell and Philip E. Converse, Editors, Russell Sage Foundation, New York, 1972, Table A. Reprinted by permission.

From Harvey Swados, *A Radical's America.* Reprinted by permission of Mrs. Harvey Swados.

From Lawrence Stassen, "The Ax and Older Workers," *The New York Times,* June 23, 1974; Robert

Sherrill, "Review of *Job Power* and *Work in America*," *The New York Times Book Review*, July 8, 1973; Daniel Bell, "The Cultural Contradiction," *The New York Times*, August 27, 1970. © 1970/73/74 by The New York Times Company. Reprinted by permission.

Table, "American Labor Force Participation by Sex, 1948–1972." Reprinted from *Work in America: Report of a Special Task Force to the Secretary of Health, Education and Welfare* by permission of the M.I.T. Press, Cambridge, Massachusetts.

From J. D. Hodgson, "The World of Work in the World Ahead," *Personnel Administration* (March–April 1972). Copyright © 1972 by the Society for Personnel Administration (now the International Personnel Management Association).

From Peter Drucker, "The Surprising Seventies," *Harper's Magazine*, vol. 243, no. 6 (July 1971), pp. 35–39. Reprinted by permission.

Chapter 7

Table, "The Fifteen Biggest Corporations in the World," *Time*, April 19, 1974; "Meanwhile, Down in Chile . . . ," *Time*, April 3, 1972. Reprinted by permission from *Time*, The Weekly Newsmagazine; Copyright Time Inc.

From Richard J. Barnet, Ronald E. Müller, and Joseph Collins, "Global Corporations: Their Quest for Legitimacy," in *Exploring Contradictions: Political Economy in the Corporate State*, eds. Philip Brenner, Robert Borosage, and Bethany Weider. Reprinted by permission of David McKay Company, Inc. and Philip Brenner.

From Ernest Fitzgerald, "The Pentagon as the Enemy of Capitalism," *World*, Febuary 27, 1973. © 1973 by *World*. Reprinted by permission.

Chapter 8

From Kenneth E. Boulding, "Reflections on Poverty," *The Social Welfare Forum: 1961* (New York: Columbia University Press, 1961) by permission of the publisher.

From Herman Miller, "Changes in the Number and Composition of the Poor," in *Inequality and Poverty*, ed. Edward C. Budd. Copyright © 1965 by Chandler Publishing Company. Reprinted by permission.

From A. Dale Tussing, "The Dual Welfare System," *Society*, vol. 11, no. 2 (January–February 1974). Prepublication, in modified form, of Chapter 4 in A. Dale Tussing, *Poverty in a Dual Economy* (New York: St. Martin's Press, 1975). Copyright © 1975 by St. Martin's Press, Inc. Reprinted by permission.

From Robert Coles, "Blaming the Victim," *American Journal of Sociology* (September 1972). © 1972 by The University of Chicago. All rights reserved. Reprinted by permission of The University of Chicago.

From Richard Sennett and Jonathan Cobb, *The Hidden Injuries of Class*. Copyright © 1972 by Richard Sennett and Jonathan Cobb. Reprinted by permission of Alfred A. Knopf, Inc.

From Harry M. Caudill, "The Permanent Poor: The Lesson of Eastern Kentucky," *The Atlantic Monthly* (June 1964). Copyright © 1964, by The Atlantic Monthly Company, Boston, Mass. Reprinted with permission.

From Oscar Lewis, "The Culture of Poverty," *Scientific American* (October 1966). Reprinted by permission of Harold Ober Associates Incorporated. Copyright © 1966 by Oscar Lewis.

Chapter 9

Chart, "The Income Gap," from *The New York Times*, July 24, 1974. © 1974 by The New York Times Company. Reprinted by permission.

From Ruben Salazar, "Stranger in One's Land," U.S. Commission on Civil Rights, *Clearinghouse* (May 1970). Reprinted by permission.

Reprinted with permission of Macmillan Publishing Co., Inc. from *The Rise of the Unmeltable Ethnics* by Michael Novak. Copyright © 1971, 1972 by Michael Novak.

Chapter 11

Excerpts from the Introduction, Chapter 7, and Chapter 14 in *Women in Sexist Society: Studies in Power and Powerlessness*, edited by Vivian Gornick and Barbara K. Moran. Copyright © 1971 by Basic Books, Inc. Publishers, New York.

From George P. Murdock, "Comparative Data on the Division of Labor by Sex," *Social Forces* (May 1937). Reprinted by permission of the University of North Carolina Press.

From Ruth E. Hartley, "American Core Culture: Changes and Continuities," in *Sex Roles in Changing Society*, eds. Georgene H. Seward and Robert C. Williamson. Copyright © 1970 by Random House, Inc. Reprinted by permission of Random House, Inc.

From Florence Howe, "Sexual Stereotypes Start Early," *Saturday Review*, October 16, 1971. © 1971 by Saturday Review, Inc. Reprinted by permission of Saturday Review/World.

From Vivian Gornick, "Why Women Fear Success," *The New York Times Magazine*, December 20, 1971. © 1971 by The New York Times Company. Reprinted by permission.

Chart, ". . . and Earn Less in All Kinds of Jobs," reprinted from *U.S. News & World Report*, May 29, 1973. Copyright 1973 U.S. News & World Report, Inc.

From Germaine Greer, *The Female Eunuch*. Copyright © 1970, 1971 by Germaine Greer. Used with permission of McGraw-Hill Book Co.

Index